The Character of
MERIWETHER
LEWIS

Explorer in the Wilderness

The Character *of*
MERIWETHER
LEWIS

Explorer in the Wilderness

Essays on One of the Most Remarkable Men in American History

Clay S. Jenkinson

The Dakota Institute Press
of the Lewis & Clark Fort Mandan Foundation

Library of Congress Control Number 2011937804
ISBN-13 978-0-9825597-2-7 (Hardcover)
ISBN-13 978-0-9825597-3-4 (Paperback)

Distributed by The University of Oklahoma Press
Created, produced and designed in the United States of America
Printed in Canada

Internal book layout and design by Margaret McCullough
corvusdesignstudio.com

The paper in this book meets the guidelines for permanence and durability
of the Committee of Production Guidelines for Book Longevity of the
Council on Library Resources.
10 9 8 7 6 5 4 3 2

The Dakota Institute Press
of the Lewis & Clark Fort Mandan Foundation
2576 8th Street South West . Post Office Box 607
Washburn, North Dakota 58577
www.fortmandan.com
1.877.462.8535

Cover Images: Captain Meriwether Lewis by
Charles Balthazar Fevret de Saint Memin (1774–1809), painted 1807; watercolor
over graphite on paper, 6 1/8 x 3 3/4 inch; accession no. 1971.125.
Collection of The New-York Historical Society

Thomas Jefferson's Instructions to Meriwether Lewis.
Manuscript Division, Library of Congress.

Publication of this book made possible by a gift from
Sheila Robinson in memory of her husband Dave.

Second printing of first edition made possible
by a gift from Warren Rockenbach.

Original art by Michael Haynes commissioned
for this book sponsored by Marvin and Luella Snyder.

MIX
Paper from
responsible sources
FSC
www.fsc.org   FSC® C016245

For Catherine Missouri Walker Jenkinson,
May you always be a butte climber,
a Missouri Walker
and an explorer
&
for Ray Frazer
with a go cup

Contents

"The most important result of all thoughtful exploration ... is to recognize in the apparent confusion and opulence of nature a quintessential unity—to study each detail thoroughly yet never be defeated by the contradiction of a mass of fact, to remember the elevated destiny of *homo sapiens* and thereby to grasp the spirit of nature, its essential meaning which lies concealed under a blanket of multifarious manifestations."

—Alexander von Humboldt

We shall not cease from exploration
And the end of all our exploring
Will be to arrive where we started
And know the place for the first time.

—T. S. Eliot

Of Meriwether Lewis

"Of courage undaunted, possessing a firmness & perseverance of purpose which nothing but impossibilities could divert from it's direction, careful as a father of those committed to his charge, yet steady in the maintenance of order & discipline, intimate with the Indian character, customs & principles, habituated to the hunting life, guarded by exact observation of the vegetables & animals of his own country, against losing time in the descriptions of objects already possessed, honest, disinterested, liberal, of sound understanding and a fidelity to truth so scrupulous that whatever he should report would be as certain as if seen by ourselves, with all these qualifications as if selected and implanted by nature in one body, for this express purpose, I could have no hesitation in confiding the enterprise to him."

—Thomas Jefferson

Foreword

David L. Nicandri

I HAVE WORKED IN THE FIELD OF THE HISTORY OF THE AMERICAN West since I emerged from graduate school in 1972. Looking back over the now almost forty years, one of my most vivid professional memories was my first introduction to Clay Jenkinson.

This happened in 1989 when my institution, the Washington State Historical Society, and like organizations in that tier of states—what might be called the Northern West—were celebrating the centennials of their admission to the Union. Included in the list, of course, was Clay's beloved North Dakota (though I was not aware of that fact at the time). I do not characterize his attachment cavalierly, for few people have as well developed a sense of respect and understanding, indeed reverence for a place, as Clay holds for North Dakota.

Coinciding with Washington's centennial, then, the Western History Association (WHA), perhaps then at the peak of its influence as a forum for ideas about the region, held its annual convention in Tacoma, the headquarters city of the Washington State Historical Society. I was the local arrangements chair, which mainly involved logistical details with the meeting venue and a field trip or two. The intellectual work of the conference was done by the program committee, chaired by John D. W. Guice of the University of Southern Mississippi, to whom I shall return later in this essay, as does Clay in his prefatory remarks. John figures in this story because he became a student of Meriwether Lewis's end days. Anyway, in those days the "Western" (as it was referred to colloquially among its habitués) reached its crescendo with a banquet on Friday night. As local arrangements chair I had the perquisite of a place on the dais, along with John Guice and a few other luminaries active in the governance of the WHA, giving me a front row seat for what was about to ensue.

The conference program noted that the banquet address would be given by Clay S. Jenkinson of Denver, Colorado, on "Thomas Jefferson and the

West." What was immediately discernable as unusual about the head table arrangement was that the speaker was not seated with us for the meal. The reason was made evident upon Clay's introduction, that is, once he strode into the banquet hall dressed in period costume as the third president of the United States. He took his spot at the podium, and, well … , anyone who has ever seen Clay in his first person re-enactment mode knows what happened. He rendered a riveting, hour-long sojourn back into the Age of the Enlightenment, complete with some interrogatories from the audience, something unaccustomed in the tradition of the convention and most banquet addresses.

About that audience: recall that the WHA, then as now, is mostly populated by academic historians, fairly dubbed as a somewhat jaded group and not, I dare say, a cohort predisposed to like something as unorthodox as first person historical interpretation. Nevertheless, Clay Jenkinson's rendering that night of Jefferson's character, philosophy, and political views was a tour de force. In fact, Clay created somewhat of a sensation. I'm confirmed in that view because many years later, in 2006 at a post-Lewis and Clark bicentennial legacies symposium in Portland, Oregon, held under the auspices of Lewis and Clark College, I was reminiscing about that evening back in 1989 with Patty Limerick. Patty is an esteemed historian of the American West who herself had rocketed to the apex of the profession with the publication of *Legacy of Conquest* in 1987. Patty also clearly recalled Clay's performance in Tacoma. She too thought that Clay's characterization of Jefferson was one of the most memorable moments in the history of the WHA and averred that she was herself inspired to experiment with historical role-playing on the theme of western land use (conducted with her University of Colorado colleague, law professor Charles Wilkinson).

The particular genius of Clay's approach is his encyclopedic grasp of the documentary record (in this first case Jefferson, but many other historical figures were to follow) and a theatrical projection of content that originated in the grand American tradition of the Chautauqua movement. Here, Clay's roots in North Dakota intersect with this story once again. Clay, with fellow Humanities scholar Ev Albers, perfected the Chautauqua format for the benefit of communities large and small across North Dakota. The great value and continued promise of this style of presentation is that it builds a bridge between the academic world with its specialized understanding of Humanities scholarship and the general public, often a remote and inaccessible audience.

Clay went on to create a national reputation (and many imitators) speaking before legislative bodies and in other distinguished settings. I did not see him again until the run-up to, and then often during, the Lewis and Clark bicentennial. In the mean time, of course, Clay had expanded and built out from his interpretive base in the form of the Jefferson character to include the president's protégé Meriwether Lewis. In this new role, if anything, Clay was even more accomplished than he was as Jefferson.

Indirectly, Clay (as "Lewis") tipped me off to an interpretive prospect that led eventually to my own book on the expedition, also published by The Dakota Institute and graced by a magnificent foreword written by Clay. The inadvertent insight based on Clay's scrupulous utilization of the documentary record, in this case the journals of Lewis, was this: Clay could only go where the Lewis record would take him. And, the few times that Clay appeared in Columbia River country, I noticed his Lewis narratives had a distinct Missouri River cast to them. This, of course, was a function of the now well-developed perception that THE major gap in Lewis's journaling occurred just as the expedition was about to voyage out onto the Columbia's westward flowing waters. Again, this was no fault of Clay's—it was that of the figure he was emulating, the fragile genius Meriwether Lewis who, as the quarterback for the Jefferson team, fumbled his pen. Lewis left much of the documentation of the voyage down the Great River of the West to a lesser writer, William Clark, the reliable fullback who kept the expedition's methodical drive westward, and its narrative, alive.

Clay Jenkinson laid down his foundation about the expedition generally, and about Meriwether Lewis specifically, in a book published in 2000, *The Character of Meriwether Lewis: 'Completely Metamorphosed' in the American West*. That slim volume, in my estimation, was one of the three or four most influential books written about the expedition during the last quarter of the twentieth century. The cohort consists of Stephen Ambrose's *Undaunted Courage: Meriwether Lewis, Thomas Jefferson, and the Opening of the American West* (1996), which, if only because of its popularity, turbocharged by Stephen's dominance of the Ken Burns & Dayton Duncan documentary for PBS, made the expedition's story a national phenomenon. The others are: John Logan Allen's *Passage through the Garden: Lewis and Clark and the Image of the American Northwest* (1975), which, though few perceive it as such, is the "master narrative" for how the expedition is typically understood; and James Ronda's *Lewis and Clark among the Indians* (1984), which offered the first contrarian view for how to consider Jefferson's western enterprise, i.e., from the (river) bank and not the (expedition's) boat.

Though the original *The Character of Meriwether Lewis* is a short book, few volumes on this topic held as many interpretive insights. With Ronda, Clay re-set the trajectory of Lewis & Clark studies. Viewed in genealogical terms, *The Character of Meriwether Lewis* served as the progenitor for Thomas Slaughter's *Exploring Lewis and Clark: Reflections on Men and Wilderness* (2003) and my own *River of Promise: Lewis and Clark on the Columbia* (2010). Jenkinson's great contribution in this regard, his key insight, is that the journals emanating from the expedition are a literary construct and not necessarily daily diaries reflecting any one-day's occurrences. In other words, there is a perceivable "dynamics of the journals" (a phrase Clay coined in his *A Vast and Open Plain: The Writings of the Lewis and Clark Expedition in North Dakota, 1804–1806* (2003)), complete with retrospective glances, indeed even meaningful silences, that inform their construction and purpose. In retrospect it seems only natural that an expert student of literature like Clay, one practiced in the art of explication, would have discovered this.

As a historian Clay was able to apply those skills to a non-fiction text, the journals, and deduced several important points. Clay was the first to hint at the fact that Lewis and Clark may have had, at times, a less than fully harmonious relationship, and he gave emphasis to Clark's role as a balance wheel that could even out some of the consequences of Lewis's aloof and prickly idiosyncrasies. He discerned that, notwithstanding Lewis's skill as a writer (when he chose to write), it is Clark's journal that provides the chronological backbone to posterity's understanding of what transpired, when, and where. Clay was the first to note that Lewis took charge at critical moments and engineered (or at least, took advantage of) circumstances that allowed him to make discoveries alone, which is to say more specifically, without Clark. He was the first scholar to question the authenticity of Lewis's grand narrative about the quest for the Shoshone, reaching the headwaters of the Missouri, and first steps into Columbia River country, citing the staged and artificial nature of Lewis's Lemhi Pass narrative. And, Clay was the first to posit that the seeds of Lewis's demise were not sown late in his post-expeditionary days but rather "out there" on the wilderness trail during 1805–1806. The corollary to this insight was that Stephen Ambrose's popularization of manic-depression as the cause for Lewis's slide had taken on overtones of popular orthodoxy and cant, and not well-established analysis.

In the original *The Character of Meriwether Lewis,* Clay, among others before and since, issued the clarion call for a fresh new reading of the journals, the modern edition under Gary Moulton's expert hand having been effectively completed in 1999. In the pages of this revised and extended edition, Clay has answered his own charge. Like the original, this new book is not a continuous narrative about the expedition, but more like a picaresque novel; a survey of several episodes that are probative as to Clay's quest: the search for clues into the mystery of Meriwether Lewis. This new book is a thoroughgoing expansion of the pre-existing body of Jenkinson scholarship and breaks much new ground. In so doing he regularly capitalizes on another vintage Jenkinsonian construct: the contrast between what he terms the "self-enclosed, micro-universe of LEWIS & CLARK" legend and lore versus the "fuller, richer, often more unsatisfying story" we find in this volume.

One of the most grating axioms that achieved some currency during the recent bicentennial was the notion that the journals had been tapped out; that is, all the stories we were ever going to glean from that record were already in hand. The premise undergirding this idea, of course, is that the journals had been truly and effectively mined in the first place. As a student of the conventions of literature and historiography, Clay has demonstrated in this new book that the modern edition of the *Journals* by Moulton can still produce precious ore.

Take, for just one example and my favorite in this book, the chapter on the grand rendezvous planned by the captains to occur on the return voyage at the confluence of the Yellowstone and Missouri rivers in the summer of 1806. This episode has long since been considered "settled history," principally because Clark's relatively carefree float down the Yellowstone is one of the least studied segments of the journey. What I mean to suggest is that the received view, held by scholars and buffs alike, is that the re-integration of the Yellowstone detachment led by Clark with the Lewis/Pryor detachment coming down the Missouri, effected hundreds of miles from where the plan was hatched at Traveler's Rest, shows either the logistical genius of the captains, or possibly magnificent good fortune, or both. But upon new and closer inspection here by Jenkinson, we have a whole new story.

Like many such insights about the expedition, the core element is the actual, as opposed to the idealized, nature of the relationship between Clark and Lewis. Here in this story specifically, and more generally throughout the book, Clay confronts Stephen Ambrose's trope about the "greatest friendship in American history." This notion, in its most refined form, appeared in Ambrose's elegy to the captains as a sidebar in the companion volume to the Burns/Duncan PBS documentary, *Lewis & Clark: The Journey of the Corps of Discovery* (1997). To wit:

> Friends never cheat each other, or take advantage. Friends glory in each other's successes and are downcast by the failures. Friends minister to each other. Friends give to each other, worry about each other, stand always ready to help. Friends will go hungry for each other, freeze for each other, die for each other. It is rarely achieved, but at its height, friendship is an ecstasy. For Lewis and Clark it was an ecstasy, and the critical factor in their great success. (page 125).

Now, about the foregoing several things might be asked or said. Did Lewis and Clark have what might be termed a brotherly love for one another? Yes. But, I ask, do siblings sometimes have strains in their relationships? After all, if the apostles, regarded literally as saints in the Christian tradition, argued with one another, are we to believe that Lewis and Clark always saw eye to eye about things? Hardly; as Clay's new story about the captains and their famed rendezvous at the Yellowstone demonstrates, by way of example.

Jenkinson, here in these pages, re-emphasizes a point made many years ago in the original version of *Character*, namely, that "one of the most tenacious myths" about the expedition is the always positive relationship between the captains. He chides Clark for his lackadaisical or indifferent demeanor about holding to a plan he had constructed with Lewis at Traveler's Rest about a meet-up at the Yellowstone/Missouri confluence. I have argued in my book that Clark had his "moments" with Lewis's comportment, failings, and foibles; here Clay argues convincingly that Lewis was quite annoyed about Clark's cavalier adherence to strategy.

The source of the problem at the Yellowstone, as Jenkinson recounts it, is Clark's inability to cope with the profusion of mosquitoes, one of nature's smallest but most aggravating species, inhabiting the confluence. Clark left the area and headed downstream before Lewis arrived, but before doing so he left a note for his fellow commander appended to a pole, one of their favorite field tactics even though more times than not it failed them. Clay's felicitous phrasing of this scene will serve here as an emblem for his colorful writing style: "A perishable note on a temporary pole in the middle of nowhere, in the heart of a game preserve in which any creature from a greedy beaver to a blundering buffalo might have torn down that casually constructed semaphore at any point in the days, weeks, or months between its erection and Lewis's putative arrival." Drawing on his command of literature of Western Civilization and helpful allusions to be gleaned from that corpus, Jenkinson suggests that the confusion at the rendezvous between the comings and goings of Clark, Lewis, and sergeants Gass and Pryor meant that "Suddenly the expedition feels more like Robinson Crusoe than the darling project of Thomas Jefferson." This is just a sample of what's in store—an imaginative excursion that shifts vantage points between serious Humanities discourse and witty conversation with the reader.

A plethora of the new stories and insights await the reader in this book. In "Meriwether Lewis's Bad Day" Jenkinson explores the theme that Lewis was best when Clark was present, but at his worst when Clark was absent. In "The Problem with Silence," Clay analyzes how Lewis compounded his difficulties by failing to communicate regularly with Jefferson and intermediate superiors. "Being First" is about Lewis's egotism and need to get to important points of discovery before Clark, or even if he fails to do that, to re-construct the narrative to make it appear he did. When Lewis was in this mode he was struggling to achieve the stature of a terrestrial James Cook. However, whereas Cook could take pride in the accomplishments associated with negative discovery, i.e., demolishing the myths of the very imperial establishment that sent him to Pacific waters, Lewis could not cope with the geo-political consequences of not finding Jefferson's desideratum of a facile cross-continental water route that would bridge Atlantic America with the Pacific Ocean. A suite of chapters, "The Problem of Silence," "Why," and "Birthdays, Holidays, Anniversaries" seriously explore the interiors of Lewis's character, strengths, and weaknesses, often in contrast to the circumstances of William Clark.

In this book Clay ranges widely across many topics in a discursive but always insightful manner. He has a particular gift for framing Sacagawea as the occasional lens through which we might more closely view the expedition as a human enterprise, as opposed to a mythic one, always with a principal view to shed light on the relationship between the captains and their role with the party. Clearly, Sacagawea came to fall within the cozy confines of what might be termed Clark's protectorate. At times Lewis can barely suffer to mention her name. As Clay notes, Clark conceded the elements of basic humanity to Sacagawea. In short, Clark and she would talk, and he benefitted from an inclination to listen to her, as happened on finding Bozeman Pass and thus the route to the headwaters of the Yellowstone. No one, in my estimation, has thought more carefully about Sacagawea, as a person or a role-player, or how we know what we think we know about her given the paucity of documentation, than Clay.

Some readers will be challenged by the boldness of some interpretations found in this book, and others may find it hard to agree with them. The Lewis and Clark saga can be at times, as Clay notes in his prefatory remarks, unsatisfying. I don't quite see Meriwether Lewis as the "iron man" of the expedition that Clay does, nor Clark a figure inclined to complain. After all, as Stephenie Ambrose Tubbs has rather succinctly stated, compared to Lewis, Clark was a man who had his act together. Nor do I share Clay's perspective on how to evaluate David McKeehan's skewering of Lewis in a famous post-expeditionary broadside prompted by the captain's presumptuous prospectus about his forthcoming but never written narrative. McKeehan is one of the best correctives we have to counter the hagiographic tendency that informs much of the popular understanding of Lewis. McKeehan may have rather enjoyed mixing vitriol with his ink, but the unvarnished critique he wrote merits respect because he either knew Lewis or knew people who did.

In the end, the purpose of scholarship is to engage the Hegelian dynamic: theses countered by antitheses that yield new syntheses. When the day comes that the body of Lewis and Clark scholars consider all matters to have been settled, that will mean the sub-discipline has died. Herein Clay Jenkinson firmly establishes himself as the most thoughtful of commentators on Lewis and his demise and the origins of the circumstances that led to his suicide (which Clay subscribes to without reservation). The story of Lewis is larger than his death, of course, but it is nonetheless the particular facet of his life that, like Captain Cook's premature death, does so much to propel interest in the expedition he led.

This revised edition of *The Character of Meriwether Lewis* is a bigger book and a more important one than the original, and building upon all of his writings about the expedition through the course of his career, Clay Jenkinson cements the new model for Lewis and Clark studies going forward. Based upon twenty years worth of reading, research and reflection, this book contains major insights about the dynamics of the journals and practical exploration that gives us a new way of seeing the expedition. For the faint of heart, be forewarned; the Meriwether Lewis here is not the ubiquitous cardboard cutout we see on the highway sign, knowledgeably and confidently pointing the way.

⌘

Life can take many unusual if not strange twists, including the fact that you never know who you might meet up with again or when. It's like meeting your neighbor, or a long-lost friend or relative at a distant airport or in the middle of Yellowstone Park. Life happens. I think of this in reflection of Clay's delightful remarks about John Guice in his prefatory remarks. Relations between scholars can be petty, especially when they disagree on matters of interpretation. It speaks highly, then, of both men that Clay wrote the introduction to a volume edited by Guice, *By His Own Hand? The Mysterious Death of Meriwether Lewis* (2006), even though he vehemently disagrees with John's "Lewis was murdered" theory. And I also pleasantly recall that in 2009 Clay, John, and I had a reunion of sorts in Olive Branch, MS, at the annual meeting of the Lewis & Clark Trail Heritage Foundation on the occasion of the 200th anniversary of Lewis's demise along the Natchez Trace. Our being first brought together in Tacoma seemed so long ago and far away, yet, improbably, there we were. I mention this now only because at that meeting, amidst much verbal jousting, John memorably stipulated that it is the duty of historians to draw inferences from the evidence before them, or lack of same for that matter. In other words, historians must dig deep, below the surface, to bring the fullest meaning possible to their stories. They may disagree about their conclusions, but they owe each other good faith, honest debate.

And so it has happened here in this book. Clay Jenkinson has assiduously employed that methodology, looking at text almost like an archaeologist, or maybe even a psychologist. With calm reason and a careful handling of the evidence, while conspicuously avoiding wild speculation, Clay has painted a new portrait of Meriwether Lewis.

David L. Nicandri

Introduction

> "Why, look you now, how unworthy a thing you make of me!
> You would play upon me; you would seem to know my stops,
> you would pluck out the heart of my mystery, you would
> sound me from my lowest note to the top of my compass, and
> there is much music, excellent voice in this little organ, yet
> cannot you make it speak. Why, do you think that I am easier
> to be played on than a pipe? Call me what instrument you
> will, though you can fret me, you cannot play upon me."
>
> *Hamlet*
> III.ii.311-18.

I CAN REMEMBER THE PRECISE MOMENT WHEN I BECAME FASCINATED with Meriwether Lewis. In 1980 I purchased a hardcover copy of David Freeman Hawke's just-published *Those Tremendous Mountains: The Story of the Lewis and Clark Expedition*. I knew the basic outlines of the story. I had read John Bakeless's *The Journals of Lewis and Clark*, a slender, but dense, one-volume compilation of the journals of the captains, and I owned a copy of Bernard DeVoto's enormously influential *Journals of Lewis and Clark* (1953). I had frankly never thought about the lives of the expedition members before or after the journey. The Lewis and Clark Expedition was, in other words, just an adventure story, albeit a very great adventure story.

I had lived most of my life in North Dakota, at the heart of the Lewis and Clark trail. I knew we had highways named 1804 and 1806 that flanked the Missouri River and that their designation somehow commemorated the expedition. I was aware of the existence of a wooden re-creation of Fort Mandan west of Washburn, ND, on the east bank of the Missouri River, though I had never actually been to it. The new Fort Mandan was completed in 1971, when I was a sophomore in high school. My understanding of Meriwether Lewis and William Clark was entirely conventional: they were the identical twins of the highway signs, co-captains and heroes who interchangeably shared the duties of the expedition. I had portrayed one of them, I cannot remember which, in a Cub Scout skit. I got to hold a BB gun in a public place and wear a coonskin cap.

Thrilled to possess a new just-off-the-press account of the Lewis and Clark Expedition, I read Hawke's *Those Tremendous Mountains* in a single day. Towards dusk I came to page 253, the beginning of a chapter called, "I Fear O! I Fear." Hawke's first sentence read, "On 11 October 1809, Meriwether Lewis, then governor of the Louisiana Territory, killed himself."

I was shocked. I had never heard that Lewis killed himself, or, for that matter, that he died just three years after his return from the journey. The moment I read Hawke's unequivocal declaration that Lewis had committed suicide, two things happened. First, I was troubled at the thought that someone I had up till that day regarded as a national hero had taken his own life, and so soon after the return of the expedition. What happened to Lewis? Even then, when I knew virtually nothing about Lewis and Clark, I regarded the interval between the expedition's return and Lewis's death to be too short to be random. If he had taken his own life twenty or thirty years after the journey, his suicide could mean just about anything. But in such tight proximity? Surely there was something extraordinary at work here. Though I could not have put it into words back then, I immediately intuited that Lewis must have had serious re-entry issues. While the expedition narrative of John Shields or William Bratton effectively ends with Clark's statement on September 23, 1806, that "we were met by all the village and received a harty welcom from it's inhabitants &.,"[1] the story of Meriwether Lewis's journey ends a full three years later in a squalid cabin in Tennessee. His expedition into the heart of darkness ended not with a land grant and double pay but with fatal gunshot wounds on the Natchez Trace seventy-two miles from Nashville.

Second, I wanted to know why. Why would someone like Neil Armstrong or Lance Armstrong commit suicide? What could possibly lead a man of such accomplishment to take his own life? That was 1980, fully thirty years ago. After giving more of my mental energy to the Lewis and Clark Expedition than to any other subject except the life and achievement of Thomas Jefferson and the poetry and prose of John Donne, and attempting more than 500 times to *inhabit* the soul of Meriwether Lewis, I still want to know why. I confess that I cannot explain to the satisfaction of others or of myself why Lewis took his own life in 1809. It's a mystery. That's why we are still talking about it.

When I read the account of Lewis's death in Hawke's book, I naturally accepted his conclusion without hesitation and without skepticism, in part because he didn't even acknowledge the existence of a rival theory. I simply assumed that Hawkes must represent the best historical thinking about Lewis. Case closed. The question was not *if* but *why*. About a year later, somebody told me that a few historians believed that Lewis had actually been murdered. So I picked up Vardis Fisher's *Suicide or Murder: The Strange Death of Governor Meriwether Lewis*. I expected the book to be a careful sorting out of the controversy, a rational weighing of the evidence on both sides in an attempt to reach a sensible and historically rigorous conclusion. What I discovered instead was a book of special pleading, bent not on finding the truth but promoting a preconceived conclusion. Like so many others who have come to the death of Lewis determined to prove that it was murder not suicide, Fisher spent most of his time trying to discredit those of Lewis's contemporaries who believed he had taken his own life, including Jefferson. The third president was an unreliable authority on the death of an American explorer, Fisher argued, because he had engaged in an adulterous relationship with the Anglo-Italian coquette Maria Cosway.

I still read everything I can get my hands on about Lewis's final days. I have debated the redoubtable John Guice, which is a bit like entering a professional wrestling ring with Andre the Giant or Mad Dog Vachon. Guice always wins Lewis debates because he is a smart, witty, and affable man, and because he is not afraid to engage when necessary in eye gouging in the public arena. At his invitation, I wrote what I hope was a dispassionate introduction to a book called *By His Own Hand: The Mysterious Death of Meriwether Lewis*, which he co-authored with James Holmberg and Jay Buckley. I try to come at the last days of Lewis from two different directions. I have, of course, studied the key documents relating to the last weeks of Lewis's life over and over, and I have read every available historical account of his death. At the same time I have read extensively in the professional literature of suicide, including Kay Redfield Jamison's superb *Night Falls Fast: Understanding Suicide*, which has an excellent chapter on Lewis.

I bring to my work a considerable fascination with the complexities of suicide. In my graduate studies at Oxford University I wrote extensively on the poetry and prose of John Donne (1572–1631). In 1608 Donne wrote *Biathanatos*, the first significant defense of suicide in the western Christian tradition. Donne's book, published after his death, was among other things a point-by-point response to the profoundly influential denunciation of suicide in St. Augustine's *City of God (AD 413ff)*. At Oxford I had the opportunity to read a great deal of literature on suicide, including Émile Durkheim's seminal classic, *Suicide* (1897).

That does not mean I am right when I conclude that the evidence in Lewis's case points to suicide, of course. But it means that I have done my homework. Like every other human phenomenon, suicide is better understood by those who have actually studied some of the professional literature than by those who presume to decide who is suicidal and why on the basis of hunches and gut feelings. It is frequently said among murder advocates that *Lewis was not the sort of man who would ever take his own life*, that *it would be out of character for him to do so*, that he *had nothing to be suicidal about*, etc. The eminent clinical psychologist Kay Redfield Jamison examined the life of Lewis carefully and came to a different conclusion. He was, she wrote, precisely the sort of man who might commit suicide.

I have no ax to grind in this book. My hero Jefferson once told a correspondent he was "not afraid to follow truth wherever it may lead."[2] If evidence were discovered that gave credibility to the murder theory, I would cheerfully embrace it as serious possibility. If some dramatic new discovery proved that Lewis was murdered, I would acknowledge my error and reassess my thinking about Lewis from birth to his untimely end. I have no dog in this fight. I wish Lewis had made it to Washington, DC, and Charlottesville in the fall of 1809, explained and exonerated himself, lived a long happy life, written his book(s), found a wife, raised children (the first of which he named William Clark Lewis), and maintained his friendship with Jefferson until the Fourth of July 1826. I agree with Jefferson that Lewis's untimely death cut us off from the most important voice of the Lewis and Clark Expedition, from whom we could have expected a lifetime of debriefings in publications and correspondence and advice to later travelers. All we know with absolute certainty is that Lewis died on the morning of October 11, 1809. Whether he was murdered or died by his own hand makes no difference to me as a historian; you follow the truth wherever it seems to lead and your private hopes for history must not be permitted to distort the lens. Personally, I wish Jefferson had not been a slaveholder, but as a historian I make no attempt to minimize his involuted lifelong complicity in the institution. I have not combed the expedition's journals and Lewis's letters for foreshadowings of suicidal moods, though my friend John Guice alleges that that is precisely what suicide theorists do.[3] In other words, I believe I would have written more or less the same book even if Lewis had been murdered on the Natchez Trace. He was, as Jefferson rightly understood, in a paroxysm of rage and anxiety at the time of his death, no matter who pulled the trigger.

I love thinking about Meriwether Lewis. I find him utterly fascinating. The fact that he was an eccentric, high strung, and sometimes-troubled man does not diminish him in my eyes. In fact, it makes him not only more interesting, but more admirable. He was a man of extraordinary intelligence and sensitivity, a superb writer and observer of nature, a natural outdoorsman with an iron physical constitution. Without perhaps intending to, he let the primordial wilderness of the American West get through his Jeffersonian defenses and into the deepest recesses of his soul. That's why I so honor Lewis. He didn't just cross the West—he ingested it, and in the end the West ingested him. I'm sure Lewis would have preferred to live a long and comfortable life, like Clark or Jefferson, but he lived a short life of *Sturm und Drang* instead. The fragmentary journals and letters Lewis left us constitute one of the most fascinating texts in American history. But in an ironic way, Lewis's unfinished life represents a text equally compelling, equally worthy of the closest study. All the obsessive talk about Lewis's last hours represents a distortion of the text we *should* be examining with all the critical faculties at our disposal. Some of those critical tools come from the realms of literature and the cultural studies movement, not the kind of linear history that has dominated the study of Lewis and Clark. The test of these relatively new methods is not whether they are clever, but whether they produce new insights about history, and help us make sense of Lewis and Clark. My hope is that readers of this book will find my analysis useful, even when they disagree with it.

The pioneers in this field have been Thomas Slaughter (*Exploring Lewis and Clark: Reflections on Men and Wilderness*, 2004), and David Nicandri (*River of Promise: Lewis and Clark on the Columbia*, 2010). The great James Ronda employed similar tools in his remarkable *Finding the West: Explorations with Lewis and Clark* (2006). Although they have very different styles and basic interests, both Slaughter and Nicandri have examined the journals of Lewis and Clark as texts rather than mines from which a tidy historical narrative can be extracted and refined. I don't always agree with their arguments, particularly Slaughter's, but I think every student of Lewis and Clark should carefully read both books before returning to the texts or the story. Slaughter's chapters, "Being First" and "Writing First" are essential reading for any understanding of Meriwether Lewis.[4] When I once told Mr. Slaughter that I admired his book but did not always agree with him, he replied, "I don't always agree with me, either." I love that spirit.

My approach to the study of Meriwether Lewis is to sift the evidence we have as carefully and imaginatively as I know how. Lewis did not write every day, but when he did write (when the switch was on) he invariably revealed something about the nature of his complex personality. This is less often the case with Clark. As the commander of the expedition and Jefferson's personal representative in the wilderness, Lewis took his role so seriously that his journal entries frequently reflect his fears that the expedition might collapse, that some setback or challenge might dishearten his crew and defeat the purposes of the journey altogether. Because he was the commander of record in one of the most important government exploration missions of the era, Lewis carried burdens of responsibility that no other member of the Corps of Discovery had to shoulder, including William Clark. Clark's role was to help the expedition get safely to the Pacific Ocean and back again. He performed that role admirably. Lewis's role was bigger. He had to try to make sense of the expedition's discoveries in the context of Jefferson's idea of America. This was no small task, in part because Jefferson was a visionary and a utopian, whom Alexander Hamilton called "an intellectual voluptuary,"[5] a radical and a revolutionary who clung to his agreeable notions with remarkable tenacity, and in part because the West (and its aboriginal inhabitants) represented a fundamental challenge to the ideals and integrity of the American republic. Lewis, but not Clark, had to carry these burdens: whether to relocate the white residents of the Louisiana Territory over on the Illinois side of the Mississippi River; where precisely the northern boundary of the Louisiana Purchase lay; how to discern and describe the flora and fauna and geographic landforms unique to the trans-Mississippi region; how to fold the existing French and Spanish cultures of St. Louis and Louisiana Territory into the paradigm of

America's republican form of government; how to square the messy reality of the watersheds of the American West with Jefferson's lovely notion that the rivers should want to interlock in a perfectly Newtonian configuration; and how to square Jefferson's concept of American Indians as untutored republicans-in-buckskin with the much rawer anthropological dynamics he was observing in his travels.

All Clark had to do was get the men home safely and complete his magnificent map. No small task, but one he was ideally suited to address. John Logan Allen has said that Clark was one of that very small percentage of people who can view a landscape as if from above, with an uncanny ability to process and visualize spatial relationships based on close observation of the landscape before them. Clark did not expect that he would ever have to answer to Thomas Jefferson. In this he was wrong. For modern readers to judge Lewis as a mentally unstable man who did not hold up as cheerfully as his partner in exploration William Clark is to create a false and unfair comparison. Clark was not carrying Lewis's burdens. In my opinion, he would not have been capable of bearing *those* burdens. He would have been the first to acknowledge that he was not well suited to be the intellectual leader of the expedition. To be sure, Lewis had problems. But many of those problems were placed on his shoulders by America's premier Enlightenment exemplar Jefferson, American's greatest optimist, one of the most intensely verbal and productive men in American history, and one of the most organized and mentally disciplined men who ever lived. Clark only answered to Lewis. Lewis answered to a man who was called by some the Lama or Sage of Monticello. That sage rewarded Lewis by appointing him to a post for which he was not suited, the tangled and controversial duties of which prevented Lewis from writing his book.

Because I am willing to look at Lewis as an imperfect man as well as an American hero, it may be thought that I do not particularly like the subject of this book. That is precisely the opposite of how I feel. I admire Lewis deeply—much more than I would if he were a better adjusted, more reliable, less tightly wound explorer. I regard Lewis as dramatically more interesting than any other member of the expedition, more multi-dimensional, more nuanced, more romantic, more complicated, more unresolved. Wallace Stegner called for a "society to match the scenery" of the American West. I believe that we also need men and women who are wired to hear the voices of the wilderness. Meriwether Lewis was just such a man. It is possible he was too much such a man. I have written this book in part because I believe that Lewis studies are caught between the Scylla of the unfortunate murder-suicide debate, and the Charybdis of historians, like Stephen Ambrose, who like to argue that Lewis and Clark were partners of such harmony that they enjoyed the "best friendship in American history." I begin my study by accepting that Lewis was a problematic individual, including problematic to his friend Clark, that he was, in the final analysis of the great Lewis and Clark scholar James Ronda, "a brash, brooding, often quite unpleasant young man," who "could be both courageous and insufferably arrogant."[6] My view is that if you want to understand the Lewis and Clark Expedition, you must wrestle with the problem of Meriwether Lewis, and not merely the manner of his death. Lewis and Clark studies should begin, I feel, by decoupling the captains and letting each one establish his own character and his own voice.

That Lewis was a man who wrestled with what Carl Jung calls *the shadow* does not diminish him in my estimation. I have found myself emboldened to probe deeper into the mysteries of the Lewis and Clark Expedition by reading the essays of James Ronda. In his book *Finding the West: Explorations with Lewis and Clark*, Ronda wrote, "And in our own time there are some who insist on recounting the journey as manly adventure wrapped in heroic courage, denying the travelers their humanity as fallible, often complaining human beings."[7] I find Buzz Aldrin more interesting than Neil Armstrong. I find George Crook more interesting than George Armstrong Custer, Samuel Taylor Coleridge more interesting than William Wordsworth, John Lennon more interesting than Paul McCartney. I find Achilles more interesting than Odysseus, though I also greatly admire "the man who was never at a loss." I find Richard Francis Burton more interesting than John Speke, Mary more interesting than Martha, and Jefferson more interesting than Adams or Madison. And I definitely find Lewis more interesting than that estimable man William Clark. I do not find anything insufficient about Clark. I greatly admire him, and I regard Lewis's hiring of Clark to be his partner in discovery as unquestionably the best decision he ever made. I would rather go on a long camping trip with Clark than with Lewis. I would trust Clark to mail an important letter before I would turn to Lewis. But I would rather attempt to tease out the mystery of Meriwether Lewis than to gaze in admiration at William Clark.

Lewis's prose speaks to me. Nobody ever wished that Lewis wrote less than he did. When he was fully engaged with the journey, when the switch was on, he easily wrote the most interesting prose of any of the journal keepers. His journal entries are precise, masterful, often lyrical. His journal entries are self-conscious in the best sense of the term. Lewis was always aware that he was not just traveling through undiscovered country west of the Mississippi River, but that he was an explorer in a tradition that extended back through James Cook and Christopher Columbus all the way to Pytheas and Herodotus. Lewis's journal entries, when he bothered to provide them, are easily the most compelling and multifaceted of any member of the expedition. Jefferson was right when he wrote, in 1813, that Lewis exhibited "a fidelity to truth so scrupulous that whatever he should report would be as certain as if seen by ourselves."[8]

It need hardly be said that history is never a settled matter. The past is not only a foreign country, but a foreign country whose *language* we seldom know how to speak.[9] History is an untidy and bewildering set of facts—to the extent that they can be uncovered and pinned down at all—upon which well meaning people attempt to impose narrative order. History is like a puzzle for which most of the pieces have been lost, and we are left to reconstruct what happened from promising but potentially misleading fragments. Ironically, this is particularly true of the Lewis and Clark expedition, in spite of the journal keepers' status as the "writingest explorers of their time."[10] Virtually every book of history makes the past seem more orderly than it actually was. At some point in the mid-twentieth century the standard narrative of the expedition got set, as if in mythological concrete. The narrative and interpretive lines were laid down principally by the great Bernard DeVoto. His abridged edition of the journals of Lewis and Clark (1953), together with his magisterial *The Course of Empire* (1952), shaped the narrative understanding of several generations of Lewis and Clark aficionados. Virtually no Lewis and Clark buff older than forty is without a copy of DeVoto's abridgement in her or his collection. It is always stunning to realize that once a narrative and interpretive line gets into the consciousness of the people, it acquires a historical tenacity that is virtually impossible to correct or displace. James W. Loewen's *Lies My Teacher Told Me: Everything Your American History Textbook Got Wrong*,[11] examines this remarkable phenomenon in great detail.

The Lewis and Clark bicentennial has come and gone. Tens of millions of dollars of funding were appropriated by Congress and state legislatures to commemorate the 1804–06 journey. Dozens of books and documentary films were released. Seminars, symposia, lecture series, conferences, exhibits, and fifteen national signature events were hosted across the United States, beginning with the commemorative launch at Monticello on January 18, 2003. It was as exhaustive and emphatic a historical commemoration as has ever occurred in American history.[12] And yet, after all that "throwing about of brains," as Hamlet puts it,[13] I now hardly ever enter into a general discussion of Lewis and Clark without hearing that *Sacagawea was their guide*, that *Lewis and Clark wouldn't have survived if it hadn't been for the generosity of the Indians*, that *Sacagawea lived to be nearly 100 and died on the Wind River Indian Reservation*, and that *those two captains fathered a bunch of Indian children all across the American West*.

Thanks to the cultural studies movement, including postmodernism, we now know that the kind of history you see and write depends on the lens you choose to wear. As historians craft their narratives of historical events, they look at them from a certain perspective. The lens they wear—and frequently don't know they wear—determines and distorts what they see. A perfect example of the benefit of new lenses is Kathleen Dalton's *Theodore Roosevelt:*

A Strenuous Life.[14] Dalton, who teaches at Phillips Academy in Andover, Massachusetts, donned a womanist lens as she researched her extraordinary biography of Theodore Roosevelt. The result was an entirely fresh look at the 26th president, with a special emphasis on the women in his world, family life, gender relations in the early twentieth century, and the social history of TR's era. Stories and dynamics that have been ignored by previous biographers— or for that matter were literally invisible to them—suddenly popped into focus. She did not challenge or dismiss the existing narrative of Roosevelt's life, but her research showed that that narrative was not the whole story. As the twenty-first century begins, more than ever before, history lends itself to a wide variety of lenses. Thanks to the pioneering work of James Ronda and the multicultural emphasis of the bicentennial, virtually everyone who studies Lewis and Clark today wears at least two lenses, one Eurocentric (the old history) and another that attempts to understand and honor the role of native cultures in the story (the new history).

I come at Lewis and Clark as a humanities scholar not as a historian per se. All of my academic work has been in English and classical literature. I think of myself primarily as a close reader of texts. Although I am deeply enamored of the Lewis and Clark Expedition, I do not regard myself as a protector of the story or of any of the participants. I like history best when it is untidy, and I am more likely to wish to re-complicate the story than to simplify it or accept the received tradition unskeptically.

What I have learned from examining the expedition's journals and letters for many years is that things that the journal keepers wrote can seldom be accepted at face value as historical writ. Given all that they experienced over twenty-eight months in at least four distinct bioregions, among dozens of Indian tribes, and in a range of climates and seasons, only a rather arbitrary fragment of their overall experience found its way to paper. At no point did any journal keeper step back to provide character sketches of the men, describe the style and physique of Sacagawea, or provide a complete portrait of even a single day in the life of the expedition. The silences of the journals—deliberate or inadvertent—are as interesting as what the journal keepers actually report. What the journal keepers do report is inevitably incomplete, Eurocentric, limited by a range of factors, and frequently biased. This does not mean that what they report is unreliable. It merely means that it does not tell the whole story. It reminds us that the work of a good historian is to attempt to bring other lenses to the experience in an attempt to tell a fuller, richer, often more unsatisfying story.

This study of Lewis and Clark has benefited greatly from a pair of little known journals kept by agents of the North West Company in 1804–05. When Lewis and Clark reached the Mandan and Hidatsa villages in today's North Dakota, they were surprised and disturbed to find a number of Canadian traders and agents *embedded* among the earthlodge Indians, particularly the Hidatsa. In the course of the expedition's long winter in North Dakota, traders representing the North West and Hudson's Bay Company came and went from trade forts along the Assiniboine River in today's Manitoba. Lewis and Clark got to know three of these men quite well: Hugh Heney, whom they would later attempt to hire as an American agent; Charles McKenzie, who wrote a fascinating and critical account of his encounters with the Americans; and François-Antoine Larocque, who actually sought permission to join Lewis and Clark on their journey west of Fort Mandan. The accounts that McKenzie and Larocque wrote of their meetings with Lewis and Clark are remarkable and historically essential documents that deserve a much larger place in Lewis and Clark studies than they have so far been accorded. Their reports are available in a scholarly edition co-edited by W. Raymond Wood and Thomas D. Thiessen.[15] The fact that many Lewis and Clark scholars have ignored these rich journals is unfortunate but not surprising. They enable us to triangulate, to see our favorite subject through a wonderful set of lenses that were worn by fellow white men who were not Americans. In *River of Promise: Lewis and Clark on the Columbia*, historian David Nicandri demonstrates how often Lewis and Clark consulted their edition of Alexander Mackenzie's *Voyages from Montreal*, which was part of the traveling library they carted to the Pacific Ocean and back again. Nicandri has written, "The American explorers emulated a number of Mackenzie's tactics, as any frontiersman may have been expected to deploy, but in addition the captains often echoed, and... even plagiarized many textual passages."[16] At times Lewis and Clark simply incorporated sentences and whole passages of Mackenzie into their journals. Their steady though often unacknowledged reference to Mackenzie's book amounts to something like an obsession, particularly in the Columbia watershed. And yet most Lewis and Clark scholars mention Mackenzie merely for the purpose of describing the "Sputnik" moment that threw Jefferson into a panic and inspired him at last to fulfill his lifelong dream of getting a reconnaissance party into the deep interior of the continent.

The fact is that Lewis and Clark scholars have generally ignored Mackenzie's journeys; the two contemporary journeys of Zebulon Pike; the incessant peripatetics of David Thompson; Nicholas Biddle's 1805 journey to Greece and the Adriatic; the visits a generation earlier of Samuel Johnson and James Boswell to the highlands of Scotland and the Hebrides; Mungo Park's contemporary exploration of Africa; the journals of Alexander Henry, Charles McKenzie, and François-Antoine Larocque; and Captain Cook's accounts of his voyages. It is past time to blow open the self-contained and self-satisfied "universe" of the Lewis and Clark story, and to place the Corps of Volunteers for North Western Discovery in a series of successively wider contexts, beginning with contemporary explorers and traders who actually mention Lewis and Clark in their journals and letters.

Nor should any study of Lewis and Clark fail to examine the journals of Prince Maximilian of Wied-Neuwied, now finally available in a superb edition published by the University of Oklahoma Press. Maximilian met Clark in March 1833, traveled with copies of the Clark's Missouri River maps and with the Biddle-Allen edition of the journals, met individuals, including Charbonneau, who remembered the 1804–06 expedition, and referred repeatedly to the experiences of Lewis and Clark.

James Ronda has long called for a wider perspective on Lewis and Clark. So has historian Elliott West. In his brilliant essay, "Finding Lewis and Clark by Looking Away," West wrote, "When we find an intriguing subject, we naturally are drawn into its flow of events. If its details are especially interesting and full of puzzles, we get caught up in chasing every lead into every evidentiary cranny. With that, we tend to lose sight of our subject's wider arena, which leaves us facing an annoying paradox. The more we concentrate on what we study, the less we understand."[17]

My approach is to use both the microscope and a wide-angle lens at more or less the same time. Most of the arguments (and I hope insights) of this book are the result of a very close reading of the journal texts. It is my opinion that scholars have spent so much time using the journals as the basis for a linear narrative of the great adventure that we have failed to examine them as rich, nuanced, perplexing, and often self-contradictory texts. At the same time we have failed to *place* Lewis and Clark in the larger context of the history of exploration, particularly what has been called "the second great age of discovery," the eighteenth and first half of the nineteenth century.

I have also given special attention in this book to Thomas Jefferson, the patron of the expedition. Although Jefferson was not the sort of man who could have ventured into the wilderness with Meriwether Lewis, his presence must have been felt by Lewis at every turn. Unlike his more robust father Peter, Jefferson never fought a bear or slept in a tree or experienced frostbite. But, like his father, Jefferson was intensely curious about the American West, and he micromanaged the Lewis and Clark Expedition as much as that was possible given the extremely primitive communications technologies of his era. The influence of Jefferson on his protégé Lewis is everywhere apparent—in Lewis's imitation of Jefferson's idiosyncratic orthography, in Lewis's concern about keeping the Federalists in Congress happy with the expedition's purposes, progress, discoveries, and expenditures, in Lewis's doomed love affair with his favorite Jeffersonian *gimcrack*, his iron framed boat *Experiment*, and in Lewis's deism and Anglophobia. It is important to remember that Lewis spent as much time living with Jefferson in the White House, sleeping in the East Room, drinking Jefferson's exquisite wines, as he did representing Jefferson in the howling wilderness, sleeping on animal skins, and enjoying "our only beverage *pure water*."[18]

Lewis even owned one of the polygraphs that Jefferson was in the habit of giving to his closest friends.

I lavish attention on Jefferson because he is inherently interesting, because Lewis belonged to the same social class of Virginia planters, because during the White House years Lewis adopted a Jeffersonian lifestyle in dramatic contrast to the buffalo and *boudin blanc* diet he subsisted on in the West, and because Jefferson not only launched the expedition but provided its bookend documents: his instructions to Lewis on June 20, 1803, and his biographical sketch of Lewis in 1813.

My thinking about Lewis has been shaped by endless reading and musing and hiking, and by three conversations. The first was with the late Stephen Ambrose (1936–2002). His daughter Stephenie Ambrose Tubbs and I are friends and fellow travelers on the Lewis and Clark Trail, particularly through the White Cliffs of the Missouri River east of Fort Benton. I got to know Steve pretty well in the last years of his life and we had a dozen or so serious conversations about Lewis and Clark, Crazy Horse and Custer, and Richard Nixon. (My father Charles E. Jenkinson was a Nixon-hater before it was cool. One of the highlights of his life was hearing Stephen Ambrose lecture on Nixon at the National Archives.) Knowing Steve was a bit like knowing Mark Twain or Theodore Roosevelt—the more you shut up and listen the more you are likely to benefit. Steve was a master storyteller, a fine historian, a celebrity, a character, and a curmudgeon, in something like that order. He was fond of the idea that Lewis and Clark developed the *greatest friendship in American history*, which is an inherently problematic thing to claim for any number of reasons, but an immensely popular notion, especially if your voice gets a little husky as you speak about it.

We were in Helena, Montana, once, eating dinner at the Montana Club, and with some trepidation I asked Ambrose—who was absolutely certain that Lewis committed suicide—whether that incident was related or unrelated to the great journey. In other words, did Lewis's suicide have something to do with the sum total of his experiences between May 14, 1804, and September 23, 1806, or did he return from the journey fully intact—and for some unrelated reason later spiraled downward into mental disarray? In his characteristically gruff and confident way, Ambrose looked at me directly and said, "Nuthin to do with the trip."

With respect to one of America's greatest historians, I disagreed with Ambrose the moment he said this, and have come to disagree much more over time. I believe that Lewis was a gifted but unstable man long before Jefferson sent him into the West, that the fissure in his soul was somehow widened by his experiences in the wilderness, that he had, as David Nicandri has argued, a kind of slow motion nervous breakdown on the return journey in 1806, and that he had severe re-entry problems following his return to civilization. Still, I have such respect for Ambrose that, since that dinner in 1999, I have never again thought about Lewis' last days without giving weight to his conclusion. That the legendary Ambrose should perish before the bicentennial really heated up is a source of great sadness to all who knew his work and his gruff and doughty spirit.

The second conversation was really a sustained dialogue with David Nicandri, the executive director of the Washington Historical Society in Tacoma, Washington. I first encountered Nicandri long, long ago in a Jefferson context, but as the bicentennial of the Lewis and Clark Expedition began to unfold we began to see each other at gatherings along the trail all over the country. I never miss an opportunity of listening to Nicandri lecture. He is always on to something interesting and he has a wonderful delivery as a lecturer, not to mention a marvelously Latinate vocabulary. He's a man after my own heart because he believes that intellectual enquiry, no matter how serious, is a form of play, that historians should take more joy in their work and express that joy in public, and that a spirit of playfulness invariably enriches the historiographical experience. Nicandri is not afraid to take historical risks. He is that rarest of beings: a very serious historian who doesn't take himself too seriously. He has a surprisingly thick skin for one of this tribe, and he is much more likely to laugh—his hearty, lusty laugh—when publicly challenged than to get his back up. He has taken me to Station Camp out near the end of the trail. There he explained everything, including the workings of the Pythagorean Theorem.

In the middle of the bicentennial I became aware that Nicandri was writing a book on Lewis and Clark on the Columbia River, the most neglected chapter in the story of the great adventure. In several different phases of that book's gestation, I had the honor of being one of Nicandri's principal advisors and peer reviewers. Eventually I became his editor in my capacity as the director of the new Dakota Institute Press at the Lewis & Clark Fort Mandan Foundation. Dave and I went through his manuscript over and over—in person and on the phone—until I knew his book just about as well as he did. *River of Promise: Lewis and Clark on the Columbia* is not primarily about Meriwether Lewis, but of course no serious book about the expedition can fail to wrestle with Lewis, and Nicandri does it with boldness, insight, and exuberance. My own thinking has been deeply influenced by Nicandri's work, his creativity, and his attempt to look with fresh eyes at a story we have all come to take for granted.

That set of sustained and mutually respectful dialogues has been one of the finest experiences of my life. You spend your entire life looking for such moments—a friendship in which you share a body of literature and can talk about it in a clever shorthand and with such mutual understanding of the breadth and intricacies of the story that it is like talking to your better self, but with a different set of lenses and perspectives. There is no element of Lewis's remarkable life that we have not discussed and sometimes debated. We are both admirers of Lewis, both suicidists, both believers that the story is far more complicated than we have been led to believe.

Nicandri has taught me more or less everything I know about Lewis's experiences between Lewiston, Idaho and Astoria, Oregon. He has challenged my conclusions about Lewis as a true intellectual friend should, and he has independently confirmed enough of my basic understanding of *the Lewis perplex* (as he might put it) to give me the confidence that I am herein at least on the right track. In particular, Nicandri has deepened my understanding of Lewis in two ways. First, he has done pioneering scholarly work on what we together call *the dynamics of the journals*. By this we mean the way in which the journals that we all know and quote came to be written, copied, and preserved. It's an immensely complicated and rich subject, but at the core of it is this insight: the journal keepers did not usually sit around the campfire at the end of the day with pen in hand writing in the journals that now repose in the vaults of the American Philosophical Society. My great mentor in the Lewis and Clark world, Stephen Dow Beckham of Lewis and Clark College in Portland, himself an avid, even obsessive, journal keeper, including field journals, has examined the originals at the APS and he concludes, unhesitatingly, that these national treasures *were never opened* on the Lewis and Clark trail, because if they had been we would find dead mosquitoes, blood, sweat, and maybe tears, water-warped pages, and other signs of actual field use, no matter how carefully Lewis and Clark tried to protect them from the elements.

An example of the problem of the dynamics of the journals is Lewis's entry for April 7, 1805, which I discuss at length in chapter one of this book. That famous passage feels not like a daily diary entry but like the first draft of the kind of book Lewis wanted to write about his travels. Did he actually compose the passage on the day that the expedition left Fort Mandan? Or did he write it during the idle winter at Fort Clatsop from his own field notes or from Clark's journal? Or when he returned to St. Louis in 1806? What relation does the grandiloquent passage bear to the actual journal that Lewis kept between April 7, 1805 and August 26, 1805? What relation does that sustained "journal" have to Lewis's daily jottings in the field? Did Lewis expect his publisher to work from his corrected journal with additions and interlineations in the manner, say, of James Boswell's manuscript of the *Life of Samuel Johnson*?[19] Of the material that we still have in Lewis's hand, how much was written in the field and how much at the times of leisure that Jefferson imagined in his instructions to Lewis? How can we possibly sort out these questions? And if we could somehow reconstruct the manner in which the final journals of the Lewis and Clark Expedition were created or assembled, what would we learn about the journey that we do not already know, if anything? These and many more questions are subsumed under the phrase *dynamics of the journals*. Nobody has done a better job than Nicandri in beginning to sort all of this out.

I do not believe that we can ever fully understand Meriwether Lewis. He was a gifted and an odd man. I believe I understand him better than most others—otherwise I would not have written this book—but I cheerfully admit that I feel flummoxed in the face of the mystery and the problem of Meriwether Lewis. That the depression that gripped him after the return of the expedition had something to do with his inability to find a wife seems to me certain, but I cannot begin to understand why he was unsuccessful in love. He was a good-looking man, a man of remarkable physical energy, and a successful explorer. He was at some level a national hero. A friend to the president of the United States, an army captain, and a man of destiny who led a company of adventurers across the American continent, should be able to find a woman who will marry him. Nowadays some people quietly reckon that Lewis must have been a homosexual. It seems more likely to me that he was asexual. Nobody knows for sure.

Nor can I understand why he couldn't write his book. He was an able writer. His mind was capacious. In spite of his own misgivings about his ability to capture in words the sublimity of the Great Falls, he had a particular gift for heightened prose. The deep melancholic Dr. Johnson (1709–84) famously said, "A man may write at any time, if he will set himself *doggedly* to it."[20] Had Lewis used the period between his return on September 23, 1806, and the day he arrived in St. Louis to take up his governorship, March 8, 1808, to work doggedly on his book, he would have been able to complete the task, or at least give himself enough momentum to be able to continue to plug away at it, no matter how busy he became. The great set pieces of Lewis's journal—first encounter with the Shoshone, the discovery and exploration of the Great Falls, particularly the magical day of June 14, 1805, the bloody skirmish with the Blackfeet on the return journey, setting out from Fort Mandan, first view of the Rocky Mountains, reaching the source of the Missouri River—are a tantalizing fragmentary indication of what his book would have been had he completed the task. In fact, it is my opinion that those passages were not field notes at all, but drafts of the book that Lewis was attempting to write, composed long after the events he describes. I do not believe that all of them were written in the field. Maybe not any of them.

The third conversation took place at Higgins Restaurant in downtown Portland in 2003. As the Lewis and Clark scholar-in-residence at Lewis and Clark College, one of my happiest responsibilities was to work with a truly remarkable woman named Sherry Manning to organize a series of four public humanities symposia on aspects of the expedition.[21] At the suggestion of our friend Christopher Zinn, we invited the great nature essayist Barry Lopez to the second of our symposia. Lopez is perhaps best known for his 1986 book *Arctic Dreams*, but I first became acquainted with his writing when a friend gave me *River Notes* and *Desert Notes* in 1985. Lopez is a man of grace. I regard him as a vatic writer and a kind of nature sage. It was with a considerable feeling of intimidation that I joined the dinner party. When we had put aside our desire for eating and drinking, as Homer puts it in the *Iliad*, I asked Lopez how he saw Meriwether Lewis. He looked off into the air for a few seconds and said, "The question is how far you can go out and still come back." There was a long pause, as if I (or he) had just consulted the Oracle at Delphi. Then he said, "It may be that Lewis ventured too far and he was unable to come back."

That has seemed to me to be one of the handful of greatest insights I have ever come upon in my study of Lewis and Clark. It immediately resonated with my special interest in Lewis's experiences between his "discovery" of the source of the Missouri River on August 12, 1805, and the council the expedition held with Cameahwait and the Shoshone Indians on August 17, 1805. It also helps to explain Lewis's re-entry issues following the safe return of the expedition to St. Louis. Lopez's insight helps us to understand Meriwether Lewis without pretending to pluck out the heart of his mystery. After all, Lewis and Clark made the same journey or very nearly so, and yet one of them clearly did not venture too far, while the other did. How two men of similar backgrounds and career paths could make the same journey differently is one of the mysteries of the human condition. I address it in the last chapter of this book, "Why?"

Mystery is the stuff of history. The life of Adolf Hitler is one of the best-documented lives of the twentieth century. He has been written about from virtually every possible point of view. His public speeches and for that matter his most banal table talk have been pored over by historians, psychologists, pathologists, philosophers, journalists, people who never met him, as well as people who knew him for years or decades, and yet we don't really know what made him what he was. As long as there is western civilization Hitler will be the subject of unending study.

We know that George Armstrong Custer was killed in Montana on June 25, 1876, when he blundered into a Lakota and Cheyenne encampment that was magnitudes larger than he had expected to find, but to this day we don't really know what happened on the bluffs overlooking the Little Big Horn River. If we knew what happened, if we discovered anachronistic satellite footage of the momentous events of that day, much of the mystery would be solved, and the Custer story would be much less compelling to professional and amateur historians alike. But we would still not know what passed through Custer's mind in those last hours, whether he would have split his command and attacked the Lakota and Cheyenne village no matter how many lodges he saw there, or whether he would have pulled back, at least long enough to permit Generals Terry and Gibbon to catch up. Did Custer throw his life away knowing that, as they say of Elvis, his death would be a *great career move*, or did he fully expect to triumph over the hostile tribes no matter how many warriors they could muster? It's a mystery.

The Lewis and Clark story is particularly rich in mystery. We don't know what happened to the dog. We don't know why Charbonneau brought only one of his two Shoshone wives with him on the journey in the spring of 1805. We don't know for sure when (or where) Sacagawea was born and we don't know for sure when (or where) she died. In fact, we don't know if Sah-cah-gar-we-a was how she pronounced her name or if that is what those who knew her best called her. We don't know what George Drouillard did in today's Iowa that offended his commanders (August 3, 1804). We don't know why Lewis was silent for extended periods of the journey. We don't know why Thomas Jefferson was uncharacteristically understated in the letters he wrote about the expedition after Lewis returned to civilization. One would have expected the Enlightenment *philosophe* of Monticello to write tens of thousands of words about the discoveries of Lewis and Clark—in cartography, in natural history, in ethnology, in geography—but in fact Jefferson wrote merely a handful of letters in response to the journey and most of them were logistical rather than substantive: e.g., have the journals been properly deposited with the American Philosophical Society?; or have you received the seeds of Arikara tobacco I forwarded to you last year?[22]

We don't know what Lewis wrote in his letter from New Madrid to William Clark on or about September 11, 1809. And of course we don't ultimately know whether he killed himself or was killed by someone else on October 11, 1809. If he did kill himself, we don't finally know why.

There is nothing mysterious about William Clark. He was a man of enormous resourcefulness. He was far more intelligent than his spelling and grammar suggest. He did more to make the expedition a success than any other person, including Lewis. In lectures I often say that in many respects it should be called the Clark and Lewis Expedition. He kept both feet on the ground throughout a long and productive life. He was a loyal friend, a superb government functionary, a level headed and rational man who made it his mission to do the right thing even when he was ill, weary, miserable, or otherwise engaged. Even his post-expedition treatment of his slaves, particularly York, and his role in helping dispossess American Indians of their homelands, are entirely predictable and—given the times in which he lived—not very surprising. Scratch a member of the Virginia gentry between 1743 and 1890 and you get: Thomas Jefferson or William Clark. Clark was a totally reliable man. We don't really know much about the inner depths of his soul because he preferred to keep that area private. He found it easy to re-enter after the journey. He was married within fifteen months of the return, and he fathered eight children over the next two decades. In other words, unlike his distinguished partner in discovery, he was possessed of a healthy and normal sexuality and he was socially well adjusted. He picked up the pieces of the publication project after Lewis's untimely death, and though he was clearly annoyed that *that task, too*, devolved on him, he saw it through with his usual good sense and discipline. It is hard to point to a single William Clark mystery. He was a man with a good head and a strong heart and a deep generosity of spirit. He faced life head on. He did not let his actions or his judgments become clouded with romanticism or an inflated commitment to the personal honor code of his era. He found it possible to live and work with difficult persons: George Rogers Clark, Meriwether Lewis, Manuel Lisa, Frederick Bates, and William Eustis. He seems to have liked Indians, both as tribes and as individuals, and he had the capacity to see them as human beings, not as Mr. Jefferson's exemplars of sylvan republicanism. He was a good keeper of records.

A man possessed of so many admirable qualities—a natural leader and a natural follower—can never be regarded as boring, but because Clark was so perfectly well-adjusted, it is hard to find him quite so interesting as the whimsical genius Jefferson, or the mercurial Lewis, or the unknowable and sometimes surprisingly opinionated Sacagawea.

In my opinion, the bicentennial of the Lewis and Clark Expedition represented an important corrective. By the time it was over, Clark's role as a key or perhaps the key player in the expedition was widely acknowledged. (At the same time, thanks to the three bicentennial biographies, by Landon Jones, William Foley, and Jay Buckley, Clark's post-expedition reputation has been permanently diminished). In the last ten years, York has ceased to be a buffoon figure, a sexual athlete and Indian village vaudevillian, and become instead a man of dignity and, in the minds of some, a kind of African-American freedom fighter. Sacagawea is more highly respected and beloved than ever, if that is even possible, now that she has ceased to be regarded as the guide of the expedition and has taken her more verifiable place as a plucky and resourceful interpreter and wilderness diplomat. Lewis and Jefferson both come out of the bicentennial diminished, Jefferson because he set in motion the twin juggernauts of American Indian policy—removal and assimilation—and Lewis both because he was edgy about so many issues, and because it is now widely recognized that without Clark he might not have been successful. Indians generally are up, white people generally are down in the public understanding of the expedition. Minor figures like John Shields and Francois Labiche have received more attention than ever before, because they are no longer regarded as interchangeable ciphers. In my own edition of the journals for the North Dakota phase of the odyssey, *A Vast and Open Plain: The Writings of the Lewis and Clark Expedition in North Dakota,* I have tried to improve the reputation of Charbonneau.

We now have excellent biographies of Clark, each sufficiently different in perspective and detail to give us for the first time a full understanding of Clark's life. Oddly enough, we still don't have an adequate biography of Sacagawea. The best book we have on that subject is Donna Kessler's *The Making of Sacagawea: A Euro-American Legend*. It's outstanding, but it is a specialist's book and a postmodern book and therefore has not been widely enough read to influence the Sacagawea discourse. Nor do we have anything like a complete biography of Lewis. Richard Dillon's biography is still essential, and Thomas Danisi and John Jackson's *Meriwether Lewis* is important for the light it sheds on the three years that Lewis lived after his return from the Pacific Ocean. But it's not so much a biography as an administrative history of Lewis's tenure as the governor of Louisiana Territory. The book deliberately ignores the great journey—which would be like writing about Shakespeare without bothering to examine the poems and plays, or about Columbus without the journeys to the New World. In my view, Danisi and Jackson have worked so hard to normalize Lewis—to reclaim him from the notion that he was a bipolar or manic depressive man, an alcoholic, and a drug addict—that they wind up over-compensating, and fail to grapple with the unmistakable fissures in Lewis's character and temperament. Stephen Ambrose's *Undaunted Courage* was marketed as a biography of Lewis, but it is in fact precisely what the public sees in it, a full account of the journey that reads like a novel. When Ambrose attempts to come to terms with the eccentricities of Lewis's life and character, he is, in my view, less interesting than when he is telling the story of the great adventure.

This book is *not* a biography of Lewis. It makes no attempt to provide a complete account of his life or provide a running narrative of the Lewis and Clark Expedition. My purpose is to examine, elucidate, analyze, and admire the life and character of Meriwether Lewis. My dream for this book is that it will come to be accepted as a careful and probing exploration of the life of an extraordinary, complicated, and problematic man. My dream—and we don't get what we don't aim for—is that this book will be regarded as required reading for anyone who wants to try to make sense of Lewis. My Lewis is a man of genius and a man of destiny, a gifted explorer and a marvelous writer. Indeed, I believe if you took Lewis out of the picture and launched the expedition into the wilderness under the sole command of William Clark, there would have been no bicentennial. A Clark Expedition would have been more interesting than the contemporary journeys of Zebulon Pike, but it would not have captured the imagination of the American people as it has done with Lewis at least technically in the lead. The expedition was the brainchild of Thomas Jefferson and no other. The first two presidents would not have sent such a "literary" expedition into the wilderness, and the next two presidents would not have done so either. Lewis was Jefferson's protégé, friend, aide de camp, errand boy, private correspondence secretary, Congressional liaison, military adviser, and—to a certain extent—surrogate son.

My method is to examine the available texts lovingly and rigorously, not for the purpose of extracting a narrative of the expedition, but to learn what I can about the character of Meriwether Lewis and in search of clues that might help us understand the mystery that hovers about him. The publication of the authoritative University of Nebraska edition of the *Journals of the Lewis and Clark Expedition*, edited by Gary Moulton, has led such scholars as David Nicandri and Thomas Slaughter, among others, to call for a completely fresh reading of the journals of Lewis and Clark and the other journal keepers. I fully agree with Slaughter's view that "If they [the journals] are less reliable guides to external events than we have long believed, they are better guides to the interior wilderness—the minds and hearts of the explorers—than we have appreciated."[23] I agree, too, with Slaughter's view that "Accepting the journals' complexities renders them no less valuable. Indeed, they are more revealing, richer, and much more useful than generally recognized. They simply merit closer readings, alert to their possibilities."[24]

That is precisely my view and, in this study, my intention.

Clay S. Jenkinson

Fractured Soul

THOMAS JEFFERSON HAD NO SON. MERIWETHER LEWIS'S FATHER William, a soldier in America's revolutionary cause, died of pneumonia in November 1779. Meriwether Lewis was five years old. His mother Lucy remarried within six months and after the war moved the family out of Virginia to the frontier along the Broad River in Georgia. We know nothing of Lewis's relations with his stepfather.

In 1801, the fifty-seven-year-old Jefferson, now the president of the United States, invited twenty-six-year-old Meriwether Lewis to move to the new national capital to serve as his private correspondence secretary. Jefferson's Monticello was located only a few miles from Locust Hill, the plantation of the Lewis family in Albemarle County, Virginia. Jefferson knew Lewis's parents and he had been aware of Meriwether's wilderness skills and interest in the American West for many years. America's greatest exemplar of the Enlightenment and the young army captain lived together in the White House for two years and three months before Lewis embarked upon his great journey. Lewis, possessed of what he called "my governing passion for rambling,"[1] had been dreaming of leading an exploration party into the American interior since he was a boy. He later called the expedition "a darling project of mine for the last ten years."

Jefferson chose Lewis to lead the expedition. Lewis, in turn, chose Clark to be his partner in discovery. It was the most intelligent decision Meriwether Lewis ever made. Together they led a group of several dozen young men and eventually a woman and child on a transcontinental journey of diplomacy and exploration and that took them all the way to the Pacific Ocean and back again, a distance of 7,689 miles. They lost only one of their recruits, Charles Floyd, to natural causes, in the first year of travel. On the return journey in 1806, Lewis and three of his subordinates killed two young Piegan Blackfeet men on the upper Marias River in today's Montana. They were acting, they believed, in self-defense.

Lewis was a tightly wound, high-strung, high-toned, self-punishing man who was prone to what Jefferson called "sensible depressions of mind."[2] He was also an enormously gifted and determined explorer, a brilliant, often lyrical writer, and a man of great integrity.

Lewis returned to what he regarded as civilization on September 23, 1806. He was soon a national hero. His boon companion William Clark lost no time in getting married and starting a family in St. Louis, where he served the Jefferson and Madison administrations as a territorial superintendent of Indian affairs. In spite of some strenuous efforts, Lewis never found a wife and never, so far as we know, fathered any children. Thus Lewis and his best friend found themselves moving in different directions in the years that followed their return.

For reasons that remain mysterious, Lewis had serious re-entry issues. In spite or perhaps because of Jefferson's importuning, he found it impossible to write his book about the great journey. He had a difficult tenure as the territorial governor of Louisiana Territory. He experienced health problems, particularly from the effects of malaria. He got crosswise with the War Department in Washington that superintended territorial affairs. He essentially broke off contact with his mentor Thomas Jefferson. Nobody knows why.

Jefferson, a man who had always cherished his private life at Monticello yet had served in virtually every public capacity the American republic had to offer, retired from the presidency in March 1809 and renounced public life, just as Lewis's personal and public difficulties reached a crisis point. Jefferson was, therefore, unable to help or protect his protégé in a dispute with the War Department that would have seemed like a routine annoyance to anyone who did not take himself as seriously or push himself as hard as did Lewis.

Meriwether Lewis died violently in a crude frontier hostelry on the Natchez Trace, on October 11, 1809, of a gunshot to his head and another to his abdomen. He was thirty-five years old. He almost certainly committed suicide.

It *is* certain that he was a fractured soul.

CHAPTER I   Getting There First

> "Companions create narrative
>
> problems for the explorer."
>
> —Thomas Slaughter, *Exploring Lewis and Clark*[1]

LONG AFTER THE DEATH OF MERIWETHER LEWIS, WHEN Nicholas Biddle was turning the raw documents of the Lewis and Clark Expedition into a publishable book, he wrote to William Clark to ask him a rather delicate question. Biddle was aware that the two leaders of the expedition had called each other co-captain and that he was publishing a book not about the Lewis expedition, as Jefferson would have considered it, but the Lewis *and Clark* expedition. Biddle was also aware that Clark had not actually been a captain in the US Army, where such titles are taken very seriously and nobody is permitted to inflate his rank just because he feels entitled to. Biddle wanted to know how Clark saw the relationship between himself and his late friend and—implicitly—how he should handle the co-captaincy issue in the publication. In a carefully periphrastic way, Biddle asked about "the exact relative situation in point of rank & command between Captain Lewis & yourself."[2] Biddle must have been apprehensive about Clark's likely reaction to the query. In an earlier draft of the letter he had written, "I am very desirous of having that matter settled, so as to prevent the possibility of any unpleasant reflections in future on the part of the friends of either of you."[3]

Clark's response was emphatic: *"equal in every point of view."*[4] Clark's full sentence reads, "You express a desire to know the exact relation which I stood in Point of Rank, and Command with Captain Lewis—equal in every point of view."[5] Given the unequivocal nature of this reply, having done due diligence on a matter of great sensitivity, and having given Clark an opportunity to insist that proper military protocols be observed, that was how Biddle wrote the story. Lewis and Clark: co-captains. That has been how Lewis and Clark have been understood ever since.

The relationship between Meriwether Lewis and William Clark was much more complicated than Biddle indicated, much more tangled, rich, nuanced, and occasionally vexed than most historians have suggested.

Had Lewis still been alive, Biddle would not have written this letter to Clark on June 28, 1811. Lewis would have borne the burden of deciding how to present the expedition's command structure to the readers of his book, a book that he intended to write largely based on Clark's journals, but apparently without any other significant input from his partner in discovery. In other words, had Lewis lived, the delicacy of clarifying the *co-captaincy* of the expedition would have devolved upon him alone.

Making sense of the relationship between Lewis and Clark depends on which lens one wears. From the perspective of the overall success of the expedition and its daily operations, Clark turned out to be the more important leader. On any given day, it was Clark who was moving the boats or the men forward toward the Pacific Coast—and back again. We cannot know how well Lewis would have managed the day-to-day logistics if Clark (or someone like Clark) had not traveled with him, but it is at least possible to wonder whether Lewis would have succeeded if getting the Corps of Discovery across the continent had been solely his responsibility. From the perspective of grand vision and overall strategy, Lewis was clearly in charge. An expedition of this sort had been a *darling project* of his for a decade at least. Clark could make no such claim. Clark was not even aware of the existence of the expedition until it was virtually underway. Lewis, not Clark, was the protégé of Jefferson, received official instructions from Jefferson, shared Jefferson's interests, and represented Jefferson's geopolitical vision. In Jefferson's eyes, Clark was the kid brother of one of his revolutionary contemporaries, the redoubtable George Rogers Clark, one of Virginia's heroes in the American Revolution. Jefferson was aware of William Clark's existence principally from a letter he received from George Rogers Clark in December 1802 saying that he had a resourceful younger brother who might be useful to Jefferson in some way or other. "He is well-qualified almost for any business," Rogers Clark wrote. "If it should be in your power to confur on him any post of Honor and profit, in this Countrey in which we live, it will exceedingly gratify me."[6] Apparently the whole family was orthographically challenged.

From the perspective of science and the agenda of the Enlightenment, Lewis was also clearly the leader of the expedition. Clark's humility about his capacities as a *writer* and *natural historian*, and his self-consciousness about his use of the English language are genuine, and a little painful to read, given what we know about his reliability, his profound sense of duty, his outstanding character, and his excellence in so many arenas, including cartography.

From the perspective of the discoveries of the expedition, including geographic discoveries, Lewis was clearly the leader. It was Lewis who first gazed upon the confluence of the Yellowstone and Missouri Rivers, not Clark. It was Lewis who discovered the Great Falls of the Missouri. It was Lewis who named the Three Forks of the Missouri after Thomas Jefferson,

Albert Gallatin, and James Madison. It was Lewis who made first contact with the critically important Shoshone Indians in southwestern Montana. It was Lewis who on August 12, 1805, drank from the "source" of the Missouri River. It was Lewis who first strode up to the continental divide at Lemhi Pass, "with a wild surmise, silent, upon a peak"[7] in Montana, and looked into the Columbia River watershed. It was Lewis who first stood on the shore of the Pacific Ocean.

In the course of the 7,689 mile, two year, four month, and nine day expedition, William Clark did not make a single major geographic discovery.

Equal in every point of view?

As the twenty-first century begins, we cannot help but think of it as the Lewis and Clark Expedition, with Lewis nominally in command, Clark technically a subordinate, but the two of them, for all practical purposes, sharing the duties of leading a reconnaissance team of volunteers from St. Louis to the Pacific Ocean. Although the forty-some members of the traveling party[8] apparently thought of Lewis and Clark as co-captains, everyone understood that Lewis was the man who had been chosen by the president of the United States to lead the expedition. Everyone knew that Lewis had lived with the president in the White House for a couple of years before the expedition began. Lewis was clearly the better educated. He was the scientist of the expedition. He was the one who collected, pressed, dried, and labeled the plants. He was primarily responsible for determining latitude and longitude.[9] And he was the one who would be expected to write the formal account of the expedition if they survived the journey. Many times in the course of the expedition, in a range of subtle ways, Lewis reminded his companions, including Clark, that he was in command. Probably Clark reinforced Lewis's primacy, too. For the enlisted men and engages Clark would have been the source of all this information about Lewis's Enlightenment credentials and his special relationship with the author of the Declaration of Independence. Surely Clark talked Lewis up at Camp Wood. That was the sort of man Clark was.

Still....

It is essential to remember that Lewis did not spend much time at Camp Wood in the winter of 1803–04, and that he was not with the flotilla on May 14, 1804, when under a "jentle brease"[10] it crossed the Mississippi River and entered what Lewis, and not Clark, called the "mighty & heretofore deemed endless Missouri."[11] In fact, Lewis did not make his appearance until May 20, a full week into the expedition, and then on horseback, accompanied by a cluster of St. Louis dignitaries. By now all the other men of the expedition, including Clark, had undergone a horrific Missouri River seven-day orientation course, a kind of seasoning, and they had earned every mile, indeed every yard, of forward progress, employing winter-softened muscles against what must have seemed to them an extremely

William Clark, the most reliable of men, without whom the expedition might not have succeeded. Courtesy of Wesley Jarvis. Acc.# 1921.55.1 Missouri Historical Society Museum Collections. N26113.

formidable river. Suddenly, just as the members of the Corps of Discovery found their Missouri River rhythm, in rode Meriwether Lewis, their commander, whom frankly they barely knew, in the company of a number of St. Louis grandees. Lewis was probably playing the gentleman that day, not the river adventurer. It is quite possible that the average enlisted man or French waterman felt some tinge of resentment towards Lewis when he made his appearance. Including, arguably, William Clark.

It is certain that, at this stage, most of the men regarded William Clark as their leader.

On May 14, 1804, thirty-two-year-old Private Patrick Gass of Pennsylvania wrote the first of his many journal entries: "[W]e left our establishment at the mouth of the river du Bois... proceeded up the Missouri on our intended voyage of discovery, under the command of Captain Clarke." Then he added, "Captain Lewis was to join us in two or three days on our passage."[12] Private Joseph Whitehouse also made it clear that so far, at least, it was Clark's expedition. "[T]his being the day appointed by Capt. Clark to Set out, a number of the Sitizens of Gotian Settlement came to See us Start. we got in readiness. Capt. Lewis is now at St. Louis but will join us at St. Charls."[13]

Sergeant John Ordway of New Hampshire, who was in his late twenties, wrote simply, "Capt Clark Set out at 3 o Clock P.M. for the western expedition."[14] Ordway made no mention whatsoever of Meriwether Lewis on May 14. On May 19 he wrote, with equal simplicity and no elaboration, "Capt Lewis arrived."[15] The other journal keeper whose records are extant, Sergeant Charles Floyd, wrote precisely what Ordway wrote for May 14, and on May 19 reported, "Capt Lewis Joined us—."[16] For (but not on) May 21, Gass wrote, "We remained at St. Charles until the 21st, where Captain Lewis arrived from St. Louis and joined us."[17] Even William Clark's official journal of the expedition reflects his primacy as the journey began: "I set out at 4 oClock to the head of the first Island... "[18]

The records indicate that Lewis spent most of his time between the end of November 1803 and the third week in May 1804, a period of five and a half months, either in Cahokia, on the Illinois side of the Mississippi, or in St. Louis, on the west bank of the Mississippi. Historian Robert E. Hartley has tallied the officers' time in camp as follows. During the 141 days between January 1, 1804, and the expedition's departure on May 14, Lewis was at Camp Wood for a total of thirty-six days. He was gone on 105 of those days. Meanwhile, Clark spent ninety-eight days in residence at Camp Wood, forty-three elsewhere.[19] David Lavender has written, "The division of responsibilities as they worked out was all but preordained by their natures. Clark, the frontiersman, would build the winter camp at Wood River, collect and pack the supplies that came in, train the men, and ready the boats for a spring start. Lewis, the more socially and politically trained of the two, would seek out men who could give him the kinds of information about Upper Louisiana that Jefferson needed for executing his Indian removal plan and that the expedition would require for carrying out its multitude of assignments."[20]

Lewis kept a half-hearted journal of his Ohio River travels from August 31, 1803, until November 28, as the expedition approached Kaskaskia, on the Illinois side of the Mississippi River. On that day he wrote only one sentence in his journal, ten words that proved to be disturbingly prophetic: "This morning left Capt Clark in charge of the Boat."[21] Lewis may not have known then that he was essentially assigning the management of the boats to Clark for the duration of the Lewis and Clark Expedition. After that single sentence, the journal of Meriwether Lewis went essentially silent for the next sixteen months. This stunning lapse is seldom emphasized by Lewis and Clark scholars, partly because Clark's journal provides a baseline narrative of the expedition's activities for that period, and partly because there has been an unfortunate tendency to collapse Meriwether Lewis and William Clark into a single composite leader called Lewis and Clark, Lewis & Clark or—in essence—*LewisandClark*. On November 28, Clark wrote the first entry in what would become an essentially continuous journal for the next two years, nine months, and twenty-six days. Thus, without ceremony, before the expedition had really begun, before the volunteers were all assembled, before Camp Wood was sited or constructed, Lewis gave Clark responsibility for the boats and the expedition's baseline journal. On December 3, 1803, Lewis left the expedition's flotilla and ventured overland for St. Louis, where, for all practical purposes, he wintered. *Equal in every point of view.*

Lewis wrote letters to Clark from St. Louis on December 17, February 18, May 2, and May 6.

Clark, now alone in practical command, spent the night of December 10 camped at today's East St. Louis on the Illinois side of the Mississippi River. The Clark party reached the mouth of Wood River on December 12. Clark, not Lewis, chose the site of Camp Wood. Clark, not Lewis, laid out the campus of the expedition's winter huts. Clark, not Lewis, presided over the crucial first weeks in which the social and organizational rhythms of the expedition began to gel, and the men began to find their niches in the formal and informal pecking order—as hunters, carpenters, skin dressers, jokesters, hard drinkers, roisterers, musicians, and dancers. Clark put the men immediately to work constructing cabins. On December 13, he wrote, "Set the men to Clearing land & Cutting logs."[22] Camp Wood was completed on Christmas Eve 1803. Lewis did not make his first appearance at Camp Wood until the end of January 1804, six weeks after Clark established the site and well more than a month after the winter compound was completed.

Lewis spent more time at Camp Wood in February 1804 than in any other month. Clark spent more time away from Camp Wood in February than in any other month. Clark's venturings to St. Louis were for the purposes of diplomacy, for the recovery of his health, for an urban break from rough camp life, and so that he could attend several balls to which the captains were cordially invited by members of the St. Louis aristocracy. In mid-January 1804 Clark wrote to his brother-in-law William Croghan in Kentucky, "I have not been from my Camp to any house since my arrival here."[23] On February 10 Lewis and Clark left Camp Dubois together for St. Louis. On February 13, Lewis returned to camp alone, leaving Clark in the city. Clark remained in St. Louis for an unspecified period of time. Lewis stayed approximately a week at Camp Dubois in Clark's absence. When he decamped to rejoin Clark, Lewis left behind a detachment order that put Sergeant John Ordway in charge when the captains were both absent. Lewis provided precise instructions for the blacksmiths, for the sawyers, for the men "making sugar," for those engaged in target practice, for the mess cooks, and for the hunters. He insisted that no man be absent without leave, and that hunters "will not extend their absence to a term by which they may avoid a tour of guard duty." He ruled that the only whiskey the men were permitted to drink would come from legal daily rations, and forbad them to buy whiskey from "the Contractor's store." He put Nathaniel Pryor in charge of the woodcutting, Charles Floyd in charge of "our quarters and store," and Ordway in charge of everything else. The detachment orders embodied the kind of stern, slightly fussy, and arguably pompous attention to detail characteristic of Lewis.[24] It is doubtful that Clark would have written such a detachment order, though he would have found a way to communicate these ideas to the men in his own more informal way.

Lewis rejoined Clark in St. Louis on February 20, 1804. When Lewis ventured back alone on February 29, Camp Wood was in chaos. Some of the men had openly defied Sergeant John Ordway, third in command of the expedition. John Colter had threatened to kill him. Lewis re-established control at the camp and expressed his sense of outrage in a stern and unrelenting detachment order of March 3, 1804. "The Commanding officer feels himself mortifyed and disappointed at the disorderly conduct of Reubin Fields, in refusing to mount guard when in the due roteen of duty he was regularly warned; nor is he less surprised at the want of discretion in those who urged his oposition to the faithfull discharge of his duty, particularly Shields, whose sense of propryety he had every reason to beleive would have induced him reather to have promoted good order ... ."[25] Some of the men could not have known what *mortified* meant. Some who did know probably snorted at such pretentious language. They probably regarded Lewis as a relative stranger, a martinet possessed of a rigid temper and a Latinate vocabulary.

Among other preachments and rebukes, Captain Lewis wrote, "The Cammanding officer is also sorry to find any man, who has been engaged by himself and Capt. Clark for the expedition on which they have entered, so destitute of understanding, as not to be able to draw the distinction between being placed under the command of another officer, whose will in such case would be their law." So *destitute*. In fact, Lewis may have been feeling a little guilty for his extended absences. In the course of his March 3 diatribe he wrote, "A moments reflection must convince every man of our party, that were we to neglect the more important and necessry arrangements in relation to the voyage we are now entering in, for the purpose merely of remaing at camp in order to communicate our orders in person to the individuals of the party on mear points of poliece, they would have too much reason to complain; nay, even to fear the ultimat success of the enterprise in which we are all embarked." *Nay*? This was quintessential Lewis, but it was decidedly not the patois of the American frontier. Many times in the course of the expedition he fretted that some situation might jeopardize "the ultimate success of the enterprise." Nothing could have induced Clark to write the words, "nay, even to fear ... " By the time this crisis had passed, probably every member of the expedition recognized the difference in leadership styles between the two captains and longed for the return of Clark. Nay, even Ordway. After describing the March 1804 discipline crisis and Lewis's stern response, biographers Thomas Danisi and John Jackson ask, "Could that be taken as a difference in command presence?"[26]

Lewis was a rigorous commander. He was something of a hothead. He preferred to read men the riot act or court-martial offenders than to handle these discipline problems informally. It is certain that William Clark could not have written the detachment order of March 3, 1804. His approach to discipline problems had the informal feel of a man who had spent a significant portion of his life on the frontier, and spoke, as Wordsworth said, "in a selection of language really used by men."[27] When some of the men got drunk and brawled on Christmas Day 1803 and on January 4, 1804, Clark merely "ordered those men who had fought got Drunk & neglected Duty to go and build a hut for a Wo[man] who promises to wash & Sow &c."[28] Lewis probably would have found that punishment insufficiently formal and professional. It worked for Clark.

Lewis biographers Thomas Danisi and John Jackson acknowledge the division of duties and headquarters of the captains during the winter of 1803–04, but they focus on Lewis's political and scientific responsibilities as the commander of the expedition rather than on the probable effect of this division on the social dynamics of the Corps of Discovery. "By superintending the soldiers and assuming responsibility for daily operations, including writing a daily journal, Clark left Lewis free to deal with more complex issues."[29] Certainly this is true. It made more sense for Lewis to interview St. Louis merchants, government officials, men who had previously ascended the Missouri River, while Clark built Camp Dubois and transformed the volunteers from hard-drinking and insubordinate raw recruits into a genuine corps of discovery.[30] The reverse would have been a much less efficient use of the winter and would have placed each of the commanders in a situation for which he was not best suited. Danisi and Jackson acknowledge that "Lewis knew that he was not temperamentally suited to the supervision of the men."[31] This is a rather serious concession. Lewis had been handpicked by the president of the United States to do just that.

Clark always underestimated his intellectual abilities. When he had to write something for public consumption, he generally asked Lewis to write the draft, and then he recopied it in his own handwriting. When the captains sent back important papers from Fort Mandan in April 1805, Clark was clearly embarrassed at the state of his journal, which he only reluctantly agreed to share with the learned president. To Jefferson, Lewis wrote, "You will also receive herewith inclosed a part of Capt. Clark's private journal, the other part you will find inclosed in a seperate tin box. This journal is in it's original state, and of course incorrect, but it will serve to give you the daily detales of our progress, and transactions. Capt. Clark does not wish this journal exposed in it's present state, but has no objection, that one or more copies of it be made by some confidential person under your direction, correcting it's grammatical errors &c."[32] What Lewis did not tell the president was that Clark's journal, however imperfect and ungrammatical, was the *only* leadership journal that had been kept during the first season of Missouri River travel.

Clark was with Lewis in St. Louis for two days in March 1804 to observe the formal transfer of the Louisiana Territory from Spain to France (March 9) and then from France to the United States (March 10). After the transfer ceremonies Lewis and Clark lingered on the Missouri side of the Mississippi River to tour Spanish military installations with Amos Stoddard, who was the official representative of the United States (and France) in the two-part transfer ceremony. Clark returned to Camp Dubois on March 21 after an absence of about two weeks. Clark was also in St. Louis for a few days beginning April 7, 1804.

The men of the expedition had spent approximately half a year getting to know the affable and pragmatic William Clark before they really had the chance to take their measure of the detached and somewhat aloof Meriwether Lewis. First impressions are important. The division of leadership duties that was established at Camp Wood created group dynamics that played themselves out for the next twenty-eight months. Clark would always be the hands-on project manager of the Lewis and Clark Expedition; Lewis would always be the acknowledged commander of the expedition, but it was clear from the beginning that he had important responsibilities that called him away from the day-to-day management of the project and, frequently enough, away from the rest of the men, including Clark. It seems clear that

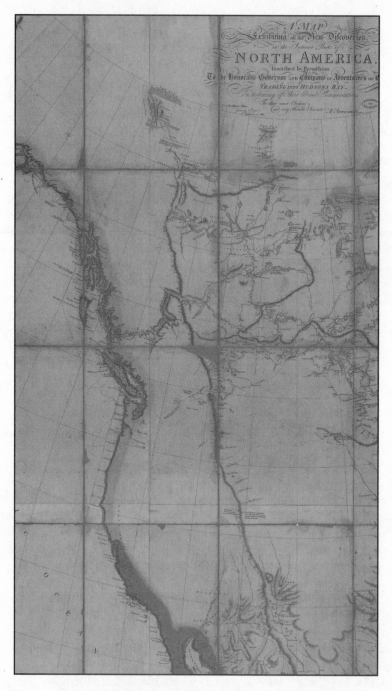

The Aaron Arrowsmith map of North America. Lewis was Jefferson's choice to begin the process of filling in the blank spaces on the map. On the left, "undiscovered" country. On the right, America's Empire for Liberty.

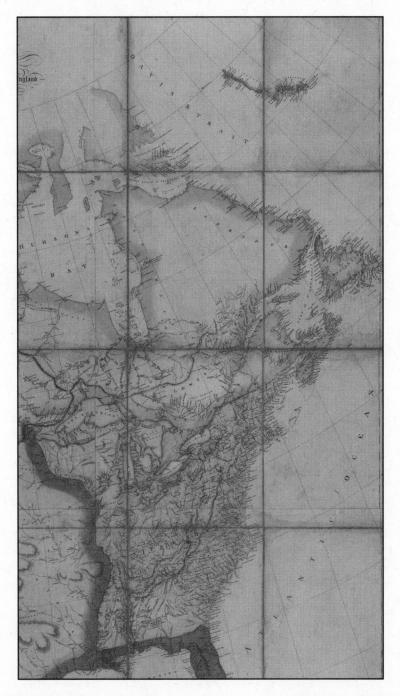

A. Arrowsmith. London: A. Arrowsmith [1802]. Courtesy of the Geography and Map Division, Library of Congress.

the men of the expedition felt great respect for Lewis. As he honestly wrote eleven months into the expedition, "not a whisper of murmur or discontent to be heard among them."[33] The only person whose journals ever even hint at implied criticism of Lewis was in fact Clark, and he never once overtly complained about his commander's choices or behavior. Still, it is clear that most of the men established a relationship with Clark that they never experienced with Lewis. As the expedition neared the Three Forks of the Missouri on July 25, 1805, Lewis wrote, "[T]he men complain of being much fortiegued, their labour is excessively great. I occasionly encourage them by assisting in the labour of navigating the canoes, and have learned to *push a tolerable good pole* in their fraize."[34] This short passage in Lewis's long journal entry for July 24, 1805, fully fourteen months into the expedition, is wonderfully, though inadvertently, revealing. Although the passage indicates that Lewis only very occasionally joined the enlisted men and the civilian watermen in their labors, it is equally clear that the men felt respect and even a kind of affection for Lewis, no matter how much they preferred the leadership of Clark. One can hear the bemused condescension of the veteran working man in granting that gentleman Lewis could, in extremis, *"push a tolerable good pole."* This is probably a direct quotation. This much is certain: William Clark could never have written that passage. He could not have felt bemusement that—deep in the American outback—he was reduced to manual labor. His temperament was wholly different from that of his co-captain, and it is certain that by now he had pushed the pole scores of times.

Lewis's absence from camp during the winter of 1803–04 may or may not have been a failure of good leadership. He certainly had important business to transact in St. Louis. He was not merely basking in the amenities and the cultivation of urban life while Clark and the rest of the men roughed it at a crude frontier outpost. But during those five-plus months, the men had a better chance to form an esprit de corps with each other and with Clark than they did with Captain Lewis, who must have seemed like a mere abstraction to most of them. Landon Jones has written, "The men had begun to bond with Clark during their training at Camp River Dubois. Lewis was frequently absent; if there was a problem, the person to go to for an answer was Clark. At St. Charles, where the expedition stopped to await Lewis's arrival overland from St. Louis, Clark asserted his authority even more convincingly."[35] When Lewis did appear during the first winter, he proved to be an austere and uncompromising commander, whose leadership and discipline methods were markedly different from those of Clark. It seems quite likely that Lewis's relationship with the men of the expedition never really recovered from the set of social dynamics established in his absence. Perhaps he did not want to have a collegial or fraternal relationship with men who were subordinate in rank to himself and from a lower echelon of the social hierarchy of the American republic. Lewis was, after all, a friend to the president of the United States. But this set of dynamics created a permanent tone and rhythm for the expedition.

When Lewis joined the expedition on May 20, 1804, and the entire Corps of Discovery was finally assembled, things quickly settled into a routine. Lewis did not keep a journal during this leg of the expedition or, if he did, it has not survived. We have five extant journals—Clark, Ordway, Patrick Gass, Joseph Whitehouse, and Charles Floyd—for the period from May 14 to August 20, 1804, and four extant journals—Clark, Ordway, Gass, and Whitehouse—for the period between August 21, 1804, and April 7, 1805, when Lewis took up his journal after an interminable silence.

Apparently, Lewis did not regard the journey from Camp Dubois to Fort Mandan as a particularly important or exciting phase of the expedition. There was little to discover and less to name. The landforms and the tributaries had all been named by previous travelers—as far up as the mouth of the Yellowstone River. Danisi and Jackson write, "For this part of the journey, rather than discovery, the corps was trailing the customary mercantile life of the middle river."[36] Lewis was probably as busy as ever during the period between May 21 and October 26, when the expedition stopped for the winter among the Mandan and Hidatsa peoples. He was collecting plants, minerals, and specimens of animals previously unknown or uncollected by American scientists. He was making celestial observations at every prominent landmark on the river. Like his mentor Jefferson, he was collecting and recording detailed weather data twice a day. He was preparing speeches to deliver to the Indians the expedition met. He was consulting every day with Clark about the larger logistics of the expedition. When discipline problems rose to a certain level, he took charge of courts-martial, using Baron von Steuben's *The Regulations for the Order and Discipline of the Troops of the United States*, published in 1779. Steuben's *Regulations* were part of the expedition's traveling library.[37] Lewis was busy, but he was not apparently keeping a journal. Lewis knew he was following the trail of previous traders and explorers. He carried with him summaries of their adventures and copies of some of their maps, particularly the James Mackay-John Evans map that was known in the United States as the "Indian Office map."[38] The expedition met with scattered white people every couple of weeks all the way to the Mandan and Hidatsa villages, where white traders and interpreters were present through the winter—and had been for more than a decade. Lewis could not honestly consider the first year of travel a journey of discovery. Probably he did not regard this first year as legitimate exploration, since the road was well-traveled and adequately mapped.[39]

Lewis came alive briefly as the expedition passed the line between tall grass and short grass prairie at the White River in today's South Dakota. On September 16 and 17, Lewis wrote exceptionally fine accounts of the birds he observed on the high plains, of the treeless vistas that now engulfed the flotilla, and of the breathtaking habits of the pronghorn antelope. These journal essays, Moulton writes, constitute "Lewis's only known daily entries—as opposed to scientific notes in the specialized journals—between May 20, 1804, and April 7, 1805."[40] The odd thing about these journal entries is that Lewis begins *in medias res*, as if he had been keeping a daily journal from the beginning, and breaks off in mid-sentence, as if he had been called away from his pen and never returned. "This morning set out at an early hour," he began, "and come too at ½ after 7 A.M. on the Lard. Shore."[41] This has the feel of a fragment extracted from a continuous journal, not a one-off excursus into journal keeping. For those who believe that Lewis surely wrote more than we now possess, this is one of the primary pieces of evidence. When these two days of journal entries ended, Stephen Ambrose wrote, "Either Lewis put down his quill, not to take it up again until April 1805—or what he wrote is lost."[42] We have no way of knowing just why Lewis broke his silence on this occasion, of course, but one is tempted to say that it was the pure majesty of the pronghorn (*Antilocopra americana*). Although the mouth of the Platte River was regarded by river men as the line of demarcation between the lower and upper Missouri River, from a geographer's or naturalist's point of view the mouth of the White River is actually a better fold in the map. Lewis and Clark began to see prairie dogs, buffalo, and pronghorn antelope in large numbers above the mouth of the White River. The expedition was now passing from a tall grass, semi-forested landscape that was essentially familiar to them to a windswept, treeless, alkaline, and seemingly endless plains country that most of the men had never seen before and not anticipated. In other words, the men of the Lewis and Clark Expedition were about to encounter the true Great Plains in a profound way.

On September 17, 1804, Lewis wrote one of his very best journal entries. It totaled 1,045 words. As was often the case after a long silence, he began by declaring that he was moving from a sedentary to an active mode. "Having for many days past confined myself to the boat, I determined to devote this day to amuse myself on shore with my gun and view the interior of the country lying between the river and the Corvus Creek— accordingly before sunrise I set out with six of my best hunters ... ."[43] *Amuse* is one of Meriwether Lewis's favorite words. It is not an expression that appears in this sense in the original journals of William Clark. Lewis was amazed to see how short true short grass can be. "[T]he shortness and virdue of grass gave the plain the appearance throughout it's whole extent of beatifull bowlinggreen in fine order."[44] A twenty-first century explorer might say it looks like a putting green, but the recreational analogy of the early nineteenth century was known as *bowls*. The countryside looked like an American Garden of Eden. "[T]his senery already rich pleasing and beatiful, was still farther hightened by immence herds of Buffaloe deer Elk and

Antelopes which we saw in every direction feeding on the hills and plains. I do not think I exagerate when I estimate the number of Buffaloe which could be compreed at one view to amount to 3000."[45]

Lewis's purpose that day was to kill a female antelope for science, but he soon lost himself in wonder at one of the most remarkable quadrupeds of North America.

> I had this day an opportunity of witnessing the agility and superior fleetness of this anamal which was to me really astonishing. I had pursued and twice surprised a small herd of seven, in the first instance they did not discover me distinctly and therefore did not run at full speed, tho' they took care before they rested to gain an elivated point where it was impossible to approach them under cover except in one direction and that happened to be in the direction from which the wind blew towards them; bad as the chance to approach them was, I made the best of my way towards them, frequently peeping over the ridge with which I took care to conceal myself from their view. ... I gained the top of the eminence on which they stood, as soon as possible from whence I had an extensive view of the country   the antilopes which had disappeared in a steep revesne now appeared at the distance of about three miles on the side of a ridge which passed obliquely across me and extended about for miles. so soon had these antelopes gained the distance at which they had again appeared to my view I doubted at ferst that they were the same that I had just surprised, but my doubts soon vanished when I beheld the rapidity of their flight along the ridge before me   it appeared reather the rappid flight of birds than the motion of quadrupeds. I think I can safely venture the ascertion that the speed of this anamal is equal if not superior to that of the finest blooded courser.[46]

Lewis concludes this famous journal entry with the words "this morning I saw" and then simply breaks off. He never finished the sentence. As Moulton indicates, Codex Ba ends abruptly with these words.[47] This would seem to be more evidence to suggest that some of Lewis's journals have been lost either on the trail itself in one of the handful of canoe accidents, in a sodden cache pit, or at some point after the expedition's return. Neither Lewis nor any other member of the expedition ever provided an explanation of just what was lost in these accidents on the water or in the flooded cache pits. It is a mystery. Lewis's silences can be clarified but never satisfactorily explained. (See Chapter 5) Some of the clues are suggestive, but none resolves the issue.

With that, Lewis went silent again for the remaining thirty-eight days of river travel in 1804. He kept no known continuous journal for the entire period (163 days) that the expedition was at Fort Mandan. That makes a total of 201 days of silence *after* the brief flurry at the mouth of the White River. Except for those two days of journal entries, and a nine-day period in February while Clark was away on a hunting expedition, Lewis was effectively silent from May 14, 1804, to April 7, 1805, a period of 328 days, 316 minus September 16–17, 1804, and February 4–13, 1805. That's little short of a year, in an expedition of the greatest importance to the government of the United States and its Enlightenment president, what Lewis later called "one of those great objects on which my mind has been unalterably fixed for many years."[48] To William Clark we owe not only the training and management of the men of the expedition, but also the baseline narrative of the journey. Up till now Clark had been *more than equal* in every respect.

The Lewis and Clark Expedition left Fort Mandan on April 7, 1805. On (or for) that day Lewis wrote what many regard as his single greatest journal entry. As far as he was concerned, the discovery phase of the expedition was finally about to begin. Everything up to this moment had been a shakedown cruise, a journey to the far edge of the known world, but still within the precinct of the known world. Now finally Lewis could regard himself legitimately as an authentic explorer. Like Captain James Cook or Christopher Columbus he believed he was about to go where no civilized man had gone before. He was ready, and he was full of heroic confidence. In a sense, with his journal entry for April 7, 1805, Lewis explained his long 1803–05 silence. There had been nothing new to report. The 1,610 miles from St. Charles to the Mandan villages might be interesting to a traveler or an ethnographer, but they were arguably boring to an explorer of the first rank. The key passage is worth quoting in full:

> Our vessels consisted of six small canoes, and two large perogues. This little fleet altho' not quite so rispectable as those of Columbus or Capt. Cook were still viewed by us with as much pleasure as those deservedly famed adventurers ever beheld theirs; and I dare say with quite as much anxiety for their safety and preservation. we were now about to penetrate a country at least two thousand miles in width, on which the foot of civillized man had never trodden; the good or evil it had in store for us was for experiment yet to determine, and these little vessells contained every article by which we were to expect to subsist or defend ourselves. however as this the state of mind in which we are, generally gives the colouring to events, when the immagination is suffered to wander into futurity, the picture which now presented itself to me was a most pleasing

Charles Willson Peale painted this portrait in 1807, before things began to come apart for Meriwether Lewis. Courtesy of the Independence National Historical Park.

one. entertaining as I do, the most confident hope of succeading in a voyage which had formed a da[r]ling project of mine for the last ten years , I could but esteem this moment of my departure as among the most happy of my life. The party are in excellent health and sperits, zealously attatched to the enterprise, and anxious to proceed; not a whisper of murmur or discontent to be heard among them, but all act in unison, and with the most perfect harmony. I took an early supper this evening and went to bed.[49]

Lewis had a right to be proud. Along with Zebulon Pike, Mungo Park, James Bruce, and many others, he was part of a worldwide movement to explore the interior spaces of the vast and still largely unknown continents of North America, Africa, and northern Asia (Siberia). The literary and scientific methods that men like Captain James Cook and Louis-Antoine de Bougainville had developed for explorations in the Pacific basin were now being applied to continental exploration. The Enlightenment geographer James Rennell (1742–1830) wrote that "the Voyages of the late Captain Cook have so far afforded gratification, that nothing worthy of research by Sea, the Poles themselves excepted, remains to be examined; but by Land, the objects of discovery are still so vast, as to include at least a third of the habitable surface of the earth: for much of Asia, a still larger proportion of America, and almost the whole of Africa, are unvisited and unknown."[50] Rennell's menu helps us understand the sheer audacity of Jefferson's vision. Lewis and Clark were biting off that "larger proportion of America" in a single expedition. An awareness of what was at stake and what was possible in the period following Cook's voyages and the success of the American Revolution was not lost on Meriwether Lewis. He was right to see himself as a man of destiny. That destiny was opportunity—and of course a mighty burden.

Even so, when Lewis wrote that he was "now about to penetrate a country at least two thousand miles in width, on which the foot of civillized man had never trodden,"[51] he knew that he was not precisely telling the truth. He knew, for example, that the newest member of the expedition, Baptiste Lepage, hired on November 2, 1804, had spent the traveling season of 1804 in the "black hills" country and had come down the Little Missouri River alone in a canoe, a journey that consumed forty-five days.[52] So Lepage had already been at the mouth of the Little Missouri River, a few score miles upriver from Fort Mandan, and presumably Lewis regarded him as a civilized man.

Three days out, on April 10, 1805, approximately at the site of today's Garrison Dam in North Dakota, Lewis wrote, "at 1 P.M. we overtook three french hunters who had set out a few days before us with a view of traping beaver; they had taken 12 since they left Fort Mandan. these people avail themselves of the protection which our numbers will enable us to give them against the Assinniboins who sometimes hunt on the Missouri and intend ascending with us as far as the mouth of the Yellow stone river."[53] It is possible, but very unlikely, that Lewis and Clark had been unaware of the fact that these three unnamed French hunters ventured into the "country at least two thousand miles in width" a day or two before the Corps of Discovery. Some conversation almost certainly occurred at Fort Mandan between the leaders of the expedition and the French trappers, who sought to work their way upriver at the same pace as the expedition in order to take advantage of the expedition's security umbrella. Lewis was not first, after all.

One week after leaving Fort Mandan, on April 14, 1805, after passing the mouth of the Little Missouri River, southeast of today's New Town, North Dakota, Lewis reckoned that now he *really was* the first civilized man in entirely undiscovered country. "[P]assed an Island," he wrote, "above which two small creeks fall in on Lard side; the upper creek largest, which we called Sharbono's Creek after our interpreter who encamped several weeks on it with a hunting party of Indians. this was the highest point to which any whiteman had ever ascended."[54] So *this* was the deepest previous penetration of white traders (not explorers) into *terra incognita*.

What Lewis did now was best reported by William Clark. After repeating in his journal that this was "the highest point on the Missouri to which a white man has been previous to this time," Clark reported that "Capt. Lewis walked out above this creek and killed an Elk ... ."[55] Forget the elk: the key word here was *above*. The moment Lewis realized that he was finally penetrating a country *at least 1950 miles in width* upon which the foot of civilized man had never trodden, he got himself on shore and hiked "above this creek," that is, up the Missouri River into previously undiscovered country. Each step that he now took up the Missouri was "the first civilized" step ever made on that ground. James Ronda has provided a wonderful explication of Lewis's phrase "foot of civilized man." "Lewis's mental image of his footprints as the first on a supposedly virgin land is powerfully evocative," Ronda writes, "perhaps reminding us of those first astronaut bootprints on the lunar surface. But of course by describing his journey in such terms, Lewis committed an act of historic and cultural erasure. On the same day that he put himself into the collective memory of other European travelers he attempted to rub out the traces of Native American explorers. ... His was to be the first imprint; all others were dismissed as uncivilized and of no account."[56] Lewis made sure he was alone and off the boats on this momentous occasion. He wanted to be first. He had also walked on shore on April 7, "ahead of the rest," as Huck Finn would later put it,[57] while behind him Clark struggled with the red and white pirogues and six new canoes. On that day Lewis got so far ahead of everyone else that towards evening he had to drop back down the river two miles to meet the rest of the men at their first encampment of the 1805 traveling season.

But it just gets curiouser. Even on April 14, when Lewis assured his readers that now *finally* he was in *terra incognita*, he had to acknowledge that he was the first "except two Frenchmen who having lost their way had straggled a few miles further, tho' to what place precisely I could not learn."[58] The journals' first editor Nicholas Biddle was apparently interested in sorting out this geographic puzzle. On that page of Lewis's journal manuscript Biddle interlineated, *"one of whom Lepage was now with us—See at Mandan."*[59] If this is not garbled somehow, Lepage was a very weak beaver man, because it would suggest that after traveling down the Little Missouri in the fall of 1804, he turned the wrong way on the Missouri River, rather than float downstream to the Mandan and Hidatsa villages where he would be likely to encounter representatives of the North West Company or the Hudson's Bay Company. Biddle almost certainly misunderstood or misreported what Clark or George Shannon told him about Lepage's movements. More to the point, in his *History of the Expedition Under the Command of Lewis and Clark*, Biddle wisely suppressed Lewis's heroic account of the April 7 departure. Biddle's official narrative prose echoed Clark's more modest language about the departure from Fort Mandan: "Having made all our arrangements, we left the fort about five o'clock in the afternoon."[60] Biddle's bland accounting of so important a moment, though strictly speaking more accurate than Lewis's, would have outraged Lewis, had he lived to read it. Biddle was writing an account of the Lewis and Clark Expedition, not the Lewis expedition. In fact, it may be said that the combination of Lewis's early death and Biddle's contractual engagement with the survivor William Clark resulted in a narrative of the journey that accorded Clark a larger place in the story than he would have enjoyed had Lewis written the book, and a narrative that told the story of the journey from an *expedition* rather than an *explorer's* point of view. On April 14, Biddle handled the *first civilized man* issue with precision but no epic invocations: "… we called Chaboneau's creek, after our interpreter, who once camped on it several weeks with a party of Indians. Beyond this no white man had ever been except two Frenchmen, one of whom (Lapage) is with us, and who, having lost their way, straggled a few miles further, though to what point we could not ascertain."[61] This is essentially Lewis's language from April 14, with the clarification Biddle obtained from Clark or Shannon.

Presumably, the next day, on April 15, 1805, near today's New Town, North Dakota, Lewis finally got ahead of the two nameless Frenchmen and, at least according to his own calculation, did now become the first white man to see country "on which the foot of civillized man had never trodden." By now the trope of getting there first must have seemed a little hackneyed even to Lewis. Nameless Frenchmen—better that they had been the pathfinders than the rascal Charbonneau.

So what did Lewis really mean to signify back on April 7 when he famously compared himself to Columbus or Captain Cook and told his readers that he was about to walk off the map of the known world? Did he know that strictly speaking he was not telling the truth? Was he engaged, as James Ronda has suggested, in a kind of posturing?[62] It is most likely that what Lewis was really saying in his wonderful and grandiloquent journal entry was that, at the time of the expedition's departure, the vast expanse of country west of the Mandan and Hidatsa villages was *effectively* or *symbolically* void of any previous white presence; that as the expedition left the Mandan and Hidatsa villages it was *essentially* walking off the map of the known world into *terra incognita*. Lewis was acknowledging that the first year of travel, from May 14 to October 26, 1804, over the 1,610 miles from the mouth of the Missouri River to its great bend in today's North Dakota, was along a well-established and previously *discovered* river road, but with the departure from Fort Mandan on April 7 the expedition was finally entering into the true discovery phase of its travels. Surely Lewis knew that the expedition's account of discovery and first contact would be more dramatic, not to mention tidier from a narrative point of view, if he made sure the undiscovered country commenced on the day he left Fort Mandan, which thus meant that the Corps of Discovery had wintered at the farthest outpost of western civilization. In other words, Lewis probably wrote his April 7 journal entry knowing full well that it was not literally true, but believing that it was true in some more important, some *essential* sense. He may also have felt that there are civilized men, and then there are *civilized* men; that Toussaint Charbonneau, Baptiste Lepage, two nameless Frenchmen, and perhaps a few other stragglers who did not know the momentousness of their actions did not really qualify in his taxonomy of genuine explorers. Lewis was the first white man worthy to be regarded as a civilizational representative and explorer in the zone west of the Mandan and Hidatsa villages. In terms of punctilious truth, the best that can really be said of Lewis was that he was almost certainly *the first white man who was keeping a journal whose words are still extant to enter the country west of the Mandan and Hidatsa villages in today's United States.* Lewis's head was probably well aware of these untidy facts, but his heart preferred to suppress them in the name of what might be called his *Captain Cook* moment. The legendary Cook had died in Hawaii, at the age of fifty, when Lewis was four years old.

In addition to all that, if Lewis had been perfectly honest, he would have had to say that he was the first civilized man to penetrate a country of nearly two thousand miles *below the 49th parallel.* He well knew that Alexander Mackenzie had been the first recorded white man to cross the American continent to the Pacific Ocean, although President Jefferson had assured Congress that Mackenzie's route took him through "a high latitude, through an infinite number of portages and lakes, shut up by ice through a long season. The commerce on that line could bear no competition with that of the Missouri, traversing a moderate climate, offering according to the best accounts, a continued navigation from it's source, and, possibly with a single portage, from the Western Ocean."[63] Lewis had Mackenzie's *Voyages from Montreal* in his portable reference library, and, thanks to the work of David Nicandri, we know that both Lewis and Clark consulted Mackenzie with considerable frequency.[64]

The more we scrutinize the famous departure passage the more Lewis's marvelous claim sounds hollow or disingenuous. Lewis had a flair for the grand gesture and the heroic pose. That's one source of his greatness. The passage he wrote on (or about) April 7, 1805, is among the best and best known in the journals of Lewis and Clark. It is both eloquent and inspiring, and it is on passages like this that the indescribable magic of the Lewis and Clark expedition largely rests. As Thomas Slaughter has shown, explorers invariably have to shape their heroic narratives from materials that seldom lend themselves to such categorical certainty.[65] First explorers explore a chaotic and contingent wilderness. Then they write about their explorations in a way that makes them seem more purposeful, more certain of precisely where they were and what they were observing, than in fact they were at any given time in the course of their travels. The two enterprises are related but distinct, even when the writing occurs at essentially the same time. The mistake is in taking the explorer's narrative at face value as if it were an objective account of the place in question and his agency in finding it. Lewis was not lying when he wrote the April 7, 1805, journal passage. He was shaping his experiences on paper for an audience who wasn't there, giving meaning to events that were inherently less meaningful. Had Lewis been aware of how dubious his future readers would be about his taxonomy of *who was civilized and who was savage*, about *what constitutes discovery* in a landscape that had been discovered, mapped, named, and made a homeland by ingenious indigenous peoples for centuries, *how unlikely it is that anyone who ever claims to be first is in fact first*, he might have written even less than he did. Lewis was no more the first civilized man to walk in western North Dakota than Charles Darwin was the first to describe the theory of evolution.

My purpose here is not to deflate Lewis's claim of being first, but to explore the character of the commander of the expedition and emphasize the inevitably problematic nature of the explorer's pose. Thomas Slaughter has written, "At the center of the paradoxes, confusions, contradictions, and lies that contribute to the explorer's construction of his journey is the inflexibility of the definition of 'explorer.' If he is second, he is nothing—a traveler at best, more likely a laughingstock who has wasted other people's money or, worse yet, a mere mortal who is ignored. He must, he will, find a way to define his journey as a 'first' and what he sees as a discovery, however far-fetched that should seem to us in retrospect."[66] We know that

Columbus was not the first European to "discover" America, and that Richard Francis Burton was not the first European to "discover" Lake Tanganyika. It is clear that Lewis was not interested in being *among the earliest* visitors to Montana, *among the first* to cross the continental divide, *among the first* to stand before the Great Falls of the Missouri River. It was critically important to him to be THE first in two ways. He genuinely wanted to be regarded as the first civilized man "to penetrate a country at least two thousand miles in width" between the Mandan and Hidatsa villages in central North Dakota and the stretch of the Columbia River below today's Corbett, Oregon, where Lieutenant William Broughton of the Vancouver Expedition camped on October 29, 1792. Being first was so important to Lewis that he was willing to write a passage that he knew to be erroneous. And yet, as a careful exemplar of the Enlightenment and a man, as Jefferson put it, with "a fidelity to truth so scrupulous that whatever he should report would be as certain as if seen by ourselves,"[67] Lewis was willing, a week later, to acknowledge that it was actually only at this juncture that he was the explorer he had described on the western portal of Fort Mandan.

The second way that Lewis needed to be first was among his colleagues, the thirty-two other permanent members of the Corps of Discovery, and particularly his partner in discovery William Clark. On April 14 when he reckoned that he had in fact reached the precise line of demarcation between land touched by white feet and undiscovered country, he got himself off the white pirogue and onto the land in question, and he quickly strode ahead of the rest of the men, including of course Clark. Clark reports that Lewis stayed out alone as long as possible that evening. Lewis "joined the boat at Dusk at our Camp on the S.S. opposit a high hill."[68] Dusk on April 14 would have been about 8 P.M.

There is something quite beautiful in this. When he finally felt sure that he was the explorer he so desperately sought to be, like Christopher Columbus (1451–1506) or James Cook (1728–1779), in a place never before trodden by the feet of white men, he stayed out as long as there was daylight to sustain him and made footsteps in undiscovered country. We can only try to imagine Lewis's solitary reverie on that spring evening of April 14, 1805, but it must have been a very heady experience. That moment, as he freely admitted on the nominal as opposed to the actual date of his triumph, must have been "among the most happy of my life." Lewis's journal entry for August 14 is understated, however. He had already written the stuff of epic a week earlier. To repeat his sense of ecstasy and destiny would be bathetic at this juncture.

If my analysis of the expedition's foray into *terra incognita* is correct, it would hereafter be wise to avoid taking any of the journals of Lewis and Clark at face value again.

Lewis and Clark knew that the Yellowstone River was the principal northern tributary of the Missouri River, and that they would encounter it a few weeks after their departure from the Mandan and Hidatsa villages. They knew of the existence of the Yellowstone before they left St. Louis, and its existence, name, and location were confirmed by both white and Indian sources during the long winter at Fort Mandan.[69] *Yellowstone* is an English translation of a French translation of a Hidatsa word meaning "Yellow Rock River." The name had entered European geographic understanding long before Lewis and Clark undertook their expedition. At Fort Mandan a white trader named Hugh Heney and the Mandan leader Sheheke-shote had on different occasions drawn them accurate maps of the lands between the mouth of the Knife River and the continental divide that clearly put the Yellowstone about where it belongs in modern geography. In other words, Lewis and Clark knew where the mouth of the Yellowstone was likely to be, and they knew when they should start scanning the western horizon for it.

As the expedition neared the confluence, in the fourth week of April 1805, Lewis found reason to strike out ahead of the flotilla. The violent winds of the spring on the northern Great Plains had detained the expedition so often in the last couple of weeks that, at one point, Lewis actually found himself wondering if the winds would ever stop howling. Nervously the captain wrote, "[T]hese hard winds, being so frequently repeated, become a serious source of detention to us."[70] One day later he lamented, "[S]o penitrating is this sand, that we cannot keep any article free from it; in short we are compelled to eat, drink, and breath it very freely."[71]

Lewis's written justification for moving ahead of the boats was to save time: "The wind had been so unfavorable to our progress for several days past, and seeing but little prospect of a favourable chang; knowing that the river was crooked, from the report of the hunters who were out yesterday, and beleiving that we were at no very great distance from the Yellow stone River; I determined, in order as much as possible to avoid detention, to proceed by land with a few men to the entrance of that river and make the necessary observations to determine it's position, which I hoped to effect by the time that Capt. Clark could arrive with the party."[72] Ascertaining latitude and longitude was tedious and painstaking work that required repeated sightings and careful record keeping. Lewis's idea was that he would get to the confluence first to perform these important but time-consuming tasks while the six small canoes and two large pirogues struggled up the circuitous river against the sharp spring winds and sandstorms, so that when Clark and the boats did arrive, there would be no further delay in the expedition's forward progress. This made perfect sense, particularly in light of the *detention* the expedition had suffered so early in its 1805 travels.

Lewis, as usual, was in a hurry and, as always, he was worried that the expedition was falling behind. Although Clark sometimes conducted celestial observations, it was Lewis who was the expedition's master of latitude and longitude. Of course, Clark might just as easily have gone ahead to make sure he had ample time to measure the two great rivers at their confluence without delaying the progress of the expedition. On April 26, Lewis reported, "Capt Clark measured these rivers just above their confluence; found the bed of the Missouri 520 yards wide, the water occupying 330. it's channel deep. the yellowstone river including it's sandbar, 858 yds. of which, the water occupied 297 yards."[73] Those measurements must have taken some time; they must have detained the expedition.

Still, from a logistical point of view, Lewis's decision was sound. It would save time if somebody ventured ahead to the confluence, and that somebody logically should be Lewis. Even at this juncture, the captains tried never to be both gone from the flotilla at the same time. It is only when Lewis's rationales begin to add up to a pattern—striking out ahead and invariably *getting there first* when the expedition was about to reach an important landmark—that one begins to wonder if Lewis felt the need—consciously or unconsciously—to secure his own place in history by making sure that he and nobody else made the principal discoveries of the expedition.

Clark explained Lewis's plans in more or less the same terms in his journal entry for April 25. "[F]inding that the winds retarded our progression for maney days past, and no apparance of an alteration, and the river being Crooked that we could never have 3 miles fair wind, Capt. Lewis concluded to go by land as far as the Rochejhone or yellow Stone river, which we expect is at no great distance by land and make Some Selestial observations to find the Situation of its mouth, and by that measure not detain the Perogues at that place any time for the purpose of makeing those necessary observations,"[74] Clark wrote. Ordway provided a more charitable view of Lewis's restlessness. By noon on April 25 the winds were so violent that the flotilla "halted for it to abate." At that point, "Capt. Lewis myself and 3 more of the party crossed over to the S. Shore to go up by land to the Mouth of the river *Roshjone* or *yellow rock* river (for observations).[75] In other words, according to Ordway, Lewis left the flotilla only when it was held up *again* by high winds.

Lewis was not entirely alone. As he struck out for the confluence, he informed his readers that he took four men with him. But he did not provide their names in his journal account of the decision. We know the names of at least three of those men: John Ordway, because he wrote about the excursion in his journal, and the indispensible George Drouillard and Joseph Field. The fourth participant might well have been Reuben Field. As time wore on in the expedition, Lewis generally chose Drouillard and both the Field brothers as his own core of the Corps of Discovery. There is nothing particularly unusual in the fact that Lewis did not provide the names of his traveling companions. Most of the enlisted men spent the entire expedition as unnamed functionaries in the journals of both captains. On the whole Clark is a little more likely to name names, but not much. Lewis and Clark were writing field notes, not a multicultural accounting of the expedition. They both regarded the thirty-one individuals with whom they were traveling as a support team, not as equals. As time went on they became what romantic historians like to think of as a family, based on Lewis's statement on August 2, 1805, that "accedents will happen in the best families,"[76] but I doubt that Lewis could have identified every individual by name even as late as Fort Clatsop. Given my thesis that Lewis sought to *get there first and get there essentially alone*, it is not surprising that he omitted the names of his companions when one of the discovery moments of the expedition was at hand.

Lewis's first view of the confluence was breathtaking. "I ascended the hills from whence I had a most pleasing view of the country, perticulary of the wide and fertile vallies formed by the missouri and the yellowstone rivers, which occasionally unmasked by the wood on their borders disclose their meanderings for many miles in their passage through these delightfull tracts of country."[77] Notice that now Lewis imagines himself alone on that ridge, even though it is virtually certain that he was not the only one who made that climb on April 25, 1805.

Lewis camped on the night of April 25 "on the bank of the yellowstone river, 2 miles South of it's confluence with the Missouri."[78] Lewis was so busy observing the landscape and hunting for fresh meat that he apparently did not undertake celestial observations until the morning of April 26, by which time the Clark party had caught up or nearly so. So much for jumping ahead to get the celestials and avoid detention. Ordway reports that Lewis "took an observation at 9 oC. and at 12 oClock, also at 4."[79]

Then Lewis wrote one of the beautiful journal passages for which he is justly celebrated: "[A]fter I had completed my observations in the evening I walked down and joined the party at their encampment on the point of land fromed by the junction of the rivers; found them all in good health, and much pleased at having arrived at this long wished for spot, and in order to add in some measure to the general pleasure which seemed to pervade our little community, we ordered a dram to be issued to each person; this soon produced the fiddle, and they spent the evening with much hilarity, singing & dancing, and seemed as perfectly to forget their past toils, as they appeared regardless of those to come."[80] This is magnificent. It is also wonderfully revealing. On the one hand Lewis speaks of "our little community." This is one of those phrases seized on by Lewis and Clark historians as an indication of the camaraderie and esprit de corps that had developed since the expedition assembled at Camp Wood. It invokes one of the central myths of American culture, best represented in our time by such films as *The Dirty Dozen* (1967), *Saving Private Ryan* (1998), and *Ocean's Eleven* and its sequels (2001, 2004, 2007). When there is a higher purpose at stake, a heterogeneous group of individualists and ne'er-do-wells can be forged into a happy and tolerant phalanx that can change the world (or at least break the bank at Las Vegas).

At the same time, Lewis explains that he joined the party "at their encampment." Although he has been separated from the Clark party for only one day, he reports that he "found them all in good health." It's as if he has not really been with the other thirty-two members of the expedition for the past three weeks. He orders a dram of whiskey to be distributed to each man as a reward for having reached "this long wished for spot," but then he makes sure that the reader pictures him at the margin of the "little community," watching as "*they* spent the evening with much hilarity," forgetting "*their* past toils" [emphasis added]. Lewis exhibits here a fascinating mingling of community and detachment. He is both part of the community and aloof from it. In some respects Meriwether Lewis and the Corps of Discovery are crossing the continent in tandem, but one of the participants is a solitary explorer and the other thirty-two are a support team that brings up the rear and hauls the gear. Journal entries such as this give the impression that Lewis was a kind of *Enlightenment man of letters in residence* with a traveling expedition led by Clark, and that Lewis did not always see the main party as his own. One wonders if he ever once joined in the "hilarity, singing & dancing" of the other men of the expedition. Did he hold himself apart because he regarded it as unprofessional to mingle that casually with his military and social subordinates? Or was Lewis just not the sort of man who found pleasure in such group activities? One wonders, too, whether Clark ever joined in the singing and dancing, the boasts and toasts, the jesting and the good-humored insults, the practical jokes and the tomfoolery of the "little community." We cannot know. If one hazarded to guess, of course, it seems much more probable that Clark would have joined the dance than Lewis. Did Lewis envy Clark's capacity for familiarity and relaxation? We cannot know.

When the boats arrived at the confluence on July 26, 1805, Clark ran into George Droulliard, who had been sent by Lewis to inform him that the explorer was "a little way up the Roche johne and would join me this evining." Clark wrote that when he heard this news, "I Sent a canoe up to Capt Lewis."[81] That's William Clark. Clark did not describe the dram or the hilarity. He did not share Lewis's flare for the dramatic. He was too much part of the little community to be able to observe it from the margins.

On the following day, April 27, Lewis and Clark had one of their rare disagreements, albeit a minor one. Lewis explored the wedge of land that formed a point at the confluence of the two rivers. Among other things, he was scouting the confluence in search of a site for a future military or trade fort. Lewis felt that the "establishment," as he called it, should be built on a high bench in the land between the rivers, far enough back from the exact confluence to be immune to flooding. Clark believed that the fort should be built on the lower benchland closer to the exact confluence. "Capt Clark thinks that the lower extremity of the low plane would be most eligible for this establishment," Lewis wrote. "[I]t is true that it is much nearer both rivers, and might answer very well, but I think it reather too low to venture a permanent establishment, particularly if built of brick or other durable materials, at any considerable expense."[82] In fact, in 1828 Fort Union was built on the north bank of the Missouri River a little west of the confluence—in other words, both of their nominations had been rejected.

On April 27, Lewis dined alone at the "long wished for spot." "[T]he wind became very hard from N.W. insomuch that the perogues and canoes were unable either to proceede or pass the river to me; I was under the necessity therefore of shooting a goose and cooking it for my dinner. the wind abated about 4 P.M. and the party proceeded tho' I could not conveniently join them untill night."[83] The expedition spent two nights at the confluence on the outbound journey. Lewis was with the little community one night and all alone on the other. The Lewis and Clark Expedition camped for the night on April 27 just inside today's Montana. Though he did not know it, Lewis had been the first member of the expedition to enter what became the forty-first state.

On May 25 and again on May 26, 1805, William Clark became the first expedition member to see the Rocky Mountains. At the beginning of his long journal entry for that day, Lewis wrote, "Capt. Clark walked on shore this morning and ascended to the summit of the river hills   he informed me on his return that he had seen mountains on both sides of the river running nearly parrallel with it and at no great distance."[84] As soon as Clark returned to the boats and made his report, Lewis got himself up on that ridge. "In the after part of the day," he wrote, "I also walked out and ascended the river hills which I found sufficiently fortiegueing. on arriving to the summit one of the highest points in the neighbourhood I thought myself well repaid for any labour; as from this point I beheld the Rocky Mountains for the first time."[85] Lewis's *fortigue* was indeed well paid. The passage he now wrote has proved to be irresistibly compelling. In fact, it is so perfect a statement of the explorer's moment that it has effectively erased the fact that it was Clark, not Lewis, who first beheld the Rocky Mountains.

[W]hile I viewed these mountains I felt a secret pleasure in finding myself so near the head of the heretofore conceived boundless Missouri; but when I reflected on the difficulties which this snowey barrier would most probably throw in my way to the Pacific, and the sufferings and hardships of myself and party in them, it in some measure counterballanced the joy I had felt in the first moments in which I gazed on them; but as I have always held it a crime to anticipate evils I will believe it a good comfortable road untill I am compelled to beleive differently.[86]

Jefferson said the earth belongs to the living. History belongs to the literate. Because Lewis wrote precisely what the explorer should write at this moment, what Clark was not temperamentally configured to write, what Clark perhaps was not capable of writing, Lewis has effectively shouldered Clark out of the story. Not purposefully—Lewis dutifully notes that Clark got to the viewing platform first, as any reader of the unabridged journals can plainly see. But the overwhelming majority of all readers of the journals of Lewis and Clark have been content with abridgements. Where space is limited, editors and historians have been incapable of resisting Lewis's superior and more romantic account of the first viewing of the Rocky Mountains. Frank Bergon gives the moment to Lewis. So does Anthony Brandt. John Bakeless garbles the authorship of Lewis's May 26 journal entry, thus making it seem as if those epic sentences were actually written by Clark. Bernard DeVoto, to his credit, includes Lewis's mention of Clark's ascent earlier in the day before printing the famous passage.[87]

Gary Moulton's outstanding 2003 abridgement of the journals he worked on for so many years also erases Clark's moment of discovery. Moulton's entry for May 26, 1805, begins with Lewis's, "In the after part of the day I also walked ... ."[88] Clark is reduced to sour grapes. His entire entry for May 26, 1805, in the Moulton abridgement reads as follows: "[T]his Countrey may with propriety I think be termed the Deserts of America, as I do not Conceive any part can ever be Settled, as it is deficent in water, Timber & too Steep to be tilled."[89] Readers of this and other abridgements inevitably think of Lewis as the first to sight the Rocky Mountains; readers of Moulton's *The Lewis and Clark Journals: An American Epic of Discovery* see Lewis in full romantic effusion and Clark adumbrating Stephen Long's *great American desert*.

Historians have been as smitten as editors with Lewis's prose. David Freeman Hawke gives the moment exclusively to Lewis.[90] Richard Dillon reports that "Lewis's spirits were recharged by the sight that greeted his eyes," from the top of the ridge.[91] Dillon makes no mention of Clark's prior observation of the Rockies. Stephen Ambrose fudged the incident. He begins by describing Lewis's first view of the Rocky Mountains, but then makes a pro forma mention of Clark. "Clark thought he had seen distant mountains the previous day; Lewis's confirmation made them the first two Americans to see the Rockies."[92] John Logan Allen correctly gave Clark the first view on May 25, but quotes from Lewis's grand prose on May 26.[93]

Pleasing President Thomas Jefferson meant a great deal to Meriwether Lewis. Not pleasing him was a source of deep disquietude—to both men. Courtesy of the Independence National Historical Park.

Even Clark's biographers succumb. William Foley writes, "Captain Clark caught a glimpse of a high mountain to the west, and by May 26 he was prepared to proclaim with certainty that the distant snowcapped peaks he had seen were in fact the Rockies, but Lewis had been the first to confront the possibility that the snowy barrier might stand astride the good comfortable road that they had expected to conduct them through the fabled passage to India."[94]

David Nicandri has carefully studied the passages in Clark's journals that essentially copy what Lewis had written on (or for) the same day. This was a security measure the captains appear to have adopted after a couple of boat accidents in the spring of 1805. Although Clark dutifully copied whatever Lewis wrote, sometimes taking on Lewis's humor, wry perspective, epic pose, and Latinate vocabulary as if in the first person, he also occasionally engaged in slight editorial adjustments as he copied Lewis's journal. The more one studies these little emendations, what might be called Clark's subtle running dialogue with his partner in the discovery, the more one learns about the differences between the two leaders. When Clark copied Lewis's May 26, 1805, first view journal entry, he effected a small but important adjustment. Lewis had written, "[F]rom this point I beheld the Rocky Mountains for the first time." Clark's copy read, "[F]rom this point I beheld the Rocky Mountains for the first time with Certainty." Nicandri concludes, "Clark dutifully copied all this Rocky Mountain Romance, but by subtly adding the words 'with Certainty' at the outset of Lewis's textual soliloquy, he quietly asserts his proper place in the story of the authoritative first sighting of the Rocky Mountains."[95]

Perhaps Clark was too subtle. Even Nicholas Biddle, who may be said to have been the first Clarkie (one who tends to prefer Clark to Lewis), gave the mantle to Lewis: "It was here that, after ascending the highest summit of the hills on the north side of the river, Captain Lewis first caught a distant view of the Rocky mountains—the object of all our hopes, and the reward of all our ambition."[96] Elliott Coues, in a footnote, quotes Lewis's passage from the journal of May 26, 1805, calling it "delightful."[97]

History belongs to the literate.

On June 13, 1805, Lewis became *the first civilized man* to see the Great Falls of the Missouri River. The story of how he got there first is fascinating.

As all students of the expedition know, the confluence of the Marias and the Missouri Rivers produced a significant geographic crisis for the captains. As Lewis put it, "An interesting question was now to be determined; which of these rivers was the Missouri, or that river which the Minnetares call *Amahte Arz zha* or Missouri, and which they had discribed to us as approaching very near to the Columbia river."[98] The captains made three efforts to determine which was the main channel and which the tributary. Lewis wrote, "[C]onvinced we were that the utmost circumspection and caution was necessary in deciding on the stream to be taken." First, on June 3, the captains "sent out several small parties by land with instructions to penetrate the country as far as they conveniently can permiting themselves time to return this evening."[99] Then, "[T]hose accounts being by no means satisfactory as to the fundamental point,"[100] Lewis and Clark each undertook a more sustained land reconnaissance "with a small party each, and ascend these rivers untill we could perfectly satisfy ourselves of the one, which it would be most expedient for us to take on our main journey to the Pacific."[101] Accordingly, Lewis ascended what turned out to be the tributary, the Marias, with Pryor, the inevitable Drouillard, Shields, Windsor, Cruzatte, and Lepage. Meanwhile, Clark ascended what turned out to be the main stem with the Field brothers, Gass, Shannon, and York. On the eve of his departure Lewis wrote, "I had now my sack and blanket happerst in readiness to swing on my back, which is the first time in my life that I had ever prepared a burthen of this kind, and I am fully convinced that it will not be the last."[102] Lewis, lest we forget, was a Virginia gentleman. The Virginia gentry did not carry their own burdens. In 1807 the liberty-loving Jefferson informed English diplomat Augustus John Foster that black men and women were "made to carry burdens."[103] Lewis ascended the Missouri River more than 2,000 miles before he ever had to carry his own gear.

The Lewis party explored the lower Marias June 4–7, and reunited with Clark at the confluence of the Marias and Missouri on June 8. Clark ascended the Missouri River valley on June 4–5, realized almost immediately that they were indeed on the main branch, and returned to the confluence on June 6. Veteran waterman that he was, he seems to have been less perplexed than Lewis. By June 8, Clark was "Some what uneasy for Capt. Lewis & party as days has now passed the time he was to have returned."[104]

Clark was utterly convinced that the south branch was the true Missouri. On June 5 he had written, "From the ridge at which place I Struck the river last, I could ... discover that the river run west of South a long distance, and has a Strong rapid Current ... as this river Continued its width debth & rapidity and the Course west of South, going up further would be useless."[105] Even so, given the fact that the rest of the men believed the north branch was the Missouri and the south branch a tributary, including Drouillard, and—as Lewis put it—that to "ascend such stream to the rocky Mountain or perhaps much further before we could inform ourselves whether it did approach the Columbia or not, and then be obliged to return and take the other stream would not only loose us the whole of this season but would probably so dishearten the party that it might defeat the expedition altogether,"[106] Lewis determined to make a third reconnaissance.

[F]inding them [everyone but the captains] so determined in this belief [that the Marias was the Missouri], and wishing that if we were in an error to be able to detect it and rectify it as soon as possible it was agreed between Capt. C. and myself that one of us should set out with a small party by land up the South fork and continue our rout up it untill we found the falls or reached the snowy Mountains by which means we should be enabled to determine this question prety accurately.[107]

Lewis reckoned he was the logical choice for this unprecedented journey. "[T]his expedition I prefered undertaking."[108]

At this critical moment Meriwether Lewis regarded himself alone as the commander of the expedition and Clark as the subordinate, albeit a nearly equal one. He did not say *Captain Clark and I, conferring on the best course of action, agreed that I should go ahead.* Why should Lewis take the lead? Because he regarded "Capt. C. best waterman &c." There was a great deal in that extended ampersand. Remember, Lewis had assigned Clark his role as the "best waterman &c." back on the Mississippi River on November 28, 1803. Lewis did not specify which men, if any, he would take with him on the reconnaissance mission. The full passage reads, "[T]his expedition I prefered undertaking as Capt. C. best waterman &c. and determined to set out the day after tomorrow," even though, as he immediately went on to explain, "I felt myself very unwell this morning."[109] Lewis was ill, Clark perfectly healthy, but in spite of that Lewis determined to undertake the mission. Clark wrote a very brief journal entry for June 9, 1805. He made no mention of the third reconnaissance whatsoever. It is, I believe, deeply significant that he did not bother to describe the additional survey Lewis *preferred* to undertake himself. For one thing, Clark was already certain that the south fork was the Missouri River. He had regarded the issue as settled on June 5. Clark ended the discursive portion of his journal entry for June 9 by embedding himself firmly in the *little community* to which he belonged more fully than Lewis. "[T]he men all engaged dressing Skins for their clothes, in the evening the party amused themselves danceing and Singing Songes in the most Social manner."[110]

On June 10, Lewis wrote, "I still feel myself somewhat unwell with disentary, but determined to set out in the morning up the South fork or Missouri leaving Capt. Clark to compleat the deposit and follow me by water with the party."[111] Lewis chose Drouillard, Joseph Field, George Gibson, and Silas Goodrich as his travel companions. Clark saw the situation a little differently. On June 10 he wrote, "[W]e deturmined to assend the South fork, and one of us, Capt. Lewis or My self to go by land as far as the Snow mountains … and examine the river & Countrey Course & to be Certain of our assending the proper river." Then he immediately added, "Capt Lewis inclines to go by land on this expedition, accordingly Selects … ."[112] *Inclines.* It's hard to know quite what to make of this. It sounds as if Clark would have liked to have undertaken the reconnaissance himself or merely to have proceeded on together in the certainty that the south branch was the true Missouri, but that Lewis had insisted upon going ahead. Clark's usual way of describing expedition decisions is to use the term *we* or to speak of *Capt Lewis and myself.* Clark's journal describes hundreds of apparently seamless joint decisions in the course of the twenty-eight-month expedition. On a few occasions he makes clear that Lewis has assumed command. This is one of them. On such occasions Clark accepts Lewis's decision, of course, but he sometimes leaves a slight verbal record—a subtle tremor—of his sense of disappointment, deflation, or annoyance. The fact that Clark tells us that "Capt Lewis inclines to go by land on this expedition" is—at the very least—an indication that Lewis made the decision and Clark simply accepted it. It could also mean that Clark felt some variety of chagrin or possibly even anger when he was told of Lewis's decision, given the fact that he had already conducted a preliminary reconnaissance of the Missouri River west of the confluence, already solved the geographic puzzle, and given the even more significant fact that Lewis was unmistakably indisposed at this juncture. All we know for sure is that, in spite of his ill health, Lewis does not indicate that he was weighing the possibility that Clark might make the trek. He *inclined* or *preferred* to make the journey. To this there was no appeal. Lewis left with his "little party" at 8 A.M. on June 11. By mid-day he was suffering from stomach cramps "with such violent pain in the intestens that I was unable to partake of the feast of marrowbones."[113] For a lover of fine food like Lewis, being deprived of such a *feast* was a serious disappointment. By evening Lewis was suffering from a high fever, so powerful that he was "unable to march," i.e., continue his hike. It was on this occasion that Lewis had a concoction of choke cherry tea made for himself. The folk remedy was so efficacious, or Lewis was so physically resilient, that "by 10 in the evening I was entirely releived from pain and in fact every symptom of the disorder forsook me."[114] On June 12 Lewis was back at his march by sunrise, after another pot of choke cherry tea. He hiked twenty-seven miles and killed a couple of grizzly bears before halting for the day a little upstream from Black Coulee in today's Chouteau County, Montana. Lewis and his four companions were now just ten miles from the falls.

In spite of his ill health, Lewis was thriving. "This evening I ate very heartily," he wrote, "and after pening the transactions of the day amused myself catching those white fish mentioned yesterday; they are here in great abundance   I caught upwards of a douzen in a few minutes."[115] Clark, the "best waterman &c.," spent the day moving the flotilla forward, trying to keep the canoes from tipping, and ministering to Sacagawea ("the interpreters wife"), who was gravely ill. "I move her into the back part of our Covered part of the Perogue which is Cool, her own situation being a verry hot one in the bottom of the Perogue exposed to the Sun."[116] Among other things, this passage reveals the generous humanity of Clark, and also that by now individuals had "assigned" seats in the boats. Because Sacagawea's assigned seat exposed her to the sun, Clark moved her temporarily to a cooler spot.

On June 13, 1805, Lewis reduced the number in his immediate party. He sent Joseph Field in one direction and Drouillard and Gibson in another, "with orders to kill some meat and join me at the river where I should halt for dinner."[117] This would seem to be the Lewis pattern, the *modus operandi* of the explorer, to reduce the number of companions to whatever is regarded as a safe and statistical minimum as the moment of discovery approaches. Lewis pressed forward alone with Silas Goodrich, a man of so little consequence that he is hardly ever mentioned in the journals. Significantly, none of the four men who accompanied Lewis were keeping journals. No Gass, no Frazer, no Ordway, no Pryor,[118] and no Clark was with Lewis on that important day.

Notice what follows in Lewis's account of the day. "I had proceeded on this course about two miles with Goodrich at some distance behind me whin my ears were saluted with the agreeable sound of a fall of water and advancing a little further I saw the spray arrise above the plain like a collumn of smoke."[119] Goodrich was not ahead of Lewis. He was not side-by-side with Lewis. He was "some distance behind me whin my ears … ." At what he regarded as one of the handful of most important moments of the expedition, indeed one of the most important moments of his life, Meriwether Lewis made sure he was alone. More to the point, perhaps, he made sure *we* knew he was alone. The care he took in making sure that history understood that Goodrich's first view of the Great Falls came behind and after his own cannot be regarded as a random detail. On June 13, 1805, the expedition consisted of thirty-three individuals. Twenty-eight of these individuals had been left behind on June 11. That was the first step. On the morning of June 13, Lewis reduced his five-man reconnaissance party to two, one of them an expedition nonentity. That was the second step. When he discovered the Great Falls just before noon, Lewis was alone in the wilderness. The last of his companions, in some respects the least of his companions, was "some distance behind." We have no idea, of course, whether Goodrich was ten steps or a thousand steps behind Lewis at that moment. In point of actual fact, we have no way to be sure that Goodrich was behind Lewis at all. Our cultural memory of the discovery of the Great Falls of the Missouri River derives solely from the journal of Meriwether Lewis. Without calling into question Lewis's integrity, I suggest that it was in Lewis's interest to write his companions out of the story of the discovery of the Great Falls and that the actual freeze-frame (satellite view) placement of Meriwether Lewis and Silas Goodrich at the moment of discovery is less important than Lewis's narrative of that moment. From an explorer's point of view, it would have been ludicrous, even insane, for Lewis to put a subordinate at the lip of the Great Falls before himself, even if it could be proven that Goodrich got there first and hallowed his commander. When Richard Francis Burton discovered Lake Tanganyika in February 1858, he made sure his readers were aware that his companion Lieutenant John Speke was temporarily blind and unable to see the immense body of water that glimmered before them. Speke was indeed blind at that moment, but it was essential for Burton to inform his readers of that fact, to insist that he, not his ambitious companion, had the first view of the massive lake.

Lewis discovered the Great Falls of the Missouri in mid-morning June 13, 1805. On or for that date he wrote one of the greatest passages in the history of exploration: "I hurryed down the hill which was about 200 feet high and difficult of access, to gaze on this sublimely grand specticle. I took my position on top of some rocks about 20 feet high opposite the center of the falls."[120] Where was Goodrich? Now, in one of the supreme moments of his life, Lewis has written Goodrich entirely out of the narrative. Was Goodrich sitting next to him or wandering around the falls or taking a nap or swimming or hunting or praying or ... ? Nobody bothered to describe his response to the discovery. Lewis sat down and wrote a long description of the falls, partly scientific, partly poetic. The smooth sheet of water that flowed on the left side of the falls impressed him, but "the remaining part of about 200 yards on my right formes the grandest sight I ever beheld," because jagged rocks below received "the water in it's passage down and brakes it into a perfect white foam which assumes a thousand forms in a moment sometimes flying up in jets of sparkling foam to the hight of fifteen or twenty feet and scarcely formed before large roling bodies of the same beaten and foaming water is thrown over and conceals them."[121]

After lamenting his incapacity with the pen—in a purely conventional way—and wishing he had the poetic capacity of James Thomson or the artistic talent of Salvator Rosa so that "I might be enabled to give to the enlightened world some just idea of this truly magnifficent and sublimely grand object, which has from the commencement of time been concealed from the view of civilized man," *until, that is, the arrival of Meriwether Lewis*, the explorer wrote, "I retired to the shade of a tree where I determined to fix my camp for the present and dispatch a man in the morning to inform Capt. C. and the party of my success."[122] *My success*. It would be interesting to know just what success Lewis was referring to here. Was it confirmation that the south branch was indeed the Missouri? Or was it the discovery of an "object, which has from the commencement of time been concealed from the view of civilized man"? Only after Lewis had "retired to the shade" to process his discovery by himself did he report that "the hunters now arrived loaded with excellent buffaloe meat." From a narrative point of view this makes perfect sense, that the others would not arrive until after

Lewis had drunk his fill of the falls. It is impossible to know whether Lewis's narrative sequencing is strictly accurate. Lewis's companions, carefully un-named, are now described as *hunters* not explorers. And Lewis immediately got rid of them. "I directed them after they had refreshed themselves to go back and butcher them [the buffalo cows] and bring another load of meat each to our camp determining to employ those who remained with me in drying meat for the party against their arrival."[123] It's hard to imagine what more Lewis could have done to insure that he was a solitary explorer when the moment came to discover the Great Falls. The next day he made sure that he was authentically—not just nominally—alone.

That night or first thing the next morning (June 14, 1805), Lewis wrote a letter to inform "Capt. C. and the party of my success in finding the falls and settle in their minds all further doubts as to the Missouri."[124] Clark had no doubts. In fact, while Lewis ventured ahead to discover the Great Falls, Clark had unhesitatingly proceeded on up the main stem of the Missouri at the usual pace. Clark received Lewis's letter at 4 P.M. on June 14. He wrote, "Capt Lewis dates his letter from the Great falls of the Missouri."[125]

Meriwether Lewis had a wonderful flare for the dramatic. Even if this dateline annoyed Clark, some part of him must have admired his romantic friend, too.

Clark's health deteriorated at the end of July 1805, just when his mo-ment of glory beckoned.

On July 18, just north of the Gates of the Mountains at today's Helena, Montana, Clark wrote, "[W]e thought it prudent for a partey to go a head for fear our fireing Should allarm the Indians and cause them to leave the river and take to the mountains for Safty from their enemies who visit them thro this rout."[126] The expedition was getting ahead of itself. Lewis and Clark were still several hundred miles from the Shoshone homelands. They probably assumed that a meeting with the Shoshone was imminent because they misunderstood something said by Sacagawea (from Hidatsa to French to English), who had been captured a few years previously by Hidatsa raiders on the Jefferson River near the Three Forks. The expedition was nearing the place where she had been captured, but it was no longer the Shoshone homeland.

At this juncture the subordinate commander asserted himself in the manner of Lewis. "I deturmined to go a head with a Small partey a few days and find the Snake Indians if possible."[127] Clark chose his slave York, Joseph Field, and John Potts as his companions. If Clark had been able to persevere in this quest, he might have been gone for several weeks or a whole month before he made first contact with the Shoshone. Unfortunately,

Clark and his companions immediately became footsore. On July 20, Clark wrote, "[T]he feet of the men with me So Stuck with Prickley pear & cut with the Stones that they were Scerseley able to march at a Slow gate this after noon."[128] He also reported, "[M]y man York nearly tired out." Lewis learned from his partner's experience. After describing Clark's ordeal and noting that "he [Clark] extracted 17 of these bryers from his feet this evening after he encamped by the light of the fire," Lewis explained that "I have guarded or reather fortifyed my feet against them [prickly pears] by soaling my mockersons with the hide of the buffaloe in parchment."[129] Lewis, writing a journal for July 20 at some later time, and thus able to explain what Clark was doing even though they were separated, said that Clark and his companions were in such pain that "he determined to encamp on the river and wait my arrival."[130] Lewis caught up with Clark on July 22, 1805, at a campsite now under the waters of Canyon Ferry Lake in Broadwater County, Montana.

That night, Lewis and Clark had some kind of confrontation. Lewis believed Clark was too exhausted and footsore to continue. He recommended that they switch roles. Clark positively refused to yield. "[A]ltho' Capt C. was much fatiegued his feet yet blistered and soar he insisted on pursuing his rout in the morning nor weould he consent willingly to my releiving him at that time by taking a tour of the same kind. finding him anxious I readily consented to remain with the canoes."[131] This is one of the most fascinating passages in the journals of Lewis and Clark. Lewis's phrase, "nor weould he consent willingly," suggests that the discussion became so heated that the only way Lewis could have prevented Clark from continuing his land reconnaissance would have been to issue a direct order to that effect. Lewis wisely chose to yield rather than force the first formal command confrontation of the expedition. *Anxious—insisted—nor weould he consent willingly*: strong words. When Nicholas Biddle read over the journals in preparing them for publication, he replaced the word *insisted* in Lewis's journal manuscript with *deturmined*, perhaps at Clark's urging, perhaps to soften the confrontation in the eyes of the reader. In his *History of the Lewis and Clark Expedition*, Biddle expunged the confrontation altogether. After explaining why it was so important for "one of us to go forward with a small party," to make contact with the Shoshone, Biddle writes, "Accordingly Captain Clark set out with three men ... ."[132]

In the last two weeks of July 1805, Clark's physical and mental reserves were sufficiently exhausted that he ran out of patience with Meriwether Lewis. If ever the two captains fell out of harmony, this was the time. It is difficult to discern the actual dynamics through the restrained and carefully constructed journal entries of this period, and even more difficult to determine the intensity of the dissension. By now the expedition had floated all the easy stretches of the Missouri River. They were a very long way from St. Louis. The discovery phase of the expedition (beginning with April 7, 1805) had brought out some interesting energies, posturings, and de facto assertions of command in Lewis. Clark had effectively been reminded that, polite fictions aside, Lewis was the real commander of the expedition and that he—Clark— was a support player, albeit an essential and much-respected one. Clark had stood by stoically and with his usual sense of forbearance while Lewis struck out ahead for the confluence of the Missouri and the Yellowstone, and while he got himself first to the Great Falls of the Missouri. Then he had twiddled his thumbs while Lewis lost precious time fussing with his pet iron-framed boat.[133] Clark was incapable of the kind of irascibility, impulsiveness, and moodiness that sometimes characterized his friend Lewis. He had learned from an early age to subordinate himself to and serve gifted men who were incapable of negotiating their way through life by themselves. Clark deported himself throughout the Lewis and Clark Expedition with remarkable equanimity and self-restraint. He knew his place. His general temperament was admirably suited to the role Lewis had crafted for him. There is no evidence that the relations between the two "captains" ever actually broke down, no evidence that they ever raised their voices at each other or reached a fundamental impasse. But the closest they ever came was in late July 1805 between Upper Portage Camp and today's Dillon, Montana.

On July 22, Clark moved on ahead, as he *determined* and *insisted*, but he was not really up to it. His body let him down at the critical moment. "I find my Self much weaker than when I left the Canoes and more inclined to rest & repose to day," he confessed. That night Clark "opened the bruses & blisters of my feet which caused them to be painfull."[134] According to Dr. David Peck, this was a serious mistake. "Intact blisters protect the underlying raw skin, giving it time to generate more surface cells that will protect yet deeper layers. Clark's self-treatment rendered the blisters into open wounds."[135] Still, Clark wrote, "I deturmined to proceed on in pursute of the Snake Indians on tomorrow and directed Jo Rubin Fields Frasure to get ready to accompany me."[136] Charbonneau requested permission to travel with Clark, probably because he found the labor of hauling the expedition's boats upstream excessive. Predictably, Charbonneau's limited stamina broke on the third day of the hiking excursion.[137] Clark resumed his journey on July 23. In spite of his physical ailments, he hiked a full twenty-five miles that day. On July 25, Clark became the first civilized man to reach the three forks of the Missouri River. Unfortunately he was too tired to lavish much attention on the moment in his journal. "[W]e proceeded on a fiew miles to the three forks of the Missouri   those three forks are nearly of a Size, the North fork appears to have the most water … ."[138] The next day Clark climbed up "to the top of a mountain 12 miles distant west and from thence view the river & vallies a head, we with great dificuelty & much fatigue reached the top at 11 oClock."[139] Unfortunately, the reader of the journals is not well repaid for Clark's extraordinary excursion. All he writes is, "[F]rom the top of this mountain I could see the Course of the North fork about 10 miles meandering through a Vallie but Could discover no Indians or Sign which was fresh."[140] Perhaps by now he knew that whatever he wrote would be trumped by Lewis anyway. When Lewis arrived with the boats on July 27 he wrote, "[T]herefore to call either of these streams the Missouri would be giving it a preference wich it's size dose not warrant as it is not larger then the other."[141] The next day Lewis wrote, "Both Capt. C. and myself corrisponded [i.e., agreed] in opinon with rispect to the impropriety of calling either of these streams the Missouri and accordingly agreed to name them after the President of the United States and the Secretaries of the Treasury and state having previously named one river in honour of the Secretaries of War and Navy."[142] Naturally, the principal stream, "that which we meant to ascend," was denominated the Jefferson River. On first glance it may seem a little surprising that Lewis included Clark in the decision to name the three branches of the Missouri after Jefferson, Madison, and Gallatin. That was a decision he almost certainly made himself. It may be that Lewis realized that the idea of naming continentally important streams after sitting members of the existing administration in Washington had the potential to create controversy back in the national political arena. One need only imagine the Federalist response to this sort of partisan nomenclature. If Lewis felt uneasy in naming the three contributing tributaries after Republican cabinet officials of an administration that, for all he knew, might not even still be in power, here was a situation in which he was all too willing to embrace Clark in the journal narrative. Safety in numbers. A joint decision on controversial nomenclature would give the names more credibility than a decision made solely by the president's protégé and family friend.

On July 26, Clark's health broke. "I was fatigued my feet with Several blisters & Stuck with prickley pears. I eate but verry little … I felt my Self verry unwell & took up Camp … ."[143] Given his weakness and his badly damaged feet, and the fatigues of York and Charbonneau, Clark had not even managed to range ahead of the slow-moving boats. On July 27 Lewis wrote an anxious account of Clark's debility.

> [A]t 3 P.M. Capt Clark arrived very sick with a high fever on him and much fatiegued and exhausted. he informed me that he was very sick all last night had a high fever and frequent chills & constant aking pains in all his mustles. this morning notwithstanding his indisposition he pursued his intended rout. … Capt. C. thought himself somewhat bilious and had not had a passage for several days; I prevailed on him to take a doze of Rushes pills, which I have always found sovereign in such cases and to bath his feet in warm water and rest himself. Capt. C's indisposition was a further inducement for my remaining here a couple of days.[144]

David Peck believes that Clark's illness was more than just fatigue. It might have been Colorado tick fever, Peck believes, or for that matter tularemia, or Rocky Mountain spotted fever. Just as easily, it might have been "run-of-the-mill viral illnesses, or wound infection from his blisters," Peck concludes.[145] Bruce Paton believes that Clark probably had tick fever.[146]

Lewis took good care of his ailing friend. He dosed him with Dr. Rush's thunderbolts, and "I had a small bower or booth erected for the comfort of Capt. C. our leather lodge when exposed to the sun is excessively hot."[147] He also now made an executive decision. Worrying that if the expedition failed to make contact with the Shoshone Indians, "I fear the successfull issue of our voyage will be very doubtfull or at all events much more difficult in it's accomplishement," Lewis announced that Clark would thereafter be relieved of the Shoshone search mission. "[H]owever I still hope for the best, and intend taking a tramp myself in a few days to find these yellow gentlemen if possible."[148] Clark accepted the decision with characteristic stoicism, perhaps because his poor health was eclipsing all other concerns at this point. "I continue to be verry unwell," he wrote on July 27, "fever verry high; take 5 of rushes pills & bathe my feet & legs in hot water."[149] Clark's health slowly improved, probably owing more to the bower than the thunderbolts.

On July 31, Clark wrote, "Capt Lewis deturmin to proceed on with three me[n] in Serch of the Snake Indians, tomorrow."[150] On August 1, Lewis set off, "as had been previously agreed on between Capt. Clark and myself," with George Drouillard, Charbonneau and Sergeant Patrick Gass who was injured, and therefore more useful on a hiking trip than as one of the expedition's boatmen. *Agreed on* is probably a serious overstatement. Clark wasn't the only member of the expedition whose health was debilitated by the heat, the prickly pears, and the labor of dragging the boats against the shallows of the Jefferson River. "[W]e have a lame crew just now," Lewis reported, "two with tumers or bad boils on various parts of them, one with a bad stone bruise, one with his arm accedently dislocated but fortunately well replaced, and a fifth has streigned his back by sliping and falling backwards on the gunwall of the canoe."[151] Lewis's health wasn't very good at this point, either. "I had taken a doze of the glauber salts in the morning in consequence of a slight desentary with which I had been afflicted for several days; being weakened by the disorder and the opperation of the medecine I found myself almost exhausted before we reached the river."[152] The accumulative strains of the expedition were beginning to take a toll on the Corps of Discovery. Everyone was exhausted. The late summer heat of Montana was debilitating, as were the extensive fields of cactus through which the expedition was slogging its way west. David Peck says, "Lewis's list of disabled read like a modern-day National Football League injury list."[153]

Still, as it turns out, Lewis had made the right choice. On August 4, as he worked his way overland towards the Shoshone, Clark, managing the boats, reported, "I could not walk on Shore to day as my ankle was Sore from a tumer on that part."[154] The captains met again on August 6, partly because Charbonneau was lame and had to be returned to the water party, partly because Lewis wanted to make sure that Clark took the correct fork at the confluence of the Big Hole and the Beaverhead. The expedition spent the next couple of days attempting to take celestial observations, drying gear that had fallen into the river in a canoe accident, including lead gunpowder canisters, "some of them had remained upwards of an hour under water,"[155] and waiting for George Shannon who—once again—was lost. Lewis's restlessness and impatience went through the roof.

> [A]s it is now all important with us to meet with those people [the Shoshone] as soon as possible," he wrote on August 8, "I determined <to leave the charge of the party, and the care of the lunar observations to Capt. Clark; and> to proceed tomorrow with a small party to the source of the principal stream of this river and pass the mountains to the Columbia; and down that river untill I found the Indians; in short it is my resolusion to find them or some others, who have horses if it should cause me a trip of one month. for without horses we shall be obliged to leave a great part of our stores, of which, it appears to me that we have a stock already sufficiently small for the length of the voyage before us.[156]

This has the ring of uncomplicated sincerity and undisguised anxiety. Lewis was now so concerned about the fate of the expedition that he actually rushed ahead at dawn's early light on August 9 to give himself some writing time before the flotilla caught up with him. "[B]y this means," he explained, "I acquired leasure to accomplish some wrightings which I conceived from the nature of my instructions necessary lest any accedent should befall me on the long and reather hazardous rout I was now about to take."[157] Just what Lewis wrote that morning is the subject of historical speculation. His reference to Jefferson's *instructions* suggests that Lewis was mostly concerned about the transfer of command authority in the event that he perished on his mission to the Shoshone. On June 20, 1803, Jefferson had written, "To provide, on the accident of your death, against anarchy, dispersion, & the consequent danger to your party, and total failure of the enterprize, you are hereby authorised, by any instrument signed & written in your own hand, to name the person among them who shall succeed to the command on your decease."[158] Everyone seemed to agree that the easiest phases of the expedition were now coming to an end. On July 31, Lewis wrote ominously, "[W]hen we have a plenty of fresh meat I find it impossible to make the men take any care of it, or use it with the least frugallity. tho' I expect that necessity will shortly teach them this art."[159]

He was right. Lewis was physically tougher than Clark, but his mental strength was much more fragile. The strain of leadership was beginning to take a toll on his mental stamina. Lewis knew that if the expedition collapsed he would be solely responsible—in the eyes of Jefferson and in the offices of the War Department—and Clark's co-captaincy would then be seen as nothing more than a polite fiction. As he prepared to venture with a dangerously small contingent of men into the unknown on "a trip of one month," if necessary, Lewis seems to have considered the possibility that he might never return. As a responsible commander, he made formal arrangements for his succession, should it come to that.

On August 9, Clark wrote, "Capt Lewis and 3 men Set out after brackft. to examine the river above, find a portage if possible, also the Snake Indians." Then he added, "I Should have taken this trip had I been able to march, from the rageing fury of a tumer on my anckle musle."[160] Clark was essentially saying that if there had been any way his body could have carried him towards the source of the Missouri River and the homeland of the Shoshone, he would have clung to his previous determination and insistence, and not permitted Lewis to veto his mission.

It is clear from the repeated references to his fevers, listlessness, digestive issues, and bruised and infected feet that Clark's health really had broken down after the heroic eighteen and a quarter-mile portage around the Great Falls. Even so, the normally pragmatic and good-humored Clark had been determined to take the lead in this situation, to ascend the final tributaries of the Missouri River and to make first contact with the Shoshone Indians. Why was this journey so important to him? The intensity of Clark's will to strike out ahead of the rest, and the unrestrained anguish he expresses after watching Lewis set off on August 9 in his place, must have great significance. There is nothing quite like it anywhere else in the expedition's journals. The explanation that makes most sense is that Clark had come to realize, somewhere between April 7, 1805, and the expedition's entrance into the Gates of the Mountains, July 19, 1805, that they were nearing the end of their Missouri River journey, and that Lewis had garnered all the firsts for himself. In other words, at some point Clark must either have realized that it was now or never on his claim to a place in the history of exploration for his discoveries on a journey whose primary mission was to explore America's new Louisiana Territory, whose boundary was getting closer every day; or he must have begun to feel something like resentment that Lewis had managed, each time plausibly enough, to think of a reason to go ahead of Clark to a landscape of discovery. If Lewis had notched the confluence of the two greatest rivers beyond the last outpost of Euro-American civilization, and the geographically and infrastructurally critical fall line of the Missouri, the only great discovery left for Clark would be the source of the Missouri River. At the same time, he must have realized that because the expedition could not get over the Rocky Mountains without the horses of the Shoshone people, whoever made historic first contact with those people was surely going to be remembered in the history of North America. Clark's anxiety—his sense of iron determination—was almost certainly born of a combination of ambition and creeping resentment. Somehow Clark had managed on this occasion to overwhelm his glory-greedy partner in discovery, even though it is clear from Lewis's journal that he found Clark's sudden assertiveness either amusing (to use his favorite term) or slightly annoying. Then, in what must have been the most frustrating element of the whole episode, Clark's body let him down just at the moment when his ego had taken care of himself for a change. Clark's August 9 statement, "I Should have taken this trip had I been able to march, from the rageing fury of a tumer on my anckle musle,"[161] is proof positive that he focused his anger on himself. The *rageing fury* was not so much about his ankle as it was about his profound sense of disappointment. The iron man Lewis, even though he was none too healthy himself, was able to make the journey with the help of his patented parchment mockersons.

One can sense Lewis's pride on August 9, 1805, when he writes, "[I]mmediately after breakfast I slung my pack and set out accompanyed by Drewyer Shields and McNeal who had been previoiusly directed to hold themselves in readiness for this service."[162]

It is quite possible that the nine days between August 9 and 17, 1805, were the greatest days of Lewis's life. When he came to have his portrait painted by Févret de Saint-Mémin (1770–1852) in the summer of 1807, Lewis chose to dress in buckskins rather than his army uniform. In fact, he had himself painted wearing the otter skin tippet he had purchased from the leader of the Shoshone Indians, Cameahwait, in late August 1805. It is a cliché of occidental exploration that the hero eventually reaches a people who have never encountered a white man before, that he faces them alone, relying on his wits alone to keep him alive in an extremely dangerous situation, and that when he has established the first calm in the encounter, he utters some variation of "take me to your leader." Lewis's quintessential explorer's moment came on August 13, 1805, near today's Tendoy, Idaho. That was the day he made contact with the three Shoshone women, a paradigmatically perfect trio consisting of an old woman, a young woman, and a child, whose "tawny cheeks," he painted with vermilion "which with this nation is emblematic of peace."[163] It was with sign language that day that he asked the three women "to conduct us to their camp that we wer anxious to become acquainted with the chiefs and warriors of their nation."[164] That was the day that Lewis advanced alone, without a gun, in the face of "about 60 warriors mounted on excellent horses who came in nearly full speed… leaving my gun with the party about 50 paces behind me."[165] That was the day Lewis was embraced again and again by the nearly naked, war-painted Cameahwait and his closest advisers, until "we wer all caressed and besmeared with their grease and paint till I was heartily tired of the national hug."[166] No wonder Lewis wanted to be painted in the Shoshone tippet. His first encounter with the Shoshone is so purely remarkable as a moment in the history of exploration, so perfectly described by the expedition's master narrative craftsman Lewis, so intelligently balanced between large gesture and minute detail, and punctuated with Lewis's odd sense of humor, *tawny cheeks*, and the increasingly annoying *national hug*, that it reads more like the formulaic fiction of exploration and encounter than an actual historical incident of August 1805. From an explorer's point of view, what could possibly be better than making successful first contact with an alien people in so vulnerable a manner? No matter how long he lived, no matter what he achieved, Meriwether Lewis could never have another moment as heightened, raw, vulnerable, uncanny, delicious, and triumphant as that one. What was Frederick Bates's greatest adventure? Or William Simmons's? Or for that matter James Madison's?

Here's the important point. Lewis not only brought a capacity for explorer's prose to this moment that neither Clark nor any other member of the expedition could have exhibited in a like situation, but something in the odd and compelling character of Lewis was peculiarly and uniquely suited to this moment. It is possible to conjecture that Clark in the same situation would have survived and made successful contact with Cameahwait, but the experience would almost certainly not have fallen out in quite this way. Clark was so much less pretentious, full of himself, and self-consciously dramatic that he might have evaporated the agony and ecstasy of the moment into something much more pedestrian and jejune. It is hard to think of Clark lifting up an old woman and painting her tawny cheeks. It is impossible to imagine Clark kvetching about the national hug of the Shoshone people. As readers of the journals of Lewis and Clark, and lovers of this American epic, we have to be grateful that Clark's feet gave out near Dillon, Montana. There is one and only one member of the Lewis and Clark Expedition who was equal to the encounter of August 13, 1805, and it was high-strung, excitable, romantic, and self-dramatizing Meriwether Lewis, not the able, affable, and straightforward William Clark. If the balance of discoveries had to be righted, it would be infinitely wiser to give Clark the confluence of the Yellowstone and the Missouri, or even the Great Falls themselves, than to substitute him for Lewis on the Shoshone encounter. Clark's discovery anguish almost cost us one of the most remarkable moments in the history of exploration and one of the greatest single passages in American literature. Only Lewis could conclude this marvelous encounter with an outburst of pique and sarcasm: "I now informed the chief that the object of our visit was a friendly one, that after we should reach his camp I would undertake to explain to him fully those objects, who we wer, from whence we had come and wither we were going; that in the mean time I did not care how soon we were in motion, as the sun was very warm and no water at hand."[167] How do you sign irony? If the encounter had gone the other way, even slightly, Lewis might have been killed or tortured that afternoon just inside Idaho. Instead he was taken back to the Shoshone camp a distinguished guest worthy of the national hug. His reaction, naturally, was haughtiness and condescension.

One day before this paradigmatic encounter, Lewis arrived at last at what he took to be the ultimate source of the Missouri River. "[A]t the distance of 4 miles further the road took us to the most distant fountain of the waters of the mighty Missouri in surch of which we have spent so many toilsome days and wristless nights."[168] In this case Lewis acknowledged his colleagues, though not by name. Everyone who now visits Sacajawea State Park near Lemhi Pass feels a sense of exhilaration to stand at or bestride the rivulet that Lewis knelt to taste on August 12, 1805, even though we now know that a great river has many capillary sources, and that the rivulet in question is certainly not the source creek farthest from the mouth of the Missouri. That "source" is now thought to be Upper Red Rock Lake some 145 miles from Lemhi Pass. Pursuing that "source" would not have taken Lewis in the direction of the Pacific Ocean, at least not without a very long detour. If it is still thrilling to bestride the Missouri River below Lemhi Pass, even though we get there entirely by way of the internal combustion engine, imagine how Lewis must have felt after earning every one of the 3,000 river miles he reckoned lay between St. Charles and Lemhi Pass.

Actually, Lewis tells us himself: "[T]hus far I had accomplished one of those great objects on which my mind has been unalterably fixed for many years."[169] Can this be true? Had Lewis "for many years" contemplated finding the source of the Missouri River? Notice that he is alone again. The men whose thighs and shoulder muscles had actually propelled him to the source are once more eliminated from the narrative. "[J]udge then," he tells the reader, "of the pleasure I felt in allying my thirst with this pure and ice cold water which issues from the base of a low mountain or hill of a gentle ascent."[170]

Now Lewis had became *the first civilized man* to drink from the source of the Missouri River.

After a short rest Lewis climbed up to the top of Lemhi Pass and enjoyed another first. He was the first American to stand on the divide between the Missouri-Mississippi and the Snake-Columbia watersheds. "[A]fter refreshing ourselves we proceeded on to the top of the dividing ridge from which I discovered immence ranges of high mountains still to the West of us with their tops partially covered with snow." Without pausing to indulge modern historians with any "Lemhi disappointment," Lewis "now decended the mountain about ¾ of a mile which I found much steeper than on the opposite side, to a handsome bold running Creek of cold Clear water. here I first tasted the water of the great Columbia river."[171]

William Clark wrote just 104 words on August 12, 1805, Lewis ten times that number. Clark's concern on the day Lewis reached the source of the Missouri was that the men were "much fatigued and weakened by being continualy in the water ... men complain verry much of the emence labour they are obliged to undergo & wish to leave the river."[172] Lewis spent the day in triumph and glory. Clark spent the day attempting to *passify* the men. On August 13, Lewis wrote 2,900 words, Clark wrote a journal entry of 185 words, including course headings. He wrote again of the suffering of the men in the shallow river and named a creek for Hugh McNeal, who was with Lewis at the time. Today it is known as Blacktail Deer Creek.

History belongs to the literate—to those with iron constitutions—and men with special footwear.

On November 14, 1805, Lewis became the "first" member of the Lewis and Clark Expedition to stand on the shore of the Pacific Ocean.

Between November 10 and 14, 1805, literally within miles of the Pacific shore, the Corps of Discovery found itself imprisoned at a place Clark came to call "the dismal nitch." The mid-November storms on the lower Columbia were so fierce that the captains did not dare venture either forward or backward in the canoes. Dismal Nitch was almost certainly the most miserable campsite on the entire trail, and there was nothing the expedition could do but wait for marginally better weather. Rex Ziak confirms that just when Lewis and Clark believed their travails were over, "the worst part of their entire expedition was still to come."[173] The men had little to eat, and their leather clothes were literally disintegrating. The waves in the lower Columbia were so gigantic that they threatened to destroy the canoe fleet and possibly even sweep men, woman, and child off their precarious perches and into the cold gray gulf. Clark called their situation "dangerous," a term he used only a handful of times in the course of the expedition.[174] David Nicandri has written, "At Dismal Nitch the detachment was effectively marooned."[175] The Dismal Nitch and its environs inspired Clark's most expressive journal language of the entire journey. "It would be distressing," he wrote, "to a feeling person to See our Situation at this time all wet and cold with our bedding &c. also wet, in a Cove Scercely large nough to Contain us."[176] Clark employed this strange locution for two purposes. First, he wanted the reader to know that the expedition members were not just miserable, but that *any other human being* possessed of the milk of human kindness would sympathize with their plight. Probably he would have said *Cempothize*. Second, it's as if Clark realized that the only way to endure such abject misery was to try to look upon the situation with detachment, as if he were a sympathetic observer *looking down from on high* at explorers cowering and shivering on the brink of a storm-tossed estuary, rather than to be one of those explorers *experiencing* that distress. At a similarly wretched campsite in the canyons of the Green River in Utah, George Bradley of the 1869 Powell Expedition wrote in his diary, "If I had a dog that would lie where my bed is made tonight I would kill him and burn his collar and swear I never owned him."[177]

Clark summarized the ordeal perfectly. "[W]e have been confined for 6 days passed," he wrote, "without the possibility of proceeding on, returning to a better Situation, or get out to hunt. Scerce of Provisions, and torents of rain poreing on us all the time."[178] In this moment of paralysis and wretchedness, the expedition was no more than a handful of miles from the western terminus of its continental journey, no more than a couple of hours by canoe if the waters had been reasonably calm. Clark rightly understood that the outbound mission was now essentially over, but Lewis realized that key members of the expedition were not yet precisely at the beach, the place where the continent gave way to the largest ocean on earth.

Lewis decided to change that. David Nicandri has written, "[N]ow he asserted himself out of restlessness, frustration, or to preserve his reputation as an explorer."[179] On November 14, Clark wrote, "Capt Lewis concluded to proceed on by land & find if possible the white people the Indians Say is below and examine if a Bay is Situated near the mouth of this river as laid down by Vancouver in which we expect, if there is white traders to find them &c. at 3 oClock he Set out with 4 men Drewyer Jos. & Reu. Fields & R. Frasure, in one of our large canoes and 5 men to Set them around the point on the Sand beech."[180] The ever-restless Lewis decided to penetrate the last few miles to something that could unambiguously be called western edge of the North American continent. Nothing less would make him Captain Cook. Lewis's reasons for undertaking this dangerous journey around the tip of what they called Point Distress and we know as Point Ellice were to make contact with any white men who might be moored just offshore in the Pacific Ocean, and to see whether George Vancouver's map of the estuary was accurate. Did Lewis take his universal letter of credit with him, protected as it surely was in a tin box or the kind of oilskin container that Jefferson had employed to conserve the ancient legal documents of Virginia? Did he take his British and French passports? Did he suit up in whatever formal military clothing he still had in reserve?

There is no question that Lewis and Clark were extremely eager to make contact with white sailors of any nation after their long and perilous journey across the continent. On November 8, Clark had written, "We are not certain as yet if the whites people who trade with those people ... are Stationary at the mouth, or visit this quarter at Stated times for the purpose of trafick."[181] The Corps of Discovery was, as Clark pointed out, essentially bankrupt of Indian trade gifts. Rex Ziak says, "Though it was not yet a matter of life or death, they were in short supply of many essentials, and this would be their only opportunity to obtain more."[182] It was essential to resupply the expedition if possible; to arrange, if possible, to send copies of the expedition's papers back to Philadelphia or Washington, DC, by water; and possibly to send some of the men home by the way of one of the two capes, the Cape of Good Hope or Cape Horn. The captains had good reason to believe traders were tantalizingly close to the expedition's wretched camp. On November 11, Clark had watched helplessly while local Indians sailed by, seemingly effortlessly, on waters so treacherous that the seasoned watermen of the expedition were afraid to ply them. "[T]hey are on their way," he wrote, "to trade those fish with white people which they make Signs live below round a point."[183] Ziak captures the excitement and anxiety of this moment: "According to these Indians, there were white people less than a mile away."[184]

Probably Lewis was worried that any further delay at Dismal Nitch might mean that the trading vessel in question would have departed by the time the expedition finally got around Point Distress. This certainly makes a kind of sense. Imagine the sense of urgency in seeming to be so close to a ship carrying civilized men, a ship filled with the fruits of civilization, after not having glimpsed a white man for more than seven months. Someone needed to strike out ahead at the earliest possibility to make sure the expedition did not *just miss* a trading ship, if one was in Baker Bay and preparing to sail away before the worst of the winter. That person could have been Clark, of course. He was purely miserable at Dismal Nitch and he seems to have experienced considerably more distress in such moments than the impervious stoic who was his partner in discovery, the iron man Meriwether Lewis. Clark called the six days at Dismal Nitch "the most disagreeable time I have experienced."[185] Does he mean the most disagreeable time he has endured recently, or in the course of the entire expedition, or *ever experienced?* The captains could quite easily have sent Joseph Field, John Ordway, Nathaniel Pryor, Patrick Gass, or any of a number of reliable members of the expedition to venture to Baker Bay.

Not surprisingly it was Meriwether Lewis who determined to make the journey. Stephen Beckham has written, "He was quick to 'jump ship' and dash for the press of discovery."[186] He was accompanied by four men, three of whom had emerged as his favorites: George Drouillard, Joseph and Reuben Field, and Robert Frazer. A five-man auxiliary crew managed to get the reconnaissance team around the point, though Clark reported that the journey had been a very difficult one. "The Canoe returned at dusk half full of water, from the waves which dashed over in passing the point."[187] Lewis was first once again.

Clark was finally able to squeeze the main body of the expedition around the point on November 16, two days after Lewis left on his reconnaissance journey. The wild weather gave him a tiny window of opportunity, and he took it. He did not go far. Clark wrote, "[P]roceeded on passed the blustering point below which I found a butifull Sand beech thro which runs a Small [river] ... I landed and formed a camp on the highest Spot I could find between the hight of the tides, and the Slashers in a Small bottom."[188] Then Clark makes a strangely weary pronouncement, borne no doubt of having been soaked to the skin for more than a week without respite: "[T]his I could plainly See would be the extent of our journey by water."[189]

After all that.

No 'thus far I had triumphed ... ' or 'the hitherto or heretofore deemed endless ... ' No 'a journey which began at ... ' Merely "[T]his I could plainly See would be the extent of our journey by water." It would be hard to compose a sentence more profoundly anticlimactic than this or more sodden with weary disillusionment. Stephen Beckham has written, "Clark, the practical navigator, wasted no words on reflection of a mission accomplished."[190] Frederick Merk wrote, "It was a custom among voyageurs to end any extended journey with a flourish."[191] Clark's *flourish* was to wring out wet clothes and take up residence in an abandoned and flea-infested camp on the beach. Rex Ziak has written, "They must have been ecstatic. After eighteen months of difficult and dangerous travel, they had finally arrived at the far side of the continent."[192] For Clark the great moment had come on November 7, when he first glimpsed what he regarded as the Pacific Ocean. On that day he had written, "Great joy in camp we are in *View* of the *Ocian*, this great Pacific Octean which we been So long anxious to See."[193] After that, his soul was too waterlogged to rise above gloom and self-pity.

Unfortunately, Lewis was silent through this entire period. Surely he would have written something more heroic than "this I could plainly See would be the extent of our journey," something fitting for the completion of a transcontinental odyssey, no matter how miserable and sodden the final week of the trek had been. The actual experience may have been purely miserable, but the writer of that experience, the explorer, must present himself as both triumphant and essentially impervious to misery. But Lewis could not be bothered to write his impressions of the Columbia River portion of the journey, even when some kind of triumphal summary statement was called for. The best account we have of the expedition's arrival at the Pacific Ocean actually comes from Patrick Gass: "We are now at the end of our voyage, which has been completely accomplished to the intention of the expedition, the object of which was to discover a passage by the way of the Missouri and Columbia rivers to the Pacific ocean; notwithstanding the difficulties, privations and dangers, which we had to encounter, endure and surmount."[194]

Lewis's prolonged silence in the period following the difficult first transit through the Bitterroot Mountains is one of the principal mysteries of the Lewis and Clark Expedition. It is much easier to make sense of his silence between May 14, 1804, and April 7, 1805. Then the expedition was still within the broad boundaries of the known world. The Missouri River from St. Charles to the Mandan and Hidatsa villages was not exactly a highway yet, but it was well enough traveled road to seem jejune to Lewis, who was bent on discovery in uncharted territory. But from the moment when the expedition left the Mandan villages, Lewis regarded himself in terra incognita. He was well aware that Broughton of the Vancouver Expedition had penetrated more than 100 miles inland from the mouth of the Columbia. But from that point (near today's Corbett, Oregon) to today's Williston, North Dakota, was Lewis's "country at least two thousand miles in width, on which the foot of civillized man had never trodden."[195] Virtually the entire Pacific watershed portion of the trail was terra incognita so far as Lewis knew. It makes no sense that he would put down his pen in a country he was effectively the first man in human history to describe.

Maybe by now everyone was so miserable, so exhausted, and so frustrated by the combination of ocean tides and a particularly nasty patch of November weather that Clark didn't care that Lewis had found a way to be first once again. It seems clear that the lowest moment of the journey for Clark was the six-day period at Dismal Nitch. Second was the Lolo Trail when snow was falling off the evergreen trees onto the heads and shoulders of the struggling men. We don't know what Lewis's mindset was during the period at Dismal Nitch. He was not keeping a journal. If he was as miserable as Clark, nobody said so.

Clark's reference to Lewis's return from his reconnaissance of the Pacific promontory on November 17 is beyond laconic, given the heroic moment they were all experiencing. "[A]t half past 1 oClock Capt. Lewis and his Party returned haveing around passd. Point Disapointment and Some distance on the main Ocian to the N W."[196] That and nothing more. Not a word about Lewis's ostensible quest for white traders. Ziak calls this a "mystery."[197] It seems more likely that Clark was by now much more concerned about getting the men dry and fed, spreading out the expedition's baggage to dry, assessing the damage of the previous week to the expedition's papers, scientific instruments, gunpowder, tools, and trade goods than he was in Lewis's grandstanding or his life as an explorer. Clark had long since come to terms with Lewis's character and habits. There was nothing new or startling here. For the most part Clark had learned to accept his role as the manager of the men, boats, and equipment, the one who was almost invariably left behind to hold the expedition together. At some point, survival is a more meaningful mission than discovery. Lewis was doing what Lewis did—and in fact what he did best. By this time, with the expedition as close to the collapse point as to the western edge of the continent, Clark probably was beyond caring about Lewis's urge to get there first and alone.

The unkindest cut of all came in a letter Lewis wrote in the last days of March 1806 and posted (actually "paisted" as he put it) in the captains' chamber at Fort Clatsop as the expedition began its long journey home. It was a letter written at large to the universe—but also to any white men who might happen along—listing the men of the party, and declaring that the expedition "did penetrate the same [the continent] by way of the Missouri and Columbia Rivers, to the discharge of the latter into the Pacific Ocean, where they arrived on the 14th November 1805, and from whence they departed... ."[198] This posting was one of the great moments of the Lewis and Clark Expedition. It is also one of the most revealing. Several agendas were at work here. Lewis was engaged in a sovereignty ritual. By pasting this document on the walls of a facility built in no man's land, Lewis was deepening the claim of the United States to what would be called the Oregon Country. As the historian Patricia Seed has written, each European nation, including now the United States, had a somewhat different protocol for laying claim to new territory.[199] The Anglo-American legal doctrine stressed the erection of buildings and fences, "improvements" to the unclaimed territory. For that reason Lewis posted his memo not at Station Camp on the north bank of the Columbia or at Baker Bay, where it would be much more likely to be noticed, but at the wooden compound the expedition erected in the wilderness. That compound, Fort Clatsop, was an unmistakable token of occupation and use. By posting his declaration there, on the walls of a wooden facility he and his men had constructed, under existing international law, Lewis had strengthened America's sovereignty claim to the lower Columbia basin.

It was also a magnificent gesture of the Enlightenment. The idealistic American republic, born of Enlightenment principles of transparency, the primacy of science, and the brotherhood of mankind, was freely sharing its basic geographic discoveries with the rest of the world. It was the same philanthropic impulse that led Jefferson to write, "He who receives an idea from me, receives instruction himself without lessening mind; as he who lights his taper at mine, receives light without darkening me. That ideas should freely spread from one to another over the globe, for the moral and mutual instruction of man, and improvement of his condition, seems to have been peculiarly and benevolently designed by nature, when she made them, like fire, expansible over all space, without lessening their density in any one point."[200] After listing the men and explaining the mission, Lewis provided the key information: "[O]n the back of some of these lists we added a sketch of the connection of the upper branches of the Missouri with those of the Columbia, particularly of it's main S. E. branch, on which we also delienated the track we had come and that we meant to pursue on our return where the same happened to vary."[201] Jefferson would have greatly admired Lewis's philanthropic gesture.

But it was also a letter about getting there first. Lewis reported that the expedition arrived at the Pacific Ocean on November 14, 1805. Actually, that was the day *he* arrived at the Pacific Ocean. On that day, Clark and most of the other men were still marooned at Dismal Nitch. Clark would not arrive at the terminus of the continent until three days later, November 17, 1805. Lewis could just as well have written November 17 in his triumphant memo. That would have been a gesture of inclusiveness, or at least of true partnership. It was not until November 17 that the entire expedition was together on the Pacific shore, not until then that the boats were all together at land's end. Had he been confronted about this final trumping of Clark, Lewis would likely have said that it was essential to record the first legitimate date of arrival to forestall any other nation's claim to the Oregon Country. If that were true, of course, he would have had to date the arrival November 13, 1805, when John Colter, George Shannon, and Alexander Willard became the actual first members of the expedition to reach the Pacific shore. On that day Clark sent the three of them around the blustery point in a canoe—just to see if it could be done—and to scout a campsite on the ocean beach. That evening Clark reported, a little uneasily, "[O]ur canoe and the three men did not return this evening."[202] Thus Colter, Shannon, and Willard were in point of fact the first members of the expedition to reach the Pacific Ocean. That, to put it mildly, was not a land's end narrative that was acceptable to Meriwether Lewis. They got to the terminus first, but they did not count.

Clark suffered a double indignity on this occasion. The "sketch of the connection" of the ways in which the upper Missouri and upper Snake-Columbia Rivers interlock was almost certainly drafted by William Clark for a document which now unapologetically made Lewis the first and more important of the two explorers. If that wasn't insult enough, Clark now performed his duty in copying out, word for word, Lewis's journal entry of March 18, 1806. What he must have thought and felt when he wrote the words, "where they arrived on the 14th day of November 1805," is unknowable. Perhaps he was grateful that at least Lewis wrote "they" rather than *I* or *the commander of the enterprise, Captain Meriwether Lewis, soon to be joined by his trusted subordinates* ...

As the expedition approached St. Louis in September 1806, Lewis was apparently in a more charitable mood. In the letter he drafted for Clark to send to his brother Jonathan, Lewis (Clark) wrote, "On the 17th of November we reached the Ocian where various considerations induced us to spend the winter."[203] That surely was how Clark wanted the narrative to read. Strangely enough, when Nicholas Biddle wrote the official narrative of the expedition, he gave the prize for reaching the Pacific Ocean first to Lewis, though rather than talk about the terminus of the continent or the possibility that ships might be anchored in Baker Bay, he merely reported that "Captain Lewis concluded to examine more minutely the lower part of the bay."[204] Biddle wrote nothing in the manner of Patrick Gass to commemorate the expedition's triumph over the North American continent.

On the return journey in 1806, Lewis reserved to himself the most interesting reconnaissance itinerary. It was Lewis who explored the overland trail that constituted "the most direct and practicable" link between navigable waters of the Columbia and navigable waters of the Missouri. He, not Clark, fulfilled the president's directive to discover the best "road" through the Missouri and Columbia corridors. It was Lewis who explored the upper reaches of the Marias River in the hopes that its source waters would drive back the Canadian border. Clark was sent on a mission (to the middle and lower Yellowstone) that could not possibly have implications for the international boundary between the United States and British North America. It was Lewis who had the most dramatic and consequential encounter with American Indians of the entire expedition. It was Lewis who suffered the most sensational wound of the journey, when he was shot in the buttocks by Pierre Cruzatte. Because of that wound, however, Lewis lost control of the six last weeks of the expedition. It was Clark who negotiated with the Mandan and Hidatsa Indians in mid-August 1806. It was Clark who paid a valedictory visit to the burned out ruins of Fort Mandan as the expedition prepared to leave the Upper Missouri forever. On August 17, 1806, he wrote, "proceeded on to *Fort Mandan* where I landed and went to view the old works the houses except one in the rear bastion was burnt by accident, Some pickets were Standing in front next to the river."[205] It was Clark who gleaned the news from the traders the expedition met between the bottom of today's South Dakota and St. Louis. It was Clark who shouted defiance to Black Buffalo and the Lakota who had tried to hold up the expedition on the outbound journey. By the time the expedition straggled back into St. Louis on September 23, 1806, it was in almost every respect Clark's expedition. Lewis had effectively abdicated even nominal command in the aftermath of his wounding on August 11, east of today's Williston, North Dakota.

Still, Meriwether Lewis got to the finish line first, after all. On October 11, 1809, at a primitive inn on the Natchez Trace in Tennessee, Lewis jumped ahead of his estimable friend to explore "the undiscovered country, from whose bourn no traveller returns."[206]

As usual, he found sufficient reason to get there first.

CHAPTER II   Meriwether Lewis's Bad Day

Which bad day?

THE THREE WORST THINGS THAT HAPPENED TO MERIWETHER Lewis occurred when he was not with William Clark. On July 26–27, 1806, he had a fatal encounter with eight young Blackfeet men on Two Medicine Creek in northern Montana and wound up killing two of them before he was able to extricate his contingent of four men (including himself) from that extremely dangerous situation. At the time, Clark was blithely floating down the Yellowstone River with about half of the Corps of Discovery, including Sacagawea and Toussaint and Jean Baptiste Charbonneau, in what came as close to being a wilderness lark as any episode of the Lewis and Clark expedition.

Just three weeks later, on August 11, 1806, Lewis was shot in the buttocks by one of his men, just east of today's Williston, North Dakota. Although the bullet missed bone and artery, and the sciatic nerve, Lewis was seriously injured, and he might have been killed. Clark was nearby, just a handful of miles down the Missouri River, alternately proceeding on at a leisurely clip and stalling to enable his estimable friend to catch up.

A little more than three years after that, on October 11, 1809, Meriwether Lewis committed suicide. According to Clark, among the last things Lewis ever said, on the road to Grinder's Inn on the Natchez Trace, seventy-two miles from Nashville, Tennessee, was that he "[c]onceipt that he herd me Comeing on, and Said that he was certain [I would] over take him, that I had herd of his Situation and would Come to his releaf."[1] At the time of Lewis's death, Clark was actually approaching the Ohio River in western Kentucky. He was not "coming on."

My thesis is very simple: none of these things would have happened if William Clark had been at Lewis's side.

It is doubtful, too, that if Clark had been at hand Lewis would have penned his famously lugubrious birthday meditation on August 18, 1805, in which he regretted that "I had as yet done but little, very little indeed, to further the hapiness of the human race, or to advance the information of the succeeding generation."[2] Lewis wrote these self-punishing words less than a week after reaching the source of the Missouri River, "one of those great objects on which my mind has been unalterably fixed for many years."[3] It seems strange, even outrageous, that at this juncture, approximately 3,000 miles up the Missouri,[4] the thirty-one-year-old Lewis "viewed with regret the many hours I have spent in indolence, and now soarly feel the want of that information which those hours would have given me had they been judiciously expended."[5] One might have expected this to be the happiest birthday of his entire life. As Lewis indulged in philosophical self-scrutiny and rededicated his life to the twin pillars of the Enlightenment—the advancement of knowledge and the promotion of the happiness of the human race—Clark was bushwhacking through the thickly forested woodlands overlooking the Salmon River, in search of the fabled *river of symmetry* in the Pacific watershed that would magically carry the Corps of Discovery to the sea. On the occasions of Clark's birthdays in the American wilderness (August 1, 1804, 1805, 1806), he wasted no time in self-scrutiny, but in fact routinely ordered the expedition's cooks to prepare him a special birthday meal.

Two weeks after Lewis was shot in the buttocks, during a hike at the big bend of the Missouri River south of today's Pierre, South Dakota, he overexerted himself and re-injured his gunshot wounds. Driven by his characteristic impatience, Lewis had not remained sedentary long enough to give his wounds time to heal completely. In his journal entry for August 27, 1806, Clark wrote, "My friend Capt Lewis hurt himself very much by takeing a longer walk on the Sand bar in my absence at the buffalow than he had Strength to undergo, which Caused him to remain very unwell all night."[6] The key phrase in this passage is *in my absence.* Clark knew well that Lewis was prone to do rash or irrational things in his absence. Although he does not say so directly, he implies here that had he been at hand, he would not have permitted Lewis to take so strenuous a walk.

The most intelligent decision Meriwether Lewis ever made was to ask William Clark to join him in the "fatigues… dangers… and honors" of the enterprise he had been entrusted to undertake on behalf of President Jefferson. That Lewis understood he could not manage the expedition alone is made clear in the letter he wrote to Clark on June 19, 1803. He offered to make Clark a genuine co-captain in substance as well as in formal army rank. He assured Clark, erroneously it turned out, that Jefferson "will grant you a Captain's commission which of course will intitle you to the pay and emoluments attached to that office and will equally with myself intitle you to such a portion of land as was granted to officers of similar rank for their Revolutionary services." Lewis assured Clark that his rank as captain would be a permanent position. And at the end of this remarkable letter, Lewis wrote, almost desperately, "Should you feel disposed not to

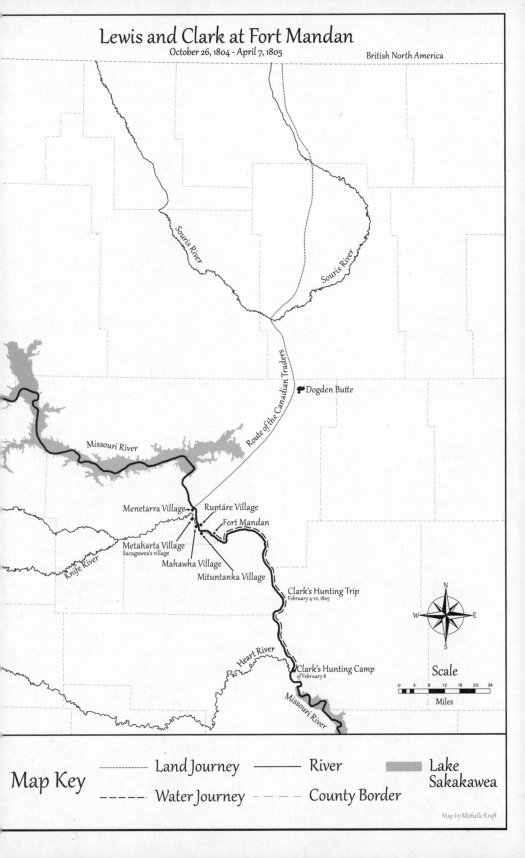

Lewis and Clark at Fort Mandan
October 26, 1804 - April 7, 1805

British North America

Souris River

Souris River

Route of the Canadian Traders

🦌 Dogden Butte

Missouri River

Menetarra Village → Ruptáre Village

Fort Mandan

Metaharta Village
Sacagawea's village

Mahawha Village

Mituntanka Village

Knife River

Clark's Hunting Trip
February 4-12, 1805

Heart River

Clark's Hunting Camp
of February 8

Missouri River

N
W · E
S

Scale

0 4 8 12 16 20 24
Miles

Map Key

········· Land Journey   ——— River   ▨ Lake Sakakawea

- - - - Water Journey   —·—· County Border

Map by Michelle Kraft

attatch yourself to this party in an official character, and at the same time feel a disposition to accompany me as a friend any part of the way up the Missouri I should be extremely happy in your company, and will furnish you with every aid for your return from any point you might wish it."[7] Lewis was determined to secure the services of William Clark in some manner because he trusted him, because he knew that no one man could manage alone all the leadership duties of the expedition, and probably because he recognized in himself certain weaknesses that only an old and trusted friend like Clark could compensate for. We take for granted that Lewis and Clark were equals, true if not technical *co-captains*, but it is important to remember that Jefferson chose Lewis, not Clark, to lead the expedition. Jefferson's War Department endorsed the hierarchy that defined Clark as Lewis's undoubted subordinate. It is commonplace to regard Lewis's offer of a co-captaincy as a sign and measure of his friendship with Clark; yet, it may well be that he made that extraordinary offer because he was willing to do anything—short of making himself actually subordinate to Clark—to secure the services of an old friend who knew him well, understood his habits and character, and complemented his leadership style. In other words, Lewis may not have been serving his friend Clark as much as himself in asking him to join the expedition—at *any level* of participation.

To explain the dynamics of the relationship between Meriwether Lewis and William Clark, I will employ a *metaphysical conceit* in the manner of the seventeenth-century British poets. Such poets as Abraham Cowley, Richard Crashaw, Andrew Marvell, George Herbert, and above all John Donne employed abstract or scientific analogies to explain such concepts as spiritual longing, love and lust, the relationship of monarchs to their courtiers, the nature of salvation or of the Trinity, friendship, travel, and the separation of lovers. England's eighteenth-century literary dictator Samuel Johnson, whose groundbreaking *Dictionary of the English Language* (1755) would have been known to both Jefferson and Lewis, grumbled that the metaphysical poets wrote verse in which "the most heterogeneous ideas are yoked by violence together; nature and art are ransacked for illustrations, comparisons, and allusions."[8] A century earlier, the seventeenth-century English poet and critic John Dryden faulted John Donne because, "He affects the metaphysics, not only in his satires, but in his amorous verses, where nature only should reign; and perplexes the minds of the fair sex with nice speculations of philosophy, when he should engage their hearts, and entertain them with the softnesses of love."[9] The most famous of all metaphysical conceits appears in John Donne's poem, "A Valediction Forbidding Mourning,"[10] in which he likens lovers separated by the travel schedule of the man to a pair of "stiff twin compasses," in other words, a geometric compass in which the man is the swiveling foot and the woman the "fixed foot."

If they be two, they are two so
As stiff twin compasses are two;
Thy soul, the fix'd foot, makes no show
To move, but doth, if th' other do.

And though it in the centre sit,
Yet, when the other far doth roam,
It leans, and hearkens after it,
And grows erect, as that comes home.

Such wilt thou be to me, who must,
Like th' other foot, obliquely run;
Thy firmness makes my circle just,
And makes me end where I begun.

When metaphysical conceits do their job well (and not, as Dr. Johnson warned, merely indulge in cleverness for cleverness' sake), they clarify complex situations and offer insights more memorable or illuminating precisely because they are startling or far-fetched.

Let that serve as a preface to the following metaphysical conceit about the relationship between Meriwether Lewis and William Clark.

I liken the friendship of Lewis and Clark to a nuclear power plant. When a nuclear plant is properly fueled and tuned, it is an engine of enormous power. But when things go wrong, the result can be disaster, as everyone who has heard of Three Mile Island, Chernobyl, or Fukushima Daiichi knows. Lewis and Clark were like the two key components of a nuclear power plant, the fuel rods and the control rods. The fuel rods are powerful, but unstable. They are made up of enriched fissile uranium, U-235. They represent Lewis. The control rods are much less powerful, but they are absolutely essential to the proper function of the nuclear plant. They are often made of an alloy of silver, indium, and cadmium, none of which can themselves generate power. They represent Clark. Only when the fuel rods and control rods are configured in proper balance does the plant produce power. If the control rods are withdrawn entirely, the reactor produces too sudden and too hot a nuclear reaction. It goes super-critical and overheats not just the enveloping water that under the correct circumstances produces productive but harmless steam, but also the entire concrete and metal structure of the power plant. Under the right circumstances it can blow up, or the internal pressure can force breaches in the protective housing through which deadly nuclear radiation escapes into the surrounding countryside. If conditions are just right, the plant can heat so rapidly to so great a temperature that the reactor burns and burrows down through the earth's surface. This is known as the China Syndrome.

Such was the relationship between Lewis and Clark. Lewis was a powerful but radioactive man. When his enormous energy was ignited, but kept from over-heating, he was an engine capable of heroic exertions—endless hikes through cactus country; long, lavish, and lyrical journal entries; disciplined scientific investigation; bold but intelligent decisions in critical situations. Clark had many capacities, but his prime importance on the Lewis and Clark Expedition was to manage his friend's radioactivity, to tamp down that which was erratic or reckless in Lewis's behavior and character. To stay close.

The control rods of a nuclear power plant work both ways. When they are withdrawn entirely, chaos ensues, as was usually the case when Clark was separated from Lewis for prolonged periods. But when the control rods are fully deployed, in closest proximity to the fuel rods, the reactor shuts down. This seems to have happened to Lewis when he and Clark were confined for long periods together in close quarters—on the keelboat, at Fort Mandan, and Fort Clatsop. Lewis was at his best when Clark was nearby but not suffocatingly near. That is why Lewis did his best work while walking alone on the shores of the Missouri River with his Newfoundland dog Seaman, his rifle, and his notebooks and collection bag. By evening he would be back with Clark in camp. By day he was close enough to Clark to act sensibly, but far enough away to build up a creative head of steam.

Notice, for example, that Lewis almost always gets energized or "lights up" when he leaves the keelboat or the White Pirogue and walks on shore by himself or with just a couple of the men, but not with Clark. Almost every time he gets off the boat after a period of stifling confinement, he writes a version of his entry for April 7, 1805: "[A]s I had used no exercise for several weeks, I determined to walk on shore as far as our encampment of this evening; accordingly I continued my walk on the N. side of the River about six miles ... ."[11] Once Lewis gets off the boat and onto the shore, earning his ascent of the Missouri valley by way of his legs and feet, he tends to enjoy great productivity and to keep a journal, in part because he always finds something interesting to observe on shore.

In close proximity to Clark, Lewis tends to go silent. He lets Clark's journal serve as a captain's log, thus depriving Mr. Jefferson and all students of Lewis and Clark of the expedition's finest, fullest, and most felicitous voice. From a documentary point of view, Lewis all but disappears during the confined keelboat journey from Camp Wood to Fort Mandan. The only time he lights up is when he leaves the keelboat on September 16–17, 1804, near the mouth of the White River in today's South Dakota. "Having for many days past confined myself to the boat," he writes, "I determined to devote this day to amuse myself on shore with my gun and view the interior of the country."[12]

Lewis is at his absolute best when he gets away from Clark for a day or two, but not so far that he cannot slip back under the umbrella of Clark's calming influence when things start to spin out of control. The best example of this is Lewis's magical day at the Great Falls in today's Montana on June 14, 1805. On that day he explored alone the four cataracts upriver from the first and greatest of the falls, which he had "discovered" and described the previous day. For June 14, Lewis wrote one of his longest and finest journal entries. But as the day unfolded in the absence of Clark, things began to get out of hand. Intending to spend the night alone on the plains of Montana, Lewis killed a buffalo, but he forgot to reload his rifle and thus left himself vulnerable to the approach of a massive grizzly bear: "[W]hile I was gazing attentively on the poor anamal discharging blood in streams from his mouth and nostrils, expecting him to fall every instant, and having entirely forgotton to reload my rifle, a large white, or reather brown bear, had perceived and crept on me within 20 steps before I discovered him; in the first moment I drew up my gun to shoot, but at the same instant recolected that she was not loaded and that he was too near for me to hope to perform this opperation before he reached me, as he was then briskly advancing on me."[13]

Lewis survived that halfhearted attack by jumping into the Missouri River and assuming a comic-heroic posture with his espontoon. "[T]he moment I put myself in this attitude of defence he sudonly wheeled about as if frightened, declined the combat on such unequal grounds, and retreated with quite as great precipitation as he had just before pursued me.   as soon as I saw him run of[f] in that manner I returned to the shore and charged my gun, which I had still retained in my hand throughout this curious adventure."[14] Later that afternoon, near the confluence of the Medicine River and the Missouri, Lewis shot at what he took to be a panther or "tyger cat,"[15] but what was probably a wolverine "looking immediately at me as if it designed to spring on me."[16] Shortly thereafter, the solitary explorer stood stock still and bolt upright while three buffalo charged toward him from approximately half a mile away. His stated reason for doing this strange, irrational, and dangerous thing was that "I thought at least to give them some amusement and altered my direction to meet them."[17] Fortunately the bulls halted, "and retreated with precipitation"[18] before they *amused* Lewis to death.

Had Clark been present on this excursion, it is doubtful that any of these incidents would have occurred. Without Clark's sensible guidance, Lewis fell into bemused reveries, lost his focus, and took unnecessary risks. Finally, Lewis became so bewildered by this sequence of eerie events that he concluded, irrationally, that "all the beasts of the neighbourhood had made a league to distroy me, or that some fortune was disposed to amuse herself at my expence."[19] There is something magical in this statement—perhaps literally.

Lewis was all alone in the heart of the American sublime. He had carried the intellectual baggage of the Enlightenment as far from Philadelphia as it could bear up. Now, in the most spectacular landscape he ever encountered, the certainties and scientific methods, the empire of reason and the linear templates of western civilization were wearing a little threadbare, like the cotton and wool clothing expedition members had been wearing since they left St. Louis. Essayist Barry Lopez asks, "How far can you go out and still come back?" The encounters Lewis experienced on June 14, 1805—with landscape, waterfalls, menacing and mysterious creatures, place and *spirit of place*—were both exhilarating and disturbing, both thrilling and unsettling. This was arguably the greatest day of Lewis's life. Certainly it was one of the handful of greatest days. This was why he had walked off the map of the known world. One is not authentically an explorer unless he carries the known so far into the unknown that he becomes unsure of which is the truer world. One is not, as Thomas Slaughter suggests, a true explorer until he becomes lost, and not merely in the physical sense of the term.[20]

No wonder Lewis had re-entry issues when he returned to civilization. How could any day between September 23, 1806, and the end of Lewis's life possibly achieve this level of heightened and enchanted consciousness? When you have stood snout to snout with a grizzly bear without a bullet in your rifle and survived the encounter using nothing but your wits, what's left to *amuse* you in St. Louis, in Washington, DC, or in Philadelphia? How do you tell your prospective bride why you cannot get over that day at the Great Falls, when it seems so unenchanted (and possibly silly) to her or anyone else when you try to explain it? When you have been alone in the heart of the wilderness of North America, surrounded by a world so real and alive with mystery and immanence that nothing before or after could ever possibly measure up, how can you take seriously the petty egotism of Frederick Bates or the pitiful and soulless bureaucracy of the clerks of the War Department? Had any other member of the expedition been at Lewis's side on June 14, 1805, the magic—the *medicine* of Montana—could not have made its appearance. Two souls are too many for a landscape of enchantment—the iron tyranny of the jejune finds safety in numbers, even if the number is only two. William Clark had no analogous experiences at the Great Falls that we are aware of. While Lewis fell into reveries that caused him to forget to reload his rifle and put him in harm's way, Clark was looking for a place to beach the expedition's flotilla and lay out a portage route.

As this succession of sublime events began to overwhelm his consciousness at the Great Falls on June 14, Lewis realized that it would be a metaphysical mistake to push his luck any further. The Enlightenment president's protégé freely admitted that he "did not think it prudent to remain all night at this place which really from the succession of curious adventures wore the impression on my mind of inchantment."[21] At this point he determined to return to camp—to Clark. At the end of a long, taxing day, Lewis walked many miles to the main expedition encampment, essentially because he no longer trusted himself to be alone in an enchanted landscape. Even here, Lewis found re-entry difficult. During the long nocturnal walk, probably no less than fifteen miles (Lewis says "about 12"), beginning after 6:30 P.M. on one of the longest summer days on the northern plains, he could not shake the enchantment. "[A]t sometimes for a moment I thought it might be a dream, but the prickley pears which pierced my feet very severely once in a while, particularly after it grew dark, convinced me that I was really awake, and that it was necessary to make the best of my way to camp."[22]

Here was a situation in which the nuclear reactor came close to going super-critical. Clark was just close enough to exert a slender moderating pressure on Lewis's erraticism. Had Clark been on the Yellowstone River that evening, who knows what might have happened. "[A]ll the beasts of the neighbourhood" might have won the battle for Lewis's soul.

The majority of the adjectives we commonly associate with Lewis are radioactive: mercurial, volatile, erratic, impulsive, romantic, heroic, moody, self-absorbed, self-punishing, reflective, brilliant, reckless, headstrong, anxious, consumed by the mission, hyper-serious, and turbulent. The adjectives we associate with William Clark are reliable, steady, pragmatic, purposeful, calm, generous, dutiful, responsible, persevering, sociable, and resourceful. Thus my metaphysical conceit in which Lewis and Clark are likened to the key components of a nuclear reactor. I believe the conceit explains a good deal and holds up under careful scrutiny. Like all metaphysical conceits, it is open to criticism. The test of this conceit, like all others, is not whether it is ingenious or clever, but whether it helps us understand something that resists straightforward analysis. The reader, of course, will decide.

Lewis and Clark were a team. They were better together than separately. This was particularly true of Meriwether Lewis, who was a high-strung, self-pushing, and self-punishing man who was sometimes capable of impulsive or erratic behavior. Clark was much more stable, but he would probably have lived out his life in relative obscurity had it not been for the invitation he received from Lewis, written June 19, 1803. With the words, "If therefore there is anything … in this enterprise, which would induce you to participate with me in it's fatiegues, it's dangers and it's honors, believe me there is no man on earth with whom I should feel equal pleasure in sharing them as with yourself,"[23] Lewis lifted William Clark to historical greatness. But for Lewis's patronage, William Clark may have just as well have been Moses Hooke. The evidence suggests that when the captains were together, Lewis was both more stable and more productive than when they were separated. Clark had a calming or stabilizing effect on Lewis. Lewis, in turn, brought out the best in William Clark. Lewis's better education, his much greater command of the English language (particularly when formal prose or official documents were called for), his connection with Jefferson and the American Enlightenment, his capacity to envision the journey as an expression of America's destiny, and his ability to situate their travels in the larger history of exploration enabled and inspired Clark's best work. In turn, Clark recognized Lewis's frailties and gave his own best energies, for a period of fourteen years between 1795 and 1809, to compensate for those weaknesses and take care of his self-destructive friend.

In the language of popular psychology, Lewis and Clark entered into a co-dependent relationship in which Lewis brought certain opportunities to the table that Clark would not otherwise have enjoyed. He got Clark as close as a friendship away from the president of the United States, made it possible for Clark to be a kind of fictional co-captain of the most important exploration mission in American history, made it possible, indeed, for Clark to explore the continent alongside one of the most gifted men of his generation. Clark's remarkable later career as a Jeffersonian governmental functionary in the Missouri River country, and his standing as one of the principal gentlemen of St. Louis, owed everything to Meriwether Lewis. It is clear that Jefferson would never have promoted Clark to these positions short of Lewis's mediation and endorsement. Still, by any rational measure, Clark gave to the relationship more than he got.

Clark propped his fragile friend up. He performed uncomplainingly a myriad of routine tasks that were required to propel the Corps of Discovery forward from St. Charles to the Pacific Coast and back again. He almost exclusively handled the cartographical work of the expedition. The map he produced was a masterpiece. He wound up being the default journal keeper for the two captains. Just how it devolved that Lewis would write in his journal when it suited him, while Clark would keep a continuous journal and maintain the "captain's log" when Lewis went silent, is unknown, but this understanding was in place before the expedition had proceeded many miles up the Missouri River in the summer of 1804. Clark personally "took on" the Charbonneau family, including Sacagawea and "my boy *Pomp*,"[24] perhaps in part because it was clear that Lewis regarded Charbonneau as a wastrel and a coward, and Sacagawea as a mere creature who would be happy anywhere on earth so long as she had three square meals a day and enough trinkets to dazzle her limited consciousness. It seems unlikely to me that Lewis would have been able to cope with Toussaint Charbonneau in the absence of Clark, or that he would have been able to keep the Charbonneau family from returning home to the Hidatsa villages when Sacagawea's health broke in July 1805, had it not been for the bond the family had formed with Clark.

Clark found it possible to accept Lewis's need to forge on ahead anytime the expedition neared one of its discovery moments—the confluence of the Missouri and the Yellowstone, the Great Falls, the source of the "heretofore deemed endless" Missouri, first contact with the elusive Shoshone, and the actual "land's end" on the tip of the state of Washington at the mouth of the Columbia River. It is possible to detect that Lewis's insistence on maintaining his own primacy as the "Columbus or Captain Cook" of the expedition at times upset Clark, but he accepted his fate with considerable grace. He seemed always to keep in mind that Lewis was the sole reason for his participation in this amazing journey.

It seems to me virtually certain that if Clark had been with him, Lewis would not have wound up killing two Blackfeet men in late July 1806. Clark would have insisted that a contingent of four was too small for a reconnaissance foray into the heart of Blackfeet country—already known to the captains as unfriendly to white intruders from the wrong direction. Clark would have handled the encounter with the Blackfeet differently, with less candor perhaps about the ways in which the expedition was proposing to disturb the existing trade infrastructure and the geopolitics of the Upper Missouri.[25] Clark would have made it possible for one of the two captains to be awake at all times during the critical night of July 26–27. Certainly, Clark would have advised against leaving a Jefferson peace medal on the chest of one of the dead Indians. He might also have persuaded Lewis not to steal the Blackfeet's horses (thus adding insult to mortal injury) after he had effectively disarmed them by burning their shields and bows and arrows.

It seems equally certain that if Clark had been with Lewis on August 11, 1806, at the Birnt Hills east of today's Williston, North Dakota, he would have advised against the captain's impulsive decision to go elk hunting in a thicket (wearing animal skins) with the least well-sighted member of the expedition, Pierre Cruzatte. That decision, born of frustration when the Lewis contingent did not reach the Birnt Hills by noon on August 11 and therefore could not *that day* ascertain the latitude and longitude of the northernmost reach of the Missouri River, seems as irrational as any decision Lewis ever made. Had Clark been at hand, he surely would have explained to Lewis that if they simply spent the rest of the day hunting, drying out their gear, and making new clothes—all desiderata—and laid over until noon, August 12, to conduct the important astronomical sightings at the Birnt Hills, nothing much would be lost, and their autumn 1806 return to St. Louis would not be derailed or even significantly delayed. Meanwhile, if Lewis insisted on working off his frustration by killing something, why not go hunting with Drouillard or one of the Field brothers, or—in short—with anyone who had a good set of eyes? Clark would have seen to all of this.

It seems even more certain that Lewis would not have committed suicide on October 11, 1809, had Clark been at his side. With his knowledge of Lewis's illness or illnesses, his rage, despair, and toxicity, surely Clark would have moderated Lewis's intake of alcohol on the overland journey. Clark would have nursed Lewis through the acute attacks of his ague or whatever fever he was enduring in those dark final hours of his life. Certainly Clark would have separated Lewis from his powder and ball and not succumbed to Lewis's demand—expressed to his free black servant Pernier—for ammunition. It is equally certain that nothing would have induced Clark to leave Lewis's side that fatal night at Grinder's Inn. If James Neelly was indeed indulging Lewis's desire for liquor, as Gilbert Russell later alleged,[26] Clark would have sent him packing in no uncertain terms. If Lewis had made it through that dark night, if Clark could have eased him back to health on the road to Nashville, or even back from the brink of suicide, Lewis would almost certainly have explained himself adequately to his critics in the War Department, would have discovered that his official and unofficial financial woes were not as grave (or degrading) as he had let himself believe when he received the bombshell letter from William Eustis (or William Simmons) on August 18, 1809, his thirty-fifth birthday. He almost certainly would have, as Clark put it, returned "with flying Colours"[27] to St. Louis or taken a leave of absence to work on the book in the more civilized and less factionalized environment of Philadelphia.

It is important to remember that Lewis and Clark first worked together in the wake of a Lewis crisis of impulsiveness. There were two types of men in the early national period: those, like Jefferson, who would not permit themselves to be drawn into an affair of honor (the workup to a duel) no matter how strenuously his antagonist provoked him, and those, like Hamilton, who were so prickly about their sense of honor that they let themselves be drawn into what was left of an ancient practice that Jefferson regarded as vulgar and barbaric. Lewis was court-martialed on November 6, 1795, for an incident that occurred on September 24, 1795, in which Lewis challenged a Lieutenant Joseph Elliott to a duel. He was acquitted. Before the incident Lewis had apparently already been transferred to a chosen rifle company commanded by William Clark, then twenty-five.[28] Clark must have immediately recognized that Lewis was an exceptional but excitable man with a fragile core and a prickly sense of honor. Sometime between 1794 and July 1796, they became friends. Just how close their friendship was at this juncture is unknown, but two things are certain. Lewis saw something in Clark—or his skill set—that gave him the confidence to invite Clark to join him on the transcontinental journey seven years later. And Clark saw something in Lewis so positive that it outweighed any sense he must have had of Lewis's difficultness.

First impressions are important.

Lewis realized how much he depended on Clark, not merely for the important work that Clark did in propelling the boats, managing the men, and making the maps, but also for helping him maintain his equilibrium. When Lewis and Clark separated in early July 1806 at Travelers' Rest near today's Missoula, Montana, Clark to find and descend the Yellowstone River, Lewis to return to the caches at the Great Falls and reconnoiter the Marias River basin, they could not know when (or for that matter, if) they would meet again. Their plan was sensible, given the impossibility of maintaining communication in a wilderness they believed they were the first to traverse. They would meet at the confluence of the two rivers sometime in late summer or fall. Lewis explained that Clark would descend the Yellowstone "to the missouri where should he arrive first he will wait my arrival."[29] Clark wrote about the separation in a calm and straightforward way, but Lewis felt apprehension. "All arrangements being now compleated for carrying into effect the several schemes we had planed for execution on our return," Lewis wrote on July 3, 1806, "we saddled our horses and set out I took leave of my worthy friend and companion Capt. Clark and the party that accompanyed him. I could not avoid feeling much concern on this occasion although I hoped this seperation was only momentary."[30] Lewis's concerns were prophetic. He was about to undertake the most personally challenging month of the expedition—for him. Clark's ensuing month was arguably the least challenging of the expedition—for him. It is quite possible that Clark's prolonged relaxation on the Yellowstone may have had something to do with his separation from the radioactive Lewis.

I have written elsewhere in this book (chapter four) about Lewis's ordeal on the upper Marias on the return journey and the strange cascade of events that followed, culminating in the shooting accident of August 11, 1806. At this juncture I wish to examine one of the most interesting periods of Lewis and Clark's residency at Fort Mandan in today's North Dakota, a nine-day period in which the captains were separated and Lewis was uncharacteristically left in sole command of the majority of the Corps of Discovery. In other words, for nine days in the heart of a Dakota winter, the world of Fort Mandan was effectively turned upside down. Clark, the nominal manager of the personnel, was off on an important hunting trip. Lewis, the generally detached commander of the expedition, was left in charge of Fort Mandan—alone—with his partner in discovery away in the howling winter wilderness. Nothing very bad happened in Clark's absence. It was a kind of hibernation period for the Corps of Discovery. The fort was secure—"cannonball proof" said one of the Canadians in the vicinity. During this short interlude, the Lakota made no attempt to attack the

Americans—either those stationed at the fort or those out hunting with Clark. No one got hurt or ill or lost. As exhibited in his own words and actions, Lewis's leadership style proved to be stern and fussy, overbearing and culturally intolerant, but the nine-day period feels to the reader of the twenty-first century more like a sitcom than a military expedition.

I'm interested in this episode for several reasons. First, the period of February 3–13 represents Lewis's only sustained journal keeping between May 14, 1804 and April 7, 1805. Starved as we are for Lewis's voice, it is important to pay attention to him when he emerges for whatever reason from his characteristic silence. Second, it was during this interlude that Sacagawea gave birth to her first child. Given her status as the first or second most celebrated Indian woman in American history, every student of Lewis and Clark cherishes the few passages in which she makes an appearance, as much as she prized blue beads. There is something exquisite—something worthy of Fred MacMurray's portrayal of Lewis in the 1955 film *The Far Horizons*—in the fact that it was Lewis, not Clark, who served as the attendant physician at the birth of Jean Baptiste Charbonneau. Third, my focus in this book is the character of Meriwether Lewis. Anything that serves as a window on his character is interesting to me. Although the nine days in question were not the most momentous of the expedition, they exhibit Lewis in wonderful and memorable relief. The fact that Lewis was in comparative repose in early February 1805 makes this set of journal entries especially revealing. In his life of Alexander the Great, Plutarch wrote,

> It must be borne in mind that my design is not to write histories, but lives. And the most glorious exploits do not always furnish us with the clearest discoveries of virtue or vice in men; sometimes a matter of less moment, an expression or a jest, informs us better of their characters and inclinations, than the most famous sieges, the greatest armaments, or the bloodiest battles whatsoever. Therefore as portrait-painters are more exact in the lines and features of the face, in which the character is seen, than in the other parts of the body, so I must be allowed to give my more particular attention to the marks and indications of the souls of men, and while I endeavour by these to portray their lives, may be free to leave more weighty matters and great battles to be treated of by others.[31]

Fourth, the presence of several Canadians at the Mandan and Hidatsa villages during this period provides a remarkable and exceedingly important lens on the Lewis and Clark Expedition in general, and Meriwether Lewis in particular. Although we need not take the Canadians' portrait of Lewis at face value, their accounts of their time at Fort Mandan represent one of the fascinating (and most neglected) portraits of the Lewis and Clark Expedition.

Clark was, all of his life, an outstanding keeper of records and a reliable journal keeper. From a point early in the great journey, he became the journal keeper of record for the Core of Volunteers for North Western Discovery. At Camp Wood and at Fort Mandan, Lewis took up the pen when Clark was absent on a side mission and he was left behind as the commanding officer of the main party. It is well known to students of the expedition that Clark has a journal entry for all but nine days of the 863 days of the journey between May 14, 1804, and September 23, 1806. Those nine days coincided precisely with his winter hunt south of Fort Mandan. Clark's absence sent Lewis to his pen. Clark was silent from February 4–12, 1805, inclusive. The remainder of this chapter is an analysis of that remarkable interlude.

Life at Fort Mandan between February 4 and 12, 1805, is one of the least studied episodes of the Lewis and Clark Expedition (except for the birth of Jean Baptiste Charbonneau on February 11). It is worth a close look for a number of reasons. First, it is a rather amusing episode in which Lewis's characteristic edginess has comic rather than tragic consequences. Second, it proves irrefutably how much better a personnel manager Clark was than Lewis. Third, it reveals a great deal about Lewis in a short space of time, during his only sustained period of journal keeping between May 14, 1804, and April 7, 1805. Fourth, it makes every reader of the journals hunger for more of Lewis's voice during the periods when he went silent, for Lewis's prose and point of view are never uninteresting. The journal Lewis wrote in Clark's absence is a fascinating document.

From February 4 to 12, 1805, Clark led a group of sixteen members of the expedition, plus two nameless Frenchmen, on a winter hunting trip south of Fort Mandan. Because he was venturing into wild country in the middle of a very harsh winter, Clark suspended his daily journal keeping for the duration of the hunt. When he returned to Fort Mandan, Clark resumed his journal keeping. In fact, on the day after he returned, Clark summarized the events of the nine days he had been gone, not in broad summary fashion in the manner of Patrick Gass, but day-by-day. The minute Clark returned, Lewis put down his pen and resumed his silence. No incident in the expedition better indicates that the modus operandi was for Clark to keep the captain's log and Lewis to assume that duty if necessary, but only if necessary. Lewis often wrote in his journal in addition to Clark's baseline narrative, but only when it suited him, except for these periods of Clark's absence from the main party.

Permanent Indian villages like those of the Mandan and Hidatsa had many advantages, but one of the downsides was that game in the vicinity tended to get hunted out. The Mandan and Hidatsa were accustomed to the

Although the Mandan treated Lewis and Clark with remarkable hospitality, Lewis found their presence within the walls of Fort Mandan mostly annoying. Karl Bodmer: Fort Clark on the Missouri (February 1834). Courtesy of the Lewis & Clark Fort Mandan Foundation, Washburn, North Dakota.

exceedingly harsh winters of today's North Dakota. Mandan and Hidatsa men hunted year around, but the women of the tribes also maintained extensive farm plots in the Missouri River bottomlands during the short growing season. With their substantial reserves of corn, beans, squash, and other produce stored underground, the Mandan and Hidatsa seldom knew starving times, but during severe winters they often lived on meager rations.

Clark's mid-winter hunting trip was born of need. "[O]ur provisions of meat being nearly exorsted," Clark wrote, "I concluded to Decend the river on the Ice & hunt."[32] He took with him a little less than half the men, three horses leased from their Canadian owners, and two specially-constructed sleighs to transport the meat. Clark later reported that his hunting party had been able to kill forty deer, three buffalo bulls, and nineteen elk during the eight-day hunt. The hunters eventually trudged their way a full forty-five miles south of Fort Mandan, to the site of today's Bismarck, North Dakota. The southernmost camp was on the east bank of the Missouri River, opposite the mouth of the Heart River south of today's Bismarck. Lewis reports that Clark was prepared "to continue his rout down the river even as far as the River bullet unless he should find a plenty of game nearer."[33] The "bullet" is the Cannonball River, which is fifty miles south of Bismarck. In other words, Clark was prepared to travel on foot, in severe weather in a sub-arctic climate, using inadequate footwear, 100 miles south of Fort Mandan in order to obtain protein for the expedition. Lewis wrote about the excursion in his characteristically formal and somewhat odd prose style. The expedition's meat supply, he said, "is now nearly exhausted" (not *exorsted*). "[A] supply of this articles is at this moment peculiarly interesting,"[34] he wrote. This was Lewis's way of saying the expedition was seriously in need of fresh meat. *Peculiarly interesting* is a strange turn of phrase. Technically it is an example of litotes, an utterance in which something is affirmed by way of deliberate understatement. Lewis was prone to this sort of expression. He went on to say the expedition needed meat "as well for our immediate consumption, as that we may have time before the approach of the warm season to prepare the meat for our voyage in the spring of the year."[35] Lewis was thinking ahead, as always. He wanted to acquire a large supply of meat for the expedition's first days or weeks beyond the Mandan and Hidatsa villages after the ice on the Missouri River broke up. He was well aware that the extreme cold of the North Dakota winter would solve the problem of preserving the meat supply in the two months before the expedition could embark.

Thus equipped with his formal prose style and bemused sensibility, Lewis stayed behind to manage the fort.

A great deal happened at Fort Mandan in Clark's absence. Lewis received important visitors: the principal leader of the Mandan people, Posecopsahe (the Black Cat); a delegation of leaders from Mituntanka, the closest of the two Mandan villages; and Charles McKenzie of the North

West Company. He changed the security arrangements at Fort Mandan. He presided over a breach of military discipline and conducted the last known court-martial of the expedition. The expedition's blacksmith John Shields did a brisk business in fancy metal work for Indian customers. And Sacagawea gave birth to her first child at or near the fort.

By the first week of February 1805, the Corps of Discovery had settled into a routine at Fort Mandan. Relations with the Mandan Indians were friendly, with the Hidatsa a little less so. Everyone was snugly housed in a v-shaped log fort constructed on the east bank of the Missouri River under the supervision of the expedition's carpenter Patrick Gass. The men of the expedition had learned how to survive the bitter cold of the northern Great Plains and, to a certain extent, how to work in such extreme weather. The captains were taking advantage of the enforced cessation of travel to prepare reports and maps for President Jefferson, and to prepare specimens for shipment to Washington, DC, in the spring. The concerns of the men of the expedition were very basic: food, fire, shelter, clothing, rest, and, if possible, female companionship. A number of the men were hiking across the windswept river to make periodic visits to the closest of the two Mandan villages to enjoy the company of Indian families and particularly women, with whom, if circumstances were right, they bedded down for the night. Food was, and was not, an issue. The friendly Mandan were famous for their hospitality. The Mandan had a cultural tradition of adopting visitors temporarily into their families. Adoption provided a measure of security for strangers, both in their persons and their property, and conferred what might be called *most favored nation* trade status for the duration of their visits. White guests were able to obtain significant quantities of corn, squash, beans, and other garden produce in exchange for pieces of metal, which Indians craved, powder and ball, cloth, awls, needles, knives, kettles, mirrors, ribbon, beads, braid, metal tools, tobacco, and trinkets.

Lewis and Clark stayed with the Mandan and Hidatsa Indians only as long as the river road was closed. They stopped for the winter on October 26, 1804. By then ice had been forming for several weeks at night on the oars and setting poles and along the shores of the Missouri River. The Missouri had frozen for the first time by November 15. In the spring of 1805, the ice of the Missouri River broke up on April 2. Five days later Lewis and Clark resumed their journey. It was fortuitous, but not inevitable, that Lewis and Clark spent their winter among the Mandan and Hidatsa. They had hoped to get all the way to the base of the "Rock" mountains in 1804. The fact that they reached the earthlodge population center of some 4,000–5,000 Indians just as the Missouri froze is nothing more than a fortunate coincidence. Among other things, it was a great boon for Plains Indian ethnography, as James Ronda has shown.[36]

February 3 (Sunday)

The principal concern of Captain Lewis as February began was the "situation of our boat and perogues."[37] When the expedition established its winter encampment in the first days of November 1804, the three heavy boats had been secured to the shore of the Missouri River, but they were not drawn up onto the benchlands above the waterline. The boats were heavy and bulky. The men of the expedition had much more pressing work to accomplish, including winter shelter, before the full severity of the winter arrived. No member of the expedition, including the ingenious captains, could have anticipated what Theodore Roosevelt later called the season "of iron desolation"[38] that grips the Dakota plains between late November and April. They must have assumed that conditions on the upper Missouri would not be greatly different from those at Camp Wood, where their principal concern about the boats had been the spring rise rather than winter ice. By the time Lewis and Clark began to understand the appalling winter climate of today's North Dakota, sometime in the first three weeks of December 1804, it was too late (and too cold!) to prevent the boats from being trapped by the frozen river. By early February, the keelboat and pirogues were "firmly inclosed in the Ice and almost covered with snow."[39] Actually, as Lewis discovered, that was the least of it. "The ice which incloses them lyes in several stratas of unequal thicknesses which are seperated by streams of water."[40] This meant that the captains could not just order the men to chop through the ice along the perimeter of the boats "because so soon as we cut through the first strata of ice the water rushes up and rises as high as the upper surface of the ice and thus creates such a debth of water as renders it impracticable to cut away the lower strata which appears firmly attached to, and confining the bottom of the vessels."[41] Lewis was afraid the boats would prove to be inextricable, and that when the ice of the river finally broke up later in the spring, the boats would be crushed by running ice or swept down the river by ice dams.

Lewis began to fret about the boats the minute he resumed his journal on February 3. It wasn't until February 26 that the men were able to free the boats after a herculean effort that included the manufacture of special iron-tipped wedging tools, the use of boiling water, and unending chopping in and through the ice-cold water. When the boats were finally extricated, they were winched up onto the dry land over a portable bed of cottonwood rollers. Once safely pulled from the river, they were turned on their sides so the spring sun and wind could dry them out and enable necessary repairs. It must have been tedious, backbreaking, frustrating, dangerous, and exhausting work. Undoubtedly, it diminished the amount of rest Lewis had hoped the men would enjoy before the rigors of the second traveling season began.

FEBRUARY 4 (MONDAY)

The hunting party left the fort. It was eighteen degrees below zero Fahrenheit, wind from the northwest. Lewis wrote exclusively about the meat supply and Clark's departure.

FEBRUARY 5 (TUESDAY)

On February 5, Lewis reported that those who remained at Fort Mandan were "visited by many of the natives who brought a considerable quanty of corn in payment for the work which the blacksmith had done for them."[42] In his addresses to Indian delegations, Jefferson liked to give homespun tutorials based on the economic theories of David Hume and Adam Smith. To Sheheke-shote of the Mandan nation, for example, Jefferson said he had sent Lewis up the Missouri because "I wished to learn what we could do to benefit them [Indians] by furnishing them the necessaries they want in exchange for their furs and peltries."[43] Commerce, Jefferson believed, would serve as the first step in civilizing American Indians: "How much better is it for neighbors to help than to hurt one another; how much happier must it make them. If you will cease to make war on one another, if you will live in friendship with all mankind, you can employ all your time in providing food and clothing for yourselves and your families. Your men will not be destroyed in war, and your women and children will lie down to sleep in their cabins without fear of being surprised by their enemies and killed or carried away."[44] Just what Sheheke-shote thought of this speech is unknown. Probably Jefferson was not aware that the peace-loving and agricultural Mandan people whom Sheheke-shote represented had, for several hundred years, occupied and managed the hub of one of the principal trade networks of North America. James Ronda has written, "[T]he Mandan and Hidatsa villagers served as brokers in an international economic and cultural trade network that faced in three directions and stretched over thousands of miles."[45] Probably Sheheke-shote could have taught Jefferson a thing or two about grain storage and corn hybridization.

At any rate, in the winter of 1805, a perfect example of Jefferson's system to provide Indians "necessaries, which we have to spare and they want," in exchange for commodities "which they have to spare and we want,"[46] was unfolding at Fort Mandan. The Mandan and Hidatsa had a modest surplus of farm produce, though they too were desperate to obtain a fresh meat supply. "I am informed," Lewis wrote on February 4, "that our Indian neighbours—suffer extreemly at this moment for the article of *flesh*."[47] They brought what they had in abundance—corn—to exchange for that which they craved—metal of any sort, and in this case, metal fashioned into battle-axes by the expedition's blacksmith John Shields. In fact, Lewis reported that the Indians "appeared extreemly pleased with the exchange." They were, he said, "extravegantly fond of sheet iron."[48]

Lewis later praised Shields for his talent as a blacksmith and gunsmith. On June 10, 1805, after Shields repaired the main spring of Lewis's air gun at the confluence of the Missouri and the Marias, Lewis wrote, "[W]e have been much indebted to the ingenuity of this man on many occasions; without having served any regular apprenticeship to any trade, he makes his own tools principally and works extreemly well in either wood or metal, and in this way has been extreenely servicable to us, as well as being a good hunter and an excellent waterman."[49] From Lewis this is virtually unlimited praise. After the expedition's return, Shields was one of just six expedition members Lewis singled out for special praise in his final personnel report to the War Department. "Nothing was more peculiarly useful to us, in various situations, than the skill and ingenuity of this man as an artist, in repairing our guns, accoutrements, &c." Lewis recommended that Shields receive a bonus for his work "as an artificer."[50]

Lewis was willing for Shields to fill these orders, but at the same time he felt the need to criticize the axe design preferred by the Mandan Indians. The preferred battle-axe is "formed in a very inconvenient manner in my opinion," Lewis wrote. For one thing the blade was too thin, "extreemly thin." For another, the handle was much too short. "[T]he handle seldom more than fourteen inches in length," he wrote, as if he were a weapons consultant brought in to assess the efficacy of the Mandan battle-axe. "[T]he great length of the blade of this axe, added to the small size of the handle renders a stroke uncertain and easily avoided, while the shortness of the handel must render a blow much less forceable if even well directed, and still more inconvient as they uniformly use this instrument in action on horseback," Lewis wrote. And that was the *improved* model of the Mandan ax. "The oalder fassion is still more inconvenient," he complained, "it is somewhat in the form of the blade of an Espantoon but is attatchd to the helve of the dementions before discribed."[51] Lewis actually took the time to draw a sketch of the inefficacious battle-axe at the end of his journal description.[52]

There is some paradox here. Lewis was an official representative of the government of the United States. The president had instructed him to promote peaceful relations among the tribes that he met. "In all your intercourse with the natives, treat them," Jefferson insisted, "in the most friendly & conciliatory manner which their own conduct will admit; allay all jealousies as to the object of your journey, satisfy them of it's innocence, make them acquainted with the position, extent, character, peaceable & commercial dispositions of the U.S. of our wish to be neighborly, friendly & useful to them, & of our dispositions to a commercial intercourse with them."[53] Nothing in Jefferson's instructions could have been construed as authorizing the Corps of Discovery to engage in arms manufacture at the Mandan and Hidatsa villages. Nor would the president have regarded such commercial exchange a specimen of *innocence*. To obtain the food they needed to get through the winter, or at least to add some vegetables to their otherwise all meat diet, the captains found themselves selling metal and metal objects to the Indians. "[T]he blacksmith's have proved a happy resoce to us in our present situation," Lewis wrote, "as I believe it would have been difficult to have devised any other method to have procured corn from the natives." Lewis said the exchange rate for unimproved iron was that "each piece about four inches square ... obtained seven to eight gallons of corn." Shields was actually cutting up a "birnt out" sheet-iron stove into convenient 4 x 4" squares. Thus, a metal stove that the Corps of Discovery had no further use for became a crude, but valuable money supply for the captains. The captains had even stepped up their manufacture of charcoal (January 24) to make sure their forge could turn out the axes being sought by the Mandan people. James Ronda writes, "This new aspect of expedition-Indian trade demanded an expansion of Fort Mandan's industrial capacity."[54] Lewis does not indicate what price was established for the battle axes, but, like all merchants, he surely understood that custom-made war implements were worth a great deal more than unimproved metal squares. The fact that Shields was manufacturing instruments of war rather than hide scrapers or other agricultural and domestic tools further increased their value. In short, more or less by accident, the Corps of Discovery had found itself at the center of a lucrative arms trade. Nobody could have anticipated this economic boon. It actually put considerable strain on the expedition's human resources. As spring, and the annual season of war skirmishing, approached, the blacksmith crew had to work overtime to fashion these weapons. On March 13, Clark reported, "[M]aney Inds. here to day all anxiety for war axes the Smiths have not an hour of Idle time to Spear."[55] Had Lewis been in a position to consult Jefferson from Fort Mandan, it is unlikely that the peace-loving president would have authorized the business. The Canadian agent of the North West Company, François-Antoine Laroque, rightly understood that Lewis and Clark were required by their government to preach peace, not help the nations they encountered prepare for war. "They made presents of a Flag, Medal, Chiefs Cloathing, tobacco, knives, Beads & other trinkets, to Every Chief of the Indian nations, which they saw, but have not given a single shot of ammunition,"[56] he wrote.

Necessity makes for strange bedfellows. At no point does Lewis have a *Star Trek* moment, in which he wrestles with the moral implications of preaching the president's continental peace policy while selling arms to the very people he is trying to wean from war. Ironically, Lewis's only comment is to express contempt for the inefficient lethality of the Mandan battle-axe design. A wider blade and a longer handle would render them much more useful and deadly, he reports. Under their current inefficient design, they deliver "a blow much less forceable if even well directed."[57]

Had Clark been keeping the journal at this point, rather than Lewis, it is unlikely that he would have wasted any time grumbling about Mandan battle-axe design. So far as we know, Lewis never actually saw the Mandan in battle. The Mandan were a comparatively pacific people, but when they fought, they exhibited great bravery and ferocity. Their later war leader Four Bears was legendary for his capacity to win honors in hand-to-hand combat. It seems unlikely that the Mandan failed to understand the dynamics of the battle-axe. It seems much more likely that they had some sensible reason for wanting these axes designed in a manner Lewis found objectionable. It may be that they were intended to be used for ceremonial purposes rather than in actual combat. We don't know.

Lewis, like his great patron Jefferson, fancied himself something of a design expert. He is said to have played a role in making a few design changes in the 1803 Harpers Ferry rifles the expedition carried. Before the expedition began, he designed his iron-framed boat the *Experiment*—his failed *Experiment,* that is. He probably helped design the lead canisters that initially carried the expedition's gunpowder supply and then could be melted down into bullets. Here he focused his design expertise on the Mandan battle-axe.

The captains' lively trade in iron at Fort Mandan may be a clue to one of the principal mysteries of the Lewis and Clark Expedition—the final disposition of Lewis's iron-framed boat. Many scholars, including the archaeologist Ken Karsmizki, believe the iron frame of the *Experiment* is still buried in the cache pit into which it was deposited on July 10, 1805, after it failed to serve the expedition's purposes. We know it was unearthed on the return journey. At Upper Portage Camp on July 14, 1806, Lewis wrote, "Had the carriage wheels dug up found them in good order. the iron frame of the boat had not suffered materially."[58] No further mention of the boat is made in any expedition journal in 1806. It is possible, of course, that Lewis's men either re-buried the iron frame, tossed it aside, or threw it into the Missouri River. Nobody knows for sure. Repeated efforts by Karsmizki to locate the boat, sometimes involving the best detection equipment available to the US military establishment, have failed to solve this mystery. Stephen Ambrose often said the iron frame represents the "holy grail" of Lewis and Clark archaeology.

It would have been severely illogical for members of the Lewis contingent to dig up the iron frame on the return journey in 1806 and then leave it in Montana. By this time the expedition was essentially bankrupt. The Mandan and Hidatsa, whose permanent villages the expedition was certain to visit on its return, were a metal-starved people, as the captains had unmistakably learned during the Fort Mandan winter. Lewis and Clark could easily have traded pieces of the iron frame for whatever they might wish or need to purchase at the Mandan and Hidatsa villages: farm produce, skin clothing, artifacts for the president, furs, and human services. If they followed this sensible course of action, nobody mentioned it in the expedition's journals. Or they might have given the metal to Toussaint Charbonneau as part of the blacksmith works they presented him on August 16, 1806. Patrick Gass is the only journal keeper who mentions the gift of the blacksmith kit.[59] It may be that the captains were too busy with diplomatic affairs to mention this extravagant gift. Lewis, of course, had ceased writing altogether following the gunshot wound he suffered on August 11. It is equally possible that the captains did not wish to call attention to their gift of United States government property to a private individual. The silence of the captains, specifically Clark, on this occasion may well have extended to the spare iron, if indeed it was extricated from the cache at the Great Falls.

February 6 (Wednesday)

On February 6, Lewis received some of the principal leaders of the Mandan nation. The leader of Mitutanka, Sheheke-shote (White Coyote), was among them, along with Sho-ta-har-ro-ra (the Coal), Oh-he-nar (Big Man), Harry Horn, and Black Man. Just what this delegation wanted is unclear. They may have just been curious about "our fashions,"[60] as Clark put it on a previous occasion. On this occasion Lewis wrote, "I smoked with them, after which they retired." This, reported Lewis, was "a deportment not common, for they usually pester us with their good company the balance of the day after once being introduced to our apartment." Here again we see Lewis's characteristic style. His general contempt for Indians is undisguised. In the midst of 4,000 Indians upon whose friendliness his life and those of his compatriots depend, in a stark subarctic place where the generosity of his hosts is essential to his comfort and possibly to his survival, Lewis describes the leaders of his host tribe as pests. He employs litotes in speaking of "their good company," by which he means *their annoying presence*. His phrase *our apartment* may be a sarcastic way of referring to everything within the stockade of Fort Mandan, or it may more specifically mean the quarters he shares with William Clark. If he means the latter, Lewis may be saying he doesn't particularly mind the presence of Indians at Fort Mandan as long as their *good company* is shared outside his private quarters. Maybe the battle-axe trade was bringing more Indian traffic to Fort Mandan than anyone wished. On February 6, even the level-headed John Ordway wrote, "[T]he Savages trouble us verry much."[61]

On February 6, the Mandan leaders may have broken with their usual habit of lingering at Fort Mandan precisely because the affable William

Clark was not in residence. In other words, their "deportment not common" may have been motivated by the lack of hospitality they experienced with the haughty and impatient Lewis, or at least by their comparative preference for the company of Clark. The proud leaders of the Mandan nation may well have sensed Lewis's contempt and left Fort Mandan as soon as their commitment to social decorum permitted. If Lewis had any inkling that the Mandan felt no warmth for him and preferred the more relaxed and genial Clark, he did not mention it in his journal. After the winter sojourn ended, Lewis said farewell to Mandan leader Posecopsahe on April 8, 1805, as the expedition began to move west towards today's Montana. "I walked on shore, and visited the *black Cat*, took leave of him after smoking a pipe as is their custom," Lewis wrote. At a different time in the same day, Clark also said farewell to Posecopsahe. "I took my leave of the great Chief of the Mandans who gave me a par of excellent mockersons."[62] You reap what you sow.

On February 6, Lewis conducted celestial observations in the morning, beginning at 7:59 A.M. and again in mid-afternoon. Apparently Clark usually served as the keeper of the chronometer during these exercises, for Lewis wrote, "I do not place great confidence in these observations, as the person who took the time was not much accustomed to the business. Capt. Clark was absent."[63]

FEBRUARY 7 (THURSDAY)

On February 7, Captain Lewis discovered a security breach at Fort Mandan. "The Sergt. of the guard reported that the Indian women (wives to our interpreters[)] were in the habit of unbaring the fort gate at any time of night and admitting their Indian visitors."[64] Night begins at about 6 P.M. in early February at Fort Mandan. An early February night would have lasted about thirteen hours at that latitude. According to Lewis's detachment orders, Indians were welcome inside Fort Mandan during daylight hours, but the gates of the fort were bolted from the inside at sunset.[65] Jusseaume's wife (name unknown) and Charbonneau's wife Sacagawea were apparently taking it upon themselves to open the gate after hours to admit their friends. Lewis immediately put a stop to the practice. "I therefore directed a lock to be put to the gate and ordered that no Indian but those attatched to the garrison should be permitted to remain all night within the fort."[66]

At this point Sacagawea was in the last stages of her first pregnancy. The evidence of the journals suggests that her health had suffered as she brought her child to term. Like all first-time mothers, she was undoubtedly scared. About the same time, back in the *civilized* world, Thomas Jefferson assured his younger daughter Maria that giving birth was really nothing more than "a knock of the elbow," a strange claim from a man who never gave birth, and whose wife died from the accumulative debilitations of child-bearing.[67] Because the father of Sacagawea's first child was a white man, she may have been worried that the birthing would be difficult or even impossible. Lewis seems to have regarded the night visits to the interpreters' wives as inessential social calls or a potential threat to the security of his company. It does not seem to have occurred to him that the nocturnal visitors may have been mid-wives or spiritual leaders or providers of Indian *medicine*. Nor did he inquire. Charbonneau was out hunting with Clark. Lewis could probably have made inquiries through Francois Labiche and Rene Jusseaume, but he chose not to. For the first time since the fort was completed on Christmas Eve, 1804, Lewis ordered tight security after dark. No journal keeper bothered to record Sacagawea's or Jusseaume's wife's reaction to the lockdown. The only person who might have been disposed to record their reaction was Clark, and he was dozens of miles downriver. It seems likely that if Clark had been at hand on February 7, he would simply have explained the expedition's security proto-cols to the interpreters and their wives, and urged the sergeant at guard to watch the front gate more closely. Without the benefit of the calming influ-ence of Clark, the irritable Lewis opted for the padlock. He did not wish to be *pestered*, especially after dark.

FEBRUARY 8 (FRIDAY)

On February 8, Posecopsahe (The Black Cat) came to visit. He was the principal leader of the upper Mandan village, Ruptare. Lewis and Clark more or less arbitrarily regarded him as the grand chief of the Mandan na-tion. It was Posecopsahe who had challenged William Clark's presumptu-ousness back on November 18, 1804, wondering why the Mandan people should hearken to the trade and sovereignty demands of the expedition's leaders "untill they were Convinced that what had been told thim by us." After all, "Mr. Evins had deceived them & we might also."[68] Posecopsahe's point was that the Mandan had heard the same story back in 1796 when the Welsh romantic traveler John Evans (1770–1799), representing the Spanish government, had urged the Mandan to sever their longstanding trade rela-tions with the French Canadians because they would thereafter be supplied from St. Louis by trade agents licensed by Spain. After a brief stay among the earthlodge villagers, Evans had gone back down the Missouri River. The traders he had promised never materialized. On November 18, Posecopsahe told Clark that the Mandan had held a council about this matter, and "it was thought advisable to put up with the resent insults of the Ossiniboins & Christonoes untill"[69] the Americans fulfilled their promise of establishing a reliable and frequent supply of trade goods from St. Louis. In other words,

Posecopsahe told Clark that the tribe had voted to continue getting its trade goods through Assiniboine and Cree intermediaries. Those tribes frequently mistreated the Mandan people, but they did reliably get them trade goods. Clark's answer on November 18 had been pretty flimsy stuff. "[W]e advised them to remain at peace & that they might depend upon Getting *Supplies* through the Channel of the Missouri, but it required time to put the trade in opperation."[70] The Canadian trader François-Antoine Larocque, embedded that winter with the earthlodge Indians, shared Posecopsahe's skepticism. "In short, during the time I was there, a very Grand Plan was schemed, but its taking place is more than I can tell although the Captains say they are well assured it will."[71]

On February 8, Posecopsahe brought Lewis a bow he had made (or commissioned) for the expedition's growing collection of Indian artifacts. He apologized that the severe winter weather had so far prevented him from completing a matching shield. Posecopsahe's wife gave Lewis two pairs of decorated moccasins to send back to Washington, DC. In return, Lewis gave the Mandan leader "som small shot 6 fishing-hooks and 2 yards of ribbon," and his wife "a small lookingglass and a couples of nedles."[72] This feels like a pretty meager "payment" for a Mandan bow and two pairs of ornamented moccasins. Lewis had paid only $8 for 2,800 fishhooks back in Philadelphia. The six fishhooks, therefore, were worth a little over one cent. The mirror for Posecopsahe's wife was worth three-and-a-half cents. Lewis had purchased 4,600 needles for $9.73. Three needles would have had a value of less than one cent. The two yards of ribbon would have been worth roughly the same. In other words, Lewis received two pairs of exquisite moccasins and a bow for well under a dollar, probably under a quarter, possibly under a dime.[73] These artifacts were of great value to the president, to Philadelphia museum impresario Charles Willson Peale, and to the Enlightenment, even then. Today they would be regarded as priceless. Whether Clark would have offered more in return for these gifts is unclear. It seems likely.

Lewis was not only stingy. He viewed Indians in an unmistakably instrumental way. Of Posecopsahe he wrote, "[T]his man possesses more integrety, firmness, inteligence and perspicuety of mind than any indian I have met with in this quarter ... ." So far so good. "[A]nd I think with a little management he may be made a usefull agent in furthering the views of our government."[74] On the one hand, this is high praise: integrity, intelligence, firmness, perspicuity. On the other hand, Lewis is clearly not interested in Posecopsahe per se, but solely as a potentially "usefull agent" in America's imperial mission. Had Posecopsahe shown any sustained resistance to the "views of our government," Lewis would have dismissed him as capricious, rascally, perfidious, or perhaps as one of the "imps of satturn."[75] (Clark's favorite negative adjective for uncooperative Indians was "sulky," which,

Lewis regarded the Indians of the lower Missouri as less interesting to his mission because they had long since had their first encounters with white emissaries. Karl Bodmer, Swiss, 1809–1893. Detail. 18, Omaha Man, paper: watercolor, pencil, sheet: 11 ⅞ x 8 ½ in. Courtesy of the Joslyn Art Museum, Omaha, Nebraska: Gift of the Enron Art Foundation, 1986, JAM 1986.49.236.

when he was really provoked, became "Sulky Bitch."[76]) Lewis can hardly contain his sense of surprise that "in this quarter" he should meet a man of such capacities, an Indian man of parts. Clark would have been far less likely to describe Posecopsahe or any other Indian in these words.

Lewis's view that Indians were chiefly valuable for their usefulness to the progress of the expedition and the geopolitical agenda of the United States extended to Sacagawea. When she almost died at the Great Falls, Lewis could barely squeeze out a hint of sympathy—"[T]his gave me some concern as well for the poor object herself, then with a young child in her arms"[77]—before he remembered what Sacagawea was good for. He did not wish to lose someone who was "our only dependence for a friendly negociation with the Snake Indians on whom we depend for horses to assist us in our portage from the Missouri to the columbia River."[78] Even when he felt genuine sympathy, Lewis could not help thinking of Sacagawea as an *object*. Clark may have shared Lewis's underlying assumptions about the capacities and the instrumental usefulness of Indians. Lewis and Clark were, after all, official and paid agents of the United States government, not disinterested anthropologists. Their mission was not to make friends, but to make progress.

February 9 (Saturday)

February 9 was an important day at Fort Mandan.

Lewis's padlock may have prevented Sacagawea and Jusseaume's wife from opening the gates of Fort Mandan after dark, and it may generally have kept unwanted Indians out of the fort in unauthorized hours, but it did not stop the seldom-mentioned Private Thomas Howard from climbing over the stockade. Lewis reported that "a man by the name of Howard whom I had given permission to go the Mandane vilage returned after the gate was shut and rether than call to the guard to have it opened scaled the works."[79] Poor Howard. He's one of the least well-known members of the expedition. He is seldom mentioned at all except in the periodic rosters and musterings. When he does rise above the radar on February 9, 1805, it is to be exposed as a man who ventured to the Mandan village Mitutanka, probably in search of sexual pleasure. His nocturnal mission ends not in satisfied sleep, but in a disciplinary incident, indeed the last known court-martial of the Lewis and Clark Expedition. He had the misfortune to be apprehended not by the flexible and understanding William Clark but by the enforcer, the sometimes-priggish Meriwether Lewis. And Captain Lewis refers to him as if he were a perfect stranger: "a man by the name of Howard." It may well be that Lewis had to ask the sergeant at guard to remind him of the name of the culprit. This is one of those important clues to the social dynamics of the expedition that only appear in close readings of the journals.

It would be interesting to know how soon after the expedition began, if ever, Lewis could identify by name each permanent member of the company, and to compare that to Clark's ready familiarity with the individuals who participated in the great journey. Back at Camp Wood Clark had famously said, "Howard—never Drink water," which was a sarcastic way of saying that Howard had a particular fondness for alcohol.[80]

The epithets, offhand characterizations, and minute revelations of personality that pop up in odd places in the journals of the expedition are manna to historians, but they may not be altogether reliable as descriptions of Thomas Proctor Howard, Peter Weiser, John Thompson, or other seldom-mentioned members of the Lewis and Clark Expedition. When the captains jotted down these slivers of characterization at random moments of the journey, they were not intending to provide a balanced assessment of William Werner or John Potts or to sum them up in a clever turn of phrase. They were merely writing up the day and noticing that which caught their attention in the midst of the hectic macro-dynamics of a transcontinental exploration mission. Historians comb the journals and letters of the expedition in a desperate search for telling details and colorful descriptors. Once George Shannon gets lost or Charbonneau cuffs his wife, they have—in the eyes of historians—locked themselves into immortality as dunderheads or brutes, like the characters in Keats' "Ode on a Grecian Urn"[81]:

> Bold lover, never, never canst thou kiss,
> Though winning near the goal – yet, do not grieve;
> She cannot fade, though thou hast not thy bliss,
> For ever wilt thou love, and she be fair!

Extrapolating whole personalities from the tiniest fragments of offhand remarks in the journals is as inevitable as it is unfair. Historians strive to make their narratives colorful and dramatic, and they feel a desperate need to differentiate one essentially identical Lewis and Clark factotum from the next. The journal keepers never stepped back to provide brief character sketches of each member of the expedition. Men like Richard Windsor and Hugh Hall spent twenty-eight months in a tight cluster of thirty-three individuals on an epic voyage across the continent without getting noticed—*at least in the journals*—more than a handful of times, but that doesn't mean they were ciphers in the social dynamics of the Corps of Discovery. Private John Newman would be an expedition nonentity had it not been for the court-martial he precipitated by way of "Mutinous expressions"[82] on October 12, 1804, near today's North Dakota-South Dakota border. Because of this grave infraction Newman was discharged from the expedition and sent back from Fort Mandan on the keelboat in April 1805. Captain Lewis, like a responsible historian, knew that Newman was a fuller, more interesting, more reliable man than the miscreant who rose above the radar at the end of the expedition's first exhausting year of travel, but he felt he could not revoke Newman's discharge without endangering the military discipline of the expedition.[83] Just as Newman was more than the articulator of *Mutinous expressions,* so Shannon was more than *the young man who got lost,* and Charbonneau was much more than the ruffian who struck his wife at dinner on August 14, 1805. Each member of the expedition was a full human being with strengths and weakness, a family somewhere, an idiosyncratic way of speaking (perhaps with a regional accent), a spiritual life, a set of stories about how he (or she) came to be on this voyage, plans for the future, attitudes towards the other members of the expedition and particularly of the leaders. Each one had dreams, quirks, styles, habits (of eating, hygiene, sleeping, snoring, laughing, expressing displeasure, loading and firing a gun, skinning a buffalo, writing his name). Three things are certain. First, if we could be dropped into the expedition's encampment on any given day after April 7, 1805, we would learn in one hour more than we have ever known about the dynamics of the Lewis and Clark Expedition. Second, what we learned would reinforce our current notions about the expedition in some respects, and almost certainly blow the doors off of our understanding in many other, and perhaps some fundamental, ways. Third, every man is the hero of his own narrative. If every member of the expedition had written a journal, it is exceedingly unlikely that we would continue to think of Howard as the man who "never Drink water," or John Collins as a *black gard* for trying to pass off a pig he poached from a neighboring farmer as bear meat at Camp Wood.[84]

James Ronda has written, "What we know about the lives of those who ventured up the Missouri 'Under a Jentle Brease' makes for thin reading. There are just hints and scraps about men like John Thompson, Moses Reed, and Silas Goodrich. They have their moments in time and then, for the most part, they are lost to us. Because we know so little, we fall back on conventional stereotypes. Here is Drouillard the hunter, Gass the carpenter, Shields the blacksmith, and Shannon the forever lost. But none of these cardboard cutouts satisfies, and we long to know these men as flesh and blood."[85]

Thus Thomas Proctor Howard (1779–1814) takes his place in history as a minor member of the Lewis and Clark Expedition who evinced a liking for alcohol and who was court-martialed for climbing the walls of Fort Mandan. Clark's statement about Howard's aversion to water was penned on January 2–3, 1804.[86] Of course Howard drank water, every day, at about the same rate of consumption as his compatriots, or he would not have lived to violate the security protocols of Fort Mandan. Howard also got a minor creek named for him in today's Montana. The expedition passed the creek on July 26, 1805, near today's Townsend (or Toston), Montana. Howard's nomenclatural fame was fleeting. Today the stream is known as Sixteen

Mile Creek. Even on the day of this brush with cartographic immortality, things went badly for poor Howard. Lewis was apparently still not quite sure who he was. He wrote, "[T]his we called Howard's Creek after Thomas P. Howard one of our party."[87] Perhaps Lewis knew Howard so little that he assumed the reader needed to be reminded that he was a bona fide, if largely invisible, permanent member of the expedition. Furthermore, Gary Moulton notes that Clark named the *wrong creek* for Howard in *Atlas* map 64.[88] Howard couldn't catch a break. On January 26, 1806, at Fort Clatsop, Lewis noted that Howard and William Werner had not returned, as expected, from an errand to the expedition's salt factory on the Pacific Coast. "[N]either of them are very good woodsmen,"[89] Lewis wrote.

Howard's crime on February 9, 1805, was not just that he scaled the walls of the fort, but that he set a very bad example in doing so. "[A]n indian who was looking on shortly after followed his example," Lewis explained. "I convinced the Indian of the impropryety of his conduct, and explained to him the riske he had run of being severely treated, the fellow appeared much allarmed, I gave him a small piece of tobacco and sent him away."[90] Howard did not get off so easily. "Howard I had comitted to the care of the guard with a determineation to have him tryed by a Courtmartial for this offence."[91] Then Lewis delivers one of those little bits of information about a member of the expedition that scholars comb the journals to obtain: "[T]his man is an old soldier which still hightens this offince."[92] Actually, Howard was only twenty-five years old at the time of this incident, but he had been in the army since 1801. Lewis meant that Howard was a veteran soldier, not one of the raw recruits inducted into the army merely as the expedition began.

February 10 (Sunday)

Howard's court-martial occurred on February 10. For some reason the commander of the expedition did not mention the trial in his journal, the official journal of the expedition. What we know about the court-martial comes from the journal of John Ordway, who also provides important details not included in Lewis's account of Howard's arrest on February 9. Lewis reported only that one Indian scrambled over the stockade, but Ordway noted "2 or 3 young Indians followed" Howard from Mitutanka to the fort, even though only "one of the Indians followed him over."[93] Ordway provided a better description of Lewis's sermon to the Indian who climbed the fence: "Capt. Lewis ordered the Indian away after Giving him a Scolding at the Same time telling him that he was not So much to blame as the white man."[94] Ordway's plain English is more detailed and evocative of the incident than Lewis's characteristically formal and Latinate description.

Ordway also explained that after finding the gate locked, Howard "went round back of the Fort and Scaled over." Fort Mandan was built at the base of the river bluffs on the eastern bank of the Missouri River. The easiest way in would be to climb over the fence at the back of the fort, where the two wings of the facility were joined by a semicircular structure that served as the expedition's principal storage room at Fort Mandan. Howard was much less likely to be caught coming in at the back of the fort, indeed much less likely to be seen by imitative Mandan Indians. The Canadian trade agent François-Antoine Laroque wrote a superb description of Fort Mandan based on direct observation. "The two Ranges of houses, do not join one another," he wrote, "but are join'd by a piece of fortification made in the form of a demi Circle, that Can defend two sides of the Fort, on the top of which they keep a sentry all night, & the lower part of that building serves as a store."[95] By climbing over the back fence, Howard avoided what Laroque called "a Range of amazing large pickets the front," but he apparently found the sergeant at guard waiting for him when he arrived at the top of the storage room.

Here, as often, the accounts of the lesser journal keepers provide essential details overlooked or omitted by the captains. Ordway's journal enables us to piece together a fuller, richer, and better-detailed account of the Howard incident. It also serves to highlight the idiosyncrasies of Lewis's prose style and to show that Lewis's formalism and pretentiousness caused him sometimes to obscure the actual events that unfolded behind his screen of verbiage. We are fortunate to have the journals of Gass, Whitehouse, and Ordway, each with a different textual and transmission history. We would be richer still if we had the undigested journal of Gass, the journal, in whatever form, of Robert Frazer, and the journal of Nathaniel Pryor, if indeed he kept one. In his letter to President Jefferson from Fort Mandan, dated April 7, 1805, Lewis reported that seven men besides himself were keeping journals. We know that Lewis, Clark, Ordway, Gass, Whitehouse, Floyd, and Frazer were keeping journals. It's not clear whether at this point Lewis was counting Floyd as one of the journal keepers, since he had died more than seven months previously, on August 20, 1804. Presumably, several other members of the expedition kept journals of some sort. We have complete journals for only three members of the expedition: Clark, Ordway, and Gass. Floyd's journal ended on August 18, 1804. Whitehouse's journal breaks off on April 2, 1806. Lewis has no extant journal for more than half of the days of the expedition. Frazer's journal disappeared in the wake of Lewis's publicly expressed hostility towards what he regarded as spurious or unauthorized publications relating to the expedition.[96]

Ordway indicates that Howard was found guilty of the offence. The court-martial began at noon local time, February 10, Ordway reported. Howard's peers rendered their verdict at sunset, which would have occurred a little before 6 P.M. "[A]t Sunset the proceedings of The court martial came out the prisoner was Sentenced 50 lashes & laid to the mercy of the commanding officer who was pleased to forgive him the punishment awarded by the court."[97] With considerable narrative sophistication, Ordway created suspense in his journal by separating the proceedings and the sentencing phase of the court-martial by way of a report on the return of Toussaint Charbonneau from Clark's extended hunting trip.

So ends the ordeal of Thomas Proctor Howard—without a whipping. Captain Lewis was apparently content to scold the unnamed Mandan Indian, rebuke Howard (complete with a *you of all people* admonishment), have him arrested (and possibly incarcerated), and shame him by way of a surprisingly protracted trial conducted by his peers. The entire incident probably stemmed from Lewis's sudden order (February 7) that a padlock be placed on the Fort Mandan gate at dusk. The fact that the men had not yet had time to become fully familiar with the new security protocol may have induced Lewis to remit the sentence, as well as to omit the trial from the expedition's orderly book and the official journal he was keeping in Clark's absence. The Lewis and Clark polymath Joe Mussulman has written that, "more than eight months into the expedition, Howard must have displayed enough redeeming qualities to justify a suspended sentence."[98]

It is impossible to know how Clark would have handled this incident. Such evidence as we have suggests that Clark maintained order in a more casual manner than the commander of the expedition. Back at Camp Wood when some of the raw recruits got drunk and fought on Christmas Day and again on January 4, Clark waited until they sobered up and then ordered them to help build quarters nearby for a woman who was performing laundry services for the expedition. During the winter at Fort Clatsop, Robert Frazer committed an infraction much graver than a nocturnal scramble over the security fence. On January 10, 1806, Clark wrote, "Rd. Frasure behaved very badly, and mutonous—he also lost his large Knife. I Sent him back to look for his knife, with Directions to return with the party of Serjt Gass."[99] Frazer's crime sounds as bad as or worse than Newman's insubordination on October 12, 1804, for which he received "seventy five lashes on his bear back"[100] and was discharged from the expedition. Yet, nothing more is said of this incident, which occurred at a time when Clark was leading a small party along an impossible route during abysmal northwest rain forest weather to get to the site of a beached whale at today's Cannon Beach, Oregon. Even Clark admitted he had rarely been as hungry as he was on this march and that he had never climbed any height so challenging as Tillamook Head. Clark wrote the words quoted above in his first journal entry for January 10, 1806. The second, more finished version of the journal stated only that "after crossing the 2d Creek frasure informed me that he had lost his big knife, here we Dined, I put frasurs load on my guide who is yet with me, and Sent him back in Serch of his knife with directions to join the other men who were out packing meat & return to the fort all together."[101] Clark appears to have shrugged the incident off once everyone was dry, fed, and rested. Indeed, he suppressed the incident from his more polished journal entry. In his annotation of the incident, Gary Moulton wrote, "Evidently Clark, perhaps after consultation with Lewis, decided that Frazer's behavior during the difficult and trying trip to and from the whale site was not serious enough to warrant disciplinary action."[102] Moulton may be right, but it would seem to me much more likely that Clark *did not* consult Lewis about the Frazer incident when he returned to Fort Clatsop that evening. Clark probably felt that he had handled the affair sensibly by separating himself from Frazer before more subversive words could be uttered, and by forcing the mutinous private to retrace his steps on the punishing trail and to retrieve the lost piece of equipment. On the Pacific Coast, in the midst of incessant rains and soggy underbrush, this was a cooling off period indeed. Had Clark informed his co-captain that Frazer had uttered mutinous expressions, Lewis would almost certainly have brought the full force of Baron von Steuben to bear on the miscreant. In my view, Robert Frazer was very lucky he uttered his incendiary words late in the course of the expedition, many miles from the ears of Captain Lewis, in the presence of a superior officer who had long since established his reputation for flexibility and an even temper.

The Howard trial was not the only big event of February 9, 1805, at Fort Mandan. That day Charles McKenzie of the North West Company came to visit Meriwether Lewis. Lewis does not specify what brought McKenzie to Fort Mandan. Possibly the Canadian trader just wanted the company of fellow English-speaking white men. McKenzie stayed overnight. He may have intended a longer stay, but cut his visit short when he realized that Clark was absent and Lewis was solely in command of the fort. The Canadian traders and company agents did not like Lewis. McKenzie later wrote, "Mr. La Roque and I having nothing very particular claiming attention, we lived contentedly and became intimate with the Gentlemen of the American expedition; who on all occasions seemed happy to see us, and always treated us with civility and kindness. It is true Captain Lewis could not make himself agreeable to us—he could speak fluently and learnedly on all subjects, but his inveterate disposition against the British stained, at least in our eyes, all his eloquence. Captain Clark was equally well informed, but his conversation was always pleasant, for he seemed to dislike giving offence unnecessarily."[103] This is a very strong differentiation of the styles of Meriwether Lewis and William Clark. Lewis, like his patron Jefferson, was an Anglophobe. As the commander of the expedition, he was aware that the Canadians were conducting a lively trade with *America's Indians* on American soil, and he was pretty sure they were saying and doing things that undermined America's dignity and sovereignty. Lewis also had intensely personal reasons for loathing the British. When he was just five years old, his father William Lewis died while defending the natural rights of the American people from the oppressions of George III and the British parliament. Not long thereafter Lewis was living in Georgia. His father was dead and his mother had quickly remarried.[104] The British had turned his whole world upside down.

Whether Lewis was glad to see McKenzie on February 9 and treated him with "civility and kindness" is unclear. Lewis's journal is spare on this subject. McKenzie's principal trade partner François-Antoine Larocque had departed for the North West Company's trade forts on the Assiniboine River on February 7. McKenzie was left behind to watch over what was left of the company's trade assortment, as it was called, at the earthlodge villages. His visit to Fort Mandan may have been merely social. It is also possible that he was seeking to associate himself with the Americans as a security measure, to help ensure that his property was not plundered or appropriated by the Hidatsa or others in Larocque's absence. Neither Lewis nor McKenzie explains.

McKenzie was a very young man in 1804–05. He may have been under twenty years old. An unflattering character sketch of McKenzie written in 1832 by a senior official of the Hudson's Bay Company has him then "about 56 years of Age. 29 Years in the Service."[105] At the time he met Lewis and Clark, McKenzie was, by his own account, "newly arrived in the Indian Country."[106] "He never advanced above the position of clerk,"[107] which suggests he was either not very capable or not much liked. In his derisive character sketch, George Simpson describes McKenzie as "A queer prosing long Winded little highland body, who traces his lineage back to Ossian and claims the Laureatship of Albany District."[108] We are fortunate that he was a "prosing long Winded" man. Ossian was the name of the narrator and supposed author of a series of epic-romantic poems, in Gaelic, that were regarded by men of letters of the eighteenth century as a northern European equivalent of the *Iliad* and *Odyssey* of Homer. The Ossianic pose was of a grieving or enraged heroic figure standing alone on the shoreline of a stormy and inhospitable sea. The poems were stark, heroic, and intensely primitive. The most famous of them was "Fingal," published in 1762 by a Scottish poetaster and fraud James Macpherson, based, he said, on Gaelic manuscripts that had fallen into his hands. Many of the smartest figures of the eighteenth century were smitten by Ossian, including Napoleon and Thomas Jefferson. The British critic and lexicographer Samuel Johnson immediately recognized the poems as frauds and publicly challenged Macpherson to produce the manuscripts and prove their authenticity. By 1805 most literate people understood that the poems were inauthentic. What makes George Simpson's characterization of Charles McKenzie interesting to us is that Jefferson was so swept up in the

Ossian craze that he wrote to Macpherson's brother Charles saying he would pay any price, bear any burden, and meet any hardship to get copies of the originals and read them in their native archaic Gaelic. "[M]y petition is, that you would be so good as to use your interest with Mr. McPherson to obtain leave to take a manuscript copy of them, and procure it to be done. I would choose it in a fair, round hand, on fine paper, with a good margin, bound in parchments as elegantly as possible, lettered on the back, and marbled or gilt on the edges of the leaves. I would not regard expense in doing this,"[109] Jefferson explained. The sage of Monticello went on to say that he would be willing to learn Gaelic in order to read "this rude bard of the North the greatest poet that has ever existed." He asked Macpherson to send him also a Gaelic grammar and dictionary, if he could procure them in Britain. No wonder Jefferson died bankrupt.

In other words, Jefferson would have liked the prosy and long-winded Charles McKenzie, if he could have met him. He would have engaged in endless conversations with him at Fort Mandan about the Ossianic epics. The French *philosophe* the Marquis de Chastellux visited Thomas Jefferson at Monticello in 1782 during his travels through America. Chastellux is the one who famously said, "Mr. Jefferson is the first American who has consulted the Fine Arts to know how he should shelter himself from the weather," and called the future president "a philosopher, in voluntary retirement from the world, and public business, because he loves the world, inasmuch only as he can flatter himself with being useful to mankind."[110] After supper on the mountaintop, they discovered they were equally enamored of Ossian. "I recollect with pleasure that as we were conversing one evening over a bowl of punch, after Mrs. Jefferson had retired, our conversation turned on the poems of Ossian. It was a spark of electricity which passed rapidly from one to the other; we recollected the passages in those sublime poems, which particularly struck us, and entertained my fellow travellers, who fortunately knew English well and were qualified to judge of their merit, though they had never read the poems. In our enthusiasm the book was sent for, and placed near the bowl where, by their mutual aid, the night far advanced imperceptibly upon us."[111] Lewis probably did not know of the highlander's interest in Ossian. As a man "not regularly educated," in Jefferson's phrase, he might not even have been aware of the existence of the Ossian craze and controversy.

Lewis may have offended the Canadians earlier in the winter with one of his characteristic bursts of sarcastic humor. McKenzie reports that Lewis visited one of the Hidatsa villages on November 25 or 26, 1804, and was treated rudely by a Hidatsa leader named Horned Weasel. In Clark's account of the incident, "[T]he Indians in all the towns & Camps treated Capt Lewis & the party with Great respect except one of the principal Cheifs *Mar par pa par ra pas a too* or (Horned Weasel) who did not Chuse to be Seen by the Capt. & left word that he was not at home &."[112] McKenzie's account agrees with what Lewis reported to Clark, but adds some interesting details and a direct quotation from Lewis. Lewis spent the night in the earthlodge of a man named the Serpent. McKenzie reports, "[N]ext morning he came to the village where I was—and observed to me that he was not very graciously received at the upper Village. 'I sent a word, said he, to inform *Le Blet qui porte le cornes* that I intended to take up my Quarters at his Lodge—he returned for answer that he was not a[t] home; this conduct surprised me, it being common only among your English Lords not to be at home, when they did not wish to see strangers. But as I had felt no inclination of entering any house after being told the Landlord would not be at home, I looked out for another lodging which I readily found.'"[113] In other words, the American republican Lewis took advantage of the opportunity to make a sarcastic comment about the haughty manners of British aristocrats. Perhaps he thought the Scotsman McKenzie would appreciate the sarcasm since it was directed at the English. Apparently he did not. Lewis's statement was actually a double insult. Not only did he satirize the manners of the British nobility, but he was also having characteristic fun in ascribing the manners and pretentions of high civilization to what he regarded as a bunch of savages. In Lewis's mind, to ascribe to a primitive aborigine whose name translates as "The Large One Who Wears Horns" the social manners of "English Lords" was inherently amusing.

McKenzie reports that the Hidatsa returned Lewis's contempt in full measure. In fact, McKenzie's journal is one of the key documents of the Lewis and Clark expedition. It has unfortunately been ignored by most historians. McKenzie and his non-American white colleagues François-Antoine Laroque and Alexander Henry provide a critically important outsiders' perspective on Lewis and Clark. Needless to say, Lewis and Clark tended to regard themselves as the heroes of their own narrative; to invest themselves with purely admirable motives and ideals; and to see every story through their own—and America's—perspective and to their own advantage. Clark in particular tends to see relations with Indians as more persuasive, harmonious, and rosier than they actually were. His statement that "the Indians in all the towns & Camps treated Capt Lewis & the party with Great respect"[114] is typical. McKenzie, describing the same diplomatic journey, reports that Lewis and Clark "held a council with the Mandanes, and distributed many presents; but most of the Chiefs did not accept any thing from them."[115] McKenzie would have known, better than Lewis and Clark, at least by the time he wrote this account, that the hospitality shown by Indian leaders set the tone for a visitor's general relations with the tribe and its individual families. If the chiefs refused gifts and chose not to be "at home" when American visitors came to call, they were engaging in a ritual rejection of the attitude or style or pricing structure of the visitors.

If Lewis sensed this Hidatsa hostility, he did not explain it to Clark when he returned from the Hidatsa villages. McKenzie reported that the Hidatsa leaders finally accepted some gifts from the Americans, "but notwithstanding they could not be reconciled to *like* these strangers as they called them."[116] McKenzie quoted the Hidatsa leadership: "'Had these Whites come amongst us, Said the Chiefs, with charitable views they would have loaded their Great Boat with necessaries. It is true they have ammunition but they prefer throwing it away idly than sparing a short of it to a poor Mandane.'"[117] McKenzie said Lewis's celebrated air gun impressed but did not delight the Hidatsa: "The Indians admired the air Gun as it could discharge forty shots out of one load—but they dreaded the magic of the owners."[118] McKenzie quoted a Hidatsa leader, probably Le Borgne (The One Eyed), as boasting, "'Had I these White warriors in the upper plains, said the *Gros Ventres* Chief, my young men on horseback would soon do for them, as they would do for so many wolves.'" Then Le Borgne delivered the unkindest cut of all: "'[T]here are only two sensible men among them—the worker of Iron, and the mender of Guns.'"[119] In other words, if McKenzie is reporting accurately, Le Borgne admired only the gunsmith and blacksmith John Shields and either Alexander Willard or William Bratton (both blacksmiths). Meriwether Lewis and William Clark were not, in Le Borgne's eyes, numbered among the "two sensible men."

These accounts are extraordinarily interesting and important. They reverse the lens of observation and discovery. James Ronda has written, "Native American explorers, struggling to understand a landscape transformed by epidemic disease, European trade goods and firearms, and the imperial ambitions of newly-arrived strangers, had their own vocabulary of images and traditions. Indians explored the explorers, making what we sometimes blandly call 'exploration' an act of mutual discovery."[120]

McKenzie reported that the Hidatsa listened to, but simply rejected, the Americans' insistence that they should thereafter fight only defensive battles. The truth of this was brought home to Clark on the return journey in 1806. When the expedition arrived back at the Hidatsa villages on August 14, 1806, Clark reported that "the Chief of the little Village of the Menetarias cried most imoderately, I enquired the Cause and was informed it was for the loss of his Son who had been killed latterly by the Blackfoot Indians."[121] In the spring of 1805 Lewis and Clark had forbidden the Hidatsa to conduct their annual raid into western Montana. The Corps of Discovery had no sooner left Fort Mandan when the Hidatsa went ahead with the raid as planned. Black Moccasin's son was killed. When he was preparing the expedition's journals for publication in 1810, Nicholas Biddle sought clarification of this incident from William Clark. Biddle reports Clark explaining that Black Moccasin's "son, contrary to our pacific advice had gone to war & been killed &c."[122]

McKenzie also took time to record an extraordinary Mandan-Hidatsa critique of the lives of white fur traders and trappers. His Indian informants told him that they would be quite happy to hunt beaver for white traders if they could chase them on horseback, but that they had no interest in "the operation of searching for them in the bowels of the earth to satisfy the avarice of the *Whites*."[123] This they regarded as degrading. Then the Indian philosopher, probably Le Borgne, asked several existential questions. "'White people, said they, do not know how to live—they leave their homes in small parties; they risk their lives on the great waters, and among strange nations, who will take them for enemies: —What is the use of Beaver? Do they preserve them from sickness? Do they serve them beyond the grave?'" Before the coming of the white man, Le Borgne said, "'we knew no wants—we were successful in war; our arrows were pointed with flint, our lances with stone; and their wounds were mortal—Our Villages rejoiced when the men returned from war; of the scalps of our enemies they brought many. The white people came, they brought with them some goods: but they brought the small pox, they brought evil liquors—the Indians Since are diminished, and they are no longer happy.'"[124] This is an amazing deconstruction of the Euro-American fur trade, one of the first global industries of the modern world. Le Borgne found it hard to believe that white people would span the globe and go to such heroic lengths to obtain the comparatively puny furs of beaver, when North America was teeming with large quadrupeds. If beaver skins had medicinal properties, served some purpose as funeral objects, or served the dead in the afterlife, it might possibly make sense. But for fashion? We are exceedingly fortunate to have Le Borgne's critique—thanks to the prosiness of Charles McKenzie and his sense of competitive distaste for the brash Americans. McKenzie's journal is as vital a Lewis and Clark document as the expedition's journals.

One wonders how Lewis would have responded to this speech, had he taken the time to get to know the Hidatsa leader and had he let himself listen carefully to his perspective. Lewis was unlikely to take this sort of critique from a man he regarded as a savage, and yet it resonates with the general cast of Lewis's thought, which frequently gravitated toward philosophical and existential reflection. McKenzie, meanwhile, was merely content to report whatever was critical of Lewis and Clark. His job was to attempt to convince Le Borgne that the men of the North West and Hudson's Bay Companies were still more desirable trading partners than the Americans.

McKenzie's narrative is a rich resource for Lewis and Clark scholars. McKenzie wrote a little summary of the expedition as it left Fort Mandan that is as good as anything in the journals. "It consisted of one large perogue; and seven small wooden Canoes—containing the commanding officers, thirty men, and a woman—the woman who answered the purpose of wife to Charbonneau was of the Serpent Nation, and lately taken prisoner by a

The Hidatsa leader Black Moccasin (Omp-he-har-ra) met Lewis and Clark in 1804–06 and, a generation later, sat for this portrait by George Catlin in 1832. Courtesy of the Smithsonian American Art Museum, Washington, DC / Art Resource, New York.

war party:—She understood a little Gros Ventre."[125] McKenzie was wrong about Lewis's "*six* small canoes and *two* large perogues," [emphasis mine] but he had the number of the permanent party correct, and he is the only source we have for Sacagawea's comparative weakness as a speaker of the Hidatsa language. Think of that. She "understood a little" Hidatsa, no English (at least at this point), and probably only a smattering of French. Aside from her sister Otter Woman, soon to be left behind, she was linguistically cut off from everyone around her, including apparently her husband Charbonneau. Furthermore, McKenzie reported that Charbonneau "did not understand English."[126]

To summarize. Lewis understood English and no other language, though he was able to toy a little with Linnaean Latin, and eventually he learned enough Indian sign language to manage simple communications. Charbonneau knew his birth language French and some simple Hidatsa, but not English. Thus, Lewis could not speak directly with Charbonneau. Sacagawea understood Shoshone, useless to the expedition until late August 1805, and a little Hidatsa, which she used to communicate with her husband Charbonneau, who also understand only a little Hidatsa. Husband and wife were thus communicating in a second language they had begun to learn comparatively late in life. Probably they were not soul mates.

McKenzie explains how the official American diplomatic party communicated with the Hidatsa Indians: "A Mulatto who spoke bad French and worse English served as Interpreter to the Captains—So that a single word to be understood by the party required to pass from the Natives to the woman, from the woman to the husband, from the husband to the Mulatto, from the Mulatto to the Captain."[127] In other words, if the Hidatsa wanted to communicate something to Captain Lewis, they spoke in their own language to Sacagawea, "lately taken prisoner by a war party," because she understood Hidatsa better than her husband, who was the expedition's *official Hidatsa interpreter*. Charbonneau then spoke in French to the expedition's Francois Labiche, "a Mulatto who spoke bad French and worse English." Labiche then spoke in his "worse English" to the captains. Thus the linguistic chain went from perfect Hidatsa to very limited Hidatsa, to good French but in the hands of a highly imperfect translator, and then through "bad French" into "worse English." The Lewis and Clark Expedition was not possessed of the linguistic sophistication of the United Nations.

If Lewis wanted to say something to Sacagawea, he had to speak in English to Francois Labiche, who spoke in French to Charbonneau, who spoke in Hidatsa to Sacagawea. None of these individuals was a professional linguist. Labiche spoke English as a second language, and Sacagawea and Charbonneau spoke Hidatsa as a second language. When Sacagawea asserted herself at the Pacific Ocean and declared that she ought to be permitted to see the great monster at the stinking lake, she spoke in

Hidatsa, Charbonneau in French, Labiche in English. The captains listened and acceded to her firm request. When we imagine the Lewis and Clark Expedition, we all—whether we know better or not—turn it into a Hollywood movie in which characters speak in their native languages for a few sentences and then, by convention, everyone agrees to speak in English for the rest of the story. Communication must have been tedious, frustrating, and rudimentary whenever the Charbonneau family was involved.

McKenzie remembered an occasion when Lewis attempted to record a Hidatsa vocabulary: "I was once present when vocabularies were making of the languages of the Mandane Villages. The two Frenchmen who happened to be the medium of information had warm disputes upon the meaning of every word that was taken down by the expedition—as the Indians could not well comprehend the intention of recording their words, they concluded that the Americans had a wicked design upon their Country."[128] This was not immediately prophetic. It's amazing that Lewis was able to record vocabularies at all, given the imprecise linguistic agents at his disposal and the inherent challenge of recording non Indo-European utterances, often intensely guttural, in the Roman alphabet, not to mention the "warm disputes" that attended the investigation of a single word from Jefferson's 250-word vocabulary list. If the Mandan and Hidatsa Indians thought there was something invidious about the vocabulary project, somehow analogous to the later sense that having one's photograph taken or visage painted was tantamount to surrendering a piece of one's soul, they may have found ways to frustrate the already preposterous enterprise.

All this, and more, we owe to the prosy and long-winded Charles McKenzie. He was the sort of man Meriwether Lewis should have prized. Had Lewis not been consumed by an "inveterate disposition against the British," he might have found a worthy winter companion in McKenzie, who was much closer in temperament and intellectual range to Lewis than either was to Clark. They were both lonely men in a far country. They probably had more in common than either acknowledged.

The other literate Canadian in residence at the Mandan and Hidatsa Indians in the winter of 1804–05 was François-Antoine Larocque (1784–1869). His first impression of Lewis was more favorable. On November 25, 1804, Larocque reported that Lewis "Invited me to his house & appeared very friendly."[129] Larocque was mostly amused, rather than offended, when the American leaders forbade him to distribute flags or peace medals, which they regarded as sovereignty tokens and therefore off limits within the boundaries of America's Louisiana Territory. Larocque said Lewis explained that his "Government, look'd upon those things, as the Sacred Emblem of the attachment of the Indians to their Country." But, said Larocque, "as I had neither Flags, nor medals, I Ran no Risk of disobeying those orders, of which I assured them."[130] Larocque parodied the captains' standard Indian speech: the

Americans told the Mandan and Hidatsa they "will protect them & supply them with all their wants, as long as they shall behave as dutifull Children to their Great Father the President of the United States &c (which has been the Continued subject of their Harangues to the Indians, throughout the Winter)."[131] This is precisely what Lewis and Clark told Indian leaders all the way up the Missouri River, the theme they emphasized especially at the Mandan and Hidatsa villages. In the parodic summary of Larocque, however, the expedition's standard Indian speech sounds pompous, presumptuous, and unrealistic. *Harangues.*

On January 18, 1805, Larocque visited Fort Mandan "in the morning, to Return a Book I had borrow'd, & to see if there was any particular news. Arrived there at 3 P.M. & Remain'd the whole day."[132] In fact, he stayed overnight at Fort Mandan. Unfortunately, Laroque did not specify the book he had borrowed from Lewis, and the journal keepers at Fort Mandan made no reference to the loan. The expedition's traveling library included Benjamin Smith Barton's *Elements of Botany* (1803), Alexander Mackenzie's *Voyages from Montreal* (1802), Richard Kirwan's *Elements of Mineralogy* (1784), Antoine-Simon Le Page du Pratz's *History of Louisiana* (1763), Patrick Kelly's *Introduction to Spherics and Nautical Astronomy* (1796), Nevil Maskelyne's *Tables Requisite* (1766), Owen's *Dictionary of Arts and Sciences* (1754–55), Benjamin Rush's *Directions for Preserving the Health of Soldiers* (1778), Baron von Steuben's *Articles of War* (1794), John Miller's *Linnaeus* (1779), and Andrew Ellicott's *Journal* (1803).[133] Lewis and Clark scholars frequently speculate on which book Larocque borrowed. If he had not yet read Mackenzie's *Voyages from Montreal*, that would, of course, be the logical choice. The most readable of the books in the expedition library would have been Owen's *Dictionary*, which was essentially an encyclopedia in two or four volumes, depending on how it was bound; but it seems unlikely that the captains, preparing reports to be sent down river in April with the keelboat, would let so valuable a reference work out of their sight. If Larocque was attempting to master celestial navigation for his projected journey of exploration in 1805, he might have borrowed Maskelyne's *Tables Requisite* or Kelly's *Introduction to Spherics.* Those books were so essential to the expedition's success, to Jefferson's prime directive delivered on June 20, 1803, that it is hard to believe they would have handed them over to a mercantile and geopolitical rival. It is, of course, possible that members of the expedition, particularly the captains, were carrying other books that were never mentioned in the journals. It seems odd, for example, that Lewis did not take along a copy of Jefferson's *Notes on the State of Virginia*, given his propensity to imitate the master. After all, *Notes on Virginia*—already regarded as an American classic—was almost certainly the kind of book Jefferson would have wanted Lewis to write upon his return. It is quite possible that someone on the expedition's roster was carrying a Bible, though no mention is ever made of one, and the only reference to the text of the Bible is Clark's joke about Jonah and the whale on January 8, 1806.[134] The title Larocque selected from the Lewis and Clark library—the first in North Dakota history—remains one of the fascinating minor mysteries of the great journey.

Larocque, unlike the more hostile McKenzie, admitted that the Indians had "grown very fond of them [Lewis and Clark] although they disliked them at first."[135] On January 30, just a few days before Clark's extended hunt began, Larocque made one of his periodic visits to Fort Mandan. He needed Lewis's help. "Went down to the American Fort to get my Compass put in order," he wrote, "the glass being broke, & the needle not pointing due north; & to see how the horses were. Arrived there at 2 P.M. Fine weather."[136] It was Clark, not Lewis, who offered that winter to take care of the horses of the Canadians representing the North West Company, to protect them from Lakota or Assiniboine raiding parties.[137] Lewis may have been an Anglophobe who regarded visitors as pests, but he was a fastidious and gifted man who had something of Jefferson's capacity for taking pains. Larocque had no doubt who was the right captain for the intricate repair of a scientific instrument.

Larocque was, in some respects, an industrial and geopolitical spy. On several occasions in the course of the winter, he requested permission to accompany Lewis and Clark on their journey west in 1805. The captains were very certain they did not intend to permit an agent of the British-Canadian fur trade to join their voyage of discovery, to attach himself to their long-planned and expensive enterprise, to see the undiscovered country west of the earthlodge villages under the security umbrella of the American government. They were not particularly happy to see agents of the North West and Hudson's Bay Company trading at the Mandan and Hidastsa villages, in *American* territory, but they were sufficiently realistic to understand that they were not really in a position to oust them and enforce the porous international borders of Louisiana Territory. Lewis and Clark fretted all winter about what the Canadians were telling the Hidatsa and the Mandan about America's purposes on the Upper Missouri and how they were characterizing the American representatives who had been sent by the Great Father to clear the road. Thanks to the accounts of McKenzie and Larocque we know a good deal about this diplomatic dance. Lewis and Clark permitted Charbonneau to serve occasionally as an interpreter for the agents of the North West Company, *on the condition* that he not translate *anything* that could be perceived as critical of the Americans. Larocque wrote that Lewis and Clark lectured Charbonneau sternly, "strictly enjoined him not to utter a word, which might any way be to the prejudice of the United States or of any of its Citizens, to the Indians, although I should order him to do so, which (say they), turning to me, we are very far from thinking you would."[138] This is exquisite. Although Lewis and Clark spent the winter on the fringes of the known world, they engaged in intricate geopolitical rituals and employed diplomatic protocols and maneuverings that would have been little different in Paris or Madrid.

When he arrived at Fort Mandan on January 30, 1805, Larocque found the captains working on their maps. He observed their actions carefully and breathlessly recorded in his journal what information he could glean from his visit: "The Captains were busy, making Charts of the Country through which they had passed, & delineating the heads of the Missouri, according to the Information they had from the Indians, who describe a River as being 4 days march west of the last navigable part of the Missouri, which River say they is very large, & the natives (whom they Call Snake Indians & Flat heads) who inhabit thereabouts, go at a Certain season of the year to that River & there live Entirely upon Fish. The Course of that River they say is nearly south & has a very placid Current. The Captains make no doubt, but that it is a south branch of the Columbia or Ouragan River." Then Larocque adds, "I think it is the Rout they will take."[139]

While Lewis fixed Larocque's compass, the clever Canadian managed to get the American commander to divulge his (and thus probably Jefferson's) interpretation of the northern boundaries of the Louisiana Purchase. "They Include in their territory as far North as River Qu'Appelle, for as it was Impossible for a Line, drawn west, from the west End of the Lake des Bois [Lake of the Woods] to strike the Missisipi, they make it Run, till it strikes its tributary waters that is the northern Branches of the Missouri, & from thence to the Pacific."[140] What Lewis meant by this is that the United States insisted that *all* of the watershed of the Mississippi and Missouri Rivers was included in the purchase; that since the source of the Mississippi was not sufficiently north to permit a line to be drawn from the headwaters due west to the Pacific without lopping off lands that were drained by the Missouri, the United States now believed that the line should angle in a northwesterly direction from the western end of Lake of the Woods until it intersected the Qu'Appelle River in today's Saskatchewan. This was geopolitical ambition indeed. The border that was finally worked out in 1818 bore some resemblance to Lewis's claim of January 1805. The US-Canadian border follows a straight line drawn west of Lake of the Woods at the 49th parallel. That line of latitude is well south of the Qu'Appelle River, but it does embrace for the United States *nearly* the entire watershed of the Missouri River, *plus* the Upper Red River basin, *and* the nipple (or angle) of northern Minnesota. The erratic peninsula of Minnesota that juts north into today's Ontario was designed to permit the United States to have continued access to vital river arteries in today's Manitoba that, in 1818, were regarded as vital to American economic (i.e., fur trade) interests in the West. The only part of the Missouri River drainage that was lopped off by the 1818 treaty is a small portion of the upper Milk River watershed in today's Saskatchewan and Alberta. Lewis would presumably have been happier if the US-Canadian border were set at the 50th parallel, though even then it would have been 200 miles south of the northern reaches of the Qu'Appelle River. By the time Secretary of State John Quincy Adams negotiated the final border in 1818, Lewis had been dead for seven years.

One can imagine Lewis bent over Larocque's compass, cleaning and repairing it in his characteristically brilliant and fastidious way while giving Larocque an informal, but sternly patriotic geopolitical lecture about a geography that for both of them was purely conjectural, and onto which the feet of Lewis, at least, would never tread. The details of this meeting, provided by Larocque but not by Lewis, deepen the Lewis and Clark story in a way that is somehow larger and more significant than the bare facts of a broken compass and a friendly visit. One likes Lewis more for this incident of scientific camaraderie, a small but important service for a fellow member of the republic of letters. Was Lewis friendly on January 30? Or supercilious? Was he talkative or taciturn? Was there "a spark of electricity which passed rapidly from one to the other"? Was Lewis glad to have the company of the literate and clever Larocque, who was in essential ways more truly an *explorer* than William Clark? In the summer of 1805 Larocque explored the Yellowstone River valley and the Big Horn Mountains with just two white companions and an escort of Crow Indians. Larocque was in fact the "first civilized man" to see a number of places in the Yellowstone basin that Clark claimed for himself—and America—in 1806. Or was it "true Captain Lewis could not make himself agreeable to us—he could speak fluently and learnedly on all subjects, but his inveterate disposition against the British stained, at least in our eyes, all his eloquence"? We cannot know. All we know is that our understanding of Lewis and Clark is the richer for Larocque's broken compass and the unknown volume he borrowed from the traveling library of the expedition.

FEBRUARY 11 (MONDAY)

Lewis's week of sole command at Fort Mandan was now almost over.

On February 11, Sacagawea gave birth to her first child. It was bitterly cold, eight degrees below zero at dawn, two below at 4 P.M., and probably much colder by the time Jean Baptiste Charbonneau "was ushered into this world of sorrow and trouble," as Charles Dickens would phrase it in 1838, the year of William Clark's death.[141] By dawn on February 12, Jean Baptiste's first full day on earth, it was fourteen degrees below zero, wind from the southeast.

Sacagawea was approximately seventeen years old at the time of this parturition. We would call her a teenage mother, but that's something of a belittling term for an era when childhood as we know it had not yet been invented, and when it was common for women of fifteen years old and sometimes younger to marry and immediately begin bearing children. Sacagawea had lived a full and eventful life *before* Lewis and Clark happened into her world and lifted her into America's known history. In fact, her time with Lewis and Clark, however perilous, was arguably one of the most secure periods of her unsettled life. She passed her first years among the Shoshone at a time when her people were doing their best to survive an arms race that had given their traditional enemies tremendous military advantage. When Lewis and Clark encountered the Shoshone in mid-August 1805, they were shocked to observe a once-proud tribe reduced to emaciation and skittishness. On August 14, 1805, Lewis reported that the Shoshone leader "Cameahwait, with his ferce eyes and lank jaws grown meager for the want of food," informed him that his people would not be starving, "if we had guns." Sacagawea's brother said, "[W]e could then live in the country of buffaloe and eat as our enimies do and not be compelled to hide ourselves in these mountains and live on roots and berries as the bear do."[142]

A few years before Lewis and Clark arrived on the Great Plains, Sacagawea had been captured by Hidatsa raiders near the three forks of the Missouri River and carried hundreds of miles to the east to the Hidatsa villages at the mouth of the Knife River. She may well have been raped during this period of her life. She was certainly traumatized, uprooted, transplanted, and thrust into an alien Indian tribal culture for which nothing in her life had prepared her. She learned to speak a little Hidatsa. Fortunately, she was not entirely alone. Her *sister*, a woman we know as Otter Woman, was with her. By 1804 she had probably been adopted into a Hidatsa clan, and she had probably been given her Hidatsa name Sah-ca-gar-we-a (Bird Woman) by the peoples who abducted her. At the Hidatsa village of Metaharta, she had, *a la façon du pays* (in the manner of the far country), somehow become the *wife* of a French-Canadian trader, interpreter, and entrepreneur named Toussaint Charbonneau. Her life as a captive alien had probably been very hard. Though it seems unlikely that she married Charbonneau of her own volition, her life was probably dramatically improved by her status as *his* and no longer the Hidatsas' woman. It was Charbonneau who offered his (and therefore her) services to Lewis and Clark almost as soon as the Americans arrived at the mouth of the Knife River in the autumn of 1804, even though at the time of Charbonneau's sales pitch, she was already six months pregnant. Until just before Lewis and Clark left Fort Mandan in April 1805, it was thought that both of Charbonneau's Shoshone wives would accompany the expedition. In the end, for reasons that are never explained, only Sacagawea made the journey. Charbonneau had some admirable qualities. He was a resourceful man who found a niche at the interface of the Hidatsa and their Euro-American visitors, traders, explorers, and occupiers, and he milked it successfully for more than forty years. Although he was perceived by most whites to be a rascal, a hanger on, a womanizer, and a brute, he made himself indispensable, and he was a man who knew how to take advantage of opportunity when it gravitated his way. We know at least one instance in which he struck Sacagawea. Lewis did not like him at all, though he occasionally found welcome comic relief in Charbonneau's cowardliness and his considerable talent as a frontier cook. In one of the expedition's strangest contrasts, Clark learned to like Charbonneau so much that he actually found it hard to say goodbye on August 17, 1806, when the Charbonneau family was formally discharged at the Hidatsa village of Metaharta on the return journey. Three days later (August 20, 1806), at the bottom of today's North Dakota, Clark wrote a strangely intimate letter to Charbonneau saying he was not ready to lose contact with the family and that he would sponsor them in St. Louis should they choose to venture down river.[143] The essential difference of personalities and styles of Lewis and Clark is nowhere better evidenced than in their wildly different responses to Charbonneau, his Shoshone-Hidatsa bride, and their son Jean Baptiste. Charbonneau is a hard man to typecast—though he is the most routinely typecast of all the members of the expedition. He was what we would call a *survivor*. And he married really well.

The thirty-seven-year-old Charbonneau had returned to Fort Mandan on February 10 to tell Lewis that the Clark party was returning and that fresh meat was on its way. It is not clear whether Charbonneau was present when his son was born on February 11. Nor do we know for sure where Sacagawea gave birth. It has long been assumed that Jean Baptiste was born in one of the cabins at Fort Mandan, but this may not be so. Back on November 22, 1804, Clark had mentioned, "the interpeters hut fire about 60 yards below the works."[144] The precise sleeping arrangements at Fort Mandan cannot be sorted out. Marginal personnel, including French voyageurs, had a different winter experience from the permanent party. Charbonneau was absent for extended periods, sometimes to serve agents of the North West Company, sometimes when he was at odds with the American captains, and once on the extended hunting trip with Clark. During some of Charbonneau's absences, Sacagawea may have returned to the Hidatsa village to be among her adoptive clan. We don't know. When her labor began she may have chosen a more secluded place than the crowded fort for her lying in. It is hard to believe that she gave birth to her first child without the benefit of Hidatsa midwives or clan sisters or a Hidatsa medicine provider of some sort. No mention is made of Hidatsa auxiliaries, however, though the silence of the journals does not prove that no Hidatsa midwives were present. The birthing of Jean Baptiste was regarded at the time as so insignificant that the usually observant John Ordway didn't even bother to mention it in his journal. Nowadays, given the apotheosis of Sacagawea in American memory, we see things rather differently. The distinguished North Dakota artist Walter Piehl has painted the Charbonneau family as a near-Biblical tableau, with something like a halo hovering over the Madonna Sacagawea. Even if Charbonneau was still at Fort Mandan on February 11, he may not have been present for his son's birth. Until extremely recently in the world's history, men of western civilization have not been present at the birth of their children. In the absence of documentary evidence, we cannot assume anything about the "bedside" of Sacagawea. Given the intense cold, it does seem certain that she gave birth indoors.

Given the genuine interest Clark later took in the entire Charbonneau family, especially in Jean Baptiste, it would have been much better, certainly more comforting to Sacagawea, if he, not the detached and awkward Lewis, had assisted in the birth. On the return journey in 1806, Lewis freely admitted that Clark was the "favorite phisician"[145] of the Indians they encountered. Clark probably would not have padlocked the Fort Mandan gate during the last days of Sacagawea's pregnancy. He almost certainly would have consulted Charbonneau—via Labiche—about how to increase Sacagawea's comfort level during the birthing. But Clark was away from Fort Mandan on February 11, somewhere near today's Mandan Lake, and he was not available for consultation.

Lewis may have been an unsympathetic scientist and military commander, but he was, at least at this juncture, the expedition's only doctor. He had undertaken a crash course in frontier medicine from America's pre-eminent physician Dr. Benjamin Rush in mid-May 1803. It was Lewis, not Clark, who on January 27, 1805, amputated the toes of an Indian boy who had slept out in a blizzard and suffered severe frostbite. Lewis was the son of a woman known for her skills as a medical herbalist. At times in the course of the expedition, Lewis addressed his own and others' medical maladies with folk and herbal solutions. If Lucy Marks was an herb doctor, she was probably also a midwife. Lewis's bedside manner may have left much to be desired, but he probably knew as much as any *non-Indian* at the mouth of the Knife River about how to help a young woman through her first birthing.

Lewis's description of the big event is worth quoting in full. "[A]bout five oclock this evening one of the wives of Charbono was delivered of a fine boy." So far so good. Lewis sounds rather pleased, maybe even proud. *Fine boy* is not a term of scientific detachment. It sounds more like Clark than Lewis. "[I]t is worthy of remark," he continues, assuming a more professional voice, "that this was the first child which this woman had boarn and as is common in such cases her labour was tedious and the pain violent."[146] Did Lewis actually witness the birth or the protracted labor? Did he administer laudanum or any of the other pharmaceuticals in his medicine kit? We have no way of knowing, but the sense one gets from studying

Lewis's later discussion of Indian reproductivity is that he was content to let nature take its course. It is quite possible that Lewis never appeared in the birthing room at all. Perhaps Jusseaume's Mandan wife and others made it clear that a white man was not welcome at so private a rite of passage. "Mr. Jessome informed me," Lewis wrote, "that he had freequently administered a small portion of the rattle of the rattle-snake, which he assured me had never failed to produce the desired effect, that of hastening the birth of the child; having the rattle of a snake by me I gave it to him and he administered two rings of it to the woman broken in small pieces with the fingers and added to a small quantity of water."[147] Notice that Lewis did not administer the rattlesnake potion himself. The syntax suggests that he did nothing more than give the whole rattle to Jusseaume, who broke it in small pieces, suspended it in water, and administered it to Sacagawea. Historian Donna J. Kessler writes, "Although he is present during her long and difficult labor, Lewis does not remain with her through the delivery."[148]

Having detached himself from the raw and bloody business in the birthing chamber by fetching the snake rattle stored among his artifacts collection, Lewis slipped happily into the voice of the pure scientist: "Whether this medicine was truly the cause or not I shall not undertake to determine, but I was informed that she had not taken it more than ten minutes before she brought forth   perhaps this remedy may be worthy of future experiments, but I must confess that I want faith as to it's efficacy."[149] This is good Enlightenment skepticism. The medical experts who have studied this incident agree with Lewis. Dr. Bruce Paton declares that the rattle of a snake is chemically similar to the substance in fingernails and therefore without the slightest efficacy in the birthing process.[150] Dr. David Peck, the author of *Or Perish in the Attempt*, agrees: "Rattlesnake rattles are made out of a substance we call keratin. Keratin is also found in fingernails, horns, and hair. It is insoluble in gastric juices, and therefore I doubt that it had any effect whatsoever on the delivery. But it makes a great story."[151]

There is no reason to dispute the authority of modern physicians, but it may be worth considering that Rene Jusseaume and his wife probably knew Sacagawea much better than any member of the Lewis and Clark Expedition did at this point; that his assurance to her that the rattlesnake potion was well known to hasten births in difficult deliveries may have had some kind of calming or placebo effect on Sacagawea. Twenty-first century birthing classes are a mixture of good obstetric science and the art of building confidence in women who are moving inexorably towards a parturition they cannot postpone or avoid. Jusseaume's bedside manner may, in fact, have been outstanding. If he believed in the efficacy of the rattlesnake potion, his own confidence may have had a calming effect on the young woman. If he was making it up, the same result may have followed his assurances. It is even possible that he told Sacagawea that the rattlesnake potion was approved by the powerful and mysterious white men, who were known to be possessed of big medicine.[152]

The last word of Lewis's journal entry for February 11, 1805, is "efficacy." Although he began by telling his readers that the wife "of Charbono was delivered of a fine boy," there is no reference to her condition following the difficult birthing, no statement of relief that she had survived the ordeal, no appreciation of her strength or pluck, no mention—in fact—even of her name. He may not have known her name at this point. She does not get *named* in the journals by Lewis until she saves light articles in the boat accident of May 14, 1805. Lewis makes no attempt to provide closure to the story of Jean Baptiste's birth. The nameless Indian woman, identified only by her social-legal relationship to her husband, "brought forth." For Lewis the story is about patriarchy and science, with a glance at the psychology of the placebo effect. Had Sacagawea returned to Metaharta to give birth, Lewis would surely not have devoted a single sentence to the event.

Lewis never bonded with Sacagawea, and he seems to have regarded Indian women as creatures (or *objects*) locked into a near-animal state of existence. Later that year, among the Shoshone, Lewis wrote a long journal entry about a trailside birthing. When one of the female Shoshone porters lagged behind the pack trail, Lewis "enquired of Cameahwait the cause of her detention."[153] The captain "was informed by him in an unconcerned manner that she had halted to bring fourth a child and would soon overtake us." An hour later the woman caught up and passed the pack train carrying her newborn child. At this point Lewis paused to reflect on birthing among American Indians. "It appears to me that the facility and ease with which the women of the aborigines of North America bring fourth their children is reather a gift of nature," he wrote, "and it is a rare occurrence for any of them to experience difficulty in childbirth."[154]

Wait. The only other birth we know he had witnessed was that of Jean Baptiste Charbonneau at Fort Mandan six months earlier. In that case, "her labour was tedious and the pain violent."[155] Kessler finds this perplexing. "Has he simply forgotten about Sacagawea's difficulties when he provides generalizations about native births months after her delivery? Or is Sacagawea, in Lewis's estimation, unlike other native women? ... Lewis displays no awareness of such contradictions in his narrative, nor does he acknowledge what they might imply about Sacagawea or about native women."[156] On this and other occasions in the journals, it is clear that Lewis carried with him from Virginia a deeply-embedded mythology about American Indians that emphasized their capriciousness, their propensity to behave like children, their fundamental unreliability, their proximity to animal creation, and the likelihood that a vast capacity for cruelty and violence lay just beneath the surface of their cultures.[157] Lewis's sustained series of actual encounters with Indians between St. Louis and the mouth of the Columbia did little, perhaps nothing, to disabuse him of this set of dark preconceptions. It is possible that his field encounters with Indians actually deepened his racist mythology and pseudo-science. Ten days before he wrote about the ease with which Indian women give birth, Lewis had witnessed the half-starved Shoshone devour a deer George Drouillard had killed, right down to the gristle and offal. After observing a young man holding "about nine feet of the small guts one end of which he was chewing on while with his hands he was squezzing the contents out at the other," Lewis informed his readers that "I really did not untill now think that human nature ever presented itself in a shape so nearly allyed to the brute creation."[158] The only indication that Lewis recognized the discrepancy between the birthing experiences of the unnamed Shoshone woman of the Bitterroot Mountains and the then-unnamed Shoshone woman of Fort Mandan was his statement, on August 26, 1805, that "I have been several times informed by those who were conversant with the fact, that the indian women who are pregnant by whitemen experience more difficulty in childbirth than when pregnant by an Indian."[159] It is certain that Clark never spoke about Indians through the dark mythological filter that Lewis routinely employed.

Because Clark was absent, he did not write a journal entry for this February 11. John Ordway, who was at Fort Mandan on February 11, wrote a thirty-five-word journal entry without ever mentioning Sacagawea, Jean Baptiste, or the birth experience. His interests on February 11 were the bitterly cold weather and food. Patrick Gass, in a journal entry written later, but dated February 5, summarized the hunting trip he took with Clark. Then he wrote, "On the 12th we arrived at the fort; and found that one of our interpreter's wives had in our absence made an addition to our number."[160] Clearly, the mother of Jean Baptiste Charbonneau had not at this point yet become the woman we recognize as the celebrated Sacagawea.

FEBRUARY 12 (TUESDAY)

Clark returned to Fort Mandan on the evening of February 12 after a very successful hunt. On that day Lewis wrote a long and fascinating journal entry on the Mandan and Hidatsa habit of lodging their horses in their earthlodges on cold winter nights. He reported that "The Indians are invariably severe riders," that they work their horses very hard in pursuing buffalo in blizzard conditions and transporting meat, and that they feed them "what seems to me a scanty allowance of wood."[161] "[U]nder these circumstances it would seem that their horses could not long exist or at least could not retain their flesh and strength, but the contrary is the fact, this valuable anamall under all those disadvantages is seldom seen meager or unfit for service."[162] The sad irony of this passage is inescapable. Lewis was more open-minded with respect to his notions of Indian horsemanship than he was about the character of Indians themselves. Lewis carried with him on his transcontinental journey traditional white notions of the severity of Indian horsemanship, but the evidence before him caused him to concede that Indian ponies appeared to thrive in spite of the harsh climate in which they passed their lives and the Spartan treatment they received from their Mandan and Hidatsa owners. Somehow he found it much easier to transcend his preconceptions about the lives of horses than the lives (and fate) of the aboriginal inhabitants of America.

With undisguised relief, Lewis closed his February 12 journal with the words, "A little after dark this evening Capt. Clark arrived with the hunting party— since they set out they have killed forty Deer, three buffaloe bulls, & sixteen Elk, most of them were so meager that they were unfit for uce, particularly the Buffaloes and male Elk— the wolves also which are here extreemly numerous heped themselves to a considerable proportion of the hunt— if an anamal is killed and lyes only one night exposed to the wolves it is almost invariably devoured by them."[163]

February 13, 1805 (Wednesday)

The always-reliable William Clark returned to Fort Mandan just after dark on February 12, 1805. He was exhausted, "much fatigued, haveing walked 30 miles on the ice and through the wood land Points in which the Snow was nearly Knee Deep."[164] The following day he wrote a detailed day-by-day account of his hunting trip. In spite of breaking through the ice on the first day out, "and got my feet and legs wet," Clark persevered on a nine-day trek that took him a full forty-five miles downriver from Fort Mandan. Opposite the mouth of the Heart River, on "a large bottom" where today's Bismarck, North Dakota, is situated, Clark built a wooden pen to secure the meat supply from wolves, coyotes, ravens, and magpies. On the seventh day out, February 10, 1805, Joseph Fields "got one of his ears frosed." That, plus the fact of "Several men being nearly out of Mockersons & the horses not returning [from Fort Mandan] deturmind me to return to the Fort on tomorrow."[165] This sentence indicates that Clark may have been keeping a cursory field journal on his hunting trip, in spite of the extreme cold and heroic exertion it entailed, and that he was transcribing it into his main journal on February 13, 1805. It is equally possible that he was casting an account written after the fact in the form of a daily journal. Clark's party had camped several nights in old or abandoned Mandan lodges in what before 1781 had been the heart of their territory. Clark admitted that "walking on uneaven *ice* has blistered the bottom of my feat, and walking is painfull to me,"[166] but he immediately took up his pen and resumed general management of affairs at Fort Mandan.

Although he took the time to write a lengthy day-by-day summary of his hunting excursion, thus bringing his journal entirely up to date, Clark did not mention that Sacagawea had given birth in his absence. In fact, Clark's first mention of Jean Baptiste Charbonneau is not until April 7, 1805, and then only in a mustering list of permanent expedition members: "Shabonah and his *Indian Squar* to act as an Interpreter & interpretress for the snake Indians—one Mandan & Shabonahs infant. *Sah-kah-gar we a*."[167] Apparently even Clark was having trouble remembering Sacagawea's name. Clark never mentions the birth of Jean Baptiste.

Lewis managed to squeeze out one last twenty-six-word journal entry on February 13, 1805. That means that the *captain's log* overlapped by a single day. Lewis provides no report on the condition of the interpreter's wife and her newborn son, and makes no mention of William Clark, now returned. He does note that he gave Posecopsahe (the Black Cat) one of the expedition's much-prized, but badly designed battle-axes, and that the great Mandan leader "appeared much gratifyed."[168] Perhaps Posecopsahe delivered the aforementioned shield on this occasion. Perhaps Lewis merely felt guilty about the niggardly recompense he had offered Posecopsahe and his wife on February 8, when they brought a bow and two pairs of moccasins to Fort Mandan.

With that, Meriwether Lewis went silent for the next fifty-three days.

CHAPTER III Birthdays, Holidays, Anniversaries

THOMAS JEFFERSON WAS A SMALL R REPUBLICAN TO THE POINT of being a bit of a prig at times. He refused as president to declare a national day of thanksgiving on the principle that the national government should not regard itself as having the authority to coordinate the people's social activities and that to name a day of thanksgiving would be a violation of the First Amendment. He steadfastly refused to divulge his birthday, partly because he was an inherently modest man, private to the point of secretive, and partly because he wanted to make sure that republican leaders did not lend any energy or legitimacy to the dangerous aggrandizement of office holding. He believed, or affected to believe, that the presidency was not really much different from jury duty, and that any tendency towards pomp and ceremony was a step towards monarchy. On March 4, 1801, he walked to his inauguration. At the White House, he sometimes met guests in his house slippers.

Accordingly, President Jefferson observed only two holidays. One was July 4, the birth date of the United States. By 1800 the Fourth of July was widely celebrated in America, even though, as John Adams would grumpily point out from time to time, the national *resolution* of independence had been adopted on July 2, 1776, while Jefferson's *declaration*—a derivative and arguably plagiarized document that he, Adams, could have written had he been less generous to his protégé Jefferson—was adopted on July 4. By 1800 the Fourth of July was firmly established as the date of the birth of the United States.

Jefferson's other holiday was New Year's Day, which the time-conscious, efficiency-loving president regarded as sufficiently secular and mathematical in nature to be worthy of an Enlightenment nation's regard. In observing New Year's, he was in some deliberately indirect sense acknowledging the existence of Christmas, or at least the holiday season, by way of a secular alternative at about the same point of mid-winter. He was also making sure the American people understood that there was no way he would officially observe a historically unverifiable birthday of a doubtful historical personage he was almost always convinced could not legitimately be regarded as the Christ.

Jefferson threw open the doors of the White House, then known as the Executive Mansion or the President's House, twice a year, on January 1 and July 4. These twice-annual receptions were famous for the president's gracefulness and his spare but eminently tasteful hospitality. Washington, DC, was a raw new national capital then, with pigs rooting along Pennsylvania Avenue and members of Congress, the cabinet, and the national bureaucracy, such as it was, huddled in a handful of unrefined boarding houses. The Federalist sarcast and bon vivant Gouverneur Morris famously said, "We only need here houses, cellars, kitchens, scholarly men, amiable women and a few other such trifles to possess a perfect city."[1] Congressmen, said one diarist, were "clustered together in eight or ten boarding-houses as near as possible to the Capitol, and there lived, like a convent of monks, with no other amusement or occupation than that of going from their lodgings to the Chambers and back again."[2] There was a great deal of grumbling, some of it good-humored. Even the agrarian Republican Albert Gallatin bemoaned the primitiveness of the federal city, which, he said, "is hated by every member of Congress without exception of persons or parties."[3] The eternal optimist Jefferson described the new capital as "a pleasant country residence, with a number of neat little villages scattered around within the distance of a mile and a half, and furnishing a plain and substantially good society."[4]

Everyone wanted to be invited to the President's House for dinners and receptions, even the Federalists who despised the man and decried his politics.

Meriwether Lewis lived with Thomas Jefferson from April 1, 1801, until July 5, 1803. He lived in the East Room, which had been partitioned to afford him both an office and a sleeping chamber. Although Jefferson brought eleven household slaves from Monticello to staff the White House, he and Lewis were usually the only white people living in the mansion. Jefferson wrote to his daughter Martha, "Capt. Lewis and myself are like two mice in a church."[5] Although we do not know the exact day-to-day whereabouts of Lewis during that twenty-seven-month period, we can be sure that he participated in several of those presidential open houses.[6] We know that Lewis carried messages between the White House and the Capitol, including Jefferson's first annual message to Congress on December 8, 1801.[7] We know that Lewis escorted Jefferson's daughters Martha Jefferson Randolph and Maria Jefferson Eppes into the national capital during their visit in the winter of 1802–03. Richard Dillon has written, "The White House served as an ideal finishing school for Lewis, thanks to the long dinner conversations in which he participated. ... No one was closer to Jefferson during his first years in the presidential office—unless it was the president's pet mockingbird. Many of Lewis's rough intellectual edges were smoothed by the cultural atmosphere of the Executive Mansion."[8] The mockingbird's name was Dick. The president sometimes let it fly around freely in the house.

Samuel Harrison Smith, the publisher of the *National Intelligencer,* wrote of the 1803 Fourth of July celebration at the White House, "Yesterday was a day of joy to our citizens and of pride to our President. It is a day which you know he always enjoys. How much more he must have enjoyed it on this occasion from the great event that occasioned it. The news of the cession of Louisiana only arrived about 8 'clock of the night preceding, just in time to be announced on this auspicious day. ... This mighty event forms an era in our history, and of itself must render the administration of Jefferson immortal."[9] Smith was right on every count. Lewis was present at that Fourth of July celebration. It must have been a heady experience for everyone. The president had just doubled the size of the United States, more or less inadvertently. The troublesome (and perennial) Mississippi River question had been settled in a way that nobody could have anticipated. Now, instead of periodically cajoling Spain and France to honor the right of American citizens to ship their commodities down the river that had formed the western boundary of the United States, the new republic suddenly owned both banks of the river—and everything beyond to the continental divide. In the spring of 1803, the French minister to the United States had said, "You have made a noble bargain for yourselves, and I suppose you will make the most of it."[10] Jefferson probably spent some part of July 4, 1803, fretting about the constitutionality of the deal his ministers in France (Robert Livingston and James Monroe) had just consummated, but he knew, too, that he had just purchased "an empire for liberty as she [the world] has never surveyed since the creation."[11] It was, Jefferson knew as well as anyone alive, the making moment of American greatness. Almost certainly Lewis (or a slave) rolled out the world's largest cheese, Jefferson's Mammoth Cheese, to deepen the conviviality of the occasion.

Lewis's patron Jefferson did not acknowledge birthdays (except the nation's), and he did not worship or observe Christian holidays—Christmas, Easter, Pentecost, Good Friday, Palm Sunday—publicly or privately. He was a deist and something of a Unitarian, but he scrupulously, even militantly, kept his religious views private. "Say nothing of my religion," Jefferson wrote. "It is known to my god and myself alone. It's evidence before the world is to be sought in my life. If what has been *honest and dutiful to society*, the religion which has regulated it cannot be a bad one."[12]

Lewis's spiritual principles are less easy to discern than Jefferson's because he was not a revolutionary ideologue or a national political figure, and because he was not nearly so prolific of prose as his great patron. Still, the limited evidence from journals and letters indicates that Lewis was, like Jefferson, a deist and a scientific skeptic. There is no evidence of any group religious activity among the expedition's membership.

None of the journals mentions prayer, public or private. Although the expedition packed a small traveling library, there is no evidence that a Bible was carried along by the captains or by individual members of the expedition. The only moment in the expedition that veered towards religious expression or ritual was the burial of Sergeant Charles Floyd on August 20, 1804, near today's Sioux City, Iowa. On this occasion Clark wrote, "Capt Lewis read the funeral Service over him after paying everry respect to the Body of this desceased man (who had at All times given us proofs of his impatiality Sincurity to ourselves and good will to Serve his Countrey)."[13] John Ordway wrote, "[W]e buried him with the honours of war. the usal Serrymony performed (by Capt. Lewis[)] as custommary in a Settlement, we put a red ceeder post, hughn & branded his name date &.C—."[14] Patrick Gass wrote the most beautiful of the expedition's journal entries about the death of Floyd. "We went on about a mile to high prairie hills on the north side of the river, and there interred his remains in the most decent manner our circumstances would admit; we then proceeded a mile further to a small river on the same side and encamped."[15] There is a Biblical simplicity to this.

William Clark was also a creature of the Enlightenment, but since he was not Thomas Jefferson's friend and not a scientist in quite the same way Lewis presented himself to be, it seems probable that he was less doctrinaire in his secularism than Lewis or Jefferson. The expedition was an official function of a self-consciously secular and republican government, a nation that assured the North African Islamic state of Tripoli in 1797 that "the Government of the United States of America is not, in any sense, founded on the Christian religion; as it has in itself no character of enmity against the laws, religion, or tranquility, of Mussulmen."[16] The expedition was launched by the nation's most prominent deist, a man widely thought to be an atheist, and the leader of the expedition was a self-conscious acolyte of the freethinking president. It would be anomalous, therefore, if there had been any organized religious activity in the course of the transcontinental journey.

My purpose in this chapter is to examine the expedition's journals for five dates per annum—Christmas, New Year's, July 4, Clark's birthday, and Lewis's birthday—to see what they reveal about the diarists, particularly the two captains. My assumption is that the diarists would have approached their journal keeping for these days with a greater self-consciousness than they would have paid on random days up and down the trail, and that a self-conscious journal keeper is going to present himself in ways that open windows on the expedition behind the surface narrative, the expedition below the radar. An examination of the ways Meriwether Lewis and William Clark observed these potentially ceremonial occasions also reveals a good deal about their styles and respective characters.

Birthdays

We don't know the birthdays of most of the men of the expedition. They all had birthdays, of course, but it seems likely that the average enlisted man lost track of time so far from the grid of the civilized world. Lewis and Clark quite probably possessed the only clock in a gigantic swath of North America, stretching at least from longitude 90° 12' 44" W (St. Louis) to the 120th meridian, and probably beyond. And their chronometer, the most expensive item in their equipage, proved to be unreliable. Thomas Slaughter has argued that the expedition frequently lost track of time, and that the seeming orderliness of the journals' time keeping is a slight of hand trick.[17] The captains, equipped with their chronometer and the expedition's small traveling library, which included actual calendars, frequently confused the date, the day of the week, and on a few occasions the month. The captains' daily briefings, if they held them at all, would not have begun with an announcement of the Gregorian calendar's designation of the day. At some point fairly early on in the expedition, precise determinations of time ceased to matter, except to the captains, who were attempting to determine the latitude and longitude of recognizable features on the landscape. Just as the men were slowly stripped of their cloth garments, boots, and other perishable markers of civilization as they ventured deeper and deeper into the wilderness, so their concept of time underwent a severe simplification. The only time that really mattered was noon (meridian), necessary for determining latitude and longitude, but noon in the wilderness before the tyranny of standard time zones was determined by careful observation of the mid-day sun. The men of the expedition worked from first light to last light and, with the help of the fire, moon, and the inspiration of Cruzatte's fiddle, frequently stretched their waking time into the darkness in a world entirely void of incandescent light. It is not clear that on any given day of the journey an average member of the expedition, Silas Goodrich or William Weiser, for example, knew what day it was, or what month, or for that matter even what year. I doubt that the captains sat down with the men at Camp Wood and took down their vital statistics, made comments on how the birthdays of the men played out across the calendar of the year, noted coincidences or near coincidences, and declared, in the manner of Facebook, that they would be sure to announce the various birthdays as the calendar unfolded.

The best recent work on the individual biographies of expedition members has been done by Larry Morris, *The Fate of the Corps: What Became of the Lewis and Clark Explorers after the Expedition*. It is on Morris's outstanding research that I base the following assessment.

We know just ten birthdays for certain. Thomas Jefferson was born on April 13, 1743, in Albemarle County, Virginia. Jean Baptiste Lepage, who joined the expedition at Fort Mandan, was born on August 20, 1761. That makes him the oldest member of the "permanent party" that left Fort Mandan on April 7, 1805. He was forty-three years old at the time of the departure. Toussaint Charbonneau was born in Montreal on March 22, 1767. He was thirty-seven when Lewis and Clark met him in November 1804. Recently discovered records indicate that he was a full ten years younger than previous generations of Lewis and Clark scholars thought. William Clark was born on August 1, 1770. Patrick Gass was born in Pennsylvania on June 12, 1771. Meriwether Lewis was born on August 18, 1774. William Bratton was born on July 27, 1778. Peter M. Weiser was born in Pennsylvania on October 3, 1781. And Jean Baptiste Charbonneau was born on February 11, 1805, at or near Fort Mandan in Louisiana Territory. Sacagawea was probably born about the time James Madison presented the Virginia Plan at the Constitutional Convention in Philadelphia in 1787.[18]

No mention is made in the journals of Jefferson's birthday, even though he was the patron of the expedition, the president of the United States, Lewis's mentor and friend, and though Lewis named a river for him in southwestern Montana. It is possible that Lewis did not know Jefferson's birthday. Jefferson did not regularly divulge what he regarded as a purely accidental notation on the calendar. It is certain that Lewis and Jefferson would not have celebrated Jefferson's birthday in the White House. Jean Baptiste Charbonneau's birth is announced with some fanfare on February 11, 1805, but nobody mentions his first birthday at Fort Clatsop. Probably nobody, including his mother, even thought about it. Sacagawea would not have been aware of her son's exact birthday. Belonging to a non-western, non-linear culture, she probably would not have found that data very interesting. She would have been disposed to mark her son's life by biological milestones, not mere calendric abstractions.

The only two birthdays ever noted in the journals of the expedition were those of Lewis and Clark. Lewis *marked* his thirtieth, thirty-first, and thirty-second birthdays in Louisiana. Clark *celebrated* or, as he likes to put it, *Selebrated* his thirty-fourth, thirty-fifth, and thirty-sixth birthdays on the journey. The two captains were quite different men in basic temperament. It is not surprising, therefore, that they observed their birthdays in quite different fashions, indeed in ways that confirm the distinctions between their personality styles. Generally speaking, Clark was the more relaxed and unselfconscious of the pair, less self-protective, less likely to wish to project a certain image of himself. Lewis took himself more seriously, had a harder time relaxing into an unconstructed expression of himself, and was less willing to exhibit or reveal himself in a genuinely spontaneous manner.

Clark wrote journal entries on each of the birthdays he passed in the course of the expedition. Lewis was entirely silent on August 18, 1804, when the expedition was approaching today's Sioux City, Iowa, and on August 18, 1806, when the expedition camped just south of today's Bismarck, North Dakota.

Lewis probably wasn't in much of a festive mood on his thirty-second birthday, since he was still nursing raw wounds from the shooting accident that occurred on August 11, 1806. Three journal keepers reported the events of August 18, 1806. It was now one week since Captain Lewis had been wounded in the posterior by Pierre Cruzatte. The last mention of Lewis in the journals had been on August 14. John Ordway reported, on the day that the expedition returned to the Mandan and Hidatsa villages, "Capt. Lewis fainted as Capt. Clark was dressing his wound, but Soon came too again.—"[19] Ordway was the only journal keeper to mention this incident. Were it not for Ordway, we would not know that Clark was serving as Lewis's doctor and changing his bandages during this difficult—and humiliating—time. After the shootout at Two Medicine Creek (July 27), the failure of the captains' rendezvous at the confluence of the Yellowstone and the Missouri (August 7), and the gun accident at the Birnt Hills (August 11), Lewis was essentially out of commission for the remainder of the expedition. It was Clark who gave the expedition's swivel cannon to the Hidatsa leader Le Borgne, Clark who recruited Sheheke-shote to accompany the expedition downriver, Clark who gave the expedition's blacksmith works to Toussaint Charbonneau.

The expedition traveled forty miles on August 18. Lewis almost certainly spent that entire time face down in a boat, cushioned against the slap of the river. It was a windy day on the upper Missouri, so windy that the expedition delayed until 8 A.M. before setting out. It must have been a painful day for Lewis no matter how carefully Clark and the rest of the men cushioned him against the "rough water." The expedition camped that night on the east bank of the Missouri River a little below the mouth of the Heart River. That evening, "after the fires were made," Clark sat down with the Mandan leader Sheheke-shote (White Coyote) and "made a number of enquiries into the tredition of his nation."[20] The expedition's records are so spotty that it is now impossible to determine where in the encampment Captain Lewis would have been positioned on a night like this. We know from one of Clark's later entries that the expedition was now entirely bankrupt of tents, tarps, and mosquito netting. The men, including the captains, were therefore sleeping entirely in the open, covering themselves with their blankets to protect themselves against the mosquitoes. So just where was Lewis while Clark and Sheheke-shote sat around the fire talking about the Mandan Indian origin story? That story, which inspired Clark to adopt Biblical cadences as he related it in his journal,[21] could only have come to Clark in a language chain beginning with Sheheke-shote in Mandan, then translated from Mandan to French by Rene Jusseaume, then from French to English by one of the French navigators, presumably Francois Labiche. Was Lewis listening? Or was he off away from the conversation nursing—or cursing—his wounds? Was he attempting to sleep nearby, or was there a somewhat detached officers' precinct at the campsite? It is possible that Lewis spent the night in one of the expedition's boats to avoid moving more than was necessary in the first critical days of his recovery. Nobody bothers to say.

Lewis 1804

Two years earlier, on August 18, 1804, the expedition was lingering at a place known as Fish Camp, south of today's Dakota City and east of Homer, Nebraska, or possibly just opposite on the Iowa side of the Missouri River. It was called Fish Camp because the expedition managed to catch 318 fish there in a single day. The Corps of Discovery remained at the camp between August 13–19, 1804. It was a very busy time for everyone. The expedition was completing its first series of councils with Indian tribes on the Missouri. It was also working its way through the most significant discipline crisis of the entire expedition.

August 18, 1804, was a monumental day for the Lewis and Clark Expedition. Lewis and Clark tried and punished a deserter, held a peace council with Indian leaders, and held a dance. Moses Reed was brought in by the posse that had been sent out on August 7 to apprehend him—literally dead or alive, according to Clark's journal. A team consisting of George Drouillard, Reuben Field, William Bratton, and Francoise Labiche brought Reed to camp, along with a number of Oto leaders they had met on the road. (The Frenchman known as La Liberte somehow escaped the posse and was never seen again). The court-martial was convened that afternoon. Reed wisely "Confessed that he 'Deserted & Stold a public Rifle Shot-pouch Powder & Bals' and requested we would be as favourable with him as we Could consistantly with our Oathes."[22] This candor and acceptance of responsibility may have saved his life. Reed was found guilty by a jury of his peers, sentenced to run the gauntlet four times, and discharged from the Corps of Volunteers for North Western Discovery. Running the gauntlet meant that the men of the expedition lined up in two rows, each man equipped with "9 Swichies," Clark said. The men were expected to beat Reed as severely as they could while he ran between the lines. Flogging in the army was outlawed by Congress in 1812, reinstated for desertion in 1833, and then outlawed unconditionally in 1861.[23] Somehow Clark regarded Reed's punishment as comparatively mild. "[W]e were [favorable to him] and only Sentenced him to run the Gauntlet four times,"[24] he wrote.

After Reed endured his "Punishment," wrote Clark, "of about 500 Lashes," the captains had a meeting with a small group of Oto Indian leaders who had been shocked at the savagery of the gauntlet and had "petitioned for Pardin for this man."[25] Clark explained "the Customs of our Countrey" to the Oto delegation and the severity of Reed's offense, after which, as he always reported in such situations, "they were all Satisfied."[26] The Oto leaders witnessed the brutal flogging with great sadness. "[A]t night we had Some talk with the Chiefs about the Cause of War between them and the Mahars," Clark wrote. The Otoes told the captains that "the object of... comeing forward is to make a peace with the Mahars thro: us__. as the Mahars are not at home this great object cannot be accomplished at this time."[27] Then, Clark wrote, the Corps of Discovery "had a Dance which lasted untile 11 oClock, the Close of Cap Lewis Birthday."[28] Because of Lewis's birthday, an extra "Gill of Whiskey" was distributed to each man. Probably the whisky served as much to calm things down after the brutalizing of Reed as to show respect to Captain Lewis. To the reader of the twenty-first century, it seems shocking or perhaps even inappropriate that the men of the expedition held a dance on the same day they meted out so grave and barbaric a punishment. We can be sure that Moses Reed did not dance that night. Was he allowed to crawl off somewhere to endure the aftermath of the blood and agony alone? Or was he required to stay close?

Clark does not report whether Lewis participated in the dance, toasted (or was toasted by) the men, or engaged in the festivities in any way. Presumably he would not have altogether avoided a celebration that was organized in honor of his birthday.

The last words Charles Floyd ever wrote were penned on Lewis's thirtieth birthday. Floyd's August 18, 1804, journal entry reads in its entirety, "[O]uer men Returnd and Brot with them the man and Brot with them the *Grand Chief* of the *ottoes* and 2 Loer ones and 6 youers of thare nathion."[29] Two days later he was dead—of a ruptured appendix or a complete collapse of his immune system.[30] If he was aware on August 18 that he was gravely ill, Floyd made no mention of it. Several weeks earlier, on July 30, 1804, Clark had reported, "Serjt. Floyd verry unwell."[31] On July 31, Floyd himself had written, "I am verry Sick and Has ben for Somtime but have Recoverd my helth again."[32] Whatever killed him swept him away virtually overnight. Clark reported that Floyd died "with a great deel of composure, haveing Said to me before his death that he was going away and wished me to write a letter."[33]

Lewis was silent on his thirtieth birthday. He was silent more or less the whole first year of travel, from May 14 to October 26, 1804, when the expedition stopped its forward progress for the winter, and indeed through the winter among the Mandan and Hidatsa Indians. August 18, 1804, was one of the most remarkable days of the entire expedition, full of rich, varied, and intensely dramatic activities. It is the kind of day that would be the ideal focus for a film or television miniseries. One can imagine the majority of the men dancing in the firelight, shaken by the grave events of the day, and at the same time relieved that someone else had received the flogging.

Meanwhile, three detached individuals hovered about the margins of the encampment: Charles Floyd, not feeling well, and beginning his sudden slide towards death by what the captains called "Beliose Cholick;"[34] Moses Reed, bloody, bruised, bludgeoned, and banished, writhing in excruciating pain and wondering, perhaps, if he would even live through the night; and Captain Meriwether Lewis, contemplating these momentous events, preparing for the council that would be conducted the following morning, and meditating on his life in the sublunary world. Unfortunately, Lewis did not take the time to write out a narrative of the incidents of the day, an analysis of the current state of the expedition and its prospects for success, or a meditation on the meaning of his life so far. In not committing these reflections to his journal, Lewis cheated posterity of what would have been a magnificent birthday journal entry.

LEWIS 1805

Students of Lewis and Clark seldom recall Clark's birthdays in the wilderness, but nobody fails to remember the famous passage that Lewis wrote on his thirty-first birthday at Camp Fortunate near today's Dillon, Montana. He had made first historical contact with the Shoshone on August 13 while Clark and the majority of the Corps of Discovery were lugging the boats to the farthest "navigable" point of the Missouri River. Clark caught up with Lewis on August 17, 1805. Sacagawea turned out to be the sister of the Shoshone leader Cameahwait. The captains were pretty sure they were going to be able to purchase the horses they would need to cross the Bitterroot Mountains. Soon they would be floating downhill for a change. The expedition's success was now virtually assured. It was a time of triumph, and it should have been an opportunity for unqualified celebration.

On August 18, 1805, Lewis wrote a journal entry of 591 words. After announcing Clark's departure that morning to examine the upper Salmon River, Lewis devoted most of his journal entry to an account of his efforts to purchase horses from the Shoshone. He met with considerable success on the first of what would be a number of days of horse trading. After reporting all of this, Lewis devoted the last 164 words to his famous birthday meditation:

> This day I completed my thirty first year, and conceived that I had
> in all human probability now existed about half the period which
> I am to remain in this Sublunary world. I reflected that I had as
> yet done but little, very little indeed, to further the hapiness of the
> human race, or to advance the information of the succeeding gen-
> eration. I viewed with regret the many hours I have spent in indo-
> lence, and now soarly feel the want of that information which those

hours would have given me had they been judiciously expended. but since they are past and cannot be recalled, I dash from me the gloomy thought and resolved in future, to redouble my exertions and at least indeavour to promote those two primary objects of human existence, by giving them the aid of that portion of talents which nature and fortune have bestoed on me; or in future, to live for *mankind*, as I have heretofore lived *for myself.*[35]

It might be useful to engage in a sustained exegesis of this journal passage, surely one of the handful of most often quoted passages in the entire literature of the Lewis and Clark Expedition. Lewis was emotionally exhausted when he penned these words—if indeed they were written at that place and at that time. As I argue elsewhere in this book, the period between August 13–17 was one of the fullest, most thrilling and troubling, and tensest episodes of the entire expedition. During that unprecedented week, more or less alone, Lewis had discovered the source of the Missouri River, made historic first contact with the Shoshone Indians, and worked tirelessly to keep Cameahwait and the Shoshones from absconding to avoid what they reckoned was some kind of ambush that Lewis was trying to draw them into down on the plains. By the time Clark caught up with him on August 17, Lewis was an emotional wreck. The previous night Lewis had expressed his anxiety with great candor: "[M]y mind was in reallity quite as gloomy all this evening as the most affrighted indian but I affected cheerfullness to keep the Indians so who were about me.   we finally laid down and the Chief placed himself by the side of my musquetoe bier. I slept but little as might be well expected, my mind dwelling on the state of the expedition which I have ever held in equal estimation with my own existence, and the fait of which appeared at this moment to depend in a great measure upon the caprice of a few savages who are ever as fickle as the wind."[36] Because the traveling season was so far advanced, and Lewis was determined to get to the Pacific Ocean before winter set in, he and Clark barely had time to shake hands before Clark left with carpentry tools and a team of men to seek navigable waters of the upper Salmon River. The next morning, Lewis was alone again, without his pragmatic, stable, and unendingly supportive partner in discovery to assure him that all would be well. His birthday meditation must be seen in this context. It is a barometric measure of the strain and fatigue of a high-strung man who regarded the success of his expedition "in equal estimation with my own existence." Lewis was alone among a refugee people who had been reduced by adverse circumstances to an existence that seemed as primitive to other Indians as those Indians seemed to white men like Jefferson, Madison, and Gallatin. Lewis was as far from the company of other civilized beings as it was possible to be.

Lewis was characteristically pretentious in speaking of life on earth as "this Sublunary world." Clark would never have used such a word in his journal. Probably he had never heard the word. In pre-Copernican cosmology, everything above the moon was thought to consist of *aether*— a pure element much more rarified than air, sometimes regarded as the breath of the gods or of God's angels. Above the moon everything was perfect, orderly, permanent, unchangeable, and incorruptible. The moon was the marker of the boundary between the superlunary and the sublunary worlds. Below the moon, everything was corruptible. The sublunary world was made up of the four elements—earth, air, fire, and water. Everything was in flux. Nothing was eternal. The earth, reckoned in pre-Copernican cosmology as the center of the universe, was a place of dross, erosion, sin, and deep imperfection.

By the time of the Enlightenment the word *sublunary* was seldom used in anything except a poetic or ironic sense. The English poet-preacher John Donne had actually meant it when he wrote, in a sermon delivered in 1631, that, "The sphear of our loves is sublunary, upon things naturally inferior to our selves."[37] By the time of Meriwether Lewis, with the heliocentric view of the universe firmly and incontestably established, nobody any longer used the term in a cosmological sense. It was now merely an archaic word employed routinely in the literature of melancholy and by those who wished to assume the pose of living in a fallen and chaotic world.

We know Lewis was wrong in reckoning that he had now reached the halfway point of his life. He could not know out on the Montana-Idaho border that he had just four years, one month, and twenty-three days left to live (a total of 1,515 days). His life was not half over, it was 87 percent over. Unfortunately, in the time he had left to him, he did "but little, very little indeed, to further the hapiness of the human race, or to advance the information of the succeeding generation." The closest he came to fulfilling that desideratum was in the natural history essays he wrote in the spring of 1806 at Fort Clatsop. They constitute a major achievement, and they indicate what Lewis was capable of when he kept himself in his chair. Unfortunately, thanks to the effective collapse of the publication project in the wake of his sudden death in 1809, Lewis's natural history essays had no impact on the scientific community, and they have seldom appeared in anything but unabridged editions of the expedition's journals, where they are seldom read. In other words, the best chance Lewis had to "advance the information of the succeeding generation" died with him at Grinder's Inn on October 11, 1809. The only way he could have accomplished his goals was to take the long view and to live through the dark night of his soul. On the Natchez Trace he was unable to dash from him the gloomy thought. In taking his own life, he broke his covenant to "live for mankind, as I have heretofore lived for myself."

In his analysis of the birthday meditation, historian Joseph Mussulman has written, "[Lewis and Clark editor Elliott] Coues read this in the light of historical hindsight as a 'sadly interesting passage, ... when we remember how near the young nobleman was to his tragic end.' The same general interpretation has largely prevailed ever since."[38] I share Mussulman's skepticism. I do not regard the passage as some kind of first draft of a suicide note, an early warning of what would transpire at Grinder's Inn. We need to be careful not to read too much back into the birthday meditation. It has a strongly conventional feel to it. It may not have been written in the heart of the American West at all. It seems more likely that it was written at Fort Clatsop—perhaps when Lewis was grinding out his natural history essays and lamenting how little formal scientific training he had obtained before the great journey began—possibly at the Long Camp on the return journey, or possibly even after the expedition had returned to St. Louis.

This much is certain. The meditation was not composed in its present form at the Shoshone village on August 18, 1805. Internal evidence alone proves that the passage could not have been written on August 18. Lewis reports that Clark departed that morning on his reconnaissance of the upper reaches of the Salmon River, and then tells us where Clark's party camped, a fact that he could not have known on the day in question. He was writing from retrospect. The birthday meditation has the polish and the feel of a carefully crafted prose set piece. In fact, it feels like something Lewis had deliberately prepared for publication. Some historians have argued that Lewis would have suppressed this personal and self-doubting passage in the book he was planning to publish about the expedition. I think it is much more likely that this passage was written precisely *for* the book. There is a fair amount of posture in it. It represents Lewis's version of Alexander Mackenzie's confession that he did not have the leisure or the scientific training to do serious fieldwork in natural history in the course of *his* transcontinental journey. Lewis is not so much a man in melancholy reflection on his life so far as a writer presenting himself as that melancholy and reflective man. However much the meditation may seem wrongheaded to twenty-first century readers of the journals, or out of sync with the known facts of Lewis's achievement between February 1801 and August 17, 1805, it has the effect of deepening and enriching the supreme episode of the journey—Lewis's arrival at the source of the Missouri and the annoyingly gratifying *national hug* he shared with the leaders of the Shoshone nation. In other words, I believe that the meditation was written for literary effect. That does not mean that what Lewis wrote was fiction. Given all we know about the character and sensibility of Lewis, it rings perfectly true as a window on his soul at what he believed was the midpoint of a journey on which the expedition was just one *darling project*. If Lewis wrote the passage at some point later than August 18, 1805, as he assuredly did, he was not writing directly from his experience that day, but reconstructing or perhaps even *constructing* that experience for the readers of his journal or his book. He was recollecting. Why didn't he suppress the meditation? He not only chose to report it, but chose to report it after the mood has passed. He wanted us to know.

Nor does the passage feel like the meditation of a depressed man. Just the opposite. After *reflecting* that he was not as well prepared for the intellectual demands of the expedition as he would like to be, and knowing that not even the traveling library was going to get him up to speed in the remaining months of the expedition, Lewis immediately *dashed* gloom aside and *resolved* to *redouble* his efforts, and to *endeavor to promote* the agenda of the Enlightenment by *giving them the aid* of his *talents*. These are all positive terms. This is not the meditation of a man thinking about ending his life. It is the resolution of a self-punishing man who has used the occasion of his meridian birthday to recommit himself to excellence and achievement. The passage does not reveal that he has no reason to go on; it declares that he intends to get more serious about his life, that he intends to bring his achievement up to the level of the great opportunities that have been extended to him.

We all know that Lewis was being too hard on himself. By our standards, his life was extraordinarily successful. He was a thirty-one-year-old man who had just reached the source of the "heretofore deemed endless" Missouri River, who had finessed his way through an exceedingly complex and frustrating encounter with the Shoshone Indians, and who was now resting in a friendly Indian camp on the other side of the continental divide after a journey of 3,000 river miles. He was, moreover, a member of America's most prestigious learned society, the friend and protégé of the celebrated Jefferson, and the commander of a congressionally authorized exploration party.

Joe Mussulman has written, "To the objective and sympathetic reader, Lewis's birthday meditation doesn't sound like a plaint of self-pity or an anguished lamentation. Even though it might have been inspired by an emotional reaction to his recent experiences among the Shoshones, it reads more like a well-rehearsed script drawn from memory, one that he has used before to regain control of himself… It reflects not weakness but nobility, not despair but strength."[39]

The great Stephen Ambrose misread the passage. After Lewis resolved "to redouble my exertions and at least indeavour to promote those two primary objects of human existence," Ambrose wrote, "[H]ere he seems to have lost his train of thought. Whatever the cause, he forgot to name 'those two primary objects of human existence.'"[40] Actually, earlier in the meditation Lewis specified that those two "primary objects" were "to further the happiness of the human race, or to advance the information of the succeeding generation." It was Ambrose who appears to have lost his train of thought.

Lewis biographer Richard Dillon merely concluded that Lewis celebrated his thirty-first birthday "with a little soul-searching."[41] James Fazio has offered an interesting summary: "Personal and poignant, it is a passage of unreasonable melancholy, perhaps even foreshadowing of the state of mind that would lead to an early death by his own hand shortly following the great expedition."[42] The medical historian Eldon Chuinard made no attempt to diagnose the neurosis or mental imbalance of Lewis at this juncture, but he did quibble with the captain's conclusions: "Lewis was wrong on both accounts. He did much to increase the happiness of the American portion of the human race and to contribute information to succeeding generations. He was also wrong in his estimate of life expectancy; he was to die at thirty-five, on October 11, 1809."[43]

David Lavender argues that Lewis's thirty-first birthday "triggered Lewis's all-too-easily induced melancholia ... he sounded like a very moody, very introspective, very youthful thirty-one. Which he was."[44] Lavender agrees with Chuinard: "Considering what he was doing for country and mankind, the self-flagellation was hardly deserved."[45] Like a New Year's resolution, Lavender says, "it may have helped stir him into filling, during the next several days, page after page of his journal with ethnographic observations about the hitherto unknown Shonshoni, or Snake, tribe. It was the sort of analysis that Jefferson wanted and that more than one 'succeeding generation' of anthropologists would find very useful."[46]

One of the most careful readers of the texts of the expedition, Albert Furtwangler, has written, "The note touched here by Lewis suggests either that he was afflicted (as [British moralist Samuel] Johnson was) with an occasional but recurring deep inner melancholy or that something in particular had very recently weighed on his mind to make him doubt his personal worth and promise. And the most noteworthy recent experience of failure was this time alone among the Shoshones, where communication was uncertain and everything he cherished seemed to hang on the cooperation of utter strangers."[47]

No analysis of the birthday meditation is altogether satisfying. The mystery abides. Lewis was an extremely intelligent, even gifted, young man who was not particularly well educated and who had not pursued his formal education with much discipline. His mentor Jefferson recognized this weakness in Lewis, but believed that his wilderness skills, his sense of responsibility, the reliability of his observations, and his unquenchable courage were ultimately more important, particularly on an exploration mission that took American soldiers so deep into the great unknown that it could not be guaranteed that Lewis and his companions would ever come back. Jefferson was a tough mentor to emulate. He had spent a significant chunk of his early adulthood reading ten to fifteen hours per day and practicing the violin for several hours per day. Lewis spent his early adulthood in the

Virginia militia and the United States Army. His letters to his mother from this period are not about books but about beef, alcohol, and camp wenches. To a considerable extent, Jefferson saw the world through books. Jefferson's extensive correspondence is, among other things, a running commentary on the books he acquired, read, and quoted, but never quite paid for. By this standard, Lewis's relationship with books was little more than average for a man of his social class. Jefferson knew seven languages, three ancient and four modern, and made a half-hearted run at German and Gaelic, too. Lewis knew English and perhaps a smattering of technical Latin. Jefferson, in the last year of his life, was reading ancient Greek histories without a dictionary or a grammar book at his side.

It is unlikely that Lewis did anything between July 5, 1803, and September 23, 1806, or for that matter between April 1, 1801, and October 11, 1809, without thinking about the likely reaction of Thomas Jefferson. If ever there was an intimidating reader standing over one's shoulder, it was Jefferson. If at the continental divide on August 18, 1805, Lewis felt he was under-prepared for the challenges he was facing, it was hardly surprising. By the standards he was employing, he was under-prepared. On the other hand, Jefferson would not have been able to endure the rigors of the Lewis and Clark Expedition for more than a handful of days. If he had brought along everything he said he could not live without—books, wine, scientific instruments, the music of Bach and Corelli—the expedition would have needed a fleet of keelboats.

No other member of the expedition mentions Lewis's birthday in 1805. He did receive a gift, however, indeed one that he cherished so much that he posed in it when he stood for his portrait by Charles Balthazar Julien Févret de Saint-Mémin in 1807. Private Joseph Whitehouse, who frequently noticed things that were reported by no other journal keeper, wrote that the Shoshone, "are tollarably well dressed with Skins Such as antelope and Mountain rams Skins &c. they have a fiew beeds and ear bobs among them. they gave Capt. Lewis a kind of an ornament which Spread around the Shoulders it was made of wezels tales & Some other ornemental afares."[48] Undoubtedly Lewis received many birthday gifts in the course of his life. This, however, is the only one that history records. He chose to immortalize it.

Thus Meriwether Lewis spent three birthdays in the wilderness. On the first, August 18, 1804, he was with the entire Corps of Discovery in Iowa or Nebraska. It was the last time he would see Charles Floyd. On that full and momentous day, the expedition distributed an extra gill of whiskey to the men and held a dance. In other words, even though it was an exceptionally tense day on the Lewis and Clark trail, Lewis can be said to have celebrated his thirtieth birthday, though the festivities were almost certainly organized by William Clark. On the second, he was essentially alone in the Shoshone Indian camp near Dillon, Montana, almost infinitely deeper into the American heart of darkness than he had been the previous year. Lewis observed his thirty-first birthday by way of one of the most famous and frequently quoted passages in all of the journals of the expedition, but he did not celebrate his birthday in any other way. Clark, who seems to have served as the master of revels of the expedition, camped that night approximately fifteen miles away from the Shoshone village.

Lewis spent his third birthday of the expedition, his thirty-second, nursing his wounds near today's Bismarck, North Dakota.

CLARK

Clark was quite willing to celebrate his own birthday, August 1. He had been born in Caroline County, Virginia, on August 1, 1770. He celebrated his thirty-fourth birthday at the Council Bluffs, north of today's Omaha, Nebraska. The contrast with Lewis could not be more complete. Clark was in a very good mood, in spite of the mosquitoes, which, as usual, he pronounced "verry troublesom."[49] He made a list of the profusion of wild fruits he observed all around the expedition's encampment, and—with his inimitable brand of English—exclaimed, "What a field for a Botents and a natirless,"[50] i.e., a botanist and a naturalist. And a dictionary. "This being my birth day," he wrote, "I order'd a Saddle of fat Vennison, an Elk fleece & a Bevertail to be cooked and a Desert of Cheries, Plumbs, Raspberries Currents and grapes of a Supr. Quality."[51] It sounds delicious. Clark does not say whether he shared this meal with his friend Lewis (probably) or whether the rest of the men of the expedition partook of the fat venison and other delights (likely). At some later point Clark crossed out the entire sentence, perhaps because in retrospect it felt self-indulgent, or because he wanted to make sure that only entries of greater official importance found their way into the book Nicholas Biddle was preparing for the press. Clark frequently used his field journal for cathartic purposes and then engaged in self-censorship in the more finished journal entry he wrote for that day sometime later. In his second version of the same journal entry for August 1, 1804, Clark removed all references to his birthday, including the birthday feast. He also removed his ejaculation about the field of study that awaited competent scientists.

CLARK 1805

If Clark was aware of his thirty-fifth birthday on August 1, 1805, he never mentioned it. Probably by now he was not really sure just what day it was, or—given how far from Louisville the expedition had now ventured— he did not much care. Still, he managed to have a special birthday meal.

The Clark party camped on the Jefferson River near today's Cardwell, Montana. He wrote, "A fine day Capt. Lewis left me at 8 oClock just below the place I entered a verrey high mountain which jutted its tremedious Clifts on either Side for 9 Miles, the rocks ragide Some verry dark & other part verry light rock the light rocks is Sand Stone. The water Swift & very Sholey. I killed a *Ibix* on which the whole party Dined ... ."[52] Clark liked to eat well. He did not share Lewis's epicurean habits or his familiarity with haute cuisine, but he definitely liked to dine well on hearty frontier fare. On this occasion, thanks to his success in killing a bighorn sheep, Clark and his colleagues dined sumptuously. So far as we know, they had no "grapes of a Supr. Quality."[53]

CLARK 1806

Clark spent his third birthday on the Lewis and Clark trail on the lower Yellowstone. He made no mention of the occasion. He was just two days from the confluence of the Yellowstone and the Missouri rivers, where he was expected either to catch up with Meriwether Lewis or wait for him to arrive as he proceeded down the Missouri from the mouth of the Marias River. The Clark party camped near today's Glendive, Montana. Clark was in a bad mood on his thirty-sixth birthday.

> We Set out early as usial the wind was high and ahead which caused the water to be a little rough and delayed us very much aded to this we had Showers of rain repeetedly all day at the intermition of only a fiew minits between them. My Situation a very disagreeable one. in an open Canoe wet and without a possibility of keeping my Self dry.[54]

The journals reveal that Clark was something of a complainer. In spite of his remarkable self-discipline and commitment to duty, he disliked discomfort and he hated to get wet. When he did get wet, he usually whined about it. The most famous occasion was September 16, 1805, in the Bitterroot Mountains. Clark wrote that the expedition was passing through, "a thickly timbered Countrey of 8 different kinds of pine, which are So covered with Snow, that in passing thro them we are continually covered with Snow, I have been wet and as cold in every part as I ever was in my life, indeed I was at one time fearfull my feet would freeze in the thin mockersons which I wore."[55] Like everyone else, as August 1806 began, he was ready to get back home to the comforts of civilization.

For two weeks Clark had been writing with awe and wonderment about the abundance of wildlife on the lower Yellowstone River, particularly of the gigantic numbers of buffalo he saw on both sides of the river. On August 1, his forward progress was actually held up by a large gang of bison. At this point in the journey, the phenomenon seems merely to have annoyed him.

[A]t 2 P.M. I was obliged to land to let the Buffalow Cross over. not withstanding an island of half a mile in width over which this gangue of Buffalow had to pass and the Chanel of the river on each Side nearly ¼ of a mile in width, this gangue of Buffalow was entirely across and as thick as they could Swim. the Chanel on the Side of the island the went into the river was crouded with those animals for ½ an hour. [*NB: I was obliged to lay to for an hour*] the other Side of the island for more than 3/4 of an hour. I took 4 of the men and killed 4 fat Cows for their fat and what portion of their flesh the Small Canoes Could Carry[56]

Probably Clark dined on a saddle of fat buffalo cow that night.

CHRISTMAS

The expedition's first Christmas in the wilderness took place at Camp Wood, eighteen miles north of St. Louis and across the Mississippi River, across from the mouth of the Missouri. Although Lewis had hoped the expedition could ascend the Missouri River a couple of hundred miles before the winter closed the road, he was prevented from entering the Louisiana Territory by the Spanish Commandant at St. Louis, Charles De Hault Delassus. By the time Delassus took his stand Lewis had come to terms with the idea of establishing a winter camp in the Illinois country, in part because this would enable him to stay in touch with the president and also learn as much as possible from Spanish or French government functionaries, fur trade capitalists, adventurers, and scientists (such as they were) in St. Louis. The opportunity to learn more—much more—about the wilderness he was about to penetrate was a significant advantage accidentally offered by the series of delays that kept Lewis from the mouth of the Missouri until May 1804.

On Christmas Day 1803, the fort at Camp Wood was nearing completion. The Clark party had reached the mouth of Wood River on December 12. Clearing of land and cutting of logs for the compound began the next day. The men were able to move in to their huts on December 19. They were probably far from finished on that date, but far enough along that the presence of the men's gear would not get in the way of final construction. Clark reported that the huts were fully covered by Christmas Eve, though the chimneys of some of the huts (perhaps all of them) were still not complete. In other words, the men woke up on Christmas Day 1803 indoors, snug in their rooms. Although Clark had apparently not begun to record weather data in a systematic way, he does report on Christmas that the weather was moderate and the sky cloudy. Fires would probably have been welcome in the huts that Christmas Day, but they were certainly not essential, given the modest size of the individual quarters and the body heat that four or six or eight strong men with large appetites could generate in a small enclosed space.

So far as we can tell, Lewis spent Christmas 1803 in St. Louis. He was certainly not at Camp Wood. In fact he had not yet been to his expedition's winter headquarters. That would not come until the last days of January 1804. Clark was the only journal keeper at Camp Wood. On Christmas morning, Clark wrote, "I was wakened by a Christmas discharge found that Some of the party had got Drunk <2 fought,> the men frolicked and hunted all day, Snow this morning."[57] Clark did not describe the Christmas meal at Camp Wood, though we can perhaps guess. Clark reported that John Shields "returned with a cheese & 4 lb butter."[58] Shields had ventured all the way over to the other side of the river to get the butter. That was at least a technical violation of the conditions set by Delassus earlier that month. Hunters killed "Several Turkey" on Christmas day. The previous day one Samuel Griffeth sold Clark "a Cargo of Turnips"[59] for $3 a bushel (an extremely high price), and the indispensible Drouillard brought in three deer and five wild turkeys. So that makes for a Christmas dinner of roasted turkey, venison, turnips, cheese, and probably some form of bread baked of wheat or corn, plus the luxury of Louisiana Territory butter. On Christmas, Clark wrote, "Three Indians Come to day to take Christmas with us."[60] Since Clark later sent the Indians off with a bottle of whiskey, one assumes that he distributed at minimum the requisite daily gill of spirits to each man, and probably a good deal more. But on this he was silent. A year later, at Fort Mandan, the captains let it be known among the Mandan and Hidatsa that they were not welcome at the fort on Christmas, because it was, they said, an important *medicine* day for white people. At Camp Dubois Indians were still a rarity, however, and therefore welcome on Christmas day. At Fort Mandan the Mandan and Hidatsa were so constant a presence that Lewis complained that they "usually pester us with their good company the ballance of the day."[61]

The expedition got the best possible Christmas gift in 1803. George Drouillard agreed to "go with us, at the rate ofd,"[62] Clark wrote. Back in November, when Lewis and Clark first met Drouillard at Fort Massac a few miles upstream from the confluence of the Mississippi and the Ohio, he had agreed to travel on their behalf to South West Point, Tennessee, to bring in recruits that had been promised to the expedition, but who had not yet arrived. At that time Drouillard had been coy about the possibility of joining the expedition once it moved up the Missouri, but now, on Christmas, he notified Clark that he would make the journey. It was a momentous decision. Three years later, Lewis singled out Drouillard for special praise in his final assessment of the expedition's personnel. In his report to the War Department, Lewis called Drouillard "a man of much merit; he has been peculiarly usefull from his knowledge of the common language of gesticulation, and his uncommon skill as a hunter and woodsman; those several duties he performed in good faith, and with an ardor which deserves the highest commendation. It was his fate also to have encountered, on various occasions, with either Captain Clark or myself, all the most dangerous and trying scenes of the voyage, in which he uniformly acquited himself with honor."[63] In Lewis's estimation, Drouillard was the third most important member of the expedition. On January 12, 1806, at Fort Clatsop, Lewis wrote, "This morning sent out Drewyer and one man to hunt, they returned in the evening, Drewyer having killed seven Elk; I scarcely know how we should subsist were it not for the exertions of this excellet hunter."[64] Drouillard was one of the handful of men that Lewis routinely chose to accompany him on special missions.

Because Lewis was characteristically silent in the winter of 1803–04, we do not know how he spent Christmas 1803, but it would not be farfetched to believe he accepted an invitation to dine with the Chouteaus, who were becoming important advisers to the journey and the future of Louisiana Territory, and who occupied a social standing at least as high as Lewis's. Towards the end of the 1803–04 winter, Clark wrote a formal statement praising the help he and Lewis had received from Auguste Chouteau: "Besides Mr. Choteaus personal merits and his claims to the attention of his fellow citizens, he has still a stronger claim upon my particular friends; arrissing from the mark politeness and attention displayed by himself, his Lady and family towards Capt. Lewis and my self during our residence in this Countrey. On our several visits to St. Louis, in the course of the Winter and Spring, we have made the house of this gentleman our home."[65] Clark was only in St. Louis for a small number of days in the winter of 1803–04. It was Lewis who chiefly benefited from the Chouteau's hospitality. Donald Jackson believes that Lewis probably wrote the draft of this statement, then Clark copied it.[66]

It would be interesting to know just how the deist Lewis spent the holiday, but neither he nor anybody else left a record of his activities on Christmas Day 1803.

CHRISTMAS 1804

The best Christmas of the expedition occurred at Fort Mandan, where Lewis and Clark spent a total of 146 nights. The Mandan leader Sheheke-shote had made good on his November 1, 1804, promise, "[I]f we eat you Shall eat, if we Starve you must Starve also."[67] In their *Estimate of the Eastern*

Indians, Lewis and Clark singled out the Mandan for special praise: "These are the most friendly, well disposed Indians inhabiting the Missouri. They are brave, humane and hospitable."[68]

Construction of the fort had begun on November 3, 1804. The two ranges of living quarters were ready to be roofed by November 11. The captains moved into their quarters on November 13. Sensing the severity of the winter that was about to envelop the northern Great Plains, the men worked until 1 A.M. on November 15–16 in an attempt to finish the living quarters. On November 16, "all the men move into the huts which is not finsihd,"[69] Clark reported. The huts were not completely roofed until November 27. Work on the security pickets had begun on or slightly before December 20 and was completed on Christmas Eve. Somehow the Corps of Discovery always managed to complete its winter forts just in time for Christmas.

For all the secularity of the expedition, and its status as a military endeavor, Christmas at Fort Mandan had something of the feel of a scene out of a Laura Ingalls Wilder novel. Patrick Gass reported that on Christmas Eve, "Flour, dried apples, pepper and other articles were distributed in the different messes to enable them to celebrate Christmas in a proper and social manner."[70] These precious items had traveled in the larder of the expedition for 1,610 river miles under conditions that must have compromised their integrity again and again. The flour, pepper, and apples were at least seven months old. It would be interesting to know when the men of the expedition had last tasted flour or apples. It was an act of extraordinary leadership and generosity of spirit for the captains to do what they could to make Christmas special at the far northwestern outpost of American civilization just as the men completed Fort Mandan. At some point between May and late December 1804, probably later rather than sooner, the captains must have discussed Christmas and determined how to celebrate the traditional holiday, if at all. It's hard to think of Lewis leading that discussion. Once they decided to observe Christmas, the captains must have gone through a mental checklist of just what they had left to distribute that was not already part of their regular mess routine. They settled on flour, pepper, dried apples, and what might be called the special reserve supply of spirits. These luxury items were more than just Christmas treats. They were precious tokens of civilization offered to exhausted and homesick men, deep in the wilderness, hundreds of miles from any possibility of resupply. Native Americans had known how to grind corn meal for centuries, of course, but no wheat had ever been grown in America before the Columbian exchange. Crab apples were ubiquitous in the temperate zones of North America, but large domesticated apples of the kind we take for granted would have existed only as far west as St. Louis and the villages that clustered near the mouth of the Missouri River. Several hundred years before the journey of Lewis and Clark, pepper—now so common as to be wholly unremarkable—had been one of the catalysts for the discovery of North America. The humble Christmas meal at Fort Mandan was not quite, as Lewis later put it, "the repast that the hand of civilization"[71] might have prepared, but it was in its own way more impressive. It was a repast that the hand of civilization could carry more than 1,500 miles up the Missouri River under very unstable traveling conditions in a leaky vessel manned by almost fifty voraciously hungry young men. Even though Lewis and Clark were on the far edge of the known world on Christmas 1804, they had brought a few items from the known world with them. It could not have failed to hearten everyone who was present that day. The Lewis and Clark Expedition was a military mission, but it was also more than that. It was already a traveling community, and it would become—at certain times and in some limited respects—what even Lewis came to call "the best [of] families."[72]

At this point in the journey, there was still an abundance of alcohol. Gass wrote, "Captain Clarke … presented to each man a glass of brandy, and we hoisted the American flag in the garrison, and its first waving in fort Mandan was celebrated with another glass.—"[73] The fort was now complete, everyone was healthy, the Mandan and Hidatsa Indians were friendly, food was abundant, and the Corps of Discovery was wintering in a dry—if appallingly cold—climate. "The men then cleared out one of the rooms and commenced dancing,"[74] Gass wrote. It was a mild winter day on the northern Great Plains. The captains recorded that it was 15 degrees above zero Fahrenheit at sunrise, snow falling, but a balmy 20 degrees above at 4 P.M., no longer snowing but cloudy. Assuming that the wind was not fierce, this was a great winter day, not quite warm enough to hold the dance outside, but balmy enough to enable the men to wander about the Fort Mandan compound quite comfortably during the course of the day. Clark, for example, noted that some of the men "went out to hunt."[75] Two weeks earlier the temperature had been so cold that Clark did "not think it prudent to turn out to hunt in Such Cold weather, or at least untill our Consts. are prepared to under go this Climate."[76] *Consts.* = physical constitutions.

"At 10 o'clock," Gass reported, "we had another glass of brandy, and at 1 a gun was fired as a signal for dinner. At half past 2, another gun was fired, as a notice to assemble at the dance, which was continued in a jovial manner till 8 at night."[77]

Gass noted that the joviality of the dance was diminished by the absence of ladies. It was Gass who paused, at the end of the Fort Mandan winter, to tantalize his readers with an invocation of the conventions of epic romance. "[S]ome readers will perhaps expect," he wrote on April 5, 1805, that, "we ought to be prepared now, when we are about to renew our voyage, to give some account of the *fair sex* of the Missouri; and entertain them with narratives of feats of love as well as of arms."[78] Gass, or his editor David McKeehan, may have been thinking of the opening books of Vergil's *Aeneid*, in which the hero Aeneas almost forgets his mission and his destiny when he encounters the Carthaginian queen Dido, who is everything he *desires*, but not what he *needs*, in a woman. Gass made it clear that he could provide his readers such titillation if he wished to, but then retreated behind the high seriousness of the Enlightenment. "Though we could furnish a sufficient number of entertaining stories and pleasant anecdotes, we do not think it prudent to swell our Journal with them; as our views are directed to more useful information."[79] On Christmas, however, Gass lamented that the men were "without the presence of any females, except three squaws, wives to our interpreter, who took no other part than the amusement of looking on."[80] Whitehouse reported that the Indian women "took no part with us only to look on."[81] The three women were almost certainly Rene Jusseaume's Mandan wife, who later made the long journey to Washington, DC, to meet President Jefferson; and Toussaint Charbonneau's two wives, both Shoshone, one named Otter Woman and the other, of course, the famous Sacagawea. It is *amusing*, as Lewis might put it, to imagine this Christmas scene. One of the 12x14 foot rooms of Fort Mandan cleared out so that the men could dance. Somewhere in the corner of the room at least one of the fiddlers, probably Pierre Cruzatte. Whitehouse said that both fiddlers played, and though he did not mention them, he surely meant Cruzatte and George Gibson. He may have been exaggerating when he said the expedition had "Two Violins & plenty of Musicians."[82] When Bernard DeVoto later imagined this scene, he envisioned "the *voyageur* Cruzatte, a mighty waterman, who played this irrecoverable Christmas music on a fiddle, while the fires blazed and the north wind howled round the fort. Boating songs, probably, and minuets and carols that had crossed the Atlantic to New France and traveled the rivers for two centuries, to be sung never more incongruously than at the Mandan villages."[83]

It is hard to imagine that more than a fraction of the men could have crowded into the dance hall at any one time. The three Indian women must have been tucked away along one of the walls. Sacagawea was seven and a half months pregnant. Just what they thought of this holiday and alcohol-heightened conviviality, the white folks' *big medicine day*, is not recorded, but this simple tableau is one of those little known but priceless glimpses into the inner workings of the Lewis and Clark Expedition. "None of the natives came to the garrison this day; the commanding officers having requested they should not, which was strictly attended to,"[84] Gass wrote. John Ordway explained their request by way of one of the few religious references in the expedition's journals. "[T]he Savages did not Trouble us," he wrote, "as we had requested them not to come as it was a Great medician day with us."[85] Ordway's account ends with a sentence worthy of Charles Dickens: "[W]e enjoyed a merry cristmas dureing the day & evening untill nine oClock—all in peace & quietness."[86] Ordway emerges in the journals as a thoughtful and decent man, with an understated but clear sense of respect and filial piety.

Dickens, by the way, had not been born in 1805. He made his appearance in 1812, when John Ordway was trying to pick up the shattered pieces of his life in the wake of the gargantuan New Madrid earthquake.[87] The author of *A Christmas Carol* (1843) and the marvelous Christmas episode in the *Pickwick Papers* (1836–37) would develop a long and fascinating relationship with America. Dickens visited America twice, once from January 22 to June 7, 1842, and again from November 19, 1867, to April 22, 1868. On the second trip, Dickens ventured as far west as St. Louis. By then William Clark had been dead for twenty-nine years. Britain's greatest novelist did not like America or its brash and restless citizens.[88] "I do not know the American gentleman," Dickens once famously quipped. "God forgive me for putting two such words together."

Joseph Whitehouse insisted that the special issue of alcohol was brandy not whiskey. He reported that the day began at 7 A.M. with a volley of small arms and the "discharge of our Swivels."[89] At 1 P.M., "our Cannon was fir'd off, as a signal for dinner," and at 2:30 P.M. "we fired off our Cannon, and repaired to the Room to dance."[90] Lots of ordinance on the white folks' big medicine day. One wonders what the Mandan people concluded.

Such was Christmas 1804 at Fort Mandan. The journals of that day—written by Clark, John Ordway, Patrick Gass, and Joseph Whitehouse—are remarkable for what they mention, but even more remarkable for what they never mention. There is not a single reference in any journal to Meriwether Lewis. Clark said, "I was awakened before Day by a discharge of 3 platoons from the Party and the french ... ."[91] Not we, but I. "[T]he men merrily Disposed," Clark wrote, "I give them all a little Tafia."[92] No mention of the expedition's commander. Ordway reported that "our officers Gave the party a drink of Taffee," but he made no specific mention of Lewis. Gass was more precise: "Captain Clarke then presented to each man a glass of brandy."[93] Whitehouse concurred. In fact, Whitehouse implied that Clark emerged from the captains' quarters, but not his partner in discovery. "Captain Clark came out of his quarters, and presented a Glass of Brandy to each Man of our party." Later, "he presented them again with another Glass of brandy."[94]

Where was Lewis? Did he spend the day alone in his hut? Did he appear in the morning with Clark, but hold back while Clark administered the gift of spirits? Did Lewis attend the dance? Did he take part in the Christmas feast? Did he greet the men at any point in the day? Even if Lewis was present at some or all of these activities, it is significant that the lesser journal keepers mentioned only Clark, not the actual leader of the expedition. We would give a great deal for Lewis's account of Christmas Day 1804. We would give even more to anyone who could provide a full account of Christmas 1804 with particular attention to the social dynamics of the day, a description of the religious rituals that took place, if any, an account of the conversations that transpired between the three Indian women as they watched all of this unfold, a report of the whereabouts and disposition of Charbonneau, and a summary of the actions and words of Meriwether Lewis, if he emerged from his quarters at all. We have a pretty full account of Christmas Day 1804 at Fort Mandan, but the journals that we have increase, rather than quench, our hunger for an authentic understanding of what really unfolded within the walls of Fort Mandan—on that and on many other occasions.

CHRISTMAS 1805

The expedition spent Christmas 1805 at Fort Clatsop. As usual the men were engaged in construction right up to the eve of the holiday. On December 23 Clark reported, "Capt Lewis and my Self move into our hut today unfinished."[95] On Christmas Eve he wrote, "[M]en all employed in finishing their huts and moveing into them."[96] On Christmas Day Lewis and Clark were visited by a Clatsop leader by the name of Cuscalah, who "come up in a Canoe with his younger brother & 2 Squars."[97] Cuscalah wanted to trade. He gave the captains "each a mat and a parcel of roots," but later demanded two of the expedition's files by way of payment. The captains declined to make the trade and returned the mats and roots. Then Cuscalah offered Lewis and Clark a very unusual—even unique— Christmas gift. "[H]e then offered a woman to each of us which we also declined axcepting of, which displeased the whole party verry much— the female part appeared to be highly disgusted at our refuseing to axcept of their favours &c."[98] Clark's phrase, "whole party," one assumes, meant the visiting Clatsops. Joseph Field also provided the captains with a special gift on December 25, 1805. Clark wrote, "Jo Fields finish for Capt Lewis and my Self each a wide Slab hued to write on, I gave a handkerchief &c."[99] To facilitate their roles as the "writingest explorers of their time,"[100] Lewis and Clark each carried portable writing desks with them on the journey. Clark's was destroyed on September 15, 1805, in the Bitterroot Mountains, when, Clark wrote, "Several horses Sliped and roled down Steep hills which hurt them verry much The one which Carried my desk & Small trunk Turned over & roled down a mountain for 40 yards & lodged against a tree, broke the Desk the horse escaped and appeared but little hurt."[101]

On Christmas Day, the rest of the Corps of Discovery moved into their winter quarters. For some reason members of the expedition seemed to be in a special Christmas spirit at the far end of the American continent. More gifts were exchanged on Christmas 1805 than in the previous two years—or at least more were reported. Clark wrote, "I recved a present of a Fleeshe Hoserey vest draws & Socks of Capt Lewis, pr. Mockerson of Whitehouse, a Small Indian basket of Guterich, & 2 Doz weasels tales of the Squar of Shabono, & some black roots of the Indians."[102] This was quite a haul. Apparently Lewis was in a giving mood this year. Joseph Whitehouse was a skin dresser, so his gift to Clark of a pair of moccasins makes perfect sense. Goodrich must have traded something for the Indian basket—it seems clear that he did not make it himself. The most remarkable—and mysterious—gift was Sacagawea's twenty-four weasel's tails for Clark. Where did she obtain them? Was she hunting on the side? What did they signify? How did she know that white people exchanged gifts at Christmas? What did her husband Charbonneau think of this extraordinary gesture? It has long been alleged that among the Shoshone a gift of weasel's tails signified romantic attachment. This is almost certainly not true, at least in this instance. It may be that the gift signified a special gratitude toward William Clark, who had long since emerged as her protector, and possibly her friend, in a company of thirty sexually deprived young men. Lewis received no such gift. That alone has significance.

Lewis was not keeping a journal during this period, so we have no idea what gifts he received, if any. No weasel's tails. Neither Clark nor any other journal keeper mentioned gifts given to Captain Lewis. Possibly he received a lump of coal.

Christmas Day began with a discharge of small arms. "This morning at day," Clark wrote, "we were Saluted by all our party under our winders, a Shout and a Song."[103] It would be wonderful to know what song they sang under the *winders*. Whitehouse wrote, "We saluted our officers, by each of our party firing off his gun at day break in honor to the day (Christmass[)]."[104]

Moving into Fort Clatsop was itself a great Christmas gift in a place where it rains 144 inches per year. Ordway tried to put the best face on life at the holiday at Fort Clatsop, but his gloom could not quite be suppressed. "[R]ainy & wet. disagreeable weather,"[105] he wrote. No surprise there. "[W]e all moved in to our new Fort, which our officers name Fort Clotsop after the name of the Clotsop nation of Indians who live nearest to us."[106] Still, as was often the case, John Ordway captured the spirit of the occasion best. "[T]hey divided out the last of their tobacco," he wrote, "among the men that used and the rest they gave each a Silk hankerchief, as a Christmast gift, to keep us in remembrence of it as we have no ardent Spirits, but are all in good health which we esteem more than all the ardent Spirits in the world. we have nothing to eat but poore Elk meat and no Salt to Season that with but Still keep in good Spirits as we expect this to be the last winter that we will have to pass in this way."[107] Notice that Ordway here regarded alcohol as the civilizational baseline of Christmas celebration. Whitehouse wrote that non-tobacco users received "a handkerchief or some other article, in remembrance of Christmass."[108] Unfortunately, he did not specify what the other articles were.

Ordway did not specify which men used tobacco and which were the recipients of handkerchiefs instead. That would be just the kind of information modern readers clutch in their desperation to humanize and differentiate the members of the expedition. Ordway, apparently using his official voice, did not even let the reader know which side of the tobacco divide he occupied. While Lewis on January 1, 1806, found himself merely longing for New Year's 1807, Ordway here seems to rule out any further sojourns in the wilderness: "the last winter that we will have to pass in this way." After the expedition, Ordway ventured to Washington, DC, with Lewis, then visited his family in New Hampshire. Thereafter, he settled down on his land grant in Missouri at New Madrid, acquired a wife and a fair amount of property, and never again ventured into the American wilderness.[109]

Joseph Whitehouse echoed Ordway's sentiment, writing that, "We had no ardent spirit of any kind among us; but are mostly in good health, A blessing, which we esteem more, than all the luxuries this life can afford."[110] Then Whitehouse provided one of the handful of religious references in the journals of Lewis and Clark: "[T]he party are all thankful to the Supreme Being, for his goodness towards us.— hoping he will preserve us in the same, & enable us to return to the United States again in safety."[111] *Supreme Being* was sufficiently ecumenical and deistic to pass muster in an expedition envisioned by Thomas Jefferson. Note that Whitehouse made no reference to the Christ. Whitehouse also reported, "We found our huts comfortable, excepting smoaking a little."[112]

Patrick Gass made no reference to Christmas at Fort Clatsop.

Clark must have liked the gifts he received, but he was unhappy with the Christmas dinner. I have already argued (see above, page 130) that food really mattered to Clark, particularly on special occasions. "Our Diner to day Consisted of pore Elk boiled, Spilt fish & Some roots, a bad Christmass diner,"[113] he wrote with unusual asperity. Clark should have listened to Ordway. Whitehouse wrote, more positively, "We have at present nothing to eat but lean Elk meat & that without Salt, but the whole of our party are content with this fare."[114] Well, almost everyone.

THE FOURTH OF JULY

Lewis and Clark spent three Independence days in the wilderness. The first occurred in today's Kansas, the second and third in today's Montana. On July 4, 1804, the expedition camped near Independence Creek on the Atchison-Doniphan county line in northeastern Kansas. Clark reported that the men of the expedition "ussered in the day by a discharge of one shot from our Bow piece."[115] Ordway said there were two firings of the bow piece, one in the morning and one in the evening, "for Independance of the U. S."[116] Clark wrote, "[W]e Closed the [day] by a Discharge from our bow piece, an extra Gill of whiskey."[117] The expedition made just fifteen miles on July 4.

It was a typically scorching American Fourth of July. Whitehouse, who often provides details not recorded by any of the other journal keepers, noted that "the day mighty hot when we went to toe the Sand [s]Calded Our [feet] Some fled from the Rope   had to put on Our Mockisons."[118] Thus in a few broken phrases, Whitehouse opened a wonderful window on the day.

Ordway wrote, "[W]e passed a Creek on the South Side about 15 yards wide. comes out of the large prarie, and as it has no name & as it is the 4 of July, Capts. name it Independence Creek   we fired our Bow piece this morning & one in the evening for Independence of the U.S."[119] The bow piece was probably one of the expedition's blunderbusses, not the swivel cannon that was given to the Hidatsa on the return journey. Perhaps because he was moved by patriotism, Ordway added that "we camped in the plans   one of the most beautiful places I ever Saw in my life, open and beautifully Diversified with hills & vallies all presenting themselves to the River."[120]

The characteristically understated Clark was so filled with pride in the American republic or so struck by the beauty of the tall-grass plains of America that he wrote one of his loftiest and most exquisite journal entries:

> The Plains of this countrey are covered with a Leek Green Grass, well calculated for the sweetest and most norushing hay —interspersed with Cops [copses] of trees, Spreding their lofty branchs over Pools Springs or Brooks of fine water. Groops of Shrubs covered with the most delicious froot is to be seen in every direction, and nature appears to have exerted herself to butify the Senery by the variety of flours… Delicately and highly flavered raised above the Grass, which Strikes & profumes the Sensation, and amuses the mind   throws it into Conjecterng the cause of So magnificent a Senerey… in a Country thus Situated far removed from the Sivilised world to be enjoyed by nothing but the Buffalo Elk Deer & Bear in which it abounds &… Savage Indians.[121]

When he came to write the final, more polished version of his journal for July 4, 1804, Clark suppressed this lovely reverie. *Leek Green Grass*—what an extraordinary phrase. Such was the difference between William Clark and Meriwether Lewis. The sort of prose that Lewis constantly strained to produce seemed to Clark—on reflection—perhaps a little too unguarded, a little too poetic, a little too personal and revealing. On the plains of eastern

Kansas, Clark wrote a passage worthy of the *Lyrical Ballads* of William Wordsworth—and then he canceled it.[122] It is at least possible that Lewis wrote the passage on which Clark's journal entry is based. *Amuses the mind* is a Lewis-like phrase.

Of this scene David Peck has asked, "Was it the Garden of Eden or the pristine American wilderness?"[123] Whichever it was, there was a serpent in paradise. The Fourth of July 1804 was not a great day for Joseph Field, one of the Nine Young Men from Kentucky. He was bitten by a rattlesnake. Gass said Field "got snake bitten but not dangerously."[124] Sergeant Floyd reported that "a Snake Bit Jo. Fieldes on the Side of the foot which Sweled much   apply Barks to."[125] Clark reported that it was Lewis who treated Field: "Jos: Fields got bit by a Snake, which was quickly doctered with Bark by Cap Lewis.[126] The *Bark* was a poultice of Peruvian bark, which contains quinine. David Peck argues that the bark "probably had no beneficial pharmacologic effect at all. Quinine and the other alkaloids in the bark act against the malarial *Plasmodium*, but not against rattlesnake venom."[127] Later in his entry, Floyd wrote, "[T]he Last mentioned prarie I call Jo. Fieldes Snake prarie."[128] Floyd's only reference to Independence Day was about naming the West: "[A]s the Creek has no name and this Day is the 4th of July we name this Independance."[129] Ordway reported that the incident occurred "under the hills near the praries on the South Side."[130]

Fortunately for historians, Clark took time on July 4, 1804, to make a list of the French engages who were helping move the boats up the Missouri River. Athough his census was a little imprecise, it has become an essential historical document. The thirty-three members of the so-called *permanent party* are well known. The engages, or temporary watermen whose job it was to propel the thirty tons of baggage to the Upper Missouri River, are less well known—almost never mentioned in the expedition's journals, considered insufficiently important to pay attention to beyond their capacity to move the boats. Clark called his roster, "The names of the french Ingishees, or Hirelens," by which he meant French engages and hirelings. The word *hirelings* did not have quite the same negative connotation it bears today. The list included *Battist de Shone, Joseph Le bartee, Lasoness, Paul Preemau, Chalo, E. Cann, Roie, Charlo Cougee, J: Le bartee, Rivee, Pieter Crousatt half Indian, and William La Beice Mallat,*[131] by which Clark appears to mean Jean-Baptiste DesChamps, La Liberte, Jean Baptiste Le Jeunesse, Paul Primeau, E. Cann, Peter Roi, Charles Caugee, Francois Rivet, Pierre Cruzatte, and Francois Labiche.[132] Such immortality as most of these Frenchmen possess comes essentially from this imperfect document. They rowed their hearts out. Most of them are utterly forgotten. In the annals of immortality, expedition non-entities like John Thompson and Peter Weiser have them beat.

JULY 4, 1805

On the Fourth of July 1805, Meriwether Lewis was too worried about his iron-framed boat to think much about American independence. By now the collapsible, eight-section, thirty-two-foot-long frame he had had made to his specifications at Harpers Ferry, Virginia, was re-assembled and covered with twenty-eight elkskins and four buffalo hides. Fully assembled, the iron frame weighed merely 176 pounds, and yet Lewis reckoned that it would be capable of carrying four tons of baggage. He had reckoned he'd be able to sew the hides so tightly that they would be watertight, or that he'd find suitable pitch or tar in the wilderness of today's Montana. He was wrong. The boat project consumed several weeks of expedition time, time that *might* have been spent crafting dugout canoes from cottonwood trees, which is what Clark and eight of the expedition's men wound up doing anyway, beginning on July 10.

On July 4, Lewis wrote, "[N]o appearance of tar yet and I am now confident that we shall not be able to obtain any; a serious misfortune. I employed a number of hands on the boat today and by 4 P.M. in the evening completed her except the most difficult part of the work that of making her seams secure. I had her turned up and some small fires kindled underneath to dry her."[133] On July 5, Lewis attempted to seal the boat's seams with a field compound of charcoal, beeswax, and buffalo tallow. "[T]he stitches," he wrote, "begin to gape very much since she has began to dry."[134] On July 9, Lewis launched the *Experiment,* as he called his pet portable watercraft. "[S]he lay like a perfect cork on the water," he said in momentary triumph. "[L]ate in the evening … we discovered that a greater part of the composition had seperated from the skins and left the seams of the boat exposed to the water and she leaked in such manner that she would not answer. I need not add that this circumstance mortifyed me not a little."[135] Lewis was embarrassed, frustrated, but philosophical. "[T]o make any further experiments in our present situation seemed to me madness … I therefore relinquished all further hope of my favorite boat and ordered… to take her in pieces tomorrow and deposit the iron fraim at this place."[136] If the boat had remained a perfect cork, Lewis would have been regarded by the rest of the men as an eccentric genius. Because it sank ignominiously, he was probably the butt of behind-the-scenes jibes and derision.

On the Fourth of July 1805 Lewis also determined *not* "to dispatch a canoe with a part of our men to St. Louis as we had intended early in the spring."[137] In the letter he wrote to President Jefferson at the end of the Fort Mandan winter, Lewis wrote, "I shall dispatch a canoe with three, perhaps four persons, from the extreem navigable point of the Missouri, or the portage betwen this river, and the Columbia river, as either may first happen."[138]

In explaining this change of plans in his journal, Lewis noted that the expedition had not yet made contact with the Shoshone and therefore could not know "whether to calculate on their friendship or hostility or friendship."[139] It would be important, therefore, to keep the expedition at full strength until the disposition of the important Shoshone could be determined. Then Lewis reverted to a pattern of thought that ran deep in his character. "[W]e fear also that such a measure might possibly discourage those who would in such case remain, and might possibly hazzard the fate of the expedition."[140] This was Meriwether Lewis.

Lewis spent some time in his July 4 journal trying to make sense of the mysterious booming sounds expedition members had been hearing in the vicinity of the Great Falls. Then he closed his account of the day with one of the most delightful passages in the journals:

> [O]ur work being at an end this evening, we gave the men a drink of sperits, it being the last of our stock, and some of them appeared a little sensible of it's effects   the fiddle was plyed and they danced very merrily untill 9 in the evening when a heavy shower of rain put an end to that part of the amusement tho' they continued their mirth with songs and festive jokes and were extreemly merry untill late at night.   we had a very comfortable dinner, of bacon, beans, suit dumplings & buffaloe beaf &c.   in short we had no just cause to covet the sumptuous feasts of our countrymen on this day.— one Elk and a beaver were all that was killed by the hunters today; the buffaloe seem to have withdrawn themselves from this neighbourhood; tho the men inform us that they are still abundant about the falls.—[141]

Baked beans on the Fourth of July in the heart of Montana. What could be more appropriate?

Clark made no mention of Independence Day 1805, but he wrote an account of the dance:

> A fine morning, a heavy dew last night, all hands employed in Completeing the leather boat, gave the Party a dram which made Several verry lively, a black Cloud came up from the S. W, and rained a fiew drops   I employ my Self drawing a Copy of the river to be left at this place for fear of Some accident in advance, I have left buried below the falls a Map of the Countrey below Fort Mandan with Sundery private papers   the party amused themselves danceing untill late when a Shower of rain broke up the amusement, all lively and Chearfull, one Elk and a beaver kill'd to day.[142]

It would be interesting to know what the private papers recorded. It is striking that on this occasion Clark did not describe the special meal that was prepared in honor of the Fourth of July. Probably he was so focused on the map he was drawing for deposit in the Upper Portage Camp cache that he did not have time to relax. His account of the convivialities of the day was cursory and, for once, detached. Nor did he mention that the whiskey had now all been consumed. As the more attentive of the two leaders to the lives and needs of the enlisted men, one would have expected Clark to make a note of the end of the whiskey supply in his journal. It is possible that Clark was annoyed with Lewis for the time he was wasting trying to perfect his iron-framed boat. Ever the pragmatist, Clark probably reckoned that the Corps of Discovery could just as easily have made boats the old-fashioned way, from the cottonwood trees in the vicinity. We cannot be sure. What is certain is that Lewis seems to have been in a much better mood on July 4, 1805, than his partner in discovery, who was uncharacteristically indifferent to the national holiday, if his journal is a fair reflection of his state of mind.

With his characteristic sense of decency and humility, Ordway wrote, "[I]t being the 4th of Independence we drank the last of our ardent Spirits except a little reserved for Sickness. the fiddle put in order and the party amused themselves dancing all the evening untill about 10 oClock in a Sivel & jovil manner. late in the evening we had a light Shower of rain but did not last long."[143]

Both of Whitehouse's accounts of the day are delightful. In the first version, he wrote, "[T]owards evening our officers gave the party the last of the ardent Spirits except a little reserved for Sickness. we all amused ourselved dancing untill 10 oClock in the evening. at which time we had a light Shower of rain, the party all in good Spirits keeping up the 4th of July &c. as Independence."[144] In the second he changed the wording a little. "Towards evening Our officers gave the party the last of the ardent Spirit that we had (excepting a little that they reserved for sickness)— We amused ourselves with frolicking, dancing &ca. untill 9 o'Clock P.M. in honor of the day."

It was nothing more than a lucky coincidence (lucky for us, not for the men) that the expedition ran out of whiskey on the Fourth of July, at the center of its transcontinental journey, in today's Montana, at the Great Falls of the Missouri River, "this truly magnifficent and sublimely grand object, which has from the commencement of time been concealed from the view of civilized man."[145] The whiskey supply may just as well have run dry on the fourth of June or the fourth of August. Somehow the story takes on deeper significance thanks to the coincidence. It is possible that the captains rationed the whiskey in the weeks leading up to July 4, 1805, so that they could give the men a special treat on that occasion.

July 4, 1806

The captains split up on July 3, 1806. Clark with twenty-two others (including Sacagawea and Jean Baptiste Charbonneau) was to approach the headwaters of the Yellowstone River, build canoes at the point of navigability, and float down the Yellowstone to its confluence with the Missouri. Lewis, with nine others, would return to the Great Falls, to the headwaters of the Marias, and then float down the Missouri to the confluence with the Yellowstone. The fact that the captains did not linger one more day at Travelers' Rest to celebrate the nation's thirtieth birthday together indicates what a hurry they were in to get home in the 1806 traveling season. One more day at Travelers' Rest would not have detained the expedition in any meaningful sense, but everyone was out of patience with the wilderness, not to mention out of tobacco and whiskey, and the divided strands of the expedition chose just to proceed on with all due speed.

Meriwether Lewis spent the Fourth of July 1806 in Missoula, Montana. He wrote a long and fascinating journal entry for July 4, 1806, but he did not mention Thomas Jefferson or America's thirtieth birthday in any way. Lewis devoted part of his journal entry to trying to sort out "the most direct & practicable" trail through the Bitterroot Mountains. He was now certain that the best route crossed the Bitterroot Mountains between today's Lewiston, Idaho, and Missoula, Montana, and that the correct way to get from Missoula to the Great Falls was over what is now known as Lewis and Clark Pass. He was about to make his way to the Great Falls by way of that previously unexplored route, which his Nez Perce guides had assured him was a good one. Lewis's reflections on "the most direct & practicable water communication across this continent for the purposes of commerce"[146] might have been expected to bring his patron Jefferson to mind, but such sentiment as Lewis had in reserve on July 4, 1806, was offered to his young Nez Perce guides. He wrote, "[T]hese affectionate people our guides betrayed every emmotion of unfeigned regret at seperating from us; they said that they were confidint that the Pahkees, (the appellation they give the Minnetares) would cut us off."[147]

As usual, Clark was the more likely to celebrate. After describing the forward progress of the day, he wrote, "This being the day of the decleration of Independence of the United States and a Day commonly Scelebrated by my Country I had every disposition to Selebrate this day and therefore halted early and partook of a Sumptious Dinner of a fat Saddle of Venison and Mush of Cows (roots)."[148] By this time in the story of the expedition, it is possible to conclude that Clark's favorite meal, at least his favorite camp meal, was "a fat Saddle of Venison," the same fare he ordered up for himself on August 1, 1804, back at the Council Bluffs in Nebraska. William Clark lived to celebrate the Fourth of July thirty-one more times in the course of his long and successful life. It is certain that he never again dined on cous roots (*Lomatium cous*). His friend Lewis apparently did not have a "disposition to Selebrate" the Fourth of July 1806. Beans and buffalo were no longer sufficient to a man who had dined regularly with the Francophile Jefferson.

Ordway and Gass both wrote journal entries for July 4, 1806. They were both traveling with the Lewis party. Neither of them mentioned the anniversary of American independence.

NEW YEAR'S

Things got a little wild on New Year's Eve at Camp Wood. Captain Clark grimly noted, in a short journal entry, that he "Issued certain & prohibited a Certain Ramey from Selling Liquor to the Party."[149] Why? In the same short journal entry, Clark wrote, "Colter Willard Leakens Hall & Colllins Drunk." Clark's concern was probably not the intoxication, though at that phase of the expedition he could not know what sorts of pranks or worse intoxicated raw recruits might succumb to, but rather the existence of an independent liquor supply that he, as the commanding officer, could not control the distribution of. Matthew Ramey took up residence in the St. Louis area in 1803, Gary Moulton notes.[150] He must have operated a still near enough Camp Wood to be in a position to haul whiskey to the fort. Clark apparently did not discipline the men in question for their intoxication. Probably he decided that interdicting the supply would effectively solve the problem. In this he was wrong. The commanders did not finally get complete control of the consumption of liquor until they were well up-river from the stills in the St. Louis area, and until after the courts-martial of Collins and Hall on June 29, 1804, when the rest of the enlisted men communicated in no uncertain terms to Hall, Collins, and other potential offenders that they would not tolerate incursions into a supply of whiskey that everyone knew would not make it all the way to the Pacific Ocean. In the June 29 incident, Collins, who was on guard duty at the time, committed the great offense by "getting drunk on his post this morning out of whiskey put under his Charge as a Sentinel." Hall was accused of "takeing whiskey out of a Keg this morning which whiskey was Stored on the Bank."[151] Found guilty by a jury of five peers—Pryor, Colter, Newman, Gass, and Thompson—Collins was sentenced to "recive *one hundred Lashes on his bear Back*, and Hall received 50 lashes."[152]

On New Year's Day 1804 Clark wrote that "a woman Come forward wishing to wash" the expedition's laundry.[153] She was never named or described, but she offered to wash the expedition's laundry "and doe Such things as may be necessary for the Detachmt,"[154] as Clark put it. Whether this was a straightforward offer of menial services or an offer of other camp consolations is not known.

New Year's proved to be a very busy day at Camp Wood, characterized more by commerce than by holiday conviviality. Not only did the prospective washer woman make her first appearance, but country marksmen brought sugar to trade. Those who were sober enough participated in the expedition's first shooting match with the locals. Clark reported that while George Gibson, who thus made his first appearance in the journals, was the best of the expedition's marksmen that day, it was the country folk who won the dollar coin that Clark, like Ahab, offered up for the winners. A man named J. Vaughan offered to supply the expedition's contractor with beef. Three other men, Thomas Lisbet and two others, offered to sell the expedition pork. Somehow this transaction would involve a man named Patrick Heneberry, who had, Clark was told, "traveled far to the north, & Visited the Mandols on Missouris, a quiet people."[155] Clark did not inform the reader whether he accepted any or all of these offers, though he did buy a quantity of sugar on January 1, 1804. Later journal entries indicate that the expedition bought an enormous quantity of pork in the course of the winter, which the men processed and stored in forty-five kegs before the expedition departed for the hog-less interior on May 14, 1804. Whether Lisbet and his colleagues provided that pork is not known.

New Year's mirth and misrule continued. In a severe shorthand, Clark reported, "R & Ws. Drunk."[156] Clark seldom wasted words, but on this occasion he provided too little information for historians of the expedition to identify the merry makers. R could be Moses Reed or it could be the Robertson mentioned on December 26. Ws. could be Peter Weiser or Richard Windsor or, for that matter, Joseph Whitehouse.

Every military expedition attracts camp followers. But once Lewis and Clark got underway in the spring, they soon passed beyond the reach of white purveyors of sustenance and mischief on the Missouri River. Their last known purchase of locally produced commodities came on May 23, 1804, at a little settlement above today's Tavern Creek, Missouri. The Field brothers were sent out to purchase an unknown quantity of corn and butter from the local farmers. After that, the expedition was on its own.

New Year's 1805

The temperature at Fort Mandan on January 1, 1805, was 18 degrees above zero at sunrise and 34 above at 4 P.M. That's a fabulous January day in North Dakota. It was warm enough that there was even a little rain in the course of the day. After sunset, it turned to snow and continued, Clark wrote, "the greater part of the night."[157] According to Gass, Lewis actually surfaced on New Year's Day. "Two shot were fired from this swivel, followed by a round of small arms, to welcome the New Year," he wrote.

That was standard holiday fare. "Captain Lewis then gave each a glass of good old whiskey; and a short time after another was given by Captain Clarke."[158] Precisely what Glass meant by this reference is unclear. Did the captains really have a stash of vintage whiskey tucked into their baggage? Whitehouse called the spirits "old ardent Spirits."[159] It may be that Lewis was following Jefferson in his preference for New Year's (a merely random day on the calendar) over a Christian saint's day for a being who may never actually have existed at all, and who certainly wasn't born on Christmas. It is impossible to exaggerate how deeply influential Jefferson was on the people he invited into his inner circle.

At this point things started to get interesting. According to Gass, "About 11 o'clock one of the interpreters and half of our people, went up, at the request of the natives, to the village, to begin the dance."[160] Whitehouse said the invitation came from the chiefs of the village, who had a "desire to see our manner of dancing."[161] Perhaps some account of the Christmas dance at Fort Mandan had gotten back to Mituntanka, and the cultural leadership of the Mandan wanted to see the bizarre dance moves of the Wasichus. Gass wrote that the advance party "were followed some time after by Captain Clarke, and three more men. The day was warm and pleasant. Captain Lewis in the afternoon issued another glass of whiskey; and at night Capt Clarke and part of the men returned from the village."[162] The phrase that follows, "the rest remained all night," embodies a world of sexual possibility.

Ordway indicated that the Fort Mandan band consisted of "a fiddle & a Tambereen & a Sounden horn."[163] The band announced its arrival by firing a round with its rifles, then making music, then firing another round. Then it marched to the center of Mituntanka, fired yet another round, and "commenced dancing." Sounds like a typical Anglo-American dance invasion. Christmas had been rather solemn, but New Year's, true to tradition, was a whoop and a holler. In the village center "a frenchman," almost certainly expedition engagé Francois Rivet, "danced on his head and all danced round him for a Short time."[164] This, the Jeffersonian equivalent of a break dance, must have been quite a spectacle. After the fancy dancing, the Clark party "went in to a lodge & danced a while, which pleased them verry much."[165] Whitehouse alone noted that "the Natives much admir'd, frequently signifying their approbation by a Whoop they gave."[166] The grateful Mandans responded to this performance by throwing a feast, "victules from different lodges & of different kinds of diet,"[167] in Ordway's words.

Clark provided a somewhat different narrative. "[W]e Suffered 16 men with their musick to visit the 1st Village for the purpose of Danceing, by as they Said the perticular request of the Chiefs of that village,"[168] he wrote. The men must have departed Fort Mandan for Mituntanka early, for at 11 A.M. Clark followed, not to dance, he made certain to note, but "to alay

Some little miss understanding which had taken place thro jelloucy and mortification as to our treatment towards them."[169] For all of his protestation of diplomatic high mindedness, Clark wound up attending the dance. "I found them much pleased at the Danceing of our men, I ordered my black Servent to Dance which amused the Croud verry much, and Some what astonished them, that So large a man Should be active &c. &."[170] Think of this scene. A huge dancing black man—the first ever seen in the history of the Mandan people—who told the Mandan that he was a wild creature, like a bear, captured and tamed by William Clark. Clark visited some of the principal men of the Mandan village "except two, whome I heard had made Some expressions not favourable towards us, in Compareing us with the traders from the north."[171] The traders of the north were François-Antoine Larocque and Charles McKenzie, employees of the North West Company, both of whom were quick to record any anti-American sentiment they picked up among their Mandan and Hidatsa hosts. Clark was assured that any such criticism had been offered "in just and lafture,"[172] i.e., in jest and laughter. Clark noted that all but six of the men returned to Fort Mandan that night. Happy New Year.

Lewis did not venture over to Mituntanka for these festivities. But he was certainly in a better mood than at Christmas, if his issue of at least two glasses of whiskey, one of them "old ardent Spirits," is any indication. Not to mention his *appearance* among the men. Probably Lewis remained at Fort Mandan as a security measure, sending no more than half of the company to the villages; and also to serve as host to Posecopsahe, the principal chief of all the Mandans, who "with his family," Clark wrote, "visited us to day."[173] It would be instructive to have Lewis's account of January 1–2, 1805. We have no description by Lewis of the village world of the Mandan or Hidatsa. Even when he went on a formal diplomatic visit to the villages, on November 25–26, 1804, Lewis provided no surviving account of his mission.

New Year's 1806

The men spent New Year's Eve in 1805 digging latrines at Fort Clatsop. The honeymoon was over.

Lewis's New Year's Day meditation in 1806 is one of the most fascinating entries in his remarkable journal. That he was writing at all is something of a surprise. He had gone silent after the expedition threaded its way through the Bitterroot Mountains. Probably the self-punishing Captain Lewis made resuming his journal his primary New Year's resolution. David Nicandri has written, "Undoubtedly the most significant development to occur at Fort Clatsop was the moment Meriwether Lewis picked up the pen and began a comprehensive set of journal entries commencing 1 January 1806. ... The timing of Lewis's resumption of literary and scientific duty smacks of a New Year's Resolution. He offers no retrospective glance other than merely to Christmas the previous week."[174] Lewis's New Year's entry is worth quoting extensively:

> This morning I was awoke at an early hour by the discharge of a volley of small arms, which were fired by our party in front of our quarters to usher in the new year; this was the only mark of rispect which we had it in our power to pay this celebrated day. our repast of this day tho' better than that of Christmass, consisted principally in the anticipation of the 1st day of January 1807, when in the bosom of our friends we hope to participate in the mirth and hilarity of the day, and when with the zest given by the recollection of the present, we shall completely, both mentally and corporally, enjoy the repast which the hand of civilization has prepared for us. at present we were content with eating our boiled Elk and wappetoe, and solacing our thirst with our only beverage *pure water*. two of our hunters who set out this morning returned in the evening having killed two bucks elk; they presented Capt. Clark and myself each a marrow-bone and tonge, on which we suped. visited today by a few of the Clotsops who brought some roots and burries for the purpose of trading with us[175]

Lewis was a great writer. He alone of the men of the expedition had the capacity to write with literary flair, to place his journal entries in a larger literary and historical context, to employ figurative language and rhetorical flourishes, and to see the world metaphorically. Here he writes a kind of sweetly melancholy parody of a New Year's entry. There is a fair amount of self-pity here, but there is also a clear sense of humor and a certain satisfaction in self-pity. After the understatement that "the only mark of rispect we had it in our power to pay this celebrated day" was a volley of small arms, Lewis appeared to be settling into a description of his New Year's meal, but, by way of metaphor, indicated that the meal consisted not so much of food as of the imagination of food—next year, "in the bosom of our friends."

Lewis was clearly homesick. The high water mark of his fascination with metamorphosing into a *perfect Indian* had occurred on August 16, 1805, among the Shoshone. Undoubtedly, Lewis had counted on meeting a trade ship at the mouth of the Columbia, from which—slapping down his universal letter of credit—he would certainly have obtained new civilized clothing had it been available, not to mention such other habiliments and comforts as "the hand of civilization" had prepared for him. By now his primitive existence in the skins of quadrupeds was no longer a compelling novelty but a kind of dreary imprisonment. It was one thing to be in a place like the Shoshone village or at the Great Falls where there was not a chance of meeting fellow white people. It was quite another to be so tantalizingly close to possible contact with fellow civilized beings, indeed civilized beings carrying trade goods, and *not* make that contact. Lewis was not just lonely and homesick on New Year's Day 1806. He was lonely, homesick, bankrupt, and a very, very long way from home. From a historian's point of view, it is both fortunate and unfortunate that the expedition met no trade ship in Baker Bay. It would be utterly fascinating to see the list of things the captains sought to purchase from visiting traders, and in what order of priority. It would tell us a great deal about the material culture of the Lewis and Clark Expedition, and it would reveal a great deal about everyone's state of mind in the winter of 1805–06, particularly the mind of the expedition's commanding officer. Because the expedition could not be resupplied, the captains were forced to exhibit a fascinating, even heroic, measure of resourcefulness on the return journey. The destitution of the expedition as it began its return journey on March 23, 1806, and the remarkable ways in which the Corps of Discovery made do with what little they had left, constitutes one of the principal ways in which the adventure deserves the title *American epic*.

Lewis spent January 1, 1806, anticipating "the 1st day of January 1807, when in the bosom of our friends we hope to participate in the mirth and hilarity of the day." It would be interesting to know precisely what he had in mind. We know that he spent that imagined day, January 1, 1807, at the White House in the bosom of America's most elegant man, whose repasts were justly celebrated and universally envied. The Lewis party, including the Mandan leader Sheheke-shote, arrived in the national capital on December 28, 1806. "Never did a similar event excite more joy through the United States," an observer wrote. "The humblest of its citizens had taken a lively interest in the issue of the journey and looked forward with impatience for the information it would furnish."[176]

Sheheke-shote had an audience with President Jefferson on December 30, 1806. Jefferson told the Mandan leader that the white people of the United States were now as aboriginal as American Indians: "My friends and children, we are descended from the old nations which live beyond the great water, but we and our forefathers have been so long here that we seem like you to have grown out of this land. We consider ourselves no longer of the old nations beyond the great water, but as united in one family with our red brethren here."[177] Jefferson explained that the French, Spanish, and English were retreating from the North American continent "never more to return to it." He assured Sheheke-shote, "We are now your fathers; and you shall not lose by the change." He thanked the Mandan people for the hospitality they had shown to Clark and "our beloved man, Captain Lewis, one of my own family." Then, reaching his rhetorical stride and slipping into what one critic of his Indian policies has called Jefferson's *Indian baby talk*, he said: "My children, you are come from the other side of our great island, from where the sun sets, to see your new friends at the sun rising. You have now arrived where the waters are constantly rising and falling every day, but you are still distant from the sea. I very much desire that you should not stop here, but go and see your brethren as far as the edge of the great water."[178] He urged Sheheke-shote and his party to visit Baltimore, Philadelphia, and New York, as long as they had come this far. And they did.

At Jefferson's annual New Year's reception at the White House, Sheheke-shote and Meriwether Lewis were the guests of honor. Although we have no precise record of the "repast" that the president offered his guests that afternoon, it was undoubtedly sumptuous—arguably better than spoiled elk and wappato roots—and the wines, French, probably from Bordeaux, were assuredly exquisite—a profound improvement on Fort Clatsop's "only beverage *pure water*." Did Lewis enjoy the reception? Did he feel *mirth* and *hilarity* on January 1, 1807? Did he enjoy, both mentally and corporally, the repast which the hand of civilization prepared for him? We have no way of knowing. What did he think about that afternoon? More to the point, what did he think about when the party ended and he was left alone with his experience?

Full of boiled elk and wappato, Lewis wrote out a long security protocol for life at Fort Clatsop on January 1, 1806. The holidays were over, construction of the fort was complete, and it was time to establish order for the couple of months the expedition must now remain on the Pacific coast before turning for home. Lewis's orders reveal a deep spiritual weariness:

> The Commanding Officers require and charge the Garrison to treat the natives in a friendly manner; nor will they be permitted at any time, to abuse, assault or strike them; unless such abuse assault or stroke be first given by the natives.   nevertheless it shall be right for any individual, in a peaceable manner, to refuse admittance to, or put out of his room, any native who may become troublesome to him; and should such native refuse to go when requested, or attempt to enter their rooms after being forbidden to do so; it shall be the duty of the Sergeant of the guard on information of the same, to put such native out of the fort and see that he is not again admitted during that day unless specially permitted; and the Sergeant of the guard may for this purpose imploy such coercive measures (not extending to the taking of life) as shall at his discretion be deemed necessary to effect the same.[179]

On New Year's Day 1806 Ordway merely reported, "The party Saluted our officers at day break this morning by firing at their quarters as a remembrance of the new year."[180] Ordway's emphasis was on the captains. Gass wrote, "The year commenced with a wet day; but the weather still continues warm; and the ticks, flies and other insects are in abundance, which appears to us very extraordinary at this season of the year, in a latitude so far north. Two hunters went out this morning. We gave our Fortification the name of Fort Clatsop."[181] Everyone was now remembering the dry, bugless, subarctic weather at Fort Mandan with a nostalgic (and ironic) fondness. Whitehouse's January 1, 1806, journal entry expressed his amazement that the climate at Fort Clatsop was so much milder than that of Fort Mandan. "Several Indians came to the fort on a visit," he wrote. "They were entirely naked, excepting a breech Cloth which they wore & Skins thrown over their Shoulders. This is the manner which the Natives in general go cloathed. The Winters here are not very Cold, & the ground has not as yet been cover'd with Snow this Winter."[182]

Clark's journal entry for January 1, 1806, was entirely unadorned. "This morning at Day we wer Saluted from the party without, wishing us a 'hapy new year' a Shout and discharge of their arms— no Indians to be Seen this morning—."[183] Clark did not expend any ink longing for home or anticipating "the 1st day of January 1807." It was not his style to write reflective or philosophical journal entries or to write purple prose. This is fortunate. If both captains had been given to literary flights, the result would probably be ponderous, even oppressive. Clark's basic English, if so it can be styled, is a welcome complement to Lewis's pretentiousness. Clark is Sancho Panza to Lewis's Quixote.

We are the beneficiaries.

Chapter IV "Damn you":

Lewis and Clark

at the Confluence

On July 3, 1806, the Lewis and Clark expedition split up. The thirty-three permanent members of the Corps of Discovery had constituted a single exploring party from April 7, 1805, until July 3, two years, two months, and two days into the expedition, at the wilderness heart of the American continent, the day before America's thirtieth birthday. Now, according to plans worked out as far back as Fort Clatsop, the captains separated, each with a contingent of the men, and Clark traveling also with the Charbonneau family—Toussaint, Sacagawea, and Jean Baptiste. How long they would be apart was unknowable.

The plan was to reunite sometime later in the summer, or perhaps in the fall, at the confluence of the Missouri and Yellowstone Rivers southwest of today's Williston, North Dakota. Whoever got there first would wait for the other traveling party. When the strands of expedition had successfully converged at the confluence, the Lewis *and* Clark Expedition would continue as a unit to the Hidatsa and Mandan villages, and then float downstream to St. Louis.

There was no plan B.

The sum total of the rendezvous plan—at least as outlined in the extant journals of the expedition—reads as follows: "Cap. C ... will build a canoe and decend the Yellowstone river with Charbono the indian woman, his servant York and five others to the missouri where should he arrive first he will wait my arrival."[1] That's it. That's a full account of the rendezvous plan written by the commander of the expedition, Meriwether Lewis, on July 1, 1806, at Travelers' Rest. And then: "[T]hese arrangements being made the party were informed of our design and prepared themselves accordingly."[2] Not only was there no plan B, but there was no way whatsoever to cross-communicate once the separation occurred at the western edge of today's Montana at the beginning of July.

Undoubtedly, there was some tacit understanding that if one of the two parties arrived at the confluence and waited, and the other party did not reach the rendezvous within some reasonable framework of time, the survivors (or perhaps just the less-delayed party) would reluctantly but resolutely make their way to St. Louis to regroup, learn what it could about up-river events, and perhaps mount a search-and-rescue party. If this understanding existed, however, the journals are entirely silent about it. The captains appear to have believed that the confluence rendezvous was both sensible and obvious, perhaps inevitable, and there is no hint in the extant journals that either one of them reckoned that anything could get in the way of the plan. By July 1806 Meriwether Lewis and William Clark understood each other implicitly. They had been on the road together for a very long time. They knew each other's leadership styles, quirks, strengths, weaknesses, personalities, and hot buttons. The fact that neither of the captains posited any alternative to the confluence rendezvous plan suggests that neither could really imagine anything going dramatically wrong in the summer and early fall of 1806. It was a sign of their supreme confidence in each other that they did not need to make a list of plans B, C, and so on. The captains' confidence may also have had something to do with their successful triumph over the Bitterroot Mountains just before the interlude at Travelers' Rest. Returning from the lean larder of the Pacific slope, through what Lewis called those "tremendous mountains," to the buffalo plains of today's Montana, Clark wrote, "is like once more returning to the land of liveing a plenty of meat and that very good."[3] The captains had made the entire transit of Montana on the outbound journey in 1805 without encountering Indians. They had never experienced hunger. They knew the Missouri River well, mile by challenging mile, and sensed that the Yellowstone would be equally navigable. They had good reason to feel confident that this would be a comparatively easy phase of their journey, particularly because they would, after a short interval, be flowing downstream towards home, together.

Still, it was an unprecedented, risky, and dramatic separation, born of the confidence of dear old friends, and hardened, field-tested frontiersmen in the twenty-sixth month of their transcontinental journey. The fissuring of the expedition was undertaken exclusively in the pursuit of Enlightenment science. Lewis did not want to return to civilization without knowing more about the principal upper basin tributary of the Missouri, the Yellowstone, especially given the disappointment of the upper Missouri as a portal into the Columbia River basin. Clark needed to explore the Yellowstone basin to insure that his map of the fur country of today's Montana was accurate.

"I took leave of my worthy friend and companion Capt. Clark and the party that accompanyed him," Lewis wrote that morning at Travelers' Rest, near today's Missoula, Montana. Then he added, "I could not avoid feeling much concern on this occasion although I hoped this seperation was only momentary."[4] This was characteristic Lewis. The president's friend and protégé, the commander of the mission, was a dedicated, anxious, high-strung man who took his responsibilities so seriously that he once wrote that he measured the worth of his existence according to the success of the expedition he was leading. During his excruciating attempt to avoid frightening off Cameahwait and the Shoshone Indians in August 1805, Lewis wrote that he had a sleepless night, "my mind dwelling on the state of the expedition which I have ever held in equal estimation with my own existence."[5]

Clark wrote a long journal entry for July 3, 1806, too. "[W]e colected our horses," he began, "and after brackfast   I took My leave of Capt Lewis and the indians and at 8 A M Set out with ____ men."[6] Clark did not express anxiety on the occasion of this separation, which would certainly last weeks, and might last for months, or for that matter, forever. Clark did not echo his friend's "much concern on this occasion." He simply collected his group of men, one of them an African American slave valet, one woman, and her child, and set out resolutely for parts unknown. That was his style.

Captain Lewis was right to express anxiety. It was a bold decision to divide and subdivide the Corps of Discovery, which primarily for reasons of security had swollen beyond President Jefferson's original prescription of "an intelligent officer with ten or twelve chosen men, fit for the enterprize and willing to undertake it, taken from our posts, where they may be spared without inconvenience."[7] In St. Louis, more or less on his own authority, Lewis had quadrupled the size of the exploration party because he was told that the Missouri River would not yield its current to a smaller force of men and because he was warned that a small party would be vulnerable to bullying (or worse) by the Dakota-Lakota people, and perhaps others. The late Stephen Ambrose understood the magnitude of what the captains now proposed to do. "Both captains would be in country they had not seen before, facing they knew not what dangers from the weather, the terrain, and the natives. Except for their rifles, scientific instruments, and journals, the men were no better equipped than the Indians, and none of the ... detachments of the Corps of Discovery would have enough firepower to drive off a determined attack from even a moderate-sized war party."[8]

The plan was relatively simple. After leaving Travelers' Rest, Clark would make his way overland to somewhere near the headwaters of the Yellowstone River, build vessels, and float through the Yellowstone Valley towards the river's confluence with the Missouri, a landmark both captains knew well from their two-day stop there in 1805. The most difficult part of Clark's journey would be the overland bushwhack from the Three Forks of the Missouri to navigable waters of the Yellowstone River. So far as he knew, no white man had ever made that journey before. Here's how Lewis described the mission: "Capt C. with the remaining ten including Charbono and York will proceed to the Yellowstone river at it's nearest approach to the three forks of the missouri."[9] The captains could not possibly know how close the waters of the Missouri and the Yellowstone approached each other

Lewis and Clark
at the Confluence

August 3 - August 12, 1806

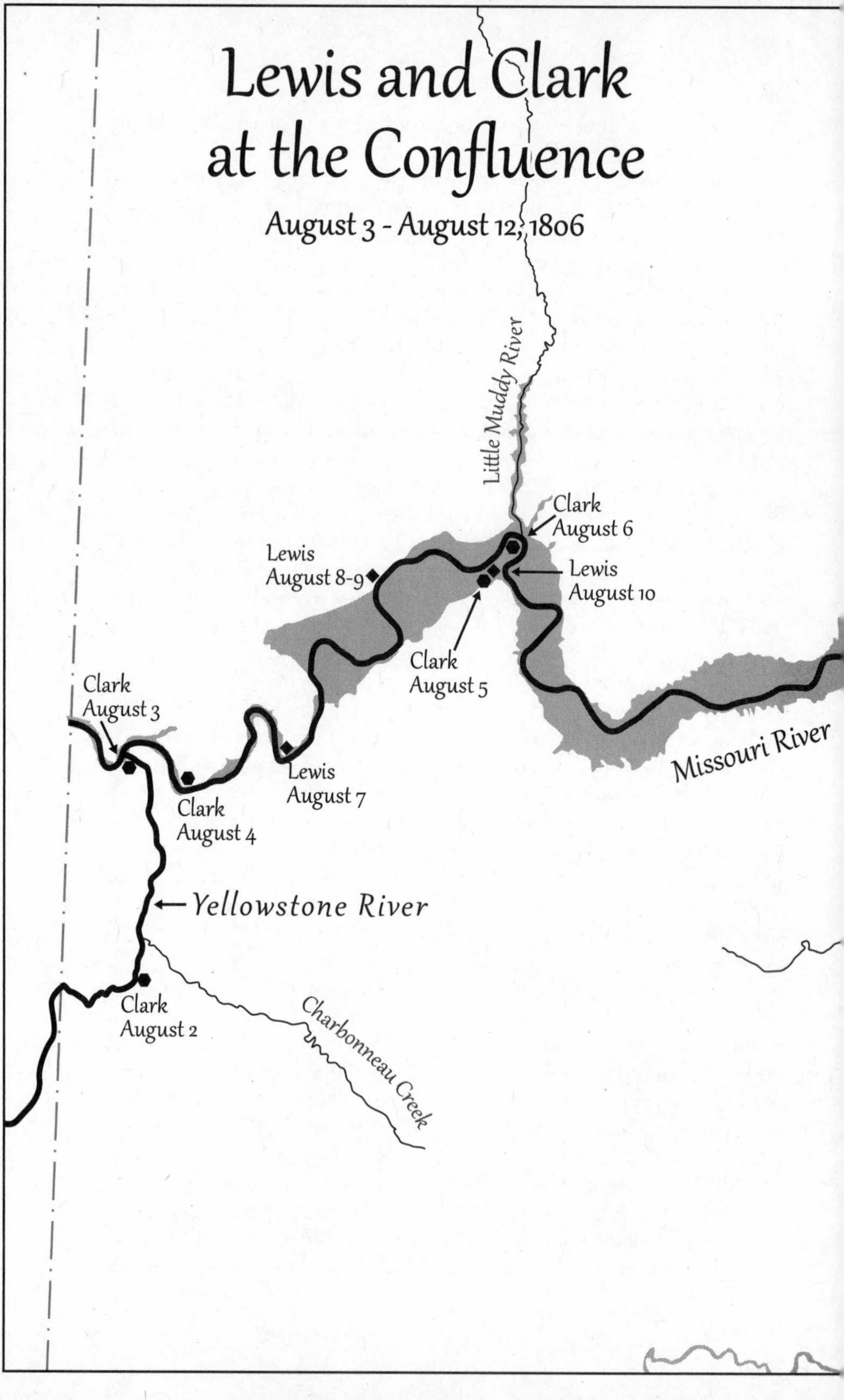

Little Muddy River

Clark
August 6

Lewis
August 8-9

Lewis
August 10

Clark
August 5

Clark
August 3

Lewis
August 7

Clark
August 4

Missouri River

Yellowstone River

Clark
August 2

Charbonneau Creek

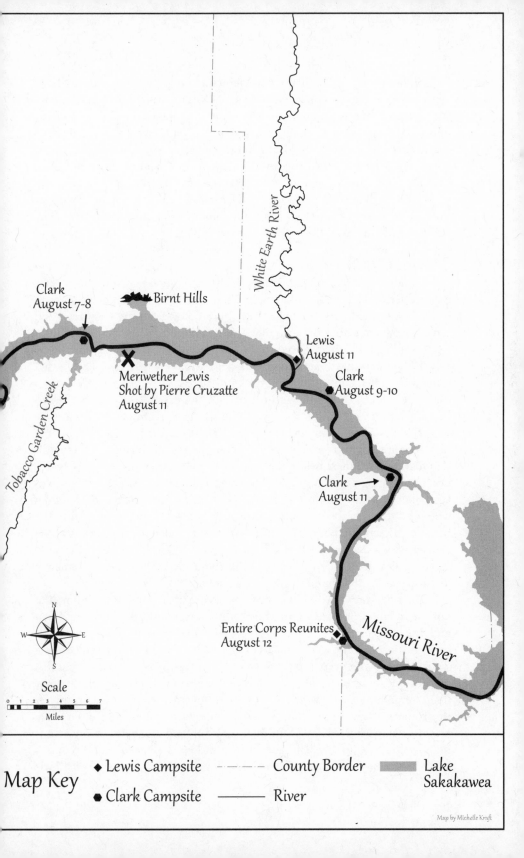

Clark
August 7-8

Birnt Hills

White Earth River

Lewis
August 11

Clark
August 9-10

X
Meriwether Lewis
Shot by Pierre Cruzatte
August 11

Tobacco Garden Creek

Clark
August 11

Clark
August 11

Entire Corps Reunites
August 12

Missouri River

N
W   E
S

Scale

0 1 2 3 4 5 6 7
Miles

Map Key

◆ Lewis Campsite   ---·--- County Border   Lake
                                                          Sakakawea
⬢ Clark Campsite   ———— River

Map by Michelle Kraft

in southwestern Montana. Meanwhile, Lewis would return to the Great Falls by a new route, the Blackfoot-Medicine River shortcut that had been vaguely suggested to them as far back as the winter among the Mandan and the Hidatsa Indians. Then he would explore the upper Marias with a party of up to six individuals before returning to the Missouri River and floating on down to its confluence with the Yellowstone.

Lewis set out from Travelers' Rest with nine men of the expedition, five Nez Perce Indian guides, and seventeen horses. The nine men were: George Drouillard, Patrick Gass, John Thompson, Silas Goodrich, William Werner, Robert Frazer, High McNeal, and Joseph and Reuben Field. The names of the five Nez Perce Indians were not recorded by any member of the expedition.

Initially, Clark traveled with twenty of his men, plus Sacagawea and Jean Baptiste Charbonneau, and fifty of the expedition's horses. Once Clark reached Ross's Hole near today's Sula, Montana, where they had met a party of Flathead Indians the previous fall, he veered off from the Lost Trail and Lemhi Pass route that the expedition had followed on the outbound journey and made his way overland to the Jefferson River and its tributaries. By July 8, the Clark party arrived at Camp Fortunate, where they had buried a number of items in a cache pit back on August 20, 1805. Clark reported that "the most of the Party with me being Chewers of Tobacco become So impatient to be chewing it that they Scercely gave themselves time to take their Saddles off their horses before they were off to the deposit."[10] What the men sought to dig up was not the medicines, plant specimens, and minerals that had been left there before the transit over the Bitterroots, but the expedition's remaining tobacco supply. The men had survived without tobacco at least since March 7, 1806, at Fort Clatsop. Clark wrote, "I gave to each man who used tobacco about two feet off a part of a role   took one third of the ballance myself and put up 2/3 in a box to Send down with the most of the articles which had been left at this place, by the Canoes to Capt. Lewis."[11] It was typical of William Clark to think about the welfare of his partner in discovery as he divvied up the remaining tobacco supply.

The next day, July 9, Clark had the expedition's canoes, built north of Fort Mandan in February and March 1805, "raised washed, brough down and drawn up on Shore to dry and repard."[12] They had been sunk in a pond back in August 1805, as the Corps of Discovery ceased temporarily to be a water journey and prepared to make its way over the Bitterroot Mountains on foot and horseback. Meanwhile, the men were not giving up on their quest for an ampler supply of tobacco. "Set Several men to work digging for the Tobacco Capt. Lewis informed me he had buried in the place the lodge Stood when we lay here last Summer, they Serched diligently without finding anything."[13] Just what happened to the Lewis tobacco cache remains a mystery. The important point is that Clark had no way to consult Lewis about this small matter on July 9, 1806. By now, Lewis was several hundred miles away. The location of the tobacco cache was of great importance to the men but of no significance to the success of the expedition. Clark, therefore, abandoned the search. The time would come during the captains' separation when communications of a much more serious nature would be rendered impossible by distance and the crude technologies of the era.

There was no plan B.

The Clark party made their way down the Beaverhead and Jefferson Rivers to Three Forks, Montana, arriving at noon on July 13. Clark lingered only long enough at the forks to regroup logistically, write a letter to Lewis that was to be delivered by Sergeant Ordway, and "to dine and let the horses feed imediately below the enterance of Gallitine."[14] The letter to Lewis has not survived.

Now Clark split up his contingent. In mid-afternoon on July 13, Sergeant John Ordway (equipped with Clark's letter to Lewis and the cache treasures intended for the Lewis party, including the precious tobacco), departed by water with John Collins, John Colter, Pierre Cruzatte, Thomas Howard, Baptiste Lepage, John Potts, Joseph Whitehouse, Alexander Willard, and Peter Weiser. Ordway's fleet consisted of six canoes. His assignment was to make his way down the Missouri River to the Great Falls. There he would supervise a reverse portage along the eighteen and one-quarter mile land detour around the five cataracts of the Great Falls of the Missouri. Fortunately, there was much less to lug over the cactus plains this time than there had been in June and July 1805. At the falls, the Ordway group would be assisted by the men of the Lewis party who did not accompany the captain on the Marias reconnaissance. Originally Lewis intended to lead a six-man party to the upper Marias. Eventually he settled on a four-man party. Once it had completed the portage, the Ordway contingent would descend the Missouri to its confluence with the Marias and wait there for Lewis and the Marias reconnaissance team to return.

What remained now of the Clark party consisted (temporarily) of Nathaniel Pryor, William Bratton, George Gibson, Hugh Hall, Francois Labiche, George Shannon, John Shields, Richard Windsor, York, Toussaint Charbonneau, Sacagawea, and Jean Baptiste Charbonneau. Sergeant Pryor and three men (Hall, Shannon, and Windsor) would soon be dispatched on an overland journey of diplomatic importance. Thereafter, the Clark Yellowstone party, reduced to its smallest strength, would consist of nine individuals: York, Sacagawea, Toussaint Charbonneau, Jean Baptiste Charbonneau, Francois Labiche, William Bratton, George Gibson, John Shields, and Clark.

Clark struck the Yellowstone River near today's Livingston, Montana, on July 15, 1806, after a two-day transit through country he had never seen before. The Shoshone-Hidatsa woman Sacagawea is credited with suggesting that Clark make his way into the Yellowstone basin not by the northerly pass he had in mind (today's Flathead Pass), but one further to the south. This turned out to be Bozeman Pass. On the basis of this relatively minor bit of good advice, for which Clark wrote that Sacagawea "has been of great Service to me as a pilot through this Country,"[15] one of the great myths of American history was born: that Sacagawea guided Lewis and Clark to the Pacific Ocean and back again. Sacagawea knew the Shoshone country of her childhood, and she either knew or intuited the geography of the Three Forks-Livingston-Dillon-Bozeman quarter of today's Montana. As an American Indian who had traveled more widely *before* the expedition than most Indian (or white) women ever traveled, she probably knew how to read landscape as well as Drouillard or Lewis. Clark, trying to punch his way through the passes between the upper Missouri and the upper Yellowstone, undoubtedly appreciated Sacagawea's geographic acumen. Clark had the capacity and will to listen to the young woman he had now known for twenty months. It's not clear that Lewis would have listened to "the interpreter's woman" with such confidence, and it is quite certain that he would not have lavished praise on her as his partner in discovery did.

Lewis and Clark are often regarded as virtually interchangeable, two men sharing a single soul, the embodiment of the most perfect friendship in American history, as the late Stephen Ambrose liked to put it. This is one of the most tenacious myths of the Lewis and Clark expedition. In fact, they were quite different men. William Clark and Meriwether Lewis did not always see eye to eye. Their perceptions were often distinct. The difference between the two captains is nowhere more evident than in their responses to Sacagawea, indeed, to the entire Charbonneau family.

Sacagawea really did guide Clark in this situation. After he led his party into a marshy bottom of the Gallatin River, in which he became "Swamped as I may Say in this bottom," Sacagawea "informed me that there was a large road passing through the upper part of this low plain from Madicins river through the gap which I was Stearing my Course to."[16] When Clark reached the Yellowstone River on July 15, he wrote, "The Distance from the three forks of the Easterly fork of Galletines river (from whence it may be navigated down with Small Canoes) to the River Rochejhone is 18 miles on an excellent high dry firm road with very incoiderable hills."[17] Crossing the divide between Missouri and Yellowstone watersheds, partly thanks to Sacagawea, had been an easy journey.

The forty days that transpired between the captains' separation at Travelers' Rest and their reunion on August 12, 1806, near today's New Town, North Dakota, could not have been a greater study in contrasts. Clark's excursion down the Yellowstone River was essentially a lark. He was almost continuously awestruck by the sheer quantity of game, particularly buffalo, in the Yellowstone Valley. Finally, on July 24, he gave up trying to count the herds: "[F]or me to mention or give an estimate of the differant Spcies of wild animals on this river particularly Buffalow, Elk Antelopes & Wolves would be increditable. I shall therefore be silent on the Subject further."[18] Well, not quite. The next day, July 25, at Pompey's Pillar, he wrote, "[A]fter Satisfying my Self Sufficiently in this delightfull prospect of the extensive Country around, and the emence herds of Buffalow, Elk and wolves in which it abounded, I decended and proceeded on a fiew miles … ."[19] July 27: "The Buffalow and Elk is estonishingly noumerous on the banks of the river on each Side."[20] Clark could not stop exclaiming over the Yellowstone country.

Food was superabundant. It was summertime and the living was easy. Clark was flowing with the current. On July 24, he had the two small cottonwood canoes lashed together into a kind of pontoon or catamaran. This made it even easier (and safer) for the nine-member party to float the Yellowstone River. Even a planned encounter with the Crow Indians failed to materialize, thus sparing Clark several days of tedious and challenging negotiation. True, on July 21, some of the expedition's horses were stolen by Indians, presumably the Crow, but that loss did not seem to upset Clark much. If ever there was a period of carefree bliss in the course of the entire Lewis and Clark Expedition, this was it.

William Clark. July 1806. Montana.

Heretical though it may sound, it seems likely that some part of Clark's unmistakable carefreeness on the Yellowstone journey was made possible by the absence of his high-strung, hyper-serious co-captain. It's hard to imagine Lewis shrugging off the Crow, the stolen horses, and the possibility of ranging the Yellowstone hills in search of mineral and plant specimens.

Contrast Clark's whimsical float trip on the Yellowstone with Captain Lewis's simultaneous catalogue of difficulties in the Missouri and Marias watersheds. First, seventeen of Lewis's horses were stolen (July 12). Not even the expedition's finest trailsman Drouillard was able to track them down. Then, when the party returned to the cache at the Great Falls, Lewis discovered (July 13) that his treasury of plant specimens had been destroyed by a rising water table. "[F]ound my bearskins entirely destroyed by the water," he reported, "the river having risen so high that the water had penitrated. all my specimens of plants also lost.   the Chart of the Missouri fortunately escaped."[21] By this stage of the expedition, Lewis was principally interested in getting home. The customary lavishness of his sense of his job description had undergone significant shrinkage somewhere between the expedition's successful transit of the Bitterroots in September 1805, and its arrival at Travelers' Rest on the return journey nine months later. At least since New Year's 1806, when (at Fort Clatsop) Lewis confessed his intense "anticipation of the 1st day of January 1807, when in the bosom of our friends we hope to participate in the mirth and hilarity of the day, and when with the zest given by the recollection of the present, we shall completely, both mentally and corporally, enjoy the repast which the hand of civilization has prepared for us,"[22] the leader of the expedition had been narrowing his focus. Had he been less weary of the mission, less homesick, less fixated on getting back to St. Louis, Lewis might have expressed serious lamentation over the loss of his precious plant specimens, the collecting, labeling, and preservation of which had cost him a world of pains. Given his spiritual exhaustion by summer 1806, he was content merely to report the loss. Nevertheless, it was a serious loss. Paul Russell Cutright concluded, "Such losses were more than minor catastrophes, resulting as they did in the defeat of prime scientific objectives and the complete vitiation of weeks and months of dedicated effort and inquiry."[23]

Then there was the collapse of Lewis's grand geopolitical hopes. He made his excursion to the upper waters of the Marias River (July 16–28) to determine if its sources were located somewhere in today's Alberta, because the Louisiana Purchase Treaty entitled the United States to all the lands watered by the Missouri River and its tributaries. A tributary with a source deep into the Canadian north would drive back the border and change the course of American history. A north-penetrating tributary would certainly please the Anglophobic president, whose standing among Federalists would be enhanced by results from the expedition that were not merely "literary." For two years Lewis had been keeping his eye open for a northern tributary. The White Earth and Little Muddy Rivers of today's North Dakota, which at first had seemed promising, proved to be minor streams and a geopolitical disappointment. By the time he and Clark spread out the completed master map at Fort Clatsop, in February and March 1806, Lewis decided that the best remaining prospect was the Marias River. This confirmed his assertion of June 8, 1805, the day he named the Marias, that "it is a noble river; one destined to become in my opinion an object of contention between the two great powers of America and Great Britin with rispect to the adjustment of the North westwardly boundary of the former."[24] Now, on the return journey, it was his duty to explore the Marias basin.

Because there were now so many demands on the Missouri River contingent, particularly in effecting the portage around the Great Falls, Lewis took merely three of his best men, three of his favorites, with him on the Marias reconnaissance: the indispensible Drouillard and the Field brothers, all three of whom he would single out for special praise in his postexpedition report to the secretary of war. The journey began on July 16. By July 21, Lewis realized—to his immense disappointment—that Two Medicine River and Cut Bank Creek were not going to drive back the border of British North America. "[T]he most northern point," he wrote, "I now fear will not be as far north as I wished and expected."[25] Lewis therefore named the site Camp Disappointment (July 26). It is interesting to consider that Lewis spent more time on the expedition fretting Canadian sources of the Missouri than he did the quest for "the most direct & practicable water communication across this continent for the purposes of commerce."[26] In other words, Lewis was at least as much concerned with the global relations between Britain and the United States as he was with establishing a water highway to the Pacific Ocean.

Then there was the disaster with the eight young Piegan Blackfeet, the only bloodshed of the Lewis and Clark Expedition, the moment when the lives of Lewis and three of his colleagues were most in danger. By the time Lewis had felt a Blackfeet bullet whistle over his bare head, killed two young Blackfeet men, deposited a Jefferson peace medal defiantly on the chest of one of the Blackfeet with a hubris worthy of Homeric chieftains, and then fled away on borrowed horses in a forced march out of Blackfeet territory that took them well more than 100 miles in less than twenty-four hours,[27] Lewis was an emotional wreck. He had hoped "to avoid an interview" with the known-to-be-hostile Blackfeet. Instead, he had not only encountered eight young Blackfeet men in the heart of their own country, but also had broken the president's prime directive to avoid armed conflict. The Marias excursion had proved to be a disappointment from every point of view. Lewis had made a fundamental mistake—and nearly a fatal one— in exploring Blackfeet country with so small a reconnaissance party. The four-man recon was arguably the biggest leadership mistake Lewis made in the course of the expedition.

By any measure, Meriwether Lewis had a hard return through Montana, Clark an amazingly relaxed and comfortable one. What follows makes sense only if we remember how different their journeys to the confluence had been, how differently they responded to the circumstances on the trail, how differently they viewed life.

As July came to an end and the final August of the expedition's travels began, the two parties began to converge on the confluence of the Missouri and Yellowstone Rivers. At the time, the traveling parties had no way of knowing that they were nearly simultaneous in their approach. Given the sheer size of today's Montana, the uncertainty of Clark's overland march to the headwaters of the Yellowstone, the variety of small missions that Lewis had undertaken once his party returned to the Great Falls, not to mention Lewis's fatal errand at Two Medicine Creek at the end of July, the fact of their nearly simultaneous convergence on the confluence is little short of miraculous. We take all of this for granted in retrospect, particularly in an era of instantaneous electronic communications, but it would not have been unusual, given the uncertainties of the plan, and the number of possibilities for delay or crisis, if the two parties had arrived weeks or even months apart.

On August 2, 1806, just inside today's North Dakota, the Clark party floated through a landscape so rich in game—elk, buffalo, wolves, bighorn sheep, and grizzly bear—that it is nearly impossible for the post-industrial imagination to keep up. Clark was drifting through what we would now call a multiple species association, in which a variety of predator and prey species live in an uneasy harmony on a common landscape. "[W]e were very near being detained by the Buffalow today which were Crossing the river we got through the line between 2 gangues," Clark wrote. The party shot one grizzly bear three times, and, Clark reported casually, it "returned to Shore badly wounded." Earlier that day Clark shot another grizzly in the head. "[T]he men hauled her on Shore and proved to be an old Shee which was so old that her tuskes had worn Smooth," Clark reported. It was, he said, "Much the largest feemale bear I ever Saw. after taking off her Skin, I proceeded on."[28]

The Lewis and Clark Expedition killed grizzly bears with abandon, not usually for the meat or the fat, and not more than occasionally for science, not usually even out of self-defense, but almost always simply because they regarded "the grizzled bear" as a dangerous nuisance, whether the bears were an immediate threat or not, and even if the party was quickly passing through the bear in question's habitat. They killed grizzly bears with indifference and abandon. This sort of mayhem sickens the twenty-first century reader, but it seemed reasonable enough to William Clark.

Clark camped on August 2 just above the mouth of Charbonneau Creek in McKenzie County, in today's North Dakota. Lewis camped on the boundary of today's Petroleum and Phillips Counties in eastern Montana, just above what was later called Horseshoe Point. The Lewis camp and Clark camp were separated by approximately 340 river miles on August 2, though neither could know this at the time, of course. In his journal, Lewis wrote, "[W]e are all extreemly anxious to reach the entrance of the Yellowstone river where we expect to join Capt. Clark and party."[29] *Extreemly anxious.*

The Clark party arrived at the confluence of the Yellowstone and the Missouri Rivers on August 3, 1806. He wrote, "at 8 A.M. I arrived at the Junction of the Rochejhone with the Missouri, and formed my Camp imediately in the point between the two river at which place the party had all encamped the 26th of April—1805."[30]

For some reason Clark was more susceptible to mosquitoes than Lewis, or at least he complained more about them. Back at Travelers' Rest, the two captains' journal entries of July 2, 1806, were a harbinger of things to come. On that day, Lewis wrote, "[T]he musquetoes have been excessively troublesome to us since our arrival at this place."[31] Clark, in the same place on the same day, wrote, "[T]he Musquetors has been So troublesom day and night Since our arrival in this Vally that we are tormented very much by them and Cant' write except under our Bears."[32] These sentences are not particularly distinct, but—it will turn out—there is a world of difference in the two captains' seemingly similar responses. Lewis acknowledged the troublesomeness of the mosquitoes, but did not elaborate. The mosquitoes were a fact of life. Clark, for his part, was not content to call the insects troublesome. He felt the need to inform us that he and the men were being "tormented," "day and night," and without pause ("Since our arrival in this Vally").[33]

One of the principal differences between Lewis and Clark is that Lewis tended to muse philosophically about the challenges of the expedition, particularly physical strains, while Clark was capable of complaining, and at times even whining. Caught in an early winter in the Bitterroot Mountains, Clark wrote, September 16, 1805, "I have been wet and as cold in every part as I ever was in my life, indeed I was at one time fearfull my feet would freeze in the thin mockersons which I wore."[34] Lewis would not have committed such a passage to his journal. Lewis's general health and physical constitution were stronger than Clark's. He brought a kind of stoicism to the physical challenges of the expedition, including "our trio of pests [that] still invade and obstruct us on all occasions"[35] (mosquitoes, gnats, and prickly pear cactus), as well as the many other difficulties of the trail. Clark had periodic bouts of ill health, principally in his feet and digestive system. His response was at times matter-of-fact and at times a kind of grousing that modern readers find delightful emanating from so competent and normally even-tempered an explorer. A comparison of Lewis's stoicism with Clark's penchant for complaint may have more serious implications than as mere indicators of trail style or rare evidence of personality distinctions between the captains. It is at least possible that Lewis's eventual breakdown and suicide can be seen to resonate with his tight repression of his soul's angst, while Clark's more natural and unguarded response to the trials of a two-year camping trip may indicate a capacity for healthy catharsis. It's hard to believe that Lewis was much of a laugher. He often found things amusing. He was frequently bemused. He had a wry and rich sense of humor. But his humor was the humor of intellectual and emotional detachment. It is not at all hard to image Clark laughing with lust and abandon. Or grumbling.

On August 2, Clark had complained about mosquitoes, but by August 3 he was so upset that he threw a little journal tantrum. "[L]ast night the Musquetors was so troublesom that no one of the party Slept half the night.   for my part I did not Sleep one hour. those tormenting insects found their way into My beare and tormented me the whole night.   they are not less noumerous or troublesom this morning."[36] Clark's "beare," i.e. bier, was his mosquito netting. By this time the protective netting was full of holes. As an officer, Clark at least *had* a bier. The rest of the party were on their own. "[T]he Musquetors were So noumerous that I could not Shute with any Certainty and therefore Soon returned to the Canoes,"[37] Clark wrote. Clark took great pride in his capacity as a hunter. Whenever he missed an important shot, or missed a shot with others watching, he pointed to some external reason (bugs, atmospheric conditions, a failure of the firearm) for missing the mark. He could not bring himself to admit that sometimes he just missed.

Clark's 3 August "journal entry" was much longer than Lewis's for the same date. In fact, Clark's entry for August 3, 1806, was almost certainly not a field jotting produced around the camp fire at the end of the Yellowstone sojourn. After summarizing the events of the day, Clark wrote a long, thorough, geographic account of the Yellowstone Valley, including the speed of the Yellowstone's current at various stages of its course, the quality of its bed, its navigability, and the nature of the countryside that it waters. This interesting and at times speculative geographic essay was almost certainly not written in that mosquito-infested camp just inside today's North Dakota. It was certainly written later and embedded into the finished journal to look like instant analysis. It shows every sign of being a synthesis arrived at much later in the expedition timeline, if not *after* the expedition returned to St. Louis. Clark notes that the party had last camped at the confluence on April 26, 1805, a fact that he assuredly would have had to look up in the expedition's records. He provides detailed statistics on the Yellowstone, including the number of miles he and his party have traveled from their embarkation point at today's Livingston, Montana. These details would have taken some time to work out, from field maps, daily course headings, and notes of distances run. This is precisely the sort of synthesis that would make perfect sense in St. Louis, where the records of the expedition could be spread out in a safe environment, distances totaled up, and maps pored over to determine how the source of the Yellowstone interlocks with that of other western American rivers.

Lewis's entry for August 3 is short. He reported that, while game was abundant, he had determined no longer to halt in the middle of the day to cook meals. Hereafter "the party should cook as much meat in the evening after encamping as would be sufficient to serve them the next day; by this means we forward our journey at least 12 or 15 miles Pr. day."[38] On this day, according to Patrick Gass, the Lewis party traveled seventy-three miles.[39] Lewis was in a hurry. It's not quite clear just why he was rushing at this point—whether he felt that he had fallen behind Clark's presumptive progress to the confluence or was just eager to get back to St. Louis, Charlottesville, and the District of Columbia, where, in the bosom of his friends, he could again "enjoy the repast which the hand of civilization has prepared for us."[40] Probably both.

There is a certain weariness in Lewis's list of the animals he saw on August 3: "a great number of Elk, deer, wolves, some bear, beaver, geese a few ducks, the party coloured covus, one Callamet Eagle, a number of bald Eagles, red headed woodpeckers &c."[41] By this point in the expedition, Lewis was reduced to mere lists. One year earlier, he would have lavished his full scientific attention on each of these creatures. Now he was in a hurry. His scientific notations have the feel of little more than due diligence.

On August 3, while Clark was safely camped on the point between the confluence of the two great rivers, Lewis and his party camped just below the mouth of Cattle Creek in Valley County, Montana, not far from the camp of May 12, 1805. The two parties were now approximately 300 miles apart, though neither knew this of the other.

The Lewis party was somewhat fractured at this point, taking risks that seem a little surprising given the skirmish with the Blackfeet just one week earlier. The Field brothers had been out hunting overnight. They came in on August 3 with "the flesh of two fine bucks, besides which they had killed two does since we passed them making in all 29 deer since yesterday morning."[42] Meanwhile the Lewis party had overtaken the beached canoe of a second pair of hunters, Colter and Collins, on the morning of August 2. Those men were away from their canoe at the time, no doubt hunting on the benches above the river. Apparently, they did not hear the men of the Lewis party hailing them from the river. Lewis therefore passed on, leaving Collins and Colter, two of his ablest men, to their fate.

On Monday, August 4, 1806, still at the confluence, Clark was entirely fed up with the mosquitoes. He began his journal entry,

Musquetors excessively troublesom So much So that the men complained that they could not work at their Skins for those troublesom insects.   and I find it entirely impossible to hunt in the bottoms, those insects being So noumerous and tormenting as to render it imposseable for a man to continue in the timbered lands and our best retreat from those insects is on the Sand bars in the river and even those Situations are only clear of them when the Wind Should happen to blow which it did to day for a fiew hours in the middle of the day.   the evenings nights and mornings they are almost indureable perticelarly by the party with me who have no Bears to keep them off at night, and nothing to Screen them but their blankets which are worn and have maney holes. The torments of those Missquetors and the want of a Sufficety of Buffalow meat to dry, those animals not to be found in this neighbourhood induce me to deturmine to proceed on to a more eliagiable Spot on the Missouri below at which place the Musquetors will be less troublesom and Buffalow more plenty.[43]

Thus, bested by the lowly mosquito, Clark left the confluence of the Missouri and Yellowstone Rivers, the sole designated rendezvous point for the scattered strands of the expedition.

Clark could have no idea how much this seemingly sensible decision would upset his estimable friend Meriwether Lewis. The two captains had only one rendezvous plan. Whichever party got to the confluence first would wait for the other. Nothing in the journals from early July 1806 indicates that either leader was free to alter the plan except in the case of a prolonged and clearly catastrophic eventuality, in which case, after a protracted delay, the survivors would continue their descent to St. Louis.

Clark soon regretted his decision. After hurriedly packing up the expedition's gear, which had been spread out to dry at the confluence, "At 5 P.M Set out and proceeded on down to the 2d point which appeared to be an eligable Situation for my purpose ... on this point the Musquetors were So abundant that we were tormented much worst than at the point. The Child of Shabono has been So much bitten by the Musquetor that his face is much puffed up & Swelled."[44] Things weren't better but worse downstream from the confluence. Now Clark's affection and sympathy for the child he later adopted played a role in his decision-making process. He continued downstream in search of a breeze or a barren.

In this remarkable passage, the journal entry for August 4, 1806, Clark referred to mosquitoes eleven times, five times by name. This continual return to the word seems to have regularized his spelling on this occasion. He spelled the word with unusual consistency: four times as *musquetors* and once as *missquetors*. According to Frances Hunter, Clark spelled mosquito nineteen different ways in the course of the expedition—but not when he was fixated on them.[45]

Given the gravity of what he was about to do—abandon the expedition's only rendezvous plan at the only place the captains had determined to reunite, with no possibility of sending a runner to the other river and the other party—Clark's instrument for letting the commander of the expedition know of his unilateral decision was nonchalant, to put it lightly. "[W]rote a note to Capt Lewis informing him of my intentions and tied it to a pole which I had Stuck up in the point,"[46] he wrote. Nothing more. A perishable note on a temporary pole in the middle of nowhere, in the heart of a game preserve in which any creature, from a greedy beaver to a blundering buffalo, might have torn down that casually constructed semaphore at any point in the days, weeks, or months between its erection and Lewis' putative arrival.

Clark woke up on August 5 just opposite today's Williston, North Dakota, fretting mosquitoes, of course. "The Musquetors was So troublesom to the men," he wrote, as if from his bedroll, "that they Slept but very little. indeed they were excessive troublesom to me. my Musquetor Bear has a number of Small holes worn through they pass in. I Set out at an early hour intending to proceed to Some other Situation."[47]

So much for Clark's alternative plan—the one he outlined in his note on the pole at the confluence.

Clark then saw a large bighorn sheep, which he attempted to kill, probably to replace the modest specimen he had collected a couple of days previously. "[T]he Misquetors was So noumerous that I could not keep them off my gun long enough to take Sight and by thair means missed."[48] This is the Clark formula.

Clark's new campsite was a sand bar, chosen to get the party as far away from the foliage as possible and out into the windiest part of the river valley. Clark wrote that he was "intending to form a Camp at this place and Continue untill Capt Lewis Should arrive."[49] But once again he soon changed his mind. When he realized that there was no adequate game in the vicinity, Clark shoved off yet again. "I detrumined to proceed on accordingly Set out at 4 P.M and proceeded on but a fiew miles." Clark's attention was briefly diverted by a huge female grizzly he managed to kill. Then he returned to his favorite subject: evading the mosquito. "I had her toed across to the South Side under a high Bluff where formed a Camp, had the bear Skined and fleaced. our Situation was exposed to a light breeze of wind which continued all the forepart of the night from the S W. and blew away the misquetors."[50] Paradise regained. One would think Clark would now settle in for the duration.

Lewis passed Big Dry Creek and the Milk River on August 4, 1806. Somehow the exhilaration of that forward progress brought out the best of Lewis that day. He described in detail a five-foot rattlesnake that the party killed, and he noted that for the first time "this season" he heard the song of the poorwill, which he called the "small whippoorwill or goatsucker of the Missouri."[51] He also reported, with the excellent narrative skill that he possessed at his best, a canoe accident involving Ordway and Willard. Delayed by their hunt, and upriver of the Lewis party campsite, the two crewmen had drifted down through a sea of sawyers in the middle of the night. Fortunately, it was a bright night. August 4, 1806, provided the night travelers a waning gibbous moon, slightly closer to full than to the last quarter. Willard was swept out of the canoe by one of the trees embedded in the river, but he managed to hold onto a sawyer for dear life, and eventually constructed a meager makeshift raft, really not much more than a wooden life preserver, with which he managed to float through the sawyer field to safety. Meanwhile, Ordway had struggled to get the canoe to shore, then ran back along the river bank to see what he could do to help his colleague Willard. Lewis had a special flare in describing dramatic incidents such as this. His account of the gunfight at Two Medicine Creek is one of the finest passages in the journals of the expedition. In this instance, Lewis writes, Ordway "at length gained the shore and returned by land to learn the fate of Willard whom he found was yet on the sawyer; it was impossible for him [Ordway] to take the canoe to his relief Willard at length tied a couple of sticks together which had lodged against the sawyer on which he was and set himself a drift among the sawyers which he fortunately escaped and was taken up about a mile below by Ordway with the canoe; they sustained no loss on this occasion."[52]

In John Ordway's account of the accident, a certain comic heroism entered the narrative. After losing Willard at the sawyer, Ordway found himself in the Missouri River's equivalent of white water. "I being in the bow of the canoe took my oar and halled the bow first one way and the other So as to clear the Sawyers and run through Safe ... ." According to Ordway, Willard, who was stranded on a tree in rushing and dangerous water, called out to determine if *Ordway* was okay: "[H]e called to me if everry thing was Safe I told him yes but he could not hear me as the water roared past the Sawyers."[53]

Lewis concluded his narrative with the laconic reflection that "it was fortunate for Willard that he could swim tolerably well."[54] We know from a variety of journal entries that some members of the expedition were poor or non-swimmers. The exact list of who could or could not swim is impossible to extrapolate from the somewhat careless way in which the captains discussed this issue, which one might have thought critical to the recruitment of a 7,689-mile *water* expedition.

The Lewis party camped on August 4 somewhere near the border of today's Valley and McCone Counties, Montana. They had traveled a distance of eighty-eight miles.

Clark's August 5, 1806, camp was just west and across the river from today's Williston, North Dakota, above the mouth of today's Little Muddy River, which Lewis and Clark continued to call the White Earth River. Lewis was still well away from the confluence on August 5. He was concerned about Collins and Colter, who had now been missing for two days. He delayed his morning start until noon in the hopes that they would catch up. At that point he concluded that they must have slipped past his camp in the dark and that he was now lagging, not they. On August 5, the Lewis party camped ten miles below today's Prairie Elk Creek in McCone County, Montana, a few miles southwest of today's Wolf Point. The main parties were now separated by 228 river miles.

Again, Lewis listed a number of species of wild animals in the region without detail, description, or even a hint of curiosity. He casually explained that Joseph and Reubin Field killed the second largest grizzly bear of the expedition that day, but aside from calling it, "the largest bear except one that I have seen,"[55] Lewis showed no engagement with his surroundings. His only moment of natural history enthusiasm was over the fact that the geese that were shedding their feathers were temporarily unable to fly, just as was a pelican he spotted "the other day in the same situation."[56] For Meriwether Lewis, except for the pesky fact that 1,800 river miles lay between himself and St. Louis, the Lewis and Clark Expedition was effectively over.

On August 6, Lewis reported that the "game is so abundant and gentle that we kill it when we please." He reported that a huge thunderstorm had swept through during the night, which made it difficult for the men to get the expedition's baggage out of the white pirogue and canoes before they filled with water. Lewis's phrase, "with difficulty I could have the small canoes unloaded," makes clear that he supervised this critical work rather than undertook it himself. "[I]n attending to the canoes I got wet to the skin," he reported, "and having no shelter on land I betook myself to the orning of the perogue which I had, formed of Elkskin, here I obtained a few hours of broken rest."[57] Notice that Lewis reported the disagreeable circumstances of this night without the slightest complaint. He made no mention of his misery, which must have been considerable, especially when the "air became very cold."[58] Lewis was an ironman.

Clark's night was no better, though he was fully 115 miles (as the crow flies) downstream from Lewis's camp. The storm must have spent part of its energy over Lewis's camp, because by the time it reached Clark it merely "Thunder and rained for about 2 hours very hard after which it continued Cloudy the balance of the night."[59] Clark's day had consisted of shooting at a large grizzly bear, but apparently without killing it, instructing Labiche to kill a large bighorn sheep, and observing the carcasses of buffalo that had drowned while attempting to cross the Missouri River. In the afternoon Clark went hunting. He was clearly stalling now to give Lewis the chance to catch up—assuming, as he apparently did, that Lewis was merely behind, not dead or wounded or mired in logistical complications.

Even on a windy day when the Clark party was spared their usual torments, Clark could not keep his mind off of the lowly mosquito. "[O]nly 2 of these deer were fat," he wrote, "owing as I suppose to the Musquetors which are So noumerous and troublesom [those two perennial words in Clark's mosquito vocabulary] that they Cannot feed except under the torments [the third perennial word] of millions of those Musquetors."[60] That was his last word for August 5.

The Lewis party reached the confluence of the Yellowstone and the Missouri on August 7, 1806. After a night of continuous rain, a night—in mid August!—when the "air was cold and extreemly unpleasant,"[61] Captain Lewis had resolved to travel no less than eighty-three miles that day. Just how he would have known that he was separated from the confluence by precisely eighty-three miles is uncertain. It is possible that he had maps and other records with him that might have indicated that distance. It is equally possible that the journal entry for August 7 was written much later. Lewis made a number of natural history notations for this day, including the observation that the landscape on the north bank of the Missouri between the Marthy's (Poplar) and Milk River "is a most beautifull level plain country; the soil is much more fertile here than above."[62]

Lewis wrote a long journal entry for August 7, in part because he had returned to what he had previously called "this long wished for spot,"[63] the confluence of the Missouri and the Yellowstone. He was just four days behind Clark. He did not know that, of course, as he "landed at the point"[64] of the confluence. For all he knew Clark could have been anywhere in Montana, or North Dakota, or dead for that matter.

Lewis had been writing short journal entries for many days. That he was keeping a journal at all is a bit surprising, given his spiritual exhaustion and his penchant for neglecting that presidential instruction. The fact is that Lewis was pretty good about keeping a journal when Clark was elsewhere. For all of his terrible and eventually fatal silences, he knew that neglecting an expedition journal altogether during days in which Clark could not cover for him would be inexcusable. Lewis usually rose to the challenge when he could find no way to evade a baseline of professionalism.

Lewis arrived at the confluence at 4 P.M. Clark was nowhere to be seen. Still, the Lewis party found unmistakable signs that Clark had already reached the rendezvous point. "I found a paper on a pole at the point which mearly contained my name in the hand wrighting of Capt. C.," Lewis wrote. Something had miscarried with Clark's explanatory note of August 4. "[W]e also found the remnant of a note which had been attached to a peace of Elk's horns in the camp; from this fragment I learned that game was scarce at the point and musquetoes troublesome which were the reasons given for his going on; I also learnt that he intended halting a few miles below where he intended waiting my arrival."[65] Apparently Clark's note of August 4 had actually consisted of two pages, with a cover sheet, on which he merely wrote Lewis's name, lest some other English-speaking white person in the vicinity pick up the wrong mail! The note was erroneous with respect to Clark's current location. He was by now far beyond "a few miles" below the confluence.

With this broken missive, William Clark set off a chain of events that would alter the nature of the Lewis and Clark Expedition and cast a shadow over Lewis's return from the wilderness.

For Lewis, suddenly confronted with this change of plans, the first order of business was to write to the other laggards, John Colter and John Collins, who were somewhere behind him either hunting, lingering, or trying to make contact with the main Lewis party. "I now wrote a note directed to Colter and Collins provided they were behind, ordering them to come on without loss of time." Lewis apparently believed that a general reunion of the entire Corps of Discovery was imminent. He was wrong. Meanwhile, he made sure his journal entry indicated how much more careful a postal officer he was than his friend Clark: "[T]his note I wraped in leather and attatced onto the same pole which Capt. C. had planted at the point."[66]

That said, Lewis immediately returned to the river—re-launched within an hour of arrival at a place that in late April 1805 he had called one of the most strategic and important locations in North America, where he and Clark had engaged in a friendly debate about the best location of the

future trade fort that was sure to be built somewhere at or near the confluence, where Lewis had conducted observations of latitude and longitude
and Clark had taken the trouble to measure the comparative widths of the
rivers. So far as we can tell from his August 7 journal entry, Lewis spent
the fewest number of minutes possible at the confluence once he determined
that Clark was now definitely ahead of him. "This being done [the letter
to Collins and Colter]," he wrote, "I instantly reimbarked and decended
the river in the hope of reaching Capt. C's camp before night."[67] No such
luck. *Instantly reimbarked.* A long series of frustrations now began to bear in
upon the commander of the expedition. Clark's epistolary assurance that he
would venture no more than "a few miles below" would prove to be illusory.
Clark was now approximately sixty-eight river miles ahead of his commanding officer. Lewis would not be reunited with Clark for a full five days—an
excruciatingly long time for a man prone to anxiety and determined to be
remembered in history as America's Captain Cook. During those five days
a great deal would happen, none of it satisfying to Meriwether Lewis.

Seven miles below the confluence on the south side of the river, Lewis
came upon tantalizing evidence that he was indeed very near Clark.
Spotting meat hung in a tree to keep it away from the wolves and coyotes,
Lewis sent the always-reliable Sergeant Ordway to investigate. Ordway
came back to report, as Lewis put it, "that he saw the tracks of two men
which appeared so resent that he beleived they had been there today, the
fire he found at the plce was blaizing and appeared to have been mended up
afresh or within the course of an hour past. he found at this place," Lewis
reported, "a part of a Chinnook hat which my men recognized as the hat of
Gibson; from these circumstances we included that Capt. C's camp could
not be distant and pursued our rout untill dark with the hope of reaching
his camp in this however we were disappointed."[68]

Exhausted from a ninety-mile day of travel, not to mention uncertainty
and anxiety, the Lewis party camped on the night of August 7 between
today's Trenton, North Dakota, and Williston. Clark's camp of that night
was not far distant, but Lewis had no way of knowing that his friend was
now less than a hard day's journey downriver.

Clark's journal entry for August 7 is his shortest of this phase of the
journey. Among other things, Clark reported that "I ... delayed untill
11 A.M. when it Stoped raining for a short time." Then, after proceeding
on for seven hours in the boats, Clark called a halt for the night. "[T]he air
was exceedingly Clear and Cold and not a misquetor to be Seen, which is
a joyfull circumstance to the Party."[69] Clark camped on August 7 opposite
Tobacco Garden Creek in northern McKenzie County, North Dakota.

As Friday, August 8, 1805, dawned, cold and disagreeable in northwestern North Dakota, both captains were now well down river from the
agreed upon rendezvous point. Each leader knew where he was, but had

no idea where the other had camped. Lewis was sure Clark was ahead, and not by many miles. Clark was pretty sure Lewis was behind; he had no idea how far. Lewis was anxious—anxious to catch up, anxious about the location and safety of Colter and Collins, anxious to get home, anxious to fulfill the last scientific desiderata of the expedition he was leading. Clark was much less anxious, at least if the journals he kept accurately record his frame of mind. He seemed to think that everything would work itself out in due time, and that his decision to drift down the Missouri at a leisurely pace would somehow result in a successful reunion of all the scattered strands of the expedition.

The day after he received the disagreeable news of Clark's departure from the confluence, Lewis suffered rapid mood swings. At first he was hot to catch up. "Beleiving from the recent appearances about the fire which we past last evening that Capt Clark could be at no great distance below I set out early,"[70] he wrote. The Lewis party rowed hard to close the gap. By mid-morning, however, Captain Meriwether Lewis, friend and private correspondence secretary to the president of the United States, sole commander of the Corps of Volunteers for North Western Discovery, Enlightenment scientist, changed his mind about the desirability of chasing his lieutenant William Clark. "[N]ot finding Capt. Clark [not finding him "a few miles below," he means] I knew not what calculation to make with rispect to his halting and therefore determined to proceed as tho' he was not before me and leave the rest to the chapter of accidents."[71] What? This was one of the strangest decisions that Lewis ever made. He knew by unmistakable evidence that Clark was only a few miles ahead of him, that it would be irrational and possibly insane to "proceed as tho' he was not before me." When did Meriwether Lewis ever leave anything "to the chapter of accidents"? A blazing fire and Gibson's Chinook hat were incontrovertible evidence that Clark was miles, rather than days, ahead of him. The still-burning fire alone should have inspired Lewis to press forward with unstinting dispatch. What induced Lewis to pull up for two full days and stop chasing his friend William Clark?

It is, I suppose, possible that Lewis believed that proceeding on at a reasonable pace made more sense than engaging in a forced march to catch up with Clark. But that explanation, though possible, does not seem plausible. Nor does it sound like Lewis. The journal entries of Lewis for the first days of August 1806 deserve to be read with the same care one gives to poems or diplomatic cables. It is difficult to explicate the last dozen entries in Lewis's remarkable and problematic journal. His behavior and his mindset were erratic, irrational, contradictory, manic, and confused. No explanation of his behavior in the wake of Clark's failure to remain at the confluence is entirely satisfying. It is clear that he was nonplussed and possibly exasperated. He was off his center of gravity. My own best sense of the journal entries of August 8–11 is that Lewis was making decisions based on pride and ego, not reason; that he was disturbed, and probably angry, that Clark had unilaterally broken the rendezvous covenant and then disregarded his epistolary pledge to drop down no more than "a few miles" from the confluence. I believe at the same time that Lewis came to regard it as undignified and possibly degrading to be put in the position of chasing his lieutenant Clark, and that he was consumed by mutually-exclusive impulses on August 8, 1806: he desperately wanted to catch Clark, re-knit the strands of the expedition, and resolve the rendezvous crisis, and, at the same time, he was determined to maintain his sense of himself, his *amour propre*, and not go scrambling down the Missouri River hugger-mugger in the wake of his errant lieutenant.

Lewis had insisted on *getting there first* throughout the expedition: first to the confluence on the outbound journey, first to the Great Falls, first to the source of the Missouri, first to the actual oceanfront in today's Washington. There can be no doubt that he wanted to be first to cross the finish line of the expedition. Nobody remembers the name of Columbus's lieutenants, or Captain Cook's. To arrive in St. Louis after William Clark would be the ultimate betrayal of "one of those great objects on which my mind has been unalterably fixed for many years."[72] Whatever he might say around the camp fire about Clark's role and irrespective of his resolution to employ the polite fiction of designating Clark *co-captain* of the enterprise, Lewis regarded himself, not Clark, as the man of destiny. Clark was co-captain only in the sense that his contributions to the success of the expedition were of inestimable importance. He was not co-captain when it came to discovery. Probably the *rational* Lewis realized that it was extremely unlikely that Clark would press on to reach St. Louis before his friend and commander, but the *irrational* Lewis seems to have felt that he might be losing control of his "darling project" to a man who was his subordinate, whom he had hired as an auxiliary, and who was not Jefferson's friend or an exemplar of the Enlightenment or a member of the American Philosophical Society.

Knowing what we know of how this strange episode played itself out, knowing what we know of Clark's devotion to Lewis and—more importantly—his lifelong capacity for subordinating himself to the strong men whose lives he helped to facilitate or fix, it seems ludicrous, bordering on incredible, to think that Lewis might have suspected that Clark would rush home to steal the glory or even allow himself to cross the finish line first. The likeliest solution to the Clark-rendezvous problem, had Lewis been thinking straight, was that Clark would under no circumstance descend the Missouri farther than the Mandan villages, where the expedition had critically important diplomatic work to attend to—including convincing a Mandan or Hidatsa leader to accompany them to St. Louis and Washington, DC. If Lewis feared—even deep in his consciousness—that Clark would return to civilization ahead of him and pluck the crown of their achievements from the rightful hero, he was doing a grave injustice to his friend's character and fundamentally misreading the situation before him. But Lewis was not thinking straight at this point in the journey, and perfidy is not unheard of or even rare among explorers. Such things happen on voyages of discovery, most notably to Richard Francis Burton in 1858, fifty-two years later, when his unquestionably subordinate lieutenant John Speke rushed back to London two weeks ahead of Burton to claim that he, not Burton, had discovered the true source of the Nile. Speke's wild and dishonorable claim shattered both of their lives. In the end, in fact, Speke's apostasy cost him his life. The controversy rocked the learned world, and it created bitterness amongst geographers and explorers that has not altogether dissipated in the 152 years that have followed.

These things can happen when the stakes are so high. Lewis, who pointedly declared that his life had meaning only insofar as he succeeded in his exploration project, must have wondered in these crowded hours just how loyal and reliable Clark really was. Why had he forged ahead in direct defiance of the only rendezvous plan the two captains had fashioned when they split the expedition at Travelers' Rest? Lewis clearly found the idea, that such a major deviation from the agreed-upon plan could be driven by the lowly mosquito, contemptible.

Some sort of betrayal fantasy seems to have percolated in the unstable brain of Lewis. On August 8, 1806, he immediately put his new plan into effect. "[A]t this place," he improvised, "I found a good beach for the purpose of drawing out the perogue and one of the canoes which wanted corking and reparing."[73] So, near enough to Clark that there has not been time for a campfire to burn out, Lewis decided to empty the boats and undertake some routine repairs—for two full days at the height of the travel season. That is not all. "[T]he men with me," Lewis wrote, "have not had leasure since we left the West side of the Rocky mountains to dress any skins or make themselves cloaths and most of them are therefore extreemly bare. I therefore determined to halt at this place until the perogue and canoe could be repared and the men dress skins and make themselves the necessary cloathing."[74] It is important to be clear about what was happening here. So far from rushing to catch Clark, or even proceeding downstream at a sensible pace in the hopes that the strands of the expedition would magically converge, Lewis now directed his party to halt their forward progress in a manner guaranteed to widen the distance between himself and William Clark. Sartorial imperatives aside, there is no way to characterize this decision as anything other than fundamentally irrational. His men had found a still-blazing fire on the banks of the river. And Gibson's hat.

Lewis followed these logistical resolutions with a philosophical observation about the mosquitoes of the region that feels—to the reader of the journals two centuries later—to be a pointed rejoinder to Clark's litanies of lament. "[W]e found the Musquetoes extreemly troublesome but in this rispect there is but little choise of camps from hence down to St. Louis,"[75] he wrote with his usual philosophical detachment. This effectively challenged the wisdom of Clark's unilateral decision to leave the confluence to get away from the press of mosquitoes. If that's your criterion for camp location, there is no difference between "a few miles below" and St. Charles, Missouri, Lewis argued. Lewis's reference to St. Louis indicates how close he regarded himself to the finish line.

Now Lewis declared his intended course of action with a mix of defiance and barely-concealed petulance. "I shall therefore when I leave this place travel at my leisure and avail myself of every opportunity to collect and dry meat untill I provide a sufficient quantity for our voyage not knowing what provision Capt C. has made in this rispect."[76] So, Lewis's best determination of how to respond to Clark's departure from the confluence was to make an unnecessary stop for the making of clothing and the repairing of the boats, followed by an amble down the Missouri in no particular hurry, "at my leisure," with frequent hunting and skin-dressing halts along the way. What Lewis resolved to do in the face of Clark's departure—fix boats, hunt intensely, make garments—was precisely what Clark should have done when he realized at the confluence that Lewis was behind him. It is Clark, not Lewis, who should have slowed his flotilla down, found a good campsite, paused to get everything ready for the encounter with the Hidatsa and the Mandan that was soon to follow. Lewis should have proceeded on with all due speed.

There is a kind of cloud-cuckoo-land quality to the Lewis and Clark Expedition at this late point in its transcontinental journey.

Lewis's tortured musings on August 8, 1806, represent one of the most fascinating entries in the journals of Lewis and Clark. My contention is that it would be impossible to make sense of this passage using any merely rational analysis. It seems clear to me that Lewis was knocked off what was left of his center of gravity by Clark's fragmentary letter at the confluence, that it threw him into some combination of panic and truculence, and that his response to Clark's departure had much more to do with pride than with good sense.

It may be worth repeating here that Lewis's instabilities increased as the twenty-eight-month expedition wore on, and that he was invariably less stable in the absence of Clark than when they were together. After the harrowing events at Two Medicine Creek, a prime example of what could go wrong when Clark was not at his side, Lewis probably needed Clark's friendship, not to mention his solidity and pragmatism, more than ever before. Lewis was counting on finding Clark at the point of land that marked the confluence of the Yellowstone and Missouri Rivers. When he discovered that Clark had departed—bested by the diminutive mosquito, on the basis of which there was "but little choise of camps from hence down to St. Louis,"[77] Lewis was sorely disappointed. He did his best to present himself to futurity and to his party of men as nonchalant in the face of this problem, but the increasing irrationality of his responses is an unmistakable indication of how disturbing he found this latest unexpected development, the last in the series (he thought), coming from the last person he would have expected to create chaos and anxiety.

In the face of this rendezvous crisis, Lewis lost his capacity to think rationally. Three days later, this kind of erratic logic would nearly cost him his life.

All sorts of interesting things happened in Clark's world on August 8, 1806. At 8 A.M., Nathaniel Pryor, George Shannon, Hugh Hall, and Richard Windsor suddenly appeared in two bullboats. The captains had dispatched Pryor (and these others) to drive the remnant of their Rocky Mountain horse herd overland to the trade forts on the Assiniboine River in today's Manitoba. There Pryor was to deliver a letter from Lewis to Hugh Heney urging the North West Company trader to organize a diplomatic mission to the Dakota-Lakota and to consider becoming an official agent of the United States government on the Upper Missouri. On Pryor's second night out on the plains of Montana, Indians, almost certainly the Crow, had stolen his entire string of horses. At that point, Pryor had intelligently decided to abandon the overland journey and descend the Yellowstone. To make this possible he and his men constructed two bullboats in the manner of the Mandan and Hidatsa Indians. The second boat was built as a backup vessel and also to make sure the small party's supply of rifles, ball, and powder was not all entrusted to a single experimental vessel. They embarked on the Yellowstone River at Pompey's Pillar east of today's Billings, Montana, and somehow managed to make those ungainly tubs float them down to the confluence—and beyond. When the Pryor party reached the confluence—sometime after August 3 and before August 7, he somehow concluded "that Capt. Lewis had passed took the note and brought it with him."[78] This, too, makes no sense, unless Pryor concluded that Lewis failed to spot the note on the point of the confluence.

All of that is very interesting, both for what it says about Pryor's resourcefulness in the face of a serious crisis (the contrast with Lewis's flustering indecision is remarkable), but also in light of the Crow Indian's nineteenth-century reputation for being the ablest horse stealers on the upper Great Plains. But what is surely most interesting about this episode is what it says about the sequencing of the various flotillas east of the confluence. Clark was in the lead with his eight companions and two canoes. Apparently Pryor's two bullboats were close behind. Lewis, with his nineteen companions and five boats, was not far behind Pryor. Given the total absence of technologies that would enable these three parties to communicate with each other, they were unable to effect the critical rendezvous in spite of the fact that the three groups were so close to each other that it is remarkable that they didn't simply bump into each other, or at least hear the report of the rifles of the different groups of hunters who were supplying meat for the three traveling parties. Thanks to the note at the confluence, Lewis knew that Clark was ahead—somewhere— but he could not be sure just where. Lewis had no idea that Pryor, Shannon, Hall, and Windsor were between him and Clark. Had he been aware of this fact, he would surely have accelerated his pace. Pryor knew Clark was ahead of him, and reckoned that Lewis was too, thanks to the note he found and irrationally appropriated at the confluence. Clark was not in a position to know where either of the other parties was during this period. He had the most reason to wonder and to fret about the whereabouts and the safety of his companions, including his mercurial commander. But his journals report no fretting and no anxiety. Although Clark paused in his August 8 journal entry to write a long explanation of how bull boats are constructed, he dispatched the *where in the world is Captain Lewis* conundrum in a single sentence! "Capt. Lewis I expect will be certain of my passing by the Sign which I have made and the encampment imediately in the point."[79] That's the sum total of Clark's speculation. Instead of sending one or two men back to the confluence to make sure Lewis knew of Clark's whereabouts—in the aftermath of Pryor's strange decision to bring with him the note Clark had written for Lewis— Clark suggests, more than a little defensively, that Lewis will probably figure things out. In a newsy journal entry of 827 words, Clark devoted precisely twenty-four words to Lewis's whereabouts. Pryor, meanwhile, was so eager to catch up with the main party that he accidentally left his diplomatic pouch behind. "Sergt. Pryor bing anxious to overtake me Set out Some time before day this morning and forgot his Saddlebags which contains his papers &c." Clark sent Pryor and Bratten back up the river "in Serch of them."[80] Had Lewis been moving forward with all due speed, he might have encountered Bratten and Pryor in the course of their retrograde motion. But Lewis was caulking boats and dressing animal skins.

That's the extraordinary thing about this fascinating set of events. Clark was completely untroubled by the situation and strangely indifferent to what would appear to have been an iron commitment to halt at the confluence until everyone else showed up. It may be that the leisurely downhill float with Sacagawea, Charbonneau, "my little danceing boy Baptiest,"[81] and the others eased Clark into a state of relaxation not so different from that of modern Montana raft parties, and that he failed to gauge either the gravity of his decision at the confluence or his friends' likely response. Pryor was so nonchalant when he reached the rendezvous point that he plucked Clark's note from the message pole for no adequate reason.

Of the three "commanders," only Lewis was fretful and disoriented, and yet he was the only one who had certain information about the whereabouts of Clark's party. He should have been able to reckon that if he accelerated his pace (as he determined to do on August 3) he could make up twelve to fifteen miles per day and that this *modus operandi* would surely enable him to catch up with Clark in the space of no more than a handful of days. That sensible course is precisely what Lewis determined *not* to do.

Clark says Pryor found Clark's note to Lewis at the confluence, decided [oddly] that Lewis had already passed that mark, and therefore [more oddly] "took the note and brought it with him."[82] There is some mystery in all of this, since Lewis reported (August 7) that he found Clark's letter at the confluence, but that it had been disturbed and parts of its contents separated. If Pryor "took the note" some time between August 3 and August 7, why was there still enough of it left at the site for Lewis to understand what Clark had decided to do? Why did Pryor conclude—counter-rationally— that Lewis had passed by the rendezvous site if the letter was still posted on the pole when Pryor arrived? The journal of Patrick Gass adds still another element of mystery. Gass was traveling in the Lewis party. When the Lewis contingent landed at the confluence on August 7, "We discovered nothing to inform us where he was gone," Gass wrote, "except a few words written or traced in the sand, which were '*W.C. a few miles farther down on the right hand side.*' Captain Lewis having left a few lines for the two men in the canoe, to inform them, if they are still behind, where we were gone, we continued our voyage."[83] Gass is the only journal keeper who wrote about a note "traced in the sand." Suddenly the expedition feels more like *Robinson Crusoe* than the Enlightenment project of Thomas Jefferson.

If I have the sequencing correct, the stretch of the Missouri River east of the confluence was a crowded stream in the first days of August 1806. If we could view the three float parties from one of the hot air balloons that Mr. Jefferson so admired, the proximity of the parties would take on an almost comic aspect.

Clark now slowed things down a little. On August 8 he sent out several hunting parties, including Shields and Gibson in the bullboats, to begin procuring deer and elk skins. "My object," he wrote, "is to precure as many Skins as possible for the purpose of purchaseing Corn and Beans of the Mandans. as we have now no article of Merchindize nor horses to purchase with, our only resort is Skins which those people were very fond the winter we were Stationed near them."[84] Lewis and Clark were both now thinking of the protocol of arriving at the Mandan and Hidatsa villages with a group of men who were very nearly destitute of clothing.

Lewis, meanwhile, had seriously begun to worry about John Colter and John Collins, who represented the fourth float party in the vicinity. They had taken a canoe to go hunting on August 3, along with several other such canoe parties, and they had not returned that night—or since. "I fear some missfortune has happened them," Lewis wrote on August 9, "for their previous fidelity and orderly deportment induces me to beleive that they would not thus intentionally delay."[85] This, too, could be read as an implied criticism of Clark. Most of the men of the Lewis party spent the day "engaged dressing skins and making themselves cloathes." Still not sure where Clark was, Lewis sent the trusty Field brothers downriver "with orders to proceed to the entrance of the White earth [i.e., Little Muddy] river in surch of Capt. C. and to hunt and kill Elk or buffaloe should they find any convenient to the river." No luck. "[I]n the evening these men returned and informed me that they saw no appearance of Capt. Clark or party."[86] They must have come close.

On August 10, the last good day of the expedition for Meriwether Lewis, his men packed everything up and departed from the skin-dressing camp at 5 P.M. The Lewis party made a few miles before dusk and camped on the south bank of the Missouri River just opposite of today's Williston.

Sleep restfully, Captain Lewis. Tomorrow night will be another story altogether.

Clark moved forward just a few miles on August 9. He took a walk through an immense bottom enclosed by the sweep of the Missouri River, ostensibly in search of elk skins. Late in the evening he killed "the largest Buck [elk] I ever Saw and the fattest animal which have been killed on the rout."[87] On that day, Sacagawea made one of her rare appearances in the journals. "The Squar brought me a large and well flavoured Goose berry of a rich Crimsin Colour,"[88] he reported. This was the 908th day of the Lewis and Clark Expedition. Clark had now known Sacagawea for two years and seven days. As the expedition wound down and she neared her Hidatsa homeland, she was still—even for William Clark—"the Squar." Lewis is usually criticized for his indifference towards Sacagawea and his purely instrumental view of her value to the expedition. It is a useful corrective to the Sacagawea mythology to realize that even Clark saw no reason to make much of her or call her by name. She brought him a bright red ripe gooseberry either because she reckoned he would be interested in it from a natural history perspective, or—more probably—because she knew gooseberries were delicious and wanted to please her principal ally in the expedition. Whatever her purposes, she had taken the time to gather up a fragile treat on the plains and to put it into the hands of Clark. This she assuredly would not have done for Meriwether Lewis. Clark acknowledged its receipt, but neither named Sacagawea nor took the time to write any sentence of appreciation for a gesture of the sort that his contemporary William Wordsworth called "little, nameless, unremembered acts of kindness and of love."[89]

On August 10, Clark made no forward progress. Clearly, he was giving Lewis time to catch up. He "finished a Copy of my Sketches of the River Rochejhone."[90] Unfortunately that map, according to Lewis and Clark editor Gary Moulton, has been lost.[91] Clark also wrote a detailed natural history note on August 10 of the pin cherry. What makes that foray into Enlightenment science strange is that Clark's journal entry actually does little more than copy the description of the pin cherry written by Lewis on August 12, 1806, *two days later*. Moreover, when Clark ostensibly wrote that description, he had not been in contact with Lewis for six weeks. He had no way of copying Lewis's journal, which wouldn't be written for another two days (and under very adverse circumstances) anyway. This is a very important piece of evidence about the way in which the journals of Lewis and Clark were constructed. I say constructed (rather than written), because it is essential for future Lewis and Clark studies that we disabuse ourselves once and for all of the idea that the journals were written, *dear diary form*, each evening at the end of the day's travels. This was undoubtedly sometimes true, but readers of the journals need to be alert to the other ways in which the journals came into their present form. It seems undeniably clear that some entries were written not on the day they purport to report, but later, perhaps days, weeks, or months later. Some entries (like this one) seem to have been jotted down at an indeterminate time in blank places in the journals, not where they belong but where they fit, where they bring maximum efficiency to the limited supply of paper in the expedition's kit, or where the journal keeper reckoned they properly belonged in the polished copy of the journal. Whenever there is a long journal entry of geographic or geopolitical analysis, it is probable that the entry was written sometime after the date of its insertion. What all of this suggests is that the journals as we have them are rarely, if ever, field journals in the naïve sense that they have seemed to represent for the last 200 years. In fact, it is quite likely that the physical journals that we have are not field journals at all, but copies of mostly-lost field journals that were kept less systematically than we like to think, and then copied and regularized at some point after the fact, either in the comparative tranquility of Fort Mandan or Fort Clatsop, or at the Long Camp among the Nez Perce, or even after the expedition returned to St. Louis, where, as Clark put it, we "Commencd wrighting."[92]

This much is certain. Clark did not write his description of the pin cherry on August 10, 1806. In fact, Clark did not *write* that description at all. He copied it at an unknown moment, but certainly *after* August 12, 1806, which was the last day that Lewis kept a journal. Clark's journal entry for August 10, 1806, is unmistakable proof that the construction of the journals is much more complicated than we like to think, and that there are few occasions when we can be sure that what we read was jotted around the camp fire on the date of its inclusion in the journals, and even then not usually in the physical journals that have come down to us.

On the fatal day to which this entire chapter has been tending, August 11, 1806, Meriwether Lewis suddenly brought an entirely new, and previously unannounced, element into the mix. He needed his men to get to a certain landmark by noon.

The Missouri River rises in southwestern Montana, then arcs its way north towards the Canadian border or (for that matter) towards the North Pole. At the top of its arc somewhere in eastern Montana or western North Dakota, the Missouri runs as close to the North Pole as it is ever going to get. Then it begins its long southeasterly sweep towards its confluence with the Mississippi River at St. Charles, Missouri. The northernmost reach of the Missouri River means nothing today except as a piece of geographic trivia, but in the age of Jefferson it was a geopolitically critical data point. At a time when the United States sought to wrest the fur trade away from its geopolitical rivals and to read the terms of the Louisiana Purchase Treaty in the most geographically expansive manner possible, ascertaining the northernmost point of the Missouri watershed—and the Missouri itself—was information essential to Thomas Jefferson and the US State Department, then directed by Jefferson's closest friend James Madison.

Using today's satellite imagery and global positioning devices, it is possible to determine the Missouri's northernmost point effortlessly. Modern maps are extremely accurate, enabling even casual geographers to determine the Missouri's northernmost reach with reasonable precision. In the late summer of 1806, Meriwether Lewis was working from William Clark's good but by no means definitive map, compiled at Fort Clatsop using a series of field sketches and field maps and incorporating—as far as it was possible—Lewis's field readings of latitude and longitude. At Fort Clatsop, after Clark's map was finished on February 14, 1806, Lewis must have spent considerable time trying to determine just where the point in question was situated.

Lewis eventually decided that the correct point was just east of today's Williston, North Dakota, at a place he called the "Birnt Hills." Gary Moulton identifies them as the Crow Hills. The latitude of the Birnt Hills is approximately 48 degrees, 10 minutes. The amazing thing about this late episode in the expedition is that Lewis was correct. Clark may have been using early nineteenth-century cartographical techniques, and mapping on the run, as it were, but he somehow managed to chart the course of the Missouri River with astonishing accuracy. In fact, there are two possible northernmost points of the Missouri River, separated by 113 miles, virtually equal in latitude. The first is at Brockton, Montana, and the other is between the mouths of Tobacco Garden Creek and Beaver Creek in today's Williams County, North Dakota. Without explaining his reasoning, Lewis ignored the Brockton stretch of the Missouri, and determined to his satisfaction that the northernmost point was the "Birnt Hills."

Accordingly, Lewis believed that he had a duty to get precise latitude and longitude coordinates of the Birnt Hills for the purposes of science. He must have been traveling with a map of the Missouri River, because it seems literally to have dawned on him on the morning of August 11, 1806, and not before, that he was getting close to the point in question. In order to get the coordinates using the techniques he had been taught, he needed to make his observations just before, precisely at, and just after noon (meridian). It was theoretically possible to make the measurements at other times of the day, but such an observation protocol complicated the business significantly and required difficult mathematical conversions. In practical terms this meant he had to take his observations at local noon, when the sun was at its zenith in the Great Plains sky. Whether Lewis had anticipated this moment for many weeks or this critical opportunity sprang upon him suddenly is unknowable, but the abruptness with which Lewis introduced the scientific errand at the Birnt Hills on August 11 is startling.

Lewis's journal entry for August 11 indicated his plan. "We set out very early this morning," he wrote. "[I]t being my wish to arrive at the Birnt Hills by noon in order to take the latitude of that place as it is the most northern point of the Missouri."[93] This is straightforward enough.

If Lewis had not been in a hurry to catch up with Clark, he would not have needed to get to the Birnt Hills by noon on August 11. He would have made his way to the spot at the usual traveling pace and then waited a day (or more if it was cloudy) until he got the latitudinal data he needed. If Lewis and Clark had achieved their rendezvous at the confluence of the Missouri and the Yellowstone Rivers, as planned, they would have been together as they neared the Birnt Hills and there would presumably have been no particular hurry about how long (within reason) it took to get the data Lewis needed. But Clark was somewhere ahead of Lewis apparently edging (perhaps racing) closer to the Mandan and Hidatsa villages and who knew where else? Lewis seems have reasoned thus: he needed to ascertain the latitude of the northernmost point of the Missouri River. That procedure needed to occur at noon (meridian). He could not afford to linger at the Birnt Hills, not even a single extra day. Therefore, he needed to churn into the spot just before noon on the day he got into proximity of the Birnt Hills, get the data he needed, and get right back into the river. He could not afford to regard this as an assignment to be fulfilled sometime in the next couple of days; he somehow talked himself into believing that the assignment must be fulfilled on August 11—or not at all. This was the logic of a man who just days earlier "determined to proceed as tho' he was not before me and leave the rest to the chapter of accidents."[94]

Lewis resumed his narrative. "[E]nformed the party of my design and requested that they would exert themselves to reach the place in time as it would save us the delay of nearly one day."[95] Here Lewis suggested that he realized that he *may* have to lay over for a day if the men do not get him to the Birnt Hills in time. But this is not what he desperately wanted to happen. "[B]eing as anxious to get forward," he wrote, "as I was [because of their homesickness, not their love of science] they plyed their oars faithfully and we proceeded rapidly." Several opportunities to hunt for much-needed food and skins (and incidentally to allow his oarsmen periods of rest) slowed the pace of the Lewis party, including a grizzly bear—"put too in order to kill it, but it took wind of us and ran off." The upshot was that when Lewis finally arrived at the Birnt Hills, "[I]t was about 20 minutes after noon and of course the observation for the ☉'s meridian Altitude was lost."[96]

So. In spite of the hard work of the men of the party and the morning rush to the Birnt Hills, Lewis lost his opportunity to get the data he needed on August 11. He would, in fact, have to endure the "delay of nearly one day" to get what he needed. Had Clark been at his side, the expedition would simply have dried out its gear, patched the leaky white pirogue, gone hunting, prepared skin clothing for the imminent encounter with the Hidatsa and the Mandan, and waited to get the celestial data at noon on August 12, 1806. But Clark was somewhere else—downstream!

In the face of this setback, had he been thinking rationally, Lewis might well have just laid over until the next day in order to get the data he needed. This would especially seem to be an acceptable option given Lewis's insistence, on August 8, that he would not chase after Clark but move forward at his own pace. Given the fact that Lewis had then stopped the expedition for two full days (August 8–9) to obtain animal skins and dry out the expedition's baggage, it would not seem unendurable for him to linger for twenty-three hours to get the latitudinal information he regarded as so important to the nation's geopolitical and scientific agenda.

Perhaps that was indeed his plan in the wake of the missed observation. But as the frustration of the unsuccessful forced march percolated in upon him in the early afternoon of August 11, and the accumulated frustrations of the summer of 1806 boiled over in the confusion that followed the intended, but failed rendezvous at the confluence, now Lewis made one of the worst decisions of his life. He decided to go hunting with the blindest man of the expedition, Pierre Cruzatte. "[J]us opposite to the birnt hills there happened to be a herd of Elk on a thick willow bar and finding that my observation was lost for the present I determined to land and kill some of them accordingly we put too and I went out with Cruzatte only."[97] William Clark would almost certainly not have permitted this to happen.

Lewis provides the best account of what happened next.

"[W]e fired on the Elk I killed one and he wounded another, we reloaded our guns and took different routs through the thick willows in pursuit of the Elk; I was in the act of firing on the Elk a second time when a ball struck my left thye about an inch below my hip joint, missing the bone it passed through the left thye and cut the thickness of the bullet across the hinder part of the right thye."[98]

In other words, the musket ball that injured Captain Lewis entered the left butt cheek high, near his hip bone, passed through his buttock below the skin and exited lower, where the buttocks meet the upper thigh. Then it creased the other buttock on the surface, cutting an open groove along the upper thigh. Since Cruzatte was using a .52 caliber ball,[99] the hole it cut through Lewis's left buttock would have been more than half an inch in diameter, and the groove in the surface of his right buttock would have been furrowed up to half an inch in depth. Lewis had suffered a very serious flesh wound.

Medical historian David Peck has written, "Lewis probably had almost no fat at all in the area, so the wound probably damaged the muscle significantly." Even so, Peck concludes, Lewis was very lucky on August 11, 1806. "Only an inch or two deeper lies the main nerve of the entire leg, the sciatic nerve."[100] Had the ball severed the sciatic nerve, Lewis, presumably, would have been paralyzed in that leg, or the leg would have needed to be amputated altogether.

The expedition's most reliable journal keeper John Ordway provided a summary view of the shooting accident. "Peter Cruzatte a frenchman went out with Capt. Lewis they Soon found a gangue of Elk in a thicket. Capt. Lewis killed one and cruzatte killed two, and as he Still kept firing one of his balls hit Capt. Lewis in his back side and the ball passed through one Side of his buttock and the ball went out of the other Side of the other buttock and lodged at his overalls which wounded him bad."[101]

Lewis immediately realized that the half-blind Cruzatte had shot him in the ass. "I instantly supposed that Cruzatte had shot me in mistake for an Elk as I was dressed in brown leather and he cannot see very well," he wrote. And yet Lewis had taken the blind fiddler hunting in a willow thicket. That, of course, raises some serious questions about Lewis's judgment. "[U]nder this impression I called out to him damn you, you have shot me, and looked towards the place from whence the ball had come, seeing nothing I called Cruzatte several times as loud as I could but received no answer."[102] John Ordway reported that Cruzatte did not hear Lewis. "[H]e instantly called to peter but Peter not answering he Supposd. it to be Indians and run to the canoes and ordered the men to their armes."[103] Ordway's explanation, it is fair to conclude, gave Cruzatte the benefit of the doubt.

When Cruzatte did not immediately step forward and fess up, Lewis descended rapidly into an Indian ambush fantasy. That Indians were essentially perfidious in nature seems to have been Lewis's core attitude. At Fort Clatsop, when the men of the expedition had gotten a little complacent about the Indians amongst whom they lived and worked, the captain had written, on February 20, 1806, without any provocation: "[A]t all events we determined allways to be on our guard as much as the nature of our situation will permit us, and never place our selves at the mercy of any savages. we well know, that the treachery of the aborigenes of America and the too great confidence of our countrymen in their sincerity and friendship, has caused the distruction of many hundreds of us."[104] And so on. Lewis's Fort Clatsop outburst slipped over the line from a commander's prudence into a racist fantasy deeply rooted in the American frontier experience—or at least in Lewis's consciousness.

Now, six months later at the Birnt Hills, Lewis "was now preswaded that it was an indian that had shot me as the report of the gun did not appear to be more than 40 paces from me and Cruzatte appeared to be out of hearing of me."[105] In spite of his correct initial assumption that he had been accidentally shot by Cruzatte (something that was likely to be regarded by Lewis as more than a specimen of the "chapter of accedents" to which all human enterprises are prone), Lewis felt immediate solicitude for Cruzatte's welfare when he imagined that he had been wounded in an Indian ambush. "[C]alling out as I ran for the first hundred paces as loud as I could to Cruzatte to retreat that there were indians hoping to allarm him in time to make his escape also."[106] In his subsequent biographical sketch of Lewis (August 18, 1813), Jefferson praised just this quality in Lewis's character. He was, Jefferson wrote, "careful as a father of those committed to his charge, yet steady in the maintenance of order & discipline."[107]

With his usual flair for the dramatic, Lewis now addressed the men of his party: "[W]hen I arrived in sight of the perogue I called the men to their arms to which they flew in an instant, I told them that I was wounded but I hoped not mortally, by an indian I beleived and directed them to follow me that I would return & give them battle and releive Cruzatte if possible who I feared had fallen into their hands; the men followed me as they were bid." This is precisely what one would expect a military commander to do. "I returned about a hundred paces when my wounds became so painfull and my thye so stiff that I could scarcely get on; in short I was compelled to halt and ordered the men to proceed and if they found themselves overpowered by numbers to retreat in order keeping up a fire. I now got back to the perogue as well as I could and prepared my self with a pistol my rifle and air-gun being determined as a retreat was impracticable to sell my life as deerly as possible."[108]

Assuming that it was an Indian attack, and that his life would be over in a matter of minutes, Lewis prepared to "sell my life as deerly as possible." In other words, he planned at minimum to discharge his rifle, his pistol, and the famous air gun, which now became a serious weapon for the first time in the course of the Lewis and Clark Expedition. Lewis was anticipating that he would get off a minimum of three shots as he was surrounded by hostile Indians. In the moment of this unprecedented crisis, Lewis provided a highly romantic narrative of his impending death. He intended to sell his life not only as *deerly* as possibly, but as romantically and dramatically as possible.

Lewis's first assumption had been right. It was Cruzatte who shot him. "[I]n this state of anxiety and suspense [I] remained about 20 minutes when the party returned with Cruzatte and reported that there were no indians nor the appearance of any; Cruzatte seemed much allarmed and declared if he had shot me it was not his intention, that he had shot an Elk in the willows after he left or seperated from me."[109]

Fair enough, by why didn't Cruzatte rush forward immediately to help his stricken commander, as Lewis surely would have done had the reverse been true? Why didn't he at least respond when Lewis first damned him and then, in solicitude, called out in alarm to him? "I asked him whether he did not hear me when I called to him so frequently which he absolutely denied."[110] Cruzatte was almost certainly lying.

Lewis rightly concluded that Cruzatte had simply panicked. "I do not beleive that the fellow did it intentionally but after finding that he had shot me was anxious to conceal his knowledge of having done so." Just to make sure Cruzatte did not persist in his denial of responsibility, Lewis engaged in instant forensic analysis. "[T]he ball had lodged in my breeches which I knew to be the ball of the short rifles such as that he had, and there being no person out with me but him and no indians that we could discover I have no doubt in my own mind of his having shot me."[111]

Assuming that the shooting was indeed an accident, Cruzatte must have wondered, when he heard Lewis shout out in pain, surprise, and anger, whether he had killed his commanding officer. Instead of rushing forward to determine the extent of Lewis's wounds and to provide what help he could, Cruzatte shrank away and kept his mouth shut—a classical panic response. His mind no doubt was racing in the minutes following the shooting. If he had killed Lewis, what then? Would Clark regard it as an accident? Would it be possible to concoct an alibi? Should he flee? Would Clark punish him for the shooting? On the other hand, if Lewis lived, how would he respond if Cruzatte assumed responsibility for his actions? Would it be possible for Cruzatte to cover up his role in the accident?

These were heady minutes in the life of Pierre Cruzatte.

That evening, the Lewis party camped just upstream of the mouth of today's White Earth River. The Clark party was camped at the mouth of the Little Knife River just west of today's New Town, North Dakota. The two camps were separated by only twenty-one river miles. They were fifteen miles apart as the crow flies. Had either of the captains known this, he would have hastened to the other. Certainly the Lewis party would have wanted to catch up with Clark on August 11, given the drama of the day, had anyone known how close the Clark camp was.

How much Lewis slept on the night of August 11 is unknown. The next day, Patrick Gass reported, "Captain Lewis is in good spirits; but his wound stiff and sore."[112] The grand reunion of the captains finally occurred in the later morning of August 12, southwest of today's New Town (and Sanish) just across from the Fort Berthold Indian Reservation. The Clark party traveled just a dozen miles that day, the Lewis party thirty-two miles.

The rendezvous site, now inundated by Lake Sakakawea (behind Garrison Dam), is now known as Reunion Bay. Clark wrote, "[A]t meridian Capt Lewis hove in Sight with the party which went by way of the Missouri as well as that which accompanied him from Travellers rest on Clarks river."[113] *Meridian*, by now, was a loaded term. What should have been a glorious reunion was marred by the news—no doubt instantly reported—of the shooting accident. "I was alarmed on the landing of the Canoes to be informed that Capt. Lewis was wounded by an accident." Note that Clark declared immediately and definitively that the shooting was *an accident*. This will be important later in this story. "I found him lying in the Perogue," Clark reported. "[H]e informed me that his wound was slight [how very Lewis!] and would be well in 20 or 30 days [Lewis was right] this information relieved me very much. I examined the wound and found it a very bad flesh wound the ball had passed through the fleshey part of his left thy below the hip bone and cut the cheek of the right buttock for 3 inches in length and the debth of the ball."[114] Clark's forensics were excellent. His is certainly the best description we have of the nature of the wound.

Then Clark reconstructed what happened as precisely as possible. "Crusat Seeing Capt L. passing through the bushes and takeing him to be an Elk from the Colour of his Cloathes which were of leather and very nearly that of the Elk fired and unfortunately the ball passed through the thy as aforesaid."[115] In this important passage, Clark's prose rises to a formality that is rare in his journals. It is as if he were writing an official report of the incident. His prose suddenly reads as if he were taking an affidavit: "as aforesaid."

Clark scrambled a little to exonerate the near-sighted Cruzatte: "This Crusat is near Sighted and has the use of but one eye, he is an attentive industerous man and one whome we both have placed the greatest Confidence in dureing the whole rout."[116] In other words, Clark concluded that there was not the slightest possibility that the shooting was intentional. With that Clark shut the book on the Lewis shooting and, as the expedition's de facto "journal of record," proceeded to summarize the wild experiences of the Lewis party from the parting at Travelers' Rest to the return of the four-man, Two Medicine Creek rendezvous team to the Missouri River on July 28. Lewis's subsequent float through the White Cliffs and Missouri Breaks sections of the Missouri—today's premier Lewis and Clark canoe zone—is dismissed with, "from thenc they proceeded without delay to the River Rochejhone."[117] Bookended by two spectacular shootings, the fabled White Cliffs of the Missouri are reduced to a mere water artery.

After this, with Lewis having now gone entirely silent, Clark turned his attention to the reunion with the Mandan and Hidatsa, to the expedition's curious and consequential encounter with Forrest Hancock and Joseph Dixon of the Illinois country, and the expedition's urgent need to get someone from the Mandan or Hidatsa world to accompany the Corps of Discovery down river to St. Louis and then on to Washington, DC, to meet "the great Chief of the Seventeen Great nations of America."[118] Lewis lingered as a journal keeper long enough to write his account of the pin cherry (see above), and then dropped the curtain on his prose writing: "[A]s wrighting in my present situation is extreemly painfull to me I shall desist until I recover and leave to my frind Capt. C. the continuation of our journal."[119]

By September 9, within today's Nemaha County, Nebraska, twenty-nine days after the shooting, Clark reported, "My worthy friend Cap Lewis has entirely recovered his wounds are heeled up and he Can walk and even run nearly as well as ever he Could." Immediately afterwards, Clark added, almost *sotto voce*, "[T]he parts are yet tender &c. &."[120]

So Lewis recovered entirely from the double-buttock wounds he received at the hands of his boatman and fiddler Pierre Cruzatte. So far as we know, he did not suffer any permanent physical damage or walk thereafter with a limp, at least not after September 9, 1806. Historically, Lewis thus joined John Colter, Nathaniel Pryor, George Shannon, and George Drouillard as the most shot-at members of the Lewis and Clark Expedition. Lewis would be shot twice more before his life ended in October 1809. One does not think of it quite this way very often, but Meriwether Lewis was shot three times in the course of his life. At least one of those shots was lethal. He also apparently narrowly missed being shot (and presumably killed) by a young Piegan Blackfeet man on July 27, 1806.

Had Lewis ever wanted to "settle the score" with Cruzatte, the moment would have come on January 15, 1807, when he provided Secretary of War Henry Dearborn a detailed assessment of the contributions of the men of the Corps of Discovery. In this fascinating document, Lewis singles out a number of men for special praise—Francois Labiche, John Shields, the Field brothers—and a couple for what amounts to rebuke. Toussaint Charbonneau, for example, is dismissed as "A man of no peculiar merit; was useful as an interpreter only."[121] (That certainly wasn't Clark's assessment). Lewis also wrote a long assessment of John Newman, who had been dismissed from the company for uttering mutinous expressions on October 12, 1804, in northern South Dakota. Lewis explained to Secretary Dearborn that while Newman had done everything in his power after the court-martial to ingratiate himself to the captains and the men of the expedition, and though he "exerted himself on every occasion to become usefull," Lewis had nevertheless felt that it would be "impolitic to relax from the sentence, altho' he stood acquitted in my mind."[122] Newman, therefore, had been sent back with the keelboat in April 1805.

Lewis might easily have written a damaging assessment of Cruzatte in the evaluation he sent to Dearborn on January 15, 1807. He might have dismissed poor Cruzatte as "a man of no peculiar merit," or he might have

The Interior of Meriwether Lewis
A Study in Illustrations

Artwork by
Michael Haynes

The Marvin and Luella Snyder Collection

The Lewis & Clark Fort Mandan Foundation commissioned
Michael Haynes to create six original paintings to illustrate
The Character of Meriwether Lewis

"FT. MANDAN WINTER"

FEBRUARY 4, 1805: "This morning fair tho' could the thermometer stood at 18° below Naught, wind from N. W. Capt Clark set out with a hunting party consisting of sixteen of our command and two Frenchmen."

"Packer Meadows"

June 11, 1806: "we have never met with this plant but in or adjacent to a piny or fir timbered country, and there always in the open grounds and glades…. it delights in a black rich moist soil, and even grows most luxuriantly where the land remains from 6 to nine inches under water untill the seed are nearly perfect."

"Grizzly On The Missouri"

June 14, 1805: "the idea struck me to get into the water to such debth that I could stand and he would be obliged to swim, and that I could in that situation defend myself with my espontoon."

"Blackfeet Encounter"

July 27, 1806: "I also retook the flagg but left the medal about the neck of the dead man that they might be informed who we were."

"At The Yellowstone"

August 7, 1806: "I landed at the point and found that Capt. Clark had been encamped at this place and was gone."

"Grinder's Stand"

October 10, 1809: Neelly reported that Mrs. Grinder, "discovering the governor to be deranged gave him up the house & slept herself in one near it."

wrestled out a mixed assessment of the fine boatman who had nevertheless shot the leader of the expedition and failed to take immediate responsibility. Instead, he merely lists Cruzatte along with most other men as a private. At the end of the roll call, Lewis steps back to speak of the men as an exploring company: "With rispect to all those persons whose names are entered on this roll, I feel a peculiar pleasure in declaring, that the Ample support which they gave me under every difficulty; the manly firmness which they evinced on every necessary occasion; and the patience and fortitude with which they submitted to, and bore, the fatigues and painful sufferings incident to my late tour to the Pacific Ocean, entitles them to my warmest approbation and thanks."[123]

Lewis apparently accepted Clark's August 12 determination that "Capt. Lewis was wounded by an accident."[124] He apparently held no grudge. Cruzatte is listed as one of the men who exhibited manly firmness, patience, and fortitude during the expedition. And it is unlikely that Lewis smiled ironically (or winced) when he wrote to Dearborn of the "painful sufferings incident to my late tour."[125] *My late tour.* The seeds of later difficulties are contained in that three-word phrase.

That would seem to be the end of this wry story of the lowly mosquito and the bungled rendezvous, but events would bring the story to the surface again, seven months later, after the expedition's safe return to St. Louis. In early April 1807, Lewis published a prospectus of his proposed multi-volume report and narrative of the expedition. Meanwhile, Patrick Gass (through an agent) announced his plans to publish his own book about the journey. Lewis, who was already sliding towards inexplicable procrastination and silence, alarmed that Gass might preempt his master narrative and undercut the sales of his definitive account of the journey, published a public notice decrying "several unauthorised and probably some spurious publications now preparing for the press," and warning the public to be "on guard with respect to such publications."[126] Lewis said that while he had authorized the publication of Robert Frazer's journal, the public needed to know that Frazer, who "was only a private," could not be expected to provide any scientific data whatsoever. Frazer's publication could not offer more than "merely a limited detail of our daily transactions," Lewis concluded. He hoped the public would patiently await his own definitive publication, "as much time, labor, and expense are absolutely necessary in order to do justice to the several subjects."[127]

Lewis's public letter sufficiently offended Gass's agent David McKeehan (and possibly Gass, too) that it precipitated one of the most vitriolic public letters in American history. McKeehan wrote an open letter to Meriwether Lewis on April 7, 1807. McKeehan did everything in his power to belittle the commander of the expedition, undermine his credibility, hint that Lewis was as corrupt as he was pompous, pretentious, and egotistical, and directly challenge Lewis's assertion that the journals of the expedition belonged to him, not to the individuals who actually penned them.

At the close of the diatribe, McKeehan turned his satirical attention to the unfortunate affair at the Birnt Hills.

> I must pass over the unhappy affair with the Indians on the plains of Maria's river, also that very affecting one of your own posteriors, and conclude with congratulating you that Mr. Gass's Journal did not fall into the hands of some wag, who might have insinuated that your wound was not accidental, but that it was the consequence of design,—that the *young hero* might not return without more scars (if not *honorable*, near the *place of honour*) to excite the curiosity and compassion of some favorite widow Wadman, who might have been languishing during his absence. In what a ludicrous situation he might have placed the *young hero* with his *point of honour* just past the *point of a rock*, with Crusatte taking aim!—perhaps there will be a representation in the plates embellishing your second volume![128]

The Widow Wadman was a character in Thomas Sterne's experimental novel *Tristram Shandy*, which—curiously enough—was one of Thomas Jefferson's favorite books. Mostly, the poisonous McKeehan was just enjoying letting his readers know that the high falutin' Captain Lewis had been shot in the ass. Nothing is more likely to deflate a national hero than to bring his "posteriors" into the equation, to reduce him to farce in the manner of Chaucer's *Miller's Tale*. Wildly, McKeehan suggests that Lewis was so urgent to be the sort of hero who returns with wounds from his adventure in the wilderness that he instructed Cruzatte to shoot him—carefully—on August 11, 1806. Just picturing that ludicrous scenario—Lewis bent over, Cruzatte aiming to wound but not mortally—gives McKeehan pleasure and removes Lewis from the realm of heroism that McKeehan rightly believed was central to his self-conception. Such wounds, says McKeehan, would have made it more likely for Lewis to win the heart of a swooning damsel back in civilization. All the muddled reference to "place of honour," "point of a rock," etc., is just scatology.

It would have been more effective, perhaps, for McKeehan to suggest that Cruzatte had indeed shot Lewis on purpose, not to provide him with a heroic adventure wound, but rather to assassinate a man who McKeehan regarded as pretentious, over-bearing, greedy, and corrupt, and assumed others did too.

Viewed from retrospect, the reuniting of the separated strands of the Lewis and Clark Expedition was accomplished with considerable efficiency and—from an overarching perspective—almost simultaneously. Four subsets of the expedition were converging on the confluence region at the same time. The strands consisted of two bullboats (the Pryor four), two canoes lashed together (the Clark nine), the trusty but by now seriously leaking white pirogue, the only vessel that dated back to the beginnings of the voyage, accompanied by five canoes, one of which lagged behind carrying the trustworthy but tardy hunters John Collins and John Colter. All of these vehicles had reached the confluence of the Missouri and Yellowstone Rivers within the space of one week, beginning with the Clark party on August 3, with the Pryor party close behind, followed by the Lewis party on August 7, and ending with Colter and Collins a day or two behind Lewis. All four strands of the expedition were reunited once and for all on August 12, 1806, at a place now called Reunion Bay near today's New Town, North Dakota. The final reunion took place approximately eighty river miles from the confluence and fifty miles as the crow flies. Everyone was alive, though Lewis had survived a life-threatening shooting accident.

If Clark had not left the rendezvous site on August 4 or if Lewis had not been a high-strung, easily rattled, and mentally weary commander, the reunion might have been uneventful. Indeed, had Lewis persisted in his initial plan to move down river at a somewhat accelerated pace, had he not inexplicably halted his progress to hunt and dress skins just downstream from the confluence, things almost certainly would have gone much better.

It's not clear how much being shot in the ass by his own man affected Lewis in the long run. The sense one gets from the journals of Ordway, Gass, and particularly Clark (the only three still writing at this late point in the expedition) is that Lewis took the accident in stride and literally got back on his feet in relatively short order. Whether he suppressed the incident in his subsequent accounts of the journey or dined out on the basis of the semi-farcical shooting is unknown. We know he never obtained the hand of the Widow Wadman, with or without the wound. He certainly did not mention the incident in his initial letter to President Jefferson when the expedition reached St. Louis on September 23, 1806. What is certain, however, is that 1806 was an unhappy year of travel for Meriwether Lewis. His increasingly erratic behavior was so uncharacteristic and unaccountable that historian David Nicandri has posited that he was undergoing a slow-motion nervous breakdown on the return journey.[129] The flare-ups with Indians of the Columbia basin, which including the famous incident in which a young Nez Perce man threw a puppy in Lewis's plate, the beatings of petty Indian thieves, and threats to burn down whole villages; the disaster at Two Medicine Creek; the shooting accident at the Birnt Hills, not to mention the geopolitical-cartographic disappointments of the upper Marias and the expedition's failure to get the latitude of the northernmost point on the Missouri, represent a rising tide of difficulties, setbacks, and failures in the life of Meriwether Lewis. No biographer or historian doubts that Lewis's life spiraled downward after the expedition returned to St. Louis and Washington, DC. Just what role the events in northwestern North Dakota played in that disintegration of hopes, confidence, projects, and opportunities cannot be determined with precision. This much, however, seems certain. Being shot in the *posteriors* did no good for a man who, soon enough, would be telling his friend Mahlon Dickerson, "I never felt less like a heroe than at the present moment."[130]

The shooting incident near Williston, North Dakota, could have occurred at any time, and anywhere, in the course of the expedition. Lewis famously said, "[A]ccidents will happen in the best of families."[131] The expedition consisted of thirty-some heavily armed men living off the land and shooting their firearms constantly in close proximity, often under circumstances of fatigue, ill health, hurry, and poor weather. Given the possibilities of drownings (on an expedition in which a number of participants didn't know how to swim), falls from horses and cliffs, chopping and butchering accidents, fevers and infections and agues (in an age before antibiotics), near-misses with rattlesnakes, the ferocity of grizzly bears, some of them deliberately provoked by hunters, the fact of uncertain encounters with more than fifty Indian tribes, with some of whom the expedition could not really communicate, it is surprising that more men of the expedition did not die in the course of a twenty-eight month, 7,689 mile journey, that Sacagawea did not die at the Great Falls of her gynecological complaint, that Bratton did not die at the Pacific Coast of a slipped disk or whatever it was that had incapacitated him, and that Lewis was not fatally wounded on August 11. That Charles Floyd died in Iowa is unfortunate but hardly surprising. That more men did not die is little short of miraculous.

Still. It seems likely to me that Lewis would not have been shot by a nearly blind man near the confluence of the Missouri and Yellowstone Rivers had Clark been at hand in the post meridian on August 11. Somehow the steadying hand of William Clark had a calming effect on the personality of Meriwether Lewis. When Clark was present, Lewis tended to make better, more rational decisions and direct the expedition with a steadier hand. When Clark was absent, things often spun out of control. It is hard to imagine that Clark would have permitted a man of such poor eyesight as Cruzatte to accompany Lewis into that willow thicket. It is equally unlikely that Lewis, had he arrived first, would have drifted down river from the confluence rendezvous, given the absence of a well-established backup plan. If he *had* departed from the confluence, it certainly would not have been in response to the tyranny of the mosquito. And if he had made a unilateral decision to depart, Lewis would certainly have provided a better method of informing his co-captain of his subsequent plans and positions.

It seems likely, too, that if Clark had waited at the rendezvous site as agreed upon, Meriwether Lewis would never have been shot. The expedition would have regrouped, obtained enough animal skins to cover their nakedness for the reunion with the Mandan and Hidatsa, and then moved downstream

Triumph: Lewis wrote this letter to President Jefferson on the day
the Corps of Discovery, looking like characters out of *Robinson Crusoe*,
returned to St. Louis. Meriwether Lewis to Thomas Jefferson,
September 23, 1806. Courtesy of the Manuscript Division, Library of Congress.

with all due speed towards St. Louis. If the expedition had arrived at the geopolitically-important Birnt Hills after its hoped-for noon sightings, Clark would surely have sent Lewis out botanizing to while away the time between the lost meridian and high noon the next day, meanwhile sending out more reliable (and steadier) teams of hunters to obtain the desired skins and meat. I believe there is virtually a direct line of consequence between Clark's decision to leave the confluence on August 4 and the shooting of Meriwether Lewis seven days later. The shooting accident was not the end of Lewis, and it certainly was not the end of the world. But it would almost certainly not have occurred had the two captains reunited at the confluence as planned.

All this was precipitated by the lowly *musquetor*—weight 2.5 milligrams.

CHAPTER IV The Problem of Lewis's Silences

"The history of exploration is not just that of people breaking new ground; it is also that of people *writing* about breaking new ground."

—Fergus Fleming
Off the Map:
Tales of Endurance
and Exploration

"Those whose lot it is to ramble can seldom write, and those who know how to write very seldom ramble."

—Dr. Johnson[715]

MY THESIS IS SIMPLE. WHAT WE HAVE HERE IS A FAILURE TO communicate. Meriwether Lewis was a great but sporadic and unreliable communicator. Virtually everything that went wrong in his life following his return to civilization in 1806 has a relation to his failure to write to those who needed to hear from him: Thomas Jefferson; the War Department; and the publishers of his book. If he had maintained even reasonably close contact with his patron Jefferson, and with the officials of James Madison's War Department, Lewis would almost certainly not have killed himself on October 11, 1809.

It's the silence that killed him. Lewis and Clark have been called "the writingest explorers of their time,"[2] and yet the principal member of the expedition was silent more often than he was writing.

Why Lewis fell into sustained silences is unclear. There are five possible explanations. 1. He was busy with other pressing duties during and after the expedition. 2. He suffered from a mental disease of some sort—perhaps manic depression or bipolar disorder—and there were times when he could just not bring himself to write. 3. He was punishing others in some way by withholding communication from them. 4. He was insecure. His lack of self-esteem led him to avoid communicating with others, because he felt somehow that anything he wrote would be inadequate, or would expose his inadequacies.[3] 5. It was a character issue. He felt that he was beyond supervision, and that he should be trusted to organize whatever was in front of him without having to answer to anyone (This was Frederick Bates's view). In other words, his silence was a form of arrogance. Possibly it was a combination of these factors. My purpose here is not to try to solve the mystery of Lewis's silences, but to describe and analyze them as best I can, and to assess the damage they did to his relations with Jefferson, the War Department, his friendships, and his career.

Lewis engaged in three types of silence in the course of his life. He failed to keep a daily journal during the expedition he led across the continent. He failed to write the book he boldly promised to the world in early April 1807. And he failed to communicate with his superiors in Washington during his time as the governor of Louisiana Territory.

To be sure, Lewis was an exceedingly busy man before, during, and after the expedition. It is possible that he was busier between March 1808 and September 1809 than at any previous period of his life, including the expedition. The administrative biography of Lewis by Thomas Danisi and John Jackson puts to rest once and for all the idea that Lewis was idle in the years following his return from the shores of the Pacific Ocean. It may be, as a number of historians have argued, that President Jefferson made a terrible mistake in appointing Lewis to be the governor of Louisiana Territory. Lewis had gone from army officer to Jefferson's aide de camp, to commander of an army exploration party, to territorial governor in the pace of seven years. Stephen Ambrose has writtten, "Jefferson's appointment of Lewis to the governorship was a frightful misjudgment. Jefferson should have found him a post in Washington or Philadelphia and given him some War Department clerks to help with the publication process."[4] Even if Lewis had been temperamentally suited for the position, he had no previous experience at that level of government administration, and his post-expedition time would have been much better spent writing the three-volume account that Jefferson and the Enlightenment regarded as the capstone and *sine qua non* of a successful journey of discovery. Thomas Slaughter has written, "The explorer often faces the greatest challenge after his welcome home. When the celebration ends, he must become a writer. This is essential for self-promoting his discoveries. He must compose himself, make order out of disorderly notes that he took in the wild before he knew what his story would be. This can be scarier than the journey. He must publish or his discoveries may perish along with him."[5]

In retrospect, we can see that Lewis took on too much during the three years and eighteen days that followed his return to St. Louis in September 1806. While it is certainly true that Governor Lewis was irresponsible in delaying his arrival in St. Louis until a full year after he had been appointed by the president and confirmed by the United States Senate, part of the responsibility for his tardiness belongs to Jefferson, who first had Lewis run a series of silly errands for him in Philadelphia[6] and then—

in September 1807—sent him to Richmond, Virginia, to monitor the Aaron Burr treason trial on his behalf. Jefferson had appointed Lewis to high office, but he continued to treat the now-famous explorer as an errand boy and aide de camp. Nor was it possible to say no to Jefferson. By the time Lewis arrived in St. Louis in March 1808, he had already effectively lost control of his own territorial administration. The multi-ethnic, even multi-national, affairs of the territory were so tangled and beset with controversy, so lacking in basic civic order, and so unprecedented as a problem of territorial administration within an emerging republican constitutional system, that Lewis was immediately overwhelmed. Concurrently, Territorial Secretary Frederick Bates let his own ambition, ego, and envy of Lewis get in the way of his work. Instead of helping Lewis succeed as governor, Bates turned his considerable talents to undermining Lewis's credibility and efficiency. Lewis worked assiduously to bring order to the territory, but he was never able to establish complete control over the jumble of public and private affairs he encountered when at last he arrived. The workload, coupled with the political and legal chaos of Louisiana Territory, effectively prevented him from making progress on his book. To write the book he would have had to leave the territory, but he did not wish to fail or resign as governor or disappoint his great mentor and patron. By early 1809 Lewis was in an essentially impossible position. If he stayed in St. Louis to try to manage the territory, there would be no book any time soon, and the outgoing president was pressing him to publish at least the first volume of his travels at the earliest possibility. If he returned to Philadelphia to write the book, he would be abdicating his territorial responsibilities (again) and worsening an already unstable situation. Instead of seeking help from Jefferson, who surely would have done whatever he could to lighten Lewis's burden and serve as his advocate and intermediary with Madison and his cabinet, Lewis foolishly went silent. In doing so he not only lost the help of the most disciplined and resourceful administrator of the early national period, but annoyed the most important person in his life.

On the transcontinental journey of 1804–06, Lewis had a great deal to attend to, even with the extraordinary William Clark at his side. Later in the nineteenth century, the polymath explorer-anthropologist Richard Francis Burton made a list of things travelers were now expected to accomplish in the field. The explorer, he wrote, "is expected to survey and observe, to record meteorology and trigonometry, to shoot and stuff birds and beasts, to collect geological specimens and theories, to gather political and commercial information … to advance the infant study of anthropology; to keep accounts, to sketch, to indite a copious, legible journal … and to forward long reports which shall prevent the Royal Geographical Society napping through its evenings."[7] Lewis was frequently silent in the course of the journey, but he was never idle. Unfortunately, his labors in determining latitude and longitude, discovering, collecting, pressing, drying, and label-ing plant specimens, discovering, collecting, eviscerating, and preserving animal specimens, collecting and classifying mineral samples, examining what he took to be ancient fortifications or the petrified bones of ancient fish (i.e., fossils), and gathering weather data twice a day at 43 below zero at Fort Mandan or 105 degrees above zero at the Great Falls, did not always lend themselves to discursive entries in the expedition's journals. The written records of Lewis's intensive scientific activities are mostly ex-tant, but they have been omitted from most publications of the expedition's journals, or marooned in appendices. The so-called *Mandan Miscellany*, for example, a series of charts and reports about the rivers and Indian tribes of the American West (broadly defined), jointly compiled by Lewis and Clark, but principally written by Lewis during the Fort Mandan winter, has been almost entirely ignored in the literature of the Lewis and Clark Expedition. The natural history essays (journal entries) Lewis wrote be-tween January and late March 1806 during the gloomy winter at Fort Clatsop have been omitted from most editions of Lewis and Clark, or re-duced to a modest sampling. Thus Lewis wrote more and more regularly than has generally been recognized—but his output must be measured in his formal reports rather than his journal. In assigning to his partner Clark the role of keeping a daily *captain's log* of the routine incidents of the journey, Lewis was freeing himself to engage in more serious intellectual pursuits. The diaspora of the specimens, artifacts, and other physical fruits of the expedition in the decades following the Corps of Discovery's return has had the effect of diminishing Lewis's achievement.[8] That scientific treasury was as important as words on a page to the Enlightenment com-munity in Philadelphia, London, Paris, Edinburgh, and elsewhere. Had the United States possessed a national museum in the age of Jefferson, the artifacts of the expedition would have found a permanent—and presumably secure—home. If they could all be magically recovered and displayed in the Smithsonian Museum, Lewis's reputation would enjoy a significant recovery.

Still, there is no question that Lewis failed to communicate in ways that frustrated those around him, particularly his mentor Jefferson and the bu-reaucrats of the War Department. After all, he wasn't the only busy man in American government. For all of Lewis's hectic activity, there is no question that he had an unfortunate propensity to go silent at critical moments in his life. If he had been as reliable a communicator as his friend and partner William Clark, he might not have spiraled down into desperation and mental collapse in 1809. Lewis was indeed extraordinarily busy, but so were William Clark and Thomas Jefferson. Indeed, Jefferson was one of the busiest men in American history, but his gift for continuous correspondence broke down only once or twice—briefly—in the course of an eighty-three-year life.

The paradox of Lewis's silences is obvious to anyone who has ever read the journals of the expedition carefully. Lewis was a gifted and accomplished writer. But more often than not he failed to keep proper written records. Clark was seldom more than an adequate and prosaic writer. But he was profoundly reliable, and reliability, it turns out, means more in human affairs than genius. The leader of the Lewis and Clark Expedition was a man who failed to fulfill the central obligation of the explorer. Fergus Fleming has written, "The history of exploration is not just that of people breaking new ground; it is also that of people *writing* about breaking new ground."[9] It doesn't do any good to be the first civilized man to leave footsteps on this or that landscape, to make first contact with this or that aboriginal tribe, to witness some "grand object, which has from the commencement of time been concealed from the view of civilized man," and not write it up, not "give to the world some faint idea of an object which at this moment fills me with such pleasure and astonishment."[10] History belongs to the record keepers. The battle of San Juan Hill was a minor episode in the Spanish-American War of 1898, but Theodore Roosevelt wrote a superbly self-referential book about it and not only became a national hero but permanently distorted the way we think about that "splendid little war," as John Hay characterized it.[11] Republican Rome's wars against Gaul (58–51 BCE) were a relatively minor event in the long, sad history of human warfare, but the masterful book that Julius Caesar wrote about those campaigns, *Comentarii de Bello Gallico* (*Commentaries on the Gallic War*), has been one of the most influential memoirs in the history of western civilization, and it has assured that every literate generation will continue to study the wars that propelled Caesar into the dictatorship that, in turn, brought about his assassination. It is certain that a number of other European men traveled into the deep interior of America before Lewis and Clark, but because they did not publish accounts of their journeys most of them are entirely unknown to history. Those few who are known at all have, thanks to their silence, condemned themselves to a miniscule place in the annals of exploration. Lewis's failure to keep adequate records of his journey not only left key episodes of the expedition entirely undescribed by anyone who was present, but reduced the written record for more than half of the expedition to the reliable but uninspired narrative written by William Clark. If Lewis had maintained a continuous journal, if he had written about his arrival at the falls of the Columbia or at the shore of the Pacific as well as he wrote about his encounter with the Shoshone or the Great Falls of the Missouri River, we would have a much richer documentary base upon which to make sense of the expedition's larger contours and purposes, and one of the key chapters in the history of white-Indian relations in American history. Indeed, the historian David Nicandri has carefully asserted that Lewis's failure to write up his journey through the Columbia watershed has made it possible for subsequent generations to wreak industrial havoc on the Columbia and the Snake that might have been chastened had Lewis lavished on that landscape the care and eloquence he delivered for his beloved Missouri River.[12] Whether the Missouri—one of the most heavily industrialized rivers in the world—has really been spared is a matter of debate; Nicandri means that the Great Falls have not been *entirely* obliterated by dams and that the stretch of the Missouri between Fort Benton and the slack waters of Fort Peck Reservoir is comparatively untrammeled.

No matter how busy Clark became, he took the time to write up his journal, either on the day that the activities occurred or relatively soon thereafter while he could still sort out the sequence of events. Clark was a very unusual man in this regard. For every thousand individuals who begin a journal on New Year's Day or their birthday, only a handful manage to sustain it through the course of an entire year, and only a very few would be able to sustain it for twenty-eight months of wilderness adventure. The English biographer and diarist James Boswell (1740–1795)—one of the most disciplined journal keepers who ever lived—once said "a man should not live more than he can record, as a farmer should not have a larger crop than he can gather in."[13] This is the other end of the spectrum from stubborn silence, but it enabled Boswell to write what is widely considered the greatest diary in human history and to mine that diary for his magnificent *Life of Samuel Johnson, LL.D.*, first published in 1791. Clark kept detailed and continuous diaries throughout his life. He was a reliable correspondent. He presented his financial vouchers to the War Department on a timely basis. He kept up with the rhythms of his life.

For whatever reasons, Lewis at times found it impossible to keep up with the rhythms of *his* life. He could not maintain a continuous journal. The longest period of sustained writing he managed on the journey was between January 1 and August 12, 1806, a period of seven months, twelve days (224 days). That long run of continuous journals ended when Lewis was shot in the buttocks by Pierre Cruzatte on August 11, 1806. The next day, near today's New Town, North Dakota, Lewis sensibly wrote, "[A]s wrighting in my present situation is extreemly painfull to me I shall desist untill I recover and leave to my frind Capt. C. the continuation of our journal."[14] Lewis's second longest period of sustained journal keeping was between April 7 and August 26, 1805, a period of four months and twenty days (142) days. That run began with the expedition's departure from Fort Mandan, and ended when the expedition began its bewildering journey along the spine of the Bitterroots in search of a gap that would deposit them on navigable waters of the Snake-Columbia river system. Between August 27 and September 23, 1805, Lewis managed a handful of journal entries, but with the expedition's arrival at Weippe Prairie on the west side of the Bitterroot Mountains, Lewis sputtered into prolonged silence.

When (September 22, 1805) he reckoned he had "triumphed over the rock-ey Mountains and [was] decending once more to a level and fertile country where there was every rational hope of finding a comfortable subsistence for myself and party,"[15] Lewis went silent for the rest of 1805. He wrote nothing from September 23 to December 31, 1805, (100 days), though it was one of the most eventful phases of the expedition and the period during which a significant number of the expedition's Indian encounters occurred.

Lewis was also silent for the entire first year of the expedition's travel, May 14 to October 26, 1804, with the exception of two days in September, and he wrote nothing through the long, cold winter at Fort Mandan, October 27, 1804, to April 6, 1805, for a total of 328 days (326 if you subtract the entries of September 16–17, 1804). In other words, Lewis did not really begin to keep a journal in earnest until the *second year* of the expedition's travels.

Lewis's journal silences are troubling but they are not inexplicable. I begin with the hiatus easiest to explain and work my way towards the more perplexing ones.

AUGUST 12-SEPTEMBER 23, 1806. Lewis had a perfectly rational reason for going silent after the shooting accident of August 11, 1806. He was in considerable pain, and he had to position his body, on land or in the boat, so that he put no pressure on his wounded buttocks. That essentially means that he was prone, face down, or bent over a bundle or keg for the month following the shooting. Meanwhile, beginning on the afternoon of August 12, the entire Corps of Discovery was together again for the first time since July 3, 1806, and Lewis knew that the always-reliable Clark could be counted on to maintain the expedition's journal, what he called "our journal"[16] and what I call the *captain's log*. Furthermore, the expedition was now in the home stretch, moving too fast for much detailed observation, through country that Lewis did not regard as having been discovered by the expedition. Everyone, not merely the two captains, just wanted to get home. Everyone, that is, except John Colter, who turned back at the Mandan and Hidatsa villages to accompany a pair of enterprising green-horns into the Yellowstone country.

SEPTEMBER 23-DECEMBER 31, 1805. By the time the Corps of Discovery stumbled out of the Rocky Mountains in late September 1805, Lewis was physically and spiritually exhausted. The accumulated stresses of leading thirty-two people, twenty-nine horses, and more than 10,000 pounds of baggage through the Bitterroot Mountains at a time when winter had already begun at that elevation, and trying to eke out enough calories from the land to keep the company alive and proceeding on, had taken a toll on the high-strung Lewis. The Bitterroot ordeal came directly on the heels of the agonizing Lost Trail detour from Lemhi Pass to Lolo Pass (August 31 to September 9), which in turn came just after the intensely nerve-wracking encounter with the suspicious and skittish Shoshone Indians (August 13–30). Lewis was the iron man of the expedition, but he had used up his physical and spiritual reserves between August 12 and September 23, 1805. The sudden shift in diet from buffalo and then horse to the salmon and roots of the Nez Perce bedeviled many members of the expedition, but none so completely as Lewis, who was so incapacitated that he had to lie down on the side of the trail to vent the flatulence brought on by the strange new food supply and its attendant bacteria. Clark, who was freely dispensing Dr. Rush's thunderclappers to all the afflicted men, wrote, "Capt Lewis Scercely able to ride on a jentle horse which was furnishd by the Chief."[17] Even though he was suffering from a gastro-intestinal disorder like everyone else during this period, the long-suffering Clark wrote, with more than a hint of annoyance, "I continu verry unwell but obliged to attend every thing."[18]

Lewis's silence during this period has another possible motive. For some reason Lewis decided he was a Missouri River explorer and not particularly a Snake-Columbia man. Somehow the Missouri River engaged his imagination much more completely than did the Columbia system. The Missouri, not the Columbia, formed the watershed of the Louisiana Purchase. The Missouri was America's river, the Columbia still a no man's land, a contested watershed. From a Jeffersonian point of view, the Missouri was a much more *rational* river, linear, with its headwaters in the geopolitically proper place, and navigable almost to its source. "I do not believe that the world can furnish an example of a river runing to the extent which the Missouri and Jefferson's river do through such a mountainous country and at the same time so navigable as they are,"[19] Lewis wrote. It must have been reaching the source of the Missouri River rather than crossing the continent that had constituted the *darling project* and the *great object* upon which Lewis's mind had been fixed for many years. He was apparently a great river source-hunter, like his contemporaries James Bruce (the Nile), Mungo Park (the Niger), and Zebulon Pike (the Mississippi and Arkansas). Once he had bestridden the "mighty & heretofore deemed endless Missouri,"[20] Lewis appears to have regarded his mission as essentially finished. Lewis's sense of fascination and discovery was entirely confined within the Louisiana Territory. He exhibited a palpable diminution of interest in the Pacific watershed. Such a discrimination makes very little sense to us, because we like to think of the Lewis and Clark Expedition as a *transcontinental* journey of discovery, extending, as Stephen Ambrose liked to put it, from "sea to shining sea." We are constantly driving the embarkation point, the "start of the journey," eastward: from the mouth of the Missouri River at St. Charles to Louisville—from Louisville to Pittsburgh—from

Pittsburgh to Charlottesville or Washington, DC,—and from those locations to the intellectual capital of the United States, Philadelphia. Even though President Jefferson instructed his protégé to seek "the most direct & practicable water communication across this continent, for the purposes of commerce,"[21] Lewis appears to have regarded his primary mission as *clearing the road* of the Missouri River and ascertaining its source.

In other words, Lewis was white America's first great lover of Montana. By the time Clark had completed his map at Fort Clatsop (February 14, 1806), Lewis was well aware that "the most direct & practicable water route across this continent" did not embrace the Gates of the Mountains, the Three Forks, or the Beaverhead River and Lemhi Pass. In its search for the source of the Missouri River, the Corps of Discovery had gone far out of its way, on a great fishhook-like detour that consumed two full months of precious time. The fact is that by the time he had portaged around the Great Falls, Lewis already had good reason to know that the most direct route was to move directly west from today's Sun River towards Missoula, then up and over Lolo Pass, along the Nez Perce "trail to the buffalo," and then down into navigable waters of the Clearwater somewhere around today's Orofino, Idaho. That's the route Lewis investigated on the return journey. Some inkling of this geographical information had been made known to him at Fort Mandan by Hidatsa cartographers. Even if Lewis had understood this essential geographic information with indisputable assurance, it seems to me extremely unlikely that he would have diverged from the course of the Missouri River before bestriding its source, no matter how much labor, delay, or inconvenience the quest for the headwaters represented. Whatever the geopolitically and commercially minded Jefferson intended, Lewis was determined to venture all the way to the source of the "heretofore conceived boundless Missouri,"[22] and quench his thirst at its fountain spring. Lewis's phrase is heroic, but it is also extremely revealing. You don't veer off a river that is "conceived boundless" or "deemed endless" before solving the mystery of its "heretofore" unknown source.

When the explorer John Wesley Powell (1834–1902) was urged by three of his colleagues to climb out of the appallingly menacing Grand Canyon at what is today known as Separation Rapids on August 28, 1869, he nearly acquiesced. Then he had a very Lewis-like moment. "But for years I have been contemplating this trip," he wrote. "To leave the exploration unfinished, to say that there is a part of the canyon which I cannot explore, having already almost accomplished it, is more than I am willing to acknowledge, and I determine to go on."[23] Powell was floating downstream, away from the source of the Colorado River, which he had never seen. The linearity of rivers has some kind of deep psychological appeal to the human consciousness. There is, apparently, something fundamentally compelling about the quest for the source. Freud is probably a better guide to source-hunting than Ptolemy, Gerardus Mercator, or Amerigo Vespucci. On the basis of human curiosity alone, it would be hard to explain the amount of money, effort, blood, and drama that was spent in the 2,000-year search for the source of the River Nile. The nineteenth century had a particular obsession with source hunting, perhaps because the primal urge to ascend (or return) to the source was buttressed by the Enlightenment's quest to know everything, in Lewis's terms "to advance the information of the succeeding generation,"[24] and by the considerable government sponsorship that was suddenly available for voyages of discovery. Lewis was a participant in source mania. He was not going to leave the Missouri River at Upper Portage Camp at the Great Falls.

By the time Lewis reached navigable waters of the Clearwater River, particularly after wandering among the labyrinthine braids of the geographically *irrational* upper tributaries of the Salmon River, he had lost interest in the Columbia watershed. With his reserves of energy, imagination, and enthusiasm now exhausted, Lewis contented himself with being a passenger on, rather than an explorer of, the Columbia River. His silence was irresponsible, but it was not inexplicable.

MAY 14, 1804-APRIL 7, 1805. Lewis's silence during this period is in many respects mystifying. Not only were Jefferson's instructions clear, but one would have thought that his excitement in setting out from St. Charles on a journey that had represented "a darling project of mine for the last ten years,"[25] after several years of earnest preparation, would have inspired Lewis to express that excitement in a sustained series of proud and eloquent journal entries. The epic of his life was at last underway. He was the leader of a band of American Argonauts threading their way into the heart of a still-mysterious continent on behalf of the philosopher-prince of Monticello. He was a man of destiny. The president himself had chosen him to explore one of the most significant chunks of unknown territory in the world. The embarkation at St. Charles would have been an appropriate place to invoke the muses of Columbus and Captain Cook, or Calliope for that matter, to wax eloquent about the mission of *civilized man*, to report that not a whisper or murmur of discontentment was to be heard among the men.

Nothing. Silence. Lewis reserved that sort of discourse for his departure from Fort Mandan. Instead we are left with Clark's basic English: "I Set out at 4 oClock P.M. in the presence of many of the Neighbouring inhabitents, and proceeded on under a jentle brease up the Missourie to the upper Point of the 1st Island ... ."[26]

In May 1804 Lewis was in perfect health, zealously attached to the enterprise, and anxious to proceed. Nobody can argue that he was physically or spiritually exhausted at this stage of the journey. All the evidence we have indicates that Lewis was always happiest when he was underway, that forward motion of any sort tended to cause his pen to flow copiously. Instructed by Jefferson to commit his observations to paper, and knowing that he would need every scrap of field information to write the book that would be the final product of the expedition, exhilarated as never before in the course of his thirty years in the sublunary world, why would Lewis travel from St. Charles to the great bend of the Missouri River in North Dakota in nearly total silence? It makes no sense.

It is possible that Lewis kept a journal for this period that was subsequently lost or destroyed. That would be the most logical explanation for his silence. Unfortunately, there is almost no evidence to support that notion. Lewis's letter to President Jefferson from Fort Mandan, dated April 7, 1805, makes it clear that he had no journal to send to the president, not even one as rough as Clark's, which he did forward, in spite of Clark's painful request that he "dose not wish this journal exposed in it's present state, but has no objection, that one or more copies of it be made by some confidential person under your direction, correcting it's grammatical errors &c."[27] Lewis promised the president that he would send a canoe and small crew back to St. Louis from "the extreme navigable point of the Missouri." With that crew, Lewis wrote, "I shal send you my journal, and some one or two of the best of those kept by my men."[28] This suggests that Lewis was planning to reconstruct (or perhaps *construct*) his journal from some set of records, either his own fragmentary field notes, or Clark's journal embellished with his own memories and reflections, during the journey from Fort Mandan to the source of the Missouri River. It seems clear that Lewis regarded Clark as a reliable field note taker and record keeper whose jottings would serve as the basis for a formal *journal* that he (Lewis) would fashion from such raw materials as he could consult during leisure moments in the journey through the undiscovered country of today's Montana. If this was his plan, it apparently broke down in the face of the strains of duty west of Fort Mandan, including his need to keep a daily journal for *that* portion of the journey.

Unless Lewis's rough journal or field notes for the first year have been lost or destroyed, the best explanation for his silence during that 328-day period of his travels is that he did not regard the journey from St. Charles to the Mandan and Hidatsa villages as a period of authentic exploration, that he was, as it were, saving himself for the moment when he actually walked off the map of the known world. Lewis was well aware that other white people had ventured from the mouth of the Missouri as far upriver as the Mandan and Hidatsa villages, and perhaps a little beyond, and that previous Europeans had both mapped and named the landscape of that 1,610-mile stretch of the Missouri River. Charles Hoffhaus has written, "During the first half of the route," of the Lewis and Clark Expedition, French voyageurs "were merely showing Lewis and Clark what had been their own backyard for over a century.... The idea that [Lewis and Clark were] 'exploring' country they and their fathers and grandfathers had traversed annually for decades would surely have struck them as a good joke."[29] All the evidence suggests that Lewis believed that the true *discovery phase* of the expedition began on April 7, 1805, when the six small canoes and two large pirogues shoved off from the portal of Fort Mandan into the great unknown. At that juncture, at what Lewis perhaps regarded as the genuine starting point of *his* journey of exploration and discovery, he began to keep a copious journal. Lewis's journal from the moment of departure from Fort Mandan through his tense and complicated encounter with the Shoshone Indians is one of the great documents of American history. If all other records of the expedition had been lost, Lewis's journal between April 7 and August 26, 1805, would still be a document of extraordinary historical and literary importance, and it would by itself capture the essence of the expedition even though it represents only one leg of the total journey.

Lewis did manage to keep a continuous journal for a little under half of the expedition, for what must have seemed to him the most important parts of the journey. Meanwhile, Clark's essentially uninterrupted baseline journal adequately covers every incident of the expedition when he and Lewis were together. Lewis's silences only represent a fundamental failure to the official mission of the expedition when he was alone at a critical time, without Clark on hand to provide a backup documentary record of those events. The first of those moments came on November 25–26, 1804, when Lewis ventured from the construction site of Fort Mandan to the Hidatsa villages a dozen miles upstream. By now the expedition had established a good working relationship with the Mandan people, whose two villages were close enough to Fort Mandan to make almost daily intercourse possible. On October 29, 1804, three days after arriving at the future site of Fort Mandan, the captains had attempted to conduct a council with Hidatsa leaders, but extremely high winds and the undisguised impatience of the Hidatsa had left everyone unsatisfied. Now, a month later, Lewis, with two interpreters and six others, set out to meet the Hidatsa leadership at their own villages at the mouth of the Knife River. His goal was to improve relations between the Corps of Discovery and the Hidatsa. It was not a very satisfying diplomatic journey. When he returned on November 27, 1804, Lewis reported to Clark that he had been able to calm Hidatsa fears— apparently stirred up by the Mandan—that "we intended to join the *Seaux* to Cut off them in the Course of the winter."[30] The clever and entrepreneurial Mandan were apparently doing everything they could to make sure that Lewis and Clark continued to trade exclusively with them and not their allies (but also mercantile competitors) the Hidatsa. Or perhaps the Hidatsa were just expressing a rationale for staying away from the brash Americans, whom they did not much like.[31] At any rate, Lewis was treated rudely by the Hidatsa leader Horned Weasel who, like a European aristocrat, had instructed his neighbors to communicate to the visiting dignitary that he "was not at home &c."[32] What little we know about this important diplomatic excursion we learn from Clark who was not a witness. Given President Jefferson's deep interest in establishing and maintaining peaceful relations with the Indians of the Louisiana Territory, one would have expected the leader of the expedition, who was traveling without Clark on this occasion, to have written a serious account of his diplomatic initiative. Lewis was silent. This seems unaccountable and inexcusable given how much was at stake.

The other moment when Lewis's silence seems officially irresponsible was when he ventured around Point Ellice on the Washington side of the lower Columbia on November 14, 1805, ostensibly to see if a white trade ship was anchored in Baker's Bay, but more probably to become the first member of the expedition to stand on the shore of the Pacific Ocean, or at least to get there before his partner in discovery William Clark. Clark followed Lewis around the stormy point late in the afternoon of the next day. One would have expected Lewis to write a lavish and self-congratulatory journal entry on or about November 14, 1805, to celebrate his triumph over the North American continent, and to establish his primacy as the expedition's principal explorer at land's end. He did not. Stephen Ambrose has written, "It is through Lewis's eyes and words that we see the White Cliffs, the Great Falls before the dams, the Gates of the Mountains, Three Forks, the Shoshones. Wonderful portraits, all. Vivid. Immediate. Detailed. They set the standard. But we don't have his description of what he saw and how he felt in his moment of triumph."[33] David Nicandri is so startled by Lewis's silence at the terminus of the continent that he gives the silent captain the benefit of the doubt: "This was such an anomaly as to suggest, though we cannot be certain, that Lewis kept an ephemeral record of some sort on that trek, but it was lost."[34]

Clark dutifully mentioned Lewis's November 14 pre-emptive venture around Point Ellice in his journal. Who knows what he thought when he later (November 17) saw that Lewis had carved his name only on a tree near the shoreline? Clark left no record of his reaction. Clark chose to describe the end of the expedition's journey in his usual understated, matter-of-fact way. If only from the perspective of America's claim to what later would be called the Oregon Country, Lewis had a professional duty to write an account of the short but important last steps of his transcontinental journey taken on November 14. America's sovereignty was at stake. In a letter to John Hawkins of May 5, 1807, Philadelphia painter and museum director Charles Willson Peale emphasized the importance of this last little excursion. "McKinsey [Alexander Mackenzie] only went to a River which ran into the South Sea," he wrote. "But... Lewis and Clark have actually visited the sea shore, and I have animals brought from the sea coast ... ."[35] Peale, though he was misreading Mackenzie's journal and shortchanging the Scottish explorer, was making an argument about American sovereignty, about Jefferson's "empire for liberty," as much as about national pride. Because of Lewis's silence, the great outbound journey ended in the journals not with a bang but a whimper. On November 15, the soggy, dispirited, and miserable William Clark was able to muster only, "[T]his I could plainly See would be the extent of our journey by water, as the waves were too high at any Stage for our Canoes to proceed any further down."[36] This is not the stuff of heroic poetry, but it beats silence. On a literary spectrum with epic grandiloquence at one end and the most pedestrian and jejune prose at the other end, Clark's weary utterance registers as far from the heroic as it would be possible to position oneself. Clark was, on this and other occasions, essentially (and perhaps deliberately) the anti-Lewis.

All students of Lewis and Clark wish, too, that Lewis had written an account of the four-day standoff with the Teton Sioux (Brule Lakota) at the mouth of the Bad River near today's Pierre, South Dakota. Clark's account (September 24–28, 1804) is outstanding, but Lewis's, had the switch been on, would have provided a triangulating second lens on one of the handful of most important incidents of the entire expedition. Furthermore, the captains were separated at key moments of the Lakota crisis, and Clark reports on Lewis's experience at the Lakota village at second hand. Lewis's later accounts of his encounters with the Shoshone (August 11–17, 1805) and with the Blackfeet (July 26–27, 1806) are so brilliant, dramatic, and masterfully crafted (if only as narratives) that one longs for his voice at other important moments of the journey, never more than during the crisis with what the captains called "the vilest miscreants of the savage race."[37] Instead, Lewis was silent.

THE BOOK

Lewis never published the two-part, three-volume book he promised the world in April 1807. After his violent death, his publishers reported to Jefferson (November 13, 1809) that "Govr. Lewis never furnished us with a line of the M.S. nor indeed could we ever hear any thing from him respecting it tho frequent applications to that effect were made to him."[38] It is common now to declare that Lewis never wrote a page (or even a line) of his book manuscript. That notion deserves to be deconstructed. It may be that what we regard as Lewis's *journal* was in fact a more polished document cast as a journal but well along the way towards a publishable manuscript, but it was certainly not anywhere near finished at the time of his death. David Nicandri goes so far as to declare that "most if not all of Lewis's account of the voyage up the Missouri from Fort Mandan to Lemhi

Pass was unquestionably a first draft of text intended for publication and not a record of proceedings made in the field."[39] I believe Nicandri overstates the case a little, but his insight is closer to the truth than the notion that Lewis's surviving journal is a simple transcript of what he actually wrote in the field. William Clark believed that Lewis was returning to the East in the fall of 1809 at least as much to "write our Book"[40] as to sort things out with the War Department. Apparently Lewis told Gilbert Russell much the same thing at Fort Pickering. He was, Russell reported, "taking with him all the papers relative to his expedition to the pacific Ocean, for the purpose of preparing and puting them to the press."[41]

Why didn't Lewis write the book? Danisi and Jackson argue that as the governor of Louisiana Territory Lewis was simply too busy with territorial affairs that he could not ignore to pay proper attention to a writing project that did not constitute one of his official duties in St. Louis.[42] Undoubtedly they are right that Lewis was consumed with official duties in St. Louis, but he had time to help launch a newspaper, to which he contributed occasional essays. He had time to create the first Masonic lodge west of the Mississippi River. He had time to attend balls and other social functions in the territorial capital. He had time to engage in an impressive and economically destabilizing series of private land transactions in the Louisiana Territory and to be one of the founders of the Saint Louis Missouri Fur Company. He had time to write Clark a teasing letter about the terminology with which the newlywed described his matrimonial bliss.

Lewis's mentor Jefferson wrote his book *Notes on the State of Virginia* in the summer of 1781, with a broken wrist, after a bad fall from a horse, in the middle of a war, under a cloud of disgrace, after the most humiliating moment of his long career, publicly accused of being a coward, with a wife who was ill, at one of the remotest white settlements in America (Poplar Forest near today's Lynchburg, Virginia). That book won immediate international acclaim and was soon regarded as an American classic. It is unlikely that the excuse of busy-ness was going to work with Jefferson.

I believe Lewis was unable to write his book for three reasons, in ascending order of importance.

First, he had not bothered to keep a comprehensive daily journal. Other members of the Corps of Discovery had made up for this deficiency with remarkable effectiveness, but their journals were on the whole rudimentary. John Ordway produced a journal entry for each day of the expedition. Clark provided a journal entry for all but nine days of the journey, and he dutifully summarized those nine days on the tenth. Of the expedition members for whom we have extant journals, Lewis was the least reliable. If Lewis had spread out all of the extant journals of the expedition before him in 1807 and 1808 and written his book from those records, he would have been able to produce a synthesis of the expedition in his own inimitable style. But for more than half of the expedition (see above) he would be writing his account from scratch rather than adapting, enhancing, clarifying, and elaborating an existing journal manuscript. Had his journal been complete from August 31, 1803, to September 23, 1806, Lewis would have been able to use that immense unpolished manuscript as the basis for his book. Almost certainly many of the finished passages in his book would have been little more than refashionings of his field journal. At least by April 1805 Lewis was aware that Clark's journal (by Clark's own admission) had so many problems as a literary document that it would have to be completely rewritten to turn it into a book. In his letter to President Jefferson from Fort Mandan, Lewis characterized Clark's journal as nothing more than "daily detales of our progress."[43] In other words, Clark's journal was no substitute for a journal kept by himself. No doubt Lewis had compelling reasons for remaining silent for long periods of the great journey and no doubt the *captain's log* arrangement made a kind of sense in the field. But when the moment came to write the book, Lewis must immediately have realized that he had dug for himself a very serious literary hole by not keeping a daily journal, by not—in a sense—writing the first very rough draft of his book in something like daily installments as he went along. At some point in 1807 or 1808, as he assessed the records in his possession and mapped out the book project, Lewis probably discovered that so much had transpired in the course of the twenty-eight-month, 7,689-mile transcontinental journey that it would be difficult, maybe impossible, to reconstruct the adventure even with the other men's journals spread out before him. *Those tremendous mountains* of experience he had embraced between 1803 and 1806—hundreds of tributary rivers, a dozen mountain ranges, more than fifty Indian tribes represented by hundreds of individuals with different names, languages, religious and economic systems, material cultures, and points of view, a morass of celestial and meteorological data, plant, animal, and mineral collections, 178 new plant species and 122 new animal species never before described by binomial science—must have daunted the literary courage of Meriwether Lewis as no grizzly bear or Blackfeet Indian had ever daunted his physical courage. It would have been hard enough to write the book had he kept comprehensive and copious field records. In the absence of those records, the project must have seemed simply overwhelming, particularly in the hectic political environs of St. Louis. To write even a relatively cursory paraphrase of the expedition's adventures kept Nicholas Biddle busy for more than a year, "seven or eight and even more hours a day," beginning at 5 A.M.[44] And Biddle had the ghostwriter's fortunate and protective detachment from the events he was paraphrasing and freedom from the inhibiting self-consciousness of the memoirist. Lewis, as the man of destiny, had burdens that no ghostwriter could experience.

Second, Lewis may have worried that the book he would have produced would disappoint his patron Thomas Jefferson. This was Stephen Ambrose's

VOCABULARY.

Fire	belly	gold	nine hundred
water	back	silver	a thousand
earth	side	copper	white
air	bubby	a stone	black
wind	nipple	wood	green
sky	thigh	gun	blue
sun	leg	a mountain	yellow
moon	foot	hill	red
star	toe	valley	good
light	shin	sea	bad
darkness	nails	lake	large
day	bone	pond	small
night	blood	river	high
heat	life	creek	low
cold	death	a spring	broad
smoak	food	grass	narrow
cloud	meat	a tree	old
fog	fat	pine	young
rain	lean	cedar	new
snow	bread	sycamore	hard
hail	Indian-corn	poplar	soft
ice	milk	ash	sweet
frost	egg	elm	sour
dew	a house	beech	bitter
a rain-bow	the mammoth	birch	hot
thunder	buffalo	maple	cold
lightning	elk	oak	dry
yesterday	deer	chesnut	wet
to-day	moose	hiccory	strong
to-morrow	bear	walnut	weak
a day	wolf	locust	pretty
a month	panther	mulberry	ugly
a year	wild-cat	a vine	sick
spring	pole-cat	tobacco	brave
summer	fox	joy	cowardly
autumn	money	sorrow	wise
winter	beaver	one	foolish
a man	raccoon	two	I
a woman	opossum	three	you
a boy	hare	four	he
a girl	squirrel	five	she
a child	flying-squirrel	six	they
father	ground-squirrel	seven	this
mother	mole	eight	that
brother	a bird	nine	to eat
sister	an eagle	ten	to drink
husband	hawk	eleven	to sleep
wife	owl	twelve	to laugh
son	turkey	thirteen	to cry
daughter	swan	fourteen	to sing
the body	wild-goose	fifteen	to whistle
the head	duck	sixteen	to smell
the hair	turkey-buzzard	seventeen	to hear
the beard	raven	eighteen	to see
the face	crow	nineteen	to speak
an eye	black-bird	twenty	to walk
the nose	crane	twenty-one	to run
the cheek	pigeon	thirty	to stand
chin	dove	forty	to sit
lip	pheasant	fifty	to lie down
mouth	partridge	sixty	to smoke a pipe
tooth	mocking-bird	seventy	to love
tongue	red-bird	eighty	to hate
ear	snake	ninety	to strike
neck	lizard	a hundred	to kill
arm	butterfly	two hundred	to dance
wrist	fly	three hundred	to jump
hand	fish	four hundred	to fall
finger	frog	five hundred	to break
		six hundred	to bend
		seven hundred	yes
		eight hundred	no

Jefferson, the Enlightenment polymath, prepared this vocabulary grid for Lewis. Notice that Jefferson wanted Lewis to record Indian words for "mammoth." Both Lewis's and Jefferson's copies of the precious vocabularies have been lost. Thomas Jefferson Vocabulary form, c. 1790–92. Courtesy of the American Philosophical Society.

explanation. "Of course, he had some real problems," Ambrose wrote, "of which the most distasteful was having to inform Jefferson that there was no all-water route or anything remotely like it across the continent, a fact reinforced by those terrible falls on the Columbia."[45] Lewis had not found "the most direct and practicable water route across this continent for the purposes of commerce."[46] Or if he had, it was nevertheless so impracticable that it would never serve as a western counterpart to the Ohio-Mississippi road system that had already proved to be so efficacious and profitable "for the purposes of commerce" in the eastern half of the United States. The mountains of the West were not symmetrical with the Alleghenies and the Appalachians in some lovely Newtonian fashion, and they were much higher and more formidable than the president had predicted. Lemhi Pass near the source of the Missouri had not proved to be Louisiana Territory's Cumberland Gap, but rather the portal into "immence ranges of high mountains still to the West of us with their tops partially covered with snow."[47] The Indians Lewis had encountered were surprisingly resistant to Jefferson's peace and commerce program, though most of them paid lip service to the preachments of Lewis and Clark while the Corps of Discovery remained in their vicinity. In fact, some of the Indians Lewis had met behaved, from his perspective, a good deal like savages. The trans-Mississippi country was certainly not a benign extension of the well-watered and gently-contoured Ohio Valley, as Jefferson at times seemed to think. In fact, Lewis discovered landscapes, particularly in eastern Montana and on the Columbia-Snake plateau, that he predicted could never be metamorphosed into benign Jeffersonian farms. The West was far more rugged, arid, treeless, and inhospitable than Jefferson had reckoned from the west portico of Monticello. The British were still tenaciously clinging to their existing trade networks—and undermining American sovereignty—well within the boundaries of the Louisiana Purchase in spite of the Treaty of Paris of 1783 and even the subsequent Jay Treaty (1794) that was specifically intended to solve that longstanding international problem. The best news Lewis had to report to Jefferson was that the "mighty & heretofore deemed endless Missouri" had turned out to be navigable nearly to its source.

These un-Jeffersonian realities of the American West are often invoked as Lewis and Clark discoveries that would have disappointed or displeased the semi-utopian Jefferson. Without wishing to show any disrespect to historians of extraordinary insight and accomplishment, I believe that the time has come to put to rest some of these traditions about Jefferson's whimsical vision of American possibilities on the other side of the Allegheny Mountains. In my opinion, these notions belong more to American mythology than to the facts of the Lewis and Clark Expedition. Jefferson developed his own mythologies, of course, and he clung to his favorite ideas with genuine tenacity, but he was above all else an Enlightenment scientist and rationalist who had been taught by Diderot that "all things must be examined, all must be winnowed and sifted without exception and without sparing anyone's sensibilities."[48] Jefferson was a mature and profoundly well-educated adult who sent Lewis into the wilderness to inventory a continent and discover the truth in a Baconian fashion, not merely seek ways to confirm Jefferson's prejudices. I'm not saying that writing for Jefferson's eyes would have been easy. Had Lewis written his book one of his challenges would have been to develop a strategy of describing the world he discovered while negotiating with Jefferson's great expectations at the same time. This would not have been easy given the deep streak of idealism and notionalism in Jefferson's character, particularly when he was envisioning the future of the American republic. But it is certain that Jefferson would have preferred to read Lewis's book, no matter how much it ran counter to his daydreams of America, than to be left in the dark about the realities of the vast region he had purchased at significant cost and some political risk from Bonaparte. Besides, Lewis informed Jefferson of some of the hard geographic truths of his journey in his letter of September 23, 1806, when the Corps of Discovery rattled into St. Louis like characters out of *Robinson Crusoe*.[49] "We view this passage across the Continent as affording immence advantages to the fur trade," Lewis wrote, "but fear that the advantages which it offers as a communication for the productions of the East Indies to the United States and thence to Europe will never be found equal on an extensive scale to that by way of the Cape of Good hope."[50] What could be more direct and unambiguous than this? In the mythology of the Lewis and Clark Expedition, Jefferson is often portrayed as an otherworldly dreamer possessed of a childlike fragility, who expected Lewis to come home leading a woolly mammoth on an elkskin leash. This was how the Federalists liked to portray Jefferson, as an "intellectual voluptuary,"[51] as Hamilton phrased it, who really believed there was a mountain of pure salt somewhere beyond the Mississippi. It's time to retire that Jefferson, the quixotic dreamer of an encounter with Welsh Indians or the lost tribes of Israel, and focus instead on the hard-headed politician and Virginia scientist who calculated eclipses and took up subscriptions to get the Potomac channelized as the gateway to the West before New York could dig a canal from the Hudson River to Lake Erie.

If Lewis actually feared that he would disappoint Jefferson, it is much more likely that he doubted his capacities as a writer of English prose than that he fretted Jefferson's likely response to the rational conclusions he drew from his transcontinental journey. Jefferson was one of the great prose stylists of American history. His letters and other writings are so lucid that it is hard to find a single sentence in the scores of volumes of his works whose meaning is not immediately clear to any serious reader. In *Notes on the State of Virginia* Jefferson had also shown that he could write prose in which the rational and the romantic, scientific description and the sublime, the grid and the grandiloquent, could coexist in perfect balance. Lewis's task was to write a book whose most important reader would be a man who never had writer's block, who seldom exhibited anything that we would call moods, who was perennially cheerful and productive, who had read more than virtually any other American of his time, and who was one of the supreme masters of the English language. The genius, erudition, and "peculiar felicity of expression"[52] that John Adams discerned in Jefferson were enough to throw any other writer into paralysis, even the voluminous Adams himself. Had Lewis, like Zebulon Pike, been writing for General James Wilkinson rather than for America's Goethe or da Vinci, his task would have been infinitely easier. Writing a book is exceedingly hard work. Writing one for the president of the United States is much harder. Writing for a man who regarded his presidency of the American Philosophical Society as a more important and honorable post than his two terms as the president of the United States, is to ensure crippling intimidation. Do we really wonder why Lewis had writer's block?

Third, if he had written his book, Lewis would have had to resolve the issue of Clark's role in the expedition. I have addressed this problem elsewhere in this book. What follows is the briefest possible expression of the problem. If Lewis insisted on being the first *civilized man* to see the confluence of the Yellowstone, the Great Falls, the source of the Missouri River, and the other side of Lemhi Pass, he was unquestionably seeking to assure his own place in the history of exploration. However generous he felt towards his partner in discovery, Lewis knew that there is room for only one Captain Cook in the annals of history. Everyone else is a subordinate, usually a nameless and forgotten subordinate. After recruiting Clark for the expedition with what turned out to be a wild promise of a true co-captaincy, and then, when the War Department ranked him no higher than second lieutenant, declaring "I think it will be best to let none of our party or any other persons know any thing about the grade, you will observe that the grade has no effect upon your compensation, which by G—d, shall be equal to my own,"[53] Lewis was hardly in a position to write Clark out of the story altogether. If he wrote the truth to the world and explained how central Clark had been to the success of the expedition, Lewis would effectively be damaging his own historical standing. If he reduced Clark in the book to subordinate status he would be betraying one of the few truly successful friendships of his life, and a promise he made in writing on June 19, 1803. It's one thing to be magnanimous in private communications or in something so pedestrian as fiscal compensation, quite another to diminish one's own stature in the annals of exploration. Unthinkable as betraying Clark may seem to us, Lewis's prospectus (ca. April 1, 1807) indicates that that is precisely what he expected to do. Although the prospectus calls the journey "Lewis and Clark's Tour to the Pacific Ocean," Lewis makes clear that he will be the sole author of the book(s). He leaves the impression with the prospective subscriber that the master map of the American West will be his (Lewis's) work, a complete reversal of the truth. In the course of the prospectus Lewis, employing the third person, speaks of the journey as "his [i.e., Lewis's] late tour" and "his late voyage."[54] Clark's name appears just three times in the prospectus, twice in titles, and once with respect to the twenty-three Indian vocabularies the captains gathered in the course of their travels. A reader of the prospectus would come away with the sense that it was Lewis's journey but that someone named Clark was somehow part of it. The prospectus indicates that the book(s) would be written by Lewis, the map was Lewis's, and that Lewis was the scientist of the expedition. Anyone who was not already familiar with Clark's role in the expedition would be left to wonder just what, besides helping collect Indian vocabularies, he did, and why he was listed in the titling for both the book and the map. Nowhere does Lewis specify Clark's role or responsibilities, or praise him for his contributions to the expedition's success. Lewis nowhere speaks of *our* late tour or *Clark's* late tour, but only of his own.

Nor is this all. David Nicandri has shown that at some point before he died, Lewis had rewritten at least one key episode of the story—the critically important reconnaissance of the upper Salmon River in late August 1805. Clark conducted that difficult search for navigable waters of the Salmon, or at minimum, some sort of practicable trail alongside the Salmon along which the expedition could pack its gear, while Lewis remained behind among the Shoshone resting, engaging in ethnographic enquiry, and attempting to purchase pack horses. Nicandri has shown that at some point after these events occurred, Lewis wrote up his journal for that period of the journey in a way that exalted his role in ascertaining the nature of the upper Salmon country and diminishing Clark's. Lewis died before he could publish that revisionist version of the story. When Clark inherited the publication project in the wake of Lewis's suicide, he discovered that his erstwhile friend had effectively written him out of this important episode. At that point, Clark actually asserted himself. Between the lines of Lewis's journal entry, Clark wrote, "This part to come in the 20th related to Capt. C. thro the interpeter."[55] What Clark meant was that he, not Lewis, learned about the tangled geography of the upper Salmon from Sacagawea linguistically (Hidatsa to French to English), not by way of Drouillard, employing sign language. Nicandri writes, "Clark saw that Lewis had expropriated geographic knowledge that Clark had actually learned the week *following* Lewis's first crossing of the divide. Clark took sufficient exception to Lewis's proto-narrative that he corrected the record, without the discomfiture of confronting his deceased partner."[56]

Whether Clark would have dared to dispute Lewis's reading of these events if Lewis were still alive is an interesting question. Probably he would not have known of Lewis's betrayal until the book was in print, and

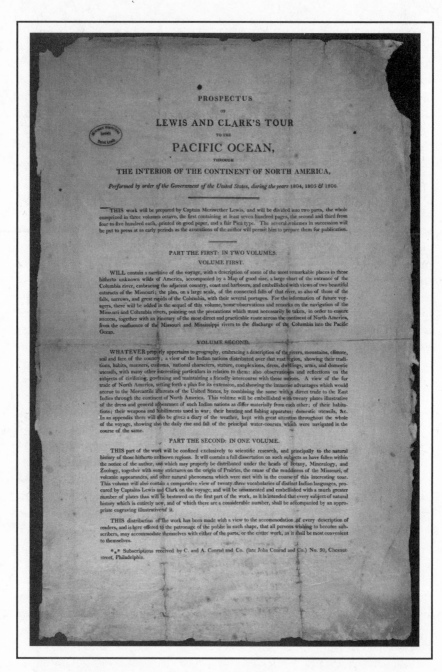

PROSPECTUS

OF

LEWIS AND CLARK'S TOUR

TO THE

PACIFIC OCEAN,

THROUGH

THE INTERIOR OF THE CONTINENT OF NORTH AMERICA,

Performed by order of the Government of the United States, during the years 1804, 1805 & 1806.

THIS work will be prepared by Captain Meriwether Lewis, and will be divided into two parts, the whole comprised in three volumes octavo, the first containing at least seven hundred pages, the second and third from four to five hundred each, printed on good paper, and a fair Pica type. The several volumes in succession will be put to press at as early periods as the avocations of the author will permit him to prepare them for publication.

PART THE FIRST: IN TWO VOLUMES.

VOLUME FIRST.

WILL contain a narrative of the voyage, with a description of some of the most remarkable places in those hitherto unknown wilds of America, accompanied by a Map of good size, a large chart of the entrance of the Columbia river, embracing the adjacent country, coast and harbours, and embellished with views of two beautiful cataracts of the Missouri; the plan, on a large scale, of the connected falls of that river, as also of those of the falls, narrows, and great rapids of the Columbia, with their several portages. For the information of future voyagers, there will be added in the sequel of this volume, some observations and remarks on the navigation of the Missouri and Columbia rivers, pointing out the precautions which must necessarily be taken, in order to ensure success, together with an itinerary of the most direct and practicable route across the continent of North America, from the confluence of the Missouri and Mississippi rivers to the discharge of the Columbia into the Pacific Ocean.

VOLUME SECOND.

WHATEVER properly appertains to geography, embracing a description of the rivers, mountains, climate, soil and face of the country; a view of the Indian nations distributed over that vast region, showing their traditions, habits, manners, customs, national characters, stature, complexions, dress, dwellings, arms, and domestic utensils, with many other interesting particulars in relation to them: also observations and reflections on the subjects of civilizing, governing and maintaining a friendly intercourse with those nations. A view of the fur trade of North America, setting forth a plan for its extension, and showing the immense advantages which would accrue to the Mercantile interests of the United States, by combining the same with a direct trade to the East Indies through the continent of North America. This volume will be embellished with twenty plates illustrative of the dress and general appearance of such Indian nations as differ materially from each other; of their habitations; their weapons and habiliments used in war; their hunting and fishing apparatus; domestic utensils, &c. In an appendix there will also be given a diary of the weather, kept with great attention throughout the whole of the voyage, showing also the daily rise and fall of the principal water-courses which were navigated in the course of the same.

PART THE SECOND: IN ONE VOLUME.

THIS part of the work will be confined exclusively to scientific research, and principally to the natural history of those hitherto unknown regions. It will contain a full dissertation on such subjects as have fallen within the notice of the author, and which may properly be distributed under the heads of Botany, Mineralogy, and Zoology, together with some strictures on the origin of Prairies, the cause of the muddiness of the Missouri, of volcanic appearances, and other natural phenomena which were met with in the course of this interesting tour. This volume will also contain a comparative view of twenty-three vocabularies of distinct Indian languages, procured by Captains Lewis and Clark on the voyage, and will be ornamented and embellished with a much greater number of plates than will be bestowed on the first part of the work, as it is intended that every subject of natural history which is entirely new, and of which there are a considerable number, shall be accompanied by an appropriate engraving illustrative of it.

THIS distribution of the work has been made with a view to the accommodation of every description of readers, and is here offered to the patronage of the public in such shape, that all persons wishing to become subscribers, may accommodate themselves with either of the parts, or the entire work, as it shall be most convenient to themselves.

⁂ Subscriptions received by C. and A. Conrad and Co. (late John Conrad and Co.) No. 30, Chesnut street, Philadelphia.

Lewis's prospectus, ca. April 1807. Lewis promised so much to the public that he virtually guaranteed the failure of the post-expedition publication project. Printed by John Conrad, Philadelphia, 3 June 1807. Courtesy Missouri History Museum Archives. Clark Family Collection. William Clark Papers. N26129.

then—like the good friend and servant he was—Clark almost certainly would have absorbed the blow in silence. We are fortunate that Clark pressed this point with Nicholas Biddle, because it reveals something important about the character of each of the captains, and it reminds us of how great a challenge Lewis faced in writing an account of "his late tour." His narrative strategy would have been to write Clark *into* the story enough to do some sort of justice to his contribution, and satisfy the claims of friendship and the tacit agreement the two had struck back in 1803. At the same time, Lewis needed to write Clark *out* of the story enough to make sure that no reader believed they were *really* co-leaders of the expedition, really equal in historical importance. This would have been particularly the case in episodes of discovery, like the reconnaissance of the upper Salmon. Lewis had to make sure his readers knew that he was the explorer and Clark the project manager, that he was the man of destiny and Clark the man of duty, that he was Aeneas and Clark the faithful Achates. There are all sorts of ironies at work here. Lewis needed to demote Clark in some fundamental ways so that he could praise him fulsomely in others. He needed to praise Clark in some easy ways—on what Lewis might regard as throwaway issues—so that he could reserve the heroic and solitary moments of exploration for himself. Lewis needed to make sure the reader understood that it was *his late tour* (and no other's), and yet not appear to be belittling or suppressing the achievement of his friend. Had Lewis hired Moses Hooke to be his second in command, he would have no problem in writing the story in a way that celebrated his own primacy. But Moses Hooke might not have been willing, like Clark, to support and cover for Lewis through the immensely challenging trek.

Lewis was not a bad man. His respect and love for William Clark were genuine. He was not the kind of explorer, like Britain's John Speke, who was eager to thrust his exploration partner off the stage. Lewis clearly understood how essential Clark had been to the expedition's success. Nor was he willing to lie outright to his readers about the leadership dynamics of the expedition. In sitting down to write his book, poor proud Lewis was walking through a narrative minefield that was much more dangerous than the Long Narrows of the Columbia. It is quite possible that the challenges of writing the complex narrative of his late tour had a paralytic effect on Lewis, who was as selfishly ambitious as he was genuinely grateful for Clark's contributions to his success.

Lewis learned instantaneously how dangerous a game he was playing when he issued his prospectus in April 1807 and warned the reading public (March 14, 1807) to beware of unauthorized publications relating to the expedition. Patrick Gass's editor and publisher David McKeehan lashed out at Lewis with such appalling viciousness that it might well have led to a duel—if McKeehan had been a gentleman, an equal, and not some common hack printer. McKeehan's principal charge against Lewis was that he was appropriating the late tour for himself, and striking out at anyone who might presume to have a story to tell about an official government expedition that involved more than fifty white people, not to mention hundreds of Native Americans. Indeed, McKeehan went so far as to question Lewis's ethics in claiming exclusive rights to the story of an expedition that was actually the *property* of the United States government. If writing Patrick Gass and Robert Frazer out of the story caused so much naked furor, what would it mean to publicly demean Clark's contributions? If Gass (and McKeehan) felt so strongly betrayed by Lewis's prospectus and his warning against spurious publications, what must Clark have thought of the prospectus? With typical forbearance, Clark left no record of his reaction.

The publication Lewis promised the world in April 1807 would have consisted of two parts spread over three volumes. The first volume would "contain a narrative of the voyage," "accompanied by a Map of good size."[57] The second volume would contain more detailed geography, all the ethnographic materials relating to the Indian tribes Lewis and Clark met, thoughts about American Indian policy, a history and analysis of the fur trade, together with suggestions about how to wrest the fur trade away from British and French rivals, and the expedition's weather diary, "kept with great attention thoughout [sic] the whole of the voyage."[58] Volume two would embrace "Whatever properly appertains to geography, embracing a description of the rivers, mountains, climate, soil and face of the country," and "a view of the Indian nations distributed over that vast region, shewing their traditions, habits, manners, customs, national characters, stature, complexions, dress, dwellings, arms, and domestic utensils, with many other interesting particulars in relation to them."[59] Volume two would also feature illustrations of Indian dress and accoutrements, and "observations and reflections on the subjects of civilizing, governing and maintaining a friendly intercourse with thouse nations,"[60] plus reflections on the future of the fur trade. Part two of the work, in one volume (volume three), would contain the formal scientific data gathered in the course of the expedition: "Botany, Mineralogy, and Zoology." It would also include an essay on the "origin of Prairies," i.e., a speculative treatise on the treelessness of the Great Plains, and other dissertations on the turbidity of the Missouri River, evidence of volcanism in the Louisiana Territory, "and other natural phenomena which were met with in the course of this interesting tour." Volume three would also contain a chart ("a comparative view") of the twenty-three Indian vocabularies "procured by Captains Lewis and Clark" on their journey, and a large number of plates illustrating the scientific discoveries of the expedition.[61]

This was an exceedingly ambitious plan. Not only was Lewis to create a comprehensive narrative of the expedition from such journals as he had in front of him, particularly Clark's, but he promised to produce a major work of Enlightenment ethnography—a field treatise of pioneering anthropology on the fifty-plus Indian tribes the expedition encountered—and a book-length analysis of the flora and fauna of a region "two thousand miles in width upon which the foot of civilized man had never trodden,"[62] plus a series of speculative essays attempting to answer questions that the new bio-regions he had encountered inspired in his curious and restless mind. Had Lewis accomplished even the majority of the things he contemplated in his prospectus he would now be regarded as a rough American equivalent of Alexander von Humboldt (1769–1859), who returned to Germany after his travels in Central and South America (1799–1804) and published more than thirty volumes of reports over the next twenty-one years. At the end of 1813 Jefferson actually found himself confessing to "My dear friend and Baron" Humboldt, that "You will find it inconcievable that Lewis's journey to the Pacific should not yet have appeared; nor is it in my power to tell you the reason."[63] By committing himself publicly to so vast and ambitious a project, Lewis virtually guaranteed his failure and probably truncated his life. The two-part, three-volume magnum opus he intended to write would certainly have silenced his critics in President Madison's War Department, or at least taken the sting out of their rebukes.

The work Lewis promised the world in April 1807 would have been precisely the sort of final product of the Corps of Volunteers for North Western Discovery that would most have pleased Thomas Jefferson. In other words, if he had been asked to describe the perfect final report, the platonic ideal of a post-expedition publication project, Jefferson would have written something very much like Lewis's prospectus of April 1807. But Jefferson surely knew that it was unlikely that Lewis could accomplish all of this in the course of his life, much less while serving as the governor of a vast, troubled, and inchoate territory 850 miles by impossible trails from the nation's capital, and 950 miles from Philadelphia. Indeed, Jefferson must have known that the not-regularly-educated Lewis was probably literally incapable of writing a three-volume work of such complexity, comprehensiveness, and scientific sophistication, no matter how much time he had at his disposal. Had Lewis pursued the publication project with genuine diligence, he would probably have produced a book that occupied some halfway position between the work promised in his prospectus and the paraphrase narrative issued by Biddle and Allen in 1814. That would have been a major contribution to American letters and Enlightenment science. Jefferson himself—a genius of organization and discipline, and a polymath—would have found it virtually impossible to write and deliver these three volumes to his friends in the international republic of letters had *he* accompanied the expedition in the manner of Britian's Joseph Banks.

Patrick Gass's editor David McKeehan pointedly challenged Lewis's scientific credentials on April 7, 1807. "Were you not afraid," McKeehan asked, "that some persons affected by your publication, might inform the public that you were not a man of science, that you were not a man of letters, and that you were not qualified for scientific research?"[64] Why Jefferson or the brilliant Albert Gallatin, the perennial realist James Madison, or the publisher John Conrad did not dissuade Lewis from promising so ambitious a publication is hard to fathom. Had Lewis simply written in timely fashion the first volume of a grand work he had formulated in his mind but not promised to the public, and then regrouped after recovering from the strain of that project and assessing the public's appetite for more, he might have produced a book or books of the greatest importance. Had he produced even a single volume of his travels, "recollected in tranquility,"[65] as Wordsworth put it, our understanding of the expedition would be enriched in countless ways, and we would have the advantage of an expedition debriefing that never occurred in a form left to posterity.

David McKeehan's savage attack on Lewis, in response to the governor's public warning (March 14, 1807) that readers should not be taken in by "unauthorized" and "spurious" publications relating to the expedition, paid due attention to the vagueness of Lewis's publication timeline. The map, McKeehan sneered (adding his own italics), "*will most probably* be published the latter end of October next; the first volume of the work *about* the first of January, 1808; and that the two remaining volumes will follow in succession, as early *as they possibly can be prepared for publication*."[66] McKeehan was making two points here. First, Lewis's timetable was so vague as to give prospective readers no clear understanding of when they would receive the books for which they were asked to prepay, *if ever*. Second, McKeehan's client Patrick Gass's book had already gone to press and would be available to the public by early summer 1807, at latest. Say what you wish about the depth of Gass's account of the journey, McKeehan jibed, at least he had actually completed the task.

Lewis's hostility to the publication of Patrick Gass's journal in 1807 and the steps he apparently took to quash publication of Robert Frazer's journal may have had less to do with prospective sales than historians have suggested. The fact that these books were appearing so soon after the expedition's return proved that it could be done, that if Lewis had moved forward on his own book with the same sense of opportunity and urgency shown by his ambitious subalterns, both of whom sought help from editors and ghostwriters in turning their raw journals into publishable form, he might have been able to get the first volume out, as Jefferson seemed to think necessary, in 1808 or 1809. The timing of the relevant letters is revealing. Lewis wrote his letter to the *National Intelligencer* denouncing spurious accounts of the expedition on March 14, 1807, *before* he had published his own prospectus. In fact, the publication of Robert Frazer's prospectus (October 1806), and the public buzz about the imminence of Gass's book (March 1807) probably forced Lewis to buckle down and issue his own prospectus (ca. April 1, 1807) before it was too late. In other words, the publication of Gass's *A Journal of the Voyages and Travels of a Corps of Discovery under the Command of Capt. Lewis and Capt. Clarke of the Army of the United States from the Mouth of the River Missouri through the Interior Parts of North America to the Pacific Ocean During the Years 1804, 1805 & 1806*, must have upset Lewis not merely because it preempted the adventure story Lewis would tell in his own book, but because it reminded him in the most pointed way that he had not only not published the first volume of his travels, but not really even begun to write them up.

When Lewis wrote his letter denouncing "unauthorized and probably some spurious publications now preparing for the press,"[67] he announced that the first volume of his travels would probably be published in January 1808. One of two things is true. Either Lewis actually believed that he would finish his work on volume one in the next nine months, or he was merely attempting to buy time with the public by proposing a publication date that knew he could not meet, but that he hoped would discourage people from buying Gass's book. The period between March 1807 and March 1808 is regarded by many historians as the lost year of Lewis's adult life. Instead of following the lead of Clark and making his way promptly to St. Louis to take up his post as territorial governor, Lewis lingered in Philadelphia, Washington, DC, and Virginia during that crucial period. Thanks to that irresponsible dallying, his governorship suffered a fatal blow. Had Lewis ground out his book during that period, it would be easy to understand why he chose to spend those months in Philadelphia, the nation's largest city and intellectual capital, home of the American Philosophical Society and the best libraries in the nation. Such a delay would not have done his governorship any good, but the president, the secretary of war, and even Frederick Bates would have been disposed to give the absent Lewis the benefit of the doubt. But after a very promising beginning, in which he signed a contract with a publisher, arranged for artists to provide illustrations, and for botanists to provide scientific descriptions of the plants he had collected, Lewis did not sit down and write his book. He seems to have spent his time drinking and carousing with his friend Mahlon Dickerson, attending meetings of the American Philosophical Society, and trying to find a suitable wife. Danisi and Jackson dismiss the idea that Lewis was irresponsibly idle during this period. The governor was sufficiently busy, they argue, in serving as Jefferson's proxy at the Burr trial, discussing territorial affairs with the former governor of Louisiana Territory James Wilkinson, who was the key prosecution witness at the trial, and looking after his personal affairs as the de facto paterfamilias of his family and the absentee manager of Locust Hill.[68] Danisi and Jackson also note that during this period, the "lost" months, Lewis wrote, or began to write, his long analysis of Indian policy in the American West, *Observations and Reflections on the Subject of Governing and Maintaining a State of Friendly Intercourse with the Indians of the Territory of Louisiana.* Danisi and Jackson call this neglected report "one of the most important documents written by Meriwether Lewis," and a proof that he was neither negligent of his territorial duties nor as silent as some biographers have alleged.[69] Unfortunately, by the time Lewis actually finished the report in St. Louis, Richard Dillon argues, "his reputation was done irreparable damage" by "his delay in transmitting it to Washington."[70] Besides, proving that Lewis was not altogether idle during this period does not explain why he made no progress on a volume he had promised to put into the hands of the American public in early 1808.

In the winter of 1807–08, Lewis and his brother Reuben finally set out for St. Louis. They were accompanied by a free mulatto servant named John Pernier, provided by Jefferson to attend to Governor Lewis's personal needs. They arrived at a natural bridge in the Ohio Military Reserve on December 20, 1807. They reached Lexington, Kentucky, on January 14, 1808. The prominent citizens of Lexington organized a reception in honor of the now-famous explorer. In mid-February the Lewis party reached Louisville. Here, according to Danisi and Jackson, the party split, with Reuben and Pernier, plus others, venturing down the Ohio River in a flat-bottomed boat with the all the baggage, while Lewis set out overland towards St. Louis by way of Vincennes and Cahokia.[71] Lewis finally reached St. Louis on March 8, 1808, precisely one year and six days after the US Senate confirmed his appointment.

The problem with announcing the likely publication date of the first volume of the book in the *National Intelligencer* was that the person most likely to read that letter was Thomas Jefferson, who was a close friend of the publisher Samuel Harrison Smith and who regarded the *Intelligencer* as a kind of house organ for his administration. In other words, in plucking an unrealistic date out of a hat to suppress the sales of rival but inferior publications, Lewis effectively thrust his head into a trap. Jefferson naturally assumed that Lewis was telling the truth about the publication timeline. When Lewis missed his self-imposed deadline, Jefferson began to fret and eventually to rebuke his protégé. Lewis's March 14, 1807, letter to the *National Intelligencer* rightly explained that "much time, labor, and expense are absolutely necessary in order to do justice to the several subjects it will embrace."[72] Unfortunately, Lewis did not give that time and labor to the project even when he was in a position to do so. By the time he finally got himself to St. Louis, he had frittered away the one significant block of time he might have used to meet his obligations to Jefferson and the reading public.

In his letter to the *Intelligencer* Lewis warned that Robert Frazer "who was only a private on this expedition," could not provide the scientific information that the Enlightenment sought. Because Frazer ("only a private") was "entirely unacquainted" with celestial observations, mineralogy, botany, zoology, or even geography, "the whole which can be expected from his Journal is merely a limited detail of our daily transactions."[73] This, of course, was an accurate, if ungenerous, assessment of what Frazer would have been able to publish had the project not collapsed, and it also correctly characterizes Patrick Gass's journal. The problem is that it also fairly characterizes Nicholas Biddle's 1814 official *History of the Expedition Under the Command of Captain Lewis and Clark to the Sources of the Missouri, Thence Across the Rocky Mountains and Down the River Columbia to the Pacific Ocean*. Biddle's book is never more than a "limited detail of our daily transactions."[74] In fact, former president Jefferson dismissed it in a letter of September 8, 1816, to William Clark, as "the travelling journal of Govr. Lewis and yourself."[75] Jefferson made it clear that what had been published so far was of limited value and told Clark he hoped "something was doing with the astronomical observations, the Geographical chart, the Indian vocabularies, and other papers not comprehended in the journal published."[76] In fact, while editing the journals, Biddle had routinely drawn red pencil lines through the scientific passages of the original journals to alert himself or others that these natural history notations were to be left out of the narrative he was crafting. It is true that Benjamin Smith Barton never got around to the analytical work he had promised to write on the plants gathered in the course of the expedition, but the only person who could have fulfilled Lewis's larger Enlightenment program for the journals was Lewis himself, and he failed. Gass and Biddle may have published nothing more than a "limited detail of our daily transactions," but that is more than Lewis ever did, and it was their narratives and their narratives alone that told the story of the Lewis and Clark Expedition between 1807 and 1905.

David McKeehan's vitriolic attack in the press was not the only negative feedback Lewis received from the public once the initial national excitement about the expedition's return faded away. New York journalist Harry Croswell, who detested Thomas Jefferson, belittled Lewis in his newspaper, *Balance and Columbian Repository*. In the summer of 1805, under the heading, "Louisiana Curiosities," Croswell wrote, "Yesterday the *Prairie dog* and Magpie, sent by Capt. Lewis, arrived at the city of Washington. The latter is precisely the Magpie of Europe; but how Mr. Lewis, or any one, in the least acquainted with classing in Zoology, came to call the *ground-fox squirrel* a dog, it is indeed difficult to imagine—It is precisely, in shape, size, colour, in the choice of its food, and in its manner of feeding by sitting up and turning handily its nuts, &c. in its paws, *a fox squirrel*; but it has lost part of the hair from its tail on the journey, *if the hair was ever as long as usual in this species of squirrel*; and this is the only novelty about it."[77] Croswell, of course, was wrong about Lewis's scientific understanding of the prairie dog (*Cynomys ludovicianus*), which he often called a "barking squirrel,"[78] but that didn't make his criticism any less condescending and dismissive.

The Monthly Anthology, and Boston Review had found the written reports sent down river from Fort Mandan in April 1805 tedious. In the December 1805 issue, the editor S.C. Thacher wrote, of the *Mandan Miscellany*, "We very much regret, that it is not in our power to insert the communication from Captains Lewis & Clark; it is extremely long and is quite as unintelligible without the assistance of a map: besides it would be very uninteresting to almost every reader, and therefore we shall proceed to the documents from Dr. Sibley and Mr Dunbar, which … may gratify a variety of readers."[79] William Dunbar and George Sibley were exploring the river systems of the old southwest at the same time Lewis and Clark were engaged in their transcontinental journey. The Sibley and Dunbar expeditions were comparatively minor in scope and neither was regarded as a successful reconnaissance. To be compared—unfavorably—to them would have been a serious affront to Lewis.

The *Monthly Anthology* of Boston printed a satirical poem in March 1807 in response to Joel Barlow's suggestion that the Columbia be renamed the Lewis River in honor of the commander of the expedition. Entitled, "On the Discoveries of Captain Lewis,"[80] the poem was mostly an attack on the supposed scientific credulity of President Jefferson. It was written by John Quincy Adams, the son of Jefferson's friend and the second president of the United States John Adams. J.Q. Adams mocked Jefferson's enthusiasm for collecting the remains of the woolly mammoth and other animals "which may be deemed rare or extinct."[81] In addition to jabs at the president's friend Thomas Paine and a mean-spirited reference to "dusky Sally" Hemings, the younger Adams wondered just what Lewis had done that was so impressive.

> I'll tell you of the mighty deeds
> Achiev'd by Captain Lewis—
> How, starting from the Atlantic shore
> By fair and easy motion
> He journied *all the way by land*
> Until he met the ocean.

Adams noted, a little inaccurately, that Lewis never met a foe, that he found no Welsh Indians, and discovered no geographic wonders outside the normal course of nature. Why then rename the Columbia for him when the results of the expedition were essentially jejune?

> Let old Columbus be once more
> Degraded from his glory;
> And not a river by his name
> Remember him in story—
> For what is *old* Discovery
> Compar'd to that which new is?
> Strike—strike *Columbia* river out,
> And put in—River Lewis!

The point of Adams' satire, aside from losing no opportunity to belittle the politics, the personal life, or the pretentions of Jefferson, was to wonder just what was so impressive about Lewis's journey across the continent. Such attacks as these probably offended or at least annoyed the thin-skinned Lewis, who may have wondered privately how well J.Q. Adams would have held up on a twenty-eight month camping trip on which a semi-excremental paunch sausage could be regarded as a wilderness delicacy.

David McKeehan made much the same point as Adams in his phillipic of April 7, 1807. "With respect to the hazardous nature of the enterprise and the courage necessary for undertaking it, candour compels me to say, that public opinion has placed them on too high ground. Mr. M'Kenzie with a party consisting of about one fourth part of the number under your command, with means which will not bear a comparison with those furnished you, and without the *authority*, the *flags*, or *medals* of his government, crossed the Rocky mountains several degrees north of your rout, and for the *first time* penetrated to the Pacific Ocean."[82] Not only had Alexander Mackenzie been first across the continent, McKeehan jibed, but he had done it with fewer men, less expense, without government funding and without the official imprimatur of the British government. What, really, had Lewis accomplished? Lewis's paltry achievement, moreover, was derivative. "You had the advantage of the information contained in his [Mackenzie's] journal, and could in some degree estimate and guard against the dangers and difficulties you were to meet."[83] In McKeehan's formulation, the credit belonged to the man who actually was the first to walk off the map of the known world. To everyone who came later, including Lewis, the journey was just sufficiently familiar enough to remove it from the realm of the heroic. In McKeehan's belittling construction, Lewis could perhaps be regarded as a traveler, but not an authentic explorer. David Nicandri has shown that Lewis was intensely self-conscious about the prior transcontinental journey of Mackenzie, that Lewis was an obsessive, if usually furtive, reader of Mackenzie's *Voyages from Montreal*.[84] McKeehan could not have known that in comparing Lewis unfavorably with Mackenzie, he had found just the right string with which to fret Jefferson's protégé.

McKeehan also criticized the compensation package Jefferson and Congress arranged for Lewis—double pay, a land grant of 1,600 acres within the very territory Lewis was to administer through "the honorable and lucrative office of Governor of Louisiana Territory!" McKeehan implied that Lewis's receiving a land grant in a jurisdiction he administered was a prima facie case of conflict of interest. "Why, sir, these grants and rewards savour more of the splendid munificence of a Prince than the economy of a republican government." Like virtually everyone else,[85] McKeehan was disgusted with the poetic strains of Joel Barlow. "I almost forgot," he sneered, "the warblings of the Muses, who have been celebrating the '*Young Hero's name.*'"[86]

McKeehan rightly criticized Lewis for his pettiness in trying to crush the publications of the lesser journal keepers. "Who could have thought that after so much liberality shewn by the country, your Excellency would have been found contending with these poor fellows, who for their small pittance were equally exposed with yourself to the toils and dangers attending the expedition, about the publication of their journals, which cost them so much trouble and anxiety to keep and preserve!"[87] McKeehan abused Lewis for not presenting his journal to the Congress of the United States in the same session in which his compensation package was voted, and intimated that some members of Congress were offended—"complain that they are called upon to legislate in the dark." McKeehan, who lived in Pittsburgh, was almost certainly making this up. The editor was essentially accusing Lewis of double dipping—pressing Congress for an extravagant compensation package without informing the government that paid for the expedition that he was planning to undertake a commercial publication project, too. Assuming the voice of Lewis, whom he called "His Excellency in embrio," McKeehan wrote, "I'll squeeze the nation first, and then raise a heavy contribution on the citizens individually." Now McKeehan directly accused Lewis of conflict of interest. "Every man of sense must agree that these journals are either *private* property of the individuals who took them, or *public* property."[88] In other words, Lewis was trying to have it both ways. If the leader of the expedition was asserting that the journals of Gass, Frazer, Whitehouse, and Ordway belonged to the government of the United States, then surely Lewis's own journal was also public property. If Lewis believed that his journal was his own intellectual property, how could he legitimately attempt to prevent the publication of the journals of other individuals, who surely had as much right to their journals as he did to his? If Lewis believed that the journals of Gass, et al., were public property, why were they not confiscated from the men "when other public property in their possession was delivered up" at the end of the expedition? Surely all public claim on those journals was "relinquished to them [the lesser journal keepers] by the act of discharge, without a demand, when the persons who had taken them were retiring from public service, to private life."[89]

McKeehan accused Lewis of "insatiable avarice" in trying to prevent Gass's journal from having the opportunity to compete with his own. If this litany of insults were not enough, McKeehan went on to predict that Gass's humble book would be a far more interesting read than Lewis's more pretentious report. "I am of opinion it will be more interesting and useful to readers generally than the volume of your work, which is to be 'confined exclusively to scientific research.' He may in some respects be considered as having the advantage; for while your Excellency was star-gazing, and taking celestial observations, he was taking observations in the world below."[90] To make his point, McKeehan quoted a passage from Alexander Mackenzie's *Voyages from Montreal* in which the Scottish explorer humbly acknowledged that he had had neither time nor proficiency to engage in serious scientific enquiry in the course of his trans-Canadian journey. McKeehan quotes Gass's "homespun account" of the muddiness of the Missouri River solely to make fun of Lewis's promise to write a full dissertation on the same phenomenon. It doesn't require a treatise, he argued, to explain that the loose sandstone bluffs of the river dissolve "like sugar; every rain washes down great quantities of it, and the rapidity of the stream keeps it mixing and afloat in the water until it reaches the mouth of the Mississippi."

As a final assault, McKeehan suggested that if Patrick Gass had been "some wag," and not a responsible expedition member and sergeant who had in fact been singled out for praise by Lewis himself, he might have insinuated that Lewis instructed Pierre Cruzatte to shoot him in the buttocks on August 11, 1806, so that "the *young hero* might not return without more scars ... to excite the curiosity and compassion of some favorite widow Wadman, who might have been languishing in his absence."[91] McKeehan could not resist ending his satirical attack with a passage calling attention to Lewis's humiliation at the Birnt Hills east of today's Williston, North Dakota. It was even more fun to suggest that Captain Lewis was so far from being a genuine hero that he had one of his own men shoot him in the posteriors late in the journey to give it some semblance of drama.

The McKeehan letter is remarkably unfair, mean, sarcastic, and irresponsible, but it is not without its moments of insight, and it must be admitted that Lewis brought it on himself in a number of respects. To the twenty-first century reader, it is as hilarious as it is unmerited. Few letters have ever so thoroughly punctured the self-importance of a serious national figure. It must have been a source of rage and humiliation to Meriwether Lewis. Given his amour propre, his prickly sense of honor, his thin skin, and his general irritability, as well as the extreme sensitivity to criticism of virtually all authors, Lewis must have suffered grievously when he read this letter in the Pittsburgh *Gazette*. The always-thorough Donald Jackson wrote in a footnote to this letter that he had not found any reprints of the McKeehan letter in other contemporary newspapers.[92] It is possible, but not likely, that Lewis never read the diatribe.

These assaults on the character of Meriwether Lewis and on the claims he was making for the expedition he led might well have had a corrosive effect on Lewis's confidence. They may have led him to wonder how the public would respond to his book(s), and it at least possible that they made him wonder if the expedition had accomplished anything worth celebrating in print. Some historians have suggested that Lewis could not write his book because he (or the public) regarded the expedition as in some sense a failure. Absurd as that proposition may seem to us, it is possible that attacks like those of Croswell and McKeehan helped to precipitate an existential crisis in Lewis. Such anti-climaxes are not as improbable as they may seem. Sir Richard Francis Burton wrote a famous passage after he became the first European to penetrate to the heart of the sacred Islamic city of Harar in 1854–55. "I had time, on top of my mule for musing upon how melancholy a thing is success. Whilst failure inspirits a man, attainment reads the sad prosy lesson that all our glories 'Are shadows, not substantial things.' Truly said the sayer, 'disappointment is the salt of life'—a salutary bitter which strengthens the mind for fresh exertion, and gives double value to the prize."[93] America's Edwin (Buzz) Aldrin became so disillusioned after his return from the moon that he found himself asking himself—in fleeting moments of confusion and gloom—if he had ever really made the journey.[94]

The historian Joseph Mussulman believes that the public glorification of the heroes of Jefferson's war against the Barbary pirates, which was at its height at the time of the expedition's return from the West, may have intimidated and depressed Lewis. "Stephen Decatur and William Eaton both had claimed more than their share of the credit for the 1805 triumph over the Barbary bashaws," Mussulman writes. "In Lewis's mind, I think, those two men were true heroes with war-won wounds as manifest evidence of their 'sacrifices,' whereas Lewis—the 'born soldier'—had only killed an Indian or two, and the only wound he wore was inflicted accidentally by one of his own men. Proud Decatur was to commit 'suicide by duel,' and self-serving Eaton was to drink himself to death. Then there was Tobias Lear's masterful orchestration of the Tripolitan bashaw Karamanli's surrender on the foredeck of the *Constitution* in the Bay of Tripoli. In the mind of every informed American, as well as his own, those three images must have trumped his trivial triumph over the destitute Lemhi Shoshonis, not to mention his diplomatic failures with the Sioux."[95]

In what sense could the Lewis and Clark Expedition be considered a failure? Jefferson's statement to Congress that the expedition "has had all the success which could have been expected,"[96] has a ring of resignation about it. I have never believed that the expedition was a failure in any meaningful sense, but those who belittle Lewis and Clark's achievement cite some combination of the following factors.

First, Lewis failed to bring back the correct latitudinal and longitudinal coordinates that mattered so greatly to Jefferson. The president's instructions of June 20, 1803, were emphatic and unmistakably clear. After reviewing the diplomatic efforts that had paved the way for the expedition, Jefferson wrote, "Beginning at the mouth of the Missouri you will take observations of latitude and longitude at all remarkable points on the river ... ."[97] Two paragraphs later, Jefferson returned to this theme to make sure that Lewis perfectly understood his duties. "Your observations [of latitude and longitude] are to be taken with great pains & accuracy to be entered distinctly, & intelligibly for others as well as yourself... . Several copies of these as well as of your other notes, should be made at leisure times, & put into the care of the most trustworthy of your attendants ... ."[98] Lewis turned out to be a surprisingly inept determiner of longitude. He had been tutored on the White House lawn by Jefferson himself, and then in specially arranged tutorials by Robert Patterson and Andrew Ellicott in Philadelphia and Lancaster, Pennsylvania. Lewis learned enough of the art of navigation to feel confident in making celestial observations along the entire route. He was so confident, in fact, that he dared quibble with David Thompson, who was in fact one of the greatest longitude men of his time. The North West Company's François-Antoine Larocque, who visited Fort Mandan on several occasions during the 1804–05 winter, reported that Lewis and Clark "differ much from Mr. Thompson, in the Longitude of this place, & say that Mr. Thompson has placed these villages, & this part of the River, a great deal too westerly, which they think is the Case, with all his observations for Longitude."[99] Lewis was wrong. He placed Fort Mandan at 99° 26' 45" W. Thompson reckoned the Mandan villages at 101° 14' 24"W. The best estimate we have, using GPS technology, is that Fort Mandan was at 101° 14' 631" W. Lewis was therefore off by almost two degrees of longitude.[100] It is well known that Lewis's accumulated celestial data proved to be so idiosyncratic or erroneous that West Point's Ferdinand Hassler pronounced it indecipherable after several months of desultory study.[101] As late as 1816 Jefferson was still fretting over the failure of the expedition to bring back the correct latitude and longitude of the Missouri and Columbia River corridors. The former president urged Clark "to correct the longitudes of the map, and to have it published thus corrected."[102] The map that appeared in the Biddle-Allen edition of the journals disappointed Jefferson because it was not graced with this essential data. In his letter to Clark, Jefferson sought to soften his criticism of the existing state of things with the words, "I hope the part I have had in this important voyage, will excuse the interest I take in securing to the world all the beneficial results we were entitled to expect from it, and which would so fully justify the expences of the expedition incurred by the United States in that expedition."[103]

Second, the "water route across this continent" that Lewis discovered proved to be anything but "direct and practicable." Although Lewis did his best to suggest that Indian porters and pack horses could be stationed on either side of Bitterroot Mountains to facilitate the exchange of goods between the watershed of the Missouri and the watershed of the Columbia River, even he had to admit that "the advantages which it offers as a communication for the productions of the East Indians to the United States and thence to Europe will never be found equal on an extensive scale to that by the way of the Cape of Good hope."[104] The Rocky Mountains proved to be an insuperable barrier to the ancient dream of a northwest passage through which boats could pass between the Atlantic and the Pacific. When he learned that Lewis was contemplating an overland journey towards Santa Fe in the winter of 1803–04, Jefferson had spelled out the primary purpose of the expedition in stern and unmistakably clear language. "The object of your mission is single, the direct water communication from sea to sea formed by the bed of the Missouri and perhaps the Oregon."[105] That water communication did not exist.

Third, the Indians of the American West were more numerous, more warlike, more wedded to their tribal cultures, and more resistant to American claims of sovereignty and peaceful trade than Jefferson had envisioned. Lewis's peace and conciliation mission could be regarded as a failure. Two tribes, the Lakota and the Blackfeet, had resisted the incursion of Lewis and Clark with a show of force. Others were passive-aggressive. Most listened more or less politely to the peace and commerce speech that Lewis liked to deliver, acknowledged the wisdom of it, made some lying promises or accepted the idea of temporary truces, waited patiently for the expedition to disappear around the next bend of the river, and then went right back to their existing habits of skirmishing, horse-stealing, raids, and blood feuds. At Fort Mandan a young Hidatsa man responded to Lewis's peace speech by asking, "[I]f they were in a state of peace with all their neighbours what the nation would do for Cheifs?, and added that the chiefs were now oald and must shortly die and that the nation could not exist without cheifs."[106]

Fourth, two of the three peace delegations arranged by Lewis and Clark came to bad ends. Instead of deepening America's alliances with western Indian tribes and creating conditions of mutual trust, these delegations set back white-Indian relations on the upper Missouri. The Arikara chief Arketarnarshar went downriver in the expedition's keelboat in the spring of 1805 and made his way to Washington, DC, to meet the great father. Unfortunately, Arketarnarshar died in the nation's capitol, and even though Jefferson informed the Arikara that "it pleased the great Spirit to take him from among us. We buried him among our own deceased friends & relatives, we shed many tears over his grave, and we now mingle our afflictions with yours on the loss of this beloved chief,"[107] Arketarnarshar's people were deeply upset and suspicious. Nathaniel Pryor's mission to return Sheheke-shote to the Mandan villages in September 1807 had to be aborted at today's North Dakota-South Dakota border after the Arikara fired on the return party. Arikara hostility to the United States lasted until well into the nineteenth century, fueled in some part by the loss of the chief who went away to the white man's world and never returned.

The Mandan leader Sheheke-shote had to be pressured to accompany Lewis and Clark to the nation's capital in the summer and fall of 1806. He did not want to make the journey. In the end, he agreed to accompany Lewis and Clark for the good of his people. He met Jefferson on December 30, 1806. The first attempt to return him in September 1807 miscarried (see above). The second attempt, undertaken at great cost, managed to return Sheheke-shote to his people on September 22, 1809, three years and one month after his departure, but that much-delayed expedition indirectly cost Meriwether Lewis his life.

Fifth, Lewis was only able to bring back a fraction of the plants he had collected in the course of the journey. The majority of his plant specimens were destroyed by high water in the cache pit the expedition dug at the Great Falls of the Missouri on the outbound journey in July 1805. When Lewis had the cache dug up on July 13, 1806, his reaction was strangely matter of fact: "[H]ad the cash opened   found my bearskins entirely destroyed by the water, the river having risen so high that the water had penitrated. all my specimens of plants also lost. the Chart of the Missouri fortunately escaped. opened my trunks and boxes and exposed the articles to dry.   found my papers damp and several articles damp."[108] Given the pains he had taken to collect, prepare, label, and preserve all those plants, one might have expected an outburst of anguish when he discovered that the specimens had not only been dampened, but in fact ruined by seepage. It was a great loss to botanical science, but Lewis assumed an attitude of stoic detachment.

Those were the disappointments of the expedition per se. In the years that followed, three equally serious setbacks followed.

First, the twenty-three vocabularies Lewis had recorded in the course of his journey were never published and no known copy of that irreplaceable data exists. Lewis had made the vocabularies a prominent feature of his proposed third volume of the post-expedition publication project. One set of the vocabularies perished when Jefferson sent his baggage home to Monticello through the Chesapeake Bay. Lewis sputtered a little but there was nothing to be done in an age when no adequate technology existed for proliferating copies of important documents. Apparently Lewis had kept a set of the vocabularies for himself. In 1816 Jefferson instructed Clark to deposit the vocabularies, if he could find them, with the American Philosophical Society, and he wrote a letter to his friend José Correia da Serra saying, "After his return, he [Lewis] asked me if I should have any objection to the printing his separately."[109] Jefferson had freely granted the request, but Lewis never followed through. Jefferson believed the vocabularies were probably among the papers of Benjamin Smith Barton, who had died on December 19, 1815. Lewis's copy of the vocabularies has never been located.

Second, Lewis never wrote the book.

Third, the expedition's artifacts never found a secure and permanent home. The artifacts of the expedition have almost all been lost or destroyed. When the Corps of Discovery returned to civilization at the end of 1806, the United States had no official place to deposit its Enlightenment treasures. Charles Willson Peale had urged President Jefferson to build a national museum of some sort, but the frugal Jefferson, who was a strict constructionist, declared that nothing of the sort could be contemplated until the national debt was paid off and, even then, it would require an enabling amendment to the Constitution. Jefferson chose a few artifacts from the expedition for his private collection at Monticello. The rest he distributed among his Enlightenment friends. Seeds went to Bernard McMahon and William Hamilton. The great majority of the larger artifacts went to Charles Willson Peale's Philadelphia Museum. In 1849, much of Peale's collection was purchased by two exhibitionists, P.T. Barnum and Moses Kimball of the Boston Museum. A fire in 1865 destroyed Barnum's American Museum in New York. The items in Kimball's museum were eventually sold or dispersed. Much of Jefferson's Lewis and Clark collection wound up at his brainchild, the University of Virginia, and virtually all of it has inexplicably disappeared.

Today all that is left of the artifact treasury are a bear claw necklace, elk horns in the lobby of Monticello, the brand Lewis fashioned for himself to blaze trees and brand horses, approximately 230 plant specimens, a few peace medals, a uniform button here and a cartographical push pin there.[110]

Lewis's personal sense of the heroic significance of his mission suffered two serious blows on the return journey. First, he was shot in the buttocks by one of his men. That cast a shadow over the return, silenced Lewis's journal once and for all, and undoubtedly degraded his sense of triumph in completing his transcontinental journey. The darling project ended with a gunshot in the commander's buttocks. Although Lewis might easily have been killed, the details of the incident lent themselves more readily to farce and ridicule than to sympathy—a fact that Gass's publisher David McKeehan was quick to exploit when the need came. Second, as the Corps of Discovery descended the Missouri River through Nebraska,

Iowa, Kansas, and Missouri, they met a large number of parties heading up the Missouri River. Donald Jackson has suggested that Lewis and Clark met at least 150 men between Fort Mandan and St. Louis.[111] These opportunists were ascending the river in spite of the relative consensus among the American people that Lewis and Clark had perished somewhere in the wilderness. On September 17 the Expedition met a trader named John McClellan, "assending in a large boat." McClellan, Clark reported, "was Somewhat astonished to See us return and appeared rejoiced to meet us. ... this Gentleman informed us that we had been long Since given out by the people of the U S Generaly and almost forgotton, the President of the U. States had yet hopes of us."[112] Apparently dead and *almost forgotten*— an appalling diminution of the American embodiment of Captain Cook. The Corps of Discovery's apparent destruction had not prevented others from cheerfully following in their footsteps. Lewis and Clark may have been opening the road to future trade, military excursions, and eventual settlement, but the rumor of their destruction does not seem to have had a significant dampening effect on men with an entrepreneurial spirit. Lewis and Clark met no search or relief party traveling upriver to learn the fate of their expedition. It is possible to conclude that if the expedition had never returned at all, the history of Louisiana Territory would have unfolded more or less as it did. What could be more deflating than to realize that the world they left behind assumed they had perished, shrugged its collective shoulders, and went about its business?

So Lewis came home a wounded and, except for Jefferson, a largely forgotten man. When, after a failed post-expedition romance, Lewis told his friend Mahlon Dickerson that he never felt less like a hero than at the present, he may have been expressing an emptiness and deflation that went well beyond his conjugal woes.

One of Jefferson's three intellectual heroes, Francis Bacon, said the three greatest inventions of the modern world, the innovations that made the modern world, were gunpowder, the compass, and the printing press.[113] They all figure in this story. Bacon died in 1626, before a useful method had been discovered for the determination of longitude, but the *compass* he cherished surely may be permitted to stand for all the improvements in navigation that followed the invention of the compass in the twelfth century. The importance of gunpowder (invented in the ninth century in China, introduced into Europe in the thirteenth century) would be impossible to exaggerate. It enabled those who had it to exert their will over those who didn't. In discussing the twilight of what he called pseudo aristocracy with his friend John Adams, Jefferson wrote, "But since the invention of gunpowder has armed the weak as well as the strong with missile death, bodily strength… has become but an auxiliary ground of distinction."[114] The one thing that Lewis had in superabundance on his transcontinental journey was powder. It has been estimated that he could have made the entire journey all over again with the supply he still had in his possession at the end of the journey. Lewis only felt fully civilized and fully confident in his dominion over the natural world when he had his rifle in his hands. At what he regarded as the most critical moment of the entire journey, when he believed that Cameahwait was about to flee to avoid being ambushed, Lewis "determined to restore their confidence cost what it might and therefore gave the Chief my gun and told him that if his enimies were in those bushes before him that he could defend himself with that gun."[115] After Lewis survived an encounter with a grizzly bear with an unloaded rifle, he reported, "My gun reloaded, I felt confidence once more in my strength."[116]

Most of the participants in the Lewis and Clark Expedition died of natural causes at some point long after the expedition's return. Charles Floyd is the only member of the Corps to die on the journey itself, though Bratton came close and so, probably, did Lewis. So far as we know, eight of the permanent party of thirty-three died violent deaths. That is slightly under 25 percent. Meriwether Lewis committed suicide. The other seven were killed—all or almost all by Indians up in beaver extraction country. The eight were, in something like chronological order, Joseph Field, John Potts, Meriwether Lewis, George Druillard, Pierre Cruzatte, Peter Weiser, John Thompson, and John Collins, who was killed by the Arikara in 1823. Nobody knows how many of these deaths involved gunpowder. At least one. Probably most of them.

It is ironic to consider that the invention that caused Lewis the most trouble was the printing press, which Jefferson confidently declared "secures us against the retrogradation of reason and information."[117] Even if a new age of barbarism arose, Jefferson wrote, "the art of printing alone, and the vast dissemination of books, will maintain the mind where it is, and raise the conquering ruffians to the level of the conquered, instead of degrading these to that of their conquerors."[118] Lewis never produced his book—the third leg of Lord Bacon's criterion of progressive modernity—upon which the Enlightenment credentials and reputation of the expedition must ultimately rest. Lewis's violent death in 1809 served as an unmistakable announcement that there would never be a great publication. We prize Nicholas Biddle's 1814 narrative, but what we are really celebrating, as Jefferson understood, is the adventure aspects of the journey, not the scientific achievements. In fact, Biddle systematically expunged the hard science in his paraphrase narrative—probably with the confidence that members of the American scientific community would undertake that technical work themselves. Lewis not only didn't write his book. He didn't even leave a rich set of raw journals behind from which a competent ghostwriter could produce that book. It is indisputable and sometimes unfortunate that the baseline narrative of the Lewis and Clark story comes from Clark, not Lewis.

The optimist and perennially loyal Jefferson seems to have felt that the expedition was at least a moderate success. That, at least, is what he wrote to others. To the French scientist Bernard Germain de Lacépède, he wrote on July 14, 1808, "And, on the whole, it is with pleasure I can assure you that the addition to our knolege, in every department, resulting from this tour, of Messrs. Lewis and Clarke, has entirely fulfilled my expectations in setting it on foot, and that the world will find that those travelers have well earned it's favor. I will take care that the Institute [the National Institute of France] as well as yourself shall recieve Govr. Lewis's work, as it appears."[119] No evidence exists that Jefferson distributed Biddle's 1814 paraphrase narrative to his friends in the international Enlightenment.

RELATIONS WITH THOMAS JEFFERSON

For reasons that have never been adequately explained, Lewis ceased to write regularly to Thomas Jefferson some time in 1807. David Lavender concludes that Lewis "wrote only three or four curt business letters to the man who had done so much for him."[120] Lavender speculates that "Lewis took deep offense at something Jefferson did or said," though he makes no attempt to specify what might have produced the breach. In the absence of evidence, I believe it is dangerous to presume that Lewis was angry with his mentor. It is possible that after his return from the West, Lewis regarded himself as a national hero who was now too important to perform the duties of the president's aide de camp. Jefferson not only asked Lewis to run routine errands for him in Philadelphia (see below), but sent him in the spring of 1807 to Richmond to observe the Burr treason trial. It is possible that Lewis may have regarded even the latter assignment as task work beneath his dignity. Lewis may also have been upset that artifacts and documents he had collected and sent to the president had been destroyed by vandals when Jefferson attempted to ship them through the Chesapeake back to Richmond and Monticello. On June 27, 1807, Lewis wrote to Jefferson about the miscarriage of these items. There is certainly a measure of irony and perhaps an expression of annoyance in his carefully chosen words. "I sincerely regret the loss you sustained in the articles you shiped for Richmond; it seems peculiarly unfortunate that those at least, which had passed the continent of America and after their exposure to so many casualties and wrisks should have met such destiny in their passage through a small portion only of the Chesapeak."[121] It would be possible to read these sentences as an intimation that Jefferson had been a little careless with priceless artifacts and papers that Lewis had managed to transport unmolested across the entire continent!

If Lewis felt humiliated to be reduced once again to Jefferson's errand boy, he must not have been aware that Jefferson routinely asked for such favors from his friends, including the father of the US Constitution, the author of the Bill of Rights and the *Federalist Papers* and the Secretary of State James Madison. When Jefferson was in Paris serving as a minister plenipotentiary to the Court of Louis XVI, he wrote to Madison requesting that he send him pecans, Pippin apples, cranberries, live opossums and live redbirds to be given away to Jefferson's friends in Parisian salon circles.[122] About the same time Jefferson wrote to Governor John Sullivan of New Hampshire asking him to send him the eviscerated remains of a moose.[123] After the expedition, Jefferson convinced Clark to venture to Big Bone Lick, Kentucky, to supervise the excavation of mammoth and mastodon bones for his cabinet of curiosities. By those standards, Lewis actually got off pretty easily.

On June 4, 1807, Jefferson wrote a short miscellaneous letter to Lewis, the principal purpose of which was to ask Lewis to check on and bring with him to Washington one or more watches that Jefferson had sent to a man named Voight in Philadelphia for repair. Jefferson concluded his letter with a sentence that indicates that Lewis was not keeping his patron abreast of his movements. "According to Mr. Cole's account we have the hope of seeing you here [Washington, DC] to the 4th of July. Accept my friendly salutations & assurances of constant affection & respect."[124] It could not have pleased Jefferson to have to rely on others for news of Lewis's post-expedition movements. Jefferson must also have been thinking it was about time for Lewis to make his way to St. Louis to take up his duties as governor, but he made no mention of territorial affairs.

Lewis replied to Jefferson's letter on June 27, 1807. He provided the president updates on the watches that Voight was repairing, and reported that he had entrusted Thomas Mann Randolph's watch and one of Jefferson's rings to Secretary of War Henry Dearborn, who was on his way to the federal capital. Lewis lamented the loss of expedition artifacts that Jefferson had sent home to Monticello by way of the Chesapeake, and reported that Charles Willson Peale was preparing the head and horns of a bighorn sheep for Jefferson's Indian museum at Monticello. Lewis closed his letter with the words, "With the most sincere and unalterable frindship Your Obt. Servt."[125]

Lewis wrote to Thomas Jefferson at least twice more in the two years, three months, and ten days before his death in Tennessee. Lewis saw Jefferson in Albemarle County, Virginia, in August 1807. How long they spent together at Monticello, and the subjects of their conversation, are unknown. Thomas Danisi and John Jackson say that Lewis "found Jefferson distracted by the trial of former vice president Aaron Burr."[126] Neither

Jefferson nor Lewis left a record of the reunion. It seems certain that they discussed territorial affairs and the unfolding Burr trial, for which the sitting president had been subpoenaed. It seems likely, too, that Jefferson pressed Lewis to complete the first volume of his book as quickly as possible. Near the end of August Jefferson sent Lewis to Richmond to serve as his informal agent—and ears—at the Burr trial. Lewis returned to Monticello in mid-September to make his report to Jefferson. Again, we have no record of their conversations. This was the last time they ever met.

On January 14, 1808, Jefferson sent a set of mammoth bones to his friend Lacépède in France (see above). Actually, Clark had collected those bones for the president at Big Bone Lick in Kentucky. Jefferson also forwarded to Lacépède specimens of the mountain goat and bighorn sheep. "Their description," he wrote, "will be given in the work of Governor Lewis, the journal & geographic part of which may be soon expected from the press; but the parts relating to the plants & animals observed in his tour will be delayed by the engravings."[127]

On July 17, 1808, the president of the United States wrote a letter of stiff rebuke to his protégé, the governor of Louisiana Territory. "Dear Sir," wrote Jefferson, "Since I parted with you in Albemarle in Sep. last I have never had a line from you, nor I believe has the Secretary at War with whom you have much connection through the Indian department." This was as angry as Thomas Jefferson knew how to get. He dispensed with what the historian Alf Mapp called "the perfunctory pleasantries:"[128] no introductory matter, no conventional enquiry into Lewis's health, no phatic language about Lewis's relatives or life at Monticello. The characteristically serene and graceful president got right to the point. *Never a line* from a young man Jefferson had plucked out of obscurity in the spring of 1801, boarded in the White House itself when they were the only two white individuals living there, trained himself in his own method of determining longitude, and sent on the most important reconnaissance mission in the history of the American republic. *Never a line* from a man he had appointed, in spite of his inexperience, to the governorship of America's newest territory. *Never a line* from a man who had been granted access to Thomas Jefferson's private library at Monticello in a room that even family members were not allowed to enter without the explicit permission of the president of the United States. *Never a line* from a man who owed everything that was remarkable in his life to Jefferson.

Jefferson was angry.

Nor had Lewis's government superiors at the War Department heard from him, not even about official business, some of which was of urgent importance. Jefferson immediately followed this reprimand with a pointed explanation of why Lewis's silence was not merely a personal annoyance. "The misfortune which attended the effort to send the Mandane chief home became

Jefferson's letter of rebuke to his protégé Lewis: "Since I parted with you in Albemarle in Sep. last I have never had a line from you, nor I believe has the Secretary at War…." Thomas Jefferson to Meriwether Lewis, July 17, 1808. Courtesy Manuscript Division, Library of Congress.

known to us before you had reached St. Louis." America's first attempt to return the Mandan leader Sheheke-shote to his village in today's North Dakota had failed dramatically when the Arikara fired upon the escort party led by expedition veteran Nathaniel Pryor in September 1807. Now Sheheke-shote, his wife Yellow Corn, their son, the Mandan interpreter Rene Jusseaume, and Jusseaume's wife and two children were all languishing near St. Louis, waiting to be returned to their homeland. By July 1808 Sheheke-shote had been gone from his home village for just under two years. Sheheke-shote had not wanted to make the journey to Washington, DC, in the first place, but, desperate for a live Mandan or Hidatsa to bring to President Jefferson, Lewis and Clark had leaned on him in August 1806 at the Mandan villages and assured him that he would be safely returned to his home in a timely fashion after his visit with the great white father. Not only had the first attempt to return Sheheke-shote ended in disaster, but as far as Jefferson knew no second attempt was underway or even planned. The inherent urgency of doing justice by Sheheke-shote was compounded in Jefferson's eyes because the last Upper Missouri Indian who had made the long journey to Washington, DC, at Lewis's invitation had never returned.

Jefferson explained to Lewis that he had not himself made arrangements for the return of Sheheke-shote and his Mandan party to North Dakota or sent instructions to the governor about return options because he assumed that Lewis would write to *him* about the unfortunate situation. "We took no step on the occasion, counting on receiving your advice so soon as you should be in place, and knowing that your knowledge of the whole subject & presence on the spot would enable you to judge better than we could what ought to be done. The constant persuasion that something from you must be on it's way to us, has as constantly prevented our writing to you on the subject. The present letter however is written to put an end at length to this mutual silence, and to ask from you a communication of what you think best to be done to get the chief & his family back."[129] Although Jefferson was too polite to make his point directly, the burden of this passage is W*hy should I have to write to YOU about getting Sheheke-shote home when YOU recruited him in the first place and it is YOUR responsibility as territorial governor to arrange his homecoming. YOU are in a much better position to solve this problem than I am, because you are THERE and I am a thousand miles away not knowing what, if anything, has been done, and wondering why you haven't even bothered to write to me about a situation of this importance and delicacy. And don't tell me how busy you are. I'm the President of the United States and yet I have found time to write to you.* Jefferson, by his own admission, was only angry a handful of times in his life. Though he manages to maintain decorum in this letter, his exasperation is unmistakable.

Here's why. "We consider the good faith, & the reputation of the nation as pledged to accomplish this [Sheheke-shote's return]."[130] Translation: *Why hasn't Sheheke-shote already been returned to his home village? This is not one of those responsibilities you can attend to at your considerable leisure. If you have in some way undertaken his return, I ought to know about it. If nothing has been done, it is even more important that I be told why.*

Having written as blistering a letter as he could in good conscience write, Jefferson took the edge off of his castigation by writing a breezy paragraph about John Jacob Astor's plans to capitalize the American fur trade, the continuing tensions with Great Britain on the high seas, and the coming presidential election. Then, at the end of the letter, Jefferson returned to his characteristic personal warmth. "I have not lately heard of your friends in Albemarle," he wrote. "They were well when I left that in June, and not hearing otherwise affords presumption they are well. But I presume you hear that from themselves."[131] One last jab.

Then, finally, a reminder that Lewis owes the enlightened world a book. "We have no tidings yet of the forwardness of your printer." Notice that Jefferson politely pretends that the delay in publication may have more to do with the printer than with Lewis's failure to write the book. "I hope the first part will not be delayed much longer. Wishing you every blessing of life & health I salute you with constant affection & respect."[132]

On August 24, 1808, Jefferson wrote again to Governor Lewis, this time from Monticello. "I am uneasy, hearing nothing from you about the Mandan chief, nor the measures for restoring him to his country. That is an object which presses on our justice & our honour. ... My letter from Washington [July 17] asked your opinions on this subject."[133] Jefferson seems to have been wondering, *How do you get this guy's attention?*

Jefferson wrote to Secretary of War Henry Dearborn on August 12, 1808. The letter was mostly about the possibility of war with Great Britain, but the president also expressed his fear that Governor Lewis had rattled the saber at the Osage Indians of today's Missouri. "I fear Governor Lewis has been too prompt in committing us with the Osages so far as to oblige us to go on," Jefferson wrote. Then he added, in mystified frustration, "But it is astonishing we get not one word from him."[134]

Lewis wrote to Jefferson in a strictly official capacity on December 15, 1808. He forwarded a treaty recently consummated with the Osage Indians, and explained that it replaced and superseded a treaty previously negotiated by William Clark. Leaders of the Osage nation had protested to Governor Lewis that they had been deceived in the original treaty deliberations, and that they had never intended to cede the amount of territory specified in that treaty. They declared that they had relinquished "no more than the privilege of hunting in that tract of country relinquished by the treaty." Knowing that a treaty in bad faith—or one characterized by fundamental misunderstanding—would create more problems than it solved, Governor Lewis had insisted that the treaty be renegotiated. Lewis believed that unspecified white traders and land speculators had stirred up

Sheheke-shote in 1807. Getting him home was the death of Meriwether Lewis.Charles Balthazar Julien Févret de Saint-Mémin. Shehek-Shote, 1807. Courtesy of the American Philosophical Society, FAP:144.

Osage discontentment to further their own financial interests, but since he had no solid proof, he declined to name the culprits, one of whom was apparently Pierre Chouteau. Lewis was able to report that the new treaty was acceptable to the Osage. "The Indians appear perfectly satisfied with this treaty, and I hope it is such as will meet your approbation."[135]

Near the end of the letter, Lewis wrote, "I shall be obliged to leave the territory shortly, for Washington and Philadelphia," and explained that he wished Clark to be given plenary powers over Indian affairs in his absence, since "Mr. Bates has very earnestly requested of me not to impose on him duties in the Indian department during my absence, alleging that it is a subject with which he is wholly unacquainted."[136] Lewis did not explain to President Jefferson just why he was coming to Washington, DC, perhaps not wishing to mingle public and private concerns in this rather formal letter, or perhaps wishing to avoid admitting to the president that his official financial affairs had become so tangled as to necessitate a personal visit to the War Department. Lewis's mention of Philadelphia signified that he intended to linger in the east long enough to make further progress on his book. That must have been good news to Jefferson.

Jefferson wrote to Lewis again on August 16, 1809, two days before Lewis's thirty-fifth birthday. Jefferson was writing a letter of introduction on behalf of the English botanist John Bradbury, who was on his way to the American West. Jefferson used the occasion to nag Lewis a little about the still unpublished book. "I am very often applied to know when your work will begin to appear; and I have so long promised copies to my literary correspondents in France, that I am almost bankrupt in their eyes. I shall be very happy to recieve from yourself information of your expectations on this subject. Every body is impatient for it."[137] This was the last letter Jefferson ever wrote Lewis. As usual, he was pleading with his protégé to communicate with him.

It is possible that Lewis wrote more than we have. It is possible that some of his letters never reached their intended recipients, though this, of course, has been one of the standard excuses of the silent since the invention of epistolary correspondence. In his letter to William Eustis of August 18, 1809, Lewis wrote a passage that somehow was garbled in Donald Jackson's *Letters of the Lewis and Clark Expedition*.[138] After defending his vouchers for cost overruns in the Missouri Fur Company's initiative to return Sheheke-shote to his homeland, Lewis wrote, "I have reason to believe that sundry of my Letters have been lost, as there remain several important Subjects on which I have not yet received an Answer."[139] Jackson's transcript reads, " … no claim will hereafter be made for that object. as there remain several important Subjects on which I have not yet received an Answer."[140] If St. Louis had been closer to Washington, DC, if the frontier postal system had been more efficient and reliable, if Lewis had sent multiple copies of his reports and letters by several routes to the federal capital, it is possible that his relations with the

War Department and patron Thomas Jefferson between 1807 and September 1809 would have been less troubled, indeed less fatal.

Lewis wrote a humorous letter to William Clark on May 29, 1808, announcing that he was sending Nathaniel Pryor with two keelboats, "one trusty Sergt. & twenty good men," to the mouth of the Ohio River (at today's Cairo, Illinois) to meet Clark and his new wife Julia Hancock and their household furnishings. This was a fine escort indeed. In a letter announcing his travel plans, Clark had spoken of his bride in close conjunction with the words "goods" and "merchandise," and Lewis chided him for "your want of Gallantry." This is the letter in which Lewis described himself as "a musty, fusty, rusty old bachelor."[141]

This letter is well known in Lewis and Clark circles. Towards the end of the letter Lewis discussed arrangements he had made to persuade Joseph Charless to begin a newspaper in St. Louis.[142] Lewis was afraid some of his correspondence had not reached the intended recipients. "I have reason to believe that this letter to Mr. Fitzhugh one to Mr. Charless and sundry other letters and valuable papers which I dispatched by the succeeding mail, remained at Cahokia several days, and were unfortunately lost when the post rider was drowned about the 15th of this month in the little Wabash."[143] It is quite possible that some of Lewis's important letters were lost in this and other incidents. One of the principal accusations of William Eustis (July 15, 1809) was that Lewis had undertaken a series of territorial initiatives, including financial outlays, without bothering to keep the War Department abreast of his actions, intentions, or rationale for making the decisions he had made. It is possible that Lewis was less culpable than he appeared to be.

Although it is possible that Lewis wrote letters during this period that never reached their intended recipients, no amount of special pleading can exonerate him from the problem of his failure to communicate. His mentor and patron Jefferson was sufficiently frustrated by Lewis's silence to chastise him in—for Jefferson—surprisingly bitter terms. Jefferson wrote to Secretary of War Henry Dearborn to express astonishment that "we hear not one word from him."[144] William Eustis (or William Simmons writing for Eustis) rebuked Lewis for his failure to inform the War Department of his actions in the field. Lewis's publishers complained to Jefferson that their repeated requests for information about the progress of his book had been *completely* ignored. Lewis himself acknowledged his failure to communicate. He apologized to President Madison for not writing on a more regular basis. He apologized to Amos Stoddard for not writing at all and never responding to "several friendly epistles which I have received from you since my return from the Pacific Ocean."[145]

Can anything be more clear than that Lewis's communications with his official and unofficial superiors, with his friends and colleagues, with his publisher and the individuals that he had commissioned to illustrate his book, had broken down more or less completely by the spring and summer of 1809? Nobody knew what to make of Lewis's silences. Everyone was bewildered (astonished!) and frustrated, and several individuals expressed their frustration directly to Lewis. The argument that Lewis was too busy to write to his superiors in the War Department or to his patron Jefferson has no credibility. It was his duty to communicate with the War Department and it was profoundly in his interest, in every possible way, to communicate with Jefferson.

The late L. Ron Hubbard developed the concept of the ARC-triangle to explain how human relationships flourish or fail. One side of the triangle represents *affinity*, the second *reality*, and the third *communication* (ARC). All three are interrelated, and they each support the others. A successful relationship requires all three to be strong. If any one of the three breaks down, the other two suffer. Example one. Thomas Jefferson and James Madison saw the world in more or less the same way. They had a nearly identical reality: they were both slaveholding Virginia plantation owners who disliked but learned to live with slavery, who were profoundly committed to religious liberty, and who envisioned an American republic with a limited and decentralized government. Because they shared this reality they established an affinity that began in 1775 and deepened through the remainder of their lives. They communicated constantly. Their correspondence has been separately edited from the rest of their papers. It consumes three dense volumes. The only time they lost affinity (and only in part) was when their communication was impaired because Jefferson was stationed in France and Madison was under a gag order about deliberations at the Constitutional Convention in Philadelphia. Once they started to communicate again, they agreed on a compromise reality and their affinity soared back to its usual heights. Jefferson and Madison: nearly perfect ARC triangle.

Example two. Thomas Jefferson and John Adams. They were two of the best communicators of their time, though not always with each other. They had deep affinity, based on their membership in the little band of brothers who wrought the revolution in 1776. But they had very different realities. Jefferson was a Virginia plantation owner, Adams a New England lawyer and hardscrabble farmer. Jefferson owned slaves. Adams was appalled by slavery. Jefferson believed in the goodness of man. Adams was a social Calvinist. After the artificial bonding of the Revolution had mostly run its course, their realities diverged so dramatically that their affinity was eventually damaged and—in 1801—their communication broke down altogether. Fortunately their core affinity was sufficiently powerful that they allowed themselves to be persuaded to resume communicating in 1812. That rebuilt their larger affinity, and—with both of them now safely out of office—their realities began to converge. They died, wary but loving friends, on the Fourth of July 1826.

Example three. Jefferson and Alexander Hamilton. No affinity. No shared reality. Little communication.

Lewis's fundamental problem was silence. Because he found himself unwilling or unable to communicate at key moments of his life, he weakened his affinity with those who shared his reality. Eventually even his closest friends and supporters lost so much affinity with Lewis that, in the end, they even came to question his reality. Secretary of War William Eustis made it clear that he did not oppose Lewis's financial arrangements per se; but because Lewis had failed to apprize the War Department of his actions in faraway St. Louis, Eustis had no reality to approve. Had Lewis kept the War Department abreast of his actions in the field with respect to returning the Mandan leader Sheheke-shote to his home village in North Dakota, had he even explained to the War Department his occasional communications with Jefferson on the subject of returning Sheheke-shote, Eustis (or his clerk William Simmons) would almost certainly not have written his stern official rebuke of July 15, 1809. When Lewis received that angry official letter on August 18, 1809, his thirty-fifth birthday, he was utterly devastated. He could accept being chastised for failing to communicate, but he could not bear having his reality so bluntly discredited. He was aware from the tone of Eustis's letter that virtually all affinity was now gone. The War Department in Washington and the territorial governor in St. Louis no longer shared a common sense of reality. What Lewis failed to realize is that he was almost wholly responsible for the breakdown, for the loss of reality and affinity, quite simply because he had failed to communicate. He had wrongly assumed that a previously established resonance of affinity and reality could withstand an almost total breakdown of communication. He was wrong. It killed him.

Lewis's problem with silence was not merely the result of post-expedition responsibilities and stresses. Way back in 1801, Tarleton Bates complained to his brother Frederick, "Meriwether Lewis is silent though he promised to write weekly."[146] From Fort Mandan Lewis sent Jefferson a long fascinating letter summarizing the expedition's first year of travel. Towards the end of the letter he confessed, "I have forwarded to the Secretary at War, my public Accounts rendered up to the present day. They have been much longer delayed than I had any idea that they would have been, when we departed from the Illinois, but this delay, under the circumstances which I was compelled to act, has been unavoidable." Lewis felt a little guilty about the delay. "I therefore did not hesitate to prefer the sensure that I may have incurred by the detention of these papers, to that of risking in any degree the success of the expedition."[147] The depth of Lewis's guilt is indicated by the length and defensiveness of his explanation: "To me, the detention of those papers have formed a serious source of disquiet and anxiety; and the recollection of your particular charge to me on this subject, has made it still more poignant. I am fully aware of the inconvenience which must have arisen to the War Department, from the want of these vouchers, previous to the last session of Congress, but how to divert it was out of my power to devise."[148] Aside from Lewis's considerable anxiety on this score, an anxiety that is wholly absent from his post-expedition correspondence, the most interesting phrase in this passage is "your particular charge to me on this subject." This surely means that Jefferson had noticed Lewis's propensity for procrastination in keeping up his official accounts during the White House years, that he had given Lewis a fatherly lecture about this subject before his protégé departed for the West. Lewis was certainly right about one thing. It was much easier to get these papers in order inside a log cabin at Fort Mandan than in an army tent or in the kind of clearing Clark sought out near White Catfish Camp on July 26, 1804, when he was trying to draw a map of the Missouri from its confluence with the Mississippi to the mouth of the Platte River: "the wind blew Verry hard all Day from the South with Clouds of Sand which incommoded me very much in my tent, and as I could not Draw in the Boat was obliged Combat with the Misqutr. Under a Shade in the woods."[149] Take your pick on the trail: clouds of sand or swarming mosquitoes.

This letter to Jefferson proves that dilatoriness, procrastination, and breakdowns of administrative reliability were habitual with Lewis, not just a post-expedition phenomenon or the result of the press of work in St. Louis.

FRIENDS AND FAMILY

Lewis wrote few personal letters during the last two years of his life. Those that he did write invariably began with an apology for his silence. Danisi and Jackson argue that the governor was simply too busy with the press of public business to take time to write to friends and family. From a certain point of view, of course, that is a ludicrous proposition. There is always time to write at least a short letter explaining why a longer one is for the moment impossible. Lewis wrote now and then to Clark when they were separated during and after the expedition (March 11, 1807 and May 15, 1807), but after March 1808, when they both lived and worked in St. Louis, he did not write again to Clark so far as we know, until the New Madrid letter of September 11, 1809, which has been lost. Nor does Lewis appear to have written to his old friend Mahlon Dickerson of Philadelphia. We know that he ignored "several friendly epistles" from his friend Amos Stoddard.[150] Possibly Lewis wrote personal letters during this period of which historians are unaware, but those few letters he did write are so apologetic that it seems unlikely that much has been lost. The unanimous and unmistakable conclusion of all those who needed or wanted to hear from Lewis during this period is that he had descended into a profound, unaccountable, annoying, and self-destructive silence.

Lewis wrote to his mother Lucy Marks on December 1, 1808, when he had been in St. Louis for nine months, approximately a year after he had last seen her in Albemarle County, Virginia.[151] So far as we know, this is the only letter he ever wrote her from St. Louis, the only letter he wrote her between their last face-to-face visit and his death on October 11, 1809. He began, inevitably, with an apology for his silence: "My life is still one continued press of business which scarcely allows me leasure to write to you. I have consequently not written to you as often as I could have wished."[152] This is conventional enough, even among correspondents who write more frequently than Lewis did. Then he provided an odd and rather tasteless variation on the conventional enquiry into the health of the recipient. "I sincerely hope you are all well tho' it seems I shall not know whether you are dead or alive untill I visit you again." Lewis was upset with his stepbrother John Marks for not writing to keep him abreast of his mother's health and family affairs. Given Lewis's problems with silence, it took more than a touch of effrontery for the governor to write, "[W]hat is John Marks and Edmund Anderson about, that they do not write to me?" Lewis no doubt felt that his silence was justified by his official responsibilities and the "one continued press of business" in St. Louis, but that his relatives, who were not agents of the United States government, had no excuse for not writing more often. Lewis used the rest of his letter to discuss his plans to bring the entire family together in the Louisiana Territory. After explaining his recent land transactions, Lewis wrote, "This place which I have selected for your residence is in the most healthy part of the country; it is an agreeable situation one with which I am convinced you will be pleased." Lewis announced to his mother that he was prepared "to sell the Ivy creek lands or at least part of them" to raise the money to relocate the entire family near St. Louis. Lewis informed his mother that he intended to return to the East "in the course of this winter." "I have been detained here much longer than I expected," he wrote, "but hope to get off shortly." Finally, Lewis put the best face he could on the state of his health: "I have generally had my health well since I left you."[153] This could not have been very encouraging news to Lucy Marks.

OFFICIAL SILENCE

On July 15, 1809, William Eustis (or someone else) wrote the letter that killed Meriwether Lewis. Eustis (1753–1825) was the US secretary of war from March 7, 1809, to January 13, 1813. The letter was a sharp, severe, and at times sarcastic official reprimand of Governor Lewis. Thomas Danisi and John Jackson have argued that Eustis was not, in fact, the author of the letter. They believe that Eustis was away from Washington, DC, on summer holiday at the time the letter was written and that it was the War Department accountant William Simmons who actually wrote the offending letter.[154] Danisi argues that Simmons worked in a separate Treasury Department unit in the War Department, and that his financial dealings with territorial officials were sufficiently separate from the work of the Secretary of War that Eustis may not have been made aware of the contents of the letter, even if he had been in the national capital at the time of its composition.[155] Simmons had been causing Lewis increasing frustration ever since Lewis first submitted his financial records of the expedition to the War Department in the spring of 1807. Simmons wrote letters to Lewis on April 15, June 17, and July 31, 1807, each less generous and understanding.[156] Because all previous accounts of this critical incident in Lewis's life have attributed the letter to William Eustis, including Donald Jackson's enormously influential *Letters of the Lewis and Clark Expedition*, in what follows I am going to designate the document as the Eustis-Simmons letter to avoid confusion. The identity of the author of the letter is less important than its devastating contents and the last paragraph, which states, "The President has been consulted and the observations herein contained have his approval."[157]

The Eustis-Simmons letter made clear that one of the principal reasons for reprimanding Governor Lewis and refusing to honor his vouchers was that Lewis had not communicated with the War Department about his decisions in St. Louis, in particular the arrangements he was making to return the Mandan leader Sheheke-shote to today's North Dakota. In fact, the accusation that Lewis had been irresponsibly and unprofessionally silent recurs in the letter like a drumbeat of rebuke. "It has been *usual to advise the Government* of the United States when expenditures to a considerable amount are contemplated in the Territorial Governments," Eustis-Simmons wrote.[158] This was immediately followed with another reprimand for Lewis's inexplicable silence. "In the instance of accepting the volunteer services of 140 men for a military expedition to a point and purpose not designated, which expedition is stated to combine commercial as well as military objects, and when an Agent of the Government appointed for other purposes is selected for the command, *it is thought the Government might, without injury to the public interests, have been consulted*."[159] Here the Eustis-Simmons letter adds sarcasm to his rebuke. Then, after informing Lewis that the US government had too little information about the proposed public-private expedition (the Shekehe-shote expedition) to authorize it, Eustis-Simmons returned to Lewis's unprofessional silence for a third time. "On another account *it was desirable that this Government should have been consulted*."[160] Eustis-Simmons explained that his department could not be sure it was complying with the intentions of Congress unless it controlled the expenditure of public moneys in the territories. Then, just to make sure Lewis understood his extreme displeasure, Eustis-Simmons returned again to Lewis's silence. "Being responsible for the expenditure of Public money & made judges in such cases whether the Funds appropriated by the Legislature are applicable and adequate to the object, it is desirable in all practicable cases that *they should be advised and consulted* when expenditure is required"[161] [emphasis added throughout].

The key information of which the War Department was not in possession was that President Jefferson, while he was still the chief executive, had instructed Lewis to do whatever it took to get Sheheke-shote home. Jefferson had said returning Sheheke-shote was a matter of the highest urgency, that the moral integrity of the government of the United States was at stake, and that as far as Jefferson was concerned, Lewis had a virtual blank check to get it done. Apparently, Jefferson did not brief his successor James Madison about the Sheheke-shote matter before he left Washington for the last time. Anticipating the likelihood that some things would fall through the cracks as Jefferson left the White House and Madison took up residence, Governor Lewis ought to have written to President Madison early in 1809 to explain the current state of affairs in Louisiana Territory, and to explain what arrangements he had made with Jefferson before the third president retired, particularly concerning the hold-over issue of the Mandan leader's return. If Madison had been aware of the arrangements Jefferson had made with Lewis for Sheheke-shote's return, or his predecessor's sense of urgency, he probably would not have authorized Eustis-Simmons to reprimand Lewis, if only out of ancient respect for his closest friend and political mentor. By failing to keep the new administration abreast of his plans, Lewis brought the wrath of Secretary Eustis and his staff down upon his head. If he had explained all these matters in a timely way, during the transition between friendly republican administrations or in the first weeks of Madison's first term, the War Department would probably have felt compelled to honor arrangements pre-endorsed by Jefferson, whose sense of urgency about Sheheke-shote had not survived (in government circles) his departure from the national capital. Even if the War Department had felt compelled to challenge Lewis's vouchers, the tone of the Eustis-Simmons letter would have been much more respectful. Lewis's silence not only prevented the War Department from understanding the complicated train of events he was trying to manage on Jefferson's behalf, but it also so frustrated Eustis and even James Madison that their fund of good will was depleted by the summer of 1809.

It is at least possible that Lewis attempted to communicate with his superiors more than they were aware. If it is true that some of his letters were lost, his fall may have been at least partly unmerited. But Lewis had failed to communicate with everyone—Henry Dearborn, Jefferson, President Madison, his friends and family, and the publishers of his book. Apparently some or all of these individuals compared notes, asked each other whether anyone (anywhere) had heard from Lewis, and concluded that, from a communications point of view, Lewis was essentially AWOL. If Lewis had been communicating regularly with any of the key figures of his life in the East, they might have alerted the others, and that may have staved off some of the trouble.

⚜

It is really this simple. If Lewis had kept a daily journal throughout the expedition, from the moment he left Pittsburgh on August 31, 1803, or *at least* from the moment the expedition left St. Charles on May 14, 1804, our understanding of the expedition would be much richer. That would have made it infinitely easier for Lewis to write his book. If Lewis had written his book, if he had fulfilled the promises of his prospectus of April 1807, the Lewis and Clark Expedition would be regarded as one of the principal episodes in the history of exploration and not merely as a very great adventure in American history. If he had written the book, it would have been impossible for official Washington to treat him as shabbily as it did, because his tardiness in getting to St. Louis and his failures to communicate regularly would have made a kind of sense, and he would have had Jefferson's support in any struggle with the War Department.

The great irony is that the only way that Lewis could rise to the level of his dreams—his grand object—was to publish an account of his journey. This was something only he could do. Danisi and Jackson have written, "Now that adventure [the expedition] was beginning to dim. To revitalize it Lewis had to write a masterpiece."[162] He might, like Cook and Mackenzie and others, have hired a ghostwriter to help him accomplish the task. To rise to the level of international fame and importance he craved was entirely within his hands. Lewis could not guarantee that he would survive the great journey itself, with its boat accidents, buffalo charging into camp, slippery gumbo slopes on the Marias River banks, encounters with grizzly bears, or accidental gunshot wounds at the Birnt Hills of Dakota. Those things were beyond Lewis's control, though good planning and reasonable prudence greatly increased the probability of survival. Lewis might well have died the day he tasted arsenic (August 20, 1804), in the tense encounter with the Teton Sioux (September 24–28, 1804), in the gunfight with the Blackfeet at Two Medicine Creek (July 27, 1806), or at the Birnt Hills (August 11, 1806). He survived. He triumphed. Once he was back in St. Louis or Philadelphia, with his notes and journals before him, good paper and pens, access to a library of North American exploration, a glass of claret before him, Lewis was entirely capable of controlling his own destiny. After the expedition's return, there were no dangers that he did not seek out himself. Thomas Slaughter has written, "As a man of action, the explorer often faces the greatest challenge after his welcome home. When the celebration ends, he must become a writer. This is essential for self-promoting his discoveries. He must compose himself, make order out of disorderly notes that he took in the wild before he knew what his story would be. This can be scarier than the journey. He must publish or his discoveries may perish along with him. He must survive this sedentary task without the stimulation of the wilderness, the adrenaline rush of physical danger, and the joy of the hunt. Now he must really work alone."[163]

Lewis's silence was his greatest failure in life. In his famous birthday meditation on August 18, 1805, he lamented the hours he had spent in indolence when he might have been filling his mind with Enlightenment taxonomies, and techniques, bodies of knowledge, and firm understandings of the history of North America. He need not have been so hard on himself. All he had to do was write up everything he saw and did, and then seek the help of professional exemplars of the Enlightenment when he returned. When he bothered to keep a journal, Lewis was always equal to the challenge of what he saw before him. With the help of Jefferson's fellow members of the republic of letters, with the assistance of the savants of the American Philosophical Society, Lewis might have written a book of genuine greatness and permanent importance in the annals of science. He chose not to write that book. For some reason he withheld himself from an eager and waiting world. The hugger-mugger thing that Nicholas Biddle produced after the death of Lewis—necessitated by the collapse of the larger publication project—was not much more than adequate.

FELIX CULPA: THE GOOD NEWS ABOUT LEWIS'S SILENCE

One of the most interesting ironies of the Lewis and Clark Expedition is that we are in some ways fortunate that Lewis did *not* write his book. Had he written the book he intended, Lewis might well have destroyed the original field journals or they might have disappeared in precisely the way Patrick Gass's original journal has disappeared in the wake of the 1807 publication of his book. Printers of this era routinely discarded original manuscripts. We have Nicholas Biddle's paraphrase edition of the journals. We are extremely fortunate. We also have all of or most of the journals that served as the basis of that narrative. Biddle's paraphrase is an essential document of the expedition, in some ways as important as the journals themselves, the letters collected by Donald Jackson, and the maps gathered in volume one of the University of Nebraska edition of the *Journals of the Lewis and Clark Expedition*. In the wake of the publication of the thirteen volumes of the University of Nebraska edition of the journals (1983–2001), the Biddle paraphrase has unfortunately come to be neglected in favor of the original journals. The original journals were first published by Reuben Gold Thwaites in 1905, but his edition had a limited distribution and it did not fully displace the Biddle paraphrase. Nicholas Biddle's many written queries, the marginal notes and interlineations he inserted onto the pages of the journals, his conversations with William Clark at Fincastle in the spring of 1810, and his continuing conversation with George Shannon, whom Clark assigned to serve as the liaison between himself and Biddle, constitute an essential lens on the expedition. Although Biddle never traveled into the American West, he was a brilliant man of letters and he was not afraid to ask questions and seek clarification when passages in the raw journals perplexed him. Biddle's fifty-four pages of queries and notes are themselves one of the most valuable documents.[164]

Had Lewis written his book he would have cast everything in careful, grammatical prose, in complete sentences. He would have regularized the spelling of such words as *musquetor* and *mockerson* and *reather* and *squar.* He would have eliminated minor details that he would have regarded as extraneous, random, or undignified, but which we cling to like historical and linguistic lifesavers. He would not have told the enlightened world that "Capt. C. thought himself somewhat bilious and had not had a passage for several days."[165] He would have eliminated or euphemized references to venereal diseases. He would have eliminated entries like Clark's October 5, 1805, report that "Capt Lewis & myself eate a Supper of roots boiled, which Swelled us in Such a manner that we were Scercely able to breath for Several hours,"[166] or cast it in such lofty or generalized language that it would have lost its specificity and its delight. Like Nicholas Biddle he would have cast Native American sexual passages into Latin. We almost certainly would have been denied our glimpse at the "aged women [of the Clatsop nation] in many of whom I have seen the bubby reach as low as the waist." And Lewis's odd and prurient admission that although "those parts [are] usually covered from familiar view, but when she stoops or places herself in many other attitudes, this battery of Venus is not altogether impervious to the inquisitive and penetrating eye of the amorite."[167] The book Lewis wrote would have been sanitized, regularized, formalized, and bowdlerized. It would have been full of high mindedness and toned up with rhetorical flourishes. It would have been a more interesting document in certain limited respects, and far less interesting in other respects. Explorers, writes Thomas Slaughter, clean up their fragmentary, inchoate, and half-understood experiences in retrospect, and impose an orderliness and narrative logic to that which in fact was disorderly and essentially random.

Lewis's book would have been a better exemplum of the detached rationality of the Enlightenment, but it would be less valuable as a document in American history. Lewis was already formal enough in his journal (or first draft) of the expedition. In his published account he would surely have strained towards an even more formal prose style. In the journals Lewis's tendency towards pretentiousness is actually an asset, because it sets him in contrast with Clark's basic English. The sudden appearance of Latinate expressions in Lewis's journal entries enliven them and keep the reader from being lulled into an uncritical reading of the journals, or a belief that what is being offered us is a set of objective facts and indisputable experiences. Lewis's self-conscious *affect* requires—or at least invites—us to read his "journals" as complex texts and not simple narratives. Such expressions as "period which I am to remain in this Sublunary world," or "a supply of this articles is at this moment peculiarly interesting,"[168]not only startle, and enliven Lewis's journal entries, but they reveal something about the way in which he thought about himself.

Lewis and Clark editor Frank Bergon rightly understands what might have been lost had Lewis completed his task. The unvarnished original journals "tell a heroic story of a people's struggles through a wilderness and the return home," he writes. "Better than more artfully constructed poems or novels or plays, they embody with the colloquial directness and power of an oral epic the mythic history of a nation."[169] In other words, in Bergon's formulation we have in Lewis and Clark a Homeric (primitive or oral) epic rather than a Vergilian (polished and self-conscious) epic. The roughness of the originals creates a kind of democratic or demotic authenticity that reflects the heart of the frontier experience of America. A more carefully crafted account by Lewis might be too polished and sophisticated for the wilderness adventure it was intended to encapsulate. Indeed, some of Lewis's more polished field journal entries, if they *are* field entries, are so grandiloquent that they feel at certain moments a little artificial, while Clark's clearly undistilled prose always strikes the reader as authentic.

We are fortunate in that we have many voices (Lewis, Clark, Clark II, Ordway, Gass, Whitehouse, Whitehouse II, Floyd) from the journey itself. It is even richer than it at first seems. We have Clark's field notes plus his somewhat more polished (and self-censoring) finished journal. We have two somewhat different versions of Whitehouse. We have Biddle's correspondence and his queries, Clark's (and Shannon's) answers, plus Biddle's paraphrase narrative. We have the voices of the Canadians in residence at the Mandan and Hidatsa villages. We have a wide range of Native American oral traditions, all of them fascinating, some of them startling, none worth dismissing just because they are oral, just because they challenge the expedition's presentation of itself, or just because some of them are mutually exclusive. And—fortunately—we have "journals" written by Meriwether Lewis that are almost certainly early drafts of the book he was writing, and therefore revelations in miniature of what sort of book he would have written, had he lived to complete the task.

What we wish we had, in addition to all of this, are Lewis's field notes, if such notes existed and have been lost or destroyed, Gass's original journal,

Frazer's journal, and Pryor's journal, if he kept one. What is extant is in some respects an embarrassment of riches—and yet no lover of Lewis and Clark ever wished the written record was smaller and briefer than it is. Every Lewis and Clark scholar imagines the day she or he finds Frazer's journal in an attic in St. Paul or Louisville, or in a mislabeled box at some state historical society along the trail.

Not surprisingly, Thomas Jefferson saw things differently. At the end of his remarkable biographical sketch of Lewis (published 1814), Jefferson wrote that, among other things, Lewis's suicide "lost too to the nation the benefit of receiving from his own hand the Narrative now offered them of his suffering & successes in endeavoring to extend for them the boundaries of science, and to present to their knolege that vast & fertile country which their sons are destined to fill with arts, with science, with freedom & happiness."[170] In other words, Jefferson understood that the raw journals represented only a tiny fraction of the impressions, observations, memories, and reflections that remained in the fertile mind of Meriwether Lewis. The book that Lewis intended to write would have used the journals as memory jogs as well as a structural foundation, as springboards for reverie, analysis, comparison and contrast, philosophical speculation, and synthesis. Lewis would have expanded his commentary on key incidents of the journey, and he would surely have provided his own *take* on many of the events for which he was silent on the journey. He would have engaged in systematic clarification and elaboration, and he would have brought his great powers of narrative to all the key incidents of the journey. With the help of reference books and the assistance of experts, he would have turned his scientific field notes into polished natural history essays, not unlike the long series of essayettes he wrote at Fort Clatsop in the spring of 1806, but with significantly greater reference to the formal standards of science of his era. He would have pulled away from the events of the journey to provide larger geographical, anthropological, and geopolitical analysis.

Jefferson understood that the bullet that entered Lewis's brain on October 11, 1809, extinguished the great mass of information and reflection that had never yet found its way to paper. Lewis's task was to use the journals as a starting point for a much larger accounting of the exploration on which he had for twenty-eight months been engaged. His task was to contextualize the fragments, to take undigested field notes and reassess them within the taxonomies of the Enlightenment and the conventions and possibilities of Euro-American travel literature. With the field notes and maps spread out before him, Lewis was expected to create a systematic synthesis of his "late tour," as he sometimes phrased it. The book(s) he would have produced would surely have been dramatically longer than the Biddle-Allen edition of the expedition's journals. In killing himself, Lewis cost the world tens of thousands of words, every one of which would today be pored over by ingenious and curious historians. For Jefferson that was an Enlightenment tragedy.

We are not so sure.

Meriwether Lewis was surprisingly talkative in the last day of his life. He told Mrs. Grinder that he needed a room, that two servants would reach the inn shortly, that another white man was some distance behind looking for lost horses. He asked his servant for gunpowder. He asked for some spirits. He paced back and forth in the clearing before the cabin in which he would spend the night, talking to himself, Mrs. Grinder said, like a lawyer. He sat down for dinner, took a few bites, then got up and spoke to himself in a violent manner. He told his host what a pleasant evening it was. He told her that he did not require a bed, that he would sleep on the floor on robes. He paced in his cabin after everyone had gone to bed, talking to himself.

When the first bullet struck his head at some point between midnight and dawn, he said, "Oh Lord." After the second pistol was fired, he said, "O madam! Give me some water and heal my wounds." After day broke he begged his servant to take his rifle and blow out his brains. He said he would give Pernier everything in his trunk.

His last recorded words were, "I am no coward; but I am so strong, so hard to die." Those words encapsulate his life exceedingly well.

Meriwether Lewis died some time after the sun rose above the trees on the morning of October 11, 1809.

The rest, as Hamlet said, is silence.

The Last Journey of Meriwether Lewis—1809

August 18 Lewis receives letter of severe rebuke
from War Department

August 26 Clark and Lewis meet for the last time. Clark: "I have
not Spent Such a day as yesterday for many years."

August 30 Lewis meets with territorial council for the last time

September 4 Departs from St. Louis by river vessel

September 11 New Madrid: writes last will and testament
and lost "suicide" letter to William Clark

September 15 Arrives at Fort Pickering after two suicide attempts;
Captain Gilbert Russell places Lewis under house arrest

September 16 letter to President Madison

September 22 letter to Amos Stoddard

September 29 Starts overland for Nashville with
Major James Neelly Pernier, and Neelly's servant

October 6 Neelly and Lewis leave Chickasaw Agency
for Nashville along Natchez Trace

October 8 Crosses Tennessee River

October 9–10 Horses stray

October 10 Neelly remains behind to search for
horses; Lewis goes on ahead

October 10 Lewis arrives at Grinder's Inn

October 11 3 A.M. gunshots to the head and abdomen; ca.
8 A.M. Meriwether Lewis dies at the age of 35.

October 18 Neelly writes to Jefferson reporting Lewis's suicide

October 28 Clark learns of Lewis's death. "I fear O! I fear"

CHAPTER VI "What a Falling Off Was There":

The Last Journey of Meriwether Lewis

MY GOALS IN THIS CHAPTER ARE THREE. THEY ARE ALMOST certainly delusional. First, I want to write the clearest account ever published of the last days of Meriwether Lewis, to assemble the facts as far as we can reconstruct them, to provide all readers with a complete, accurate, and reliable account of the events of September 4-October 11, 1809, and their aftermath.

Second, I want to write about the death of Lewis in a way that everyone will regard as fair—the murder theorists (hereafter murderists) and the suicide theorists (hereafter suicidists) and everyone in between. My hope is that even those who disagree with my conclusions will respect my narrative and my analysis.

Third, I want to make the case for suicide as carefully and as humbly as I possibly can, not as a lawyer marshals evidence on behalf of the conclusion he wishes you to reach, but as a dispassionate humanities scholar who has been led to the conclusion of suicide by the evidence of the case. In other words, I have no ax to grind, no bias that I am aware of, and my mind is open, so far as I can tell. If new evidence would make it seem more rational to conclude that Lewis was murdered, I would cheerfully follow those findings to their logical conclusion.

Here's what we know. Lewis was appointed governor of Louisiana Territory on February 28, 1807. He did not arrive in St. Louis to take up his duties until May 8, 1808. He was in residence in St. Louis for a year and a half—actually, one year, five months, and twenty-seven days. By the summer of 1809, his world was beginning to fall apart. He was by now in an open breach with his lieutenant, Territorial Secretary Frederick Bates. In fact, their struggle brought them to the first stage of an *affair of honor* that might have led to a duel, if William Clark had not carefully stalled the process and ratcheted things down until Lewis was under greater self-control. The War Department in faraway Washington, DC, had begun to refuse to honor some of Governor Lewis's vouchers, a few of them for very large sums of money, and the tone of correspondence from functionaries in the War Department to Lewis had become reproachful. The word had gotten around the territorial capital that Lewis's official finances were being challenged at the highest levels of the United States government. This had the effect, as Lewis ruefully acknowledged, of causing his personal creditors to crowd in on him for payment. His personal solvency was in a perilous state. Rumors had begun to circulate to the effect that Governor Lewis would be recalled or at least not re-appointed, that the new Madison administration had lost confidence in him.

That was the public face of things. Lewis's private world was also in disarray. Not for lack of determined trying, he had found it impossible to find a wife. Immediately after the expedition's return, his friend William Clark had effortlessly courted and married Julia Hancock of Fincastle, Virginia, whose only fault was being the daughter of a Federalist. With comic lugubriousness, Lewis had come to think of himself as a "musty, fusty, rusty old bachelor."[1]

Lewis and Clark biographer John Bakeless, who is a murderist, summarizes the state of Lewis's life at this juncture perfectly; excellently. "He was certainly ill. He had had difficulties with Bates, a singularly irritating individual. His personal finances were in a bad way. He had been drinking heavily. His reappointment was in doubt. His accounts were disputed by Washington auditors."[2] To be perfectly fair, we have no way of knowing for sure that Lewis was *drinking heavily*.

In August 1809 Governor Lewis decided to make the long journey to Washington, DC, to defend his territorial actions and expenditures in a face-to-face meeting with the bureaucrats of the Madison administration. He also intended to visit his mother Lucy Marks and his patron and friend Thomas Jefferson in Albemarle County, Virginia, then venture to Philadelphia to move his book closer to publication. Attempts have recently been made to suggest that Lewis was not mentally disturbed at the time he left St. Louis in early September 1809. Lewis's most recent biographers, Thomas Danisi and John Jackson, have provided extensive details of his professional activities in the spring and summer of 1809 in an effort to prove he was both busy and undeniably in possession of his rational faculties.[3] Vardis Fisher summarizes the same burst of administrative activity and concludes: "All this—his handwriting during these last days in St. Louis, his clear and orderly record of his debts, and his investing three friends with the power of attorney, to sell his property during his absence, if creditors should demand it—all this certainly does not look like the behavior of a man in a paroxysm."[4] Danisi and Jackson write, "Taking the time to tidy up a difference of opinion with his former mentor [Jefferson] showed that Meriwether was in complete command of his faculties." With his packet of reports and vouchers, Lewis was going east to "convince those chair-bound bureaucrats that a frontier government required immediate decisions. Louisiana could not be directed at long distance over an imperfect system of communication."[5] Danisi and Jackson go so far as to say, "[T]he governor of Louisiana had lost confidence in the present administration."[6] This, in my opinion, is precisely the reverse of the truth.

It may be worth remembering two things here. First, Lewis engaged in this burst of administrative activity solely because he was about to journey to Washington to face his accusers in the War Department. He was trying on the eve of his departure to bring order to the neglect and disarray that had gotten him into trouble in the first place. Any chance of being exonerated or vindicated in Washington would involve presenting in person the documents and detailed justifications of his actions that he had not taken the time to send to the War Department previously. All of these documents and reports should have been forwarded long since. It was their absence that led Madison administration officials, including the president himself, to question Lewis's competence, ethical probity, and fitness for territorial office. In other words, the unusual burst of activity described by Danisi and Jackson was not a representative sample of Lewis's administrative life in St. Louis. On the contrary, it was an emergency response to a period of significantly less focused activity. Second, Lewis did not accomplish these things alone. His closest friend William Clark worked side by side with him to put his affairs into something like order. Even if Clark didn't actually create the documents in question, it was essential that he was at Lewis's side to calm the governor and keep him focused on the tasks before him. Clark's account of the final day he and Lewis spent together is profoundly sad. To his brother Jonathan, Clark wrote, "I have not Spent Such a Day as yesterday for maney years.... took my leave of Govr. Lewis who Set out to Philadelphia to write our Book, (but more perticularly to explain Some matter between him and the Govt.[)] Several of his Bills have been protested and his Crediters all flocking in near the time of his Setting out distressed him much, which he expressed to me in Such terms as to Cause a Cempothy which is not yet off—I do not beleve there was ever an honest er man in Louisiana nor one who had pureor motives than Govr. Lewis. if his mind had been at lease I Should have parted Cherefully ... ."[7] This is not the portrait of a man who is calmly and routinely attending to business in preparation for a long leave of absence.

Clark's "I have not Spent Such a Day as yesterday for maney years" can only refer to the similar efforts he made in the late 1790s to bring some kind of order to his alcoholic brother George Rogers Clark's equally tangled legal and financial affairs. Clark had been familiar with Lewis's temper, impulsiveness, and penchant for self-drama for fifteen years. He had lived in closest proximity with the mercurial Lewis for three years on the trail from Falls of the Ohio to the Pacific Ocean and back again. For Clark to notice and describe this level of distress in Lewis, "expressed to

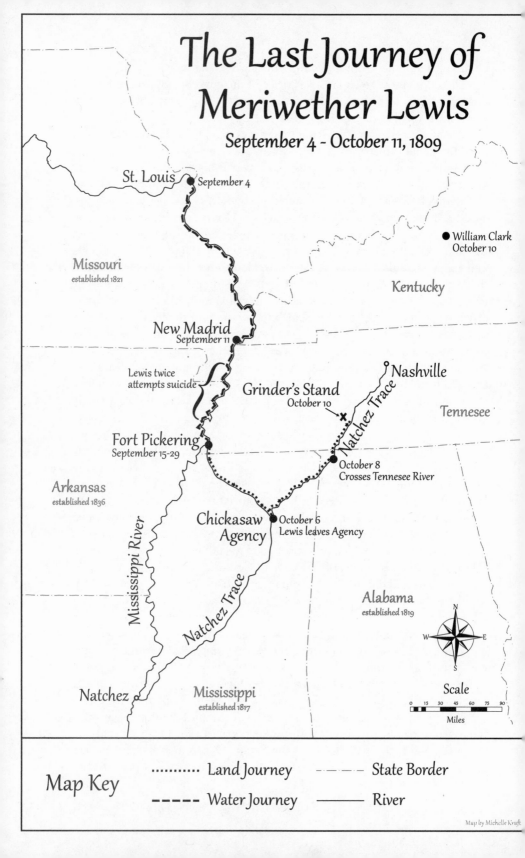

me in Such terms as to Cause a Cempothy which is not yet off," suggests Lewis was indeed in a paroxysm of rage, bitterness, self-punishment, and self-pity at the time he departed from St. Louis. Clark's reference to Lewis's honesty and the purity of his motives makes clear that Clark was aware that the War Department had accused Lewis of dishonesty and impure motives with respect to the public-private mission to return Mandan leader Sheheke-shote to his home village in today's North Dakota. It would be hard to imagine Clark describing Lewis's state in terms of greater alarm and sorrow. This remarkable passage in a private letter by Lewis's best friend refutes all the lists that could possibly be made of Lewis's professional activity in the late summer of 1809. Danisi and Jackson say, "Although exasperated by the difficulties that the accounting process was creating, he was not hysterical."[8] Actually, it sounds like he was. The great Bernard DeVoto wrote, "[I]t is clear that he was in a very nervous state when he left St. Louis."[9] Jefferson himself wrote that, "He was in a paroxysm of one of these [sensible depressions of mind] when his affairs rendered it necessary for him to go to Washington."[10]

On July 8, 1809, six weeks before he received the bombshell letter from the War Department that precipitated his final journey to the national capital, Lewis wrote to an unknown friend that the Madison administration's rejection of his vouchers was causing him great distress. "[T]his occurrence has given me infinite concern," he wrote, "as the fate of other bills drawn for similar purposes to a considerable amount cannot be mistaken; this rejection cannot fail to impress the public mind unfavourably with rispect to me, nor is this consideration more painfull than the censure which must arise in the mind of the executive from my having drawn for public monies without authority, a third and not less imbarrassing circumstance attending the transaction is that my private funds are entirely incompetent to meet those bills if protested."[11]

Lewis met with the Governor's Council in St. Louis for the last time on August 30.

Lewis left St. Louis on September 4, 1809. The *Missouri Gazette* wrote that the governor "set off in good health for New Orleans on his way to the Federal City."[12] John Bakeless has said, "[T]he emphasis of the statement [by the *Gazette*] faintly suggests official propaganda."[13] Lewis's original intention was to take passage on a flatboat or keelboat all the way down the Mississippi River to New Orleans. From there he planned to take passage on a ship through the Gulf of Mexico, around the southern tip of Florida, and then up the East Coast to the Chesapeake, where he would find additional water conveyance either up the James River to Charlottesville (likely) or up the Potomac River to the federal capital.

Lewis's baggage consisted of: a pair of red slippers; five vests; two pairs of pantaloons; one pair of black silk breeches; two cotton shirts; one flannel shirt; two pairs of cotton stockings; three pairs of silk stockings; a broadcloth coat; a silver tumbler; a tomahawk; a pistol case; a silver watch; several bundles of maps; "Two small bundles containing silk for dresses—for Mr. Clark"[14]; three knives; a sword; a "pike blade" with a broken shaft (probably his espontoon); a sea otter skin; a supply of medicines; all of his official papers, including "One small bundle of Letters & Vouchers—of consequence"[15]; and all the papers relating to his transcontinental journey, including the expedition's journals.

One of the three men to whom Lewis had entrusted his private affairs during his absence, his friend William C. Carr, wrote a letter to his brother on August 25, 1809: "Our Governor left us a few days since with his private affairs altogether deranged. He is a good man, but a very imprudent one—I apprehend he will not return."[16] Things were that bad.

Lewis arrived in New Madrid on September 11, 1809, approximately 250 miles downstream from St. Louis. He sent his free black servant Pernier ashore to collect food for supper and to obtain a competent legal witness. In New Madrid Lewis wrote his will. He left his estate, after all debts had been paid, to his mother Lucy Marks. Sometime before he reached New Madrid, Lewis decided to leave the Mississippi River and venture overland to Virginia. The reasons usually alleged for this change of plans are that Lewis was warned that fever was raging in the lower Mississippi River, or he feared that his papers, which included the journals and other documents relating to the expedition, might fall into the hands of the British, who were patrolling the Gulf of Mexico and boarding American vessels.

There may have been a third reason; Lewis was always most confident when he was in control of his own motion. In the course of the expedition, he frequently left the flotilla to walk on the shores of the Missouri River. When his own body was engaged in forward progress, he was invariably more optimistic, more productive, and more likely to write in his journal. Idleness and passivity were apparently destructive to his mental health. During the long delay at Camp Chopunnish on the return journey, on the Pacific side of the Rocky Mountains, Lewis wrote (on May 17, 1806) of "that icy barier which seperates me from my friends and Country, from all which makes life esteemable.—patience, patience."[17] On June 14, 1806, he wrote, "[W]e have now been detained near five weeks in consequence of the snows; a serious loss of time at this delightfull season for traveling. ... every body seems anxious to be in motion ... ."[18]

In September 1809, it must have been difficult for Governor Lewis, who once had led an expeditionary force 7,689 miles to the Pacific Ocean and back again, now to be reduced to the status of a mere passenger on a vessel making its way slowly down the Mississippi River. Danisi and Jackson write, "For Meriwether Lewis a lazy drift nodding in the warm sun should have been a welcome rest. Actually the tortuous pace prolonged his tension. In a fog of daily boredom and increasing pain Lewis tried to contain his growing sense of urgency, but the slow trip gave him too much time to churn matters over and over."[19] David Lavender has said, "Lewis had too much time in which to brood, drink—and twice attempt to take his life."[20] Lewis was a naturally restless and impatient man. He may have decided, after a week of frustrating passivity, that he would rather travel overland to Washington, DC, than continue as a mere passenger on other people's vessels. He was a man, as Jefferson put it, "habituated to the hunting life,"[21] used to command, and impatient of all restraints.

In short, Lewis may have decided to leave the river because he had a sense that he would be better off, physically and mentally, on land, setting his own pace and directing his own movements.

At New Madrid, Lewis also wrote a letter to William Clark. That letter has been lost. From Clark's characterizations of it after the death of Lewis, it seems to have struck Clark, after the fact, as a kind of suicide note, or a letter of such personal anguish that it essentially corroborated Lewis's suicide. It probably also provided an explanation of the steps needed to complete Lewis's book project, should Lewis perish on the journey to Philadelphia. In other words, the letter to Clark was written in the same mood that inspired Lewis to write his last will and testament at New Madrid. Clark may have lost the letter, along with a number of others he mentioned to his brother Jonathan in his letter of October 28, 1809.[22] It may also have been suppressed.[23]

Sometime before he disembarked at Fort Pickering, at today's Memphis, Tennessee, from the boat that was carrying him down river, Lewis had twice attempted to commit suicide. In an affidavit or deposition recorded two years after Lewis's death, on November 26, 1811, Gilbert Russell, who had been in command of Fort Pickering when Lewis arrived, stated, "[T]he Commanding officer of the Fort on discovering his situation, and learning from the Crew that he had made two attempts to Kill himself, in one of which he had nearly succeeded, resolved at once to take possession of him and his papers, and detain them there untill he recovered, or some friend might arrive in whose hands he could depart in safety."[24] Neither Russell nor any other contemporary provided any more precise details of these incidents. No historian has ever ascertained just how Governor Lewis tried to commit suicide during his journey from St. Louis to Fort Pickering. More likely these suicide attempts occurred between New Madrid and Fort Pickering. Russell's statement, "in one of which he had nearly succeeded," is perplexing. It's hard to believe this can refer to a suicide attempt involving pistols. No witness noticed any wounds on Lewis's body before the final night at Grinder's Inn. It is possible that, in a drunken or deranged state, Lewis brandished weapons—guns, his knife, his razor—and announced his intention to kill himself, but was physically subdued until he calmed down, passed out, or fell asleep. It is possible that he attempted to drown himself. For a man of his physical strength, however, that would be easier said than done. Thomas Danisi and John Jackson argue that these "suicide" attempts were responses to a severe bout of ague or malaria. "Unable to bear it any longer," they write, "in a complex state of inescapable pain and intoxication, stepping over the side into the enveloping waters may have seemed the only way to end the torture."[25] This is a little melodramatic, but so indeed was Lewis. The phrase, "two attempts to Kill himself," can cover a lot of ground, from the drunken ravings of a self-pitying man to a genuine attempt to take one's own life. Improbable though all this sounds, there is no good reason to doubt Russell's testimony. This is the sort of thing one might exaggerate, but not make up.

At any rate, Lewis arrived at Fort Pickering about two in the afternoon on September 15, with this damaging information hovering about him. Captain Russell immediately realized that the governor was ill and mentally unstable. He placed Lewis under arrest, put the distinguished guest under the care of the surgeon's mate W.C. Smith, and installed Lewis in the captain's own quarters. In his letter to former president Jefferson of January 4, 1810, Russell wrote, "He came here on the 15th September last. ... His condition rendered it necessary that he should be stoped until he would recover which I done."[26]

In his November 26, 1811, deposition, Captain Russell wrote, "On the morning of the 15tht of September, the Boat in which he was a passenger landed him at Fort pickering in a state of mental derangement, which appeared to have been produced as much by indisposition as by other causes."[27] Russell meant that on September 15, at least, Lewis exhibited signs of mental illness, mental instability, or perhaps delirium principally because he was suffering from a severe physical ailment, probably malaria. Russell wisely placed Lewis under a kind of friendly house arrest, confined him to quarters, restricted Lewis's intake of alcohol, and took care of his distinguished guest until the worst symptoms of the malaria passed and his toxicity (no doubt a combination of alcohol and medicines, including laudanum) diminished. In his letter to Jefferson of January 4, 1810, Captain Russell wrote, "[I]n a short time by proper attention a change was perceptible and in about six days he was perfectly restored in every respect and able to travel."[28] Although Russell deplored the subsequent death of Lewis, he rightly told Jefferson, "[A]s it has turned out I shall have the consolation that I discharged those obligations towards him that man is bound to do for his fellows."[29]

Thomas Danisi and John Jackson have done an important service to Lewis and Clark studies, and particularly our understanding of Lewis, by documenting how seriously he suffered from bouts with malaria in the post-expedition period. Although I believe they wrongly played down Lewis's mental instability and his sense of bitter rage during the weeks (August 18-October 11, 1809) following his receipt of the harsh rebuke from the War Department, Danisi and Jackson have presented the facts of Lewis's sufferings at the hands of malaria so thoroughly that no future Lewis biographer will be able to ignore their findings or regard Lewis's derangement as exclusively psychological in nature. It is certain that Lewis was in significant pain as he descended the Mississippi River in September 1809, and that his physical pain was alone sufficient to reduce his mental clarity.

DERANGEMENT

The words that recur most often about Lewis's condition in the last weeks of his life are *deranged* and *derangement*. The *Oxford English Dictionary* defines *deranged* as "disordered in mind; insane," and cites several useful examples from the era in question.

Captain James House, for example, wrote a letter from Nashville on September 28, 1809, about what he had heard on the road about the indisposition of Governor Lewis. Lewis's friend Amos Stoddard had told House that, near Chickasaw Bluffs, he had encountered someone "who informed him, that Governor Lewis had arrived there ... in a State of mental *derangement*—that he had made several attempts to put an end to his own existence, which the patroon had prevented, and that Cap Russell, the commanding officer at the Bluffs had taken him into his own quarters where he was obliged to keep a strict watch over him to prevent his committing violence on himself and had caused his boat to be unloaded at the ferry to be secured in his stores."[30] House went on to sound very much like Clark: "I am in hopes this account will prove exaggerated—tho' I fear there is too much truth in it" [emphasis added throughout this section]. This letter is an important document in the suicide-murder debate, because it proves that the story of Lewis's suicide attempts on the lower Mississippi River did not surface *after* Lewis's death by way of adding ex post facto credibility to the reports of his suicide. House's letter was written at the end of Lewis's stay at Fort Pickering, and eleven days before the incident at Grinder's Inn.

In his letter announcing Lewis's suicide to former President Jefferson, dated October 18, 1809, James Neelly wrote, "[O]n our arrival at the Chickasaw nation I discovered that he appeared at times *deranged* in mind. we rested there two days and came on ... ." Neelly informed Jefferson that at Grinder's Inn, "a woman [Priscilla Grinder] who discovering the governor to be *deranged* gave him up the house & slept herself in one near it." [31]

Captain John Brahan wrote, "No person being at home but the wife of Mr. Grinder the woman discovering the Governor to be *deranged* gave him up the house and slept herself in another house near it."[32]

Gilbert Russell wrote several accounts of the two weeks he spent taking care of the ailing Lewis in September 1809. Three of those narratives are extant. In the first of those accounts, a letter to Thomas Jefferson dated

January 4, 1810, Russell, who knew of Lewis's suicide, reported that when he arrived at Fort Pickering Lewis was suffering from a "situation that rendered it necessary that he should be stoped until he would recover, which I done & in a short time by proper attention a change was perceptible and in about six days he was perfectly restored in every respect & able to travel."[33] Russell did not specify just what the *situation* was in the letter. In the second account, a letter to Jefferson dated January 31, 1810, Russell explained that Lewis's death was precipitated by "the free use of liquor," [34] which Russell had prohibited Lewis at Fort Pickering, but which James Neely had permitted and apparently encouraged on Lewis's overland journey towards Nashville. This is the letter in which Russell blamed Neely for Lewis's death. On November 26, 1811, Russell produced his last extant account of the decline and death of Lewis. "On the morning of the 15th of September," he wrote, "the Boat in which he was a passenger landed him at Fort pickering in a state of mental *derangement*, which appeared to have been produced as much by indisposition as other causes."[35] Thanks to Russell's careful ministrations and his refusal to give Lewis access to alcohol, "on the sixth or seventh day," Russell wrote, "all symptoms of *derangement* disappeared and he was completely in his senses and thus continued for ten or twelve days."[36] Unfortunately, once Lewis had resumed his journey, "in three or four days he was again affected with the same *mental disease*, [emphasis added]" perhaps because "By much severe depletion during his illness he had been considerably reduced and debilitated, from which he had not entirely recovered when he set off," because "that country being yet excessively hot and the exercise of traveling [was] too severe for him," and because "He had no person with him who could manage or controul him in his propensities."[37]

On November 26, 1809, Clark wrote to his brother Jonathan about the disposition of Lewis's papers. "I have just receved letters from Capt. Russell," he reported, "who Commands at the Chickasaw Bluffs that Govr. Lewis was there detain by him 15 Days in a *State of Derangement* most of the time and that he had attempted to kill himself before he got there."[38] Apparently Clark received letters from Gilbert Russell that have subsequently disappeared. Those letters confirmed the two prior suicide attempts, the house arrest at Fort Pickering, and Lewis's mental derangement.

In his biographical sketch of Lewis of August 18, 1813, Jefferson wrote, "Mr. Neelly, agent of the U.S. with the Chickasaw Indians arriving there [Fort Pickering] two days after, found him extremely indisposed, and betraying at times some symptoms of a *derangement of mind*."[39]

In 1845, the New York *Dispatch* published a retrospective article on Lewis's death, drawn from a newspaper called the *North Arkansas*, published in Batesville, Arkansas. Although the article reported Priscilla Grinder telling a somewhat different account of Lewis's death, it confirmed her observation "that Mr. Lewis was *mentally deranged*" on the evening of October 10, 1809.[40]

Thus the overwhelming testimony of Lewis's contemporaries was that in the last month of his life he was mentally ill, that his mental illness was related to and exacerbated by a severe physical indisposition (almost certainly malaria), and that his mental illness was worsened by "the free use of liquor which he acknowledged verry candidly," and vowed to curtail, according to Gilbert Russell. Although some of these observations would be regarded as hearsay and derivative in a court of law, three of these contemporaries, Gilbert Russell, James Neely, and Priscilla Grinder, had the opportunity to observe Lewis directly between September 15 and October 11. They all used the word *derangement* in describing Lewis's behavior. Jefferson's account must have been based in part on James Pernier's face-to-face report at Monticello sometime later in the autumn of 1809.

It seems quite likely that Lewis's *derangement* was partly the result of a severe bout of malaria. Gilbert Russell explicitly considered that possibility. In other words, Lewis's mental illness may not have been solely mental in nature, but a combination of physical and metaphysical factors. In his last letters, Lewis spoke of his *indisposition* and his state of *exhaustion*, but not of mental or physical derangement. Vardis Fisher argues that Lewis's ability to write coherent letters to Madison and Stoddard "suggests that on his arrival at the fort he was delirious, or otherwise 'deranged,' because of heat and fever, and not that he had gone out of his mind because of his financial and other troubles."[41] Danisi and Jackson do their best to ignore the evidence of Lewis's mental derangement and emphasize his physical illness instead. Thus: "Commanding officer Capt. Gilbert Russell was appalled to see a man who was obviously so sick. ... Captain Russell was no doctor but he had seen many men, himself included, suffer from the ague."[42]

On September 16, the ailing Lewis, now under house arrest at Fort Pickering, wrote a letter to President Madison. Much has been made of the visual quality of this letter, which has been called "incoherent," "garbled," and "chaotic," by various historians. John Bakeless says, "[I]ts sprawling and uncertain hand and the constant striking out of words and interlineation of others, to no particular purpose, show clearly that ... he was far from being his usual bold and decisive self by the time he reached Chickasaw Bluffs."[43] Bakeless blames malaria for the mental confusion: "The best explanation of his odd conduct is probably malaria, as it is well known that fever of any kind invariably made him light-headed."[44] Danisi and Jackson argue that the orthographical confusion of the letter he wrote can be explained by way of Lewis's malarial *indisposition* alone. The letter is undeniably jumbled in its visual presentation, but it is unobjectionable when viewed in a linear transcript.

Lewis informed the president of his change in itinerary. He indicated that he was bringing his financial records, "which when fully explained, or reather the general view of the circumstances under which they were made I flatter myself they will recieve both sanction & approbation and sanction." Then Lewis apologized for having been a poor communicator: "My anxiety to pursue and to fullfill the duties incident to the internal arrangements incident to the government of Louisiana has prevented my writing you more frequently."[45] Finally, Lewis noted that he was enclosing a copy of the laws of Louisiana, which he had printed in St. Louis. Danisi and Jackson argue that this publication "was Lewis's answer, sent ahead, to those State Department bills that Madison continued to refuse, a matter of honor and withheld respect as much as accounting."[46]

This was perhaps not the most lucid or eloquent letter that Lewis ever wrote, but it cannot be called incoherent. In short order he conveyed everything he wanted the president of the United States to know. Fisher is certainly right to conclude, "There seems to be no sign of insanity or mental derangement in the letter to Madison, but only signs of exhaustion and debility."[47]

The last letter Lewis wrote, dated September 22, 1809, was to his old friend Amos Stoddard, now the commander at Fort Adams on the lower Mississippi River. After providing a routine apology for his prolonged and inexplicable silence, Lewis explained that he would not now be descending the Mississippi River as planned, but traveling overland to the national capital. The only reason he gave for this change was "my indisposition." He stated that he was on his way to Washington to explain some protested vouchers. "[A]n explaneation is all that is necessary I am sensible to put all matters right." The actual purpose of the letter was financial. Because his personal finances had been compromised by his public difficulties, Lewis called on Stoddard to send him $200 that Stoddard was holding for him. Finally, he explained that in January "I expect I shall be on my return to St. Louis."[48]

Apparently Lewis was well enough that he could have resumed his journey sometime around September 21 or 22, but he delayed his departure for another week to accommodate Gilbert Russell, who attempted to get a leave of absence to permit him to make the same journey. Russell, too, had protested vouchers to clear up with the War Department. Eventually, the leave was denied. Russell wrote, "[H]e waited six or eight days expecting I would go with him, but in this we were disappointed."[49]

Lewis left Fort Pickering on September 29. He was traveling with his free black servant Pernier and with Major James Neelly, the US agent to the Chickasaw Nation, and Neelly's servant, whose name is unknown. Neelly had arrived at Fort Pickering on September 18. He was bound for Nashville. So far as we know he had never previously met Lewis. When it became clear that Russell could not accompany Lewis, Neelly apparently offered to travel with Lewis as far as Nashville and watch over him. Russell later regretted that decision. "He [Neely] seem'd happy to have it in his power to serve the Govr," Russell wrote on January 31, 1810, "& but for making the offer which I accepted I should have employ'd the man who packed the trunk to the Nation to have them taken to Nashville & accompany the Govr. Unfortunately for him this arrangement did not take place, or I hesitate not to say he would this day be living."[50] In other words, Russell believed a more reliable chaperon chosen by himself would have delivered Lewis safely to Nashville, kept liquor and gunpowder away from him, and made a special effort to keep him safe. Ideally the chaperon would have been Russell himself. Next best would have been "the [unnamed] man who packed the trunk to the [Chickasaw] Nation." Neelly proved to be precisely the wrong man for the job, in Russell's opinion.

Captain Russell lent Lewis ca. $100 and sold him two horses on credit. In return, Lewis signed a promissory note for $379.58, payable on or before January 1, 1810. Russell wrote that Lewis "set off with two Trunks which contained all his papers relative to his expedition to the Pacific Ocean."[51] Russell said Lewis's baggage now included "Gen'l Clark's Land Warrant, a Port-Folio, pocket book Memo and note Book together with many other papers of both public and private nature and two horses two saddles and bridles a Rifle gun pistols pipe tommy hawk & dirk, all ellegant and perhaps about two hundred and twenty dollars, of which $99 58/100 was a Treasury check on the U.S. Bank of Orleans endorsed by me. The horses one saddle and the check I let him have."[52] In turn, Lewis, who was unable to transport by land as much baggage as he had put on board the vessel on which he was descending the Mississippi River, left at Fort Pickering "two Trunks a case and a bundle which will now remain here subject at any time to your order or that of his legal representative,"[53] Russell informed Jefferson.

The first leg of this last journey took the party from Fort Pickering to somewhere in the Chickasaw Nation. The Lewis party of four (Lewis, Pernier, Neelly, Neelly's servant) may have traveled with some Chickasaw Indian "chiefs." The only reference we have to these Indians is from the affidavit Russell wrote two years later. Most scholars have assumed that Neelly took Lewis first to the Chickasaw Agency near today's Houston, Tennessee, where Neelly attended to some business and where they intersected the Natchez Trace, but Danisi and Jackson have argued that it is more likely that Neelly and Lewis traveled due east from today's Memphis to an intersection with the Natchez Trace. "Taking the Chickasaw Nation statement at face value meant an unnecessary detour that would have required a fifty-mile-a-day pace to reconcile with the known timeline."[54] For a variety of reasons, I believe Danisi and Jackson are wrong and that Lewis and Neelly indeed traveled from Fort Pickering to the Chickasaw Agency, remained there a couple of days, then rode the Natchez Trace all the way to Grinder's Inn (see footnote).[55] At the Chickasaw Agency the party intersected the

Natchez Trace, a narrow, but well-traveled trail carved out of the wilderness between Nashville, Tennessee, and Natchez, Mississippi. The Natchez Trace was one of America's first government-sponsored highways. One of its purposes was to provide American farmers and entrepreneurs an alternative road for traveling between the lower Mississippi and the East Coast at a time when Spain was obstructing or threatening to obstruct traffic on the Mississippi River. Elliott Coues wrote that the trace was "cut to facilitate the movement of troops and the transportation of supplies to and from the newly acquired 'Spanish country.'"[56] General James Wilkinson concluded a treaty in 1801 with the Chickasaw Nation, permitting the US government to construct the highway through Chickasaw territory.

By the time the party arrived at "the Chickasaw nation," according to Neelly, Lewis "appeared at times deranged in mind." He was also drinking again—thanks entirely to the enabler Neelly, Gilbert Russell later alleged.[57] Because of Lewis's relapse, indisposition, and derangement, the party rested two days at "the Chickasaw nation," probably at the agency. Neelly explained to Jefferson that "we rested there two days & came on."[58]

On October 5 or 6, the party resumed its journey, now on the Natchez Trace. On October 8, Neelly and Lewis crossed the Tennessee River and camped near today's Collinwood, Tennessee. On the night of October 9–10, two of the party's horses strayed from the camp. Restless as ever, Lewis ventured ahead on his horse, "with a promise to wait for me," James Neelly wrote to Jefferson, "at the first house he came to that was inhabited by white people."[59]

On the afternoon of October 10, Lewis rode up alone to a frontier establishment known as Grinder's Inn or Grinder's Stand, located seventy-two miles from Nashville near today's Hohenwald, Tennessee. Neelly says it was "about sun set."[60] The inn was owned by Priscilla and Robert Grinder. Priscilla Grinder was approximately thirty-five years old. Robert Grinder was somewhere else that evening—probably at the Grinders' settlement at Duck River, more than twenty miles away. It seems likely that Priscilla Grinder was at the inn alone with her two or three young children, and her twelve-year-old slave girl Malinda. Neelly said that when Lewis arrived there was "no person there but a woman."[61] Much has been made of the apparent discrepancy, but probably Neelly meant that Mrs. Grinder was the only responsible adult at the inn.

Grinder's Inn consisted of two cabins linked by a fifteen-foot covered breezeway. This common connecting structure was known as a *dogtrot*.

Lewis was wearing a loose fitting blue-and-white striped cloak when he arrived. He asked Mrs. Grinder "if he could stay for the night" [Grinder-Wilson 1811] (see explanatory footnote).[62] "[N]o person [was] there," Neelly reported, "but a woman who discovering the governor to be deranged gave him up the house & slept herself in one near it."[63] Lewis carried his saddle into the cabin assigned to him. Priscilla asked Lewis if he was traveling alone. That would have been unusual.[64] Lewis replied that two servants were somewhere behind him on the Trace, and that they would soon arrive. "He called for some spirits, and drank very little" [Grinder-Wilson 1811].

The two servants rode up. One of them was Lewis's free black servant (not slave) John Pernier (also known as Pernia). Actually, Pernier was a mulatto, like so many other free black individuals of this era. The name of the other servant is not known. He may have been a slave. He was Neelly's attendant. Mrs. Grinder says one of the servants was "a negro" [Grinder-Wilson 1811]. It may be that Pernier was white enough to "pass." It is possible, but not likely, that Neelly was attended by a white servant.

Lewis asked Pernier about his gunpowder, saying he was sure he had some in a canister. According to Priscilla Grinder, Pernier seemed reluctant to answer Lewis's question. "The servant gave no distinct reply" [Grinder-Wilson 1811]. The servants unsaddled their horses and led them toward the stable, located about two-hundred yards away from the cabins. That was where the servants spent the night. Lewis's behavior soon struck Mrs. Grinder as erratic. For one thing, he began pacing back and forth in front of one of the cabins, muttering to himself. "Sometimes, she said, he would seem as if he were walking up to her; and would suddenly wheel round, and walk back as fast as he could" [Grinder-Wilson 1811].

Priscilla Grinder fed her guest. She reported that Lewis "had eaten only a few mouthfuls when he started up, speaking to himself in a violent manner" [Grinder-Wilson 1811]. The governor's fits came and went. He raged, grew calm, then flared up again, his face "flush as if it had come on him in a fit" [Grinder-Wilson 1811]. Eventually, Lewis pulled a chair to the door of the cabin, lit his pipe, and gazed out at the Tennessee wilderness. "[I]n a kind tone of voice," Lewis said, "Madam, this is a very pleasant evening" [Grinder-Wilson 1811].

He smoked for some time, but quitted his seat and traversed the yard as before. He again sat down to his pipe, seemed again composed, and casting his eyes wishfully toward the west, observed what a sweet evening it was. "Mrs. Grinder was preparing a bed for him; but he said he would sleep on the floor, and desired the servant to bring him the bear skins and buffaloe robe, which were immediately spread out for him" [Grinder-Wilson 1811].

Just why Lewis chose to sleep on the floor is unknown. It may be that he found Mrs. Grinder's accommodations unacceptable. Bed linens were seldom changed in those days, and it was not uncommon for a variety of people in various stages of cleanliness to sleep in the same linens, sometimes at the same time.[65] According to one version, Lewis explained to his host that he had not slept in a bed since his late tour. It's very hard to believe that can be true.

"[I]t being now dusk the woman went off to the kitchen, and the two men [the servants] to the barn, which stands about two-hundred yards off" [Grinder-Wilson 1811].

Dusk on October 11 would have come at approximately 7:30 P.M. If Pernier and Neely's servant went off to the barn, that puts Governor Lewis alone in one small log cabin, with his bear and buffalo robes taking up much of the floor, and Priscilla Grinder, who was the same age, preparing to sleep in some makeshift bed, fifteen-to twenty-feet away in the other cabin. If her children and slave were with her, as seems overwhelmingly likely, it was a snug fit in the cabin that doubled as a kitchen. Mrs. Grinder was unable to sleep.

"The kitchen is only a few paces from the room where Lewis was, and the woman being considerably alarmed by the behaviour of her guest could not sleep but listened to him walking backwards and forwards, she thinks for several hours, and talking aloud, as she said, 'like a lawyer'" [Grinder-Wilson 1811].

So far Priscilla Grinder's report squares perfectly with everything we know about Meriwether Lewis's last journey. Periods of distraction and soliloquy alternated with periods of calm and civility. Fits came on him, flushed his face, consumed his attention, and then ebbed away. His symptoms were both physical and mental. Courtliness was juxtaposed with lawyerly argumentation. The same mental suffering and emotional intensity that had roused William Clark's *Cempothy* in late August, the same violent interior dialogue that Gilbert Russell had witnessed at Fort Pickering, the fits and imposition that had been observed by Russell and Neelly, recurred at Grinder's Inn on the last night of Lewis's life. Nothing in Priscilla Grinder's testimony to Alexander Wilson in 1811 is at odds in any way with what we know about Lewis's behavior between August 25 (his last meeting with William Clark) and October 10 (his last moments with James Neelly). Nor was Mrs. Grinder's behavior in any way unusual or improbable. She was alone (at least essentially alone) at a rustic frontier outpost with an erratic and intense man just a few yards away whose first words to his servant that evening had been a request for gunpowder. If Lewis really arrived around sunset, all of these events unfolded in a surprisingly brief period of time. Now the ill and deranged governor was in the room just across the breezeway, and instead of settling down for the night, thereby letting Mrs. Grinder relax into sleep, he was pacing about the floor talking violently to himself. The phrase, "she thinks for several hours," suggests that Mrs. Grinder drifted in and out of sleep between the hours of 8 P.M. on October 10 and 3 A.M. on October 11.

"She then heard the report of a pistol, and something fall heavily on the floor, and the words, 'O Lord.' Immediately afterwards she heard another pistol, and in a few minutes she heard him at her door calling out '*O madam! Give me some water, and heal my wounds*' [Grinder-Wilson 1811].

Neelly explained to Jefferson that "the woman reports that about three o'Clock she heard two pistols fire off in the Governors Room" [Grinder-Neelly 1809].

Virtually all historians agree with the Grinder-Neelly and the Grinder-Wilson account of the events of October 10, 1809, so far. The governor arrived in the late afternoon or evening. His behavior was erratic and it upset Mrs. Grinder, who was the only white adult at the inn. She put Lewis in one room for the night and took the other for herself. *He* could not sleep because he was pacing and talking to himself, almost certainly about his struggles with the War Department or about Frederick Bates and his other detractors in St. Louis.[66] *She* could not sleep because her guest was making a lot of noise, and his strange behavior had thrown her off of her center of gravity. Deep into the night, at approximately 3 A.M., Mrs. Grinder heard two shots go off in close succession. Somehow she recognized them as pistol shots.[67] She heard something or someone (presumably Lewis) "fall heavily on the floor" [Grinder-Wilson 1811]. She heard the wounded man (presumably, but not yet certainly Lewis) say, "O Lord!," and "O madam! give me some water, and heal my wounds" [Grinder-Wilson 1811].

At this point the story begins to braid a little. Alexander Wilson wrote, "The logs being open, and unplastered, she saw him stagger back and fall against a stump that stands between the kitchen and room. He crawled for some distance, raised himself by the side of a tree, where he sat about a minute. He once more got to the room; afterwards he came to the kitchen door, but did not speak; she then heard him scraping the bucket with a gourd for water" [Grinder-Wilson 1811]. All accounts emphasize Lewis's thirst in the aftermath of the shooting. In his letter to Jefferson, Neelly wrote, "[S]he heard two pistols fire off in the Governors Room: the servants being awakened by her, came in but too late to save him. He had shot himself in the head with one pistol & a little below the Breast with the other" [Grinder-Neelly 1809]. Proponents of the murder theory (murderists) argue that Priscilla Grinder could not possibly have seen Lewis staggering around the breezeway and the yard of the inn. The night of October 10–11 was, they correctly indicate, a time of a virtually new moon (new moon, October 9), and even that sliver of the moon had set long before folks at Grinder's Inn went to bed. Thus Priscilla Grinder could not possibly have actually seen Lewis staggering about in the faint starlight, unless he was illuminated by candles or a lantern, neither of which are mentioned in any account of the incident.[68] It is, of course, quite possible that Lewis had lit a lantern or candle in his unchinked quarters. Without illumination neither Lewis (nor any putative assassin) would have been able to take careful aim in the darkened cabin. The argument from lunar data, frequently played as a kind of trump card to discredit Mrs. Grinder's testimony, raises as many questions as it settles. Whatever else is true, we can be certain that October 10–11 was a very dark night on the Natchez Trace.

Just how long Priscilla Grinder waited before she roused the servants (her own or those traveling with Lewis), and just when she first looked in on the stricken governor are matters that have precipitated feverish historical debate. Neelly's timeline has Mrs. Grinder awakening the servants immediately after hearing the gunshots—if not in real time, certainly in the narrative he sent to Jefferson. "[T]wo pistols fire off in the Governors Room: the servants being awakined by her, came in but too late to save him" [Grinder-Neely 1809]. Much more time passes in the account provided by Alexander Wilson. "As soon as day broke and not before, the terror of the woman having permitted him to remain for two hours in this most deplorable situation, she sent two of her children to the barn, her husband not being home, to bring the servants" [Grinder-Wilson 1811]. Wilson was angry that Mrs. Grinder had done nothing to help the dying Lewis: "[I]t appears that this cooling element [water] was denied the dying man!" [Grinder-Wilson 1811]. Wilson was emphatic that Mrs. Grinder waited until daybreak *and not before* to rouse the servants.

Note that Lewis's friend Alexander Wilson did not in any way, with any language—vague, implied, or direct—dispute Mrs. Grinder's story that Lewis had committed suicide. That Wilson was angry during or after his interview with Priscilla Grinder is certain, but his anger was confined to her seeming indifference to the needs of a dying man.

Murderists are more incredulous than outraged by Mrs. Grinder's apparent timidity. Fisher says, "[I]t takes a lot of credulity to believe that a frontier woman, used to hardship and living in a dangerous wilderness, on a trail infested with bandits, would wait until morning before going herself to the barn, or sending children, to summon the servants, when a mortally wounded man was crawling around and begging for help."[69] No matter what the motive, Bakeless concludes, "Lewis was left alone in agony all night or at least most of the night."[70]

At some point Mrs. Grinder summoned Pernier and Neelly's servant, either herself or by way of her children. It seems likely that Wilson's version of the aftermath of the shootings is the more accurate of the two, not only because it is longer and more detailed, but because Mrs. Grinder told the story to Wilson in a way that did not put herself in a very good light; an account unfavorable to the teller is almost always more credible than one that exonerates or aggrandizes the teller. If the servants came shortly after first light, they were able to see for themselves not necessarily *what* had happened, but the results of what had happened:

> [T]hey found him lying on the bed; he uncovered his side and showed them where the bullet had entered; a piece of the forehead was blown off, and had exposed the brains, without having bled much [Grinder-Wilson 1811].

Neelly's report has less detail, but it does not in any way contradict the story Priscilla Grinder told Wilson sixteen months later: "[H]e had shot himself in the head with one pistol & a little below the Breast with the other" [Grinder-Neely 1809]. Meriwether Lewis died of a gunshot wound to the head and another to the abdomen ("his side"). In neither of her contemporary reports did Mrs. Grinder speak of razor cuts or knife wounds. Neelly, who came upon the scene later in the morning of October 11 and had the opportunity to observe Lewis's body, did not speak of knife or razor slashings, at least in his letter to Jefferson. The lurid account, provided by Gilbert Russell on November 26, 1811, that, after shooting himself, Lewis "got his razors from a port folio which happened to contain them and Seting up in his bed was found about day light, by one of the Servants, busily engaged in cutting himself from head to foot,"[71] finds no corroboration in the near-eyewitness accounts of Mrs. Grinder and James Neelly, or in Alexander Wilson's account of his interview with the Grinders. Sensational stories tend to breed exaggeration, elaboration, and wild rumor. It cannot be ruled out that Lewis slashed his body "in the most cool desperate and Barbarian-like manner,"[72] as Russell put it in 1811, however. The apparent written source of the story was the Nashville *Democratic Clarion*, the newspaper that broke the Lewis suicide story on October 20, 1809. The account in the Frankfort *Argus* that William Clark read on October 28, 1809, was based on the article in the Nashville *Clarion*.[73] The account in the *Clarion* was based upon direct communication with Neelly. Because the *Clarion* reported that Lewis, at the time of his death, "was cutting himself with a razor,"[74] it is possible, even likely, that Neelly was the source of that information. It may be that Neelly remembered that detail, or learned it from Pernier, on his journey from Grinder's Inn to Nashville. It may be that Neelly omitted that detail in his brief letter to Jefferson to spare the former president sensational details of the incident or because he realized that—whatever else was true—it was the *pistol shots* that killed Lewis. It may be that Neelly invented the slashings to make the story he told more melodramatic and sensational. It may be that a reporter for the *Democratic Clarion* embellished the story for effect. We have no way of knowing. Whatever their source, and irrespective of their accuracy, once the knife and razor cuts got into the informal network of frontier newspapers, it was impossible *not* to include that lurid detail of the incident. That's the story as President Madison heard it. In a letter of October 30, 1809, to Jefferson, the president wrote, "[H]e had recourse to his Dirk with wch he mangled himself considerably. After all he lived till the next morning, with the utmost impatience for death."[75] What could be better than a *dirk* in a sensational story of frontier suicide? A dagger or a bare bodkin perhaps.

Lewis's last words were also variously reported. Neelly had him saying to Pernier, "I have done the business my good Servant give me some water" [Grinder-Neelly 1809]. Wilson reported that Lewis "begged they would take his rifle and blow out his brains, and he would give them all the money he had in his trunk. He often said, 'I am no coward; but I am so strong, so hard to die.' He begged the servant not to be afraid of him, for that he would not hurt him" [Grinder-Wilson 1811].

Gilbert Russell, who was not at Grinder's Inn on October 11, 1809, later reported, "He again beged for water, which was given him and so soon as he drank, he lay down and died with the declaration to the Boy [i.e., Pernier] that he had killed himself to deprive his enemies of the pleasure and honor of doing it."[76] Neelly reported, "He [Pernier] gave him water, he survived but a short time" [Grinder-Neelly 1809].

Nobody doubts that Meriwether Lewis died on October 11, 1809, sometime after first light, that he died primarily and perhaps exclusively of gunshot wounds, that he was—like most victims of gunshot wounds—exceptionally thirsty in the last hours or minutes of his life, and that he lived long enough to speak to his servant Pernier and others. Wilson's direct quotation, derived from Mrs. Grinder, "I am no coward; but I am so strong, so hard to die" [Wilson-Grinder 1811], has the ring of truth. It echoes something Lewis wrote on May 11, 1805, just inside today's Montana when the expedition recognized for the first time the profound life force of the grizzly bear: "[T]hese bear being so hard to die reather intimedates us all; I must confess that I do not like the gentlemen and had reather fight two Indians than one bear."[77] It is hard to know how Mrs. Grinder or Wilson would have been able to invent words that so closely resonated with Lewis's own particular phraseology.[78]

So Governor Meriwether Lewis died sometime after sunup on Wednesday, October 11, 1809. He was thirty-five years old. He was 738 miles from Washington, DC. He was 618 miles from Locust Hill and Monticello. He was 1,905 miles from the source of the "mighty & heretofore deemed endless Missouri" River.[79] Most important of all he was 223 miles from his friend and protector William Clark, who spent the night somewhere near Hardinsburg or Radcliffe, Kentucky.

James Neelly, who had stayed behind to round up the stray horses, apparently camped out on the night of October 10–11 somewhere not far from Grinder's Inn. When he arrived at the inn on the morning of October 11, Lewis was dead. "I came up some time after, & had him as decently Buried as I could in that place" [Neelly 1809].[80] Unfortunately, Neelly does not supply more detail about matters of great importance to us: the disposition of the corpse, including the exact placement of the bullet wounds and any other evidence of violence; the location and condition of Lewis's pistols; the location of the gunpowder canister Lewis had inquired about the previous evening; the location of the grave, the depth, and grave markings; and whether Lewis was buried in his clothes or in some other form of shroud.[81] When Wilson visited Grinder's Inn early in 1811, he reported, "He lies buried close by the common path, with a few loose rails thrown over his grave. I gave Grinder [Robert, not Priscilla] money to put a post fence round it to shelter it from the hogs, and from the wolves; and he gave me his written promise he would do it" [Wilson 1811].

Danisi and Jackson attempt to put physical closure on the incident: "Most accounts discreetly overlook what those secondary victims of the tragedy had to do. There was a grim search for enough boards to cobble together a crude box. The shredded, blood-crusted clothing had to be removed, the wounded body washed, and the corpse redressed in something suitable for a tolerable burial. That was just what frontier countrymen of the period would have done for a deceased relative or neighbor."[82]

So far as we know, no one witnessed the death of Meriwether Lewis. Lewis's servant Pernier was sleeping in a barn or stable approximately 200 yards from the cabin in which the shooting occurred. So was Neely's servant. If Mrs. Grinder is to be believed, the servants apparently did not hear the gunshots. Mrs. Grinder was close at hand, across the breezeway, trying to sleep in the other cabin about fifteen feet away, but she did not claim to witness the gunshots. James Neelly was camping somewhere near, but not at Grinder's Inn. Priscilla Grinder was an ear-witness to the shooting. She heard the shots, and she heard someone fall heavily to the floor of the other cabin. She claimed to have seen Lewis staggering around in the vicinity of the inn shortly after the shooting. In none of the accounts we have did she claim to have seen the body after Lewis's death, though she almost certainly did. Nor is it clear from the accounts we have whether she was present in the room at the time of Lewis's death. Probably she was.

The story of Lewis's death works its way out from whatever actually happened at Grinder's Inn through a handful of individuals, not one of whom is regarded as an unimpeachable witness. Everyone agrees that something happened at Grinder's Inn at about 3 A.M. on October 11, 1809. Priscilla Grinder was as close to an eyewitness as exists in this troubled story, but she did not actually see what transpired. The next two to learn what happened and see the result were Lewis's servant Pernier and Neelly's unnamed servant. They seem to have had an exchange of words with the dying Lewis, who was still alive when they were summoned to the scene. When James Neelly rode up sometime later in the morning of October 11, Priscilla Grinder told him what she believed—or wanted him to believe—had happened. Neelly accepted her account and supervised the burial of Governor Lewis, though probably the physical labor was performed by black men. Neelly wrote to former president Jefferson on October 18, 1809, one week after Lewis's violent death. John Bakeless has written, "The entire suicide story, therefore, depends entirely on what the people at Grinder's Stand that night told Neeley [sic] the next day, with some possible confirmation from Lewis's two servants."[83] Only one was Lewis's servant.

Vardis Fisher has called Neelly's letter to Jefferson "one of the most unsatisfactory documents in all of history."[84] That is something of an exaggeration. Neelly's letter does not tell us all *we* would like to know about the death of Lewis, but it told Jefferson all *he* needed to know, and in clear terms. Neelly's first sentence got right to the point: "It is with extreme pain I have to inform you of the death of His Excellency Meriwether Lewis, Governor of upper Louisiana who died on the morning of the 11th Instant and I am Sorry to Say by Suicide."[85] What could be more clear and concise than this? Neelly went on to provide a few details. He also accounted for Lewis's trunks and papers, and asked the former president where they should be sent. That would have been one of Jefferson's primary concerns. Indeed, Jefferson would have regarded the security of Lewis's papers as more important at the time than further details about the shooting. Like Clark, Jefferson's next thought after absorbing the terrible news of Lewis's death would have been, as Clark put it, "[W]hat will be the Consequence? what will become of my his paprs?"[86]

The key player in this sad story was Priscilla Grinder. Dee Brown has called her "history's sole source for the last hours of Meriwether Lewis's life."[87] Unfortunately, neither Mrs. Grinder nor Pernier nor Neelly's servant ever wrote a first-person account of Lewis's death, so far as we know.[88] Neelly was not an eyewitness. His account of the death of Lewis was based primarily on the testimony of Mrs. Grinder, to a certain degree on the testimony of Pernier and his own servant, and partly on his own direct observation of the desperate tableau that awaited him at Grinder's Inn when he arrived on the morning of October 11.

The key documents pertaining to the death of Lewis are, in descending order, Priscilla Grinder's account as told by Neelly in his October 18, 1809, letter to former president Jefferson; Alexander Wilson's account of his interview with Mrs. Grinder, dated May 18, 1811; and three documents created by Gilbert Russell. These documents included two letters to Jefferson, dated January 4, 1810, and January 31, 1810, and the affidavit or deposition he gave on November 26, 1811. Although Russell was not at or near Grinder's Inn on October 10–11, 1809, he had an opportunity to observe Lewis at Fort Pickering for two full weeks between September 15 and September 29, 1809. Because Russell felt the need to place Lewis under friendly arrest at Fort Pickering, and because he reported that Lewis had twice attempted to commit suicide on the Mississippi River ride between St. Louis and today's Memphis, his testimony represents an essential part of the story.

An incident for which there was no known eyewitness can never be entirely cleared of mystery.

Much has been made of Robert Grinder's absence on the night of the shooting, but such things happen. Grinder had no way of knowing that Lewis was approaching his hostelry. His absence does not automatically make him a suspect in the case. The murderists find Priscilla Grinder's fear and trembling, her delay in rousing Lewis's attendants, deeply suspicious; but there is no adequate reason to discredit her testimony merely because she was paralyzed by fear after the shooting and waited until daylight to send for help. Such things happen. How many historians have been awakened in the middle of a dark night in the middle of nowhere by a shooting incident in their family's private quarters? Murderists find Neelly's absence at the time of the shooting suspicious, particularly because he turned up so soon after Lewis's death on the morning of October 11. On that score, President Madison's explanation is as good as any: "As soon as they had passed the Tennessee [River], he [Lewis] took advantage of the neglect of his companion [Neelly], who had not secured his arms, to put an end to himself."[89] In other words, the separation of Neelly and Lewis was not the work of Neelly but of Lewis, who insisted on riding ahead to the first white settlement on the Natchez Trace while Neelly remained behind to scour up the stray horses.

Unfortunately, as in virtually all cases of violent death, none of the core players can be regarded as entirely reliable. Mrs. Grinder changed her story over time. By 1839, thirty years after the incident, in her last known account of the death of Lewis, she stated that, "About dark two or three other men rode up and called for lodging. Mr. Lewis immediately drew a brace of pistols, stepped towards them and challenged them to fight a duel. They not liking this salutation, rode on to the next house, five miles."[90] Even Vardis Fisher, who was determined to undermine the credibility of any suicide witness, dismissed the 1839 account as preposterous. "That Lewis rushed out and challenged two or three men to a duel merely because they asked for lodgings is so fantastically improbable that we must assume either that Mrs. Grinder invented it to support her story of derangement, or got Lewis mixed up with another lodger on another occasion."[91]

James Neelly was not the villainous character most murderists make him out to be, but he did appropriate a number of Lewis's personal objects at the time of Lewis's death. He "returned" a few of them only when Lewis's brother John Marks directly confronted Neelly's wife in Nashville in January 1812, and apparently never returned some of Lewis's personal effects to his family. He had the effrontery to make a financial claim against Lewis's estate, in spite of his failure to protect the safety of the distinguished man he had agreed to escort. He may also have pocketed the cash Lewis was carrying on his last journey. Neelly's mismanagement of Lewis's drinking problem between Fort Pickering and Grinder's Inn earned him the wrath of Gilbert Russell, who told Jefferson that Neelly was essentially responsible for Lewis's death: "[T]his Agt. being extremely fond of liquor, instead of preventing the Govr from drinking or keeping him under any restraint advised him to it & from every thing I can learn gave the man every chance to seek an opportunity to destroy himself."[92] Neelly was unceremoniously dismissed from his post as US Indian agent in 1812, a fact that murderists seldom fail to cite in their indictment of his character. In retrospect, Gilbert Russell believed that almost anyone else would have been a more responsible chaperon of Lewis than Neely.

If Meriwether Lewis was murdered at Grinder's Inn, Priscilla Grinder was either one of the conspirators, or—after the killer(s) fled—she wrongly concluded that Lewis had killed himself. If she had a role in the murder, James Neely was either a fellow conspirator, or he was a man so simple-minded that he accepted her suicide story without skepticism when he rode up later that morning. These notions frankly strain credulity. If Neely and Mrs. Grinder were co-conspirators, they either committed the crime without Pernier and Neely's servant knowing what they had done, or they included the servants in the conspiracy, or they intimidated them into lifelong silence about what actually transpired at Grinder's Inn. By the time Pernier reached Thomas Jefferson later that fall, he was sufficiently far away from Neely that he would have felt secure in telling Jefferson the truth, the whole truth, and nothing but the truth.

The two most important men in Lewis's life, Thomas Jefferson and William Clark, had the same reaction to the news. They were shocked, but they were not surprised. Jefferson could not have been more categorical if he tried. In a public account of the life of Lewis, Jefferson wrote, "About 3. oclock in the night he did the deed which plunged his friends into affliction and deprived his country of one of her most valued citizens."[93] William Clark, learning of Lewis's suicide from a frontier newspaper, wrote, "[I]t Says that Govr. Lewis killed himself by Cutting his Throat with a Knife, on his way between the Chickaw Saw Bluffs and nashville, I fear this report has too much truth, tho' hope it may have no foundation—my reasons for thinking it possible is founded on the letter which I recved from him at your house, in that letter he Says he had Some intintion of going thro' by land ... . I fear O! I fear the waight of his mind has over come him, what will be the Consequence? what will become of my his paprs?"[94] Notice that Clark did not question the suicide. What he sought was confirmation that Lewis had changed his plans and traveled overland towards Nashville.

Neither Jefferson nor Clark rejected the suicide story as preposterous or even unlikely. That is exceedingly significant. If either of them had the slightest doubt, they would have expressed their resistance to the news in one way or another. If Clark had felt there was any possibility that Lewis had been murdered, if he had sensed anything suspect in the stories radiating out from Nashville, he would have gone to Grinder's Inn himself to investigate. It is, in fact, more than a little odd that he never in the course of his long life made the pilgrimage to Lewis's lonely grave. Perhaps he could not bear to visit the scene of such desperation. Perhaps he was ashamed of his friend, or ashamed of himself for not doing more to help Lewis during his last struggle.

The two most important men in Lewis's life accepted the suicide story because it rang true—it squared with what they knew about the troubled soul of Meriwether Lewis; how completely he embodied the external strains and challenges of his life; how sensitive he was to criticism; how hard he was on himself; how dramatic and even melodramatic he tended to be; and how self-punishing he was when he felt that he was not meeting his own or the world's expectations. For Clark, Lewis's suicide made sense in light of the last letter he received from Lewis, in light of his last meeting with Lewis on August 25, 1809, in St. Louis, after which Clark confessed that "I have not Spent Such a Day as yesterday fer maney years ... if his mind had been at ease I Should have parted Cherefully."[95] That *that* Meriwether Lewis might have taken his own life did not surprise William Clark, however deeply he grieved for his fallen friend. For Jefferson, Lewis's suicide made sense given Lewis's bewildering silence in the last fifteen months, his failure to write the book, and the difficulties he had put himself in with the War Department in Washington. Jefferson remembered observing "sensible depressions of mind"[96] during the White House years, and he was aware of the "constitutional source"[97] from which they sprang in both branches of the Lewis family.

These great men—both individuals of extraordinary integrity—accepted Lewis's suicide. They had more heart and soul invested in Meriwether Lewis than any historian can muster two centuries after the fact. If Jefferson and Clark found Lewis's suicide all too plausible, how is that we have such trouble accepting it? If they accepted the story without protest, how can a modern biographer declare, "If there is such a person as the anti-suicide type, it was Meriwether Lewis. By temperament, he was a fighter, not a quitter. Much has been made of his introspection. ... Sensitive he was; neurotic he was not. Lewis was one of the most positive personalities in American history"?[98]Doubting Neelly and Mrs. Grinder is a painless enterprise, even if it is unfair. Doubting Thomas Jefferson and William Clark requires amazing temerity. Clark and Jefferson did not believe that Lewis was the "anti-suicide type." Just the reverse.

The only close friend of Lewis's who visited the gravesite was Alexander Wilson, the American ornithologist whom Lewis met in 1807 after returning from the great journey. Wilson made his pilgrimage to Grinder's Inn in the spring of 1811. He loved Lewis. After his interview with the Grinders, he stated, "I left this place in a very melancholy mood, which was not much allayed by the prospect of the gloomy and savage wilderness which I was just entering alone."[99] Wilson subsequently wrote a remarkable poem about Lewis's disintegration and demise. Wilson, like Jefferson and Clark, was an unambivalent suicidist.

Wilson was no patsy. In his letter to Alexander Lawson, May 28, 1811, he expressed anger at Priscilla Grinder's failure to succor Lewis as he lay dying on October 11. He had sternly instructed Robert Grinder to take something like adequate care of the late governor's grave, made him sign a letter promising to do so, and sealed the contract with an advance payment of cash. Wilson interviewed Priscilla Grinder. He recorded her story in considerable detail. It does not vary in any significant way from James Neelly's more cursory account of Lewis's death. Danisi and Jackson, though they are not quite suicidists and emphatically not murderists, rightly acknowledge the credibility of Wilson's report and the unvarnished authenticity of Mrs. Grinder's narrative. "His interview with Mrs. Grinder recovered the best first-person account of the fatal night. It seems unlikely that the authenticity of the vivid details that he took down were colored by sympathy or retelling."[100]

Wilson was Lewis's friend and advocate. If he had felt the slightest doubt about the veracity of Mrs. Grinder's story, if he had suspected that she had anything to hide or was omitting any material facts of the case, he would have challenged her directly or at least written of his suspicions and frustrations when he had gotten clear of the grumpy Robert Grinder and Grinder's Inn. His moving account of the death of Lewis accepts the suicide story unhesitatingly. So does his poem.

These would seem to be insuperable problems for the murderists. Thomas Jefferson, patron and father figure to Lewis, was publicly certain it was suicide. William Clark, partner in discovery and closest friend, was unhesitatingly convinced it was suicide. Alexander Wilson, the scientific friend who undertook a pilgrimage to the lonely grave and interviewed the woman who was the nearest thing we have to an eyewitness, was entirely convinced it was suicide. None of them ever wrote a single sentence giving Lewis's death the benefit of the doubt or suggesting any possibility of an alternative theory of his death.

Strangely, the enormous weight of these three men's testimony has not prevented some historians from preferring that he was murdered at Grinder's Inn.

Melodramatically, Lewis's distinguished biographer Richard Dillon wrote, "Was Meriwether Lewis murdered? Yes. Is there proof of his murder? No. Could Lewis's death have been a suicide? Yes. Not only because the analysts today will insist that *anyone* is capable of self-destruction, given the right set of circumstances, even a man of courage like Lewis, but because the Governor was fatigued, depressed, sick and, at times, delirious ... . And, where there was no proof of murder, there was 'evidence' of suicide at Grinder's Stand."[101] Consider the logic of this. There was *evidence of suicide*, there was *no proof of murder*, the governor was *fatigued, depressed, sick and, at times, delirious*, but "Was Meriwether Lewis murdered? Yes." It is hard to imagine historiography more colored by wishful thinking than this.

Given all that he conceded in his analysis, it would seem that Dillon, an outstanding historian and biographer, would be forced by his own scrupulousness to pronounce Lewis's death a suicide, but he concluded, "If there is such a person as the anti-suicide type, it was Meriwether Lewis. By temperament, he was a fighter, not a quitter."[102]

Dillon's suspects include Pernier (perhaps to recover "the money which his master owed him"), Neelly's servant ("bribed or terrified into lasting silence, or an accomplice"), Neelly ("certainly stole the Governor's rifle, horse, pistols, dagger, and pipe-tomahawk"), the Grinders ("the inn-keeper, lurking in the woods, or his hard-bitten woman"), possibly even Gilbert Russell ("no paragon of virtue").[103] In the end, having sifted the evidence against all of these individuals, Dillon opts for someone else, however: "His assassin, I am convinced, was either an unknown land pirate of the ilk of the Harpe brothers of bloody Natchez notoriety, or the mysterious Runnion, suspected by Whiteside's coroner's jury because his moccasin tracks and the impression of the butt of his unusual rifle were found in the dirt near Lewis's cabin."[104] "Is there proof of his murder? No."

Although the great Lewis and Clark editor Elliott Coues was inclined to vote for murder, he freely admitted that "the fragmentary evidence which has come down to us [indicating murder], moreover, does not hang together well."[105] He freely acknowledged that one of the principal problems for the murder theory was Jefferson's public declaration that Lewis took his own life. The murder theory is "offset," Coues admitted, "by the unqualified statements of Mr. Jefferson, a wary and astute man of the world, accustomed to weigh his words well; one who must have been satisfied in his own mind that he had the facts of a case beyond his personal knowledge; and one who had every imaginable reason—personal, official, or other— to put the matter in the most favorable light."[106] Coues admitted that the principal reason to wish it were murder is "to clear so great a name from so grave an imputation."[107] That would seem to be the essential motive of the majority of murderists.

Dr. Eldon Chuinard rejected suicide on the basis of forensics. A man shooting himself with .69 caliber bullets is not going to have the strength to wander about the yard and breezeway of Grinder's Inn. "The second shot," Chuinard wrote, "would be expected to have killed Lewis instantly, or have disabled him ... What do the supporters of suicide think that this second shot would have done to the heart, lungs, aorta and/or intestines? Certainly Lewis would have been in dire shock and soon have bled to death or perhaps paralyzed from spinal cord injury."[108]

More recently, Dr. David Peck has disputed Chuinard's conclusion. The internal trauma and bleeding "could have definitely gone on for two hours prior to his death, not causing the 'instant death' that Dr. Chuinard believes it would have,"[109] Peck wrote.

Peck believes Lewis was suffering from the milder of the two forms of malaria. He would not have been able to travel if he had been suffering from the more severe strain which caused low blood sugar, anemia, and kidney failure, causing the victim to die "within days."[110] He also doubts that the milder form of malaria would have caused him to commit suicide. "I find it difficult to imagine that symptoms of fever, chills, headache, and nausea he had experienced previously would have caused Lewis to take his own life at this time."[111] Peck believes it is more likely that Lewis's suicide was brought on by a combination of the malaria, opium addiction, alcoholism, and "other psychological problems."[112]

David Lavender, like Stephen Ambrose, was certain that Lewis committed suicide. "There was no doubt in Jefferson's mind—or in Clark's who heard the news in Louisville while on another trip East with Julia and their eldest son, the infant Meriwether Lewis Clark—that the death was suicide and not murder, a theory that keeps insistently cropping up to explain, in more palatable form, the death of a national hero."[113] For Lavender, the murder theory is not based on evidence, but on the psychology of the American public. Suicide is a shameful way for a national hero to die. Murder is "more palatable," because would enable us to believe Lewis was mentally stable at the time of his death.

The list of contemporaries who believed that Lewis committed suicide is monumental: Thomas Jefferson, William Clark, Alexander Wilson, Gilbert Russell, James Neelly, John Pernier, Priscilla Grinder, John Brahan, and the anonymous friend who wrote Lewis's obituary.[114] The list of contemporaries who believed that Lewis was murdered is… well, entirely blank, with the possible exception of Lewis' mother Lucy Marks. The list of twentieth century authors who are convinced that Lewis committed suicide is enough to daunt the courage of any murderist: Donald Jackson, Gary Moulton, James Ronda, James Holmberg, Kay Redfield Jamison, Stephen Ambrose, Thomas Slaughter, David Lavender, Stephen Dow Beckham, M.R. Montgomery, Harry Fritz, David Freeman Hawke, David Nicandri, Paul Cutright, Jonathan Daniels, Dayton Duncan, William Foley, Landon Jones, Stephenie Ambrose Tubbs, Carolyn Gilman, Larry Morris, Dawson Phelps, David Peck, and a host of others.

The list of historians who favor the murder theory is also impressive: John Guice, Richard Dillon, Elliott Coues (?), Reuben Gold Thwaites, John Bakeless, Bernard DeVoto, Vardis Fisher, Eldon Chuinard, Olin Wheeler, Kira Gale, and James Starrs.[115]

John Bakeless, though he was a murder advocate, acknowledged, "The evidence for murder is not very strong, and the stories from Fort Pickering strongly suggest suicide, but none of the evidence is really conclusive."[116]

The leading exponent of the murder position is John Guice, an emeritus professor of history at the University of Southern Mississippi and an expert on the history of the Natchez Trace. He has written and lectured extensively on this subject. In the endless debate over the death of Meriwether Lewis, Guice and the murderists have one enormous advantage; it is impossible to refute their main assertion. Guice has written, "No one knows whether or not Meriwether Lewis committed suicide. No one witnessed the firing of the two .69 calibre pistol balls that caused the fatal wounds."[117]

Guice has summarized the murderist position in a delightful and at times playful thirty-two-page essay, "Why Not Homicide?" in *By His Own Hand? The Mysterious Death of Meriwether Lewis*. Guice's historiography—at least in this essay—is remarkable and perplexing, to say the least. He spends a full thirty pages attempting to punch holes in the suicide theory, and just a page and a half making the case that Lewis might have been murdered. By my count, Guice offers forty arguments against suicide. (See footnote)[118] The essence of his argument is twofold: first, that the "evidence" for suicide is not nearly as compelling as it has been made to appear, and almost every piece of suicide "evidence" is capable of being read another way; second, because it is impossible to know definitively that Lewis committed suicide, historians should be much more even handed and agnostic about this sensitive and important question. Guice argues that the authority of three men has unfairly distorted the debate: Dawson Phelps, who wrote an influential article for the *William and Mary Quarterly* in 1956; Donald Jackson, whose magisterial *Letters of the Lewis and Clark Expedition* (1978) has made him seem like the final authority on Lewis and Clark questions; and Stephen Ambrose, whose *Undaunted Courage* (1996) has sold "millions of copies and who did far more than any other single writer to convince Americans that Lewis killed himself."[119] Guice argues that if historians were more rigorous and less impressionable—less in the thrall of Ambrose and Jackson—they would admit the suicide-murder debate is far from resolved. He suggests that responsible historical analysis must acknowledge, at the very least, that in the absence of an eyewitness, we can never be 100 percent sure that Lewis took his own life. In that regard, Guice has performed an important service to Lewis and Clark studies.

John Guice makes many useful points in his essay. He argues that there is no good reason to conclude that Lewis was depressed after the expedition merely because he was dilatory in getting to St. Louis. Not only did Lewis make considerable progress on the publication project in the nation's intellectual capital, Philadelphia, in 1807, but he got a well-deserved vacation in which he "cavorted with the girls."[120] Guice also rightly contextualizes Lewis's drinking habits. Heavy drinking in the early national period was not unusual. W.J. Rorabaugh's *The Alcoholic Republic: An American Tradition* is a useful study of the heavy consumption that was commonplace on the American frontier. Guice concludes, "The amount of whiskey drunk on the southern frontier seems astronomical by modern standards."[121]

Guice also insists that while Lewis's administrative difficulties in St. Louis were serious and to him exasperating, they were not particularly unusual on the western frontier in that era. US government functionaries in and out of the army routinely had trouble getting their vouchers honored by faraway Washington bureaucrats. As Danisi and Jackson convincingly prove, Lewis was busy, productive, and professionally engaged throughout his time in St. Louis, in spite of the backbiting insubordination of his assistant Frederick Bates, in spite of the manifold complexity of land titles and social and legal authority in the period of transition between European colonial administration of Louisiana and the regimen that the new sovereign, the United States, was attempting to impose on an outspoken and unruly population far from the national capital.[122]

Guice joins a chorus of writers, best represented by the late Stephen Ambrose, in arguing that "It would have been utterly unrealistic" for President Jefferson to believe that Lewis could administer the raw new territory and, at the same time, write a multivolume account of his travels. It is far from clear, Guice argues, that Lewis felt any significant guilt or despondency in not having completed the book.[123]

Guice is much less convincing when he faults Gilbert Russell for not providing details about Lewis's two alleged suicide attempts on board the boat that brought him from St. Louis to Fort Pickering. Guice implies that Russell's failure to specify the nature of the suicide attempts undermines his credibility. Guice fantasizes that Lewis might simply have lost his balance and fallen (twice?) from the deck of the ship "due to wind and current on one of the world's greatest rivers."[124] This is not a convincing argument. Nor does Guice make a convincing argument that Russell's affidavit of November 26, 1811, is inauthentic.[125]

Guice rightly argues that Lewis's letter to President Madison from Fort Pickering, dated September 16, 1809, is the work of a man essentially in control of his rational faculties (see above, page 285–286). The fact that the extant copy of the letter is riddled with corrections and deletions is not necessarily evidence that Lewis was deranged. It may have been a draft of the letter Lewis actually sent. He was writing to the president of the United States at a moment when his entire future was at stake. Lewis was physically ill. The document we have is a mess. But the letter is anything but incoherent.[126]

Guice spends more time trying to puncture peripheral arguments for suicide than analyzing the facts of October 10–11 themselves. In the course of his thirty-two-page essay, he is unable to shake the credibility of Priscilla Grinder, the key "witness" in the story. The best he can do is raise the possibility that Mrs. Grinder claimed, after the shots were fired, she saw more than would actually have been possible on a moonless night. His attempts to weaken the authority of Jefferson's and Clark's immediate and lifelong acceptance of the suicide story are unconvincing. He joins Vardis Fisher in arguing that because Jefferson's integrity (on some issues) has been called into question by biographers and historians, the former president's declaration that Lewis committed suicide should not be accorded automatic credibility. Jefferson apparently anticipated Guice's skepticism. At the end of his biographical sketch of Lewis, he wrote, "To this melancholy close of the life of one whom posterity will declare not to have lived in vain I have only to add that all facts I have stated are either known to myself, or communicated by his family or others for whose truth I have no hesitation to make [myself] responsible."[127] One of those "others" was John Pernier, who traveled to Monticello after Lewis's death to provide a personal report to Jefferson. Guice is even weaker on Clark's "I fear O! I fear" letter to his brother Jonathan dated October 28, 1809. If Clark really believed Lewis committed suicide, he argues, why didn't he write more about Lewis's death during the remaining nineteen years of his life?[128] This argument is essentially incoherent. If Theodore Roosevelt really believed that his first wife died on Valentine's Day 1884, why did he steadfastly refuse to talk or write about her for the rest of his life?

Guice is at his best when he calls for skepticism and agnosticism, at his worst when he publishes absurdities in the hope of nibbling the opposition to death. Even so, it is possible to grant many of Guice's arguments without joining him in the conclusion that the suicide theory is weak or baseless. The sum total of Guice's argument is this: We cannot prove Lewis committed suicide. He might have been murdered. Therefore he was murdered.

Guice gives the overwhelming bulk of his energy to the mission of weakening the suicide theory. Only in the last page and a half of his essay does he actually make the case for murder, and then rather half-heartedly. First he nominates as potential assailants James Neelly, John Pernier, and Robert Grinder, but without providing any details or even suggesting motives. Then he cites one of his university students who irresponsibly suggested that Lewis made sexual advances towards Priscilla Grinder, after which she shot him dead. Next he offers two vague indictments of the notorious James Wilkinson. In the first, Wilkinson, a spy and a traitor, wanted Lewis dead (no motive provided) and somehow convinced Lewis's servant Pernier to do the wet work. In the second, Jefferson helped Wilkinson cover up the crime.[129] At least it can be said that not even Guice is convinced by the wild argument that Jefferson was part of the conspiracy. Finally, in the last sentence of the essay, Guice provides his entire case for murder. I quote John Guice's murder theory in its entirety: "A perfect target for outlaws, Lewis was probably their victim."[130] That, and nothing more.

As Hamlet said, "Is this a prologue, or a posy of a ring?"[131]

In addition to their insistence that Lewis's death is too mysterious to declare a suicide, the murderists advance six principal arguments. The review that follows is not meant to be an endorsement.

First, the problem of forensics. How could a master marksman bungle his suicide? Assuming that Lewis was using .69 caliber pistols, how could he miss with the first shot? Lewis was a superb marksman, so the argument goes, and if he wanted to blow his brains out he would surely have been able to do so. Even if we accept that somehow the first shot miscarried and removed a portion of his skull without killing him, what followed, according to the evidence we have, strains credibility. How could a man suffering from a severe head wound have the capacity to shoot himself a second time? After he shot himself in the head, the murderists argue, he would have been unable to regroup and shoot himself in the side. Assuming he was—somehow—able to shoot himself in the side, he would have died more or less immediately. If somehow he lived on after the second shot, he would not have had the strength to crawl about the premises and the yard at Grinder's Inn. If we really want to know the truth, why not exhume the body and subject Lewis's remains to rigorous twenty-first century forensic analysis? Murderists claim that the suicidists are hiding behind the protocols of the National Park Service, because they know that exhumation would confirm that Lewis was murdered.

Second, the problem of mixed messages. Why would a suicidal man tell Amos Stoddard that he intended to return to St. Louis? Why would Lewis tell Gilbert Russell he intended to go to Philadelphia to finish his book if he planned to kill himself? Why would a suicidal man make plans to move his mother to Missouri? Why would Clark say he reckoned Lewis would return with flying colors if he knew Lewis was in steep decline?

Third, the problem of narrative inconsistency. What should we make of the conflicting testimony of Priscilla Grinder in the years (decades) after Lewis's death? Was she alone or wasn't she? Did she see Lewis lurching around on a moonless night, or did she make that up? If Lewis slashed himself with a knife or razor, why didn't Neelly mention that in his letter to Jefferson? Were there other travelers at or near the inn that night? What actual evidence do we have that Lewis tried twice to kill himself on the journey from St. Louis to Fort Pickering? Are Russell's letters authentic?

Fourth, the problem of credibility. How can we trust Major Neelly if he stole some of Lewis's personal items and refused to return a few of them to the Lewis family after his death? How can we trust the Grinders? All three of them were perfect strangers to Meriwether Lewis. All three are shadowy figures who would not merit even a footnote in history were it not for their association with Lewis at the worst moment of his extraordinary life. They may have been speaking the truth as they knew it, but none of them actually witnessed the death of Lewis, unless they were his assassins or co-conspirators with his assassins, in which case their testimony would, of course, be tainted. If Jefferson had an adulterous affair with Maria Cosway and tried to seduce his friend John Walker's wife, how can we trust him as a biographer of Lewis? Isn't there some evidence that Clark may have changed his mind later in life?

Fifth, the problem of character. Lewis had no adequate reason to kill himself. "If there is such a person as the anti-suicide type, it was Meriwether Lewis."[132] All the alleged symptoms of Lewis's mental instability, gleaned both from the journey itself and from the years after his return, are deliberately taken out of context and heaped together to create the portrait of a neurotic and suicidal man. Guice wrote, "Interpretation of those … [incidents] as evidence of suicidal tendencies is farfetched, to say the least, unless one starts with the premise of suicide … Where is the hard evidence that Lewis suffered from depression?"[133]

Sixth, the problem of the tenacity of the murder theory. It is not true, as the suicidists claim, that the murder theory didn't spring up until the mid-nineteenth century. Local folks from the Hohenwald have always suspected the suicide story. Although the written records are lost, oral tradition tells us of inquests, widespread suspicion of Robert Grinder, the possibility of bandits whose names are preserved, the rumor that Lewis had a map of a gold mine he had discovered in Montana, and much more. The 1848 Monument Committee in Tennessee would not have declared, without evidence, "The impression has long prevailed that under the influence of disease of body and mind Governor Lewis perished by his own hands. It seems to be more probable that he died by the hands of an assassin."[134] Where there is smoke, there's fire. Oral tradition that points towards murder circulated immediately after the crime, and it continues to percolate in rural Tennessee in the twenty-first century.

The most recent contribution to the debate has been offered by Thomas Danisi and John Jackson in their 2009 administrative biography of Meriwether Lewis. Their view is that Lewis was suffering from an extremely severe form of malaria in the last weeks of his life. After twice attempting to kill himself on the river journey between St. Louis and Fort Pickering, Lewis did in fact take his own life at Grinder's Inn. His death was not suicide in the manner of a desperate or *deranged* man taking his own life, but an extreme response to extreme pain. It was, as they put it, "a strange and tragic form of self-surgery, not suicide."[135] In other words, Lewis killed himself but did not commit suicide.

This is an extraordinarily ingenious argument. It effectively *solves* the problem of Lewis's violent death. Now the overwhelming evidence for what the poet John Donne called "self slaughter" can be accepted, but the stigma of suicide is removed. Good historians that they are, Danisi and

Jackson found it impossible to explain away the documentary evidence for suicide. They did not engage in John Guice's quixotic attempt to undermine the foundation for suicide plank by plank, with good argument and bad. In my opinion, no competent historian, not even the formidable Guice, has been able to dispose of the evidence for suicide in a convincing way. Danisi and Jackson acknowledge the validity of the documents and oral traditions available to us. At the same time they do not believe Lewis was, in psychological terms, a suicidal man. Danisi and Jackson write, "It was the failure of his body, not his mind, nor his dedication, that cut him down. Lewis was simply unable to continue treating a lifelong, incurable illness. His death cannot be attributed, as many have tried to do, to personal weakness or to the failure to rise to a challenge. It was the result of unforgiving nature, the work of an impartial centuries-old protozoa as indifferent and final as a bullet."[136]

The often-repeated analogy to the *self-slaughter but not suicide* theory is the fate of the workers in the World Trade Center towers who jumped out of the skyscrapers' windows after the September 11, 2001, attacks. Those individuals unquestionably jumped to their deaths that morning, but they cannot justly be regarded as people who committed suicide. They were not suicidal. Like Lewis, they killed themselves, but they did not commit suicide.

Given the slender basis for concluding that Meriwether Lewis was murdered, what fuels the persistence and vehemence of the murderists? I think literary historian Albert Furtwangler gets it exactly right. In his remarkable book *Acts of Discovery: Visions of America in the Lewis and Clark Journals*, Furtwangler writes, "No matter how one takes these lines [from Neelly's letter to Jefferson], as artless report or contrived cover story, they make a demeaning end for a man like Lewis. ... One wants his death to be a fitting conclusion to his life, but it reads as a travesty of Lewis's days on the trail—an incongruous, discontinuous perversion of his career at his height."[137] Furtwangler notes that in the last journey of his life, Lewis was not leading, but led, chaperoned by a man as far beneath him as James Neelly. The man who bestrode the source of the Missouri River ended his life in a roadside inn so squalid that he preferred to sleep on the floor. During Lewis's terrible derangement, one of the expedition's supreme riflemen "bungles even as a marksman."[138]

This seems like an essential insight into the perseverance and the vehemence of the suicide-murder debate. Elliott Coues admitted that one must prefer murder "to clear so great a name from so grave an imputation."[139] David Lavender explained that the murder theory "keeps insistently cropping up to explain, in more palatable form, the death of a national hero."[140]

I have in this chapter tried in every possible way to be careful, rational, analytical, and generous. I have described the events of October 10–11, 1809, as objectively and fairly as possible. I end by paraphrasing Richard Dillon.

Was Meriwether Lewis murdered? Let the reader decide. Did Meriwether Lewis commit suicide? Let the facts be submitted to a candid world. As the master himself put it in the Virginia Statute for Religious Freedom:

[T]ruth is great, and will prevail if left to herself; that she is the proper and sufficient antagonist to error, and has nothing to fear from the conflict, unless by human interposition disarmed of her natural weapons, free argument and debate; errors ceasing to be dangerous when it is permitted freely to contradict them.[141]

Meanwhile, rest, rest perturbed spirit.

CHAPTER VII   Why?

"It is impossible to form any correct conjecture whatever could have produced so horrid a determination in the mind of a man, whose respectability and talents were so pre-eminent as those of the deceased."

Unidentified Nashville newspaper, 1809

IF MERIWETHER LEWIS COMMITTED SUICIDE ON OCTOBER 11, 1809, why did he do it?

There is no way to come to a definitive answer to that question. Lewis did not leave a suicide note. The key document, the closest thing we have to a suicide note, is missing. When his friend William Clark learned in the newspapers that Lewis had apparently committed suicide, he wrote to his brother Jonathan on October 28, 1809, from Shelby County, Kentucky: "I fear this report has too much truth, tho' hope it may have no foundation—my reasons for thinking it possible is founded on the letter which I recved from him at your house."[1] At New Madrid, on his river journey from St. Louis to Fort Pickering, Lewis had written his last letter to Clark. The letter must have been written on or about September 11, 1809, at the same time that Lewis wrote his last will and testament. Something in that letter suddenly made sense to Clark in the wake of Lewis's suicide, or something he had understood (and perhaps dismissed) as a kind of rhetorical posturing had now proved to be true.

Later in the same letter Clark wrote, "I fear O! I fear the waight of his mind has over come him, what will be the Consequence?"[2]

The waight of his mind. If ever a single phrase could sum up the demise of Meriwether Lewis, this is it.

When he heard the news, William Clark was shocked but not surprised. It is possible, of course, that the reports of Lewis dying by his own hand were erroneous. What is striking, however, is that Clark found nothing to doubt in the reports he was hearing; the news seemed plausible enough. Clark did not dismiss the story as beneath contempt or as an irresponsible absurdity. He went straight to "the waight of his mind" in his first attempts to make sense of the sudden and violent death of his old friend and partner in discovery.

Two days later, on October 30, 1809, from Lexington, Kentucky, Clark wrote a second letter to Jonathan confirming that Lewis was dead. He returned to the contents of the New Madrid letter: "I wish much to get the letter I receved of Govr. Lewis from N. madrid, which you Saw it will be of great Service to me. prey Send it to Fincastle as Soon as possible."[3] It seems clear from the context of this letter that what Clark most needed from the New Madrid letter, the part that would be of "great Service to me," was whatever Lewis wrote in it about the current state of the book he was writing about the expedition. Clark immediately added, "I wish I had Some conversation with you about our Book. the plans of Govr." Clark understood already, just two weeks after Lewis's death, that if there were ever going to be an official published account of the expedition, he would now be playing some sort of role in getting it done. Earlier in the letter Clark said, "I have wrote to judge Overton of Nashville about his papers."[4]

If the missing Lewis letter ever turns up, it may prove to be a disappointment. I'm guessing it communicated three main points. First, Lewis had decided to travel overland to Washington, DC, rather than continue down the Mississippi. Clark most wanted to confirm that fact by rereading the September 11 letter. If Lewis wrote that he was intending to change his itinerary and travel overland to the national capital, that would give credence to the stories swirling about Kentucky and Tennessee. Second, Lewis probably wrote that should anything happen to him, Clark should take certain steps to get the book published. Third, Lewis probably said something to the effect of: *it would be better if I destroyed myself rather than give my enemies the satisfaction of doing it.* This is pure speculation, but it is based on my close reading of the letters Clark wrote to his brother in the aftermath of Lewis's death and the testimony of Captain Gilbert Russell of Fort Pickering. The *proximate* cause of Lewis's mental disturbance was the letter of stiff rebuke he had received in mid-August from William Eustis (or a clerk) of the War Department. Nobody can know why Lewis took his own life. The September 11 letter has emerged in recent Lewis and Clark historiography as the potential key to our understanding Lewis's suicide. But even if Lewis's letter to Clark surfaced, it would be unlikely to clear things up. I doubt that it was a suicide note in any direct sense of the term.

One consequence of Lewis's sudden death, no matter what the cause, was that the all-important book project was now in complete disarray. Clark had no idea who had been hired to help with any part of the book or what the current status was of projected illustrations, corrections of longitudinal notations, analyses of scientific data, or drafts of the book itself. With his characteristic sense of responsibility, Clark turned immediately from Lewis's state of mind to the fate of the publication. "[W]hat will become of my his paprs?" he wrote to Jonathan. "I must write to Genl. Robinson or Some friend about nashville to enquire about him, and Collect and Send me his papers, if he had any with him."[5] At this moment, just two weeks after Lewis's death, Clark could not know that he would become responsible for seeing the publication project through to completion, but already he knew that it was his duty to make sure that Lewis's papers, wherever they might be, were adequately secured in the wake of his death. That was William Clark.[6]

What follows in this chapter is inevitably speculative. That does not mean that it is an improper or necessarily fruitless enterprise, however. The job of the historian is to bring to every historical problem her or his best sense of what must have, or at least what might have happened. I do not pretend to be able to "pluck out the heart" of Lewis's mystery.[7] I do believe that after many years of puzzling over his demise, sorting the thin stream of available evidence, and trying to make sense of his character, his moods, his doubts, his anxieties, his ambitions, his state of health, his outlook on life, and his experiences in the wilderness, that I might be able to make a useful contribution to the debate. My plan here is to assemble all of the theories of why he killed himself, to attempt to ground them in such evidence as we have, and to create, if possible, a profile of Lewis's suicide.

I hope what follows will be useful even to those who believe that Lewis was murdered on the Natchez Trace. The purpose of this book is to explore the character of Meriwether Lewis, to help myself and others understand the complexities of his soul, to listen carefully to his voice and read his texts with great care and sensitivity, in the hope that for me and for others something will *click into place*, and we will gain new insight into Lewis and into the Lewis and Clark Expedition. The portrait I will attempt to draw in this chapter is not meant as an autopsy, but as the profile of a complex man, an explorer in the wilderness.

The murder theory faces two seemingly insuperable problems. First, there is no serious evidence for murder. Second, it fails to account for the mental ordeal that was consuming Meriwether Lewis as he made his way down the Mississippi River and then overland on the Natchez Trace. Even if he was murdered, Lewis was in disarray at the time of his death—physically ill certainly, terribly upset by his difficulties with the territorial secretary Frederick Bates in St. Louis and the War Department in faraway Washington, DC, anxious about the book he had not finished, and probably suffering from chemical toxicity. By now he was, to a considerable extent, alone in life, and he may have been lonely. He may have been drinking heavily.

My aim here is to provide the most accurate and fair assessment I can of Lewis's state in the first week of October 1809. The man who arrived at Grinder's Inn on the evening of October 10, 1809, was not well. His post-expedition life had become a shambles. Lewis had returned to civilization on September 23, 1806, an American hero, and in the three years that followed, his life had spiraled out of control. This was particularly true of the period between March 8, 1808, when he arrived in St. Louis, and September 4, 1809, when he left the provincial capital for the last time.

Speculation is inevitable in the writing of history, in spite of the complaints that most historians make about *others'* speculations. David

Lavender, for example, in his superb *The Way to the Western Sea*, offers the following psychological reading of Lewis's stop at Fort Pickering on September 15, 1809: "Conceivably, another subconscious wish was involved. In 1797, as a young ensign, Lewis had supervised the building of, and had been briefly in command at, Fort Pickering. Did he welcome being put ashore in a blurred hope of again gaining command, this time of himself?"[8] The late Stephen Ambrose wrote a two-page speculation on what Lewis must have been thinking as he sat in the open doorway of Grinder's Inn on October 10, 1809, gazing wishfully towards the west. Earlier Ambrose speculated on what prompted Lewis to write his melancholy birthday meditation on August 18, 1805, and why he went silent for significant periods in the course of the expedition.[9] John Guice engages in speculation throughout his essay, "Why Not Murder?" in *By His Own Hand: The Mysterious Death of Meriwether Lewis*. He speculates, for example, that Jefferson may have accepted the accounts that Lewis had committed suicide not because they were true, but because "acceptance of suicide was a 'clean' way to handle the situation."[10] He speculates that the editor of the Jefferson Papers, Julian Boyd, had a personal vendetta against the novelist and historian Vardis Fisher.[11] Where there is mystery there will be speculation. When biographers and historians aren't sure of what happened at key moments in history, they have no choice but to reconstruct the past by way of careful speculative analysis. We will probably never know precisely whether the assassination of John F. Kennedy on November 22, 1963, was the work of a lone gunman or a conspiracy. Every biographer of Kennedy, every scholar of the assassination, engages in unavoidable speculation. That's how history works.

The late Stephen Ambrose had absolutely no doubt that Lewis committed suicide. Without being quite as categorical as Ambrose, I share his analysis. After describing the last hours of Lewis's life, Ambrose wrote, "There is a considerable literature on the possibility that Lewis did not commit suicide but was murdered … The literature is not convincing. … Had William Clark entertained the slightest suspicion that his friend had been murdered, can anyone doubt that he would have gone to Tennessee immediately to find and hang the murderer?"[12] *Hang the murderer*—quintessential Ambrose.

Explorers not infrequently have troubled homecomings. Some don't come home at all. Although he was the greatest explorer of the eighteenth century and an Enlightenment celebrity, Captain James Cook was killed in Hawaii on his third voyage in 1779. Mungo Park was killed by African natives at Bussa rapids on the Niger River in 1806, at the same time Lewis and Clark were returning from the Pacific coast. Columbus returned to

Spain in chains in 1500 after he alienated the Spanish colonists and adventurers on Hispaniola. His fourth voyage (1502–04) was a failure. He died in disarray in 1506, discredited, nearly blind, and unaware that he had discovered a new world. To this date, seventeen American astronauts (or cosmonauts) have died in their capsules, three on the ground and fourteen in space. A number of astronauts have had trouble adjusting to the sublunary world after their time in space, most notably Edwin Eugene (Buzz) Aldrin. The second man on the moon had been reduced, by 2010, to participating in the ABC television series *Dancing with the Stars*. Explorers, if they make it home at all, like Coleridge's ancient mariner, have stories to tell that can only be fully understood by themselves. The public can never really comprehend. When Neil Armstrong and Buzz Aldrin walked on the moon on July 21, 1969, CBS news commentator Eric Sevareid said, "We're always going to feel, somehow, strangers to these men. They will, in effect, be a bit stranger, even to their own wives and children. Disappeared into another life that we can't follow. I wonder what their lives will be like, now. The Moon has treated them well, so far. How people on Earth will treat these men, the rest of their lives, that gives me more foreboding, I think, than anything else."[13]

Disappeared into another life that we can't follow.

Lewis is the most important, but he certainly is not the only member of the Lewis and Clark Expedition who did not die quietly in his sleep. Joseph Field was killed in 1807, just a year after the expedition returned. John Potts and George Drouillard were killed by Blackfeet Indians, one in 1808 and the other in 1810. So far as we know, eight of the thirty-three permanent members of the Corps of Discovery endured violent deaths.

Clark returned from the wilderness in 1806 not diminished by the great adventure but strengthened. He had no known re-entry issues. He began to court Julia Hancock of Fincastle, Virginia, just a few weeks after the expedition's return, and married her on January 8, 1808. She was just fifteen years old. They had met when she was just twelve. Clark was so interested in securing her hand in marriage that he missed the official Washington, DC, ball (January 14, 1807) celebrating the success of the expedition. Together they had five children. Julia died on June 20, 1820. The ever-resilient Clark found it possible to remarry just a year and five months later, on November 28, 1821. His second wife Harriet Kennerly Radford bore him three more children. Clark succeeded as the Indian superintendent in Louisiana Territory, managed to pick up the pieces of the expedition's inchoate publication project after the death of Lewis, served as governor of Missouri from 1812–1820, and signed a tenth of all the treaties ever negotiated with the Indians of America.[14] He built for himself a private museum, a *cabinet of curiosities,* which had greater actual influence than Jefferson's much more famous Indian museum in the entrance hall of Monticello. Clark advised subsequent travelers on the Missouri River, including Prince Maximilian of Wied-Neuwied and Karl Bodmer. The *St. Louis Directory* reported, "The Council Chamber of Gov. William Clark, where he gives audience to the Chiefs of the various tribes of Indians who visit St. Louis, contains probably the most complete Museum of Indian curiosities, to be met with any where in the United States; and the governor is so polite as to permit its being visited by any person of respectability at any time."[15]

By all accounts, Clark returned from the twenty-eight-month transcontinental sojourn with greater confidence, prominence, and promise than when he signed on in the summer of 1803. He made the most of his long and eventful career. It would be hard to imagine a more successful and satisfying post-expedition life than Clark's. By the time Washington Irving visited him in 1832, Clark was a Missouri patriarch. In his notes, Irving wrote, "Genl arrives on horseback with dogs—guns. His grandson on a calico poney hallowing & laughing—Genl on horseback—gun on his shoulder—cur—house dog—bullying setter."[16] Irving's portrait of Clark at sixty-two is brilliant.

Clark's funeral in 1838 was the most heavily attended event in the early history of Missouri. His nephew wrote, "People lined the streets for blocks to watch the cortege led by a military band... Last, before the carriages which held the family and friends, the General's horse was led by his servant, both in black. Clark's pistol, holster, and sword were laid on the saddle and his spurred boots were reversed in the stirrups."[17] A young tradesman in St. Louis wrote, "[I]f eccessive toil and Peril, and a life of Laborious Servitude spent in the service of his country entitle a man to honours, there are none more deserving than Gen. Clark."[18]

Sometime on October 10 or 11, 1809, the body of Meriwether Lewis was buried in a shallow grave near a squalid inn in the middle of nowhere on the Natchez Trace. So far as we know there was no burial ceremony of any sort. At most a handful of individuals watched as the governor of Louisiana Territory, the protégé of Thomas Jefferson, and the hero of the Core of Volunteers for North Western Discovery was laid to rest, in a grave so shallow, so hugger-mugger, that within a year, pigs had disturbed the bones of the man who once bestrode the source of the "mighty & heretofore deemed endless Missouri."

The contrast is staggering. David Lavender has written, "Clark's concluding years were the antithesis of Lewis's."[19]

By 1809 Lewis had made a hash of virtually every aspect of his life. He was alone in the world. He had not been able to find a wife. His brother Reuben Lewis was engaged in the fur trade far up the Missouri River. His mother Lucy Marks was back in Albemarle County, Virginia. His closest friend had moved into the self-imposed intimacy of a successful marriage in its first flush. Lewis was at open war with his secretary Frederick Bates. The War Department in Washington, DC, had lost confidence in him.

He was, he and others believed, in danger of being recalled or at least not reappointed as governor of Louisiana Territory. His official finances were being challenged by bureaucrats in Washington, DC, and he had been accused by a War Department official of mismanagement, conflict of interest, and possibly worse. His private finances were in considerable disarray, and his creditors were crowding in upon him. He had even managed to earn the rebuke of his patron and friend Jefferson—and it was not easy to anger one of the most understanding and gracious men of the early national period. Lewis was physically and probably also mentally ill in October 1809. His body chemistry was, thanks to a medley of opium, alcohol, and other medicines, in a state of advanced toxicity. He had not written his book. He had largely stopped writing anything.

The most authoritative contemporary to write about the last days of Meriwether Lewis was former president Thomas Jefferson. On August 18, 1813, Jefferson wrote the first sustained biographical sketch of Meriwether Lewis. Because it served as the foreword to Nicholas Biddle's *History of the Expedition Under the Command of Captain Lewis and Clark to the Sources of the Missouri, Thence Across the Rocky Mountains and Down the River Columbia to the Pacific Ocean*,[20] because Jefferson knew Lewis intimately, and because of Jefferson's authority as a founding father of the United States, the former president's sketch of Lewis has been enormously influential.

Jefferson's response was unhesitating: "About 3. oclock in the night he did the deed which plunged his friends into affliction and deprived his country of one of her most valued citizens."[21] Attempts have been made to discredit Jefferson, either by pointing to moments in his life when he lacked integrity (Vardis Fisher[22]) or by suggesting that he was part of the conspiracy that destroyed Lewis (David Leon Chandler[23]), or that he was old and winding down and simply chose to close the books on the incident (Guice[24]). These allegations are not really about Jefferson. They are attempts to weaken the suicide theory by lessening the credibility of the author of the Declaration of Independence and the Virginia Statute for Religious Freedom, the creator of the University of Virginia, the designer of the Virginia state capitol, the father of American paleontology, the architect of Monticello and Poplar Forest, America's first wine connoisseur, the father of the first Republican Party, the US minister to France, the governor of Virginia, and the de facto midwife of the Bill of Rights.

Jefferson was a collector of protégés. He was extremely loyal to his friends. He was gracious, generous, and likelier to give the benefit of the doubt than to jump to conclusions. It would have been much easier for Jefferson to write simply that Lewis had died tragically young than to endorse the suicide story. He told the story of Lewis's suicide not to embrace a clean and tidy way of handling a complex situation, but because he was genuinely convinced that was how Lewis died. He felt the need to explain to readers of the Biddle-Allen paraphrase edition of the journals why Lewis had not published the Enlightenment treatises he had promised in his prospectus of April 1807. Jefferson was not one to expatiate on the private difficulties of other men—at least if they were his friends.[25]

Jefferson wrestled with the implications of Lewis's self-destruction, and asked himself—as every survivor who has been close to the victim does—could this have been foreseen, were there warning signs, am I in some way partly responsible for what happened?[26] Jefferson addressed each of those concerns. He had indeed seen warning signs. In his 1813 public biographical sketch of Lewis, Jefferson wrote, "Governor Lewis had from early life been subject to hypocondriac affections. It was a constitutional disposition in all the nearer branches of the family of his name, & was more immediately inherited by him from his father. They had not however been so strong as to give uneasiness to his family."[27] The *Oxford English Dictionary* (OED) defines the adjective *hypochondriac* as "consisting in, or having the nature of, a settled depression of spirits." This is precisely the sense in which Jefferson used the term. The OED defines the noun *hypochondria* as "a morbid state of mind, characterized by general depression, melancholy, or low spirits, for which there is no real cause."

In their recent biography of Lewis, Thomas Danisi and John Jackson have attempted to exonerate Lewis from the stigma of mental illness by redefining *hypochondria* as "a cluster of chronic illnesses manifested by a fever stemming from an unknown cause."[28] The most they are willing to concede is that "a 'disorder of the mind' is an effect of intermittent fever."[29] Although they have correctly defined one clinical meaning of the word *hypochondria*, they have engaged in a curious form of special pleading. "Far from being the melancholic disposition that gave rise to imaginary illnesses, as American doctors had latterly considered it, the hypochondriasis that afflicted Meriwether Lewis was a debilitating complication of chronic untreated malaria," they argue.[30]

The context of Jefferson's reference to hypochondria proves that the Danisi-Jackson argument is baseless. Soon after reporting that Lewis had "from early life been subject to hypocondriac affections," Jefferson reports that during the White House years, "I observed at times sensible depressions of mind" in Lewis. The phrase *sensible depressions of mind* is Jefferson's own parsing of his diagnosis that Lewis suffered from "hypochondriac affections," i.e., melancholia. For Danisi and Jackson to pluck the phrase out of context and give it a reading that is palpably at odds with the clear meaning of the paragraph written by Jefferson, a man who chose his words with enormous care, is misleading. Jefferson immediately added, "It was a constitutional disposition in all the nearer branches of the family of his name." This could not possibly be a reference to malaria. Jefferson is either asserting that members of the Lewis family were subject to constitutional melancholia or that a streak of mental illness ran in the Lewis family. Some Lewis descendants have protested that Jefferson's assessment of the family malady was inaccurate and unfair. Perhaps so, but it was nonetheless Jefferson's assessment—that Meriwether Lewis's mental illness was not a condition unique to himself. Jefferson knew Lewis's father William Lewis (1733–79). He asserts that the "hypocondriac affections" were "more immediately inherited by him [Meriwether] from his father." Here, Jefferson implies that he had observed something of the same hypochondria (melancholia) in William Lewis, his neighbor in Albemarle County, Virginia.

Those who are convinced that Lewis was murdered invariably ask why Jefferson would entrust a transcontinental journey of such importance to a man he knew to be unstable. Jefferson himself must have been asked that question, or asked it of himself, because he provides an answer in his biographical sketch of Lewis: "I estimated their course [i.e., how serious the problem was] by what I had seen in the family." Translation: Lewis had a streak of melancholy, but Jefferson did not regard it as severe enough to jeopardize the success of the expedition. Other members of the Lewis family had been able to function adequately while suffering from the same malady, including the Revolutionary War veteran William Lewis. Jefferson also indirectly faced the question of his own possible responsibility for Lewis's suicide. If he knew Lewis to be a man prone to depression, how could he have sent him on so stressful a mission? Wouldn't that just make things worse? "During his Western expedition," Jefferson wrote, "the constant exertion which that required of all the faculties of body & mind, suspended these distressing affections."[31] It was only after his return to civilization that the old demons reappeared. "[A]fter his establishment at St. Louis in sedentary occupations they returned upon him with redoubled vigor, and began seriously to alarm his friends."[32]

This statement is perfectly in line with Jefferson's general attitude to depression—hectic activity leads to mental health, sedentary idleness produces ennui. To his eldest daughter Martha he wrote in 1787, "[N]othing can contribute more to it (moral rectitude always excepted) than the contracting a habit of industry and activity. Of all the cankers of human happiness none corrodes it with so silent, yet so baneful a tooth, as indolence. Body and mind both unemployed, our being becomes a burthen, and every object about us loathsome, even the dearest. Idleness begets ennui, ennui the hypochondria, and that a diseased body."[33] Notice that for Jefferson the mind leads the body, not the other way around.

To his younger daughter Maria, who possessed a retiring spirit, Jefferson wrote,

> I think I discover in you a willingness to withdraw from society more than is prudent. I am convinced our own happiness requires that we should continue to mix with the world, and to keep pace

with it as it goes; and that every person who retires from free communication with it is severely punished afterwards by the state of mind into which they get, and which can only be prevented by feeding our sociable principles, I can speak from experience on this subject. From 1793. to 1797. I remained closely at home, saw none but those who came there, and at length became very sensible of the ill effect it had upon my own mind, and of it's direct and irresistible tendency to render me unfit for society, and uneasy when necessarily engaged in it. I felt enough of the effect of withdrawing from the world then, to see that it led to an antisocial and misanthropic state of mind, which severely punishes him who gives in to it: and it will be a lesson I never shall forget as to myself.[34]

This letter was written on March 3, 1802. Jefferson may as well have been writing to Meriwether Lewis six years later.

If Jefferson said so boldly and unambiguously that Meriwether Lewis committed suicide, it is certain that Jefferson believed that is precisely what happened at Grinder's Inn. If Jefferson had believed Lewis was murdered, he would either have convinced his protégé President James Madison to launch a War Department investigation into the events of October 10–11, 1809, or expressed his doubts about the received narrative or at least qualified his statements in his biographical sketch. He could easily have written, 'Although his friends accepted the initial accounts of his suicide, subsequent reflection and the unanimous opinion of those who knew him best raise the possibility that some other explanation may ... .' Almost four years had passed since Lewis's death. The rumors and sensational reports swirling about the American frontier in the immediate aftermath of Lewis's death had been sifted and clarified in the years that followed. Lewis's servant John Pernier had visited Jefferson at Monticello to provide a first-person report of what happened at Grinder's Inn. Alexander Wilson had visited Lewis's grave and interviewed the Grinders. Jefferson had met personally with Clark and exchanged letters with him. James Neelly's letter to Jefferson announcing Lewis's death had been confirmed and deepened in letters to Jefferson from President James Madison, fellow members of the American Philosophical Society, and Captain Gilbert Russell, who had spent two weeks with Lewis at the center of his final journey. The fact that Jefferson wrote a categorical confirmation of Lewis's suicide, and then specifically vouched for the reliability of his account, should be enough to convince anyone of Jefferson's sincerity and certainty. "I have only to add," Jefferson wrote in 1813, "that all facts I have stated are either known to myself, or communicated by his family or others for whose truth I have no hesitation to make [myself] responsible."[35]

SUPPORT STRUCTURES

All modern understanding of suicide is indebted to Émile Durkheim's seminal *Suicide* (1897). Durkheim argued that the presence of intact social support structures greatly reduced the likelihood of suicide. Among the support structures he cited were birth family, marriage, parenthood, religious involvement, voluntary associations, friendship, and employment. When *any one* of these props is in place, suicide is dramatically less likely. It is only when an individual feels alone in life, indeed alone in the universe, that suicide becomes a real—not merely a rhetorical—possibility. It will be important to review each of these areas of Lewis's life in some detail.

In the course of a life, almost everyone has periods of struggle and difficulty. On April 8, 1816, Jefferson wrote to John Adams, "There are, I acknolege, even in the happiest life, some terrible convulsions, heavy set-offs against the opposite page of the account."[36] Although Jefferson was a disciplined stoic and one of the most cheerful men of American history, he understood melancholia, traces of which he had discerned in himself and a larger strain in his daughter Maria. "There are indeed," he wrote Adams, "gloomy and hypocondriac minds, inhabitants of diseased bodies, disgusted with the present, and despairing of the future; always counting that the worst will happen, because it may happen." Jefferson might have been describing the Meriwether Lewis of 1809. His response? "To these I say How much pain have cost us the evils which have never happened? My temperament is sanguine. I steer my bark with Hope in the head, leaving Fear astern. My hopes indeed sometimes fail; but not oftener than the forebodings of the gloomy."[37] It is quite possible that this characteristically upbeat attitude of Jefferson's was part of what made it impossible for Lewis to write to him when he could not steer his own bark with hope in the lead. The depressed and disturbed Lewis may have felt that the serene, productive, and preternaturally self-controlled Jefferson could not possibly understand his woes, or that he would simply respond with one of his *cankers of indolence* letters. Jefferson was a man of great friendliness and generosity of spirit, but his responses to the difficulties of others always bore a kind of generalized sympathy and stoic detachment. The historian James Ronda has written, "Euro-American explorers in the Age of Thomas Jefferson and Sir Joseph Banks might have thought themselves Reason's children, but passion was everywhere in their lives."[38] Jefferson always preferred the company of *Reason's children*.

John Adams suffered from serious but not crippling self-doubt all of his life. He poured out his anxieties and conviction that the world never quite recognized his greatness in diaries, anonymous newspaper articles, letters to virtually anyone who would accept his friendship (or just the letter!), to his many real and perceived enemies, and in political commentaries on the books he devoured and almost inevitably quarreled with. In one of his public essays, the long-suffering Adams compared himself to "an animal I have seen take hold of the end of a cord with his teeth, and be drawn slowly up by pulleys, through a storm of squils, crackers, and rockets, flashing and blazing around him every moment." Though the "scorching flames made him groan, and mourn, and roar, he would not let go."[39] Fortunately, Adams had married one of the most extraordinary women of American history. Abigail Adams, though she knew her husband's weaknesses better than anyone else in the republic, loved him, believed in him, and caressed him through his periods of gloom. Adams also nurtured his son John Quincy to be a reader, diplomat, and statesman in his own image. The result of those Pygmalion parental efforts was to create a son who was every bit his father's equal in knowledge and mindset, someone who became virtually another self for Adams to consult as he hacked and grumbled his way through life. Furthermore, Adams's almost unbearably prolific output of words must have served as a powerful catharsis for his mental woes. Plus he had a superb sense of humor, including the crucial ability to laugh at himself. These qualities Lewis lacked.

In 1782–3, five years before he became the principal creator of the greatest constitution in human history, James Madison courted a woman less than half his age. Madson was thirty-one and Catherine (Kitty) Floyd was fifteen. When she fell in love instead with a nineteen-year-old medical student named William Clarkson and sent Madison a Dear John letter, the future president guardedly poured out his troubles to his closest friend and mentor Jefferson. In reply, Jefferson wrote one of the letters for which he is justly regarded as the most graceful man of the age: "I sincerely lament the misadventure which has happened, from whatever cause it may have happened. Should it be final however, the world still presents the same and many other resources of happiness, and you possess many within yourself. Firmness of mind and unintermitting occupations will not long leave you in pain. No event has been more contrary to my expectations, and these were founded on what I thought a good knowlege of the ground. But of all machines ours is the most complicated and inexplicable."[40]

Even the stoic Jefferson buried four of his six children in their childhoods, and a fifth, Maria Jefferson Eppes, just a few weeks before the Lewis and Clark Expedition ventured into the mouth of the Missouri River. After the death of his wife Martha on September 6, 1782, Jefferson contemplated suicide, at least rhetorically. To his sister-in-law Elizabeth Wayles Eppes, Jefferson wrote, "This miserable kind of existence is really too burthensome to be borne, and were it not for the infidelity of deserting the sacred charge left me, I could not wish it's continuance a moment. For what could it be wished? All my plans of comfort and happiness reversed by a single event and nothing answering in prospect before me but a gloom unbrightened with one chearful expectation."[41] Jefferson was probably posing a bit in his contemplation of suicide, but he rightly explained that his children were reason enough to carry on. When the worst moment of his life came, Jefferson had friends, siblings, an extensive kinship network, meaningful work, and the responsibilities of parenting to lean on. Not to mention more than 200 slaves for whom he felt a paternalistic responsibility. His closest friend Madison soon convinced Congress to send Jefferson to Paris to serve as minister plenipotentiary and later America's minister to France. Madison rightly understood that Jefferson needed to be removed from the theater of his grief in order to recover his spirits. These support structures arguably saved Jefferson's life. Certainly they hastened his emotional recovery.

Loss, grief, unrequited love, career setbacks, unscrupulous colleagues, breakdowns of communication, misunderstandings, and random accidents are the stuff of the human condition. Hamlet's famous list of burdens on humanity includes bearing fardles, the pangs of despised love, the oppressor's wrong, the whips and scorns of time, the law's delay, the insolence of office, and the spurns that patient merit of the unworthy takes. Man, says Hamlet, is the receiver of "the slings and arrows of outrageous fortune," the "heartache, and the thousand natural shocks that flesh is heir to."[42] Any rational being would commit suicide, Hamlet argues, if he could only be sure that death were the Big Sleep. And yet only a tiny fraction of humans their "quietus make with a bare bodkin."

Jefferson was right. There are, "even in the happiest life, some terrible convulsions." But humans are enormously resilient. Even those, like Jefferson in the fall of 1782, who are convinced that they have no reason to live any longer, almost always find a way to go on. Many who feel prostrated by the burdens of life survive to achieve genuine happiness. Suicide rates vary according to climate and nation state, but in the United States the rate has been remarkably steady over time, about 11 per 100,000 or .01 percent. The natural resilience of humankind is nearly miraculous.

In 1809, Meriwether Lewis was certainly suffering from some of the shocks on Hamlet's list. He knew the pangs of despised love at the hands of such women as Letitia Breckenridge and others. The bureaucrats in James Madison's War Department had given him a full dose of the insolence of office and the spurns that patient merit of the unworthy takes. He had borne his share of fardles in the Bitterroot Mountains, and his colleague Pierre Cruzatte had delivered one of the unnatural shocks that flesh is heir to by way of a .52 caliber musket ball.

For those who are reasonably familiar with the biography of Meriwether Lewis, particularly the well-documented period between 1801–1809, any examination of the clinical, psychological, or sociological literature on suicide creates what has been called the "shock of recognition." Any examination of the known risk factors for suicide suggests that Lewis was precisely the sort of person who commits suicide, not the very epitome of "the anti-suicide type," as Richard Dillon, John Guice, John Bakeless, and others of the murder school have argued.[43] Those who argue that what we know of Lewis's personality proves that he is decidedly the kind of man who *does not commit suicide* seem not to have read the relevant literature. The following are common risk factors for suicide:[44]

✓ Suicide is far more common among those who are not married than among married individuals. The risk factor increases for those who have been unsuccessful in their courting lives, and individuals of doubtful sexual identity. Clark married fifteen months after the expedition returned to St. Louis. Lewis never married and never achieved a successful romantic relationship, so far as we know.

✓ Suicide is more common among those who have lost a parent early in life than for those whose parents die after their children have reached full maturity. The risk factor increases for those whose parents die suddenly or violently. Lewis's father William Lewis died in November 1779, when Meriwether was just five years old.

✓ Suicide is more common for those who live away from their blood relatives. In 1809 Lewis's brother John Marks was living in Virginia. His brother Reuben Lewis was stationed on the Missouri River in today's Montana, and his mother Lucy Marks was living in Albemarle County, Virginia. He had not seen his mother since late 1807, a period approaching two years.

✓ Suicide is more common among those who are away from their home country than for those who remain in the country of their birth. Although Louisiana Territory was technically part of United States in 1809, it was still largely foreign territory. The majority of residents were Native Americans, particularly Osage Indians, and French and Spanish nationals. Though most of these "others" reluctantly acknowledged the technical sovereignty of the United States, many still regarded St. Louis as a French or Spanish community and the United States as an occupying power. One of the vouchers that the War Department challenged was the cost Lewis incurred in having the laws of Louisiana Territory translated into French for the benefit of citizens whose presence pre-dated the Louisiana Purchase.[45]

✓ Suicide is more common among the childless than among those with children. In fact, studies have shown that the more children a couple have, even if the strain of feeding and raising those children is debilitating, the less likely either parent is to commit suicide. Clark eventually had eight children.

✓ We know that untreated depression is today's number one cause of suicide. Lewis was almost certainly experiencing a low point in life from his serious legal problems, rejection by love interests, and feelings that he had not lived up to his mentor's expectations, among other issues.

Lewis and Clark each brought a personal companion along on their transcontinental journey.[46] Clark brought his personal slave and valet York. Our view that slavery is an odious and morally repugnant institution must not obscure the fact that masters and slaves frequently managed to form relationships of mutual concern, affection, and dependency. York had been assigned to young Bill Clark at very early age, and he became Clark's actual property in 1799 after the death of William's father John on July 29, 1799. They had spent an enormous amount of time together by the time they ventured up the Missouri River. Clark was sufficiently dependent on York that he took the liberty of taking him along on an official US Army expedition. Beginning on April 7, 1805, York slept with the captains in the "official" leadership tipi rented from Toussaint Charbonneau. He frequently carried a gun and · frequently was trusted to venture away from the boats alone.

Lewis came from the same slaveholding class of Virginia and Kentucky gentry that produced William Clark, but he did not bring a black slave with him on the journey. He seems to have had a more enlightened view of slavery than his partner in discovery. After the expedition, when Clark was so frustrated by York that he thrashed him and threatened to sell him, Lewis carefully intervened. On December 7, 1808, Clark wrote to his brother Jonathan, "Govr. Lewis has insisted on my only hireing him out in Kentucky which perhaps will be best.... I do not wish him again in this Country until he applies himself to Come and give over that wife of his."[47] Clark's unenlightened post-expedition relations with his slave York have been explored in excruciating detail in each of the recent biographies of William Clark.[48]

Lewis's personal companion on the journey was a Newfoundland dog named Seaman. Seaman gets mentioned in the expedition journals frequently and more lovingly than virtually any other participant. Lewis spoke on more than one occasion of the "segacity of my dog,"[49] which impressed Indians up and down the Lewis and Clark trail. Clark typically handled the boats while Lewis wandered on shore with his rifle, notebook, collection bag, and Seaman. Lewis apparently purchased the dog for $20 in Pittsburgh some time before the keelboat was completed in late August 1803. That's probably an important detail of the Seaman story. He was purchased as an expedition dog—almost as a mascot. His usefulness may have begun in Pittsburgh on

August 31, 1803, and ended in St. Louis on September 23, 1806. That doesn't quite square with our sentimental view of Seaman's place in American mythology, but it accommodates those facts that have come down to us.

Nobody is quite sure what happened to Seaman. All we know for sure is that the dog made its last appearance in the journals on July 15, 1806, on the return journey, and was never mentioned by any journal keeper again. On that day Lewis wrote, "the musquetoes continue to infest us in such manner that we can scarcely exist; for my own part I am confined by them to my bier at least ¾ths of my time. my dog even howls with the torture he experiences from them, they are almost insupportable, they are so numerous that we frequently get them in our thrats as we breath.——"[50] Nor is Seaman ever mentioned in the letters and newspaper accounts that followed the return of the expedition. Lewis did not mention Seaman when he discussed St. Louis living arrangements with William Clark in his letter of May 29, 1808. People who have genuinely bonded with pets almost never abandon them. In fact, in modern times, people who are dying or need to die frequently go to elaborate lengths to make arrangements for their pets in the aftermath of their deaths.

What I am about to suggest will amuse some and perhaps offend others, but I believe that Lewis would probably not have killed himself if his dog had been with him on the Natchez Trace in October 1809. Studies show that many people are suicidal but comparatively few commit suicide. A whole series of factors need to converge into a kind of perfect psychic storm before someone takes his or her own life. The presence of any ameliorating factor generally forestalls the suicide. That factor can be something as seemingly trivial as the need to care for a pet. The unconditional love and physical affection of a dog might provide just enough reassurance, affirmation, and attention to get a desperate person like Lewis through the dark night of the soul. People who suffer from physical maladies or mental illness are frequently able to rouse themselves to care for a pet. The simple fact of having some other living thing to care for livens and in some cases actually prolongs the life of individuals in decline. Had Seaman survived the journey, or lived long enough to be Lewis's companion in St. Louis between March 8, 1808 and September 4, 1809, it is unlikely that Lewis would have spiraled downward as he did.

At the risk of inviting still more disbelief, I believe that the three most important relationships in Lewis's life were with his mother Lucy Marks, his partner in discovery William Clark, and with his dog Seaman. In the short list of those "members" of the expedition who receive favorable mention in the journals of Meriwether Lewis, Seaman ranks virtually as high as Drouillard, and well higher than John Shields, Hugh McNeal or Nathaniel Pryor. During the critical last months of his life in St. Louis, Lewis makes no mention of Seaman. Nor does anyone else. It seems likely that Seaman was gone or dead long before Lewis left St. Louis for the last time. The total absence of any mention of the dog in the three years that followed the expedition's return suggests that Seaman was no longer Lewis's companion. Lewis's mother lived almost a thousand miles away. Clark was absorbed in his marriage, in the birth of his first child, and in his career. Assuming that Seaman was no longer with him, Lewis was effectively cut off from two of those crucial intimate relationships, and the nature of the third—with Clark—had been fundamentally redefined by marriage.

The evidence from the journals suggests that Lewis had a much warmer, or more warmly expressed, feeling for animals than he did for his fellow human beings. He frequently wrote about the sufferings of animals with great sympathy. It's hard to believe Lewis would be capable of jettisoning Seaman without a paragraph of tribute in his journal or an explanation of why he could no longer take responsibility for the dog. It is possible that during the extremely hectic period of the return journey between July 3-August 12, 1806, Seaman died or wandered off, and nobody had time to record the fact in the expedition's journals. That seems pretty unlikely. It is odd that no journal keeper mentioned Seaman in any capacity between July 15 and September 23, 1806. But the silence of the journal keepers is more likely to signify that Seaman did nothing especially remarkable during that period of the journey and that the journal keepers were so preoccupied with their approaching homecoming that they did not find time to write about the dog. Far the most likely scenario is that Seaman survived the full journey but slipped below the radar of journal notice in the hectic summer of 1806, then either died or remained behind in St. Louis when Lewis traveled to Monticello, Washington, DC, and Philadelphia. It's hard to imagine Lewis, Mahlon Dickerson, and Seaman cavorting together in the intellectual capital of America in 1807.

We simply don't know. But the evidence suggests that Seaman was not with Lewis in the last weeks of his life. Had the dog been with him, it seems likely that he would have survived the night of October 11, 1809.

One of the persistent popular traditions about Lewis and Clark is that Seaman was with Lewis on his last fateful journey, and that after his master's death in Tennessee, Seaman lingered on Lewis's grave until his own death. The story has the feel of being apocryphal. In the absence of any contemporary documentation of the dog's disposition at the end of the expedition or the end of Lewis's life, it is impossible to credit the legend of Seaman's presence at Grinder's Inn.[51]

WOMEN AND SEXUALITY

Meriwether Lewis never married. So far as we know he never had a sustained relationship with a woman. If the journals of the expedition are candid and complete, Lewis abstained from sexual relations with American Indian women in the course of the journey, even when it was a diplomatic affront to decline the unusual hospitality gestures of his Indian hosts.[52] In all of the documentary record that has been left to us, there is no evidence that Lewis had sexual intercourse at any point in his life. It seems unlikely that he was a lifelong celibate, but it is at least possible. Larry Morris has written, "By 1809, Lewis by all rights should have been living prosperously, publishing books, and preparing for marriage. Instead, he was deep in debt, unpublished, and alone, with no prospects for marriage, battling a host of personal and political problems."[53]

Why didn't Lewis get married and start a family like his friend Clark?

We know that Lewis thought about women in the course of his journey. He named a geopolitically important river in Montana for his cousin-once-removed Maria Wood, who had been thirteen years old when he last saw her in Virginia.[54] With the awkwardness that characterized his discussions of women generally, Lewis wrote on June 8, 1805, at the mouth of the Marias River: "[I]t is true that the hue of the waters of this turbulent and troubled stream but illy comport with the pure celestial virtues and amiable qualifications of that lovely fair one; but on the other hand it is a noble river; one destined to become in my opinion an object of contention between the two great powers of America and Great Britain with rispect to the adjustment of the North westwardly boundary of the former; and that it will become one of the most interesting brances of the Missouri in a commercial point of view ... ."[55] One hopes he did not send this endorsement to Miss Wood. Probably Lewis thought he was being courtly or gallant or perhaps just witty in writing this passage, but a man who begins a tribute to a woman by invoking the adjectives *turbulent* and *troubled* is not on the road to matrimonial bliss. Danisi and Jackson rightly conclude, "The naming of Maria's River must have been more sentimental than romantic."[56]

The oddity of Meriwether Lewis's sexual persona was even more in evidence on the Pacific Coast when he observed the negligent clothing style of coastal women. He wrote,

[W]hen this vest is woarn the breast of the woman is concealed, but without it which is almost always the case, they are exposed, and from the habit of remaining loose and unsuspended grow to great length particularly in aged women in many of whom I have seen the bubby reach as low as the waist. The garment which occupys the waist, and from thence as low as nearly to the knee before and the ham, behind, cannot properly be denominated a petticoat, in the common acceptation of that term ... . the whole being of sufficient thickness when the female stands erect to conceal those parts usually covered from formiliar view, but when she stoops or places herself in many other attitudes, this battery of Venus is not altogether impervious to the inquisitive and penetrating eye of the amorite.[57]

The *ham*. It is important to remember that, by the time he wrote these words, Lewis had not had sexual relations or even the company of a civilized woman for more than two years. Perhaps any young man (he was thirty-one) so deprived of sexual contact would develop, in the presence of largely naked aborigines, "the inquisitive and penetrating eye of the amorite," but not everyone would include such a revelation in his journal. There is, moreover, a strange humor at work here, which is easier to point to than analyze. Lewis confesses that observing the sexual organs of Indian women is not inadvertent. When he writes that their "battery of Venus is not altogether impervious" to his sight, he is, of course, admitting that he had to strain to catch a glimpse of the Indian women's pudenda. A view which he then finds repulsive. "I think," he writes, "the most disgusting sight I have ever beheld is these dirty naked wenches."[58] Meriwether Lewis was a complicated and fastidious man. No doubt Freud would say he was merely a man.

Clark never wrote about women in the strange manner of his partner in discovery. He did not write of women's *hams,* and he never called Sacagawea an *object.* Clark married—twice. Lewis was a lifelong bachelor.

Danisi and Jackson rightly note that Lewis and Clark were, when they returned from the wilderness, "essentially strangers to society beyond their immediate families."[59] Three years of travel where the foot of civilized man had never trodden had removed them from the circles in which they would have been expected to nurture relationships with women that might have led to marriage. Clark was fortunate to reconnect with Julia Hancock in Fincastle, whom he had last seen when she was just ten or eleven years old, and after whom he named an un-turbulent and un-troubled river in Montana. By all accounts, Clark quickly settled into a happy marriage.

Lewis was not so fortunate. Danisi and Jackson write, "He was the reigning national hero whose exploits exploring a vast wilderness could be read in prestigious newspapers. And he was a handsome, well-cut bachelor who danced well at the balls he attended. But something didn't click."[60] Although his extant correspondence mentions a number of women, most of them represented by ellipses so severe that his biographers have not been able to ascertain whom he was pursuing, Lewis seems never to have advanced even to the far suburbs of an authentic romance. There was something in his approach to women that remained perpetually adolescent, immature, inauthentic. Off. The women he pursued may have recognized this. If he spoke to women as strangely as he wrote about them in his journal, his relations with *damsels,* tawny or otherwise, must have been *turbulent* and *troubled,* indeed. Probably the *battery of Venus* held. In his letter congratulating Clark on the progress of his courtship of Julia Hancock, for example, Lewis briefly addressed his own prospects. He essentially informed Clark that he wasn't really interested in hearing his raptures on the beauties of

Julia Hancock or the success of his courtship. "I must subjoin a wish that you would make your disertations on the subject of _____ to Miss _____ as short as is consonate with your amorous desires, for god's sake do not whisper any attachment to Miss _____ or I am undone."[61] Given the Latinate vagueness and puerility of the letters Lewis wrote about his romantic life during this period, it is no wonder no woman chose to *subjoin* him. Danisi and Jackson call this sort of love discourse "quaintly evasive."[62]

Lewis spent several months in Philadelphia in the spring of 1807. He resumed a friendship he had begun with Mahlon Dickerson back in 1802. Mahlon's diary is the source of a number of important details about Lewis's post-expedition life. On November 3, 1807, he wrote a remarkable letter to Dickerson. After asking Dickerson to help supervise his brother John Marks's education, Lewis wrote:

> So much for business, now for the *girls*. My little affair with Miss A___n R____ph has had neither beginning nor end on her part; pr. Contra, on my own, it has had both. The fact is, that on enquiry I found that she was previously engaged, and therefore dismissed every idea of prosecuting my pretentions in that quarter, and am now a *perfect widower with rispect to love.*[63]

The identity of Miss A___n R____ph has not been determined. It is quite possible that Lewis was referring to President Jefferson's granddaughter Ann Randolph. Miss Randolph married a man named Charles Bankhead in 1808, so her age and her engagement to Bankhead make her a likely candidate. If Lewis was courting Ann Randolph, two things are true and another possible. First, the published family correspondence of Jeffersons and the Randolphs makes no mention of Lewis as a potential beau for Ann. The romantic, shy, awkward, and sometimes unrealistic Lewis may have felt an attraction that he never expressed, or his protestations may not have been regarded as serious by the Randolph family. Second, Ann would have been better off with Lewis than with Charles Bankhead, who was a brutish and alcoholic man who beat his wife and stabbed his brother-in-law on the streets of Charlottesville. Third, it is at least possible that Lewis pursued Ann Randolph in a way that offended her family, including Jefferson, and that the supposed post-expedition breach between Jefferson and Lewis, or at least the awkward silence that grew between them, was related to tensions emanating from some unpleasant courtship incident or confrontation. About this time, Dickerson wrote cryptically in his diary, "my Friend Capt. L. in trouble."[64] This could mean almost anything, but it is unlikely to have signified a positive development in Lewis's life. All of the above is fairly wild conjecture, but it certainly cannot be ruled out that one of the young women who caught Lewis's eye was the granddaughter of the president.

Whatever happened with A___ R____ph had a destabilizing effect on Lewis. His letter to Dickerson continues:

Thus floating on the *surface of occasion*, I feel all that restlessness, that inquietude, that certain indiscribable something common to old bachelors, which I cannot avoid thinking my dear fellow, proceeds, from that *void in our hearts*, which might, or ought to be better filled. Whence it comes I know not, but certain it is, that I never felt less like a heroe than at the present moment. What may be my next adventure god knows, but on this I am determined, *to get a wife*.[65]

It's impossible to gauge the emotional tone of this letter. It may be playful. It may be dead serious. It may be both at once. It may be that Lewis was attempting to cast a genuine romantic setback and a severe disappointment into the rhetoric of lugubrious comedy, a kind of devil-may-care bemusement at his romantic ineptitude. It may be that he meant precisely what he wrote: that he felt serious restlessness and disquietude, that he feared he would remain a bachelor forever, that there was an unmistakable void in his heart that he knew needed to be filled, that it meant little to be a national hero if he couldn't even leverage that fame into a successful sexual and romantic relationship with a woman, and that he was, now more than ever, determined to find a woman who would marry him. The pose of lightheartedness in this letter may be nothing more than a coping mechanism for a seriously unhappy and lonely man who was watching his best friend and partner in discovery prosper in romance while he failed miserably. In light of the fact that Lewis remained a restless "old bachelor," and in light of the sense of "restlessness … inquietude … and indiscribable something," that led to his suicide, we have no choice but to read this letter as a cry of anguish by a man whose life was seriously off track. This is as revealing, and self-revealing, a letter as Lewis ever wrote.

At the end of the same letter to Dickerson, Lewis wrote:

Do let me hear from you as frequently as you can and when you have no subject of more importance, talk about *the girls*. You see already from certain innate workings of the spirit, the changes which have taken place in my dispositions and that I am now so much unlike my former self that I speak of those bewitching gipsies as *a secondary consideration*. I sincerely wish, my dear fellow, that candour would permit me to say as much with respect to Miss E___ B___y of Philadelphia, whose memory will still remain provokingly important in spite of all my philosophy. Have you heard from her? Have you seen her? How is she? Is she will, sick, dead or married? Oh! I had forgotten you have no particular acquaintance with her. Ask your coadjutor, R. Rush, and tell me.[66]

This is the stuff of arrested adolescence. Thomas Jefferson stopped writing letters like this one when he was twenty-four years old.

In the winter of 1807–08, as he made his way slowly in the direction St. Louis, Lewis met Letitia Breckenridge (aged sixteen) and her younger sister Elizabeth at the home of Clark's father-in-law George Hancock. Lewis was smitten. His brother Reuben reported that Miss Breckenridge was "one of the most beautiful women I have ever seen, both as to form & features."[67] Lewis—somehow—drove her away. Reuben wrote, "[U]nfortunately for his Excellency she left the neighborhood 2 days after our arrival so that he was disappointed in his design of addressing her." When she learned "of the Governours intention of Coarting her" she declared that "if she remained it would look too much like a challenge."[68] To escape Lewis's apparently unwanted attention, Letitia accompanied her father on a journey to Richmond. Reuben confessed, "I should like to have her as a sister."[69] William Preston, Julia Hancock's brother-in-law, suggested that Lewis pay court to Elizabeth Breckenridge, instead. He declined. "I consider Miss E B a charming girl," he wrote, "but such was my passion for her sister that my soul revolts at the idea of attempting to make her my wife, and shall not consequently travel that road in quest of matrimony."[70] Lewis had integrity.

That Lewis knew how to appreciate female beauty is certain. On November 23, 1803, at Cape Girardeau, as the expedition ascended the Mississippi River towards St. Louis, he dined at the home of the French Canadian patriarch Louis Lorimer. Lewis wrote, "Lorimer has a large family of very handsome Children three of which have attained the age of puberty; the daughter is remarkably handsome & dresses in a plain yet fashonable stile or such as is now Common in the Atlantic States among the respectable people of the middle class. she is an agreeable affible girl, & much the most descent looking feemale I have seen since I left the settlement in Kentuckey a little below Louisville."[71] Apparently nothing came of the encounter.

So far as we know Lewis proposed to women, or came close to proposing, twice in his life. The first was to Letitia Breckenridge, who left town rather than face that prospect. The second was to an unidentified woman. In March 1807 Clark wrote to Lewis discussing some loose ends of the expedition, several of them involving Robert Frazer. After dispatching official business and announcing that "I shall proceed without delay to St. Louis," Clark announced that Julia Hancock had agreed to marry him early in 1808, at which time he would "be in possession of what I have never yet experienced." The prompt and dutiful Clark, who took up his post in St. Louis in April 1807, hoped "my absence from the Louisiana will not be displeasing to the govermt." Then Clark turned to Lewis's marital prospects. "My F. [friend] your choice is one I highly approve, but should the thing not take to your wish I have discovered a most lovly girl Butiful rich possessing those accomplishments which is calculated to make a man hapy—inferior to you—but to few others the Daughter of C—His politicks is in opposition to yours."[72] The identity of the butiful Miss C—, the daughter of a vile Federalist, is unknown. "The thing" with Lewis's unidentified "choice" did not take. Had she or Miss C___ or Letitia Breckenridge or anyone else agreed to marry him, the entire story of his post-expedition life might have been different. It is hard to imagine Lewis committing suicide if he had not been, at the time of his collapse, "a musty, fusty, rusty old bachelor."[73]

Donald Jackson concludes, "Lewis's search for a wife was dogged and inexplicably futile."[74] John Bakeless' conclusion reflects the old western history, not the new: "What, after all, is a woman, compared to solitude in the wilderness, Indians, the bright face of danger, the high adventure of the Rockies, canoes in foaming rapids, a grizzly hunt, or sword blades flashing in the sun, a flag that flutters over steel-tipped columns, the cadenced tramp of doughboys at your back, and polished brass and bugles, calling, calling, and rifles crashing smartly to 'Present'?"[75]

LEWIS'S MOTHER LUCY MARKS

John Bakeless's theory was that perhaps no woman could measure up to the standard set by Lewis's mother Lucy. "What mere girl could approach the grace, the charm, the intelligence, and the tremendous vigor of his fascinating mother?"[76] The sole extant painting of Lucy Marks clearly exhibits her intelligence, but grace and charm make no appearance. Because of the early death of his biological father, Lewis may well have developed a strong but ambivalent relationship with his mother, particularly after her relatively quick remarriage, followed by the relocation of the family from the nation's premier state to godforsaken Georgia.

The letters we have from Lewis to his mother exhibit nothing but filial respect and affection. In his letter from Fort Mandan, dated March 31, 1805, Lewis assured his mother, "So far, we have experienced more difficulty from the navigation of the Missouri, than danger from the Savages." Most of the letter is a summary of the navigation challenges of the Missouri River, in terms rather detailed and technical for a missive to one's mama. Towards the end of the letter Lewis wrote, "You may expect me in Albemarle about the last of next September twelve months. I request that you will give yourself no uneasiness with rispect to my fate, for I assure you that I feel myself perfectly as safe as I should do in Albemarle; and the only difference between 3 or 4 thousand miles and 130, is that I can not have the pleasure of seeing you as often as I did while at Washington."[77] This from a man who believed he was about to walk off the map of the known world.

Lewis's mother Lucy lived at the other end of the country at a time when it was extremely difficult to maintain communication over so vast a territory, particularly in a frontier separated from the contiguous settlements of the United States by hundreds of miles. If, as most commentators say without much proof, the relations between Lewis and his mother were very close, they had not seen each other very much in recent years. From July 1803 until December 1806 they were separated. During this period Lewis wrote her several letters, including the superb one from Fort Mandan in April 1805. He had seen her for a few days on his triumphant return to Charlottesville in December 1806 before he left for his official national homecoming in Washington, DC. Probably he saw her in 1807 and possibly even in early 1808, but he did not see her ever again after the first days of 1808. He arrived in St. Louis on March 8, 1808, and remained there until his fatal last journey. Lewis was planning to bring his mother to St. Louis to live with or near him. His last known letter to her was written on December 1, 1808. Aside from informing his mother that "I have been detained here much longer than I expected but hope to get off shortly. You may expect me in the course of this winter," Lewis wrote mostly about land transactions, particularly the plantation he had purchased to accommodate her when she moved to St. Louis.

> I entend giving you [the new plantation] for your relinquishment of dower to the lands on Ivy creek. it was my intention to give you a life estate in that property but if you wish it I have no objection to convey it to you in fee simple. This place which I have selected for your residence is in the most healthy part of the country; it is an agreeable situation one with which I am convinced you will be pleased. I have paid about three thousand dollars for the lands which I have purchased, fifteen hundred dollars more will become due in May and twelve hundred more on the 1st of May 1810 – to meet these engagements it will be necessary to sell the Ivy creek lands or at least a part of them, and for this purpose I shall shortly inclose to Mr. Dabney Car[r] a power of attorney to dispose of them.[78]

Even today, with a breathtaking array of pharmaceutical amelioratives available to people suffering from depression and mental illness, separation from loved ones can be a prerequisite for suicide. Dr. Thomas Joiner argues that even when a person's primary relationships are close and healthy, physical separation greatly increases the likelihood of suicide.[79] In the last hours of his life, Lewis was isolated from the most important beings in his life. Jefferson was at Monticello. Lucy Marks was at Locust Hill in Albemarle County, Virginia, only a dozen miles from Monticello. Reuben Lewis was among the Mandan. John Marks was either in Virginia or Pennsylvania. And Clark, who was closest to hand, was in Kentucky approaching his family's estates at Louisville. He was not "Comeing on," and he would not "Come to his releaf,"[80] as Lewis apparently hoped and expected.

The Problem of Deism

Lewis seems to have been a deist, like his master Jefferson. Although Lewis was certainly capable of thinking for himself, he tended to ape Jefferson's ways. He adopted Jefferson's orthographic peculiarities, including his tendency to start sentences without the benefit of a capital letter. He was, like Jefferson, an ardent Republican; Clark mock-apologized to him for marrying the daughter of a Federalist. Lewis kept daily weather logs. He was a thoroughgoing Anglophobe. Like his master, Lewis knew how to "enjoy the repast which the hand of civilization has prepared for us."[81]

Never once in the journals does Lewis address himself to God or to Jesus. His few invocations of the concept of divine providence are philosophically detached. On July 15, 1806, for example, after McNeal narrowly escaped being killed by a grizzly bear, Lewis wrote, "[T]hese bear are a most tremenduous animal; it seems that the hand of providence has been most wonderfully in our favor with rispect to them, or some of us would long since have fallen a sacrifice to their farosity.   there seems to be a sertain fatality attatched to the neighbourhood of these falls, for there is always a chapter of accedents prepared for us during our residence at them."[82] This is not the God of the Christian tradition. Fate and destiny make their appearance from time to time. When things seem to Lewis extra-rational, he is capable of musing, "It now seemed to me that all the beasts of the neighbourhood had made a league to distroy me, or that some fortune was disposed to amuse herself at my expence," and that the landscape of Montana "from the succession of curious adventures wore the impression on my mind of inchantment."[83]

The best evidence we have of Lewis's deism is his account of his "discovery" of the source of the "mighty & heretofore deemed endless Missouri," on August 12, 1805, just below Lemhi Pass. Lewis drank from the fountain of the great river and congratulated himself on fulfilling a longstanding dream. At the end of his famous journal entry, he wrote, "[T]wo miles below McNeal had exultingly stood with a foot on each side of this little rivulet and thanked his god that he had lived to bestride the mighty & heretofore deemed endless Missouri."[84] *His god.* The god of the lower case. McNeal was almost certainly a Catholic. There is an intriguing narrative strategy at work here. Lewis might easily have omitted any reference to McNeal's actions at the source of the Missouri River. That would have been more in keeping with his need to be alone at key moments of triumph and discovery. Lewis wants us to know that *he* did not himself bestride the source rivulet of the Missouri. At the same time he knows that McNeal's dramatic gesture adds a charming sense of epic grandeur to the moment. Lewis makes sure we know that *he* did not thank God for permitting him to reach the source of the endless river, but that such gratitude was appropriate .

for a man of different (and lesser) religious sensibilities. Probably Lewis felt a certain level of condescension towards poor McNeal, a throwback to papal credulity and superstition in the brave new world of science and reason. But McNeal's prayer nevertheless deepens the moment when Lewis finally reached the source of the Missouri, so long as he can both invoke the gesture and distance himself from it at the same time. In other words, in a certain sense Lewis gets it both ways. McNeal becomes his stand-in for a more traditional response to reaching the source of the great river, a kind of serio-comic doppelganger Lewis can simultaneously borrow from and gently sneer at. The moment is characteristic of Lewis's emotional detachment from other members of the Corps of Discovery. It's almost as if Lewis wishes he were the kind of man who could let himself bestride the source rivulet of the Missouri and pour out his sense of triumph and relief in unguarded terms. But he is trapped in his own persona, forced to articulate even the most powerful personal satisfaction in the conventional language of high-mindedness and heroic achievement. It's hard to know which of the two men had the more satisfying experience at the source of the Missouri, but McNeal was certainly the more humble and probably the more candid. Lewis, a scientist, a rationalist, a deist, and a Jeffersonian, had no one to thank, not even his patron. His exaltation was all about himself—*I* had accomplished one of those grand objects upon which *MY* mind had been fixed for many years. Judge then of the pleasure *I* felt.

When Scottish explorer Mungo Park finally reached the banks of the Niger River after a hard journey in 1796, he wrote a passage strikingly similar to Lewis's at the source of the Missouri: "Looking forwards, I saw with infinite pleasure the great object of my mission—the long sought for majestic Niger, glittering in the morning sun, as broad as the Thames at Westminster, and flowing *to the eastward*. I hastened to the brink, and having drunk of the water, lifted up my fervent thanks in prayer to the Great Ruler of all things, for having thus far crowned my endeavour with success."[85] Lewis would not have been capable of those last words.

Mungo Park was as much a representative of the second great age of discovery as Lewis. He was a physician and a member of the Scottish Enlightenment. That he was a deist is proved by his preference for "Great Ruler" over "God." But he took time to thank the ruler of all things, even so. Lewis not only couldn't let himself do that, but the manner in which he distanced himself from poor superstitious McNeal suggests that he found the incident a little embarrassing. Or perhaps he would have liked to have invoked providence on that momentous occasion, but he just couldn't let down his rationalist guard to do so. The same Lewis who determined always to be the first to reach the great discovery points of the expedition, and who seldom named his colleagues on such missions, here is content to let a subordinate engage in the histrionics of exploration.

When Park was set upon by banditti and stripped to his trousers and his boots, "five hundred miles from the nearest European settlement," he prayed for deliverance and put himself under "the protecting eye of Providence."[86] At no point in the course of the Lewis and Clark expedition did Lewis pray—so far as we know. In the one moment of the expedition when prayer would seem inevitable, at the funeral of Charles Floyd on August 20, 1804, the text the captains were working from was Baron von Steuben's *Regulations for the Order and Discipline of the Troops of the United States* rather than the Bible. So far as we know, no copy of the Bible was included in the traveling library of the expedition or the kit of any participant.

The problem of deism is that it depersonalizes God and denies the divinity of Jesus. The deist God is a kind of celestial Newtonian mechanic or physicist who created a clock-like universe, suspended the planets in the firmament, left the law of gravitation in charge, and walked away. That left no God or god to pray to. The deist God is exalted (and reduced) to "Thou Great First Cause," in Alexander Pope's *Universal Prayer* of 1738.[87] Deists tended to view Jesus as a great ethicist and moral reformer, but not the Son of God. In a letter to his nephew Peter Carr, Jefferson described Jesus as "a man of illegitimate birth, of a benevolent heart, enthusiastic mind, who set out without pretensions to divinity, ended in believing them, & was punished capitally for sedition by being gibbeted according to the Roman law which punished the first commission of that offence by whipping, & the second by exile or death *in furca*."[88] There is little room for the universal redeemer for the sins of mankind in that formulation. The deist's Jesus is thus a man to emulate, but not to pray to.

In one of his late letters to Jefferson, John Adams summarized a modified deism perfectly. "I could express my Faith in shorter terms," he wrote. "He who loves the Workman and his Work, and does what he can to preserve and improve it, shall be accepted of him."[89]

Modern studies of prayer indicate that it is efficacious and spiritually comforting even to people who have serious doubts about the existence of God. It is a form of self-humbling, self-catechizing, and surrender that enables a troubled person to re-center her or himself. The centrality of God (or a Higher Power) in twelve-step programs is not about redemption but about surrendering any lingering sense of being master of one's life. In other words, prayer can be an important ritual of self-soothing even to those who skeptically wonder if anyone is listening. So far as we know, the adult Lewis never engaged in prayer, even when his life had collapsed into genuine disarray. Had he been a practicing Christian, Lewis might have been better able to cope with his troubles. Among other things, he would have had access to ministers, whose concern for their pastoral flock has dimensions that extend far beyond Christian doctrine.

The cliché is that there are no atheists in foxholes. It is, of course, possible that Lewis had a richer spiritual life than is indicated in his writings. It seems unlikely, however, for when the trouble came, he had nowhere to turn, no God to pray to, no redeemer or intercessor to call upon, no Christian consolation, no minister to lean on, and no sacred text to scrutinize for comfort or answers. The problem with being a deist is that it leaves you alone in a universe that deserves praise and veneration but answers no calls—not from the source of the Missouri or the heart of the Natchez Trace.

No Children

Lewis never had any children that we can be sure of. He did in some sense *adopt* one of the children of Rene Jusseaume, the French Canadian who served as the expedition's Mandan interpreter at Fort Mandan. Thirteen-year-old Toussaint Jusseaume had accompanied his parents and the Mandan leader Sheheke-shote to Washington, DC, in the autumn of 1806. When the United States finally sent the Sheheke-shote and Jusseaume families home in the summer of 1809, Toussaint stayed behind in St. Louis. On May 13, 1809, Lewis entered into a formal indenture with the boy. It is not clear how often Lewis saw Toussaint, who was partly French and partly Mandan. It is possible, even probable, that in "adopting" Toussaint Jusseaume Lewis was merely fulfilling Jefferson's instructions of June 20, 1803, in which the president wrote, "If any of them should wish to have some of their young people brought up with us, & taught such arts as may be useful to them, we will receive, instruct & take care of them."[90] The evidence suggests that Lewis never developed the kind of attachment for young Jusseaume that Clark had established with Jean Baptiste Charbonneau, whom he dandled on the trail and affectionately called "my little dancing boy."[91] Lewis appears to have "adopted" Toussaint Jusseaume as a matter of American Indian policy, not as a matter of the heart.

If Lewis fathered any children on the trail, as is sometimes alleged, he never acknowledged them and never met them.

When the trouble came, Lewis had no children whose very existence would force him to attend to something other than his own concerns, no children to provide him a fund of unconditional love, no children to remind him that life advances inexorably on from generation to generation.

Once he had finally arrived in St. Louis, Lewis rented an expensive home for himself *and* Clark on the corner of South Main and Spruce streets. In a letter to Clark of May 29, 1808, he outlined his proposed living arrangements. Lewis described the house he had rented from a Mr. Campbell in lavish detail, the way one might describe a newly-discovered house to one's absent spouse. Then, as if catching himself in the realization that he and Clark were no longer bachelor roommates, Lewis added, "Should wee find on experiment that we have not sufficient room in the house, I can obtain an Office somewhere in the neighborhood and still consider myself your messmate."[92] The experiment turned out precisely as Lewis predicted. Once William and Julia Hancock Clark were settled into the residence, it became clear that Lewis was a supernumerary. The Clarks were still in the first flush of their marriage, after all, and Lewis no doubt exhibited "that restlessness, that inquietude, that certain indescribable something common to old bachelors," that made him a less than desirable housemate. Besides, as everyone who has ever been married knows, for the marriage bond to deepen into an unassailable sacrament, all prior associations, including those with one's parents, must be redefined in a way that does not undermine the harmony of the couple. Lewis and Clark had literally slept in close proximity for many years: in their quarters at Fort Mandan, in the tipi that Charbonneau sold to them, in their quarters at Fort Clatsop, and under the stars at innumerable campsites up and down the Missouri and Columbia Rivers. David Freeman Hawke has written, "There is no reason to imagine sexual overtones in the close bond between them, yet the relationship did resemble that of a successful marriage where the partners accommodated themselves without attempting to change one another."[93] No responsible historian has ever suggested that Lewis and Clark were lovers, but they clearly loved each other and had developed a deep intimacy, born of friendship and a magnificent shared adventure. Through their shared sense of mission and sustained physical proximity, they had developed a familiarity that few modern unmarried Americans ever achieve. After the Clarks arrived in the frontier capital in the early summer of 1808, Lewis and Clark certainly did not sleep together in the old way. Probably they did not even remain messmates very long.

In some genuine sense of the term, Lewis and Clark *broke up* when Clark married Julia Hancock.

Beneath the humor of Lewis's May 29, 1808, letter there is a vein of wistfulness and envy. "I must halt here in the middle of my communications and ask you if the matrimonial dictionary affords no term more appropriate than that of *goods*, alise *merchandize*, for that dear and interesting part of the creation? It is very well Genl., I shall tell madam of your want of Gallantry; and the triumph too of detection will be more compleat when it is recollected what a musty, fusty, rusty old bachelor I am."[94] Clark had entered into marriage so pragmatically that Lewis teasingly accused him of writing about Julia Hancock as if she were goods and merchandise. Lewis made sure Clark knew that of the two keelboats he had sent to the mouth of the Ohio to accommodate the Clarks' furniture, he had taken pains to make sure that at least one of the vessels "is well covered and sufficiently capacious to accommodate *the ladies* comfortably." In other words, Lewis would not treat a woman as merchandise to be transported across the country, but as a delicate creature to be protected from the elements in every possible way. Lewis was essentially warning Clark not to take his young wife for granted. In threatening to "tell madam of your want of Gallantry,"

Lewis was humorously insinuating that he knew better how to cherish a woman than his rough and ready friend Clark. In calling himself a "musty, fusty, rusty old bachelor," Lewis contrasted himself with his best friend, who had proceeded on in his life while Lewis, prematurely old, had locked himself in an emotional attic. The melancholy of this is the more pointed when we remember that Clark was a full four years older than Lewis.

In seeming to celebrate the nuptials of Clark, Lewis was all too well aware of the growing differentiation between his life and that of Clark. They were men of about the same age and with similar military experience, who came from the same social class and the same region of the United States. They were both men with a strong pre-expeditionary interest in and familiarity with the American West. Modern Americans tend to see them today as doppelgangers, a virtually interchangeable pair of enlightened frontiersmen. The phrase *Lewis and Clark*, or *Lewis & Clark*, is so formulaic as to form a hendiadys, which the *Oxford English Dictionary* defines as "a figure of speech in which a single complex idea is expressed by two words connected by a conjunction." But if their lives were ever truly parallel, their lifelines began to diverge late in 1806. Clark almost immediately married; Lewis remained a bachelor, though perhaps not by choice. Clark quickly fathered children; Lewis, so far as we known, never fathered a child. Like most upwardly mobile Americans, Clark moved into steadily larger and more expensive houses; Lewis took temporary lodgings with others. Clark fulfilled one career role after the next with intelligence and success; Lewis floundered. Clark became a kind of informal patron to later voyages up the Missouri River; Lewis could not complete the book that would have constituted not only an indispensable guide to later travelers but would have given him an unassailable place in the history of exploration. Clark communicated with everyone on a timely basis; Lewis failed to be a faithful communicator even when it was critically important.

William Foley recognizes the poignancy in Lewis's letter to Clark about the living arrangements once the entire Clark family (William, Julia, Ann Anderson, and household slaves) arrived in St. Louis. "Lewis's somewhat poignant letter suggests that the lonely bachelor was somehow hoping that he and his former partner might be able to pick up where they had left off at the end of their Pacific journey," Foley writes. "But Clark was now married and prepared to move on to a new life, while Lewis sadly seemed more focused on recapturing the 'most perfect harmony' that he had once shared with Clark and their little traveling family. While the two old friends would once again have an opportunity to work together, it was never to be quite the same."[95]

By the summer of 1809, the "parallel" lives had diverged to the point that Clark found himself unable to help Lewis in any conclusive way. He felt *Cempothy*, but he could not fix Lewis's troubles. He lamented the decline of his fellow adventurer and dear friend, but there was little he could do to prop him up. Whether Julia ever developed anything like her husband's affection and respect for Lewis is unclear. If something in his character or behavior was repellant to other women, it would be unusual if Julia were impervious to it, even out of respect for her new husband's longstanding friendship with the governor.

At the end of his May 29, 1808, letter to Clark, Lewis wrote, "I trust you do not mean merely to tantalize us by the promise you have made of bringing with you some of your Neices, I have already flattered the community of S Louis with this valuable acquisition to our female society."[96] By now, at the age of thirty-three, Lewis had taken himself out of the matrimonial lottery.

On November 16, 1808, Lewis published an essay in the *Missouri Gazette* entitled, "The True Ambitions of an Honest Mind." It is a rather stilted and pretentious essay written for effect rather than revelation. Lewis informs the reader that he "would be happy in a few but faithful friends," that he would choose his house for "convenience rather than state," that he wanted "business enough to secure me from indolence, and leisure enough always to have an hour to spare." Although he wrote that he "would be happy in a few but faithful friends," he made no mention of marriage and family. The closest he came was a strange reference to the passions, which was probably a way of indirectly abusing Frederick Bates. "As to my passions, since we cannot be wholly divested of them, I would hate only those whose manners rendered them odious, and love only where I knew I ought." Lewis probably thought he was being a good stoic Jeffersonian in this strange view of passions. Would he really have preferred to be "wholly divested" of the passions of love? There is a clumsy echo here of Jefferson's famous letter to Maria Cosway in which the Head insisted that, "The art of life is the art of avoiding pain: & he is the best pilot who steers clearest of the rocks & shoals with which he is beset.... The most effectual means of being secure against pain is to retire within ourselves, & to suffice for our own happiness. Those, which depend on ourselves, are the only pleasures a wise man will count on: for nothing is ours which another may deprive us of."[97]

Voluntary Associations

Lewis was a member of the American Philosophical Society, but he could not attend their meetings. Lewis had been elected to membership in the APS in November 1803. (Jefferson was so honored to be elected president of the APS in 1797 that he declared—probably a little disingenuously—that it was a greater honor than being elected vice president of the United States in the same year.) Nor could Lewis keep up with the learned society's transactions. Had he been as disciplined and obsessive a correspondent as his patron Jefferson, he might have been able to maintain his place in the republic of letters. From a steady communication with fellow lovers of science and nature, Lewis might have taken great solace. Fellow members of the APS would surely have encouraged Lewis's great writing project, answered his queries, and sent him materials with which to finish his manuscripts. Instead of doing what he could to keep up with these savants, many of whom stood in awe of him, Lewis went silent.

He was also a serious Mason. Freemasonry was a more philosophically sophisticated organization in the eighteenth century than it became in the early twenty-first century. It was intimately associated with the Enlightenment. A number of the Founding Fathers were freemasons, including George Washington, Benjamin Franklin, Rufus King, and John Hancock. Lewis joined the Virtue Lodge Number 44 of Albemarle County, Virginia, on January 28, 1797. By October 1797 he was a Royal Arch Mason. Although attempts have repeatedly been made to discover that Jefferson was a Freemason, no evidence has ever been unearthed to prove that he joined the organization. Jefferson was, in Dr. Samuel Johnson's words, not a *clubbable* man. As one of the busiest and most private of men, and the nation's foremost advocate of democratic equality, Jefferson subscribed to most of the views and doctrine of Freemasonry but apparently resisted joining an organization with an exclusive membership.

When he finally reached St. Louis in the spring of 1808, Lewis helped to establish a Masonic Lodge, the first in the Louisiana Territory. He was installed as the lodge's first Master on September 16, 1808. It proved to be a bitter association for Lewis. The solace that he would probably have gained from his association with Freemasonry was damaged by the fact that his enemy Frederick Bates was also a member. In fact, the great public quarrel between Lewis and Bates occurred at a Masonic ball on June 24, 1809, a celebration of the Festival of St. John the Baptist.[98]

A Masonic apron alleged to have been owned by Meriwether Lewis is one of the treasures maintained by the Grand Lodge of Ancient Free and Accepted Masons, in Helena, Montana.

Madison was President

Thomas Jefferson served two terms as president of the United States. Although he was encouraged to stand for a third term in 1808, including by moderate Federalists who had once been his political enemies, like William Plumer of New Hampshire, he chose "to retire to my family, my books and farms," he informed his old *philosophe* friend Pierre Samuel Du Pont de Nemours on March 2, 1809, two days before he yielded the presidency to his closest friend James Madison. "Never did a prisoner, released from his chains, feel such relief as I shall on shaking off the shackles of power."[99] Like the first president of the United States, indeed like nearly all the landed gentry of that day, Jefferson regarded himself as an American Cincinnatus, called from the plow to lead his people in troubled times, serving only long enough to save the republic, but panting all the while for the soft joys of a rural retirement. Jefferson retired in 1809 partly because he wanted to reinforce President Washington's precedent of two terms only for an American head of state.

Jefferson was famous for declaring that government did not have a perpetual claim on its most talented citizens. To his protégé James Monroe, Jefferson wrote, "If we are made in some degree for others, yet in a greater are we made for ourselves. It were contrary to feeling & indeed ridiculous to suppose that a man had less right in himself than one of his neighbors or indeed all of them put together. This would be slavery & not that liberty which the bill of rights has made inviolable and for the preservation of which our government has been charged."[100] Jefferson knew something about slavery. If he can be believed, he never aspired to be president of the United States in the manner of virtually all modern presidential candidates. By March 4, 1809, he had served as a member of the Second Continental Congress, the Virginia House of Delegates, as the governor of Virginia, a Virginia representative in the national Congress under the Articles of Confederation, the American minister to France, the nation's first secretary of state, the vice president of the United States, and (for two terms), the president of the United States. This was public service enough. Men like Jefferson and George Washington actually worried that if they accepted too many public offices in the course of their lives, they would be despised as career politicians and men of ambition. Jefferson told his friends that he would stand for a third term *only* if some international emergency endangered the survival of the American republic, but he never seriously contemplated staying on after 1809, and there can be no doubt that by then, at the age of sixty-five, he really did ache for rural retirement. To Du Pont, he explained, "Nature intended me for the tranquil pursuits of science, by rendering them my supreme delight."[101]

If Lewis had finished his book in anything like a timely fashion, Jefferson would still have been president of the United States at the time of publication. Whatever difficulties Lewis might have had with the War Department, then or later, would have presumably been worked through or papered over to everyone's satisfaction, however much *internal* frustration might have been expressed by War Department functionaries. Once Lewis was perceived to be a problematic hero, however, a less than masterful territorial governor, a poor official communicator, a man given to unilateral decision making in a nation that took deep pride in being a participatory republic, an unauthorized user of public funds, and an individual who could not write a book, men who were essentially anonymous—mere functionaries—who would have been overawed by Lewis had he continued to achieve success, felt emboldened to find fault with him given his post-expeditionary troubles.

Unfortunately, Jefferson retired just when the life of his protégé Meriwether Lewis fell apart.

By now Lewis had also effectively lost Jefferson. Biographers and historians have made more of the "breach," if it can be called that, than the evidence suggests. That Jefferson was frustrated by Lewis's silences and his inability to see the book project through to completion is certain. Jefferson's rebuke of July 17, 1808, is as close to an unalloyed declaration of anger as Jefferson ever wrote. (Even his denunciations of George III are articulated with Newtonian grace and balance.) But even when he was seriously upset with Lewis, Jefferson ended his letter with friendly salutations. The cause of Lewis's breach with Jefferson is less important than the effect. Had Lewis written Jefferson on a timely basis, he would not only have had a loyal advocate in his relations with James Madison and his struggle with the War Department, but he would have enjoyed the attention of one of the most important and generous men of the era. The confidence of a man receiving frequent letters from Thomas Jefferson cannot be undermined very much or very long by comparative insects like Frederick Bates or William Simmons. By cutting himself off from Jefferson, Lewis lost one of the best supporters a man could ever have—a Renaissance man specifically and assiduously interested in his welfare.

Jefferson handpicked his successor. In fact he handpicked his first two successors. In 1808, when a political contest appeared to be looming between Madison, who was TJ's presumptive successor, and Monroe, who was the junior partner of the Virginia triumvirate in every sense, Jefferson intervened with his characteristic grace and indirection. To Monroe he wrote, "I see with infinite grief a contest arising between yourself and another, who have been very dear to each other, and equally so to me."[102] That was all it took to move Monroe out of the way and seat Madison in the presidential mansion first. Monroe would get his turn. If Monroe had been elected in 1808, he would almost certainly have taken a more favorable view of Lewis and his erratic vouchers. Monroe had a much deeper interest in the American West than Madison. In late 1802, when Americans of the trans-Allegheny region were pressing Jefferson to do something about the closing of the Mississippi River by the Spanish Intendant of New Orleans, Jefferson leaned hard on Monroe to travel to Paris to try to sort things out.

Knowing that Monroe would be reluctant to accept the mission, Jefferson poured on his famous charm.

> I am sensible ... that it will be a great sacrifice on your part, and presents from the season and other circumstances serious difficulties. But some men are born for the public. Nature by fitting them for the service of the human race on a broad scale, has stamped them with the evidences of her destination and their duty.[103]

Notice that Jefferson, now the president of the United States, took a position on public service precisely opposite to that which he had expressed to the same—though much younger—Monroe twenty years previously. If Jefferson was aware of the irony of his claim that "some men are born for the public," he did not express it to his protégé. Monroe reluctantly accepted the assignment, made his way to France, and arrived in Paris just as Robert Livingstone consummated the Louisiana Purchase. Monroe's reward for hearkening to Jefferson's hypocritical insistence that some men were fitted by nature for "the service of the human race on a broad scale" was that history has given him much more credit for the Louisiana Purchase than he deserved.

James Madison was one of the most brilliant men in American history, but he was a much more eastern-looking statesman than his famous friend from Monticello. Madison, who was something of a hypochondriac (in the modern sense of the term), a man of such diminutiveness and self-described frailty that his own wife could call him "the great little Madison," could not thrill like his mentor to the ideas of grizzly bears or Indians living in something like a state of nature. Although Madison handled the diplomatic protocols of the Louisiana Purchase and the purchase treaty's progress through the United States Senate with his usual administrative mastery, he regarded Louisiana principally as a bulwark to America's geopolitical security rather than a windfall for the Enlightenment. Madison's contributions to Jefferson's June 18, 1803, instructions to Meriwether Lewis were negligible. His mindset was administrative not imperial.

When Jefferson left the presidency (March 4, 1809), he left Washington, DC, forever (March 11) and walked away from power like a character out of his beloved Plutarch. He made a big point of not attempting in any way to interfere with the work of his successor. He remained in the environs of Monticello for the remaining seventeen years of his life, and could barely be induced to visit faraway Richmond, Virginia, seventy miles away. Indeed, Jefferson all but abdicated the presidency during his last year in office, particularly in the wake of the political disasters attending the various Embargo acts, and left to his successor important decisions and political appointments that should have been resolved during his own last days as president. Jefferson pre-determined to wash his hands of the defilements of power once and for all, and never to meddle in his successor's administration. The principal victim of that Plutarchian resolution was Meriwether Lewis.

If Jefferson had still been president in the spring of 1809, he would almost certainly have protected his protégé from the bad-tempered accountants of the War Department. He would probably have been frustrated with Lewis's silences and his failure to consult the War Department on key and costly issues, but he would not have countenanced the sort of letter that was written to Lewis on July 15, 1809, and received by Lewis on his thirty-fifth birthday, August 18, 1809. That was not Jefferson's style. Furthermore, it was Jefferson who had instructed Lewis that it was absolutely essential that the Mandan leader Sheheke-shote be returned safely and at the earliest convenience to the earthlodge villages in today's North Dakota. In his chiding letter of July 17, 1808, Jefferson wrote, "We consider the good faith, & the reputation of the nation as pledged to accomplish this."[104] Although Jefferson was eager to avoid "any considerable military expedition in the present uncertain state of our foreign concerns," he authorized Lewis to get the Mandan leader home "if it can be effected in any other way & at reasonable expence."[105] *Any other way* and *at reasonable expence.* This amounts to a kind of frugal blank check, delivered to a "beloved man" and trusted protégé who, at the president's insistence, had carried a universal letter of credit on his transcontinental journey. In other words, President Jefferson had granted Lewis so much independence and discretionary latitude during the heroic years that it was natural for Lewis to believe that he was still entitled to make his own decisions, independent of bureaucratic review, including decisions involving public expenditure, and particularly in tying up loose ends from the expedition, many hundreds of miles and a world away from the District of Columbia.

Lewis knew more about the conditions of the Missouri River corridor than any living person, certainly more than Jefferson, Madison, Madison's cabinet members, or any government functionary in the faraway War Department. After the debacle of the first attempt to return Sheheke-shote to the Mandan villages, Lewis was not about to send an undermanned and underfunded escort party with him the second time. Given Jefferson's unreserved sense of moral urgency, his written instruction that Lewis should get the Mandan leader home, come what may, and the professional habits Jefferson and his protégé had established over the previous seven years, it is not surprising that Lewis planned the impressive and expensive Sheheke-shote expedition that left St. Louis in the early summer of 1809, and indeed successfully returned the Mandan leader to his home village. William Eustis and his clerk William Simmons may have felt that Lewis's arrangements to return Sheheke-shote were excessively expensive and smacked either of conflict of interest or worse. But if Jefferson had still been president, it is unlikely that Henry Dearborn would have regarded the plans as disproportionate to the problem Lewis was trying to solve, particularly if Dearborn had discussed the issue with Jefferson, the man who had to write the letter of condolence to the Arikara nation after their leader Arketarnarshar died in Washington, DC, during his visit to meet the great father. By almost any standard of reason, Eustis and Simmons were more at fault than Lewis in the Sheheke-shote affair. In my view, they bear a considerable responsibility for Lewis's death.

President Madison must not have known of Jefferson's sense of urgency about Sheheke. It is possible that he did not see the issue in the same way as his predecessor.

Nor was Madison's Secretary of War William Eustis a man of his predecessor Henry Dearborn's capacities. Madison's biographer Ralph Ketcham concludes that Madison, in 1809, "saddled himself with one of the weakest cabinets in American history." He writes that William Eustis had such good Republican social connections that "he apparently did not need to have any particular talents or experience qualifying him for the War Department." As the War of 1812 loomed, the mediocrity of Eustis, whom Madison liked personally, became a serious issue. By 1813, Madison had replaced Eustis with another Jefferson protégé James Monroe. "The weak appointments in the War and Navy departments might in normal, Jeffersonian times have been of little consequence; attending to a few hundred soldiers at frontier posts and directing a handful of frigates were not demanding jobs," Ketcham concludes.[106] William Foley calls Eustis a "tightfisted New Englander."[107]

The letter that precipitated the death of Lewis, written by Secretary of War William Eustis (or his clerk William Simmons) closed with what Lewis would have regarded as the unkindest cut of all: "The President has been consulted and the observations herein contained have his approval."[108] James Holmberg has written, Lewis "took the rejection as a denunciation by the Madison administration."[109] Given the letter's invocation of President Madison, it would have been hard for Lewis to read it otherwise. If President Madison really endorsed the contents of the July 17, 1809, letter, Madison committed a grave error of judgment.

Even though Jefferson and Madison were best friends and the most successful political collaborators in American history, the departure of Jefferson in March 1809 left Lewis vulnerable in Washington for the first time. We cannot know what Madison's relationship with Lewis was, but we can imagine how alien to Madison Lewis must have seemed even in 1801, when they lived together in the White House for a number of weeks. Madison was one of the best-educated men of his generation; Lewis, said Jefferson, was "not regularly educated."[110] Madison was a shrimp, a sedentary man, and a hypochondriac (in our sense of the term); Lewis was a man who in his boyhood had stared down charging bulls. Madison was an individual who exhibited almost infinite self-control throughout a long and productive life; Lewis was an impulsive, proto-romantic figure who, Attorney General Levi Lincoln warned, "will be much more likely, in case of difficulty, to push to far, than to recede too soon. Would it not be well to change the term, 'certain destruction' into probable destruction & to add—that these dangers are never to be encountered, which vigilance percaution & attention can secure against, at a reasonable expense."[111] Madison never shot a buffalo and ate it steaming from the kill. It is not certain that he ever shot anything. He could never have gushed over the delectability of Toussaint Charbonneau's boudin blanc. It would be hard to find two of Jefferson's protégés, both Virginia plantation owners and slaveowners, who were more unlike than James Madison and Meriwether Lewis.

If Thomas Jefferson had accepted a third term in 1809, Lewis would not have received the sort of rebuke that William Eustis or William Simmons wrote on July 15, 1809. Had that letter been written in some form, it could not possibly have contained the devastating final declaration that it had been endorsed by the president of the United States. If Jefferson had stood for a third term, Lewis probably would not have taken his own life.

BLOCKAGE ON THE BOOK

When Mungo Park returned from his first extended exploration of northwest Africa just before Christmas 1797, he paid a visit to the impresario of British exploration Joseph Banks, who had given him up for lost. Banks was thrilled. He wrote a letter to the German polymath Johann Blumenbach outlining Park's principal experiences along the Niger. Blumenbach, one of the pioneers of the emerging science of ethnography, wrote back, "How ardently I long to see once Mr Park's own extensive Account of his wonderful & highly interesting Travels."[112] Lewis lived in a time when the learned world waited *ardently* for such accounts of travel and discovery, encounters with aboriginal peoples, and scientific surveys of the previously unknown world. Richard Van Orman has written, "Explorers and philosophers were the heroes of that period, the foremost citizens of a volatile age, and among the first great personalities on the world stage."[113]

That Lewis could have written a splendid account of what he called "my late tour" is certain. One need only read through his journal entries from the Montana portions of the journey to see what his prose was capable of. Whether he could have written "*his own* extensive Account of *his* wonderful & highly interesting travels," given the co-captaincy he created in the summer of 1803, is another question [emphasis added]. Blumenbach perfectly recognized the intensely personal nature of a journey of this sort, no matter who comes along as an auxiliary. I believe that one of the main reasons that Lewis never wrote his book is that he did not know how to handle the problem of Clark's leadership (see passage in Chapter 5). The only way the travels could conform to the convention of the solitary explorer is if Lewis were seen as essentially alone in the vast wilderness of the trans-Mississippi West. To produce a literary classic, he would have had to write Clark out of the book. But Lewis was too good a friend to write Clark out of the story entirely, and he was surely aware that Clark was as important to the success of the expedition as he was, perhaps, in strict justice, more. What makes Mungo Park's *Travels* so wonderful & highly interesting is his existential aloneness. Park really *was* alone on the Niger. His two auxiliaries were a guide named Johnson, formerly a slave in Jamaica and then a freed man in service in England, and Demba, a sprightly African slave boy, whose freedom Park promised to purchase after their successful return. Lewis's thirty auxiliaries included such independently interesting men as Robert Frazer and Patrick Gass, both of whom announced their plans to publish independent accounts of the journey, the most famous Indian woman in American history, and of course Clark.

The western historian Patricia Limerick has said that Meriwether Lewis was suffering from "the greatest case of writer's block in American history."[114] After Lewis's death his Philadelphia publishers sent a bewildered and frustrated letter to former president Jefferson: "Govr. Lewis never furnished us with a line of the M.S."[115] If Lewis had a book to publish in 1809, he hadn't bothered to let his publisher know.

After his return from the mission, Lewis did important preliminary work towards the publication for which his patron Jefferson so eagerly awaited. He signed a contract with a printer in Philadelphia, published a prospectus of the three volumes he had in mind, including a timeline of their expected release. That prospectus was subsequently reprinted. On the strength of that public announcement of an ambitious and timely publication project, subscriptions began to trickle in and—more to the point—the expectations of the learned world and the general public were aroused. In Philadelphia in the spring of 1807 Lewis entered into a series of agreements to get the celestial data corrected by a competent mathematician; to get illustrations made of some of the animals he had discovered, and the Great Falls of the Missouri River; and to have the plants he had discovered properly and technically described. He did everything one might expect a serious explorer to do—except write the book.

Describing Lewis's state of mind as he prepared to leave St. Louis late in the summer of 1809, Larry Morris confidently writes, "After two years, Lewis had not written a single word of the new work."[116] It is impossible to know if this is true. It may be that Lewis was farther along than his biographers think. Just because he had not supplied his publishers with a single page of his manuscript does not mean that he had not written portions of the book. It seems clear that Lewis was intending for the first volume of the book to be heavily based on, and in many instances taken directly from, the final version of the journals, which was probably produced by Lewis some time after the expedition's return. In other words, Lewis appears to have intended to have the book set from the journals themselves, with interlineations, emendations, marginalia, and additional passages attached in some way to the actual pages of the journals. Such a plan would explain many of the interlinear markings on the original journals in pencil, including red pencil. That certainly was the plan after Lewis's death. Lewis's uncle William D. Meriwether wrote to William Clark that the ghostwriter would work from the original journals, "correct the gramatical [sic] errors that it may contain, and to strike out the minutia, that may make it tedious to the reader."[117] Such a procedure would not have been unusual in Jefferson's era. James Boswell's celebrated *Life of Samuel Johnson*, for example, was in many episodes assembled directly from Boswell's journal, which he regarded as too reliable and too extensive to rewrite or even recopy as he produced his great biography.[118] Certain passages in the journals of the Lewis and Clark Expedition have the feel of having been polished up or entirely re-written not as field journal entries, but as drafts of what was meant to be the book.[119] At Fort Pickering, according to Stephen Ambrose, Lewis told Captain Gilbert Russell "that all the work on the journals had been completed and they were ready for the press."[120] It may be that Lewis was not altogether lying about the progress of the book. Still, in September 1809 there was much more to do to prepare even a straightforward expedition narrative for the press, much less all the other modules Lewis had promised the reading public.

In August 1809, Clark assured his brother Jonathan that Lewis's journey to the East would not only clear away his difficulties with the War Department, but enable him to finish the book. Still, biographer William Foley claims that Clark was frustrated by Lewis's inability to write the book. "Clark," he writes, "at one point privately complained that his [Lewis's] procrastination had likely lessened their chances for profiting from the sales of their journals."[121] The Clark letter in question was written in November 1808. Clark merely wrote, "Govr. Lewis is here and talks of going to philadelphia to finish our books this winter, he has put it off So long that I fear they will [not] bring us much."[122]

In December 1838, a man named Henry Bechtle wrote, in a history of Cincinnati, that he had encountered Governor Lewis on the Natchez Trace back in 1809 and travelled with him for a full day. He called Lewis the "greatest man in the world." He said that Lewis had given him a prospectus of the book he was writing, "& had promised to send him one of his large ones when Printed."[123] There is no reason to doubt the credibility of this reminiscence, since a complete stranger who had never previously met Lewis would hardly be capable of inventing a story so specific about a by now long-forgotten book project. Even in the last dark week of his life, Lewis was still intending to complete his book, vindicate his governorship, and somehow turn his troubled life around. That didn't happen. Peter Kastor has written, "Lewis's downfall occurred in no small part because he found himself unable to write his way out of trouble."[124]

Lewis's inability to write his book is one manifestation of a larger problem he had with writing. For a man of such linguistic gifts and such volubility (when the switch was on), Lewis was surprisingly prone to silence and broken communications. This theme is developed fully in Chapter 5.

PHYSICAL ILLNESS

Meriwether Lewis had an iron constitution. His body had held up amazingly well on the transcontinental journey. He worked through bouts of malaria and dysentery, and he was generally much less discombobulated by such routine annoyances as mosquitoes, gnats, cactus, sleet, wind, wet clothes, and cold feet than his partner in discovery William Clark or other members of the expedition. He was only slowed to a stop twice in the course of the expedition, first by the transition from a buffalo to a salmon and roots diet among the Nez Perce in late September 1805, and then by a bullet wound east of today's Williston, North Dakota, on August 11, 1806. Even when he was wounded by a musket ball, Lewis recovered so fast that less than a month later Clark wrote, with a kind of wonder, "My worthy friend Cap Lewis has entirely recovered his wounds are heeled up and he Can walk and even run nearly as well as ever he Could.[125] Jefferson rightly declared that the expedition had been good for Lewis both mentally and physically. At the end of the Fort Mandan winter, Lewis wrote to his mother, "For myself individually I [enjoy] better health than I [have] since I commenced my [voyage]."[126]

After the expedition's return, Lewis settled into a comparatively sedentary life. The mission had been accomplished. He was now quite content to "enjoy the repast which the hand of civilization has prepared for us,"[127] as he put it on New Year's Day at Fort Clatsop. No longer propelled by the need to proceed on up the river no matter what the weather conditions, no matter how he or his men felt, Lewis lost some of his physical edge. Stephen Ambrose wrote of "too many balls with too many toasts."[128] If Lewis was depressed and beset by re-entry issues, he was likely more sedentary than was good for his physical constitution. By the summer of 1809 he was quite ill. He certainly was suffering from malaria. Lewis's account book indicates that he was purchasing an unusual amount of medicine: "pills of opium and tartar," "antibillious pills." Bakeless wrote, "The size of his bill for medicine shows that Lewis was in poor health, or thought he was; and there is no doubt that he was taken genuinely ill on the [last] journey."[129]

We know that Lewis was drinking. How heavily, and with what impact on his health, is a much-debated question. See below page 362–365.

We know too that he was taking laudanum. Lewis wrote that he was taking opium pills of one gram. Although a one-gram pill certainly did not contain a full gram of opium, according to Dr. David Peck, "[H]e was ingesting an unknown quantity of morphine, codeine, and several dozen other pharymacologically active substances produced within the cells of the magic poppy."[130] Peck believes he might have been addicted. If Lewis ran out of an opium supply somewhere between St. Louis and Grinder's Inn, the withdrawal effects would not have been greatly different from heroin withdrawal in our time. "Opioid withdrawal produces an intense craving for more of the substance, nausea, cramps, a depressed mood, inability to sleep, increased sensitivity to pain, and increased anxiety."[131] Alcohol would have magnified these symptoms.

Lewis was certainly suffering from some sort of illness at the time of his death. In his letter to Amos Stoddard of September 22, 1809, Lewis acknowledged that "my indisposition has induced me to change my route ... ." On September 16, 1809, he explained to President Madison that he was "very much exhausted from the heat of the climate, but having taken medicine feel much better this morning."[132] Most scholars understand Lewis's indisposition to have been malaria, from which Lewis suffered off and on throughout his adult life.

Danisi and Jackson have exhaustively documented Lewis's pre-expedition and post-expedition struggle with malaria. They believe that severe bouts of malaria, not mental illness or derangement, were the principal cause of Lewis's violent death.[133] They believe that Lewis was suffering from "the most dangerous" of the three strains of malaria in America, the *falciparum* strain, which produced "intermittent high fevers, with a severe retro-orbital headache, parched throat, and diffuse body aches."[134] Dr. Peck disputes the Danisi-Jackson thesis that Lewis was suffering from cerebral malaria. "I find it difficult to imagine that symptoms of fever, chills, headache, and nausea he had experienced previously would have caused Lewis to take his own life this time."[135] In other words, if Lewis was suffering from severe malaria in September 1809, it was not for the first time. Since he had successfully weathered previous storms, either he had an adequate coping regimen or he was *not*, at the time of his death, suffering from a strain of malaria severe enough for him to shoot himself in the head *merely* to extinguish the pain. Peck wrote, "I think it is more likely that the malaria, added to the effects of opium addiction, alcoholism, and other psychological problems, combined" to precipitate the suicide.[136]

Dr. Reimert Ravenholt has argued that Lewis was suffering from the advanced stages of syphilis at the time of his death.[137] If true, this would have amounted to both a physical and a mental illness. Given Lewis's fustiness and the captains' steadfast refusal to accept Indian women as hospitality gifts in the course of their travels, this theory seems unlikely. It is possible that Lewis contracted syphilis before or after the expedition, of course, or that the protestations of the captains about native women were deceptive or occasionally breached, but few historians have accepted Dr. Ravenholt's thesis, particularly because he goes so far as to nominate the most likely moment at which Lewis might have contracted his STD. On August 13, 1805, Lewis had made a successful first encounter with the Shoshone people on the Idaho-Montana border west of today's Dillon, Montana. Dr. Ravenholt's argument is that Lewis was so overcome with joy at having made that critical contact with the people whose horses would get the expedition safely over the Bitterroot Mountains that he let down his guard and had sexual relations with a willing Shoshone woman (unnamed, and of course unmentioned in Lewis's journal). The fact that Clark was elsewhere that night, and Lewis had only three of his men with him in the Shoshone camp, makes it more likely, according to Dr. Ravenholt, that Lewis could have indulged himself (just once!) without the possibility of embarrassment or recrimination.

The medical books written about the Lewis and Clark expedition are uniformly skeptical of Ravenholt's thesis. David Peck argues that the symptoms cited by Ravenholt as pointing towards syphilis are equally indicative of other diseases, including malaria, and concludes, "It is very presumptive to assume that Lewis caught syphilis anywhere along the route."[138]

Finding a precise diagnosis to Lewis's real or perceived physical illness(es) in the fall of 1809 is less important than our understanding that he was seriously indisposed between September 4 and October 10, 1809. Because Lewis was physically ill, his mental reserves were also diminished. If he was, as seems certain, taking large quantities of medicine to treat his illness(es), his mental stability would have been further impaired. No historian doubts that Lewis's physical illness was a factor in the downward spiral that consumed him in the fall of 1809. Just how much his physical illness(es) contributed to his death is unknown. Dr. Peck, David Nicandri, Stephenie Ambrose Tubbs, and other historians believe that Danisi and Jackson have overstated their case.

Mental Illness

The frontier between physical and mental illness is porous. If Lewis was suffering from an even more severe flare up of malaria than he had suffered earlier in his career, and dosing himself with medicines, including laudanum (an opium derivative), his reason may have been seriously impaired in September and October 1809. Laudanum is a dangerous and addictive narcotic, especially when taken in heavy doses. If Lewis was also drinking heavily in the last weeks of his life, severely enough to be arrested and dried out by Gilbert Russell at Fort Pickering, his mental clarity would have been seriously impaired by that alone.

I am not at all fond of ex post facto diagnoses of illustrious figures from history. It is both dangerous and unfair to throw conveniently anachronistic labels at historical figures who are not available for professional clinical diagnosis. It is also inherently reductionist. It is fashionable in our time for people with no actual training in psychology or psychoanalysis to decide that this or that person suffered from bipolar disorder, or exhibited symptoms of manic depression, or showed signs of obsessive-compulsive disorder.

At the same time, the recent quest to *normalize* disorder (e.g., calling a handicapped person *otherwise advantaged*) has led well-meaning people to make lists of famous men and women who have suffered from this or that malady and yet lived lives of remarkable achievement. It has recently become fashionable, for example, to suggest that Abraham Lincoln was suffering from a disease known as Marfan Syndrome; that Beethoven, Winston Churchill, and Theodore Roosevelt suffered from bipolar disorder; and that Isaac Newton, Theodore Roosevelt, and Prince Albert were stutterers. These may be accurate identifications, but they feel exploitative and intrusive.

Still, it seemed clear to many of his contemporaries, including Thomas Jefferson, that Lewis suffered from some sort of mental illness. The terms of choice in the Enlightenment were *hypochondria* and *melancholia*. At least in the last weeks of his life, he was suffering sufficiently from derangement "seriously to alarm his friends."[139] Lewis's acute derangement may have been exacerbated by physical illness, more likely malaria than syphilis, but it was not solely grounded in his physical condition. Although scientifically rigorous clinical psychology had not yet been born, there was a distinguished literature on melancholia available to physicians and Enlightenment scientists, including the Renaissance classic of the genre, Richard Burton's *The Anatomy of Melancholy, What it is: With all the Kinds, Causes, Symptomes, Prognostickes, and Several Cures of it. In Three Maine Partitions with their several Sections, Members, and Subsections. Philosophically, Medicinally, Historically, Opened and Cut Up*, first published in 1621. More recently, the works of Samuel Johnson and the diaries and biographies of James Boswell had comprised an extensive, if unsystematic, exploration of melancholy. Virtually everyone who encountered Lewis in his last weeks of life spoke of his *derangement* (see 283–285). It seems to me virtually certain that if Lewis were available for psychological profiling by today's credentialed experts, he would be found to be suffering from one of the following maladies: bipolar disease, manic depression, psychiatric disorder, or post traumatic stress disorder. It is at least possible, as Stephenie Ambrose Tubbs alleges, that he was suffering from Asperger's Disease.

Dr. David Peck concludes, "Captain Lewis went progressively downhill from the time he reentered society in 1806."[140] Peck believes that Lewis was "suffering from depression greatly worsened by the use of alcohol and opium."[141] The late Stephen Ambrose was certain that Lewis suffered from manic depression. He believed that Lewis was a manic depressive at the time he became the president's aide de camp, that Jefferson had recognized Lewis's problem, but selected him anyway for the great expedition. Jefferson's confidence was vindicated by Lewis's field performance. Ambrose argued that "it was his [Lewis's] special triumph that he seldom let his emotional state take over, and then only momentarily. Whether he was high or low, his emotional state played no role in daily decision-making for two and a half years."[142] Ambrose believed that Lewis's depressions recurred with renewed severity after he returned from the journey, and that he exacerbated the problem by consuming inordinate amounts of alcohol. Ambrose broached the question of Lewis's mental illness while attempting to explain his unaccountable silences, particularly as the expedition finally approached the Pacific coast in mid-November 1805.

Ambrose's daughter Stephenie Ambrose Tubbs has made the best case she can for Asperger's in her book, *Why Sacagawea Deserves the Day Off and Other Lessons from the Lewis and Clark Trail*. She points to Lewis's incapacity to find a mate, his detachment from the lives of the men under his command, his lack of empathy for some of the people around him and for Sacagawea and her son Jean Baptiste in particular, his preference for the company of his dog Seaman over that of other humans, his inability to bond with a woman, his propensity to count things in nature, like the 176 scuta on the rattlesnake that he found near his bedroll on the morning of June 14, 1805, and his clear annoyance at being repeatedly subjected to the "national hug" of the Shoshone people.

Such *symptoms* do resonate with what we know of Asperger's, first diagnosed in 1944 by Austrian pediatrician Hans Asperger, but they make for a pretty thin diagnostic gruel, and this behavior set, taken singly or together, can be explained by a variety of other analyses. Enlightenment scientists loved to count things—that was their Baconian method of exploring and classifying the unknown world. Ambrose Tubbs makes much of Lewis's distaste for the "national hug." Any familiarity with the extensive literature on personal space indicates that virtually nobody would be pleased to be swept into a tight full body hug by a complete stranger, a mostly naked man who might be an enemy, whose body was covered with pigmentation and bear grease.[143] Like all good explorers, Lewis was willing to honor the peculiar hospitality codes of his Shoshone hosts up to a point, but eventually he lost patience with the oily full-body "handshake": "we wer all carressed and besmeared with their grease and paint until I was heartily tired of the national hug."[144] It's hard to imagine *anyone* who would not share Lewis's discomfort, though Clark probably would not have felt the need to express his displeasure in such wonderfully prissy terms.

Ambrose Tubbs wisely concludes her essay with the acknowledgement that "We will never know whether Meriwether Lewis suffered from Asperger's syndrome or what caused him to take his own life."[145]

I see two problems with the Asperger's thesis. First, it is not a great fit for Meriwether Lewis. He was not particularly beset by rigidity of character, nor was he as fond of counting and list making as Ambrose Tubbs implies. The Asperger's label actually fits Lewis's patron Jefferson better than Lewis himself. Jefferson, not Lewis, was the zealous advocate of the grid and the questionnaire, though that principally revealed his complete enamorment with the taxonomical methodologies of the Enlightenment. It was Jefferson, not Lewis, who had obsessively rigid personal habits, as evidenced in his letter to Vine Utley on March 21, 1819.[146] It was Jefferson who had a hard time making eye contact—at least until he decided he could trust a new acquaintance. It was Jefferson who felt the need to count everything in his world, and to work out the dimensions for the build- ings he was designing to four and five decimal points of precision. It was Jefferson who responded to great emotional pain by throwing himself into something that involved detailed measurement.[147] But if Jefferson had Asperger's, then virtually everyone on earth should yearn to suffer from the malady; Jefferson was one the most productive, gifted, creative, per- suasive, lucid, organized, thoughtful, efficient, generous, and influential men who ever lived.

The second problem with the Asperger's thesis is that, even if it helps us understand Lewis, it doesn't explain why he committed suicide. Ambrose Tubbs makes no claim that those who suffer from Asperger's commit suicide at a higher than normal rate. That would seem to be the key to making the case for Lewis and Asperger's. Although the available literature suggests that people with various forms of autism have a higher incidence of suicidal feelings than the general population, there is no conclusive evidence that the actual suicide rate is higher. In other words, even if it could be proved that Lewis suffered from Asperger's, that does not mean that he committed suicide. Still, the Asperger's diagnosis covers Lewis's known behavior traits better than bipolar disease or manic depression, and it is used by Ambrose Tubbs and others in a more careful way than her father's broad psychoana- lytical brush was employed.

All that we can say is that Apserger's cannot be ruled out. Whether it gets us any closer to understanding the life and meaning of Meriwether Lewis is a different question.

In the end we are left with Jefferson's careful and astute analysis. "Lewis had from early life been subject to hypocondriac affections." Hypochondria ran in the family, but most of the Lewises were nevertheless functional. He had noticed, when they lived alone like two church mice in the White House, "sensible depressions of mind." Lewis's mental problems were "suspended" by "constant exertion" during the great adventure. When he returned to "sedentary occupations" his depressions "returned upon him with redoubled vigor." Because of his troubles in St. Louis the accumulative stresses brought on what Jefferson called a "paroxysm." It was in the grip of that paroxysm that Lewis "did the deed which plunged his friends into affliction."[148] No member of the American Philosophical Society, including America's first psychologist Benjamin Rush, would have found this hasty or insufficiently precise and detailed.

LEWIS'S GOVERNORSHIP

One of the myths of Lewis and Clark studies is that Lewis was a failure as the governor of Louisiana Territory. Like most myths, it is not without a foundation of truth. Carolyn Gilman has written starkly, "The appointment of Lewis to a political post was a colossal blunder. He was an introvert accustomed to commanding others rather than beguiling them, and he was unsuited to the deal-making of political life in a town where an entrenched mercantile oligarchy clashed with turbulent new populist factions."[149]

There were three essential problems of Lewis's governorship. First, he was insufficiently communicative with his superiors in the American government and with his patron and protector Thomas Jefferson. Second, he was tardy in getting himself to St. Louis. Dillon concludes, "Meriwether Lewis's year-long procrastination in assuming his duties as Governor was absolutely inexcusable. In a very real sense he was as responsible as Bates for the deterioration and chaos of Indian affairs."[150] During that inexcusable delay, his secretary Frederick Bates served as acting governor, made a series of decisions that Lewis later felt the need to clarify or reverse, and established his own primacy in territorial affairs. Third, he was, as Bates insightfully concluded, too accustomed to military command to understand the yeasty brew of frontier politics. Danisi and Jackson have written, "For a year while Lewis attended to more pressing matters, Territorial Secretary Bates was the only authority in Louisiana. But those distractions had dragged on too long, and the subordinate developed a proprietary interest in his temporary authority. It was unfortunate that they had gotten off on a sour note causing Bates to turn sulky, then belligerent, and finally insulting."[151]

If Bates had been a more generous man, if Lewis had gotten himself to St. Louis as promptly as Clark did after their appointments, had he possessed some of Clark's good humor, tolerance, and flexibility, if Lewis had made communication with the home government in Washington, DC, a priority, he would assuredly have had a better tenure as governor of Louisiana Territory.

It's hard for a reader of the twenty-first century to understand the chaos and turmoil of what became Missouri in 1808. Four different *tribes* had to find some way to co-exist. The *Americans* were technically in charge, though they were still in the minority, but the other populations were at best reluctant to respect American sovereignty. The *French* had founded the city back in 1765, and they had continued to represent the social aristocracy of the district even under Spanish and now American control. The *Spanish* had owned the vast Louisiana Territory from 1768 until 1800, when it was returned to France in the secret Treaty of San Ildefonso. The Americans purchased the Louisiana Territory in 1803, and formal transfer occurred on March 10 1804, with Amos Stoddard and Meriwether Lewis presiding. Add to these the fourth tribe, the *Osage Indians*. In addition to the significant differences in social style between the Europeans and the Americans, and between the French and the Spanish for that matter, the three Euro-American peoples had to face the challenge of treating and trading with, governing (to some degree), and systematically dispossessing the aboriginal inhabitants of Louisiana. The country west of St. Louis was really *their* land, of course, now occupied by Euro-Americans who simply presumed that they represented a superior brand of civilization and that their mission was to extinguish Indian title to any lands that Euro-Americans were ready to settle. After observing United States Indian policy at first hand in the last years of Clark's life, the French traveler Alexis de Tocqueville famously wrote, "It would be impossible to destroy men with more respect for the laws of humanity."[152] The first treaty that Clark concluded with the Osage was so confiscatory that Lewis insisted that it be renegotiated. Later in life Clark confessed that if he went to hell, it would be because of his agency in negotiating the Osage treaty.[153]

Frederick Bates was almost certainly right in concluding that Lewis, who habits were "altogether military," was not well suited to be the republican governor of a raw and tumultuous new territory. In light of all of this, it is hard to take Jefferson's summary seriously. "The even-handed justice he administered to all soon established a respect for his persona & authority, and perseverance & time wore down animosities and reunited the citizens again into one family."[154]

Still, Lewis had a productive governorship. He concluded treaties with the Osage Indians highly advantageous to the United States. He did what he could to restrain illegal preemption of mining claims and claim jumping. He enacted a law to permit villages to incorporate. He completed an important position paper on Indian policy. He laid out a road from St. Louis to Ste. Genevieve, Cape Girardeau and New Madrid. He helped organize expeditions to build trade factories at Forts Osage and Madison. He published the laws of the territory in English and had the laws translated into French for the benefit of that important community. As one of the first US citizens of St. Louis, he helped to start the first newspaper in the territory. He helped to create the first Masonic lodge west of the Mississippi River. He wrote occasional articles for the *Missouri Gazette*.

Lewis accomplished all of this with a passive-aggressive, back-biting, and undermining territorial secretary, while attempting to write a book and at the same time wrap up the last loose ends of the expedition, the most important of which by far was getting the Mandan leader Sheheke-shote back home to the Mandan villages in today's North Dakota. I have written about this problem elsewhere in this book. The point I wish to make here is that returning Sheheke-shote was a huge problem for which there was no satisfying solution. After the first return expedition was turned back by the hostile Arikara within 125 miles of its goal, at the cost of a number of lives and the loss of George Shannon's leg, it was clear that an expedition powerful or intimidating enough to get through Arikara country at the mouth of the Grand River on today's North Dakota-South Dakota border would have to be enormous. It would also be extremely expensive. There was no adequate military population in Louisiana Territory to accomplish the goal. Under the circumstances, it would have to be a public-private partnership, and, with the possible exception of Manuel Lisa, whom Lewis detested, there was no adequate commercial entity in place to undertake the mission or partner with a military contingent. Lewis and Clark (and others) had to invent the St. Louis Missouri River Fur Company before they could get Sheheke-shote home, and then pay it a massive sum to enter into an ethically dubious contract with the US government, as represented by Lewis (who was a silent partner in the same fur company), and then supplement that sum at the last moment, in the hopes of over-awing the Arikara and reaching the Mandan villages. All this to get seven Indians to the great bend of the Missouri River. Meanwhile, Sheheke-shote was restless and feeling aggrieved. According to Frederick Bates, after having been escorted to Washington, DC, by Lewis and being presented to the "great Chief of the Seventeen great nations of America,"[155] Sheheke-shote had come to "believe that he is the 'Brother' and not the 'Son' of the President."[156]

Lewis's efforts to get the leader of the Mandan people home, at a cost of almost four times the amount that Congress initially appropriated for the Lewis and Clark Expedition, consumed much of his time, money that the United States did not wish to spend in that manner, and almost all of his political capital. Nor was it certain that even the enormous public-private enterprise Lewis assembled to transport a handful of increasingly restive Indians would succeed in getting past the Arikara, if indeed it got *that far* up the Missouri River. There must have been times when Lewis sorely regretted the full-court effort he and Clark had undertaken in mid-August 1806 to convince Sheheke-shote to accompany them to the nation's capital.

The simple fact is that if Lewis had not had the responsibility of arranging for Sheheke-shote's return, an urgent moral imperative for the government of the United States, Jefferson said, he would not have offended the sensibilities of the staff of the War Department sufficiently to receive the bombshell rebuke and repudiation of July 15, 1809. Had he not received that profoundly destabilizing letter ... .

It seems certain (to us) that the mercurial Lewis overreacted to the rebuke he received from Eustis or one of his lieutenants. John Bakeless has spoken of "the wire-drawn ingenuity of Washington's official bumbledom."[157] This sort of bureaucratic second-guessing was a common frustration in the life of frontier administrators. Bakeless wrote, "His accounts were disputed by Washington auditors. But though the government's financial methods drive men to distraction, they rarely drive them to suicide."[158] Gilbert Russell wanted to accompany Lewis along the Natchez Trace to the nation's capital to explain several of *his* protested vouchers, and even the always-reliable Clark received a letter from the blustery Eustis, not long after Lewis's departure in early September 1809, rebuking him for what Eustis regarded as an unnecessarily inflated budget in Clark's Indian agency. Eustis wrote, "[I]t does not appear to be necessary that the expense attending our Relations with the Indians in the Territory of Louisiana should be four times as much as the whole expense of supporting its civil government."[159]

Thus Lewis was not the only frontier official whose vouchers were being challenged by the penny-pinchers of Madison's War Department. Nor were his field expenditures as irresponsible as the letter of July 15, 1809, alleges. It seems unlikely that Eustis and his clerk William Simmons were aware of the general arrangement established between President Jefferson and his protégé about the way decisions should be made in the field, or of the sense of urgency with which Jefferson instructed Lewis to find a way to get Sheheke-shote home to the Mandan villages. Eustis and Simmons probably did not know (or if they knew, agree with) the virtually unlimited grant of financial discretion President Jefferson had provided Lewis during the course of his transcontinental journey. In his letter inviting Clark to join the expedition, written in Washington, DC, on June 19, 1803, Lewis made a list of the factors that ensured the expedition's success. After explaining that he had the authority to requisition both equipment and men from establishments of the US Army, he said, "I am likewise furnished with letters of credit, and authorized to draw on the government for any sum necessary for the comfort of myself or party."[160] Here Lewis referred to the universal letter of credit that Jefferson supplied him, authorizing him to purchase anything he needed to further the success of the expedition at any emporium, operated by factors of any nation, anywhere on earth, including trade ships at the mouth of the Columbia. Lewis sorely wished to make use of that letter of credit during the expedition's winter stay at Fort Clatsop, either to resupply the Corps of Discovery with Indian trade items, whiskey, tobacco, clothing and shoes, and such luxuries as mosquito netting, or to send part or all of the men home by way of Cape Horn, but he literally had no where to draw on the credit line. During the long winter in today's North Dakota, Canadian trader François-Antoine Larocque wrote, "They have likewise Letters of Credit from the American Government for the payment of any draughts, they should draw upon it."[161] After the first attempt to deliver Sheheke-shote to his homeland failed, Jefferson wrote several letters to Lewis expressing the moral urgency of getting the Mandan leader home. In the first of those letters, dated July 17, 1808, Jefferson rebuked Lewis for his silence on the subject and then wrote, "We consider the good faith, & the reputation of the nation as pledged to accomplish this. We would wish indeed not to be obliged to undertake any considerable military expedition in the present uncertain state of our foreign concerns, & especially not till the new body of troops shall be raised. But if it can be effected in any other way & at reasonable expense we are disposed to meet it."[162]

It would have been perfectly rational for Lewis to regard Jefferson's letters on this subject as a kind of carte blanche to get Sheheke-shote home. It was certainly a large grant of authority to find a way to return the Mandan leader, and Jefferson rightly realized Lewis would be in a better position than anyone in Washington, DC, to know what that would entail. Lewis would have been perfectly within reason to assume he was authorized to cobble together what we would call a public-private partnership to accomplish the task, particularly because the frugal and peace-loving Jefferson stated specifically that he would rather not "undertake any considerable military expedition."

Had William Eustis or James Madison been in possession of Jefferson's letters, they would have been much less likely to have challenged the contract he undertook with the Saint Louis Missouri Fur Company or to imply that Lewis was arrogating to himself an authority he did not possess. In particular, had Eustis or Madison been aware of Jefferson's sense of urgency and his aversion to a military expedition to return Sheheke-shote, they would not have made the outrageous accusation that Lewis was engaged in some sort of public-private conflict of interest or that the intended expedition might be some sort of illegal or disloyal filibustering mission like the one undertaken by Aaron Burr in 1806. It was these irresponsible accusations that drove Lewis to the frenzy that ended his life. In fact, the mission that Lewis organized to return Sheheke-shote cannot be regarded as counter to the grant of authority that Jefferson—the sitting president of the United States—provided in his letters of July 17, 1808, and August 24, 1808. Lewis was doing precisely what he was told.

Lewis's unilateral decision to augment the $7,000 flat fee granted to the Saint Louis Missouri Fur Company with additional moneys totaling $500 and $440 was perhaps a mistake, given the seemingly gigantic amount of the original contract and the fact that the expedition intended to engage in commercial trade once it had deposited the Mandan leader at his home village. But he knew the facts on the ground as no one back East could possibly know them; he had been instructed by Jefferson in no uncertain terms to accomplish the mission *in any practicable way*; and he had taken care to make the additional sums conditional on developing conditions on the Upper Missouri. If things turned out to be more peaceful than he expected, Pierre Chouteau was required by contract to return the money. The Sheheke-shote affair was an unexpected emergency in a volatile geography[163] a very long distance from Washington, DC. Lewis believed he was making responsible, indeed necessary, decisions that could not wait for specific approval from the War Department, given the turnaround time of such communications and America's tardiness in getting Sheheke-shote home.

For the three years between July 1803 and September 1806, Lewis had been almost entirely on his own in a far country. He had had no choice but to make all of his own decisions from the moment he left St. Charles until he returned twenty-eight months later. No doubt he would have sought Jefferson's advice many times in the course of his transcontinental journey, had that been possible, but he had literally walked off the edge of the known world without the slightest possibility of receiving communications from the government of the United States. Now, in the summer of 1809, although he was technically back in "civilization," Lewis could not get authorization for any act or decision in less than two months, and possibly a great deal longer. The only instructions he had about Sheheke-shote came from Jefferson, and they were unambiguous.

DRINKING

Historians routinely declare that Lewis was drinking heavily in the last months of his life. The usually fastidious William Foley writes, "As the amiable redhead [Clark] slipped comfortably into his new post-expedition life, his close friend and associate Meriwether Lewis began drinking heavily and descended ever further into despondency."[164] Ambrose writes, "Lewis was drinking heavily, using snuff frequently, taking his pills, talking wildly, telling lies."[165] Harry Fritz is emphatic and unambiguous. "Lewis had a problem with alcohol. ... He took 120 gallons of distilled spirits up the Missouri River in 1804. Excessive drinking most assuredly contributed to his suicide in 1809."[166] It may be so, but the documents relating to the last year of Lewis's life do not themselves indicate heavy consumption.

A number of the murderists, led by John Guice, have argued that Lewis's drinking, even if excessive, was not particularly unusual for the early national period on the American frontier. Citing W.A. Rorabaugh's book, *The Alcoholic Republic: An American Tradition* (1979), they argue that if Lewis was drinking heavily, he was probably not much different from his frontier contemporaries, and that twenty-first century readers, living in a much different era with adequate water treatment facilities and a wide variety of superb non-alcoholic beverages to choose from, tend to make too much of such evidence as we have of Lewis's drinking. Fair enough.

This cuts both ways, of course. If heavy drinking was so commonplace in the era that it is hardly worth mentioning, then when Lewis's heavy consumption is mentioned by his contemporaries, it must have been sufficiently serious to have attracted notice. Several key individuals close to Lewis volunteered that he was not just drinking heavily, but that he had a drinking problem. In 1810 Jefferson wrote, "He was much afflicted and habitually so with hypochondria. This was probably increased by the habit into which he had fallen and the painful reflections that would necessarily produce in a mind like his."[167] It is generally assumed that Jefferson is here referring to Lewis's habit of drinking, but the veil of discreteness that Jefferson threw over Lewis's behavior leaves open the possibility that the former president was referring to some other debilitating habit: whoring, masturbation, addiction to laudanum, sleeping through the day, or for that matter keeping to himself and avoiding the company of others. There is no way to know precisely what Jefferson had in mind as he wrote this sentence, except that he regarded it as sufficiently shameful as to require a veiled reference.

Assuming that Jefferson was referring to excessive drinking, he was quite right that the worst thing a depressive individual can do is self-medicate with alcohol. Jefferson was in a better position to observe Lewis's behavior than most others. They had lived together, virtually the only two white people in the White House, between April 1801 and July 1803. The president, who was famous for the exquisite wines he served at his thrice-weekly dinner parties, would have had plenty of opportunities to observe Lewis's drinking habits. At the same time, it is important to remember that Jefferson was an exceedingly moderate drinker. Although he could say, "Good wine is a daily necessity for me,"[168] Jefferson limited himself to a couple of small glasses of wine per day, those frequently diluted (in the European fashion) with water. After his college years, it would be a mistake to assume that Jefferson was ever again intoxicated in the course of his long life. Lewis's "habit" might have seemed much less problematic—or even noticeable—to Andrew Jackson or any other of Jefferson's hard-drinking contemporaries. Jefferson prided himself on never losing control of his famous Stoic equanimity. He certainly did not understand the manners that prevailed in the US Army in his era. In a letter to his mother Lucy Marks written from Winchester, Virginia, on October 4, 1794, at the age of twenty, Lewis boasted, "We have mountains of beef and oceans of whiskey, and I feel myself able to share it with the heartiest fellow in camp."[169] The profoundly disciplined and sober Jefferson, who found fault with his distant cousin Chief Justice John Marshall in part for what he called "his lax lounging manners," and frequent visits to taverns, was not perhaps the best person to pass judgment on Meriwether Lewis's habits.[170]

Still, Jefferson was sufficiently convinced that Lewis's difficulties were exacerbated by alcohol that he implied that it contributed to Lewis's demise both chemically and by way of the feelings of guilt and remorse it awakened in him. Jefferson's assertion that Lewis felt guilty about his drinking is corroborated by Gilbert Russell, who reported that, once he had dried out, Lewis vowed that he would never drink again. In his January 1810 letter to Jefferson, Russell wrote, "The fact is which you may yet be ignorant of that his untimely death may be attributed solely to the free use he made of liquor which he acknowledged verry candidly to me after he recovered and expressed a firm determination never to drink any more spirits or use snuff again both of which I deprived him of for several days & confined him to claret & a little white wine."[171] This squares precisely with Jefferson's assessment.

Russell continued, "But after leaving this place by some means or other his resolution left him & this Agt. being extremely fond of liquor, instead of preventing the Govr from drinking or keeping him under any restraint advised him to it & from every thing I can learn gave the man every chance to seek an opportunity to destroy himself. … I cannot help to believe that Purney was rather aiding & abeting the murder than otherwise."[172] The agent (Agt.) was James Neelly, who accompanied Lewis from Fort Pickering to Grinder's Inn, and who apparently was a heavy drinker himself. By *murder*, Russell means either self-murder, or that Neelly and Pernier in a sense murdered Lewis by encouraging him to drink heavily when they knew he was physically and mentally impaired.

The letter Gilbert Russell wrote to Thomas Jefferson on January 31, 1810, was an angry denunciation of Neelly. Russell regretted that he did not send a different chaperon with Lewis to Nashville, because Neelly permitted and even encouraged Lewis to resume drinking, which precipitated the state of mind in which Lewis killed himself on October 10–11. Neelly also appropriated some of the personal effects of the dead governor "for some claim he pretends to have upon his estate."[173] Russell declared that Neelly "can have no just claim for any thing more than the expenses of his interment unless he makes a charge for packing his two Trunks from the nation."[174] Russell heaped contempt on Neelly's claim that "he lent the Govr money which cannot be so as he had none himself & the Govr had more than one hund. $ in notes & specie besides a check I let him have of 99.58 none of which it is said could be found."[175] Even so, Russell authorized the payment of Neelly's "pretended claim" in order to recover Lewis's pistols, "which will be held sacred to the order of any of the friends of M. Lewis free from encumbrance."[176] We know that Neelly somehow evaded that transaction and that Lewis's pistols and dirk were never returned.

On the other hand, it is certainly worth noting that nobody on the Lewis and Clark expedition ever accused Captain Lewis of having a drinking problem, and none of the extant journal keepers ever mentioned seeing Lewis intoxicated. In fact, no single journal entry in Moulton's thirteen-volume comprehensive edition of the journals could by the most ungenerous reader be tortured into hinting that Lewis was drinking any significant quantity of alcohol. When the captains wrote about alcohol consumption on the trail, it was usually to note that the enlisted men had been weaned from consumption so completely that even a small quantity of whiskey made them tipsy. On July 4, 1805, for example, at the Great Falls of the Missouri, Lewis wrote, "[O]ur work being at an end this evening, we gave the men a drink of sperits, it being the last of our stock, and some of them appeared a little sensible of it's effects the fiddle was plyed and they danced very merrily untill 9 in the evening when a heavy shower of rain put an end to that part of the amusement tho' they continued their mirth with songs and festive jokes and were extreemly merry untill late at night."[177]

Nor did Lewis's enemy Frederick Bates include drunkenness in his litany of charges against the governor. We can be sure that Bates would not have failed to note any drinking problem he perceived in his superior.

AFFAIR OF HONOR

An affair of honor is a conflict between two individuals (usually men) of more or less the same social class, in which one person affronts or confronts the other in such a way that it creates a fundamental crisis of honor or self-identity. The affronted individual believes that his honor has been deliberately degraded, that his social standing has been damaged, and that he has no choice, as a man of honor, but to demand some sort of satisfaction—either an apology or a clarification that reduces the offensiveness of the initial statement or action. If no apology or clarification is forthcoming, or either of those gestures is regarded as insincere or inadequate, the affair of honor might end in a duel. Duels were relatively common in the early national period, particularly in the southern states and territories. The most famous duel of the era was conducted at Weehawken, New Jersey, on July 11, 1804, between Alexander Hamilton and Aaron Burr, both of New York. In fact, one of the first pieces of news that Lewis and Clark learned on their homeward journey was that Hamilton had been killed in a duel. On September 3, 1806, near today's Sioux City, Iowa, a trader named James Aird informed the captains that the former secretary of the treasury, "Genl. Hambleton" had been cut down on the west bank of the Hudson River by Vice President of the United States Aaron Burr.[178]

Affairs of honor were much more common than duels. Even the pacific and rational President Jefferson was involved in one in 1805. His old college friend, now enemy, John Walker demanded that Jefferson clarify the nature of his relations with Walker's wife Elizabeth back in 1768, when Walker had been called away from Albemarle County on diplomatic business. He had asked Jefferson to look after his family. Apparently Jefferson either seduced or tried to seduce Betsy Walker, or they engaged in a consensual extra-marital relationship. Nobody knows for sure. The affair of honor was resolved, well this side of a duel, when Jefferson wrote to his secretary of the navy, but for Walker's eyes, "[W]hen young and single I offered love to a handsome lady. I acknolege its incorrectness."[179]

The great Hamilton scholar Joanne Freeman has written, "For twentieth-century onlookers far removed from the culture of honor, the duel was a ritual of violence whose purpose was to maim or kill an adversary. But to early national politicians, duels were demonstrations of manner, not marksmanship; they were intricate games of dare and counterdare, ritualized displays of bravery, military prowess, and—above all—willingness to sacrifice one's life for one's honor."[180]

Lewis was involved in three affairs of honor in the course of his life.

The first, beginning on September 24, 1795, involved a fellow officer in the US Army. On that day, at Greenville, Ohio, Lewis issued a challenge to Lieutenant Joseph Elliott. Apparently Lewis had behaved in an aggressive and provocative way in Lieutenant Elliott's quarters. Elliott, who was offended that Lewis had disrupted the harmony of a private party, chastised Lewis in front of his peers. Lewis withdrew—angry and mortified—and later that day sent a letter to Elliott demanding satisfaction. This led Elliott to file formal charges against Lewis. Five weeks later, on November 6, 1795, Lewis was court-martialed. Six days later Lewis was exonerated of all charges and "acquitted with honor."[181]

The second affair of honor was between Lewis and Frederick Bates. When it became clear that they could not learn to like each other, Lewis told his subordinate, "Well, do not suffer yourself to be separated from me in the public opinion. When we meet in public, let us, at least, address each other with cordiality."[182] This was precisely the right way for a territorial governor and gentleman to behave. Lewis gave his subordinate excellent advice. On July 14, 1809, Bates informed his brother that he intended to honor Lewis's request. "However I may have disapproved and continue to disapprove the [official] measures of the Governor, as a man I entertain good opinions of him."[183] This was probably not altogether candid. Nor did Bates honor his agreement.

Unfortunately, Bates is the only source we have for the crisis that followed. It is like a scene out of a Jane Austen novel. Bates may have been a miscreant, but he wrote colorful letters full of superb detail. The affair of honor began in earnest at a Masonic ball in celebration of the Festival of St. John the Baptist in late June 1809. Bates wrote,

> There was a ball in St. Louis. I attended early, and was seated in conversation with some Gentlemen when the Governor entered. He drew his chair close to mine—There was a pause in the conversation—I availed myself of it—arose and walked to the opposite side of the room. The dances were now commencing.[184]

In the tautly civil world of the early nineteenth century, among the gentry, in Virginia or on the raw frontier, Bates's sudden withdrawal was an intolerable breach of social decorum. In spite of his agreement to be civil and respectful to Governor Lewis in public, by his own testimony Bates engaged in an unmistakable act of public disrespect. Lewis's sense of honor and dignitas were so wounded by Bates's rudeness that he felt he had no choice but to challenge his lieutenant's behavior. If Bates had informed Lewis that he would only speak to him about official affairs, and that he was not prepared to be civil to Lewis in St. Louis social circles, his behavior at the ball might have been understandable. But he had agreed "in public [to] address each other with cordiality." Nor can it fairly be said, even according to Bates's testimony, that Lewis "thrust himself" into Bates's circle at the ball. It would have been impolite for Lewis *not* to sit down with Bates at a public event, at least briefly.

Bates continued:

> *He* also rose—evidently in passion, retired into an adjoining room and sent a servant for General Clark, who refused to ask me out as he foresaw that a Battle must have been the consequence of our meeting.[185]

In the ratcheting up of aggressive behavior that might, if taken to its logical extreme, put two combatants on the field of honor, Bates had committed the first overt act. He had publicly shunned and dishonored his superior and a fellow gentleman. Lewis left the room "evidently in passion." In this context, *evidently* means visibly, unmistakably, publicly. Lewis did not conceal his anger. He chose Clark to be his second. When Clark arrived, Lewis explained the affront to his colleague and dearest friend: "[H]e complained to the general that I had treated him with contempt & insult in the Ball-Room and that he could not suffer it to pass." Lewis was certainly right about the public insult; Bates confirmed the charge in his letter to his brother. If Clark had been a less loving and careful friend, he might have served notice to the odious Bates that Lewis was challenging him to a duel. Clark refused, "as he foresaw that a Battle must have been the consequence of our meeting." In this, Bates was probably lucky. Lewis was a fearless and extremely accurate gunman. It's hard to imagine any actual duel in which Bates would not have been killed, wounded, or treated with socially crippling contempt.

Bates continued:

> He knew my resolutions not to speak to him except in business and he ought not to have thrust himself in my way. The thing *did pass* nevertheless for some weeks when General Clark waited on me for the purpose of introducing me to make some advances.[186]

In other words, after permitting a cooling off period, Clark visited Bates and urged him to find a way to reconcile with Governor Lewis. In addition to short-circuiting the possible duel, Clark now made overtures to Bates to try to repair his relationship with the mercurial Lewis. That's the kind of man Clark was. Bates rejected Clark's overture: "You come ... as *my* friend, but I cannot separate you from Gov Lewis—You have trodden the *Ups* & the *Downs* of life with him, and it appears to me that these proposals are made solely for *his* convenience."[187] Bates refused to reconcile and refused to regard Clark as an impartial intermediary.

> I replied to him, "NO, the Governor has told me to take my own course and I shall step a *high* and a *proud* Path. He has *injured* me and he must *undo* that injury or I shall succeed in fixing the stigma where it *ought* to *rest*."[188]

In other words, Bates refused to restore the social equilibrium, when Clark had given him a perfect opportunity to do so. Instead, Bates now indicated that it was Lewis who had set in motion the affair of honor by injuring him in some way. In publicly spurning Lewis, Bates was defending his own honor. Poor Clark was trying to neutralize the antagonists and resolve the affair of honor before it got out of hand. He began by refusing to serve as his friend's second while he was in the throes of his passion at the St. Louis ball. In giving Lewis enough time to get his emotions under control, Clark prevented what might have been a fatal encounter. He waited a number of weeks, and then he went to work on Bates in a careful and indirect way. At this point, he was essentially serving as Bates's second. Bates rejected the careful overtures. Fortunately, the affair of honor petered out in some way that neither Bates nor Clark nor Lewis ever explained. Probably Clark's stall tactics had been the key to a non-violent conclusion. Once again, the remarkable William Clark had cleaned up after his hot-tempered and volatile friend.

The focus of our understanding of the demise of Meriwether Lewis is usually his deteriorating physical and mental condition, and his struggle with President Madison's War Department. But the situation with Bates deserves more attention than it has received. The failure of Clark's diplomatic mission to the territorial secretary meant that Bates and Lewis were now open and public enemies. Their agreement to be publicly respectful of each other— essential for the orderly government of the territory, essential for the social harmony of St. Louis, essential for their individual political futures—had collapsed at a public dance. A ball in the early national period was a kind of social tableau that publicly displayed and reinforced social norms: the class hierarchy, the distinction between masters and servants and masters and slaves, the sanctitude of matrimony, the eligibility of unmarried men and women for each other, the acceptable level of public displays of affection, the distinction between government functionaries and citizens, and between military men and the civilian population. A ball was not a dance in our sense of the term. It was a choreographed public visualization of the social register.

In Shakespeare, broken rituals (marriages, funerals, feasts) inevitably signal the breakdown of the social order. That order must be restored for life to go on in King Lear's primitive England or Othello's Venice or for that matter Meriwether Lewis's Louisiana Territory. It was essential that Lewis and Bates find some way of working together and maintaining social decorum until one or both of them moved on or was reassigned. The collapse of their public *and* private relations in the summer of 1809 created an irreparable social breach. Not even Clark, who spent his life patching up the personalities of difficult people, could find a way to repair things.

It's hard to imagine how things could have gone on in St. Louis in the face of this struggle. It would have been hard enough to govern Louisiana Territory with an administration as harmonious as Jefferson's cabinet in Washington, DC. But to display before the enemies of order (and there were many in St. Louis in 1809) a public dispute between the famous but difficult governor and his able but unprofessional subordinate was essentially to destroy the credibility of the territorial government and to let any unscrupulous entity—individual or corporate—play the two top officers of the territory off each other, to capitalize on the quarrel to advance their own claims or just to carry on knowing that there was not sufficient solidarity in the government to enforce the laws and codes of the territory.

If Lewis had ventured to Washington, DC, and Philadelphia and then returned to Louisiana "with flying colors," as Clark predicted, how would he have solved the problem of Bates? The only solution that would have worked—and then not necessarily entirely—would have been to secure Bates's reassignment or recall. It is just possible that Lewis might have convinced President Jefferson that nothing short of the departure of Bates could fix the problem, but Jefferson was now happily (and militantly) in retirement at Monticello, and Lewis's credibility with Jefferson had suffered significantly in the post-expeditionary period. Since it was Bates who had served as acting governor during Lewis's unpardonable absence, and since Bates continued to serve as the communication arm of the territorial government with the world back East, it would have been hard for even Jefferson to side unhesitatingly with his famous protégé. And if Lewis's credibility with his friend and patron Jefferson had suffered a series of setbacks, his standing with President Madison was comparatively negligible. Lewis may have been the injured party in his struggle with Bates, but he had damaged his righteousness by frustrating everyone who believed in him, including Jefferson and Clark, and by frustrating even more those not disposed to give him the benefit of the doubt. In other words, Lewis was the author of his own gubernatorial crisis, no matter how badly history judges the behavior of Frederick Bates. Surely Lewis knew this.

The third affair of honor pitted Lewis against William Eustis and the US War Department. When Eustis (or William Simmons) sent his letter of severe rebuke on July 15, 1809, he did far more than disallow several of Lewis's territorial vouchers. Such financial challenges were common in the early national period. Eustis went much farther than that. He leveled three profoundly upsetting charges at Governor Lewis. First, he accused Lewis of engaging in a serious conflict of interest in awarding a lucrative contract to a private fur company to return Sheheke-shote to today's North Dakota. "In the instance of accepting the volunteer services of 140 men for a military expedition to a point and purpose not designated, which expedition is stated to combine commercial as well as military objects, and when an Agent of the Government appointed for other purposes is selected for the command, it is thought the Government might, without injury to the public interests, have been consulted."[189]

Second, he hinted that the Missouri Fur Company might be involved in some sort of illegal filibustering mission into the far northwest not so different from the treasonous conduct of Aaron Burr in the southwestern borderlands of the United States. "As the object & destination of this Force is unknown, and more especially as it combines Commercial purposes, so it cannot be considered as having the sanction of the Government of the United States, or that they are responsible for the consequences."[190] This was an insult of such magnitude and such irresponsibility that I believe it precipitated Lewis's final breakdown. It had been bad enough to have Secretary Bates undermining his reputation and nipping at his heels with increasing recklessness. But to have a high official of the government of the United States imply that Lewis, the hero of the Corps of Volunteers for North Western Discovery and the friend and protégé of the former president of the United States, was no better than Aaron Burr, a scoundrel and traitor, was intolerable.

Third, the letter accused Lewis of violating the terms of the US Constitution by permitting himself as a member of the executive branch to spend tax dollars without a congressional appropriation.

The tone of Eustis's letter was so personal and so ungenerous that it could not be dismissed as a routine administrative matter. The accusations were leveled at Lewis in categorical terms. He was not asked to clarify his decisions, but bluntly accused of malfeasance in office. Eustis (or his clerk) made no effort to give Governor Lewis the benefit of the doubt. The letter includes no statement of the Madison administration's general confidence in the territorial governor, coupled with a statement that when proper explanations have been provided, the War Department feels certain that Governor Lewis's decisions will make more sense and vindicate his judgment. The language of respect and accommodation was deliberately withheld from the War Department letter. These accusations and the tone in which they were articulated in the July 15, 1809, letter were so hostile and so direct that Meriwether Lewis could *only* regard the letter as an unambiguous professional and personal attack on his competence, his integrity, his honesty, and his honor. And if the letter had not been sufficiently damning and damaging to Lewis's sense of himself, the author added an appalling final note: "The President has been consulted and the observations herein contained have his approval."[191]

It is sometimes said that the English romantic poet John Keats died from the harsh criticism his poetry received in his lifetime. He was just twenty-five years old at the time of his death in 1821. It seems to me unmistakable that this irresponsible letter contributed to Meriwether Lewis's death at the age of thirty-five. It seems to me that Lewis could not help but regard the letter as a direct assault on his character and his honor. It was the kind of letter that, under other circumstances, could start the chain of events that might lead to a duel. But one does not fight a duel with the secretary of war or the president of the United States. Lewis had been assaulted—with words—in a way he had *not* been affronted by Joseph Elliott or Frederick Bates, with both of whom he entered into an affair of honor. When the government you serve expresses its official judgment of no confidence in your work, you have no choice but to absorb the blow, if you are permitted to hold on to your office, or defend yourself with a barrage of letters, documents, and memos. You cannot issue a challenge. In the early national period, the outlet for the kind of rage and humiliation that a letter like the Eustis-Simmons letter of July 15, 1809, stirred in its recipient was a duel. Barbaric as dueling seemed to reasonable men like Jefferson and Madison, the ritual enabled men to vent their spleen in extreme situations, to salve their wounded egos, to preserve their sense of identity, and to reestablish their place in the social and political hierarchy. In spite of his instincts to fight back and to fight for his own honor, Lewis had to abase himself in his reply to Eustis and in his letter to James Madison. He had to address a man he regarded as a scoundrel, a man Clark called "a green pompous new englandr,"[192] in respectful and defensive terms, merely because he was the secretary of war. He had to address the president, a man who had permitted his name to be used as the final authority in a letter of open character assassination, as a respected sovereign.

I believe that it is certain that Lewis's rage, indisposition, depression, and derangement were the measure of the sense of outrage he felt at the way he was being treated by government clerks who knew nothing of the grizzly bear and the Shoshone national hug, men who had scarcely been west of the Appalachians and never even dreamed of drinking from the source of the "mighty and heretofore deemed endless Missouri." Lewis could not have them whipped, as he would have done for a puppy like Simmons or a nonentity like Eustis, had they spoken disrespectfully to him anywhere between St. Charles and Astoria. He could not brandish his tomahawk over their faces, as he had when the Nez Perce boy threw an Indian puppy on his plate. He could not shoot Eustis or Simmons, as he had when a brave young

Blackfeet man tried to steal the captain's horses in north-central Montana. He had to take their abuse, and he could not respond in kind. He had now completely lost control of his life.

Gilbert Russell of Fort Pickering said that Lewis arrived at Grinder's Inn "where in the apprehension of being destroyed by enemies which had no existence but in his wild immagination, he destroyed himself, in the most Cool desperate and Barbarian-like manner, having been left in the house intirely to himself."[193] Lewis let it be known that it would be better to kill himself than to give his enemies the satisfaction of doing it on his behalf.

I believe that between August 18, 1809, and October 11, 1809, Lewis was involved in an affair of honor that left him enraged, humiliated, bitter, deranged, and degraded in the eyes of the public and the class of American gentry to which he belonged—in other words, far down the path towards a duel in an affair of honor. But there was no antagonist he could meet on the field of honor. I believe that, at the very least, this one-sided affair of honor put Lewis into such a paroxysm (to use Jefferson's word) of impotence and rage that it made him feel more completely alone than at any previous moment of his life. In other words, at the very least, the quarrel helped to create the conditions that led to his suicide. But it may be deeper still. It is possible that in putting a bullet to his head in the early morning hours of October 11, 1809, Lewis was killing the only available person who bore any responsibility for what had happened to his life and career. In other words, in some strange but genuine sense, Lewis fought a duel between St. Louis and Grinder's Inn, and vented his profound sense of having had his identity, his integrity, his character, and his honor damaged by shooting himself. Had Eustis been a *former* secretary of war as Hamilton was a *former* secretary of the treasury, he might have paid for his misuse of power and verbal abuse with his life. Because he was a sitting member of the Madison administration, because he could hide behind the *great little Madison*, Eustis was allowed to live, and in his place died one of the most gifted and promising men of American history.

Buzz Aldrin Syndrome

Edwin (Buzz) Aldrin was the second man on the moon. After he returned to earth, Aldrin found himself in a post-expedition depression. He found that he was unable to relate to his friends and family in the old way. Eric Sevareid's prediction, intoned while Aldrin and Armstrong were still *on* the moon, proved to be insightful. "We're always going to feel, somehow, strangers to these men. They will, in effect, be a bit stranger, even to their own wives and children," Sevareid said.[194] Aldrin had trouble finding work that was meaningful in the shadow of his expedition to the moon. In his first book,

Return to Earth (1973), Aldrin wrote, "I had been on the first lunar landing and what could I possibly do to improve on that?"[195] He was now automatically overqualified for almost any job on earth and paradoxically at the same time overlooked for some positions that were equal to his celebrity but for which he was not well suited temperamentally. He had an extra-marital affair. Things became so difficult that he began to see a psychologist—taboo in NASA and military circles. Eventually he was hospitalized for depression. His marriage broke up. He suffered a nervous breakdown. "I had gone to the moon. What to do next? What possible goal could I add now? There simply wasn't one, and without a goal I was like an inert Ping-Pong ball being batted about by the whims and motivations of others. I was suffering from what poets have described as the melancholy of all things done ... "[196]

Aldrin's willingness to acknowledge his mental problems may have saved his life. In *Return to Earth,* he wrote, "It is my devout wish to bring emotional depression into the open and so treat it as one does a physical infirmity. I want my children to know so that if they too become ill they will see the symptoms and seek help. It doesn't truly matter whether or not the cause is genetic or environmental. The point is that it must be treated, the sooner the better."[197] Craig Nelson has written, "In time, Buzz became one of the bravest of all of America's astronauts by publicly revealing his mental illness."[198]

Aldrin has been fortunate. We live in a time when psychiatric counseling is widely available—even to heroes—and modern chemistry has developed a range of drugs more ameliorative than Rush's Thunderbolts, laudanum, or grain alcohol. Public tolerance for depression has never been greater. Because he was willing to work with ghostwriters, Aldrin has been able to publish half a dozen books about his explorations and his re-entry problems. His obsessive return to the same theme once every five years or so suggests that the catharsis each book provides is only temporary, however. His most recent book, *Magnificent Desolation* (2010), is essentially nothing more than an elaboration of his first, *Return to Earth.* Aldrin, unlike Lewis, has found plenty of women willing to give him solace and unlimited affection. He's neither fusty nor rusty.

When you have been to the moon, what's left?

Lewis did not seek professional help for his mental problems. He did not hire a ghostwriter to finish the book, vastly more important to the success of his mission and to his post-expedition reputation than any book written by any twentieth century astronaut. There were no adequate pharmaceuticals to treat mental illness in his time. Laudanum was nothing but an addictive painkiller. Lewis was unable to find women to soothe his perturbed spirit. Letitia Breckenridge left town to avoid him.

Richard Van Orman has written, "The hero-explorer found that one of the most difficult parts of the exploratory experience was the return and reintegration into society, where he was often confronted with jealousy, skepticism, and misunderstanding. The difficult experiences that Bruce, Park, Lewis, Speke, and Stanley faced on their return paralleled the mythical hero's return ... .The explorer was a stranger not only to natives but, in a sense, to his own society, especially if he had been away for a long time or had undergone significant changes."[199]

John Speke, the discoverer of the source of the Nile, died of self-inflicted gunshot wounds on September 15, 1864, one day before he was to square off with his arch-rival Richard Francis Burton for a debate about the Nile question. Speke was a superb hunter. Although the shooting was ruled an accident, most historians have regarded it as a species of suicide, even if technically it could be understood as a mishap. Speke's open betrayal of Burton divided the British geographical community and took away his satisfaction for having discovered—more or less by accident—the source of the Nile. Speke won the prize, but he wore his crown in bitterness and defensiveness until his untimely death. He was thirty-seven years old.

After his rescue in 1709, Alexander Selkirk, marooned for four years on the island of Juan Fernandez off the west coast of South America, lived like a hermit and slept in a cave. Before his rescuers would take him back to England, they forced him to run down and kill an island goat, just to prove that he was telling the truth about how he had fed himself through his long ordeal. Selkirk was the inspiration for Daniel Defoe's *Robinson Crusoe*.[200]

James Bruce spent six years exploring Africa between 1768 and 1773. When he returned to London in 1774, he was greeted by an incredulous public, one of whom, Samuel Johnson, accused him of telling tall tales about his travels. The story that amused and alienated the British public was Bruce's claim that Ethiopians cut beefsteaks out of live cattle. The public sneered at what it regarded as a whopper, but Richard Francis Burton later confirmed that it was true. Asked at a dinner party whether the Ethiopians possessed musical instruments, Bruce said they had the lyre. A wag at the table said, sotto voce, "I am sure there is one less since he came out of the country."[201] Bruce was so hurt by these jibes and the general skepticism of the British public that he retired in sore bitterness to his home at Kinnaird in Scotland. In 1790 he was finally prevailed upon to publish his remarkable *Travels to Discover the Source of the Nile, In the Years 1768, 1769, 1770, 1771, 1772 and 1773*, but that multi-volume masterpiece of travel literature was widely and at times acerbically criticized for a lack of "veracity," "his mis-statements," "his pretensions to an almost intuitive knowledge of the languages of the country," and "the unpardonable concealment" of some facts about his journeys. His principal detractor was Henry Salt, the author of *A voyage to Abyssinia, and travels into the interior of that country, executed under the orders of the British government in the years 1809 & 1810*.[202] That Bruce's essential accuracy has been confirmed by later travelers was, of course, little consolation to him.

When presidential explorer Theodore Roosevelt returned from his ordeal on the River of Doubt in 1914, having lost a quarter of his body mass and nearly died in the jungles of the Amazon basin, he was appalled to discover that skeptics in British geographic circles were discounting his achievement. The English explorer Henry Savage-Landor proclaimed that a river as large as the one Roosevelt described could not exist. Roosevelt's response was characteristically strenuous. "To be accused by him is to have an iron enter my soul," he said.[203] At the height of his jungle fever, Roosevelt had repeated over and over the first lines of Coleridge's *Kubla Khan*, "In Xanadu did Kubla Khan a stately pleasure dome decree, where Alf the sacred river ran, through caverns measureless to man, down to a sunless sea." Now, after his return to the United States, Roosevelt found himself more in the guise of Coleridge's Ancient Mariner, telling anyone who would listen that he really had explored the last uncharted major river of the Amazon watershed, that it had been an adventure worthy of the Argonauts, that he really had almost perished, that ... .

Lewis faced some of the same public skepticism and derision (see Chapter Five). His homecoming was as problematic as that of many other explorers. If the story is true that he had not slept on a bed for the three years following his return, it would not strike a historian of exploration as especially unusual.

When you have been to the source of the "mighty and heretofore deemed endless Missouri," what's left?

THE BARRY LOPEZ QUESTION

The distinguished essayist Barry Lopez gave a lecture at Lewis & Clark College in Portland, Oregon, at the height of the bicentennial of the Lewis and Clark Expedition. The question he asked at the beginning of his lecture was, "How far can you go out and still come back?" Lewis, said Lopez, apparently ventured too far. Lewis traveled almost precisely the same number of miles as his estimable friend William Clark, but somehow they were not on quite the same journey.

Is it possible to ascertain the moment at which Lewis had ventured *too far*?

One way to look at the story of Lewis and Clark is that in the course of their transcontinental journey they were stripped of layer after layer of the thin integument of civilization until they were essentially naked in the wilderness. On the return journey, as the various strands of the expedition approached the confluence of the Yellowstone and the Missouri, the captains realized that they were too naked to present themselves to their civilized countrymen, or even to the semi-civilized Mandan Indians. They paused to kill as many elk and deer as possible in the shortest time possible and to dress the skins to cover their nakedness. There is an uncanny echo of Genesis 3:6-7 in this: "She took of the fruit thereof, and did eat, and gave also unto her husband with her; and he did eat. And the eyes of them both were opened, and they knew that they *were* naked; and they sewed fig leaves together, and made themselves aprons." Lewis and Clark were, so far as they knew, the only civilized human beings in today's Montana. Since there was no one observing them who mattered, they did not mind being essentially naked. But when they realized that they would soon be "the observed of all observers,"[204] first by the 4,500 residents of the Mandan and Hidatsa villages, and then by whatever white traders they met on the Missouri that fall, they found ways to cover their nakedness. It was indeed the end of innocence—not perhaps for the men of the Lewis and Clark Expedition, but certainly for Montana.

A careful examination of the expedition's journals reveals the Corps of Discovery's slow-motion striptease. First their boots gave out and were replaced by moccasins, which were a highly imperfect footwear for young men pushing thirty tons of baggage up the Missouri River. Then their cloth shirts and trousers gave out. Late in the journey, Lewis petulantly reported the loss of his dress uniform coat. Just before the expedition left Fort Clatsop for the return journey, Lewis found that "nothing excep this coat would induce them to dispose of a canoe which in their mode of traffic is an article of the greatest vale except a wife, with whom it is equal, and is generally given in exchange to the father for his daughter. I think the U' States are indebted to me another Uniform coat, for that of which I have disposed on this occasion was but little woarn."[205] On July 4, 1805, the last of the whiskey was distributed to celebrate the American republic's twenty-ninth birthday. The flour ran out, and the smoked pork.[206] At some point at Fort Clatsop the tobacco supply had been fully consumed.

Like all exploration missions, the Lewis and Clark Expedition wrestled with what might be called the paradox of payloads. The men of the expedition couldn't possibly carry with them everything they would need to cross the continent—twice. They had to take the bare minimum. If they added more men to the roster in order to be able to force more baggage against the current of the Missouri River, they would have to bring provisions for those men, too. That's the paradox. They were fortunate in that the wilderness through which they passed was teeming with protein—buffalo, elk, deer, beaver, and salmon. The most efficient baggage they carried on the journey was thus rifle, powder, and ball, and they even maximized the efficiency of that supply by packing their gunpowder in lead canisters that could later be melted down into bullets. As long as they had serviceable rifles, they were bound to eat well, at least in the Missouri watershed. The expedition could not possibly carry enough whiskey, tobacco, mosquito netting, flour, pork, shirts, trousers, coats, and shoes, to make the entire journey. Thanks to the resourcefulness of such men as Joseph Whitehouse, a skin dresser, they were able to make replacement clothing on the trail. By the time they got home on September 23, 1806, they looked, said an observer, like characters out of *Robinson Crusoe*.[207] The first thing the captains did the following day was visit a tailor. Clothes make the man.

The genius Jefferson addressed the paradox of payloads by slipping into their baggage a document that weighed far less than one pound. The universal letter of credit he prepared for Lewis would have enabled him to purchase tons of supplies at the mouth of the Columbia River, or passage home around the southern tip of South America. It's a kind of Lewis and Clark parlor game to make a list of things Lewis would have purchased if he had come upon a trade vessel or series of trade vessels on November 14, 1805, when he ventured around Point Ellice into Baker Bay. Surely he would have purchased salt, tobacco, and whiskey, clothing, shoes, and as many trinkets and trade goods as the ship factors would have permitted the men to cart away. Whether the weary Lewis would have chosen to return to the Chesapeake by water is an interesting question. Probably not, since he had not yet found "the most direct & practicable water communication across this continent for the purposes of commerce."[208]

In 1845 Henry David Thoreau built himself a modest little cabin at Walden Pond near Concord, Massachusetts, to conduct an experiment in minimalism. He was attempting to slough off the superfluities of life, to simplify radically, and to see who he was when he drove life into a corner and reduced it to lowest terms. Thoreau was attempting to determine three things. First, what were life's absolute necessities, what he called our "grossest groceries." After food, shelter, clothing, pen and paper, and a few choice books, what were the prime desirabilities of life? Second, he wanted to know how many work days per year would be needed to provide himself those grossest groceries, and then to calculate on an item by item basis what luxuries he might wish to add to his kit, knowing in each case how much of his freedom and leisure he would have to give up to obtain them. Third, he wanted to prove to himself and his readers that a life of radical simplicity actually created greater satisfaction and soulfulness than one clogged with unnecessary stuff and complexity. Thoreau knew, of course, that he could give up the experiment at any time and move back into a more comfortable life in Concord.

Meriwether Lewis did not venture into the American West to perform a similar experiment. If he had been able to use his universal letter of credit at Fort Mandan, and Fort Clatsop, and places in between, he would assuredly have done so. In other words, he did not, like Thoreau, volunteer to reduce life to its lowest terms. He had several dozen subordinates to carry his baggage, and he carried with him as much as he could possibly transport. But in spite of the size of his company and the number of items he was able to carry into the wilderness, his life was eventually reduced to lowest terms by circumstance, and by the sheer distance he launched the capsule of his brain into the unknown.

The key week of Lewis's life occurred between August 12 and August 17, 1805. It was during that week that he "accomplished one of those great objects on which my mind has been unalterably fixed for many years,"[209] by reaching the source of the Missouri River. It was during that week that he made first contact with the Shoshone Indians. That, he knew, was the last of the expedition's Louisiana Territory quests. The Shoshone lived on the far western edge of the Louisiana Purchase. It was during that week that he peeped into the Oregon country for the first time and drank from a tributary stream of the Columbia River. It was during that week that his life was reduced to its lowest terms. It was during that week that he became as vulnerable and unprotected as he had ever been or ever would be in this sublunary world.

Lewis believed that the expedition would either succeed or fail depending on whether he could make successful first contact with the Shoshone Indians, whose horses he believed the expedition needed to get over the Bitterroot Mountains. He knew that if for some reason he scared the Shoshone off his chances for success would be very seriously diminished. The fact that the expedition had not seen an Indian (except for Sacagawea and her son) since April—they had not seen an Indian in the entire state of Montana—made Lewis anxious. Had they been routinely encountering Indian tribes in Montana the way they had between St. Louis and the Mandan and Hidatsa villages, he would have felt more confident. Given the total absence of Indian contact since April 10, 1805, Lewis had no way of sending Indian individuals on ahead as emissaries, no way of consulting neighbor tribes about the likely disposition and response of the Shoshone, no hope that the news of his presence and peaceful intentions would reach the Shoshone before he did. It is a commonplace of Lewis and Clark studies that the Shoshone were skittish in August 1805. But so was Meriwether Lewis. Even before he saw his first Shoshone individual on August 11 he was on edge. By the time Clark caught up with him on August 17, he would be a nervous wreck.

On August 11, 1805, Lewis and his three companions—George Drouillard, John Shields, and Hugh McNeal—approached a lone Shoshone man on horseback. Drouillard was far off on his right, Shields an equal distance off to the left, McNeal next to him. Because the two flankers failed to halt at the proper moment, Lewis believed, the lone Shoshone man "turned his hose [horse] about, gave him the whip leaped the creek and disapeared in the willow bush in an instant and with him vanished all my hopes of obtaining horses for the preasent."[210] Lewis lost his temper. "I now called the men to me and could not forbare abraiding them a little for their want of attention and imprudence on this occasion."[211] It would have been very interesting to hear an independent account of the tone, volume, and intensity of Lewis's upbraiding. This was not just another encounter with Indians. This was *the* encounter. The success of the entire expedition was at stake—at least in the brain of Captain Lewis.

On August 12, Lewis drank on the same day from what he regarded as the source of the Missouri and one of the sources of the Columbia, "in surch of which we have spent so many toilsome days and wristless nights."[212] "[J]udge then of the pleasure I felt in allying my thirst with this pure and ice cold water which issues from the base of a low mountain or hill of a gentle ascent for ½ a mile."[213] This was quite possibly the great day of Meriwether Lewis's life.

On August 13, Lewis made first contact with the Shoshone Indians. After a tantalizing near-miss with two women, a man, and some Shoshone dogs, which Lewis tried to catch in hopes that he could tie handkerchiefs with trinkets around their necks, the four Americans happened upon three paradigmatic Shoshone women digging roots, one old, one young, and one in between. What followed was one of the supreme moments in the history of exploration. "[W]e had not continued our rout more than a mile when we were so fortunate as to meet with three female savages."[214] The woman in her early adulthood sprinted off in terror. The other two, "an Elderly woman and a girl of about 12 years old remained," frozen in fear and crouched into the smallest physical space possible "as if reconciled to die which the[y] expected no doubt would be their fate." Lewis lifted the old woman up by the hand, "repeated the word *ta-ba-bone*," which he thought meant something like *friend* or *white man*, and "strip up my shirt sleve to s[h]ew her my skin; to prove to her the truth of the ascertion that I was a white man for my face and ha[n]ds which have been constantly exposed to the sun were quite as dark as their own." He gave "these women some beads a few mockerson awls some pewter looking-glasses and a little paint." Lewis had Drouillard sign to the elderly one to call back the woman who had bolted. To Lewis's enormous surprise, "the fugitive soon returned almost out of breath." Lewis "now painted their tawny cheeks with some vermillion which with this nation is emblematic of peace."[215]

Lewis's description of this scene is one of the classics of American literature. His use of detail is magnificent. One can see the scene—four virile and heavily armed white men in buckskins, three Native American women in deerskin dresses, in the pristine mountains just inside Idaho, everyone on edge, the women wondering if they were going to live out the day, the men glancing around nervously, rifles ready, Lewis, feeling continental success within his grasp but intensely fearful that something might still go terribly wrong, daubing vermilion powder with his fingers on the faces of women he has never met and with whom he could himself communicate, vociferating a word that he thinks means *friendly white man* and they probably regard as either *stranger* or just plain gibberish. Lewis says it was a hot, dry, sunny day. One can picture the scene. Anyone who has been out in the foothills of Montana during the dog days of summer can feel the moment, remember dust in one's nostrils, the little stirrings of the summer breeze, the intense soundlessness of the heart of the wilderness, the big, big sky.

Then Lewis spoke the quintessential words of the explorer:

> after they had become composed I informed them by signs that I
> wished them to conduct us to their camp that we wer anxious to
> become acquainted with the chiefs and warriors of their nation.
> they readily obeyed and we set out ... .[216]

Take us to your leader.

The leader, it turns out, was already on his way.

Half an hour later ("2 miles"), "we met a party of about 60 warriors
mounted on excellent horses who came in nearly full speed."[217] Here at last
was the defining moment of Lewis's life. Two days earlier he had feared that
he had blown his chance to meet the Shoshone and he had *abraided them a
little.* The day before he had drunk from the source of the Missouri River and
crossed the continental divide. Today he was about to take the greatest physical risk of his life. "I advanced towards them with the flag leaving my gun
with the party about 50 paces behind me."[218] As usual, in the great moments of
the expedition, Lewis was essentially alone. He was unarmed, the Shoshone
heavily (albeit primitively) armed. Lewis was on foot. The Shoshone were on
horseback. In the event of a skirmish, Lewis and his three men could not possibly escape. With their single shot rifles and Lewis's pistols (if he had them
with him), they could probably have killed or seriously wounded half a dozen
of the Shoshone warriors before they were cut down, but they could not possibly have escaped a determined Shoshone assault. Lewis was a stranger in a
strange land. The Shoshone were at home.

We take that moment for granted because it ended happily and with
repeated expressions of the national hug. The scene is dramatic for us, but
it was literally a life and death moment for Lewis. We know Cameahwait
will turn out to be friendly, that he will escort Lewis back to his camp, that
Sacagawea will come along in a few days and that she will discover that the
Shoshone leader is her brother. *We* know that Lewis and Clark will be able
to trade for the horses they need to cross the Rocky Mountains. But Lewis
had no such assurance as he advanced alone toward the sixty armed warriors
on horseback. That moment had to be one of the purest moments of Lewis's
life. We his readers have never experienced anything like it. Neil Armstrong
and Buzz Aldrin never had such a moment, because they did not meet alien
beings. It was intense, exhilarating, thrilling, terrifying. Overwhelming.
Exhausting. Unforgettable. Untoppable. *The melancholy of all things done.*

> [T]he chief and two others who were a little in advance of the main
> body spoke to the women, and they informed them who we were
> and exultingly shewed the presents which had been given them

these men then advanced and embraced me very affectionately in their way which is by puting their left arm over you wright sholder clasping your back, while they apply their left cheek to yours and frequently vociforate the word *âh-hi'-e, âh-hi'-e* that is, I am much pleased, I am much rejoiced.[219]

A few days earlier Lewis had written that he "had no doubt of obtaining a friendly introduction to his nation provided I could get near enough to him to convince him of our being whitemen."[220] Now he had done just that. Later on August 13, at the Shoshone camp, he reported, "[A]ll the women and children of the camp were shortly collected about the lodge to indulge themselves with looking at us, we being the first white persons they had ever seen."[221]

Success. The mission would not collapse after all. Meriwether Lewis had survived his civilization's first encounter with an alien people who could have snuffed him out with impunity in their contested homeland. He was a man of destiny. He was now an explorer in the profoundest sense. Vastly outnumbered, he had survived (and indeed mastered) a supremely volatile situation by way of his wits alone. This is the very essence of the explorer's work. Now, as the great accumulated tension broke, the strange character of Meriwether Lewis emerged:

[B]othe parties now advanced and we wer all carresed and besmeared with their grease and paint till I was heartily tired of the national hug.[222]

Success and survival are immediately followed by condescension and sarcasm. *The national hug*, later denominated the *fraternal hug*. Just after the most vulnerable moment of his life, Lewis reasserted his cultural superiority by way of a sentence dripping with distaste and discomfort. Lewis, through Drouillard, now informed Cameahwait of how he wanted the rest of the day to play out:

I now informed the chief that the object of our visit was a friendly one, that after we should reach his camp I would undertake to explain to him fully those objects, who we wer, from whence we had come and wither we were going; that in the mean time I did not care how soon we were in motion, as the sun was very warm and no water at hand.[223]

More sarcasm. Lewis was hot, thirsty, and ready to proceed on to the Shoshone camp, *I did not care how soon*.

Anyone who does not believe that Meriwether Lewis was a very strange man should try to explicate this scene. Clark would have been entirely incapable of writing a journal entry like this one—he could never have gathered into prose the actions and details that make this one of the world's quintessential encounter moments, but he equally could never have belittled his hosts just moments after averting a bloody encounter. In fact, when Clark met Cameahwait and other leaders of the Shoshone nation on August 17, he simply wrote, "the Three Chiefs with Capt. Lewis met me with great cordialliaty embraced and took a Seat on a white robe."[224] Apparently, the national hug did not especially upset him.

On the night of August 12, 1805, Lewis tasted Pacific salmon for the first time in his life. The Shoshone threw a celebration dance that lasted "nearly all night." Lewis retired for the night about midnight, "leaving the men to amuse themselves with the Indians." "I was several times awoke in the course of the night by their yells but was too much fortiegued to be deprived of a tolerable sound night's repose."[225] At least he didn't get up in the night, march to the edge of the dance circle, and tell the Shoshone to keep the noise down, thank you very much.

On August 14, Lewis got the first of several geography lessons from Cameahwait and an unnamed Shoshone man from another village. He asked Cameahwait to accompanying him the following day to the head of navigation on the Missouri River system to meet Clark.

On August 15, Lewis discovered that most of the Shoshone people believed that he was trying to lure them into an ambush at the rendezvous site. "I readily perceived that our situation was not entirely free from danger as the transision from suspicion to the confermation of the fact would not be very difficult in the minds of these ignorant people who have been accustomed from their infancy to view every stranger as an enimy."[226] Lewis found himself shaming Cameahwait, calling into question his courage and the depth of his leadership among the Shoshone, in order to keep him committed to accompanying Lewis towards the rendezvous site. "I soon found that I had touched him on the right string; to doubt the bravery of a savage is at once to put him on his metal."[227] Lewis got his way, but it was emotionally exhausting to have to harangue and shame his host in this way. Later he vented his spleen in his journal: "[T]his may serve in some measure to ilustrate the capricious disposition of those people who never act but from the impulse of the moment. they were now very cheerfull and gay, and two hours ago they looked as sirly as so many imps of satturn."[228]

August 16 was another exceedingly tense day for Meriwether Lewis. First, the expedition's outstanding hunter George Drouillard managed to kill a deer at some distance ahead of the Cameahwait-Lewis party. When a breathless runner returned to announce the kill, Lewis, who did not understand what the Shoshone messenger was reporting, first feared that there had been an ambush after all, "that by some unfortunate accedent that perhaps some of there enimies had straggled hither at this unlucky moment."[229] When it became clear that Drouillard had killed a deer, the semi-starving Shoshone hurtled down the mountain to the site of the kill. "[I]n an instant they all gave their horses the whip and I was taken nearly a mile before I could learn what were the tidings."[230] When he finally reached the place where Drouillard was butchering the deer, Lewis saw humankind reduced to its grossest groceries indeed. The Shoshone "dismounted and run in tumbling over each other like a parcel of famished dogs each seizing and tearing away a part of the intestens which had been previously thrown out."

> [O]ne of the last who attacted my attention particularly had been fortunate in his allotment or reather active in the division, he had provided himself with about nine feet of the small guts one end of which he was chewing on while with his hands he was squezzing the contents out at the other. I really did not untill now think that human nature ever presented itself in a shape so nearly allyed to the brute creation. I viewed these poor starved divils with pity and compassion.[231]

Lewis had left civilization so far behind him, he had ventured so far into the heart of American darkness, that he was now, for the first time in his life, seeing humanity reduced to its lowest terms, "so allyed to the brute creation." Lewis's reaction was identical to King Lear's when he encountered the naked bedlam beggar in the storm on the heath: "Thou art the thing itself; unaccommodated man is no more but such a poor bare, forked animal as thou art."[232] Lear's impulse was to strip himself of his remaining clothes and join Poor Tom in the rawest form that humanity can take. Lewis felt repulsion and compassion.

We are now in the zone of Barry Lopez' great question, "How far can you go out and still come back?" And Lewis's day was not yet over.

When they got close to the rendezvous site Cameahwait demanded a brief halt.

> [W]e now dismounted and the Chief with much cerimony put tippets about our necks such as they temselves woar I redily perceived that this was to disguise us and owed it's origine to the same cause already mentioned [i.e., fear of an ambush]. to give them further confidence I put my cocked hat with feather on the chief and my over shirt being of the Indian form my hair deshivled and skin well browned with the sun I wanted no further addition to make me a complete Indian in appearance the men followed my example and we were son completely metamorphosed.[233]

It is as if Meriwether Lewis was able to peer into one of the pewter looking glasses he was handing out to the Shoshone. Three thousand river miles from St. Louis, he looked like an Indian. He was as tan as an Indian. He ate what Indians ate. He slept on the ground as Indians slept. He eliminated his bodily wastes like an Indian. He had now placed on the head of Cameahwait the only part of his costume that differentiated him from the Indians he was among. In draping a Shoshone tippet over Lewis's shoulders the Shoshone leader had made sure that it would be impossible for an enemy to differentiate him from a Shoshone. Lewis was about to hand his rifle—ironically, the very last token of his status as a civilized man—to a "savage," to Cameahwait. Lewis realized that the only way he could accomplish his mission was to *exchange identities* with the Shoshone leader, at least temporarily. Lewis was now *completely metamorphosed* in the American West. He was now in Lopez land, a place without opera or Latin orations or the minuet or the exquisite suavity of a Parisian salon. No wigs or diamond-studded buckles on the borderlands of the Louisiana Territory, no Linnaean binomial classification, no Corinthian columns or polygraphs or calendar clocks or orreries. *Unaccomodated man.*

I believe that this moment simultaneously completed Meriwether Lewis and emptied him. He had become a "perfect Indian." I'm guessing that was not one of the goals he had been harboring for the last ten years. It was a logical but unintended consequence of the immense journey he had made across "a country at least two thousand miles in width, on which the foot of civillized man had never trodden."[234] He was, at this moment, as fully alive as he had ever been or would ever be. And yet he was in a perfectly elemental state. The only thing that marked him as a civilized man was his gun, and he was about to hand that over to someone he had never heard of until two days ago.

No wonder Lewis had Saint-Mémin paint him in that tippet. If he had been the kind of soldier-explorer who could return effortlessly to civilization after a foray into the wilderness, he would have had himself painted in full dress uniform or an eighteenth century gentleman's suit. But that man was the US Army captain and presidential aide de camp who had set out from St. Charles, Missouri, in May 1804. That man, like the gorgeous uniform he wore, disappeared somewhere out in the vast and open plain of Montana. The man who could rage at the bungling of his dress uniform in 1803 ("Of all the damned pieces of work, my coat exceeds. It would take up three sheets of paper, written in shorthand, to point out its deficiencies or, I may even say, deformities."[235]) was now eating—and relishing—roasted deer's intestines. Saint-Mémin painted Lewis at the moment when he was perfectly poised between two incompatible and mutually exclusive worlds. As he stood next to Cameahwait on the far border of Louisiana, Lewis was as close to being an Indian as he was ever going to be. He did not, like other mountain men, *go native*. But he was never going to be the same when he returned to civilization, no matter how exquisite Mr. Jefferson's 1784 Château d'Yquem might be.

Lewis found it nearly impossible to sleep that night, partly because after all the buildup with Cameahwait, Clark had not yet reached the rendezvous site. Lewis had had to lie to Cameahwait about the contents of the note he [Lewis] had left at the site a few days earlier. It worked, after a fashion, but Lewis, who prided himself on his integrity, confessed that it "set a little awkward"[236] in his conscience. Lewis could not be sure where Clark was that night or whether he was safe and secure.

> I now entertained various conjectures myself with rispect to the cause of Capt. Clarks detention and was even fearfull that he had found the river so difficult that he had halted below the Rattlesnake bluffs. I knew that if these people left me that they would immediately disperse and secrete themselves in the mountains where it would be impossible to find them or at least in vain to pursue them and that they would spread the allarm to all other bands within our reach & of course we should be disappointed in obtaining horses, which would vastly retard and increase the labour of our voyage and I feared might so discourage the men as to defeat the expedition altogether. my mind was in reallity quite as gloomy all this evening as the most affrighted indian.[237]

Completely metamorphosed. Now he had the mind of an Indian, too.

> but I affected cheerfullness to keep the Indians so who were about me. we finally laid down and the Chief placed himself by the side of my musquetoe bier.[238]

Almost completely metamorphosed. Lewis, unlike the Shoshone leader next to him, had a section of mosquito netting. He was still a little civilized after all.

> I slept but little as might be well expected, my mind dwelling on the state of the expedition which I have ever held in equal estimation with my own existence, and the fait of which appeared at this moment to depend in a great measure upon the caprice of a few savages who are ever as fickle as the wind.[239]

On August 17, Clark turned up and "we had the satisfaction," Lewis wrote, "once more to find ourselves all together, with a flattering prospect of being able to obtain as many horses shortly as would enable us to prosicute our voyage by land should that by water be deemed unadvisable."[240]

It had been quite a week for Meriwether Lewis. Although no doubt he slept well under his mosquito netting on the night of August 17, with Clark at hand and the expedition at full strength in both senses of the term, I do not think that Lewis ever fully recovered from this cluster of un-precedentedly intense moments his soul had to absorb between August 12 and August 17, 1805. Even if I am wrong, one thing is certain. Meriwether Lewis was never going to have another week like August 12–17, not if he had lived his threescore and ten, not if he had lived as long as Methuselah. Nothing in Albemarle County, Washington, DC, Philadelphia, or St. Louis was ever going to match this. He had peaked out on the Montana-Idaho line within a few miles of the source of the endless Missouri. He was re-lieved, triumphant, and spiritually exhausted. He would soon go silent for the remainder of 1805.

Lopez asks why Lewis and Clark made the same journey, and yet Lewis ventured too far to come back and Clark somehow didn't. Think of how differently they spent the week of August 12–17, 1805.

While Lewis wrestled with a series of existential questions—how do you tell a civilized man from a savage if they wear the same clothes? How close can you come to brute creation and still be human? Who are you when you give your rifle to a potential enemy in the middle of nowhere? When you have reduced yourself to brute creation, can you ever climb fully back into a Jane Austen novel?—all Clark had to do was drag the boats over the gravel shoals of the extreme upper Missouri, surrounded by cursing, belching, whining, farting, joking, confessing, jesting, boasting, praying, and bickering men, who probably never all went silent in the wil-derness at the same time, even when they were sleeping. The sheer amount of chatter and carnal noise that Clark endured for twenty-eight months had the effect of reducing his capacity to hear the voices of the wilderness. By abandoning the boats on November 28, 1803, to Clark, and leaving the main party whenever a discovery moment was at hand, Lewis made it pos-sible for himself to have a fundamentally different journey from that of his co-captain, to luxuriate in the solitude of the American wilderness at the moment when it would present itself as untainted by Euro-American civi-lization as it would ever be. The historian of exploration Alan Moorhead has spoken of "the fateful moment when a social capsule is broken open, when primitive creatures, beasts as well as men, are confronted for the first time with civilization."[241] Surely Lewis understood that he was the man of destiny who was doing the cracking. Clark was able to reenter American life successfully because although he had logged the same number of miles, he had been on a very different journey. Clark was the nominal leader of a group exploration of the American West. Lewis was in many respects a solo explorer who was semi-attached to an immense support and supply train, managed by the best and most supportive of friends William Clark.

On the occasions when he got off on shore by himself, Clark was a remarkable explorer. In Iowa he was so overwhelmed by the beauty of the landscape that he actually forgot what his mission was.

[A]fter assending and passing thro a narrow Strip of wood Land, Came Suddenly into an open and bound less Prarie, I Say bound less because I could not See the extent of the plain in any Derection, the timber appeared to be confined to the River Creeks & Small branches, this Prarie was Covered with grass about 18 Inches or 2 feat high and contained little of any thing else, except as before mentioned on the River Creeks &c, This prospect was So Sudden & entertaining that I forgot the object of my prosute and turned my attention to the Variety which presented themselves to my view.[242]

At Tillamook Head, at a precipice now known as Clark's Point of View, Clark wrote, "[W]e Set out early and proceeded to the top of the mountain next to the which is much the highest part and that part faceing the Sea is open, from this point I beheld the grandest and most pleasing prospects which my eyes ever surveyed, in my frount a boundless Ocean; to the N. and N.E. the coast as far as my sight Could be extended, the Seas rageing with emence wave and brakeing with great force from the rocks of Cape Disapointment as far as I could See to the N.W."[243] Lewis was somewhere else. Clark was not lugging boats and managing men. His imagination had one of its rare moments.

On the return journey on the Yellowstone in 1806, the volume of the nine members of the Clark party, including Clark, was sufficiently lowered, and Lewis's tightly-wound personality was sufficiently far away, that Clark wrote some of his most lyrical journal passages, particularly when he was overwhelmed with awe at the sheer quantity of game that grazed and rumbled before him. He frequently fell into reveries that are almost wholly absent from his journal entries when the expedition is at full strength.

Still, I do not believe that even if their roles had been reversed, if Lewis had managed the day-to-day aspects of the journey and Clark had been free to wander the wilderness, that he would have experienced what Lewis did in the course of the expedition. Clark was, like Odysseus, a man whose feet were always firmly planted on the ground. He kept his balance. He let much more in than Lewis in a routine human way, and much less in an existential way. In other words, Clark was the kind of man who could remain grounded no matter what he encountered, and Lewis was the kind of man who gravitated toward experiences that destabilized him. He processed his journey in such a way that he could become completely metamorphosed in the American West.

I don't think Lewis ever got over August 12–17, 1805. When you have lived through that week, what's left? How do you explain to Miss A___ R__ of Richmond or Fincastle or Philadelphia or Cape Girardeau what that week meant to you, to your country, to the history of exploration, to the human project? How could any Virginia or Kentucky belle do anything— no matter how remarkable she was—but shudder at Lewis's experiences and reduce them to Lilliputian dimensions. The most one could hope for is a wife like Desdemona. Othello says,

> My story being done,
> She gave me for my pains a world of sighs.
> She swore, i'faith, 'twas strange, 'twas passing strange;
> 'Twas pitiful, 'twas wondrous pitiful.
> She wished she had not heard it; yet she wished
> That heaven had made her such a man. She thanked me;
> And bade me, if I had a friend that loved her,
> I should but teach him how to tell my story,
> And that would woo her. Upon this hint I spake.
> She loved me for the dangers I had passed,
> And I loved her that she did pity them.[244]

I'm guessing that Lewis would have accepted the hand of Desdemona, who defied her father to marry the exotic Moor and who insisted that she be permitted to travel with him on his campaign to Cyprus, in spite of Othello's firm belief that it was a bad idea. Unfortunately, Lewis met no such woman in the course of his life, or, if he did, he drove her away to Richmond. Othello wound up killing both his wife and then himself.

Could Jefferson have understood the elemental and existential moments of Lewis's journey? Jefferson, who never camped out a night in his life, never ate anything raw, never raised his voice, never admitted even his daughters Martha and Maria or his closest friends into the *sanctum sanctorum* of his soul? 'Have another glass of Montrachet, Mr. Lewis, and tell me if the Shoshone have a word in their vocabulary for mastodon.' Could even William Clark understand what Lewis encountered away from the boats? The true explorer, like Odysseus, self-selects himself to venture out past the last outpost of civilization into the heart of the heart of the great mystery. He shouts ahead (the literal meaning of the word *explorer*) a little comically from a lunar perspective, as he ventures beyond the boundaries of safety, security, identity, and the reassuring power of his home civilization's habits of the heart. Many explorers venture so far that they never return at all: Magellan, Cook, Park. Of those who return, more turn out to experience difficulties similar to those of Lewis than the longevity and the diurnal joys of William Clark.

Of course, if you are lucky, you can physically *still go back*, in Lopez' words. Thomas Slaughter has written, "Vision quests, the Plains Indians knew, do not work for everyone. Lewis was already dead; only his body was still alive."[245] Dead to a normal life. And if somehow you could return to normalcy and simply be re-absorbed into the diurnal world of courting by coy convention, drinking healths to falsely cheerful strangers, getting the presidential pocket watch fixed, making arch comments to the shining faced members of the American Philosophical Society, then what was the point of venturing so far from those manifold comforts in the first place? The explorer wants to return a bit strange, even to those who know and love him best, wants forever to travel with an aura of mystery hovering almost visibly over his head, to be widely known as a man who cannot quite explain all that happened out there. The explorer wants, in Sevareid's terms, to have disappeared into another life that we can't quite follow.

At the Great Falls on June 13, Lewis wrote a rather conventional journal entry about the indescribability of a sublime waterfall. No doubt he was sincere in his confession that "after wrighting this imperfect discription I again viewed the falls and was so much disgusted with the imperfect idea which it conveyed of the scene that I determined to draw my pen across it and begin agin, but then reflected that I could not perhaps succeed better than pening the first impressions of the mind,"[246] but he was also participating in a well-worn literary convention known as the *inexpressibility topos*. He had not seen Indians devour an entire deer raw at this point, down to the very hooves, and he had not yet looked in the pewter looking glass at himself as *a perfect Indian*. He had not yet seen the effective collapse of his sense of himself as an exemplar of civilization. He could not know it as he sat at the base of the Great Falls on June 13, 1805, but the sublime waterfall before him turned out to be nothing more than a minor indescribability. The essential indescribability of reducing yourself to lowest terms and becoming indistinguishable—except in your own consciousness—from a naked "savage" had not yet come to Lewis. When it did, he discovered that it was not something that could be communicated in Enlightenment prose. The greatest mystery of life is to make sense of the person you see before you in the mirror. The paradox is that men go exploring to look at themselves with open eyes for the first time. Like Odysseus you have to go so deep into the interior that the natives cannot make sense of your habits, habiliments, or accoutrements. What Lewis saw near the source of the Missouri River was someone who was never again going to be happy running errands for the president of the United States.

If Lewis had come home and written his book, he might—like Buzz Aldrin—have gotten some of the ineffable out of his system, no matter how much he decried the gap between his actual experience and his account of that experience. Had he married Letitia Breckenridge or Miss C___ or some Kentucky Desdemona, he might have discovered that the wilderness of a deep human intimacy is as mysterious and compelling as anything out at the other source. For some reason or other, he never was able to surrender himself to a woman. Anyone who can finds one.

In taking his own life, Lewis behaved in a shockingly selfish way. Jefferson rightly understood that Lewis had thus denied the world access to the vast treasury of his reflections and remembrances. Lewis began his suicide by blasting a ball two-thirds of an inch in diameter into the brain that held those memories, impressions, theories, ironies, sarcasms, lyricisms, and Latinate phraseology. In doing so, he voted for silence. He took the concept of indescribability to its logical conclusion. Why some people find it impossible to fathom that Lewis killed himself, I do not understand. It seems perfectly—if horrifyingly—explicable to me.

Conclusion

No matter which of these possible explanations you reject or diminish in significance, it seems to me indisputable that by the summer and fall of 1809 Lewis was suffering from the accumulated stresses of physical and spiritual maladies that were far graver and more debilitating than malaria or alcoholism. A lot of territory can be covered by such convenient labels as Post Traumatic Stress Disorder or Bipolar Disorder, but what I have attempted to do here is explore Meriwether Lewis as much as possible in his own experiences and in his own words. He was, in my view, a great man with a great, troubled soul. The accumulation of the fractured personality he brought to the White House on April 1, 1801, the experiences and the strains of the great journey, and the many difficulties of the post-expedition period wore down his spiritual immune system until it was extremely fragile. Just at that time, when his governorship was in some disarray, his personal life unsatisfying and unresolved, and the book unfinished, and Jefferson playing Candide, he received the bombshell letter of July 15, 1809, from the War Department.

Such evidence as we have points to likelihood that Meriwether Lewis committed suicide on October 11, 1809. The murder theorists are unable to point to a single piece of positive evidence that indicates Lewis was murdered. Suicide is mystery even when the individuals in question write explicit suicide notes. Because the letter Lewis wrote to Clark from New Madrid has been lost, and because we have no other document in Lewis's hand that explains the precise nature of his desperation in the last weeks of his life, we will never know for certain why he killed himself. I have tried in this essay to explore as rigorously as possible all of the explanations that I have read or heard in twenty years of thinking about this great man. Almost certainly a combination of some of these motives led Lewis to put a gun to his head at Grinder's Inn. It is possible that the letter to Clark will turn up at some point in the future. If it does, I expect that my explanation of its contents (see page 311–312 above) will be confirmed and that it will get us closer to an understanding of what went wrong without unmistakably solving the mystery. What I have attempted to do in this book is provide a basis for continuing conversation and debate about the character of

Meriwether Lewis and his untimely death. My own hunches are probably of importance to nobody but myself, but if I had to articulate my analysis in a few sentences I would say that the proximate cause of Lewis's suicide was the affair of honor forced upon his sensitive soul by William Eustis, James Madison, and the War Department; coupled with a toxic mix of physical, mental, and spiritual illness; exacerbated by excessive use of alcohol; and deepened by a sense that he had failed to meet the expectations that Jefferson and his own ambition had set for himself. My view is that Lewis was a high-strung man with a fracture in his basic sense of himself; that that fissure had been widened in the wilderness; and that he had fundamental reentry issues when he returned in the fall of 1806. I believe that Lewis was suffering from the Buzz Aldrin Syndrome and a sense that a wilderness once discovered and cracked open immediately became something more pedestrian and less romantic.

My own best analysis is that Lewis committed suicide for precisely the reason that Mrs. Grinder reports, that it was better to kill himself than to give his enemies the satisfaction of doing it. When Clark read the New Madrid letter for the first time, he must have regarded it as typical of Lewis's penchant for over-dramatizing his situation. But after he learned of Lewis's actual suicide, Clark appears to have realized that for all of his hyperbole, Lewis had truthfully intimated the way he intended to close the journey.

In the end we cannot know just what happened at Grinder's Inn on October 11, 1809, and we cannot know why Lewis did what he did. The mystery abides, in spite of the best labors of a range of thoughtful historians, psychologists, and biographers.

I like mystery.

ACKNOWLEDGEMENTS

The paintings that grace this book are far more than illustrations. When I began this project I asked Michael Haynes if he would be willing to undertake a series of paintings of the *interior* Lewis, paintings of Lewis not in the mode of American adventure, but as a solitary Enlightenment explorer at the heart of the continent. It gave me immense joy when he agreed to paint the scenes. We had a couple of conversations, and I sent him several memos about Lewis's sometimes-lonely journey. The results speak for themselves. His paintings are, in my opinion, as much a part of the meaning of this book as the 195,000 words I have written. I cannot adequately express my gratitude to Michael Haynes, who more than anyone else has created America's modern visual understanding of the Lewis and Clark world. Not only do Haynes' paintings deepen the meaning of my book, but I believe they take his art to a new level of interpretive mastery.

This book would not have been finished, more or less on schedule, had it not been for a week I spent this spring at the University of Vermont at Burlington. I have the great honor to be a James Marsh Professor-at-Large at UVM. I go there every year for a week or so. The history department and the honors program put me to work spot lecturing in humanities classes, advising honors students, meeting with faculty groups, and sometimes making presentations around Vermont. This year, because I landed in Burlington just before a whopper winter snowstorm, some of my off-campus activities were canceled. I spent the week mostly in my "office" in the Cyber Café of the Bailey/Howe Library writing the backbone of a couple of chapters of this book. I wish to thank Melanie Gustafson and President Daniel Fogel and his staff for providing me such perfect hospitality during my annual visits, which I wish could continue to the crack of doom. Thanks, too, to the history department for its generosity and insights. Because of my Marsh fellowship, I have had the unique advantage of being able to talk through and "field test" the themes of this book with the students and faculty at UVM. *The Character of Meriwether Lewis* was not finished at UVM, but there, like my hero Lewis, "I thought myself well repaid for my labour; as from this point I beheld the Rocky Mountains for the first time … I felt a secret pleasure in finding myself so near the head of the heretofore conceived boundless Missouri."[1] Precisely. It was at UVM, to shift metaphors, that I saw the light at the end of the tunnel in this immense and sometimes daunting project, the result of many years of thinking about Lewis and several years of hard writing. Even so, like Lewis, "when I reflected on the difficulties which this snowey barrier would most probably throw in my way to the Pacific, and the sufferings and hardships of myself and party in them, it in some measure counterballanced the joy I had felt in the first moments in which I gazed on them."[2] Indeed. It turned out that the territory between my

Vermont prospect and the completion of this book was filled with impassable rivers and cyclopean monsters of the deep. But again, Lewis had it right: "[A]s I have always held it a crime to anticipate evils I will believe it a good comfortable road untill I am compelled to beleive differently."[3]

Michael Mooney, then president of Lewis & Clark College in Portland, invited me in 2003 to join Sherry Manning and Steve Beckham in creating bicentennial programming at and for the college. Mike Mooney is a scholar of the Enlightenment, a man of grace and extraordinary integrity. He read my earlier monograph on this subject and urged me to expand it into a full book. I shall never forget the night we passed at a dude ranch in Idaho where we swam in the stock pond and I revealed to Mike the recently discovered "secret diary of Sacagawea."

I owe thanks, too, to my Lewis and Clark College colleagues Elizabeth Safran, Steve Tufte, Curtis Johnson, Doug Erickson, Paul Merchant, Jeremy Skinner, Holly Bard (Otter Woman), and the uproarious Roger Wendlick. But it is Sherry Manning and Stephen Dow Beckham to whom I owe the biggest debt. Sherry held all the projects together.

At Lewis & Clark College I had the opportunity to help create a thirteen-hour, thirteen-part public radio documentary called *Lewis and Clark: the Unfinished Journey*. It was broadcast on more than 100 public radio stations throughout the United States. It is still available at www.shoppbs.org. It is one of my proudest achievements. Among other things, I had the opportunity to interview just about everyone who had something to say about Lewis and Clark. One of my rewards for *The Unfinished Journey* was a hard drive that stores every interview and all the commentary of the documentary project, uncut and unedited. Needless to say, I learned more from the remarkable people I had the opportunity to interview than I have ever known myself.

Mike Carrick of Oregon provided important wisdom on guns. Thomas Danisi shared some of his recent research with me, and put into my hands several important letters by Meriwether Lewis that I had not previously seen. I am most grateful. Stephenie Ambrose Tubbs managed to overcome her aversion to poor Mr. Lewis long enough to do some ready research for me on a few occasions when I was beyond the reach of wireless. She also read several chapters with generosity and made useful suggestions.

I owe an immense debt of gratitude to two historians. First, to James Ronda, who wrote what I regard as the best book ever published about Lewis and Clark, *Lewis and Clark Among the Indians* (1984), and who proved to everyone in the Lewis and Clark community that the story you see depends on the lens you choose to wear. My friend David Nicandri has improved this book in three ways. He read the manuscript as it chugged out of my printer and provided precisely the kind of thoughtful feedback every scholar desires. He encouraged me to take risks that I might otherwise not have been willing to take. And by reading my previous book on this subject with deep generosity and incorporating some of my ideas into his own excellent book on Lewis and Clark, he gave me the confidence that I was on the right track. One never knows. Nicandri's affirmation has made all the difference in my writing and my life.

In the summer of 2010, I had the good fortune to lead a group of thirty-one modern adventurers on an eight-day odyssey on the Lewis and Clark trail in Montana and Idaho. It was my ninth Lewis and Clark cultural tour. We floated the White Cliffs stretch of the Missouri River for three days with Missoula outfitter Wayne Fairchild and his band of merry young men and women, some of them excellent campfire musicians. Then we camped up on the Lolo Trail in the most pristine section of the Lewis and Clark Trail. It was a glorious and whimsical journey, except for the climb straight up Wendover Ridge, which led my bombastic friend Sam to cough up a lung and ask how Lewis and Clark could discover the source of the Missouri but not switchbacks. It is true that my partner in discovery Rebecca Cawley tried to drown me somewhere near Judith Landing, and nearly succeeded, but "I dash from me the gloomy thought,"[4] and choose to forgive her, though the key reference books I have consulted in writing this study of Lewis are now warped and muddied beyond recognition and I can almost detect the odor of sagebrush and the Hole in the Wall as I separate the blown pages of John Logan Allens's *Passage Through the Garden* and volume two of Donald Jackson's *Letters of the Lewis and Clark Expedition*. By the time you read this book, I will have exacted sweet revenge. Special thanks to the tree dork and L&C comedian Chad Jones and Alison R. (the poet).

My friends and colleagues David Borlaug and Wendy Spencer of the Lewis and Clark Fort Mandan Foundation have encouraged this book at every turn, and shown saintly patience in the face of its delays. There were a few times when I wondered if I might not be channeling my hero Lewis in the art of procrastination. Like Lewis, I am never actually idle, but it is amazing how many tasks of immediate importance can displace a big longer-term project like this one. And there is always a David McKeehan lurking somewhere in the equation. David Borlaug has given me the opportunity to fulfill many of my Great Plains dreams. There is no way to express my thanks for that gift. Kevin Kirkey of the staff of the Fort Mandan Foundation did exemplary work in tracking down the illustrations and getting legal permission to reproduce them in this book. My friend Sarah Trandahl helped get the manuscript ready for the press. I am immensely grateful. Thanks, too, to Nancy Krebsbach, Laura Gardner, and Ethel Mart. Thanks to Arik Spencer who may one day make good on his promise to take me to the heretofore deemed chimerical sole waterfall in North Dakota.

My administrative assistant Nancy Franke holds my little universe together. And she only whups me now and then. It is literally the case that without her this book would never have been written.

Thanks to Michelle Kraft of Bismarck State College for creating the maps that grace this book. As any study of William Clark proves, making of a map is an interpretive act, a way of reading the landscape and interpreting it for others. The dapper Larry Skogen, President of Bismarck State, read parts of the book and helped me talk through many of its themes. He's a Clark guy, of course, and he likes Neil better than Buzz, Odysseus better than Achilles, Wordsworth better than Coleridge, and Red Cloud better than Crazy Horse. I have taken President Skogen to several of the sources of the "mighty & heretofore deemed endless Missouri."[5] Like Clark, he is easily overcome by *musquetors*. He hustled away to wash the dust off of his car every time we found a town with a car wash.

My mother Mil Jenkinson has been my estimable friend through life. At some point about twenty-five years ago, we discovered a shared delight in Lewis and Clark. We have gone to trail heritage annual meetings together, explored Lewis and Clark sites in Dakota and Montana, talked endlessly in an unsystematic fashion about every aspect of the Lewis and Clark story, and found the second great bond in our life on the trail of Lewis and Clark. The first involved cowboys and the Dakota badlands, the campground at the Summit, and the terrifying road down to the Nelson spread on the Little Missouri River. Like her son, Mother is a Lewisite not a Clarkie. Like her son, she is drawn to the dark romantic Meriwether Lewis more than that steady and reliable problem solver William Clark. Nothing can be more pleasing than having an adult friendship with your parent(s). If my mother didn't enjoy the Lewis and Clark world so much, it wouldn't be half as much fun for me.

Joe Mussulman of Missoula, Montana, is one of my favorite people in or out of the Lewis and Clark world. He is a brilliant antiquarian in the manner of the seventeenth century's John Aubrey. There is no subject that he cannot make more precise with his exceedingly careful research and ready wit. He convinced me once to drive with him in a single day from Missoula to Upper Red Rock Lake southeast of Dillon in search of a particular specimen of cactus—and back again to Missoula in time for supper, the most quixotic research journey of my entire life. And yet he objected to my driving with my knee! We found the cactus and it clung to us. Then we met a trio of pests for dinner. Joe Mussulman embodies the word genial. It's an honor just to know such a man.

My friend and former wife Etta L. Walker once asked the perfect Lewis question: "How can you say that Lewis loved the American wilderness if he didn't particularly like the indigenous people who lived naturally in that wilderness?" Etta is never anything but completely interesting, no matter what the subject.

Thanks also to Sheila Schafer, Kent Conrad, Valerie Naylor, Janie Guill, David Swenson, Dusty Anderson, Cindy Lewis, the late Gary Davis,

Tom Cordingly, Leon Basler, Ken Rogers, Jess Godfrey, Larry Epstein, James Holmberg, Robin McQuinn, Harry Fritz, Wendy Raney, Lanny Jones, Jim Merritt, Fred and Gerard and Byron Baker, Robert Moore, Bryant Boswell, Bud Clark, John Fisher, John Guice, Jim Fuglie, and Lillian Crook. Special thanks to Violet Wether for her assistance in assembling a ping pong ball schematic of the arrival of various parties of the expedition at the confluence of the Yellowstone and Missouri Rivers. Special thanks to my friends Richard McCallum and Sharon Kilzer of Dickinson State University for their preternatural patience. And Stacy and Simon Cordery, and their son Gareth, who has the winsome integrity of George Shannon.

My friend Kimberly Jondahl did the copy editing of the manuscript with her usual excellence and good humor. Two years ago, she wrote a banned book. What could be better than that?

My dear friend Melanie Carvell took me to the drop point for my errand in the wilderness. In 2005 I hiked the Little Missouri River from Marmarth, North Dakota, to the north unit of Theodore Roosevelt National Park. Melanie walked with me along the ridges around Bismarck every day for six months to get me ready for my 173-mile trek. And then, on the hottest day of the hottest summer in North Dakota history, she dropped me off at my beloved Marmarth. Because she claimed to cherish my health, she stole from my pack the Cloverdale Tangy Summer Sausage that I had purchased as my one indulgence for that journey. I will not repeat what I said to the universe when I discovered her vile and pitiful crime, but it translates into *Lewis-and-Clark-speak* as, "the vilest miscreant of the savage race."[6] At Marmarth my wonderful chain-smoking friend Patti Perry, the mayor, cooked me a splendid last supper before I lurched off with my sixty-five-pound pack. I remember just two things from Patti's goodbye hug at the bridge over the Little Missouri River on U.S. 12. First, she continued to puff away at her cigarette through the national hug. Second, as I walked away she said, "Hey, the rattlesnakes are shedding their skins early this year because of the drought. They are in a really bad mood right now. Have a great trip." I did blunder face first into the coil of the largest rattlesnake I ever saw, on day four, but it declined combat.

Thanks too, to Laura McClanathan, Wes Jackson, the late, great Everett C. Albers, Kris Wallman, Marv Kaiser, Kathleen Tigan, Aaron Meyer, Jane Atkinson, Maggie Covall, Rodney and Greg Jacobs, Rob Reynolds, Dennis McKenna, William Foley, Susan Shinneman, Miss Redwood, Jan Daley, Rick Collin, Merl Paaverud, Claudia Berg, Christopher Zinn, Marianne Keddington Lang and Bill Lang, Harry Fritz, Anne Rawlinson, Jan Donalson, Ken Altergott, Ken Berkemeyer, Tom Ronk, Jim Wallace and Neal Corey of the Discovery Expedition of St. Charles (DESC) boat crew, Joni Kinsey, Timothy Billings, Jack Gladstone, and Mariah Gladstone, a young woman of powerful medicine. Very special thanks for a wide range of reasons to Dan Jordan. And to the best professor I ever encountered, Thomas Clayton, who represents all that is good in the tradition of the humanities.

Thanks to all the wonderful people who have joined me on my Lewis and Clark cultural tours, led by the miscreant Rebecca Cawley of Lewiston, Idaho.

Thanks, too, to Lynn Miyauchi, Cindy Crain, Seldon Hale, Claudia Stravato, Marge Larson, Melanie Tolliver, Judith Powell, Frank and Sandee Beaman, Dianne Brown, Charlotte Shirven, Neil and Bonnie Voskuil, Galye Gilbert, Henry Heuser, Nuncle Wesley, Annie Hall, Joanne and Robbie Bock, Craig and Tomese Buthod, Diane McKanna, Marti Clark, Diana Tang, John and Marsha Henderson, Lynn Moran, Gene Mahalko, Debra Juchem, Pat Brodin, Jessy Cawley, Pat and Suzanne Haney, Arik Spencer, Francie Berg, Sid and Melissa Easley, Robin McQuinn. And the seven-continent marathoner George Neil and his wife Doreen.

And so many more.

Clay S. Jenkinson

BIBLIOGRAPHY

Aldrin, Edwin E. "Buzz," Jr., with Wayne Warga. *Return to Earth*. New York: Random House, 1973.

Allen, John Logan. *Lewis and Clark and the Image of the American Northwest*. 1975. Reprint, New York: Dover, 1991.

Ambrose, Stephen. *Undaunted Courage: Meriwether Lewis, Thomas Jefferson, and the Opening of the American West*. New York: Simon and Schuster, 1996.

Arnebeck, Bob. *Through a Fiery Trail: Building Washington 1790–1800*. Lanham: Madison Books, 1991.

Asma, Stephen T. *Stuffed Animals & Picked Heads: The Culture and Evolution of Natural History Museums*. Oxford: Oxford University Press, 2001.

Augustine, *Concerning the City of God against the Pagans*, trans. Henry Bettenson. (Middlesex: Penguin Books, 1972)

Bakeless, John. *The Journals of Lewis and Clark*. New York: New American Library, 1964.

———. *Lewis and Clark: Partners in Discovery*. New York: William Morrow & Company, 1947.

Beckham, Stephen Dow. *Lewis & Clark: From the Rockies to the Pacific*. Portland: Graphics Arts Center Publishing, 2002.

———, et al., *The Literature of the Lewis and Clark Expedition: A Bibliography and Essays*. Portland: Lewis and Clark College, 2003.

Belyea, Barbara, ed. *Columbia Journals: David Thompson*. Seattle: University of Washington Press, 1999.

Bergon, Frank, ed. *The Journals of Lewis and Clark*. New York: Penguin Books, 1989.

Betts, Edwin Morris and James Adam Bear, eds. *The Family Letters of Thomas Jefferson*. Columbia: University of Mississippi Press, 1966.

Betts, Robert B. *In Search of York: The Slave Who Went to the Pacific with Lewis and Clark*. Boulder: University Press of Colorado, 2001.

Biddle, Nicholas. *History of the expedition under the command of Captains Lewis and Clark, to the sources of the Missouri, thence across the Rocky Mountains and down the River Columbia to the Pacific Ocean, Performed during the years 1804–5 –6, by order of the government of the United States*. Ed. Paul Allen. Philadelphia: Bradford and Inskeep, 1814.

Brandt, Anthony. *The Journals of Lewis and Clark: Meriwether Lewis and William Clark*. Washington, DC: National Geographic Adventure Classics, 2002.

Brandt, Anthony. *The Man Who Ate His Boots: The Tragic History of the Search for the Northwest Passage*. New York: Alfred A. Knopf, 2010.

Brodie, Fawn. *The Devil Drives: A Life of Sir Richard Burton*. New York: Norton, 1967.

Bruce, Susannah Ural. *The Harp and the Eagle: Irish-American Volunteers and the Union Army, 1861–1865*. New York: New York University Press, 2006.

Buckley, Jay H. *William Clark: Indian Diplomat*. Norman: University of Oklahoma Press, 2008.

Burroughs, Raymond Darwin. *The Natural History of the Lewis and Clark Expedition*. East Lansing: Michigan State University Press, 1961.

Cappon, Lester J., ed. *The Adams-Jefferson Letters: The Complete Correspondence between Thomas Jefferson and Abigail and John Adams*. Chapel Hill: University of North Carolina Press for the Institute of Early American History and Culture at, Williamsburg, Virginia, 1959.

Carter, Clarence E., ed. *The Territorial Papers of the United States. Volume XIV, The Territory of Louisiana-Missouri 1806–1814*. Washington, DC: US Government Printing Office.

Chastellux, Francois Jean, *Travels in North-America in the Years 1780–81–82*. New York: [s.n.], 1828.

Chuinard, Eldon G. *Only One Man Died: The Medical Aspects of the Lewis and Clark Expedition*. Glendale: A.H. Clark Company, 1979.

Coues, Eliott, ed. *The Lewis and Clark Expedition*. 3 vols. Philadelphia: J.B. Lippincott Company, 1961.

Criswell, Elijah H. *Lewis and Clark: Linguistic Pioneers*. Columbia: University of Missouri Press, 1940.

Cutright, Paul Russell. *A History of the Lewis and Clark Journals*. Norman: University of Oklahoma Press, 1940.

———. *Lewis and Clark: Pioneering Naturalists*. Urbana: University of Illinois Press, 1969.

Dalton, Kathleen. *Theodore Roosevelt: A Strenuous Life*. New York: Vintage, 2004.

Danisi, Thomas C., and John C. Jackson, *Meriwether Lewis*. Amherst: Prometheus Books, 2009.

DeVoto, Bernard. *The Course of Empire*. Boston: Houghton Mifflin, 1952.

———, ed. *The Journals of Lewis and Clark*. New York: Houghton Mifflin, 1953.

Dillon, Richard. *Meriwether Lewis: A Biography*. New York: Coward-McCann, 1965.

Dolnick, Edward. *Down the Great Unknown: John Wesley Powell's 1869 Journey of Discovery and Tragedy through the Grand Canyon*. New York: Harper Collins, 2001.

Donne, John. *Biathanatos: A Modern Spelling Edition*. Ed. Michael Rudick and M. Pabst Battin. New York: Garland Pub., 1982.

———. *Poetical Works*. Ed. Herbert J. C. Grierson. Oxford: Oxford University Press, 1929.

———. *The Sermons of John Donne*. Ed. George Potter and Evelyn M. Simpson. 10 vols. Berkeley: University of California Press, 1953.

Dryden, John. *A Discourse Concerning the Original and Progress of Satire*, 1693.

Duncan, Dayton. *Out West: A Journey Through Lewis and Clark's America*. Lincoln: University of Nebraska Press, 2000.

———. *Scenes of Visionary Enchantment: Reflections on Lewis and Clark*. Lincoln: University of Nebraska Press, 2004.

Durkheim, Émile. *Suicide*. [*Le suicide: Étude de sociologie*]. Paris: F. Alcan, 1897.

Eliot, T.S. *The Complete Poems and Plays, 1909–1950*. New York: Harcourt Brace & Company, 1950.

Ellis, Joseph. *Passionate Sage: The Character and Legacy of John Adams.* New York: Norton, 1993.

Fazio, James R. *Across the Snowy Ranges: The Lewis and Clark Expedition in Idaho and Western Montana.* Moscow: Woodland Press, 2001.

Fisher, Vardis. *Suicide or Murder: The Strange Death of Governor Meriwether Lewis.* Chicago: A. Swallow, 1962.

Fleming, Fergus. *Off the Map: Tales of Endurance and Exploration.* New York: Grove Press, 2004.

Foley, William E. *Wilderness Journey: A Life of William Clark.* Columbia: University of Missouri, 2004.

————. *The Genesis of Missouri: From Wilderness Outpost to Statehood.* Columbia: University of Missouri, 1989.

Freeman, Joanne B. *Affairs of Honor: National Politics in the New Republic.* New Haven: Yale University Press, 2001.

Fritz, Harry William. *The Lewis and Clark Expedition.* Greenwood Guides to Historic Events, 1500–1900. Westport: Greenwood Press, 2004.

Furtwangler, Albert. *Acts of Discovery: Visions of America in the Lewis and Clark Journals.* Urbana: University of Illinois Press, 1993.

Gass, Patrick. *A Journal of the Voyages and Travels ... to the Pacific Ocean.* Pittsburgh: David McKeehan, 1804. Reprint. Minneapolis: Ross and Haines, 1958.

Gilman, Carolyn. *Lewis and Clark—Across the Divide.* Washington, DC: Smithsonian Books, 2003.

Goetzmann, William H. *New Lands, New Men: America and the Second Great Age of Discovery.* New York: Viking, 1986.

Gough, Barry. *First Across the Continent: Sir Alexander Mackenzie.* Norman: University of Oklahoma Press, 1997.

Guice, John. *By His Own Hand: The Mysterious Death of Meriwether Lewis.* Norman: University of Oklahoma Press, 2006.

Hailman, John. *Thomas Jefferson on Wine.* Jackson: University of Mississippi Press, 2006.

Hartley, L.P. *The Go Between.* London: Longman, 1991.

Hartley, Robert E. *Lewis and Clark in the Illinois Country: the little-told story.* Westminster: Xlibris and Sniktau Publications, 2002.

Hawke, David Freeman. *Those Tremendous Mountains: The Story of the Lewis and Clark Expedition.* New York: Norton, 1980.

Hoffhaus, Charles. *Chez les Canses, Three Centuries at Katsmouth: The French Foundations of Metropolitan Kansas City.* Kansas City: Lowell Press, 1984.

Holmberg, James, ed., *Dear Brother: Letters of William Clark to Jonathan Clark.* New Haven: Yale University Press, 2002.

Hunter, Frances. *The Fairest Portion of the Globe.* Austin: Blind Rabbit Press, 2010.

Jackson, Donald. *Among the Sleeping Giants: Occasional Pieces on Lewis and Clark.* Urbana: University of Illinois Press, 1987.

————. *Thomas Jefferson and the Stony Mountains: Exploring the West from Monticello.* 1981. Reprint, Norman: University of Oklahoma Press, 1993.

————. *Letters of the Lewis and Clark Expedition, with Related Documents, 1783–1854.* 2nd ed. 2 vols. Urbana: University of Illinois Press, 1981.

Jamison, Kay Redfield. *Night Falls Fast: Understanding Suicide.* New York: Alfred A. Knopf, 1999.

Jefferson, Thomas. *The Life and Selected Writings of Thomas Jefferson.* Ed. Adrienne Koch and William Peden. New York: Modern Library, 1993.

————. *The Papers of Thomas Jefferson.* Ed. Julian Boyd. Princeton: Princeton University Press.

————. *Thomas Jefferson: Writings.* Ed. Merrill Peterson. New York: Library of America, 1984.

————. *The Writings of Thomas Jefferson.* Ed. Albert Ellery Bergh. Washington, DC: Thomas Jefferson Memorial Association, 1903.

Jenish, D'Arcy. *Epic Wanderer: David Thompson and the Mapping of the Canadian West.* Toronto: Doubleday Canada, 2003.

Jenkinson, Clay S., ed. *A Vast and Open Plain: The Writings of the Lewis and Clark Expedition in North Dakota, 1804–1806.* Bismarck: State Historical Society of North Dakota, 2003.

Johnson, Samuel, Allan Massie, and James Boswell. *A Journey to the Western Islands of Scotland, with The Journal of a Tour to the Hebrides.* New York: Knopf, 2002.

————. "Life of Cowley." In *Samuel Johnson: Selected Poetry and Prose*, edited by Frank Brady and W.K. Wimsatt, 348. Berkeley and Los Angeles: University of California Press, 1977.

Joiner, Thomas. *Myths About Suicide.* Cambridge: Harvard University Press, 2010.

————. *Why People Die By Suicide.* Cambridge: Harvard University Press, 2005.

Jones, Landon Y. *William Clark and the Shaping of the West.* New York: Hill and Wang, 2004.

Kastor, Peter J. *William Clark's World: Describing America in an Age of Unknown.* New Haven: Yale University Press, 2011.

Keats, John. *Keats: The Complete Poems.* Ed. Miriam Allott. London: Longman, 1970.

Kennedy, Dane. *The Highly Civilized Man: Richard Burton and the Victorian World.* Cambridge: Harvard University Press, 2005.

Kerouac, Jack. *On the Road.* New York: Viking, 1997.

Kessler, Donna J. *The Making of Sacagawea: A Euro-American Legend.* Tuscaloosa: University of Alabama Press, 1996.

Koch, Adrienne and William Peden, eds. *The Life and Selected Writings of Thomas Jefferson.* New York: Random House, 1993.

Kukla, Jon. *A Wilderness So Immense: The Louisiana Purchase and the Destiny of America.* New York: Knopf, 2003.

Lavender, David. *The Way to the Western Sea: Lewis and Clark Across the Continent.* Lincoln: University of Nebraska Press, 2001.

Least Heat Moon, William. *River Horse: Across America by Boat*. New York: Penguin, 1999.

Loewen, James W. *Lies My Teacher Told Me: Everything Your American History Textbook Got Wrong*. New York: New Press, 1995.

Mapp, Alf J. *Thomas Jefferson: Passionate Pilgrim: The Presidency, the Founding of the University, and the Private Battle*. Lanham: Madison Books, 1991.

Miller, John Chester. *The Wolf By the Ears: Thomas Jefferson and Slavery*. New York: Free Press, 1977.

Miller, Robert J. *Native America, Discovered and Conquered: Thomas Jefferson, Lewis & Clark, and Manifest Destiny*. Westport: Praeger, 2006.

Moore, Robert J. *Tailor Made, Trail Worn: Army Life, Clothing and Weapons of the Corps of Discovery*. Helena: Farcountry Press, 2003.

Moorehead, Alan. *The Fatal Impact: An Account of the Invasion of the South Pacific, 1767–1840*. New York: Harper & Row, 1966.

Morris, Larry. *The Fate of the Corps: What Became of the Lewis and Clark Explorers after the Expedition*. New Haven: Yale University Press, 2004.

Moulton, Gary E., ed. *The Journals of the Lewis & Clark Expedition*. Vols 1–13. Lincoln: University of Nebraska Press, 1983–2001.

———, ed., *The Lewis and Clark Journals: An American Epic of Discovery*. Lincoln: University of Nebraska Press, 2003.

Nelson, Craig. *Rocket Men: The Epic Story of the First Men on the Moon*. New York: Viking, 2009.

Nelson, W. Dale. *Interpreters with Lewis and Clark: The Story of Sacagawea and Toussaint Charbonneau*. Denton: University of North Texas Press, 2003.

Nicandri, David. *River of Promise: Lewis and Clark on the Columbia*. Washburn: Dakota Institute Press, 2010.

Nisbet, H.B., and Claude Rawson. *The Cambridge History of Literary Criticism. Volume Four: The Eighteenth Century*. Cambridge: Cambridge University Press, 2005.

Nisbet, Jack. *Sources of the River: Tracking David Thompson Across Western North America*. Seattle: Sasquatch Books, 1994.

Oglesby, Richard Edward. *Manuel Lisa and the Opening of the Missouri Fur Trade*. Norman: University of Oklahoma Press, 1965.

Osgood, Ernest Staples. *The Field Notes of Captain William Clark: 1803–1805*. New Haven: Yale University Press, 1964.

Paton, Bruce C. *Lewis & Clark: Doctors in the Wilderness*. Golden: Fulcrum Publishing, 2001.

Peck, David J. *Or Perish in the Attempt: Wilderness Medicine in the Lewis and Clark Expedition*. Helena: Farcountry Press, 2002.

Peterson, Merrill, ed. *Thomas Jefferson: Writings*. New York: Library Classics of the United States, 1984.

Phelps, Dawson A. "The Tragic Death of Meriwether Lewis." *William and Mary Quarterly*, 3:13 (July 1956): 305–318.

Plutarch. *The Life of Alexander*, in John Dryden, ed., *The Lives of the Noble Grecians and Romans*. New York: Modern Library, 1932.

Potter, Tracy. *Sheheke, Mandan Indian Diplomat: The Story of White Coyote, Thomas Jefferson, and Lewis and Clark*. Helena: Farcountry Press and Fort Mandan Press, 2003.

Powell, John Wesley. *Exploration of the Colorado River and its Canyons*. New York: Dover Press, 1961.

Queen, Edward L., Stephen R. Prothero, and Gardiner H Shattuck. *Encyclopedia of American Religious History*. New York: Facts on File, 1996.

Ronda, James. *Finding the West: Explorations with Lewis and Clark*. Albuquerque: University of New Mexico Press, 2001.

———. *Lewis and Clark Among the Indians*. Lincoln: University of Nebraska Press, 1984.

———, ed. *Voyages of Discovery: Essays on the Lewis and Clark Expedition*. Helena: Montana Historical Society Press, 1998.

——— and Nancy Tystad Koupal, eds. *Finding Lewis and Clark: Old Trails, New Directions*.

Roosevelt, Theodore. *Ranch Life and the Hunting Trail*. 1888. Reprint, Lincoln: University of Nebraska Press, 1983.

Sarasohn, David. *Waiting for Lewis and Clark: The Bicentennial and the Changing West*. Portland: Oregon Historical Society Press, 2005.

Schlicke, Paul, ed. *Oxford Reader's Companion to Dickens*. Oxford: Oxford University Press, 1999.

Seed, Patricia. *Ceremonies of Possession in Europe's Conquest of the New World, 1492–1620*. Cambridge: Cambridge University Press, 1995.

Sheehan, Bernard W. *Seeds of Extinction: Jeffersonian Philanthropy and the American Indian*. New York: Norton, 1974.

Sisman, Adam. *Boswell's Presumptuous Task: The Making of the Life of Dr. Johnson*. New York: Farrar, Straus, and Giroux, 2000.

Slaughter, Thomas. *Exploring Lewis and Clark: Reflections on Men and Wilderness*. New York: Knopf, 2003.

Sobel, Dava. *Longitude: The True Story of a Lone Genius Who Solved the Greatest Scientific Problem of His Time*. New York: Walker and Company, 1995.

Stafford, Barbara Maria. *Voyage into Substance: Art, Science, Nature, and the Illustrated Travel Account, 1760–1840*. Cambridge: MIT Press, 1984.

Starrs, James E., and Kira Gale. *The Death of Meriwether Lewis: A Historic Crime Scene Investigation*. Omaha: River Junction Press, 2009.

Steffen, Jerome O. *William Clark: Jeffersonian Man on the Frontier*. Norman: University of Oklahoma Press, 1977.

Thwaites, Reuben Gold, ed. *Original Journals of the Lewis and Clark Expedition, 1804–1806*. 8 vols. New York: Dodd, Mead & Company, 1904–05.

Tubbs, Stephenie Ambrose. *Why Sacagawea Deserves the Day Off and Other Lessons from the Lewis & Clark Trail.* Lincoln: University of Nebraska Press, 2008.

———, and Clay Straus Jenkinson. *The Lewis and Clark Companion: An Encyclopedic Guide to the Voyage of Discovery.* New York: Henry Holt, 2003.

Twain, Mark [Samuel Langhorne Clemens]. *Adventures of Huckleberry Finn: an authoritative text, backgrounds and sources, criticism.* Eds. Sculley Bradley, Richmond Croom Beatty, E. Hudson Long, and Thomas Cooley. New York: Norton, 1977.

Van Orman, Richard A. *The Explorers: Nineteenth Century Expeditions in Africa and the American West.* Albuquerque: University of New Mexico Press, 1984.

Viola, Herman J. *Diplomats in Buckskins: A History of Indian Delegations in Washington City.* Washington, DC: Smithsonian Institution Press, 1981.

Wallace, Anthony F.C. *Jefferson and the Indians: The Tragic Fate of the First Americans.* Cambridge: Belknap Press of Harvard University Press, 1999.

Wishart, David J. *The Fur Trade of the American West, 1807–1840.* Lincoln: University of Nebraska Press, 1979.

Wood, W. Raymond. *Prologue to Lewis and Clark: The Mackay and Evans Expedition.* Norman: University of Oklahoma Press, 2003.

———, and Thomas D. Thiessen. *Early Fur Trade on the Northern Plains: Canadian Traders Among the Mandan and Hidatsa Indians, 1738–1818.* The American Exploration and Travel Series, no. 68. Norman: University of Oklahoma Press, 1985.

Wordsworth, William. *Poetical Works.* Ed. Thomas Hutchinson. Oxford: Oxford University Press, 1936.

———. *Selected Poems and Prefaces by William Wordsworth.* Ed. Jack Stillinger. Boston: Houghton Mifflin, 1965.

Ziak, Rex. *In Full View: A True and Accurate Account of Lewis and Clark's Arrival at the Pacific Ocean, and their Search for a Winter Camp along the Lower Columbia River.* Astoria: Moffitt House Press, 2002.

Notes

Preliminary Note

I have attempted to annotate this book as lightly as possible. Most of the references are to the University of Nebraska edition of *The Journals of the Lewis & Clark Expedition,* 13 vols., edited by Gary E. Moulton (Lincoln, 1983-2001). Hereafter cited as *JLCE.* In most cases I transcribe the text just as it appears in the printed version of *JLCE,* though occasionally I remove bracketed material, including Nicholas Biddle's editorial intrusions and Professor Moulton's internal corrections and annotations, to preserve the clarity of the original journal entry. I have tried, wherever possible, to reproduce gaps and blank spaces in the journal texts, even when they seem inexplicable from a strict grammatical or syntactical point of view. When I have italicized words or phrases in original quotations for emphasis, I always note that at the end of the sentence or passage in question with brackets: e.g., [emphasis added]. I use the convention [sic] only when absolutely necessary, so that the reader knows that a misspelling in an *unexpected place* was so written in the original. To use [sic] every time Clark, Lewis, Jefferson, or some other writer deviated from orthographic or usage standards of our time would make me a killjoy rather than a lover of the more informal standards of the early nineteenth century, and it would reduce the raw readability of the journals. Note that Jefferson—while strictly consistent—routinely spelled knowledge as knolege and reversed our conventions of the possessive its (which he spelled it's) with the contraction it is (which he spelled its). Most of the footnotes in this book are purely referential. In the few instances where I develop an argument or provide further information in a footnote (endnote), I note that in the text.

Introduction

[1]   Gary E. Moulton, ed., *The Journals of the Lewis & Clark Expedition,* 13 vols. (Lincoln, 1983–2001), JLCE, VIII:371. Hereafter cited as *JLCE.* I prefer to refer to the volume number in Roman numerals and the page number in Arabic numerals. Thus *JLCE,* VIII:371 rather than *JLCE,* 8:371.

[2]   Jefferson to William Roscoe, December 27, 1820. See Adrienne Koch and William Peden, eds., *The Life and Selected Writings of Thomas Jefferson* (New York, 1993), p. 641.

[3]   John Guice, "Why Not Homicide," in John Guice, ed., *By His Own Hand: The Mysterious Death of Meriwether Lewis* (Norman, 2006), pp. 77, 88. Hereafter cited as Guice, *By His Own Hand.*

[4]   Thomas Slaughter, *Exploring Lewis and Clark: Reflections on Men and Wilderness* (New York, 2003), pp. 27–64. Hereafter cited as Slaughter, *Exploring Lewis and Clark.*

[5]   Quoted in John Chester Miller, *Alexander Hamilton and the Growth of the New Nation* (Brunswick, 2004), p. 348.

[6]   James Ronda, *Finding the West: Explorations with Lewis and Clark* (Albuquerque, 2001), p. 27. Hereafter cited as Ronda, *Finding the West.*

[7]   Ronda, *Finding the West,* p. xvii.

[8]   Donald Jackson, ed., *Letters of the Lewis and Clark Expedition with Related Documents: 1783–1854,* 2nd ed. (Urbana, 1978), p. 590. Hereafter cited as Jackson, *Letters.*

[9]   L.P. Hartley, *The Go Between* (London, 1991), p. 1.

[10]   Jackson, *Letters,* p. vii.

[11]   James W. Loewen, *Lies My Teacher Told Me: Everything Your American History Textbook Got Wrong* (New York, 1995).

12   See David Sarasohn, *Waiting for Lewis and Clark: The Bicentennial and the Changing West* (Portland, 2005).

13   *Hamlet*, II,ii.350-351. Alfred Harbage, ed., *William Shakespeare: The Complete Works* (London, 1969).

14   Kathleen Dalton, *Theodore Roosevelt: A Strenuous Life* (New York, 2004).

15   W. Raymond Wood and Thomas D. Thiessen, eds., *Early Fur Trade on the Northern Plains: Canadian Traders Among the Mandan and Hidatsa Indians, 1738–1818: the Narratives of John Macdonell, David Thompson, François-Antoine Larocque, and Charles McKenzie* (Norman, 1999). Hereafter cited as Wood and Thiessen, *Early Fur Trade*.

16   David Nicandri, *River of Promise: Lewis and Clark on the Columbia* (Washburn, ND, 2010), p. 205. Hereafter cited as Nicandri, *River of Promise*.

17   Elliott West, "Finding Lewis and Clark by Looking Away," in eds. James P. Ronda & Nancy Tystad Koupal, *Finding Lewis & Clark: Old Trails, New Directions* (Pierre, 2004), p. 174.

18   *JLCE*, VI:152.

19   See Adam Sisman, *Boswell's Presumptuous Task: The Making of the Life of Dr. Johnson* (New York, 2000), pp. 147–170.

20   Samuel Johnson and James Boswell, *A Journey to the Western Islands of Scotland, with The Journal of a Tour to the Hebrides* (New York, 2002), p. 169.

21   2003: *Unveiling the World in 1800*; 2004: *Encounters*; 2005: *Rivers*; 2006: *Legacies*.

22   Jackson, *Letters*, pp. 389, 619.

23   Slaughter, *Exploring Lewis and Clark*, p. 64.

24   Slaughter, *Exploring Lewis and Clark*, p. 64.

PROLOGUE: FRACTURED SOUL

1   Thomas C. Danisi and John C. Jackson, *Meriwether Lewis* (Amherst, 2009), p.35. Hereafter cited as Danisi and Jackson, *Meriwether Lewis*.

2   Jackson, *Letters*, pp. 591–592.

CHAPTER I

1   Thomas Slaughter, *Exploring Lewis and Clark* (New York 2004), p. 29.

2   Quoted in Landon Y. Jones, *William Clark and the Shaping of the West* (New York, 2004), p. 199. Hereafter cited as Jones, *Shaping of the West*.

3   Jones, *Shaping of the West*, p. 200.

4   William E. Foley, *Wilderness Journey: The Life of William Clark* (Columbia, 2004), p. 70. Hereafter cited as Foley, *Wilderness Journey*.

5   Foley, *Wilderness Journey*, p. 70.

6   George Rogers Clark to Jefferson, December 12, 1802. Donald Jackson, *Letters of the Lewis and Clark Expedition* (Chicago, 1978.), pp. 7–8. Hereafter cited as Jackson, *Letters*.

7   John Keats, "On First Looking into Chapman's Homer," in *The Poems of John Keats*, ed. Miriam Allott (London, 1970), 60–62.

8   Somewhere in the upper 40s, possibly 46, from St. Charles on May 14, 1804; 33 in the permanent party that left Fort Mandan, including the two captains. See Gary E. Moulton, ed., *The Journals of the Lewis & Clark Expedition*, 13 vols. (Lincoln, 1983–2001), II:509–529. Hereafter cited as *JLCE*.

9   See Moulton's footnote, *JLCE,* II:122. "As far as we know, Lewis was Clark's only instructor" in taking celestial observations.

10   *JLCE* II:227.

11   *JLCE,* V:74.

12   *JLCE,* X:1.

13   *JLCE,* XI:1.

14   *JLCE,* IX:14.

15   *JLCE,* IX:6.

16   *JLCE,* IX:374.

17   *JLCE,* X:8.

18   *JLCE,* II:215.

19   Robert E. Hartley, *Lewis and Clark in the Illinois Country.* (Westminster, 2002), p. 164.

20   David Lavender, *The Way to the Western Sea: Lewis & Clark Across the Continent* (Lincoln, 2001). Hereafter cited as Lavender, *The Way to the Western Sea.*

21   *JLCE,* II:117.

22   *JLCE,* II:133.

23   Quoted in William Foley, *Wilderness Journey,* p. 65.

24   *JLCE,* II:174–175.

25   *JLCE,* II:178.

26   Danisi and Jackson, *Meriwether Lewis,* p. 79.

27   William Wordsworth, *Preface to the Lyrical Ballads,* in *Selected Poems and Prefaces by William Wordsworth,* ed. Jack Stillinger (Boston, 1965) p. 446.

28   *JLCE,* II:152.

29   Danisi and Jackson, *Meriwether Lewis,* p. 77.

30   James Ronda, "'A Most Perfect Harmony': The Lewis and Clark Expedition as an Exploration Community," in Ronda, ed., *Voyages of Discovery: Essays on the Lewis and Clark Expedition* (Helena, 1998), pp. 77–78. Hereafter cited as Ronda, *Voyages of Discovery.*

31   Danisi and Jackson, *Meriwether Lewis,* p. 77.

32   Jackson, *Letters,* pp. 231–239.

33   *JLCE,* IV:10.

34   *JLCE,* IV:423.

35   Jones, *Shaping of the West,* p. 125.

36   Danisi and Jackson, *Meriwether Lewis,* p. 88.

37   For the traveling library see Stephen Dow Beckham, *The Literature of the Lewis and Clark Expedition: A Bibliography and Essays* (Portland, 2003), p. 25–42. Hereafter Beckham, *The Literature of the Lewis and Clark.*

38   Foley, *Wilderness Journey,* p. 66.

39   See W. Raymond Wood, *Prologue to Lewis and Clark: The Mackay and Evans Expedition* (Norman, 2003), p. 7. Hereafter cited as Wood, *Prologue.*

40   *JLCE,* III:79n.

41   *JLCE,* III:76.

42   Stephen Ambrose, *Undaunted Courage: Meriwether Lewis, Thomas Jefferson, and the Opening of the American West* (New York, 1996), p. 168. Hereafter cited as Ambrose, *Undaunted Courage.*

43   *JLCE,* III:80.

44   *JLCE,* III:80.

45   *JLCE,* III:81.

46   *JLCE,* III:81–82.

47   *JLCE,* III:85n.

48   *JLCE,* V:74.

49   *JLCE,* IV:9–10.

50   Quoted in Richard A Van Orman, *The Explorers: Nineteenth Century Expeditions in Africa and the American West* (Albuquerque, 1984), p. 78.

51 *JLCE*, IV:9.

52 *JLCE*, III:226; IV:36.

53 *JLCE*, IV:20.

54 *JLCE*,IV:36.

55 *JLCE*, IV:39.

56 Ronda, *Finding the West*, p. 22.

57 Samuel Clemens, *The Adventures of Huckleberry Finn*, ed. Sculley Bradley, Richmond Croom Beatty, E. Hudson Long, and Thomas Cooley (New York, 1977), p. 229.

58 *JLCE*, IV:36.

59 *JLCE*, IV:36n.

60 Elliott Coues, ed., *The History of the Lewis and Clark Expedition* (Philadelphia, 1961), I, p. 253.

61 Coues, *The History of the Lewis and Clark Expedition*, I, p. 272.

62 Ronda, *Finding the West*, p. 17.

63 Jackson, *Letters*, p. 12.

64 David L. Nicandri, *River of Promise: Lewis and Clark on the Columbia* (Bismarck, 2009), pp. 203–217. Hereafter cited as Nicandri, *River of Promise*.

65 Slaughter, *Exploring Lewis and Clark*, pp. 47–64.

66 Slaughter, *Exploring Lewis and Clark*, p. 31.

67 Jackson, *Letters*, p. 590.

68 *JLCE*, IV:39.

69 See *JLCE*, III:258, 269, 276.

70 *JLCE*, IV:64.

71 *JLCE*, IV:65.

72 *JLCE*, IV:66.

73 *JLCE*, IV:71.

74 *JLCE*, IV:68.

75 *JLCE*, IX:137.

76 *JLCE*, V:32.

77 *JLCE*, IV:67.

78 *JLCE*, IV:67.

79 *JLCE*, IX:137.

80 *JLCE*, IV:70.

81 *JLCE*, IV:73.

82 *JLCE*, IV:77.

83 *JLCE*, IV:77–78.

84 *JLCE*, IV:200–201.

85 *JLCE*, IV:201.

86 *JLCE*, IV:201.

87 Frank Bergon, ed., *The Journals of Lewis and Clark* (New York, 1989), pp. 137–138; Anthony Brandt, ed., *"The Journals of Lewis and Clark* (Washington, DC, 2002), p. 160; John Bakeless, ed., *The Journals of Lewis and Clark* (New York, 1964), p. 153; Bernard DeVoto, ed., *The Journals of Lewis and Clark* (Boston, 1953), pp. 117–118.

88 Gary Moulton, ed., *The Lewis and Clark Journals: An American Epic of Discovery* (Nebraska, 2003), p. 114. Hereafter cited as Moulton, *The Lewis and Clark Journals*.

89 Moulton, *The Lewis and Clark Journals*, p. 114.

90 David Freeman Hawke, *Those Tremendous Mountains: The Story of the Lewis and Clark Expedition* (New York, 1980), p. 118. Hereafter cited as Hawke, *Those Tremendous Mountains*.

91 Dillon, *Meriwether Lewis*, p. 175.

92 Ambrose, *Undaunted Courage*, p. 226.

93 John Logan Allen, *Lewis and Clark and the Image of the American Northwest* (New York, 1996), p. 266.

94 Foley, *Wilderness Journey*, p. 108.

95   Nicandri, *River of Promise*, p. 179.
96   Coues, *The History of the Lewis and Clark Expedition*, I, p. 328.
97   Coues, *The History of the Lewis and Clark Expedition*, I, p. 328 fn.
98   *JLCE*, IV:246.
99   *JLCE*, IV:246–247.
100 *JLCE*, IV:250.
101 *JLCE*, IV:250.
102 *JLCE*, IV:250.
103 Quoted in John Chester Miller, *The Wolf By the Ears: Thomas Jefferson and Slavery* (New York, 1977), p. 57.
104 *JLCE*, IV:267.
105 *JLCE*, IV:259.
106 *JLCE*, IV:246.
107 *JLCE*, IV:271.
108 *JLCE*, IV:271.
109 *JLCE*, IV:271.
110 *JLCE*, IV:274.
111 *JLCE*, IV:275.
112 *JLCE*, IV:277.
113 *JLCE*, IV:278.
114 *JLCE*, IV:278.
115 *JLCE*, IV:280.
116 *JLCE*, IV:281.
117 *JLCE*, IV:283.
118 Whether Nathaniel Pryor was keeping a journal, as the sergeants had been instructed to do, is one of the mysteries of the expedition. We know that Pryor was not illiterate because of the report he sent to William Clark after the failure of his mission to return Sheheke-shote to the Mandan villages in September 1807. See Jackson, *Letters*, pp. 432–438.
119 *JLCE*, IV:283.
120 *JLCE*, IV:283.
121 *JLCE*, IV:284.
122 *JLCE*, IV:285–286.
123 *JLCE*, IV:286.
124 *JLCE*, IV:286.
125 *JLCE*, IV:295.
126 *JLCE*, IV:401.
127 *JLCE*, IV:401.
128 *JLCE*, IV:410.
129 *JLCE*, IV:404.
130 *JLCE*, IV:408.
131 *JLCE*, IV:417.
132 Coues, *The History of the Lewis and Clark Expedition*, II, p. 421.
133 Stephen Ambrose, following the lead of Arlen Lange, believed that the futile whimsicality of Lewis's iron-framed boat experiment may have "caused a rift between the captains. If so it was the only one." Ambrose, *Undaunted Courage*, p. 249.
134 *JLCE*, IV:418.
135 David Peck, *Or Perish in the Attempt: Wilderness Medicine in the Lewis and Clark Expedition* (Helena, 2002), p. 174. Hereafter cited as Peck, *Or Perish in the Attempt*.
136 *JLCE*, IV:418.
137 *JLCE*, IV:428.
138 *JLCE*, IV:428.
139 *JLCE*, IV:432.

140 *JLCE*, IV:432.
141 *JLCE*, IV:435–436.
142 *JLCE*, V:7.
143 *JLCE*, IV:432.
144 *JLCE*, IV:436.
145 Peck, *Or Perish in the Attempt*, p. 177.
146 Bruce C. Paton, *Lewis and Clark: Doctors in the Wilderness* (Golden, 2001), 134–35.
147 *JLCE*, V:8.
148 *JLCE*, IV:437.
149 *JLCE*, IV:438.
150 *JLCE*, V:20.
151 *JLCE*, V:18.
152 *JLCE*, V:25.
153 Peck, *Or Perish in the Attempt*, p. 179.
154 *JLCE* V:43.
155 *JLCE*, V:53.
156 *JLCE*, V:59.
157 *JLCE*, V:61.
158 Jackson, *Letters*, p. 66.
159 *JLCE*, V:18.
160 *JLCE*, V:62–63.
161 *JLCE*,V:62–63.
162 *JLCE*,V:61.
163 *JLCE*, V:78–79.
164 *JLCE*, V:79.
165 *JLCE*, V:79.
166 *JLCE*, V:79.
167 *JLCE*, V:79.
168 *JLCE*, V:74.
169 *JLCE*, V:74.
170 *JLCE*, V:74.
171 *JLCE*, V:74.
172 *JLCE*, V:75–76.
173 Rex Ziak, *In Full View: A True and Accurate Account of Lewis and Clark's Arrival at the Pacific Ocean, and their Search for a Winter Camp Along the Lower Columbia River* (Moffitt ouse Press, 2001), p. 7.
174 See Nicandri, *River of Promise*, p. 168.
175 Nicandri, *River of Promise*, p. 168.
176 *JLCE*, VI:42.
177 Quoted in Edward Dolnick, *Down the Great Unknown: John Wesley Powell's 1869 Journey of Discovery and Tragedy through the Grand Canyon* (New York, 2001), p. 18.
178 *JLCE*, VI:49.
179 Nicandri, *River of Promise*, p. 172.
180 *JLCE*, VI:47.
181 *JLCE*, VI:36.
182 Ziak, *In Full View* p. 12.
183 *JLCE*, VI:40.
184 Ziak, *In Full View*, p. 31.
185 *JLCE*, VI:48.
186 Stephen Dow Beckham, *Lewis and Clark: From the Rockies to the Pacific* (Portland, 2002), p. 64. Hereafter cited as Beckham, *From the Rockies to the Pacific*.
187 *JLCE*, VI:46.

[188] *JLCE*, VI:49–50.

[189] *JLCE*, VI:50.

[190] Beckham, *From the Rockies to the Pacific*, p. 64.

[191] Quoted in Ziak, *In Full View*, p. 9.

[192] Rex Ziak, *In Full View*, p. 6.

[193] *JLCE*, VI:33.

[194] *JLCE*, X:171.

[195] *JLCE*, X:YY.

[196] *JLCE*, VI:60.

[197] Ziak, *In Full View*, p. 65.

[198] *JLCE*, VI:429.

[199] Patricia Seed, *Ceremonies of Possession in Europe's Conquest of the New World, 1492–1620* (Cambridge, 1995).

[200] Jefferson to Isaac McPherson, August 13, 1813. See Koch and Peden, *The Life and Selected Writings of Thomas Jefferson*, pp. 576–577.

[201] *JLCE*, VI:430.

[202] *JLCE*, VI:44.

[203] Jackson, *Letters* p. 329.

[204] Coues, *The Lewis and Clark Expedition*, II. P. 478.

[205] *JLCE*, VIII:306–307.

[206] *Hamlet*, III.i.79–80.

Chapter II

[1] Clark to Jonathan November 26, 1809. See James Holmberg, *Dear Brother* (New Haven, 2002), p. 228. Hereafter cited as Holmberg, *Dear Brother*.

[2] *JLCE*, V:118.

[3] *JLCE*, V:74.

[4] Clark named 3000 Mile Island on August11, 1805. *JLCE*, V:72.

[5] *JLCE*, V:118.

[6] *JLCE*, VIII:325.

[7] Jackson, *Letters*, p. 60.

[8] Samuel Johnson, "Life of Cowley," in *Samuel Johnson: Selected Poetry and Prose*, ed., Frank Brady and W.K. Wimsatt (Berkeley and Los Angeles, Univ. California Press, 1977), p. 348.

[9] John Dryden, *A Discourse concerning the Original and Progress of Satire*, p. 1693.

[10] John Donne, *Poetical Works*, ed. Herbert J. C. Grierson. Oxford. (Oxford University Press, 1929), P. p. 44–45.

[11] *JLCE*, IV:9.

[12] *JLCE*, III:80.

[13] *JLCE*, IV:292.

[14] *JLCE*, IV:292.

[15] *JLCE*, IV:294.

[16] *JLCE*, IV:293–294.

[17] *JLCE*, IV:294.

[18] *JLCE*, IV:294.

[19] *JLCE*, IV:294.

[20] Slaughter, *Exploring Lewis and Clark*, pp. 29–31.

[21] *JLCE*, IV:294.

[22] *JLCE*, IV:294.

[23] Jackson, *Letters*, p. 60.

[24] William Clark to Toussaint Charbonneau, August 20, 1806. Clay Jenkinson, ed.,

A Vast and Open Plain: The Writings of the Lewis and Clark Expedition in North Dakota (Bismarck, 2003), p. 431. Hereafter cited as Jenkinson, *A Vast and Open Plain.*

25   James Ronda, *Lewis and Clark Among the Indians* (Lincoln, 1984), p. 241. Hereafter cited as Ronda, *Lewis and Clark Among the Indians.*

26   Gilbert Russell to Thomas Jefferson, January 31, 1810. See James Starrs and Kira Gale, *The Death of Meriwether Lewis* (Omaha, 2009), p. 246. Hereafter cited as Starrs and Gale, *The Death of Meriwether Lewis.*

27   Holmberg, *Dear Brother*, p. 210.

28   For a new analysis of the sequences of events that led to Lewis's friendship with Clark, see Thomas Danisi's forthcoming book, *Uncovering the Truth about Meriwether Lewis* (New York: Prometheus Books, 2012).

29   *JLCE*, VIII:74.

30   *JLCE*, VIII:83.

31   Plutarch, *The Life of Alexander*, in John Dryden, ed., *The Lives of the Noble Grecians and Romans* (New York, 1932), p. 801

32   *JLCE*, III:285.

33   *JLCE*, III:286.

34   *JLCE*, III:286.

35   *JLCE*, III:286.

36   Ronda, *Lewis and Clark Among the Indians*, pp. 113–132.

37   *JLCE*, III:284.

38   Theodore Roosevelt, *Ranch Life and the Hunting Trail* (Lincoln, 1983), p. 73.

39   *JLCE*, III:284.

40   *JLCE*, III:284.

41   *JLCE*, III:284–285.

42   *JLCE*, III:286.

43   Thomas Jefferson "To the Wolf and People of the Mandan Nation," in Merrill Peterson, ed., *Thomas Jefferson: Writings* (New York, 1984) pp. 564–566. Hereafter cited as Peterson, *Thomas Jefferson: Writings.*

44   Peterson, *Thomas Jefferson: Writings*, pp. 564–566.

45   Ronda, *Lewis and Clark among the Indians*, p. 75.

46   Jefferson to William Henry Harrison, February 27, 1803. Peterson, *Thomas Jefferson: Writings* pp. 1118.

47   *JLCE*, III:286.

48   *JLCE*, III:288.

49   *JLCE*, IV:275.

50   Jackson, *Letters*, p. 367.

51   *JLCE*, III:286–287.

52   See *JLCE*, III:287 for the illustration.

53   Jackson, *Letters*, p. 64.

54   Ronda, *Lewis and Clark among the Indians*, p. 103.

55   *JLCE*, III:313.

56   Wood and Thiessen, *Early Fur Trade*, p. 139.

57   *JLCE*, III:287.

58   *JLCE*, VIII:108.

59   *JLCE*, X:268.

60   *JLCE*, III:237.

61   *JLCE*, IX:113.

62   *JLCE*, IV:14.

63   *JLCE*, III:289.

64   *JLCE*, III:289.

65   *JLCE*, III:289.

66 *JLCE*, III:289.
67 Quoted in Alf Mapp, *Thomas Jefferson: Passionate Pilgrim* (Lanham, 1991), p. 75.
68 *JLCE*, III:237.
69 *JLCE*, III:237.
70 *JLCE*, III:237.
71 Wood and Thiessen, *Early Fur Trade*, p. 140.
72 *JLCE*, III:290.
73 Jackson, *Letters*, pp. 93–95.
74 *JLCE*, III:289.
75 *JLCE*, V:97.
76 *JLCE*, VII:139.
77 *JLCE*, IV:299.
78 *JLCE*, IV:299.
79 *JLCE*, III:290.
80 *JLCE*, II:148.
81 Keats, *Ode on a Grecian Urn*, in Miriam Allott, ed., *Keats: The Complete Poems* (London, 1970), p. 535
82 *JLCE*, III:167.
83 Jackson, *Letters*, p. 365.
84 *JLCE*, II:148.
85 "'A Most Perfect Harmony:' The Lewis and Clark Expedition as an Exploration Community." Ronda, ed., *Voyages of Discovery*, p.78.
86 *JLCE*, II:148.
87 *JLCE*, IV:430.
88 *JLCE*, IV:433 n.
89 *JLCE*, VI:237.
90 *JLCE*, III:290.
91 *JLCE*, III:290.
92 *JLCE*, III:290.
93 *JLCE*, IX:113.
94 *JLCE*, IX:113.
95 Wood and Thiessen, *Early Fur Trade*, p. 143.
96 See *JLCE*, II:530–548, and Jenkinson, *A Vast and Open Plain*. pp. 549–552.
97 *JLCE*, IX:114.
98 Joe Mussulman, www.lewis-clark.org, *Discovering Lewis and Clark*, "A Man By the Name of Howard."
99 *JLCE*, VI:195.
100 *JLCE*, III:170.
101 *JLCE*, VI:195.
102 *JLCE*, VI:198 n.
103 Wood and Thiessen, *Early Fur Trade*, p. 238.
104 *Hamlet* I.ii.180–181: "The funeral baked meats did coldly furnish forth the marriage tables."
105 Wood and Thiessen, *Early Fur Trade*, p. 222.
106 Wood and Thiessen, *Early Fur Trade*, p. 230.
107 Wood and Thiessen, *Early Fur Trade*, p. 222.
108 Wood and Thiessen, *Early Fur Trade*, p. 222.
109 Jefferson to Charles McPherson, February 25, 1773, in Merrill Peterson, ed., *Thomas Jefferson: Writings*, p. 746.
110 Marquis de Chastellux, *Travels in North America in the Years 1780–81–82*, New York, 1828, p. 228.
111 Basil Hall, ed., *Chastellux's Travels in North-America in the Years 1780–81–82*, p. 229.
112 *JLCE*, III:241.

113   Wood and Thiessen, *Early Fur Trade*, p. 232.
114   *JLCE*, III:241.
115   Wood and Thiessen, *Early Fur Trade*, p. 232.
116   Wood and Thiessen, *Early Fur Trade*, p. 232.
117   Wood and Thiessen, *Early Fur Trade*, p. 232.
118   Wood and Thiessen, *Early Fur Trade*, p. 232.
119   Wood and Thiessen, *Early Fur Trade*, pp. 232–233.
120   Ronda, *Finding the West*, p. xiv.
121   *JLCE*, VIII:298.
122   See *JLCE*, VIII:300 n. See also Jackson, *Letters*, p. 522.
123   Wood and Thiessen, *Early Fur Trade*, p. 234.
124   Wood and Thiessen, *Early Fur Trade*, p. 234.
125   Wood and Thiessen, *Early Fur Trade*, p. 238.
126   Wood and Thiessen, *Early Fur Trade*, p. 238.
127   Wood and Thiessen, *Early Fur Trade*, p. 238.
128   Wood and Thiessen, *Early Fur Trade*, pp. 238–239.
129   Wood and Thiessen, *Early Fur Trade*, p. 137.
130   Wood and Thiessen, *Early Fur Trade*, p. 138.
131   Wood and Thiessen, *Early Fur Trade*, p. 138.
132   Wood and Thiessen, *Early Fur Trade*, p. 149.
133   For an outstanding account of "The Expedition's Traveling Library," see Beckham, *The Literature of the Lewis and Clark Expedition*, pp. 25–54.
134   *JLCE*, VI:184.
135   Wood and Thiessen, *Early Fur Trade*, p. 150.
136   Wood and Thiessen, *Early Fur Trade*, p. 151.
137   Wood and Thiessen, *Early Fur Trade*, p. 149.
138   Wood and Thiessen, *Early Fur Trade*, p. 138.
139   Wood and Thiessen, *Early Fur Trade*, p. 151.
140   Wood and Thiessen, *Early Fur Trade* 152.
141   Charles Dickens, *Oliver Twist* (New York, 1993), p. 17.
142   *JLCE*, V:91.
143   For the text of this extraordinary letter, see Jenkinson, *A Vast and Open Plain*, pp. 431–432.
144   *JLCE*, III:239.
145   *JLCE*, VII:209.
146   *JLCE*, III:291.
147   *JLCE*, III:291.
148   Donna J. Kessler, *The Making of Sacagawea, A Euro-American Legend* (Tuscaloosa, 1996), p. 54. Hereafter cited as Kessler, *The Making of Sacagawea*.
149   *JLCE*, III:291.
150   Paton, *Doctors in the Wilderness*, p. 109.
151   Peck, *Or Perish in the Attempt*, p. 134.
152   Wood and Thiessen, *Early Fur Trade*, p. 232.
153   *JLCE*, V:xxx
154   *JLCE*, V:171.
155   *JLCE*, III:291.
156   Kessler, *The Making of Sacagawea*, p. 55.
157   See, for example, Lewis's dark fantasy of Indian perfidy on February 20, 1806. *JLCE*, VI:332.
158   *JLCE*, V:103.
159   *JLCE*, V:171.
160   *JLCE*, X:72.

[161]   *JLCE*, III:292.
[162]   *JLCE*, III:292.
[163]   *JLCE*, III:292.
[164]   *JLCE*, III:293.
[165]   *JLCE*, III:294.
[166]   *JLCE*, III:293
[167]   *JLCE*, IV:11.
[168]   *JLCE*, III:293.

CHAPTER III

[1]   Quoted in John Hailman, *Thomas Jefferson on Wine* (Jackson, 2006), p. 260.
[2]   Quoted in Henry Adams, *History of the United States During the Administrations of Thomas Jefferson* (New York, 1986), p. 24.
[3]   Quoted in Bob Arnebeck, *Through a Fiery Trial: Building Washington 1790–1800* (Lanham, 1991), p. 610.
[4]   To Joel Barlow, May 3, 1802. See Albert Ellery Bergh, *The Writings of Thomas Jefferson* (Washington, D.C., 1903), p. 321. Hereafter cited as Bergh, *Writings*.
[5]   Quoted in Ambrose, *Undaunted Courage*, p. 63.
[6]   Interestingly, Lewis spent almost precisely the same amount of time in Jefferson's White House as he did on the transcontinental journey.
[7]   Danisi and Jackson, *Meriwether Lewis*, p. 42, say Lewis carried 27 messages altogether.
[8]   Richard Dillon, *Meriwether Lewis* (Lyfayete, CA, 2003), pp. 28–29. Hereafter cited as Dillon, *Meriwether Lewis*.
[9]   Quoted in Leandra Zim Holland, *Feasting and Fasting with Lewis & Clark: A Food and Social History of the Early 1800s* (Emigrant, MT, 2003), p. 73.
[10]   Quoted in Danisi and Jackson, *Meriwether Lewis*, p. 63.
[11]   Jefferson to Madison, April 27, 1809. See Bergh, *Writings*, vol. XII, p. 277.
[12]   Jefferson to John Adams, January 11, 1817. See Lester J. Cappon, ed., *The Adams-Jefferson Letters: The Complete Correspondence Between Thomas Jefferson and Abigail and John Adams* (Chapel Hill, 1959), p. 506. Hereafter cited as Capon, *The Adams-Jefferson Letters*.
[13]   *JLCE*, II:495.
[14]   *JLCE*, IX:41.
[15]   *JLCE*, X:29.
[16]   See Edward L. Queen, Stephen R. Prothero, and Gardiner H. Shattuck, *Encyclopedia of American Religious History* (New York, 1996), p. 511.
[17]   Slaughter, *Exploring Lewis and Clark*, pp. 57–62.
[18]   Larry Morris, *The Fate of the Corps: What Became of the Lewis and Clark Explorers After the Expedition* (New Haven, 2004), pp. 187–202.
[19]   *JLCE*, IX:350.
[20]   *JLCE*, VIII:308.
[21]   See Moulton, *JLCE*, VIII:309 n.
[22]   *JLCE*, II:489.
[23]   Susannah Ural Bruce, *The Harp and the Eagle: Irish-American Volunteers and the Union Army, 1861–1865* (New York, 2006), p. 32.
[24]   *JLCE*, II:489.
[25]   *JLCE*, II:488–489.
[26]   *JLCE*, II:489.
[27]   *JLCE*, II:488.
[28]   *JLCE*, II:488.
[29]   *JLCE*, IX:395.

30 Peck, *Or Perish in the Attempt*, pp. 102–106.
31 *JLCE*, II:429.
32 *JLCE*, IX:391.
33 *JLCE*, II:495.
34 *JLCE*, II:492.
35 *JLCE*, V:118.
36 *JLCE*, V:106.
37 George Potter and Evelyn M. Simpson, eds., *The Sermons of John Donne* (Berkeley, 1953), I, p. 200.
38 Mussulman, www.lewis-clark.org, *Discovering Lewis and Clark.*
39 Mussulman, www.lewis-clark.org, *Discovering Lewis and Clark.*
40 Ambrose, *Undaunted Courage*, p. 280.
41 Dillon, *Meriwether Lewis*, p. 204.
42 James R. Fazio, *Across the Snowy Ranges: The Lewis and Clark Expedition in Idaho and Western Montana* (Moscow, 2001), p. 23.
43 Eldon G. Chuinard, *Only One Man Died: The Medical Aspects of the Lewis and Clark Expedition* (Glendale, 1979), p. 311.
44 Lavender, *The Way to the Western Sea*, p. 254.
45 Lavender, *The Way to the Western Sea*, p. 255.
46 Lavender, *The Way to the Western Sea*, p. 255.
47 Albert Furtwangler, *Acts of Discovery: Visions of America in the Lewis and Clark Journals*, 132.
48 *JLCE*, XI:276.
49 *JLCE*, II:434.
50 *JLCE*, II:433.
51 *JLCE*, II:433.
52 *JLCE*, V:29.
53 *JLCE*, II:433.
54 *JLCE*, VIII:268.
55 *JLCE*, V:209.
56 *JLCE*, VIII:268.
57 *JLCE*, II:140–141.
58 *JLCE*, II:141.
59 *JLCE*, II:140.
60 *JLCE*, II:141.
61 *JLCE*, III:288.
62 *JLCE*, II:141.
63 Jackson, *Letters*, pp. 368–369.
64 *JLCE*, VI:199–200.
65 Jackson, *Letters*, p. 178.
66 Jackson, *Letters*, p. 179 n.
67 *JLCE*, III:225.
68 *JLCE*, III:403.
69 *JLCE*, III:237.
70 *JLCE*, X:67.
71 *JLCE*, VI:152.
72 *JLCE*, V:32.
73 *JLCE*, X:68.
74 *JLCE*, X:68.
75 *JLCE*, III:261.
76 *JLCE*, III:256.
77 *JLCE*, X:68.
78 *JLCE*, X:75.

79 *JLCE*, X:75.

80 *JLCE*, X:68.

81 *JLCE*, XI:114.

82 *JLCE*, XI:114.

83 Bernard DeVoto, "Christmas to Christmas with Lewis and Clark," in Ronda, *Voyages of Discovery*, p. 91.

84 *JLCE*, X:68.

85 *JLCE*, IX:106.

86 *JLCE*, III, IX:106.

87 Morris, *The Fate of the Corps*, pp. 102–104.

88 See Paul Schlicke, ed., *Oxford Reader's Companion to Dickens* (Oxford, 1999), pp. 14–18.

89 *JLCE*, XI:114.

90 *JLCE*, XI:114.

91 *JLCE*, III:261.

92 *JLCE*, III:261.

93 *JLCE*, X:68.

94 *JLCE*, XI:114.

95 *JLCE*, VI:135.

96 *JLCE*, VI:136.

97 *JLCE*, VI:136.

98 *JLCE*, VI:136.

99 *JLCE*, VI:136.

100 Jackson, *Letters*, p. vii.

101 *JLCE*, V:206–207.

102 *JLCE*, VI:137.

103 *JLCE*, VI:137.

104 *JLCE*, XI:407.

105 *JLCE*, IX:262.

106 *JLCE*, IX:262.

107 *JLCE*, IX:262.

108 *JLCE*, XI:407.

109 See Morris, *The Fate of the Corps*, pp. 101–105.

110 *JLCE*, XI:407.

111 *JLCE*, XI:407.

112 *JLCE*, XI:407.

113 *JLCE*, VI:137.

114 *JLCE*, XI:407.

115 *JLCE*, II:347.

116 *JLCE*, IX:20.

117 *JLCE*, II:348.

118 *JLCE*, XI:34.

119 *JLCE*, IX:20.

120 *JLCE*, IX:20.

121 *JLCE*, II:346–347.

122 Wordsworth, *Poetical Works*, ed. Thomas Hutchinson (Oxford, 1904), p. 86.:

> She dwelt among the untrodden ways
>
> Beside the springs of Dove,
>
> A Maid whom there were none to praise
>
> And very few to love.

A violet by a mossy stone

Half hidden from the eye!

Fair as a star, when only one

Is shining in the sky.

She lived unknown, and few could know

When Lucy ceased to be;

But she is in her grave, and, oh,

The difference to me!

123 David Peck, *Or Perish in the Attempt*, p. 89.

124 *JLCE*, X:18.

125 *JLCE*, IX:385.

126 *JLCE*, II:347.

127 Peck, *Or Perish in the Attempt*, p. 92.

128 *JLCE*, IX:385.

129 *JLCE*, IX:385.

130 *JLCE*, IX:20.

131 *JLCE*, II:347. I have made no attempt to reproduce the list in the vertical form used by Clark. Because I have violated an exact reproduction of the list in Clark's journal, I have placed these names in italics rather than enclosed them in quotation marks.

132 See Morris, *The Fate of the Corps*, p. 202.

133 *JLCE*, IV:359.

134 *JLCE*, IV:363.

135 *JLCE*, IV:369.

136 JCLE, IV:369.

137 *JLCE*, IV:359.

138 Quoted in Jenkinson, *A Vast and Open Plain*, p. 359.

139 *JLCE*, IV:359.

140 *JLCE*, IV:359–361.

141 *JLCE*, IV:362.

142 *JLCE*, IV:362.

143 *JLCE*, IX:179.

144 *JLCE*, XI:218.

145 *JLCE*, IV:285.

146 Jackson, *Letters*, p. 61.

147 *JLCE*, VIII:88.

148 *JLCE*, VIII:163.

149 *JLCE*, II:142.

150 *JLCE*, II:143 n.

151 *JLCE*, II:329–330.

152 *JLCE*, II:329–330.

153 *JLCE*, II:144.

154 *JLCE*, II:144.

155 *JLCE*, II:144.

156 *JLCE*, II:144.

157 *JLCE*, III:267.

158 *JLCE*, X:68.

159 *JLCE*, XI:115.

160 *JLCE*, X:68.

161 *JLCE*, XI:115.

162 *JLCE*, X:68.
163 *JLCE*, IX:107.
164 *JLCE*, IX:107.
165 *JLCE*, IX:107.
166 *JLCE*, XI:116.
167 *JLCE*, IX:107.
168 *JLCE*, III:266.
169 *JLCE*, III:267.
170 *JLCE*, III:267.
171 *JLCE*, III:267.
172 *JLCE*, III:267.
173 *JLCE*, III:267.
174 Nicandri, *River of Promise*, p. 236.
175 *JLCE*, VI:151–152.
176 Quoted in Morris, *The Fate of the Corps*, p. 26.
177 Jefferson "To the Wolf and People of the Mandan Nation," in Merrill Peterson, ed., *Thomas Jefferson: Writings*, p. 564.
178 Jefferson, "To the Wolf and People of the Mandan Nation," p. 564–565.
179 *JLCE*, VI:157.
180 *JLCE*, IX:263.
181 *JLCE*, X:185.
182 *JLCE*, XI:409.
183 *JLCE*, VI:153.

CHAPTER IV

1   *JLCE*, VIII:74.
2   *JLCE*, VIII:74.
3   *JLCE*, VIII:77.
4   *JLCE*, VIII:83.
5   *JLCE*, V:106.
6   *JLCE*, VIII:161.
7   Jackson, *Letters*, pp. 12–13.
8   Ambrose: *Undaunted Courage*, p. 379.
9   *JLCE*, VIII:74.
10   *JLCE*, VIII:172.
11   *JLCE*, VIII:172.
12   *JLCE*, VIII:173.
13   *JLCE*, VIII:173–174.
14   *JLCE*, VIII:179.
15   *JLCE*, VIII:180.
16   *JLCE*, VIII:181–182.
17   *JLCE*, VIII:185.
18   *JLCE*, VIII:219.
19   *JLCE*, VIII:225.
20   *JLCE*, VIII:237.
21   *JLCE*, VIII:107.
22   *JLCE*, VI:151–152.
23   Paul Russell Cutright, *Lewis and Clark: Pioneering Naturalists* (Urbana, 1969), p. 313. Hereafter cited as Cutright, *Pioneering Naturalists*.
24   *JLCE*, IV:266.

25 *JLCE*, VIII:121.
26 Jackson, *Letters*, p. 61.
27 The four men rode 63 miles between dawn and 3 P.M. on July 27. They rested for an hour and a half. Then they rode another 17 miles before dark. At this point they killed a buffalo and had supper. Then they rode their horses at a walk through a plains thunderstorm—thunder and lightning but no rain—until 2 A.M. Now the party of four slept for a couple of hours. At first light Lewis had his men up and back in the saddle. After a journey of just 12 miles, they reached the Missouri, just as Ordway's canoe party floated into sight of the confluence of the Missouri and the Marias. See Ambrose, *Undaunted Courage*, 394.
28 *JLCE*, VIII:272–273.
29 *JLCE*, VIII:146.
30 *JLCE*, VIII:276.
31 *JLCE*, VIII:79.
32 *JLCE*, VIII:80.
33 *JLCE*, VIII:80.
34 *JLCE*, V:209.
35 *JLCE*, IV:423.
36 *JLCE*, VIII:275.
37 *JLCE*, VIII:276.
38 *JLCE*, VIII:146,
39 *JLCE*, X:262.
40 *JLCE*, VI:152.
41 *JLCE*, VIII:146.
42 *JLCE*, VIII:146.
43 *JLCE*, VIII:280.
44 *JLCE*, VIII:281.
45 Frances Hunter, *The Fairest Portion of the Globe* (Austin, 2010).
46 *JLCE*, VIII:281.
47 *JLCE*, VIII:281.
48 *JLCE*, VIII:281.
49 *JLCE*, VIII:282.
50 *JLCE*, VIII:282.
51 *JLCE*, VIII:147.
52 *JLCE*, VIII:147–148.
53 *JLCE*, IX:345.
54 *JLCE*, VIII:148.
55 *JLCE*, VIII:148.
56 *JCLE*, VIII:148.
57 *JLCE*, VIII:149.
58 *JLCE*, VIII:149.
59 *JCLE*, VIII:282.
60 *JLCE*, VIII:283.
61 *JLCE*, VIII:149.
62 *JCLE*, VIII:150.
63 *JLCE*, IV:70.
64 *JLCE*, VIII:150.
65 *JLCE*, VIII:150.
66 *JLCE*, VIII:150.
67 *JLCE*, VIII:150.
68 *JLCE*, VIII:151.
69 *JLCE*, VIII:283.
70 *JLCE*, VIII:152.

71 *JLCE*, VIII:152.
72 *JLCE*, V:74.
73 *JLCE*, VIII:152.
74 *JLCE*, VIII:152.
75 *JLCE*, VIII:152.
76 *JLCE*, VIII:152.
77 *JLCE*, VIII:152.
78 *JLCE*, VIII:285.
79 *JLCE*, VIII:285.
80 *JLCE*, VIII:285.
81 Jenkinson, *A Vast and Open Plain*, p. 432.
82 *JLCE*, VIII:285.
83 *JLCE*, X:263.
84 *JLCE*, VIII:285.
85 *JLCE*, VIII:153.
86 *JLCE*, VIII:153.
87 *JLCE*, VIII:286.
88 *JLCE*, VIII:286.
89 Wordsworth, "Lines composed a few miles above Tintern Abbey, on revisiting the banks of the Wye during a tour," in Thomas Hutchinson, ed., *Poetical Works*, p. 164.
90 *JLCE*, VIII:287.
91 *JLCE*, VIII:288 n.
92 *JLCE*, VIII:371.
93 *JLCE*, VIII:154.
94 *JLCE*, VIII:152.
95 *JLCE*, VIII:154.
96 *JLCE*, VIII:154.
97 *JLCE*, VIII:154–155.
98 *JLCE*, VIII:155.
99 I am sincerely indebted to Lewis and Clark firearms expert Mike Carrick for his judgment that the ball that damaged Captain Lewis's posteriors was .525 caliber, not .54 caliber as is usually suggested. Carrick notes that a .54 caliber rifle can, however, shoot a .535 caliber ball. Thus Moulton rightly indicates that Lewis was probably shot by a ".54 caliber Model 1803 rifle." See *JLCE*:VIII:157 n.
100 Peck, *Or Perish in the Attempt*, p. 276.
101 *JLCE*, IX:347.
102 *JLCE*, VIII:155.
103 *JLCE*, IX:347.
104 *JLCE*, VI:331
105 *JLCE*, VIII:155.
106 *JLCE*, VIII:155.
107 Jackson, *Letters*, p. 590.
108 *JLCE*, VIII:155.
109 *JLCE*, VIII:155–156.
110 *JLCE*, VIII:156.
111 *JLCE*, VIII:156.
112 *JLCE*, X:266.
113 *JLCE*, VIII:290
114 *JLCE*, VIII:290.
115 *JLCE*, VIII:290.
116 *JLCE*, VIII:290.
117 *JLCE*, VIII:295.

118 Jackson, *Letters*, p. 204.
119 *JLCE*, VIII:158.
120 *JLCE*, VIII:354.
121 Jackson, *Letters*, p. 369.
122 Jackson, *Letters,* p. 365.
123 Jackson, *Letters*, p. 369.
124 *JLCE*, VIII:290.
125 Jackson, *Letters*, p. 369.
126 Jackson, *Letters*, p. 385.
127 Jackson, *Letters*, pp. 385–386.
128 Jackson, *Letters*, p. 407.
129 Nicandri, *River of Promise*, pp. 248–266.
130 Quoted in Danisi and Jackson, *Meriwether Lewis*, p. 173.
131 *JLCE*, VI:32.

Chapter V

1 Fergus Fleming, *Off the Map: Tales of Endurance and Exploration*, (New York, 2004), p. 3. Hereafter cited as Fleming, *Off the Map*. Samuel Johnson letter to Mrs. Thrale, quoted in James Boswell, *The Life of Samuel Johnson, LL.D. (*Boston, 1832), p. 272.
2 Jackson, *Letters*, p.vii.
3 Lavender, *The Way to the Western Sea*, p. 380: "At first he may have been frozen by plain old writer's block, rising from a deep, inner fear of the inadequacies that McKeehan chanced to hit on ... The same feelings of inadequacy may have kept him loafing around Philadelphia when he should have been following Clark to St. Louis. ... Later, drink may have added its chains to his paralysis of will, for it is known that by 1809 he was indulging heavily."
4 Ambrose, *Undaunted Courage*, p. 483.
5 Slaughter, *Exploring Lewis and Clark*, pp. 31–32.
6 See, e.g., Jefferson to Lewis, June 4, 1807. Jackson, *Letters*, p. 415.
7 Richard Francis Burton, *Zanzibar: City, Island, and Coast*, II, pp. 223–24. Quoted in Van Orman, *The Explorers*, p. 71.
8 Cutright, "The Fate of the Lewis and Clark Booty," *Pioneering Naturalists*. pp. 349–392.
9 Fleming, *Off the Map,* p. 3.
10 *JLCE*, IV:285.
11 The sarcast Mr. Dooley said it should be titled not *The Rough Riders*, but rather *Alone in Cuba*.
12 Nicandri, *River of Promise*, pp. 123–136. Nicandri makes the point with greater piquancy in his superb lectures.
13 James Boswell, "On Diaries," quoted in H.B. Nisbet and Claude Rawson, *The Cambridge History of Literary Criticism*, vol. 4, *The Eighteenth Century* (Cambridge, 2005), p. 314.
14 *JLCE*, VIII:158.
15 *JLCE*, V:229.
16 *JLCE*, VIII:158.
17 *JLCE*, V:232.
18 *JLCE*, V:249.
19 *JLCE*, V:65.
20 *JLCE*, V:74.
21 Jackson, *Letters*, p. 61.
22 *JLCE*, VI:201.
23 John Wesley Powell, *Exploration of the Colorado River and its Canyons* (New York, 1961), pp. 279–289.

24 *JLCE*, V:118.

25 *JLCE*, IV:10.

26 *JLCE*, II:227.

27 Jenkinson, *A Vast and Open Plain*, p. 359.

28 Jenkinson, *A Vast and Open Plain*, pp. 359–360.

29 Charles Hoffhaus, *Chez les Canses, Three Centuries at Kawsmouth: The French Foundations of Metropolitan Kansas City*, p. 127; quoted in Wood, *Prologue*, p. 138.

30 *JLCE*, III:241.

31 Wood and Thiessen, *Early Fur Trade on the Northern Plains*, p. 232: "They [the Hidatsa] could not be reconciled to *like* these strangers as they called them."

32 *JLCE*, III:241.

33 Ambrose, *Undaunted Courage*, p. 312.

34 Nicandri, *River of Promise*, p. 232.

35 Jackson, *Letters*, pp. 410–411.

36 *JLCE*, VI:50.

37 *JLCE*, III:418.

38 Jackson, *Letters* p. 469.

39 Nicandri, *River of Promise*, p. 216.

40 Clark to Jonathan Clark, August 26, 1809. See Holmberg, *Dear Brother* p. 210.

41 Deposition of Gilbert C. Russell, November 26, 1811. Quoted in Guice, "Why Not Homicide?," *By His Own Hand*, p. 159.

42 Danisi and Jackson, *Meriwether Lewis*, pp. 189–212.

43 Jenkinson, *A Vast and Open Plain*, p. 359.

44 Paul Russell Cutright, *A History of the Lewis and Clark Journals*, (Norman, 1976), p. 60.

45 Ambrose, *Undaunted Courage*, p. 311.

46 Jackson, *Letters*, p. 61.

47 *JLCE*, V:74.

48 Denis Diderot, *Encyclopedia*, in *Rameau's Nephew and Other Works*, translated and edited by Jacques Barzun and Ralph H. Bowen, (Indianapolis, 1964), p. 297.

49 The *Baltimore Federal Gazette* reported an eyewitness who said that the men of the expedition "really have the appearance of Robinson Crusoe—dressed entirely in buckskins." See Betty Houchin Winfield, he Press Response to the Corps of Discovery: The Making of Heroes in an Egalitarian Age," in *Journalism & Mass Communication Quarterly* 80.4 [2003]: pp. 866–883.

50 Jackson, *Letters,* p. 321.

51 Quoted in John Chester Miller, *Alexander Hamilton and the Growth of the New Nation* (Brunswick, 2004), p. 348.

52 Quoted in John E. Ferling, *John Adams: A Life* (Oxford, 1992), p. 272.

53 Jackson, *Letters*, p. 179.

54 Jackson, *Letters*, pp. 394–397

55 Quoted in Nicandri, *River of Promise*, pp. 34–36. See also *JLCE*, V:94 n.

56 Nicandri, *River of Promise*, p. 38.

57 Jackson, *Letters*, pp. 394–395.

58 Jackson, *Letters*, p. 395.

59 Jackson, *Letters*, p. 395.

60 Jackson, *Letters*, p. 395.

61 Jackson, *Letters*, pp. 395–396.

62 *JLCE,* IV:9.

63 Jackson, *Letters*, p. 596.

64 Jackson, *Letters*, p. 406.

65 William Wordsworth, *Preface to the Lyrical Ballads*, in *Selected Poems and PrefacesSelected Poems and Prefaces by William Wordsworth*, ed. Jack Stillinger (Boston, 1965), p. 460.

66   Jackson, *Letters,* p. 400.
67   Jackson, *Letters,* p. 385.
68   Danisi and Jackson, *Meriwether Lewis,* pp. 184–185.
69   Danisi and Jackson, *Meriwether Lewis,* p. 186.
70   Dillon, *Meriwether Lewis,* 311.
71   Danisi and Jackson, *Meriwether Lewis,* p. 190.
72   Jackson, *Letters,* pp. 385–386.
73   Jackson, *Letters,* p. 386.
74   Jackson, *Letters,* p. 386.
75   Jackson, *Letters,* p. 619.
76   Jackson, *Letters,* p. 619.
77   Mussulman, www.lewis-clark.org, *Discovering Lewis & Clark.*
78   *JLCE,* Februiary 25, 1806
79   Mussulman, www.lewis-clark.org, *Discovering Lewis & Clark.*
80   The poem is quoted in Dillon, *Meriwether Lewis,* pp. 275–277.
81   Jackson, *Letters,* p. 63.
82   Jackson, *Letters,* pp. 401–402.
83   Jackson, *Letters,* p. 402.
84   Nicandri, *River of Promise,* pp. 203–217.
85   John Bakeless has called Barlow's celebratory verse "an excruciatingly bad poem." See John Bakeless, *Lewis and Clark: Partners in Discovery* (Mineola, 1947), p. 380. Hereafter cited as Bakeless, *Partners in Discovery.*
86   Jackson, *Letters,* p. 402.
87   Jackson, *Letters,* p. 402.
88   Jackson, *Letters,* p. 403.
89   Jackson, *Letters,* p. 404.
90   Jackson, *Letters,* p. 405.
91   Jackson, *Letters,* p. 407.
92   Jackson, *Letters,* p. 408 n.
93   Richard Francis Burton, *First Footsteps in Africa,* pp. IX, 364–65. Quoted in Fawn Brodie, *The Devil Drives* (New York, 1967), pp. 113–114.
94   See Buzz Aldrin and Ken Abraham, *Magnificent Desolation: The Long Journey Home from the Moon* (New York, 2009).
95   Joseph Mussulman, personal correspondence, March 17, 2011.
96   Jackson, *Letters,* p. 352.
97   Jackson, *Letters,* pp. 61–62.
98   Jackson, *Letters,* p. 62.
99   Wood and Thiessen, *Early Fur Trade,* pp. 151–152.
100 See Jenkinson, *A Vast and Open Plain,* p. 115 n.
101 Ferdinand Hassler to Robert Patterson. Jackson, *Letters,* pp. 556–569.
102 Jackson, *Letters,* p. 619.
103 Jackson, *Letters,* p. 619.
104 Jackson, *Letters,* p. 321.
105 Jackson, *Letters,* p. 137.
106 *JLCE,* V:160.
107 Jackson, *Letters,* p. 306.
108 *JLCE,* VIII:107.
109 Jackson, *Letters,* pp. 611, 619.
110 Cutright, "The Fate of the Lewis and Clark Booty," *Pioneering Naturalists,* p. 349–392.
111 Donald Jackson, *Among the Sleeping Giants: Occasional Pieces on Lewis & Clark* (Urbana, 1987), p. 31.
112 *JLCE,* VIII:363.

113 Brian Vickers, *Francis Bacon: The Major Words* (Oxford, 2008), p. 36. Quoted in Ronda, *Finding the West*, p. 21.

114 Jefferson to John Adams, October 28, 1813. See Cappon, *The Adams-Jefferson Letters*, p. 388.

115 *JLCE*, V:104.

116 *JLCE*, IV:293.

117 Jefferson to Monsieur Paganel, April 15, 1811. See Bergh, *Writings*, pp. 36–37.

118 Jefferson to John Adams, September 12, 1821. See Cappon, *The Adams-Jefferson Letters*, pp. 574–576.

119 Jackson, *Letters*, p. 443.

120 Lavender, *The Way to the Western Sea*, p. 381.

121 Jackson, *Letters*, p. 418.

122 Jefferson to Madison, September 17, 1787. See Julian P. Boyd, ed., *The Papers of Thomas Jefferson*, vol. XII, August 1787 to March 1788 (Princeton, 1950), pp. 136–137. Hereafter, Boyd, *Papers*.

123 Jefferson to John Sullivan, January 7, 1786. See Boyd, *Papers*, vol. IX, January 7, 1786, p. 160.

124 Jackson, *Letters*, p. 415.

125 Jackson, *Letters*, p. 418.

126 Danisi and Jackson, *Meriwether Lewis*, p. 183.

127 Jackson, *Letters*, p. 443.

128 Alf J. Mapp, Jr.,. *Thomas Jefferson: Passionate Pilgrim: The Presidency, the Founding of the University, and the Private Battle*, p. 73.

129 Jackson, *Letters*, p. 444.

130 Jackson, *Letters*, p. 444.

131 Jackson, *Letters*, p. 445.

132 Jackson, *Letters*, p. 445.

133 Quoted in Ambrose, *Undaunted Courage*, p. 456. See Clarence E. Carter, ed., *The Territorial Papers of the United States*, vol. XIV, *The Territory of Louisiana-Missouri 1806–1814* (Washington, D.C., 1949), p. 222. Hereafter cited as Carter, *Territorial Papers*.

134 Jefferson to Henry Dearborn, August 12, 1808. See Bergh, *Writings*, vol. XI, p. 125.

135 Lewis to Thomas Jefferson, December 15, 1808. I wish to thank Thomas Danisi for reminding me of the existence of this letter and making a photocopy of it available to me. See ASP, *Indian Affairs* 1:766–767.

136 ASP, *Indian Affairs* 1:766–767.

137 Jackson, *Letters*, p. 458.

138 I am indebted to Thomas Danisi for pointing out the garbled passage in Jackson, *Letters*, and for providing the omitted words.

139 Carter, *Territorial Papers*, p. 292. See also Jackson, *Letters*, p. 461.

140 Jackson, *Letters*, p. 461.

141 Quoted in Jones, *Shaping of the West*, p. 163.

142 I am indebted to Thomas Danisi for reminding me of this passage in Lewis's letter to Clark.

143 Carter, *The Territorial Papers*, p. 221.

144 Jefferson to Henry Dearborn, August 12, 1808. See Bergh, *Writings* vol. XII, p. 125.

145 Jackson, *Letters*, p. 466.

146 Quoted in Ambrose, *Undaunted Courage*, p. 449.

147 Jenkinson, *A Vast and Open Plain*, pp. 360–361.

148 Jenkinson, *A Vast and Open Plain*, p. 361.

149 *JLCE*, II:420.

150 Jackson, *Letters*, p. 466.

151 I am indebted to Thomas Danisi for providing me a copy of this letter.

152 Lewis to Lucy Marks, December 1, 1806. Meriwether Lewis Collection, Missouri Historical Society.

153   Lewis to Lucy Marks, December 1, 1806. Meriwether Lewis Collection, Missouri Historical Society.

154   Danisi and Jackson, *Meriwether Lewis*, p. 274.

155   Conversation with Thomas Danisi, March 10, 2011.

156   See Jackson, *Letters*, pp. 408–409, 416–417, and 419.

157   Jackson, *Letters*, p. 457.

158   Jackson, *Letters*, p. 457.

159   Jackson, *Letters*, p. 457.

160   Jackson, *Letters*, p. 457.

161   Jackson, *Letters*, p. 457.

162   Danisi and Jackson, *Meriwether Lewis*, p. 288.

163   Slaughter, *Exploring Lewis and Clark*, pp. 31–32.

164   Jackson, *Letters*, pp.496–547; 550–555.

165   *JLCE*, IV:436.

166   *JLCE*, V:246.

167   *JLCE*, VI:435.

168   *JLCE*, V:118; III:286.

169   Bergon, *The Journals of Lewis and Clark*, p. x.

170   Jackson, *Letters*, p. 592.

CHAPTER VI

1   Quoted in Jones, *Shaping of the West*, p. 163.

2   Bakeless, *Partners in Discovery*, pp. 425–426.

3   Danisi and Jackson, *Meriwether Lewis*, p. 287.

4   Vardis Fisher, *Suicide or Murder? The Strange Death of Governor Meriwether Lewis* (Athens, OH, 1993), p. 73.

5   Danisi and Jackson, *Meriwether Lewis*, p. 287.

6   Danisi and Jackson, *Meriwether Lewis*, p. 287.

7   Holmberg, *Dear Brother*, p. 210.

8   Danisi and Jackson, *Meriwether Lewis*, p. 277.

9   De Voto, *The Journals of Lewis and Clark*, p. li.

10   De Voto, *The Journals of Lewis and Clark*, p. li. Jackson, *Letters*, p. 592.

11   Lewis to an unknown correspondent, July 8, 1809. Quoted in Danisi and Jackson, p. 268.

12   Quoted in Ambrose, *Undaunted Courage* p. 470.

13   Bakeless, *Partners in Discovery*, p. 412.

14   Jackson, *Letters*, p. 471.

15   Jackson, *Letters*, p. 470.

16   Quoted in Danisi and Jackson, *Meriwether Lewis*, p. 279.

17   *JLCE*, VII:267.

18   *JLCE*, VIII:24.

19   Danisi and Jackson, *Meriwether Lewis*, p. 289.

20   Lavender, *The Way to the Western Sea* p. 384.

21   Jackson, *Letters*, p. 590.

22   Holmberg, *Dear Brother*, p. 218. Clark: "I have left all my letters which I received from defferent persons at your house' or lost them, they are not with my baggage. will you be So good as to examine and enquire for them, and if you get them Send me them to me by John, or John Croghan."

23   Homberg, *Dear Brother,* p. 221 n: "One wonders if the letter revealed so much of Lewis's troubled mental state that Clark may have even destroyed it to protect his friend."

24 Quoted in Fisher, *Suicide or Murder?*, p. 82, and Starrs and Gale, *The Death of Meriwether Lewis*, p. 251.

25 Danisi and Jackson, *Meriwether Lewis* p. 291.

26 Quoted in Fisher, *Suicide or Murder?*, pp. 81–82. I have italicized the word *condition* because the manuscript is nearly illegible.

27 Quoted in Fisher, *Suidice or Murder?*, p. 82.

28 Quoted in Fisher, *Suicide or Murder*, p. 82.

29 Quoted in Starrs and Gale, *The Death of Meriwether Lewis*, p. 244.

30 Quoted in Fisher, *Suicide or Murder?*, p. 87.

31 Jackson, *Letters*, p. 467.

32 Quoted in Fisher, *Suicide or Murder?*, p. 140.

33 Quoted in Starrs and Gale, *The Death of Meriwether Lewis*, pp. 243–244.

34 Quoted in Starrs and Gale, *The Death of Meriwether Lewis*, p. 246.

35 Quoted in Starrs and Gale, *The Death of Meriwether Lewis*, p. 251.

36 Quoted in Starrs and Gale, *The Death of Meriwether Lewis*, p. 251.

37 Quoted in Starrs and Gale, *The Death of Meriwether Lewis*, p. 252.

38 Holmberg, *Dear Brother*, p. 228.

39 Jackson, *Letters*, p. 592.

40 Quoted in Starrs and Gale, *The Death of Meriwether Lewis*, p. 259.

41 Fisher, *Suicide or Murder?*, p. 85.

42 Danisi and Jackson, *Meriwether Lewis*, p. 291.

43 Bakeless, *Partners in Discovery*, p. 412.

44 Bakeless, *Partners in Discovery*, p. 413.

45 No two transcripts of this letter agree. I have made my own here from the facsimile of the original letter in Guice, *By His Own Hand?*, pp. 146–147.

46 Danisi and Jackson, *Meriwether Lewis*, p. 291.

47 Fisher, *Suicide or Murder?*, p. 81.

48 Quoted in Fisher, *Suicide or Murder?*, p. 83.

49 Quoted in Starrs and Gale, *The Death of Meriwether Lewis*, p. 244.

50 Quoted in Starrs and Gale, *The Death of Meriwether Lewis*, p. 246.

51 Quoted in Fisher, *Suicide or Murder?*, p. 89.

52 Quoted in Fisher, *Suicide or Murder?*, p. 89.

53 Quoted in Fisher, *Suicide or Murder*, p. 89.

54 Danisi and Jackson, *Meriwether Lewis,* p. 305 fn.

55 The Danisi-Jackson theory has many problems. Given the fact that Captain Russell's man prepared a trunk for the "Nation," and that Neelly was the US Agent to the Chickasaw Nation, it seems likelier that Lewis and Neelly did take that "detour." Neelly's chronology has them crossing the Tennessee River on October 8, losing the horses on the night of October 9–10, Neelly waiting behind to find the horses on the 10th, and Lewis going on ahead to Grinder's Inn. It would have been virtually impossible for them to cross the Tennessee on the Tennessee-Mississippi border and remain on Neelly's timeline. Furthermore, if they took a direct route from Memphis to the Natchez Trace they would have had to swim their horses and baggage across the Tennessee River, or build or borrow some sort of boat. That would have been a huge risk given the fact that Lewis's trunks included all of his official government papers and vouchers *and* the precious expedition journals. If Neelly and Lewis intersected the Natchez Trace at the Chickasaw Agency, they would have been able to take George Colbert's ferry across the Tennessee River on October 8. Given Lewis's indisposition and the preciousness of his baggage, it seems infinitely likelier that he took advantage of the well-established trail from Memphis to the Chickasaw Agency, and the Natchez Trace from the agency to Grinder's Inn, with the assurance of a ferry ride across the Tennessee River, than that he and Neelly

bushwacked across the Mississippi and Tennessee wilderness. I am indebted to historian Tony Turnbow and my friend John Guice for their confirmation of my analysis.

56 Coues, *The History of the Lewis and Clark Expedition*, p. lii.

57 Starrs and Gale, *The Death of Meriwether Lewis*, p. 246.

58 Jackson, *Letters*, p. 467.

59 Jackson, *Letters*, p. 467.

60 Jackson, *Letters*, p. 467.

61 Jackson, *Letters*, p. 467.

62 To give the reader as precise an account of what happened at Grinder's Inn as possible, and to sort out as much as possible the various strands of historical *testimony*, I have put in brackets after each statement of contemporary testimony the source of the information and the date. Because all accounts of the death of Lewis begin with Priscilla Grinder, I include her when referring to the letter of Alexander Wilson on May 18, 1811, the letter of James Neelly on October 18, 1809, etc. Once Neelly has arrived at the scene on the morning of October 11, 1809, *after* Lewis's death, I cite Neelly alone in brackets. The presumption in criminal cases is that the witnesses closest to the event in place and time are usually the most reliable witnesses, even when their testimony is in some ways unreliable, self-protective, or biased. Hereafter [Grinder-Wilson] refers to Alexander Wilson's letter of May 28, 1811, Guice, *By His Own Hand?*, pp. 157–158; and [Grinder-Neelly] refers to James Neelly's letter to Jefferson on October 18, 1809, Jackson, *Letters*, pp. 467–468.

63 Jackson, *Letters*, p. 467.

64 Guice, *By His Own Hand?*, p. 90: "The trace was still so dangerous in 1809, however, that the rough, tough boatmen always rode or walked up it in convoy. Travelers seldom ventured down the trace from Nashville to Natchez alone."

65 Bakeless, *Partners in Discovery*, p. 417: "Soldier and explorer, he had slept that way often enough and probably preferred it to the rather dubious beds of such an establishment."

66 Dillon, *Meriwether Lewis*, p. 332. Lewis was "wrapped in thought and anger as he rehearsed his upcoming confrontation with Secretary of War Eustis."

67 Fisher, *Suicide or Murder?*, p. 151. "No one has explained how the woman knew it was a pistol instead of a rifle: are we to assume that after she entered the cabin she looked at the weapons?"

68 Guice, *By His Own Hand*, p. 94.

69 Fisher, *Suicide or Murder?*, p. 151.

70 Bakeless, *Partners in Discovery*, p. 418.

71 Quoted in Starrs and Gale, *The Death of Meriwether Lewis*, p. 252.

72 Quoted in Starrs and Gale, *The Death of Meriwether Lewis*, p. 252.

73 See Danisi and Jackson, *Meriwether Lewis*, p. 302.

74 Quoted in Danisi and Jackson, p. 303.

75 Quoted in Danisi and Jackson, *Meriwether Lewis*, p. 304.

76 Quoted in Starrs and Gale, *The Death of Meriwether Lewis*, p. 252.

77 *JLCE*, IV:141.

78 Bakeless, *Partners in Discovery*, p. 419: "The last words must be an exact quotation— they are the very words Lewis applies to a wounded grizzly in the Journals."

79 *JLCE*, V:74.

80 At this point, Neelly's testimony becomes his own. See Jackson, *Letters*, pp. 467–468.

81 Dillon, *Meriwether Lewis*, p. 336: "It is not known ... whether he examined the body for powder burns, which would have strongly suggested suicide; whether he even examined the Governor's pistols to see if they had taken his life."

82 Danisi and Jackson, *Meriwether Lewis*, pp. 301–302.

83 Bakeless, *Partners in Discovery*, p. 415.

84   Fisher, *Suicide or Murder?*, p. 128.
85   Jackson, *Letters*, p. 467.
86   Holmberg, *Dear Brother*, p. 218.
87   Dee Brown, "What Really Happened to Meriwether Lewis?" in *Columbia Magazine*, Winter 1988. Vol. 1, #4.
88   Dillon, *Meriwether Lewis* , p. 337: "But not one word, alas, of Jefferson's conversation with the Creole [Pernier] has come down to us. Certainly, however, Pernia confirmed Neelly's claim of suicide (whether rightly or wrongly), so that Jefferson never even considered murder to be a possibility."
89   Quoted in Danisi and Jackson, *Meriwether Lewis*, pp. 303–304.
90   Quoted in Fisher, *Suicide or Murder?*, p. 155.
91   Fisher, *Suicide or Murder,* pp. 155–156.
92   Quoted in Starrs and Gale, *The Death of Meriwether Lewis*, p. 246.
93   Jackson, *Letters*, p. 592.
94   Quoted in Holmberg, *Dear Brother*, pp. 216–218.
95   Quoted in Holmberg, *Dear Brother*, p. 210.
96   Jackson, *Letters*, p. 592.
97   Jackson, *Letters*, p. 592.
98   Dillon, *Meriwether Lewis*, p. 344.
99   Quoted in Guice, *By His Own Hand*, p. 158.
100 Danisi and Jackson, *Meriwether Lewis,* p. 343.
101 Dillon, *Meriwether Lewis*, p. 344.
102 Dillon, *Meriwether Lewis*, p. 344.
103 Dillon, *Meriwether Lewis*, p. 345–347.
104 Dillon, *Meriwether Lewis*, p. 348.
105 Coues, *The History of the Lewis and Clark Expedition*, p. lvi.
106 Coues, *The History of the Lewis and Clark Expedition*, p. lvii.
107 Coues, *The History of the Lewis and Clark Expedition*, p. lvi. Fisher, *Suicide or Murder?*, p. 251, acknowledges that Coues and Olin Wheeler "found themselves unable to reach a conclusion."
108 Quoted in Peck, *Or Perish in the Attempt*, p. 293
109 Peck, *Or Perish in the Attempt*, p. 293.
110 Peck, *Or Perish in the Attempt*, p. 294.
111 Peck, *Or Perish in the Attempt*, p. 295.
112 Peck, *Or Perish in the Attempt*, p. 295.
113 Lavender, *The Way to the Western Sea*, p. 385.
114 For the obituary, see Danisi and Jackson, *Meriwether Lewis*, p. 329.
115 Couse, Thwaites, and DeVoto, it must be acknowledged, were half-hearted murderists, at best. Each of them preferred murder but was aware that Lewis might well have killed himself. None was willing to dismiss suicide out of hand.
116 Bakeless, *Partners in Discovery*, p. 423.
117 Guice, *By His Own Hand*, p. 74.
118 1. There were no eyewitnesses; 2. Too much is made of Lewis's state of mind during his last days in St. Louis; 3. He was busier, less idle and dissipated in Philadelphia than historians have suggested; 4. Lewis was not the first man who has had a hard time finding a wife; 5. Claims that Lewis was an alcoholic have been greatly exaggerated; 6. What evidence do we have that Lewis was despondent about his inability to finish his book?; 7. Considering the complexities of his work in St. Louis, he was not a bad governor of Louisiana Territory; 8. Frederick Bates was not a reliable or credible source for describing Lewis's difficulties or unpopularity in St. Louis; 9. His financial difficulties have been exaggerated. He was in trouble economically, but he had considerable equity in land, and he was far from bankrupt; 10. Writing one's will is

hardly an indication that he is about to kill himself; 11. It is hard to take seriously Gilbert Russell's statement that Lewis had twice tried to kill himself given how vague his statement is; 12. Lewis's letter to President James Madison was clear, upbeat, and rational; 13. Lewis's letter to Amos Stoddard was hardly the kind of letter one would write who did not intend to return to St. Louis; 14. Russell's November 26, 1811, deposition may not be authentic; 15. James Neelly's statement that Lewis was deranged may only indicate physical exhaustion or a bout of drunkenness; 16. Jefferson would not have hired Lewis or sent him west if he thought he was mentally unstable; 17. Stephen Ambrose was inconsistent—earlier in his career he praised Dillon's biography, but later became an unambiguous advocate for suicide; 18. Jefferson's acceptance of the suicide story was a "clean" way to handle a difficult situation; 19. Jefferson was capable of self-deception and duplicity; 20. Jefferson's view that mental hypochondria ran in the Lewis family has been refuted by family members; 21. Too much has been made of Clark's acceptance of the suicide story—wild rumors were swirling around the American frontier; 22. The fact that Clark never wrote about Lewis's death after 1809 is very odd—suggests that he was less sure it was suicide than we think; 23. Reliance on Clark's single letter written immediately after the event is not proof that Clark was *always* convinced that Lewis killed himself; 24. Historians have read too much into Lewis's birthday meditation of August 18, 1805, including that whippersnapper Clay Jenkinson; 25. The gaps in Lewis's journal are not an indication that Lewis was suffering from depression—perhaps Clark was just the more natural journal keeper; 26. The Natchez Trace was not really as safe as historian Dawson Phelps claimed; 27. Dr. Ravenholt's syphilis theory is implausible; 28. Dr. Chuinard was sure that Lewis could not have survived the second gunshot wound; 29. Lewis was suffering from malaria, not depression; 30. Lewis's pistols would have made it difficult to shoot himself, particularly the second (abdominal) shot; 31. It was too dark that night for Mrs. Grinder to have seen Lewis struggling about the yard, and there is no mention of a candle or lantern; 32. In 1848 the Tennessee committee reckoned that Lewis had been murdered—it is worth taking that seriously; 33. Dawson Phelps's conclusion is irrational and illogical—just because there is no evidence that Lewis was murdered does not mean that he *wasn't* murdered; 34. The *William and Mary Quarterly* should have published Grace Lewis Miller's fine refutation of Dawson Phelps; 35. What happened to Lewis's money if he committed suicide?; 36. Vardis Fisher was not taken seriously primarily because he was a novelist; 37. Donald Jackson's authority has been too influential in the suicide-murder debate; 38. Stephen Ambrose's obsession with Lewis's supposed suicide has more to do with his first wife's suicide than with the facts of the Lewis shooting; 39. Why not dig Lewis up and do proper forensics tests?; 40. Richard Dillon makes a convincing argument that Lewis was not the kind of man who commits suicide.

[119] Guice, *By His Own Hand?*, p. 100.
[120] Guice, *By His Own Hand?*, p. 77.
[121] Guice, *By His Own Hand?*, p. 78.
[122] Danisi and Jackson, *Meriwether Lewis*, pp. 213–251.
[123] Guice, *By His Own Hand?*, p. 79.
[124] Guice, *By His Own Hand?*, p. 81.
[125] Guice, *By His Own Hand?*, p. 83.
[126] Guice, *By His Own Hand?*, p. 82.
[127] Jackson, *Letters*, p. 593.
[128] Guice, *By His Own Hand?*, p. 87.
[129] Guice, *By His Own Hand?*, p. 102.
[130] Guice, *By His Own Hand?*, p. 102.
[131] *Hamlet*, III.ii.143.
[132] Dillon, *Meriwether Lewis*, p. 344.

133 Guice, *By His Own Hand?*, pp. 88, 89.

134 Quoted in Guice, *By His Own Hand?*, p. 95.

135 Thomas Danisi, "The 'Ague' Made Him Do It," in *We Proceeded On* 28, no. 1 (February 2002): pp. 10–15.

136 Danisi and Jackson, *Meriwether Lewis*, p. 342.

137 Furtwangler, *Acts of Discovery*, pp. 224–225.

138 Furtwangler, *Acts of Discovery*, pp. 224–225.

139 Coues, *The History of the Lewis and Clark Expedition*, p. lvi.

140 Lavender, *The Way to the Western Sea*, p. 385.

141 Jefferson, *A Bill for Establishing Religious Freedom*, Peterson, *Thomas Jefferson: Writings*, p. 347.

CHAPTER VII

1 Holmberg, *Dear Brother*, pp. 216–218.

2 Holmberg, *Dear Brother*, p. 218.

3 Holmberg, *Dear Brother*, p. 224.

4 Holmberg, *Dear Brother*, p. 224.

5 Holmberg, *Dear Brother*, p. 218.

6 James Neely sent the expedition journals to Jefferson, who sent them on to President Madison. By January 10, 1810 Clark had received the papers. See Cutright, *A History of the Lewis and Clark Journals*, p. 54.

7 *Hamlet*, III.ii,51.

8 Lavender, *The Way to the Western Sea*, p. 384.

9 Ambrose, *Undaunted Courage*, pp. 474–475, 280.

10 Guice, *By His Own Hand*, p. 85.

11 Guice, *By His Own Hand*, p. 98.

12 Ambrose, *Undaunted Courage*, pp. 477–478.

13 Quoted in Craig Nelson, *Rocket Men: The Epic Story of the First Men on the Moon* (New York, 2009), p. 324. Hereafter cited as Nelson, *Rocket Men*.

14 Jay Buckley, *William Clark: Indian Diplomat* (Norman, 2008), p. 235. Hereafter cited as Buckley, *Indian Diplomat*.

15 Quoted in Morris, *The Fate of the Corps*, p. 167.

16 Quoted in Morris, *The Fate of the Corps*, p. 169.

17 Quoted in Morris, *The Fate of the Corps*, p. 170.

18 Quoted in Foley, *Wilderness Journey*, p. 266.

19 Lavender, *The Way to the Western Sea*, p. 386.

20 Hereafter Biddle's narrative or Biddle-Allen's edition of the journals.

21 Jackson, *Letters*, p. 592.

22 Fisher, *Suicide or Murder?*, pp. 171–177.

23 See David Leon Chandler, *The Jefferson Conspiracies: A President's Role in the Assassination of Meriwether Lewis* (New York, 1994).

24 Guice, *By His Own Hand?*, p. 85.

25 See Joanne B. Freeman, *Affairs of Honor: National Politics in the New Republic* (New Haven, 2001), pp. 62–104.

26 Foley, *Wilderness Journey*, p. 182: "He [Clark] seems never to have doubted that it was suicide, and one suspects that he asked himself what, if anything, he might have done to prevent this terrible tragedy."

27 Jackson, *Letters*, pp. 591–592.

28 Danisi and Jackson, *Meriwether Lewis*, p. 308.

29 Danisi and Jackson, *Meriwether Lewis,* p. 309.

30 Danisi and Jackson, *Meriwether Lewis,* p. 309.

31   Jackson, *Letters*, p. 592.

32   Jackson, *Letters*, p. 592.

33   Jefferson to Martha Jefferson, March 28, 1787. See Boyd, *Papers,* vol. 11, p. 250.

34   Jefferson to Maria Jefferson Eppes, March 3, 1802. See Edwin Morris Betts
and James Adam Bear, Jr., eds., *The Family Letters of Thomas Jefferson*
(Columbia, 1966), p. 219.

35   Jackson, *Letters* p. 593.

36   Jefferson to John Adams, April 8, 1816. Cappon, *The Adams-Jefferson Letters*, p. 467.

37   Jefferson to John Adams, April 8, 1816. Cappon, *The Adams-Jefferson Letters*, p. 467.

38   Ronda, *Finding the West*, p. xvi.

39   Quoted in Joseph Ellis, *Passionate Sage: The Character and Legacy of John Adams*
(New York, 1993), p. 77.

40   Jefferson to James Madison, August 31, 1783. See James Morton Smith, ed., *The
Republic of Letters: The Correspondence between Thomas Jefferson and James Madison
1776–1826*, vol. 1, p. 264.

41   Boyd, *Papers*, vol. 6, p. 198.

42   *Hamlet*, III.i.56–90.

43   Dillon, *Meriwether Lewis*, p. 344.

44   I am heavily indebted to the work of Thomas Joiner in my analysis of the risk factors
for suicide. See, *Why People Die By Suicide* (Cambridge, Mass., 2005) and *Myths about
Suicide* (Cambridge, Mass., 2010).

45   See Danisi and Jackson, *Meriwether Lewis*, p. 253.

46   For another view of the unfortunate analogy between master-slave and master-
Newfoundland, see Slaughter, *Exploring Lewis and Clark*, p. 121.

47   Quoted in Jones, *Shaping of the West*, p. 170.

48   Jones, *Shaping of the West;* Foley, *Wilderness Journey;* and Buckley, *Indian Diplomat.*

49   *JLCE*, V:112.

50   *JLCE*, VIII:110–111.

51   Legend has it that a dog collar was found long after Lewis's death bearing the
inscription: "The greatest traveler of my species. My name is SEAMAN, the dog of
captain Meriwether Lewis, whom I accompanied to the Pacifick ocean through the
interior of the continent of North America." The book that recorded the inscription
explained, "The fidelity and attachment of this animal were remarkable. After the
melancholy exit of gov. Lewis, his dog would not depart for a moment from his lifeless
remains, and when they were deposited in the earth no gentle means could draw him
from the spot of interment. He refused to take every kind of food, which was offered
him, and actually pined away and died with grief upon his master's grave!" The
wild improbability of this story is self-evident. Neither Gilbert Russell nor Priscilla
Grinder nor Neelly nor Alexander Wilson ever mentioned Seaman. See Guice,
By His Own Hand, pp. 136–137 n.

52   See, e.g., *JLCE*, VI:136.

53   Morris, *The Fate of the Corps*, p. 56.

54   Danisi and Jackson, *Meriwether Lewis,* p. 168.

55   *JLCE*, IV:266.

56   Danisi and Jackson, *Meriwether Lewis,* pp. 168–169.

57   *JLCE*, VI:435.

58   *JLCE*, VI:436.

59   Danisi and Jackson, *Meriwether Lewis*, p. 169.

60   Danisi and Jackson, *Meriwether Lewis*, p. 172.

61   Quoted in Danisi and Jackson, *Meriwether Lewis*, p. 169.

62   Danisi and Jackson, *Meriwether Lewis*, p. 170.

63   Quoted in Danisi and Jackson, *Meriwether Lewis*, p. 172.

[64] Quoted in Danisi and Jackson, *Meriwether Lewis*, p. 172.

[65] Quoted in Danisi and Jackson, *Meriwether Lewis*, pp. 172–173.

[66] Quoted in Dillon, *Meriwether Lewis*, pp. 285–286. Also Danisi and Jackson, *Meriwether Lewis*, p. 173. The transcriptions are slightly different in the two accounts of this episode.

[67] Quoted in Dillon, *Meriwether Lewis*, p. 286.

[68] Quoted in Ambrose, *Undaunted Courage*, p. 440.

[69] Jackson, *Letters*, p. 721.

[70] Jackson, *Letters*, p. 721.

[71] *JLCE*, II:108.

[72] Jackson, *Letters*, p. 388.

[73] Quoted in Jones, *Shaping of the West*, p. 163.

[74] Jackson, *Letters*, p. 721.

[75] Bakeless, *Partners in Discovery*, p. 386.

[76] Bakeless, *Partners in Discovery*, p. 385.

[77] Jenkinson, *A Vast and Open Plain*, pp. 257–260.

[78] Lewis to Lucy Marks, December 1, 1806. Meriwether Lewis Collection, Missouri Historical Society. I am indebted to Thomas Danisi for providing me a transcript of this letter.

[79] Thomas Joiner, *Why People Die By Suicide*, p. 122–127.

[80] Quoted in Holmberg, *Dear Brother*, p. 228.

[81] *JLCE*, VI:152.

[82] *JLCE*, VIII:110.

[83] *JLCE*, IV:294.

[84] *JLCE*, V:74.

[85] Mungo Park, *Life and Travels of Mungo Park in Central Africa* (Teddington, 2006), p. 116. Hereafter cited as Park, *Life and Travels*.

[86] Park, *Life and Travels*, p. 143.

[87] Alexander Pope, *The Universal Prayer*, in John Butt, ed., *The Poems of Alexander Pope*, pp. 247–248.

[88] Jefferson to Peter Carr, August 10, 1787. See Merrill Peterson, ed., *Jefferson: Writings*, p. 903.

[89] John Adams to Thomas Jefferson, June 28, 1812. See Cappon, ed., *The Adams-Jefferson Letters*, p. 310.

[90] Jackson, *Letters*, p. 64.

[91] Jenkinson, *A Vast and Open Plain*, p. 432.

[92] Quoted in Foley, *Wilderness Journey*, p. 167.

[93] Hawke, *Those Tremendous Mountains*, p. 250.

[94] Quoted in Ambrose, *Undaunted Courage*, p. 448.

[95] Foley, *Wilderness Journey*, p. 167.

[96] Quoted in Ambrose, *Undaunted Courage*, p. 448.

[97] Jefferson to Maria Cosway, October 12, 1786. See Peterson, ed., *Thomas Jefferson: Writings*, p. 872.

[98] See Danisi and Jackson, *Meriwether Lewis*, pp. 260–261.

[99] Jefferson to P.S. Dupont de Nemours, March 2, 1809. See Peterson, ed., *Thomas Jefferson: Writings*, p. 1203.

[100] Jefferson to James Monroe, May 20, 1782. See Peterson, ed., *Thomas Jefferson: Writings*, p. 779.

[101] Jefferson to P.S. Dupont de Nemours, March 2, 1809. See Peterson, ed., *Thomas Jefferson: Writings*, p. 1203.

[102] Jefferson to James Monroe, February 18, 1808. See Bergh, *Writings* vol. XI, pp. 443–444.

103   Jefferson to James Monroe, January 13, 1803. See Bergh, *Writings* vol. X, p. 345.

104   Jackson, *Letters*, p. 444.

105   Jackson, *Letters*, p. 144.

106   Ralph Ketcham, *James Madison: A Biography* (New York, 1971), pp. 482–483.

107   Foley, *Wilderness Journey*, p. 179.

108   Jackson, *Letters*, 457.

109   James Holmberg, "The Case for Suicide," in Guice, *By His Own Hand*, p. 26.

110   Jackson, *Letters*, p. 18.

111   Quoted in Ambrose, *Undaunted Courage*, p. 93.

112   Quoted in Richard Holmes, *The Age of Wonder* (New York, 2008), p. 221.

113   Van Orman, *The Explorers*, p. 61.

114   Lecture in Durango, Colorado, *Lewis and Clark Teacher Institute*, the Colorado Endowment for the Humanities, June 1999.

115   Jackson, *Letters*, p. 469.

116   Morris, *Fate of the Corps*, p. 57.

117   Jackson, *Letters*, p. 489.

118   See Adam Sisman, *Boswell's Presumptuous Task* (New York, 2001), pp. 147–170

119   This would seem to be the case, at minimum, for the following journal entries. Lewis, April 7, 1805; Lewis August 12, 1805; Lewis, January 1, 1806; Lewis July 26–27, 1806. And others.

120   Ambrose, *Undaunted Courage,* p. 471. I have not been able to find anything in Russell's writings to authenticate this claim.

121   Foley, *Wilderness Journey*, p. 180.

122   Holmberg, *Dear Brother,* p. 172.

123   Quoted in Fisher, *Suicide or Murder?,* p. 116.

124   Peter J. Kastor, *William Clark's World: Describing America in an Age of Unknowns,* (New Haven, 2011), p. 130.

125   *JLCE*, VIII:354.

126   Quoted in Jenkinson, *A Vast and Open Plain*, p. 259.

127   *JLCE*, VI:152.

128   Ambrose, *Undaunted Courage*, p. 436.

129   Bakeless, *Partners in Discovery*, p. 411.

130   Peck, *Or Perish in the Attempt,* p. 291.

131   Peck, *Or Perish in the Attempt,* pp. 291–292.

132   See Guice, *By His Own Hand?,* pp. 146–149. My transcriptions.

133   Danisi and Jackson, *Meriwether Lewis,* passim. See especially pp. 307–325.

134   Danisi and Jackson, *Meriwether Lewis,* p. 315.

135   Peck, *Or Perish in the Attempt,* p. 295.

136   Peck, *Or Perish in the Attempt,* p. 295.

137   Reimert T. Ravenholt, "Triumph Then Despair: The Tragic Death of Meriwether Lewis," in *Epidemiology* 5 (May 1994), pp. 366–379.

138   Peck, *Or Perish in the Attempt,* p. 298.

139   Jackson, *Letters*, p. 592.

140   Peck, *Or Perish in the Attempt,* p. 290.

141   Peck, *Or Perish in the Attempt,* p. 290.

142   Ambrose, *Undaunted Courage*, p. 312.

143   See Edwad T. Hall, *The Hidden Demension* (New York, 1966) and *The Silent Language* (Garden City, 1959).

144   *JLCE*, V:79.

145   Stephenie Ambrose Tubbs, "I Grew Heartily Tired of the National Hug: Meriwether Lewis Under the Microscope," in *Why Sacagawea Deserves a Day off and Other Lessons from the Lewis & Clark Trail* (Lincoln, 2008), p. 88.

[146] Jefferson to Vine Utley, March 21, 1819. See Peterson, ed., *Jefferson: Writings*, pp. 1416–1417.
[147] See Fawn Brodie, *Thomas Jefferson: An Intimate History* (New York, 1974), p. 169. Hereafter cited as Brodie, *Thomas Jefferson*.
[148] Jackson, *Letters*, p. 592.
[149] Carolyn Gilman, *Lewis and Clark Across the Divide* (Washington, D.C., 2003), p. 317.
[150] Dillon, *Meriwether Lewis,* p. 296.
[151] Danisi and Jackson, *Meriwether Lewis*, p. 261.
[152] Quoted in Simon Young, *Trouble with Tradition: Native Title and Cultural Change* (Sydney, 2008), p. 379.
[153] Foley, *Wilderness Journey*, p. 174.
[154] Jackson, *Letters*, p. 591.
[155] Jackson, *Letters*, p. 204.
[156] Jackson, *Letters*, p. 438.
[157] Bakeless, *Partners in Discovery*, p. 409.
[158] Bakeless, *Partners in Discovery*, pp. 425–426.
[159] Quoted in Jones, *Shaping of the West*, p. 176.
[160] Jackson, *Letters*, p. 58.
[161] Wood and Thiessen, *Early Fur Trade*, p. 138.
[162] Jackson, *Letters*, 444.
[163] Already this region had become what historian Elliott West calls "contested plains." See Elliott West, *The Contested Plains: Indians, Goldseekers, and the Rush to Colorado* (Lawrence, 1998).
[164] Foley, *Wilderness Journey*, p. 161.
[165] Ambrose, *Undaunted Courage*, p. 471.
[166] Harry Fritz, *The Lewis and Clark Expedition* (Westport, 2004), p. 108.
[167] Quoted in Hawke, *Those Tremendous Mountains*, p. 255.
[168] Quoted in Thomas Pinney, *A History of Wine in America: From the Beginnings to Prohibition* (Berkeley, 1989), p. 127.
[169] Quoted in Danisi and Jackson, *Meriwether Lewis*, p. 34.
[170] James F. Simon, *What Kind of Nation: Thomas Jefferson, John Marshall, and the Epic Struggle to Create a United States* (New York, 2002), p. 35.
[171] Starrs and Gale, *The Death of Meriwether Lewis*, p. 246.
[172] Starrs and Gale, *The Death of Meriwether Lewis,* p. 246.
[173] Starrs and Gale, *The Death of Meriwether Lewis*, p. 246.
[174] Starrs and Gale, *The Death of Meriwether Lewis*, p. 246.
[175] Starrs and Gale, *The Death of Meriwether Lewis*, p. 246.
[176] Starrs and Gale, *The Death of Meriwether Lewis*, p. 247.
[177] *JLCE*, IV:362.
[178] *JLCE*, VIII:347.
[179] Quoted in Brodie, *Thomas Jefferson: An Intimate History*, p. 76.
[180] Joanne Freeman, *Affairs of Honor: National Politics in the New Republic* (New Haven, 2001), p. 167.
[181] Lewis biographer Thomas Danisi has recently discovered the original handwritten transcription of the court martial, which will be part of his new book: *Uncovering the Truth of Meriwether Lewis* (New York, Prometheus Books, 2012).
[182] Quoted in Ambrose, *Undaunted Courage*, p. 464.
[183] Frederick Bates to Richard Bates, July 14, 1809.
[184] Danisi and Jackson, *Meriwether Lewis*, p. 260.
[185] Danisi and Jackson, *Meriwether Lewis*, p. 260.
[186] Danisi and Jackson, *Meriwether Lewis*, pp. 260–261.
[187] Foley, *Wilderness Journey*, p. 183.
[188] Danisi and Jackson, *Meriwether Lewis*, p. 261.
[189] Jackson, *Letters,* p. 457.
[190] Jackson, *Letters,* p. 457.

191   Jackson, *Letters*, p. 457.
192   Foley, *Wilderness Journey*, p. 183.
193   Guice, *By His Own Hand?*, p. 159.
194   Quoted in Nelson, *Rocket Men*, p. 329.
195   Buzz Aldrin, *Return to Earth*, (New York, 1973), p. 22. Hereafter cited as Aldrin, *Return to Earth*.
196   Nelson, *Rocket Men*, p. 200.
197   Aldrin, *Return to Earth*, pp. 306–307.
198   Nelson, *Rocket Men*, p. 329.
199   Van Orman, *The Explorers*, p. 132.
200   Van Orman, *The Explorers*, p. 701.
201   Quoted in Van Orman, *The Explorers*, p. 68.
202   Orman, *The Explorers*, p. 68.
203   See Patricia O'Toole, *When Trumpets Call: Theodore Roosevelt after the White House* (New York, 2005), p. 258.
204   *Hamlet*, III.i. 154.
205   *JLCE*, IV:426.
206   Even so, astonishingly, Lewis still reported some pork and a few pounds of flour as late as August 21, 1805. See *JLCE*, V:133.
207   See Betty Houchin Winfield, "The Press Response to the Corps of Discovery: The Making of Heroes in an Egalitarian Age," in *Journalism & Mass Communication Quarterly* 80.4 [2003]: pp. 866–883.
208   Jackson, *Letters*, p. 61.
209   *JLCE*, V:74.
210   *JLCE*, V:70.
211   *JLCE*, V:70.
212   *JLCE*, V:74.
213   *JLCE*, V:74.
214   *JLCE*, V:78.
215   *JLCE*, V:78–79.
216   *JLCE*, V:79.
217   *JLCE*, V:79.
218   *JLCE*, V:79.
219   *JLCE*, V:79.
220   *JLCE*, V:69.
221   *JLCE*, V:81.
222   *JLCE*, V:79.
223   *JLCE*, V:79.
224   *JLCE*, V:114.
225   *JLCE*, V:83.
226   *JLCE*, V:96.
227   *JLCE*, V:96.
228   *JLCE*, V:97.
229   *JLCE*, V:103.
230   *JLCE*, V:103.
231   *JLCE*, V:103.
232   Shakespeare, *King Lear*, III.iv.101–102
233   *JLCE*, V:104.
234   *JLCE*, IV:9.
235   Quoted in Dillon, *Meriwether Lewis*, p. 23.
236   *JLCE*, V:105.
237   *JLCE*, V:106.
238   *JLCE*, V:106.

[239] *JLCE*, V:106.
[240] *JLCE*, V:109.
[241] Alan Moorehead, *The Fatal Impace: An Account of the Invasion of the South Pacific, 1767–1840* (New York, 1966).p. xiii.
[242] *JLCE*, II:394.
[243] *JLCE*, VI:182.
[244] Shakespeare, *Othello*, I.iii.158–168.
[245] Slaughter, *Exploring Lewis and Clark*, p. 20.
[246] *JLCE*, IV:285.

ACKNOWLEDGMENTS

[1] *JLCE*, IV:204.
[2] *JLCE*, IV:204.
[3] *JLCE*, IV:204.
[4] *JLCE*, V:118.
[5] *JLCE*, V:74.
[6] *JLCE*, III:418.

Index

A

Achilles xvii
Achilles xvii
Adams, Abigail 322
Adams, John xvii, 113,
230, 240, 249–250,
260, 321–322, 337
Adams, John Quincy
103, 240–241, 322
Aeneas 136, 233
Affairs of Honor 68, 275,
342, 365–372, 391
Air gun 95
Aird, James 365
Alcohol 86, 128, 132,
135, 137, 140, 147,
330, 351, 364
in early national
period 303, 362
Alexander the Great 70
Aldrin, Buzz xvii,
244, 315, 372–375,
380, 389
Allegheny Mountains 228
Allen, John Logan xvi, 29
Allen, Paul 235,
245, 270, 318
Ambrose, Stephen
xxii–xxiii, xxix,
14, 29, 79, 126,
159, 164, 212, 223,
226–227, 301, 302,
303, 304, 314, 350,
351, 354–355, 362
Ambrose Tubbs,
Stephenie xxii,
302, 353, 354
American flag 135
American Philosophical
Society xxiv, xxvii,
126, 179, 230, 237,
248, 320, 341–342,
356, 389
American Revolution 18

Anderson, Edmund 263
Appalachian Mountains
228
Arikara Indians
xxvii, 246–247,
255, 358–359
Arketarnarshar
(Arikara) 246–247
Armstrong, Lance xii
Armstrong, Neil xii,
315, 372, 380
Assiniboine Indians
82, 101
Assiniboine River
xx, 92, 182
Astor, John Jacob 256
Astronauts xii, 244, 315,
372–375, 380, 389
Augustine, Aurelius
(Saint) xiii
Austen, Jane 366, 386

B

Bacon, Francis 229,
249, 250, 355
Bad River 224
Bakeless, John xi,
29, 276, 279, 285,
292, 295, 302, 324,
333, 351, 359
Baker Bay 49, 52,
53, 152, 223, 377
Bankhead, Charles 330
Banks, Joseph
235, 321, 348
Barbary Pirates 244
Barlow, Joel 240, 242
Barnum, P. T. 248
Barton, Benjamin
Smith 100, 239, 248
Bates, Frederick xxviii,
45, 64, 212, 213, 237,
258, 261, 275, 276, 291,

304, 313, 316, 341, 342,
344, 357, 358, 359, 365,
366–369, 370, 371
Bates, Tarleton 261
Battle-axe 77–80, 111
Beaverhead River
42, 163, 219
Bechtle, Henry 350
Beckham, Stephen Dow
xxiv, 49, 50, 302
Beethoven, Ludwig
von 354
Bergon, Frank 29, 269
Bible 100–101, 116,
337, 375–376
Biddle, Nicholas
xx, 20, 31, 38, 53,
95, 129, 226, 233,
235, 239, 245, 250,
251, 267, 268, 269,
270, 317, 318
Handling of the
Captain Clark issue 1
Big Bone Lick,
KY 252, 253
Big Dry Creek 173
Big Hole River 42
Birnt Hills
(northernmost point
on the Missouri) 67,
187, 188, 191, 203,
205, 208, 243, 266
Birthdays 117–131
Bismarck, ND 73,
110, 119, 129
Bitterroot Mountains
50, 109, 122, 130,
146, 150, 158, 162,
165, 168, 216, 217,
246, 323, 353, 378
Black Buffalo (Lakota) 54
Black Cat
(see Posecopsahe)
Black Coulee 34

Simpson, George 92
Sioux City, IA
116, 119, 365
Sixteen Mile
Creek 87–88
Slaughter, Thomas
xv, xxx, 22, 64,
117, 212, 266–267,
268, 302, 388
Smith, Adam 76
Smith, Samuel
Harrison 115
Smith, W.C. 282
Southwest Point 132
Sovereignty
protocols 52, 99
Spanish-American
War 215
Speke, John xvii, 36,
180, 233, 374
Sputnik xx
Stanley, Henry 374
Star Trek 78
Starrs, James 302
Station Camp xxiii, 52
Sterne, Thomas 204
Steuben, Baron von
13, 91, 100, 337
Stoddard, Amos 9,
259, 262, 283, 285,
286, 306, 352, 357
Suicide, defense of
(John Donne) xiii
Suicidists xxiv, 275,
299, 300, 302
Sula, MT 162
Sullivan, John 252
Sun River 219

T

Tavern Creek 148
Tendoy, ID 44
Tennessee River 288
Terry, Alfred
Howe xxvii

Thacher, S.C. 240
Thiessen, Thomas D. xx
Thompson, David
xx, 245
Thompson, James 36
Thompson, John 86, 87,
142, 147, 162, 250
Thoreau, Henry
David 377
Three Forks 2, 12, 37,
39, 159, 163, 164,
219, 223
Three Mile Island 61
Thwaites, Reuben
Gold 268, 302
Tillamook Head,
OR 90, 357
Tippet 44–45, 128,
383–384
Tobacco xxvii, 74,
78, 88, 139, 140,
146, 162, 163, 360,
376, 376, 377
Tobacco Garden
Creek 177,187
Tocqueville, Alexis
de 358
Tosten, MT 87
Townsend, MT 87
Traveler's Rest 69,
146, 158, 162, 164,
165, 168, 180, 193
Traveling Library xx,
13, 22, 117, 126
Treaty of Paris 228
Treaty of San
Ildefonso 357
Treelessness 13
Trenton, ND 177
Tripoli 116, 244
Tristram Shandy 204
Twain, Mark xxii, 19
Two Medicine Creek
57, 119, 166, 167, 173,
181, 193, 205, 266

U

Universal Prayer 337
Upper Portage Camp
39, 79, 145, 220
Upper Red Rock
Lake 46

V

Van Orman, Richard
348, 373
Vancouver expedition
23, 48, 51
Vaughan, J. 148
Vergil 135–136
Vespucci, Amerigo 220
Vincennes, IN 238

W

Walker, Elizabeth 307, 365
Walker, John 307, 365
War Department xxxiv,
59, 64, 68, 76, 133,
211, 212, 214, 216,
225, 230, 235, 253,
258, 259, 260, 261,
263, 265, 266, 275,
277, 278, 279, 282,
286, 291, 299, 312,
313, 316, 320, 323,
324, 343, 344, 345–
346, 347, 350, 359,
361, 368, 369, 370, 391
Washington, George
342, 343
Weippe Prairie 216
Weiser, Peter 86, 117, 118,
142, 148, 163, 250
Werner, William 86, 162
West, Elliott xxi
Wheeler, Olin 302
Whiskey 27, 121,
128, 132, 134, 141,
144–145, 147, 149,
150, 363, 364

More Praise for:

Clay Jenkinson's book on Meriwether Lewis is everything we would expect from him—intelligent, shrewdly perceptive and masterfully grounded in the historical record—but its defining quality is its intimacy, the close and compassionate engagement of a fine historian with his subject. Jenkinson's examination of this famous explorer is itself a kind of bold exploration into the man's elusive character and his deeply troubled spirit."

—Elliott West
Author of *The Last Indian War: The Nez Perce Story* and
*The Contested Plains: Indians, Goldseekers, and the
Rush to Colorado*

"Meriwether Lewis is the mystery man of American history. Intellectually brilliant and physically robust—but also emotionally brittle, impatient, and self-aggrandizing—Lewis was crammed with contradictions that have fascinated us ever since he died on the Natchez Trace in 1809. In his astonishing and insightful deep reading, Clay Jenkinson restores Lewis's essential humanity, with all his strengths and flaws displayed, and reveals previously unexamined human dramas hidden within the voluminous documentary record left by the two captains and their men. By refusing to take their writings at face value, Jenkinson has firmly yanked Lewis and Clark out of the hands of received wisdom and required us to look at the explorers as if we see them in their landscape for the first time."

— Landon Jones
Author of *William Clark and the Shaping
of the West* and *The Essential Lewis and Clark*

If you love and yearn to understand Meriwether Lewis, Read this Book! Not only does Jenkinson thoroughly explore the many forces which led to Lewis's tragic and untimely end, he does so in a manner which forces the reader to reconsider long held assumptions about the complex Captain of the Corps of Northwestern Discovery. A skilled and insightful portrait of a man who has puzzled historians for generations.

— Stephenie Ambrose Tubbs
Author of *Why Sacagawea Deserves the Day Off*